Praise for *Teaching at Its Be*

"*Teaching At Its Best* is a truly comprehensive resource for any teacher, faculty developer, or instructional designer to work on the why, what and how of teaching. It answers 99.9% of the questions we deal with in our daily practice to improve student learning, and weaves in current discussions around inclusivity, belonging, and community building – on site and online. This book will guide countless teachers to teach at their best!"

—Janina Tosic,
Consultant, Center for Teaching and Learning,
Ruhr West University of Applied Sciences

"An essential and easy-to-use resource for novice and experienced faculty alike, Zakrajsek and Nilson's *Teaching at Its Best* includes the opportunity for self-reflection as well as concrete teaching tips that are sure to increase student completion and success. The edition covers the newest developments in evidence-based teaching practices in important areas such as course design and development, along with immediately applicable techniques in crucially current areas such as classroom inclusivity, academic integrity, and preventing classroom incivility."

—Stacey S. Souther,
Professor of Psychology and College-wide
Faculty Development Coordinator, Cuyahoga Community College

"I have leveraged *Teaching at Its Best* in college teaching courses and faculty development settings since the second edition. This fifth edition offers a major leap forward, one that is deeply evidence-based, that will prove essential for higher education faculty as well as faculty developers who wish to improve teaching practice as well as student learning outcomes."

—C. Edward Watson,
Associate Vice President for Curricular and Pedagogical Innovation,
American Association of Colleges and Universities (AAC&U), and
co-author of *Teaching Naked Techniques: A Practical Guide to Designing Better Classes*

"Todd Zakrajsek has done a masterful job updating Linda Nilson's canonical research-based teaching resource. This edition includes invaluable information from new research findings and is a must read for everyone desiring to teach at their best and anyone who wants students to learn at their best."

—Saundra Yancy McGuire, Ph.D.,
Director Emerita, Center for Academic Success,
Professor Emerita of Chemistry & (Ret)
Assistant Vice Chancellor, Louisiana State University

Teaching At Its Best is an absolute gem. Whether you are new to teaching in higher education or have been doing it for a while, you will find this book's evidence-based advice on a wide range of teaching issues to be very helpful. The style is engaging and the breadth is impressive. If you read only one book this year to help you improve your teaching, this one should be it!

—Dan Levy,
Senior Lecturer at Harvard University and
author of *Teaching Effectively with Zoom*

TEACHING AT ITS BEST

A Research-Based Resource for College Instructors

Fifth edition

Todd D. Zakrajsek
Linda B. Nilson

JB JOSSEY-BASS™
A Wiley Brand

Jossey-Bass
A Wiley Imprint
111 River St, Hoboken, NJ 07030
www.josseybass.com

Jossey-Bass books and products are available through most bookstores. To contact Jossey-Bass directly, call our Customer Care Department within the U.S. at 800–956–7739, outside the U.S. at +1 317 572 3986, or fax +1 317 572 4002.

Wiley also publishes its books in a variety of electronic formats and by print-on-demand. Some material included with standard print versions of this book may not be included in e-books or in print-on-demand. If this book refers to media such as a CD or DVD that is not included in the version you purchased, you may download this material at http://booksupport.wiley.com. For more information about Wiley products, visit www.wiley.com.

Library of Congress Cataloging-in-Publication Data
Names: Zakrajsek, Todd, author. | Nilson, Linda Burzotta, author.
Title: Teaching at its best : a research-based resource for college
  instructors / Todd Zakrajsek, Linda B. Nilson.
Description: Fifth edition. | Hoboken, NJ : Jossey-Bass, 2023. | Includes
  index.
Identifiers: LCCN 2022047646 (print) | LCCN 2022047647 (ebook) | ISBN
  9781119860228 (paperback) | ISBN 9781119860242 (adobe pdf) | ISBN
  9781119860235 (epub)
Subjects: LCSH: College teaching. | Effective teaching.
Classification: LCC LB2331 .N55 2023 (print) | LCC LB2331 (ebook) | DDC
  378.1/7–dc23/eng/20221102
LC record available at https://lccn.loc.gov/2022047646
LC ebook record available at https://lccn.loc.gov/2022047647

Cover Design: Wiley
Cover Image: © Studio-Pro/Getty Images
SKY10052094_072723

To my husband Greg, who has backed me all the way.
—Linda

To my wife Debra, without whom I would have been so much less.
—Todd

and

To everyone who stands before learners with the recognition that our profession comes with never-ending struggles and exhilarating wins, often with the same student. We wrote this book to assist you on your quest to advance as many students as possible by teaching at your best.

CONTENTS

Part 4
TOOLS AND TECHNIQUES
TO FACILITATE LEARNING   233

Linda B. Nilson, PhD, is the founding director of Clemson University's Office of Teaching Effectiveness and Innovation. Her career as a full-time faculty development director spans more than 25 years. Along with four editions of *Teaching at Its Best: A Research-Based Resource for College Instructors* (1998, 2003, 2010, 2016), she has authored three other books: *The Graphic Syllabus and the Outcomes Map: Communicating Your Course* (Jossey-Bass, 2007); *Creating Self-Regulated Learners: Strategies to Strengthen Students' Self-Awareness and Learning Skills* (Stylus, 2013); and *Specifications Grading: Restoring Rigor, Motivating Students, and Saving Faculty Time* (Stylus, 2015). She also co-authored *Online Teaching at Its Best* (Jossey-Bass, 2018) with Ludwika A. Goodson.

She has also co-edited several books: *Enhancing Learning with Laptops in the Classroom* (with Barbara E. Weaver, Jossey-Bass, 2005) and volumes 25 through 28 of *To Improve the Academy: Resources for Faculty, Instructional, and Organizational Development* (with Douglas Reimondo Robertson, Anker, 2007, 2008; with Judith E. Miller, Jossey-Bass, 2009, 2010). *To Improve the Academy* is the major publication of the Professional and Organizational Development (POD) Network in Higher Education.

Her other publications include articles and book chapters on a range of topics: validity problems with student ratings, ways to measure learning in a course, the instability of faculty development careers, teaching with learning objects and mind maps, designing a graphic syllabus, improving student-peer feedback, teaching large classes, fostering critical thinking, and graduate student professional development.

Dr. Nilson has given well over 450 webinars, keynotes, and live workshops at conferences, colleges, and universities nationally and internationally on dozens of topics related to college teaching and academic career success. Her repertoire of speaking topics spans every chapter in this book, as well as early faculty career management and scholarly writing and publishing.

Before coming to Clemson in 1998, she directed the Center for Teaching at Vanderbilt University and the Teaching Assistant Development Program at the University of California, Riverside. At the latter institution, she developed the disciplinary cluster approach to training teaching assistants (TAs), a cost-effective way for a centralized unit to provide disciplinary-relevant instructional training. Her entrée into educational development came in the late 1970s while she was on the sociology faculty at UCLA. After distinguishing herself as an excellent instructor, her department selected her to establish and supervise its Teaching Assistant Training Program. As a sociologist, she conducted research in the areas of occupations and work, social stratification, political sociology, and disaster behavior. Her career also included a few years in the business world as a technical and commercial writer, a training workshop facilitator, and the business editor of a regional magazine.

Dr. Nilson is a member of the POD Network, which honored her work with the 2000 Innovation (Bright Idea) Award, and the Canada-based Society for Teaching and Learning in Higher Education. She has held leadership positions in the POD Network, the Southern Regional Faculty and Instructional Development Consortium, the Society for the Study of Social Problems, Toastmasters International, and Mensa.

A native of Chicago, Dr. Nilson was a National Science Foundation fellow at the University of Wisconsin, Madison, where she received her PhD and MS degrees in sociology. She completed her undergraduate work in three years at the University of California, Berkeley, where she was elected to Phi Beta Kappa.

Todd D. Zakrajsek (Zuh-CRY-sick), PhD, is an associate professor in the Department of Family Medicine at UNC–Chapel Hill and president of the International Teaching Learning Cooperative. At UNC–School of Medicine, he is a co-associate director of an early career faculty development fellowship program, providing resources for early career doctors on various topics related to teaching/learning, leadership, and scholarly activity. He is also the President of the ITLC, which presents four national Lilly Teaching Conferences annually, and manages the *Scholarly Teacher* blog. Todd has directed faculty development efforts for 16 years and has served as the director of interdisciplinary teaching conferences, both in the United States and abroad, for over 20 years.

Todd recently authored the third edition of *The New Science of Learning* (Stylus, 2022). He is currently working on a book for faculty new to higher education. Todd has also co-authored *Teaching for Learning* (with Claire Major and Michael Harris, first and second editions; Routledge, 2022), *Advancing*

Online Learning (with Kevin Kelly; Stylus, 2021), and *Dynamic Lecturing* (with Christine Harrington; Stylus, 2017). He is the series editor for a 10-volume collection of books (in development) related to teaching and learning.

His other publications include articles and book chapters on a variety of topics, including the scholarship of teaching and learning, teaching large classes, postpandemic teaching, teaching students how to learn, active learning, effective lecturing, humor in the classroom, time management, and teaching students who are neurodivergent. He has also published on the topic of faculty and educational development: possible programs to offer, documenting and assessing faculty development efforts, managing budgets, using evaluation data to improve teaching.

Todd has delivered and facilitated over 400 keynotes, workshops, conference presentations, and webinars across 49 US states, 12 countries, and four continents. His recent presentation topics include: the scholarship of teaching and learning, teaching in a post-COVID environment, active and engaged learning, teaching to encourage student motivation, avoiding teaching myths, overcoming bias in teaching, and universal elements of all learning. Throughout his career, Todd has presented on topics that can be found in every chapter of the fifth edition of *Teaching at Its Best*.

Todd began his career in higher education teaching at Southern Oregon State College, where he was a tenured associate professor of psychology. The courses he taught included the psychology of learning, history of psychology, human memory, cognitive psychology, social psychology, educational psychology, human relations, and behavior modification. He founded centers for teaching and learning and built faculty development efforts at Southern Oregon State College (now University), Central Michigan University, and the University of North Carolina at Chapel Hill. Todd has served on many educationally related boards and work groups, including *The Journal of Excellence in College Teaching, International Journal for the Scholarship of Teaching and Learning, College Teaching,* and *Education in the*

Health Professions. Todd has consulted with organizations such as The American Council on Education (ACE), Lenovo Computer, Microsoft, and the Bill and Melinda Gates Foundation.

Todd is a native of Michigan, earning a BS in psychology from Lake Superior State College (now University). He received his MS and PhD degrees in Industrial/Organizational Psychology from Ohio University, and an Honorary Doctorate in Humane Letters from Lake Superior State University. Follow and connect with Todd on Twitter @toddzakrajsek and LinkedIn.

I met Linda Nilson in 1998 at a national meeting of faculty developers—the POD Network. I had recently read her new book, *Teaching at Its Best*, and I told her that it was the best book to support faculty members and their teaching I had ever read. As a new faculty developer, I bought copies for new faculty members to read and use as a guide. In the fourth edition of this book, Linda commented that she never dreamed she would be revising and updating the book nearly 20 years later. It is a tremendous honor to be asked to write a third, fourth, and now fifth edition of any book, but especially a book that impacts so many individuals. That is a testament to the foundational ethos of this book. It is not only a bestseller, but the inspiration for countless unsolicited emails from faculty members thanking Linda for helping them survive and thrive in their early years of teaching. I know what it means to them; I also struggled in my first years of teaching.

In the fall of 2021, I was asked if I would consider working on *Teaching at Its Best*, fifth edition. Linda was moving into phased retirement from writing, but her book had become so foundational that it was important work to continue. I eagerly accepted, and began working on what I consider one of the finest resources for anyone teaching a course in higher education. I believe what we have in this fifth edition is very special.

This edition, like its predecessors, is meant for a broad audience of both new and experienced faculty members who teach at all types of postsecondary institutions. It is especially useful for those teaching relatively young students in a traditional classroom or hybrid environment. Many of the strategies in this book transfer smoothly to online courses, but that is more by happy accident than design. As you read through the teaching strategies in this book, we hope you see that many elements of good teaching are effective regardless of the delivery modality. For example, creating a community conducive to learning is important in courses that are onsite, online, hybrid, hyflex, remote, or anything else. If humans come together to learn, community is important in facilitating that learning. In this book, you will see the community theme repeated across many concepts and teaching strategies.

One thing that every faculty member shares is a lack of discretionary time, and when time and resources are strained, professional development is among the first luxuries to be eliminated. Aware of that unfortunate aspect of teaching in higher education, we designed this new edition for people, like you, who likely don't have time to read a book from front to back with granular explanations of detailed nuances of teaching, students, and learning. To preserve your time, the writing is concise and informal, the paragraphs fairly short, the 27 chapters generously sectioned, and the table of contents detailed with chapter section headings. In addition, the five major parts are sequenced according to your likely chronological need for the material. Still, you can read the chapters in any order you find most helpful, and the text often cross-references other chapters that elaborate on a given subject. You can casually browse or quickly locate specific topics, and easily skip over with whatever you are already familiar. Everything about this book is designed to facilitate your use of new tools, resources, and strategies right away.

The research on college-level teaching, called the scholarship of teaching and learning (SoTL), provides the foundation and inspiration for this book. This fertile body of literature continues to expand the toolbox for both classroom and technology-enhanced instruction. As with physical tools, you have to find the right tool for the job, but you can choose from among several right tools for any given teaching job. And realize that no tool works in every situation. This book offers plenty of alternatives for facilitating student learning, enhancing instructor-student rapport, managing the classroom, and assessing student achievement. And it avoids playing champion for certain methods over others and for the latest innovations over the well-proven ones. You will find the how-to's and why-do's for many teaching tools, along with their trade-offs, just as the research reports them. This is what you need to make your own choices and execute them with confidence.

Because quite a few colleges and universities use this book in extended new-faculty orientations and college teaching courses, you will find at the end of every chapter two Reflection Questions and one Concept Into Practice item. The Reflection Questions are designed to be conversation starters based on the information in the chapter. The Concept Into Practice items are activities to try and then discuss the results. Of course, you may certainly have a discussion pertaining to material in any chapter using the following general questions:

1. What common problems faced by faculty members does the chapter try to prevent or solve? How well do the recommendations in the chapter prevent or solve these problems?
2. What practices explained in the chapter do you already implement? What have your results been?
3. What new practices explained in the chapter do you want to try? What reservations, if any, do you have?
4. What practices explained in the chapter do you think wouldn't work well for you, and why? Would this be due to your students' expectations, values, knowledge or skill background, or level of maturity; or your class sizes, time pressures, or teaching style; or some other reason? Can you think of any ways around these roadblocks?

These general questions direct readers to the main purpose of this book: practical ways to maximize student learning, promote productive instructor-student relationships, and make the life of faculty members easier and more rewarding.

While preserving the most appreciated features of the fourth edition, this fifth edition has an extensive amount of new material, including a chapter on becoming an inclusive teacher. The material throughout the book focuses on teaching to help faculty members develop the best educational experiences possible. In addition, you will find extensive evidence-based updates on major topics and line-by-line editing to further improve the writing and flow of the information. Following is a synopsis of the book so that you can quickly get a sense of all that is included and perhaps even decide where you'd like best to begin.

Part One, "Teaching Preparation," guides you through the decisions you have to make and the tasks you have to complete before the term begins. As understanding your students and how they learn anchors all your plans, this topic is featured in the first chapter. The section on how people learn brings in more principles and findings from cognitive and educational psychology, as well as more concrete implications for teaching. Chapter 2 on designing outcomes-centered courses provides extensive information on types of outcomes and how to write and sequence them. Four very well-established frameworks are provided to help guide you in developing outcomes as you design your courses. Chapter 3 gives you strategies for incorporating critical thinking into your course design. Most importantly, it clears the fog around critical thinking, a teaching topic that has been clouded by a polyglot of competing schools of thought that rarely, if ever, cross-reference each other. This chapter identifies common ground among them, presents lists of critical thinking outcomes suitable to various disciplinary groups, and lays out concrete questions and tasks from the different schools that engage students in critical thinking. Because instructional technology changes so quickly, Chapter 4 focuses on strategies for identifying when and which technology to use. As technology is changing at an ever-increasing rate, this chapter primarily focuses on how to think about technology, although some specific educational technology solutions are also included. Chapter 5, on the syllabus, focuses on creating an encouraging learning environment, elucidating the relevance of the course material, and explaining the alignment among the outcomes, learning experiences, and assessments. Examples of the graphic syllabus are also provided. Finally, Chapter 6 translates copyright guidelines into plain language to help you to understand what is permissible and how to get permission when it is needed. New to this edition is information on the growing area of Creative Commons.

Part Two, "The Human Side of Teaching," deals with ways to bring out the best in your students. It opens with Chapter 7 on creating the ever-important positive learning community. The community you establish will impact nearly every aspect of the course, starting with the first day of class. Chapter 8 is a new chapter on the ongoing work of becoming increasingly inclusive in your instructional role. It includes strategies to make a course more inclusive and ways to reduce inequities in and out of the classroom. Chapter 9 on enhancing student motivation includes seven theories of motivation and 50 practical strategies related to student motivation. Chapter 10 contains extensive information to ensure students get as much as

possible out of working in groups, whether they are short-term, ad hoc groups used in a single class or those used for long-term, team-based learning. Chapter 11 addresses the uncomfortable situation of classroom incivilities. This chapter contains a wide variety of approaches for preventing classroom incivility and features a comprehensive section on how to respond to the most frequently reported incivilities. Finally, Chapter 12 provides updated data on the prevalence of cheating, the students most likely to do it, and the reasons that they do it. This chapter also includes 40 ways to discourage cheating.

Part Three, "Tried-and-True Teaching Methods," opens with Chapter 13, which provides advice on selecting the teaching formats, methods, and moves that, according to the research, best help students achieve specific cognitive outcomes. This chapter also has a graphic view of course and curriculum alignment and two curriculum design tools: Davis and Arend's (2013) model of learning outcomes, ways of learning, and teaching methods and Fink and Fink's (2009) three-column planning grid for developing a well-aligned course. Chapters 14 through 18 describe instructional methods that have proven their worth over many decades when implemented and managed properly: lecture, discussion (including questioning techniques), experiential learning, inquiry-guided methods, and case-based learning. These chapters discuss new ways to think about the active learning versus lecture debate, effective lecture strategies, ways to combine lecture with active learning, strategies to facilitate effective discussions, methods to encourage participation during class discussions, and questioning techniques. There is new information on role-playing, Reacting to the Past, simulations, and resources about service-learning. Chapters 17 and 18 also provide strategies and suggestions to make inquiry-guided methods effective. In these two chapters you will find information on just-in-time teaching, project-based learning, problem-based learning, and designing and teaching case-based strategies.

Part Four, "Tools and Techniques to Facilitate Learning," covers the major mental processes involved in learning and memory. Chapter 19 makes the case that learning is something that learners ultimately must do themselves and presents questions that self-aware, self-regulated learners ask themselves as they study or complete an assignment. After presenting evidence that self-regulated learning greatly increases student achievement, it describes almost 30 short assignments and activities that will acquaint your students with their learning process, enhance their learning, and demonstrate the benefits of self-regulated learning, while adding little or nothing to your grading workload. Chapter 20 provides updates on STEAM education research. Previously known more commonly as STEM, STEAM demonstrates that science is heavily assisted, and in many ways influenced, by art. This chapter includes information about why we are losing STEM majors and ways to help students to be more successful in these courses, including teaching students better learning strategies and engaging students with more effective teaching strategies.

Chapter 21 addresses the many reasons that students don't prepare for class, some of which are beyond their control. This chapter includes methods to help students come to class prepared, including strategies to hold them accountable for assigned work. In view of clear research discrediting the value of teaching to a given learning style, Chapter 22 now includes a new section focused on the learning style myth. This chapter also contains a great deal of information on visual modes of learning. Humans process visual information extraordinarily efficiently, which makes it very important in the learning process. After summarizing in depth why our feedback to students can fail, Chapter 23 examines ways that feedback facilitates learning. This chapter also presents research pertaining to metacognition and student peer feedback. In addition, examples are given of classroom assessment techniques, which give fast feedback to both us and our students.

Finally, Part Five, "Assessment and Grading," showcases best practices in helping students prepare for exams (Chapter 24). The goal of having students in our courses is for them to learn. To know the extent to which they are learning, we engage in a variety

of assessments, ensuring that the students understand them and their purpose. Chapter 25 provides extensive research pertaining to construction and use of different types of assessments. One of the most challenging and time-consuming parts of teaching is grading. Chapter 26 explains grading strategies, including the increasingly popular specifications (*specs*) grading. This concept has gained traction as research suggests that it raises academic standards, motivates students to do higher-quality work, increases their sense of responsibility for their grades, and reduces faculty members' grading time. New sections in this chapter include automated scoring and ungrading. These topics have a mixed reception at the moment, but have strong potential to impact higher education in a positive way. The final chapter in this section, and the book, is Chapter 27, with a focus on how you are assessed as an instructor—specifically, what teaching effectiveness means, how institutions evaluate it, and how to document yours for review purposes. Research increasingly demonstrates that student ratings of instruction (aka student evaluations) do a poor job of measuring teaching effectiveness. They are in fact unrelated to learning (they used to be somewhat related), more biased than in the past, and factually inaccurate much of the time. Unfortunately, nearly every institution in higher education continues to use them to evaluate faculty teaching. As a result, they have created an unsustainably disjointed state of affairs: prioritizing and measuring student learning for accrediting agencies but rewarding and sanctioning faculty members primarily on student satisfaction.

Because many of us depend on high teaching evaluations to stay employed, Chapter 27 has a section on what you can (and cannot) do to improve your ratings. Fortunately, several of the instructor behaviors that raise ratings also promote learning. In addition, this chapter suggests a wide range of ways that you can document student learning in your courses, the criterion on which institutions *should* assess faculty members to be consistent with how accrediting agencies assess institutions, colleges, and programs.

Although there is a wide variety of topics in this book, there are a few that we purposely left out. For example, not included are many of the "high-impact practices" that Kuh (2008) recommends. They are wonderful practices that encourage student persistence and retention, but they tend to grow out of institutional, departmental, and program decisions and initiatives. This book focuses on what *you*, the individual faculty member, can do, so it covers just a few high-impact student experiences like service-learning, collaborative assignments and projects, and building communities of learners. Another topic not dealt with here is how to conduct research on the scholarship of teaching and learning (SoTL) and the scholarship of educational development (SoED). There is a well-established literature on these topics, and it is impossible to give you any meaningful way to begin this work in a page or two of this book.

Several purposeful choices were made regarding word choice. You will note that in many places the term *teaching* is used where others might prefer the phrase *teaching and learning*. We see *teaching*, not *teaching and learning*, as the best description of what we faculty members *do*, and this book is all about what we *do*. We certainly hope our teaching results in student learning, but the students are the ones to learn. Try as we might, we cannot make them learn. You will also see the terms *faculty*, *instructors*, and occasionally *professors* to refer to those who teach at the postsecondary level, with the word *teachers* typically reserved for those at the K–12 level. Only recently has the term *teacher* been attached to faculty members in higher education. The word *college* is regularly used to represent all institutions in higher education. It is awkward to write "college and university" repeatedly. Finally, we have adopted the use of *they* and *them* as singular pronouns. This removes the need to write he/she, removes the concern as to whether we have balanced the number of male and female examples, and removes potentially delicate issues of using he or she to refer to something negative. APA, MLA, and the New Oxford Dictionary of English all encourage the use of the singular pronoun. Plus, after a few uses, one realizes how easy it is to write more inclusively.

Our gratitude for the support and help given us while writing the book extends to so many people. First, recognition to the tens of thousands of faculty members who have influenced our work. This newest edition would not be possible without their influence. Thank you, all of you throughout higher education, who are dedicated to teaching at its best. Not just because you may buy this book, but because you are working—tirelessly and devotedly for endless hours, despite modest recognition and remuneration—to improve the fates of multiple generations and ultimately the entire world. As Todd Whitaker is credited with saying, "Teaching is the profession that makes all professions possible." You are that profession and for that reason this edition of the book continues to be dedicated to you.

Thank you, Christine O'Connor, our managing editor at Wiley, along with Natalie Muñoz (Associate Editor, Jossey-Bass), Mary Beth Rosswurm (Editorial Assistant, Jossey-Bass), and everyone else who worked on this project. It takes a team to create a book such as this and we had a truly outstanding team.

Thank you also to McKenzie Baker, who read every word of the draft manuscript for this edition (approximately 200,000 of them), making suggestions and asking clarifying questions all the way through. This book is much better for her efforts and encouragements.

Finally, we thank our families and devoted pets. It is because of their patience, their willingness to pick up duties left as we wrote, and their constant encouragement that this edition of the book came into existence. Writing is an arduous process, made possible by those who never type a single word, but through their sacrifices allow and encourage every word to emerge. Thank you.

TODD D. ZAKRAJSEK
Durham, North Carolina

LINDA B. NILSON
Clemson, South Carolina

TEACHING PREPARATION

CHAPTER 1

Understanding Your Students and How They Learn

What do you teach? You have likely been asked that question many times. Think about how you answer. Most faculty members list their areas of expertise: psychology, biology, physics, English, business, and so on. That is fine. We all worked very hard to become experts. We would like for you to begin to verbalize a typically unspoken, but critical element of teaching. The next time someone asks you *what* you teach, give them the name of your discipline and add, "But also extremely important is *who* I teach—students."

This is an important addition in thinking. Most of us have learned the intricacies of a discipline and been granted a degree and a faculty appointment, whether full time or part time, because of that work. Teaching at its best has, for too long, been a secondary consideration. We would like to shift that thinking. Still considering the disciplines in which we gained expertise, let's shift our focus to the plethora of factors that must be learned to gain a second area of expertise, teaching. Our hope is not merely that you teach, but that you teach as if what you

do is exceedingly important in maximizing student learning, because it is.

When done well, teaching introduces students to ideas, topics, and information they may not have otherwise experienced. Such teaching also holds the promise of unleashing the potential of the human mind and impacting future generations. Faculty members skilled in educational practices hold the ability to help students achieve things they themselves previously thought not possible. As you will see throughout this book, everyone who teaches can get better at teaching. Teaching well is nuanced and impacted by many factors. There will be many opportunities for you to learn concepts and strategies to help you become the educator you desire to be.

■ THE STUDENTS IN YOUR COURSE

The first challenge all faculty members face is understanding the students in their courses. This is no small

3

feat, as there is wide variability among students, and student composition changes constantly. Who you teach this semester will be different than who a colleague at another institution is teaching. Similarly, check in regularly on the composition of the students at your institution, as subtle changes can take place from year to year. If you stop checking in on who your students are, you will walk into a classroom one day filled with individuals who are very different than you expected. If you don't have it already, your institution's admissions or student affairs office is a good place to begin collecting the student data you need. The student affairs office can give you distributions and percentages on a wide number of variables, such as age, gender, race, ethnicity, marital and family status, socioeconomic background, employment status, campus residents versus commuters, domestic versus international, geographical mix, and special admissions. This information is very helpful. For example, if your students are older, research suggests that they often prefer to talk about and apply their work and life experience in class, discussion forums, assignments, and group work, so draw on and refer to those experiences frequently. Because they know the world to be complex, adult learners typically expect to learn multiple ways of solving problems and to have discretion in applying the material. Those learners appreciate the opportunity for reflection after trying out a new application or method. In addition, they want the material to have immediate practical utility and relevance (Aslanian, 2001; Vella, 1994; Wlodkowski, 1993). Adult learners are often highly motivated, eager participants, and well prepared for class.

It is also helpful to know your students' level of academic preparation and achievement. Although many colleges and universities no longer use SAT and ACT scores for application packets (Koljatic et al., 2021), you can find the percentage of students ranked at varying percentiles of their high school graduating classes, the percentage of National Merit and National Achievement Finalists (over 5% is high), and the percentage that qualified for Advanced Placement credit (over 33% is high). For

several hundred American colleges and universities, almost all of this information is published every summer in the "America's Best Colleges" issue of *U.S. News and World Report.*

Your institution's career center can provide the percentage of students planning on different types of graduate and professional educations, as well as the immediate employment plans of the next graduating class. Often, departments and colleges collect follow-up data on what their students are doing a few years after graduation. Adult learners are usually seeking a promotion or a new career.

If you are new to the institution, your department colleagues are an excellent resource for providing a good snapshot of the students in the department. When learning about students from colleagues, keep in mind that different faculty members often have different perceptions of students. Therefore, it is typically a good idea to ask a few individuals for input. A final source of information, perhaps one of the best, is the students themselves. During the first week of classes, consider administering an anonymous survey regarding the characteristics of interest to you, or carve out a bit of time and have a discussion with students about how they see themselves as learners and what they prefer.

As you collect information about your students in order to become better positioned as a teacher, it is important to keep in mind that researchers, offices, and administrators talk about students in terms of averages (e.g., average GPAs, proportion of first-generation students, most prevalent ethnicities, number of National Merit Finalists). You don't teach averages, proportions, and numbers; you teach individuals. Knowing the composition of your students will help you create better learning opportunities for them. This is the starting point for teaching at its best and the start to creating inclusive classrooms.

In addition to knowing important characteristics of the student population in your course, so that you can better develop the best learning opportunity for them, another important consideration is how the human mind learns. Some ways of receiving and processing new knowledge are easier for people to attend to, grasp, and remember. Yet in spite of the fact that we are all responsible for encouraging human minds to learn, too few of us know how the human mind works.

HOW PEOPLE LEARN

Although each student is unique, there are well-researched principles about how people learn that apply to a wide variety of learners. That research is described throughout the book. Following is an introductory list of 15 robust findings about learning along with an example or two to illustrate how these principles can be applied in nearly any course.

1. People have an insatiable curiosity and are learning all the time. They absorb and remember untold billions of details about their language, the people around them, objects in their environment, and things they know how to do (Spence, 2001). Individuals find it much easier to learn what they regard as relevant to their lives (Ambrose et al., 2010; Bransford et al., 1999; Persellin & Daniels, 2014; Svinicki, 2004; Winne & Nesbit, 2010; Zakrajsek, 2022; expanded on in Chapter 19). Explain to your students the relevance of your material to their current and future careers, consumer decisions, civic lives, and personal lives as well as real-world problems. Use examples and analogies out of their lives and generational experiences. Also ask them how they can apply the material.

2. People learn by thinking about the meaning of the new knowledge and connecting it to what they already know and believe (Ambrose et al., 2010; Bransford et al., 1999; Tigner, 1999; Zull, 2002; expanded on in Chapters 17 and 20). Ask students to connect new knowledge to what they already know and believe either in class or in a brief writing assignment such as a self-regulated learning exercise (Chapter 19).

3. People learn more when they are motivated to do so by the inspiration and enthusiasm of their instructors or other people in their lives (Herrando & Constantinides, 2021; Hobson, 2002; expanded on in Chapters 7 and 9). Express your enthusiasm and passion for your material, your process of teaching, and your students.

4. People often learn more efficiently when they are actively engaged in an activity (Freeman et al., 2014; Hake, 1998; Jones-Wilson, 2005; Spence, 2001; Svinicki, 2004; Theobald et al., 2020). Group work generally increases engagement (Persellin & Daniels, 2014; expanded on in Chapters 10 and 16). Allow students to work in groups some of the time, especially on the most challenging tasks, but also inform them that learning is ultimately an inside job—that is, it requires them to focus their mind on the material and their progress in comprehending and recalling it (see Chapters 10 and 19).

5. People learn new material best when they actively monitor their learning, reflect on their performance, and make appropriate adjustments. This process is called *metacognition* or *self-regulated learning*. People are responsible for their learning; it is very challenging to *make* someone learn (Ambrose et al., 2010; Hattie, 2009; Nilson, 2013a; Winne & Nesbit, 2010; Zakrajsek, 2022; Zimmerman et al., 2011; expanded on in Chapter 19). Start your course with a pretest, which will also serve as (1) a diagnostic test to tell you what your students do and do not know; (2) the first half of a self-regulated learning activity, to be repeated at the end of the term; and (3) the baseline for measuring your students' learning at the end of the term (see Chapters 19 and 27). Teach your students how to learn your material, and build in self-regulated learning activities and assignments that make them observe, analyze, and assess how well they are learning (see Chapter 19).

6. People learn most easily when their cognitive load is minimized by reducing distractions and helping learners to chunk information

(Feldon, 2010; Sweller, 1988; Winne & Nesbit, 2010; expanded on in Chapter 19). Minimize cognitive load by (1) reducing extraneous load (information that doesn't contribute to students' understanding or problem-solving facility); (2) integrating explanatory text into visual materials; (3) scaffolding new material (e.g., modeling and providing explicit instructions, step-by-step procedures, and partially worked examples (Feldon, 2010; Kirschner et al., 2006; Mayer, 2009; Mayer & Moreno, 2003); and (4) helping students identify patterns and similarities and thereby *chunk* material into categories, concepts, and the like (Gobet et al., 2001). Minimize student distractions in class, the most tempting of which are technological (see Chapter 4).

7. People learn best when they receive the new material multiple times but in different ways, which uses different parts of their brain (Hattie, 2009; Kress et al., 2006; Vekiri, 2002; Winne & Nesbit, 2010; Zakrajsek, 2022; Zull, 2002; expanded on in Chapter 22). Give students the opportunities to read, hear, talk, write, see, draw, think, act, and feel new material into their system. In other words, involve as many senses and parts of the brain as possible in their learning. If, as is commonplace, students first read or listen to the material, have them take notes on it, discuss it, concept-map it, freewrite about it, solve problems with it, or take a quiz on it (see Chapter 22).

8. Reviewing learned material spaced over time facilitates learning better than does cramming in one long session (Brown et al., 2014; Butler et al., 2014; Cepeda et al., 2006; Dunlosky et al., 2013; Hattie, 2009; Rohrer & Pashler, 2010; Winne & Nesbit, 2010). This is called *spaced* or *distributive* practice (see principle 10). Build in activities and assignments that have students review and practice retrieving the same material at spaced intervals.

9. People learn better when newly learned information is *interleaved* with other information (Butler et al., 2014; Dunlosky et al., 2013; Rohrer & Pashler, 2010). Interleave this review-and-retrieval practice by having students work with old material as they are learning new material.

10. People strengthen their memories of newly learned information when they practice retrieving the information, such as self-quizzes (see principle 18) (Brown et al., 2014; Dunlosky et al., 2013; Karpicke & Blunt, 2011; Roediger & Karpicke, 2006; Rohrer & Pashler, 2010; Winne & Nesbit, 2010).

11. Learning is facilitated by targeted feedback to improve performance in more practice (Ambrose et al., 2010). Build into your course plenty of opportunities for feedback, including low-stakes quizzes, practice tests, in-class exercises, and homework assignments that can both tell students how much they are really learning and give them retrieval practice. Provide timely, targeted feedback that students can use to improve their performance (see Chapter 23).

12. People learn from making and correcting mistakes (Najafi et al., 2014). Persuade students that errors are memorable learning opportunities by sometimes giving them the chance to correct their errors (see Chapter 19).

13. People can remember newly learned information longer when they have to work harder to learn it—a research area called *desirable difficulties* (Bjork, 1994; Bjork & Bjork, 2011; Brown et al., 2014; McDaniel & Butler, 2010). Integrate *desirable difficulties* into your students' learning. These can help them generate multiple retrieval paths and stretch their abilities (Persellin & Daniels, 2014). Methods include having students recast text material into a graphic format such as a concept map; giving them frequent quizzes; varying the conditions and location of their practice opportunities; having them transfer new knowledge to new situations; assigning especially creative, inventive, and challenging tasks to small groups; and

holding your students to high standards (e.g., refusing to accept or grade work that shows little effort). However, be reasonable and don't use yourself as the standard. Very few students will learn your field as quickly as you did or choose the life of the mind as you have.

14. People learn better when the material evokes emotional involvement (Leamnson, 1999, 2000; Mangurian, 2005; Zull, 2002, 2011). Motivate and reinforce learning with emotions. Make a learning experience dramatic, humorous, surprising, joyous, maddening, exciting, or heart-wrenching. Integrate engaging problem-solving and experiential learning opportunities into your courses. Let students reflect, debate, consider multiple viewpoints, record their reactions to the material, and work in groups on gripping material.

15. People learn better when they have adequate sleep; exercise regularly; and feel they are in a safe, fairly stress-free environment (Zakrajsek, 2022; expanded on in Chapter 7). Be sure your students are aware of these biological imperatives to learning.

When even some of these research-based principles are employed in a course, students attend classes at a higher rate, are more engaged, and learn twice as much as students in a lecture-based course taught by a seasoned instructor (Deslauriers et al., 2011).

■ HOW STRUCTURE INCREASES LEARNING

Every field of study has a system of patterns that make up a structure. An essential aspect of being an expert is to identify and then use that structure to advance the field. Even not knowing your area of expertise, we do know it has structure. Without some kind of structure, there would be no way to organize newly learned information or even know which information to learn. As an example, stop reading for 30 seconds and look around the room where you are

working, taking in any sound you hear; everything you see; and what you feel, from sitting or from your hands on the desk. Take a moment to process your discoveries. Then, look around the room again, but this time imagine you are an interior designer. What new elements jump out at you? What if you looked as a carpenter, a custodian, or a thief? Each person processes the same space differently, according to a particular field's structure, which helps the viewer decide which information in the environment to attend to and how it fits together with other information. This is true for looking at a room and true for anyone learning in a given field. One of the largest, and arguably most critical, challenges in teaching is to help novices see the structure of your field as professionals do, in a way that makes sense professionally and personally, and ultimately helps them to organize future information for easy access and understanding.

With the proliferation of information on the internet, and the speed at which information is increasing, it is becoming very easy to find isolated bits of information. When we (the authors of this book) began teaching (which we admit was before the internet was available to the public), much of our job as faculty members was to teach students the information of our field. That is no longer necessary. Students are experts at finding "information." Students can find people's phone numbers, the capitals of countries, the years of historical events, directions from one place to another, an area's major industries, election results, and just about anything you mention in class. Suppose you and your 17-year-old child are sightseeing and walking through a historic district and begin to think about finding a place to eat. You stop in front of a restaurant, look in the window to see how busy they are, and then glance at the posted menu by the door. You turn to your teenager (who is looking at their phone) and say, "This place looks pretty good." Your child replies, "They have great reviews, and they have some specials that sound fantastic. They are a bit busy tonight, but I just got us a reservation for 30 minutes from now. They have a link to a statue in a park right around the corner that looks interesting. We could check it out and be back in 30 minutes." The amazing thing is that this is not an exaggeration. Tell your students this hypothetical and ask them if this seems realistic. However, finding and learning individual bits of information is not the same as acquiring knowledge.

Our challenge, as educators, is to facilitate the acquisition of knowledge in our fields, knowledge as a structured set of patterns that we have identified through careful observation, followed by reflection and abstraction—a grid that we have carefully superimposed on a messy world so we can make predictions and applications (Kuhn, 1970). Knowledge comprises useful concepts, agreed-on generalizations, well-grounded inferences, strongly backed theories, reasonable hypotheses, and well-tested principles and probabilities. Without knowledge, science and advanced technology wouldn't exist. With knowledge, there are no limits.

When students first begin to learn about a given area, they start to amass foundational information, struggling to identify what information is important and what is irrelevant. Be patient with them, as this is a necessary challenge before a structure is identified. From this perspective, memorization as a learning strategy makes sense. If our course instruction stops there, too many students leave the course viewing the material as disconnected facts and technical terms, no more meaningful, nor memorable than a set of websites full of information. The information they worked so hard to learn will be quickly forgotten.

One of our first tasks is to dispel misconceptions and faulty models students hold regarding the subject matter (Hansen, 2011; Svinicki, 2004). As novices, they are unable to identify central, core concepts and principles (Kozma et al., 1996), typically wandering through a body of information, picking up and memorizing what may or may not be important facts and terms, and using trial and error to solve problems and answer questions (Glaser, 1991). It would be challenging for anyone to figure out how to classify and approach problems at the conceptual level when all they see is a bunch of loosely related factoids (Arocha & Patel, 1995; DeJong & Ferguson-Hessler, 1996).

It is quite possible that your students have some accurate and foundational knowledge about the area being taught. This is good news, as learning is strongly dependent on preexisting knowledge. The brain is an amazing thing. When learning new material, you quickly look for elements that match some preexisting structure of information stored as a memory. If there is a close enough match, the new information is folded into the preexisting structure. This may happen in seconds, and without you even realizing it. If there is no similar preexisting structure (no prior relevant prior knowledge), students will struggle to comprehend and retain the new material (Bransford et al., 1999; Hanson, 2006; Svinicki, 2004; Wieman, 2007).

Another amazing thing about how humans process information is that we have the ability to extrapolate information to fill in the blanks in our understanding of phenomena. Some of these made-up connections stand up to scrutiny and testing and may be elevated to science. Charles Darwin, for example, did not observe mutations happening in nature; rather, he hypothesized their occurrence to fill in the explanatory blanks for species diversity. No one was around to watch the big bang, but the theory fills in quite a few missing links in cosmology. Astronomers have never directly observed dark matter (undetectable matter or particles that are hypothesized to account for unexpected gravitational effects on galaxies and stars), but they believe it makes up 30% of the universe. Not all imagined connections, however, stand the test of time or science. Superstitions and prejudice exemplify false patterns. Humans have been trying to influence natural phenomena for thousands of years, with any number of specialized behaviors. Many stereotypes about individuals in marginalized groups have been perpetuated based on a chance occurrence or willfully ignoring relevant information or context. This illustrates the importance of learning the proper way to use structures to create knowledge based on the systematic study of information, rather than randomly grasping at bits of information.

The kind of deep, meaningful learning that moves a student from novice toward expert is all about acquiring the discipline's hierarchical organization of patterns that make up its mental structure of knowledge (Chi et al., 1982; Royer et al.,1993). By their very nature, knowledge structures are hierarchical. The general terms, core concepts, and propositions serve as a foundation for knowledge that is conditional, specific, and derivative. Experts understand and exploit the complexity of this hierarchy.

Given the amount of time students are in our course or courses, it is highly unlikely we can help them to become experts in a year or two, or even four. So, what can you do? One very solid option is to make the organization of our knowledge explicit by providing our learners with an accurate, ready-made structure for making sense of our content and storing it. Following are some strategies you can adopt and adapt to help you help your students begin to learn the structures of your field. In so doing, you can begin to move students from being purely information-seekers to being individuals who better understand how information fits into a well-defined structure that will aid their learning and help them develop content knowledge:

- At the beginning of the term, ideally in the first week, surface their understanding of the material they are about to learn. This can be done with a background knowledge probe (Angelo & Cross, 1993). Ask questions that require students to retrieve, articulate, and organize what they already know (or think they know) about your course material. This will allow you to address misconceptions in a supportive way at the appropriate time, explain why their position is incorrect, and show them a mental model that is more plausible, useful, and convincing (Baume & Baume, 2008; Taylor & Kowalski, 2014).
- Give students the big picture as early in the course as possible. The clearest way to show this is in a graphic syllabus (see Chapter 5). Carry through by presenting your content as an integrated whole, that is, as a cohesive system of interpreting phenomena rather than an aggregate of small, discrete facts and terms. Keep referring back to how and where specific topics fit into that big picture.
- Help students to see an overall structure for the course material by providing the logical sequencing of your learning outcomes for them. A flowchart of the student learning process for a course is called an *outcomes map* (see Chapter 2).
- Help students see the difference between information and knowledge. The previous discussion of the topic, as well as the next section of this chapter, supplies some useful concepts and vocabulary for explaining the difference.
- Teach students the thinking structures that your discipline uses—for example, the scientific method, the diagnostic process, the rules of rhetoric, basic logic (the nature of fact, opinion, interpretation, and theory), and logical fallacies. Where applicable, acquaint them with the competing paradigms (metatheories) in your field, such as the rational versus the symbolic interpretive versus the postmodern perspectives in English literature, pluralism versus elitism in political science, functionalism versus conflict theory in sociology, and positivism (or empiricism) versus phenomenology in social science epistemology.
- Show your students some of the fundamental patterns in your discipline and teach students about chunking to help them become more proficient in managing the landslide of new material. These thinking processes will help them identify conceptual similarities, differences, and interrelationships while reducing the material to fewer, more manageable pieces (Hanson, 2006; Wieman, 2007).
- Visuals are powerful learning aids (Hanson, 2006; Wieman, 2007). Whenever possible, furnish students with graphic representations of theories, conceptual interrelationships, and knowledge schemata—concept maps, mind maps, diagrams,

flowcharts, comparison-and-contrast matrices, and the like. It is also helpful to have students develop graphic representations of material to clarify their understanding of the material.

THE COGNITIVE DEVELOPMENT OF UNDERGRADUATES

Many believe that education is primarily about content. It starts in early school years with the question after school, "What did you learn today?" Content is certainly important, but it is even more important to learn the processes necessary to think more deeply. Most students, even the brightest of students, often begin their studies with serious misconceptions about knowledge in general and the discipline specifically (Hansen, 2011). Dispelling these misconceptions is an important part for students to mature intellectually. As an instructor, you have the opportunity—some would say the responsibility—to lead them toward epistemological maturity.

Psychologist William G. Perry (1968, 1985) formulated a theory of the intellectual and ethical development in which college students progress through four major stages on their way to the apex of cognitive functioning. The four stages are subdivided into nine positions, but for this introduction we will stick to the four stages. Students begin college in the stage of dualistic perspective and may, depending on their instruction, advance through the stages of multiplicity, relativism, and commitment (definitions are given in what follows). The research supporting the model accumulated rapidly, making Perry's theory a leader in cognitive development of undergraduates.

Perry developed his theory using a sample of mostly male students, but some years later, researchers, notably Baxter Magolda (1992), focused on female students. Baxter Magolda identified four levels of knowing—absolute, transitional, independent, and contextual—roughly parallel to Perry's stages. One important difference is that the females in

Baxter Magolda's studies followed a more relational pattern, whereas the males in Perry's work were more abstract in their thinking. Table 1.1 displays both models.

Although Perry's framework of development applies across disciplines, a student's level of maturity may be more advanced in one discipline than another. For example, we shouldn't assume that a cognitively sophisticated senior in a physical science major has a comparable understanding of the nature of knowledge in the humanities. How far and how rapidly students progress through the hierarchy depends largely on the quality and type of instruction they receive. It is this flexible aspect of Perry's theory that has made it particularly attractive and useful. The schema suggests ways that we can accelerate undergraduates' intellectual growth although there is no guarantee that everyone will reach the top.

We begin with *dualism*, the lowest of the Perry's stages of cognitive development. Many first-year students enter our courses in this state. (Of course, there are people at all ages stuck in this stage.) Perry used the term *dualism* to describe students' thinking at this stage because they perceive issues in the world as fitting into one of two options: black or white, up or down, day or night. Dualism makes life simple. With only two options, there is little uncertainty. Learning, by this view, is simply accumulating the facts, as they look to be cleanly identified. Unfortunately, simplicity comes with a high cost. Much detail is lost when we cognitively put concepts into one of two boxes. To move students to a higher cognitive level, we teach them that although issues can be simplified by thinking of only the two extremes, the world is much more complex than that.

Students who advance in their learning leave dualism and enter the cognitive stage of *multiplicity*, where they realize there are conflicting opinions from others, and it is best to trust one's "inner voice." Students come to realize that the field they are studying rarely has definitive answers. Early in the stage of multiplicity individuals believe that

Table 1.1 Stages or Levels of Student Cognitive Development

Perry's Stages of Undergraduate Cognitive Development	Baxter Magolda's Levels of Knowing
1. *Duality*: Black-and-white thinking; authorities rule	Absolute knowing
⇩	
Uncertainty	
2. *Multiplicity*: Poor authorities or temporary state	Transitional knowing
⇩	
Uncertainty as legitimate, inherent	
3. *Relativism*: Learn to evaluate solutions	Independent knowing
⇩	
Standards of comparison	
4. *Commitment* (tentative): Best theory available	Contextual knowing

everyone has a right to an opinion. This is the stage where people might "agree to disagree" and move on. Some students believe that, for coursework, an instructor's exercise is simply designed to ultimately lead them to the one true answer. As students advance through multiplicity, they accept the notion that genuine uncertainty exists, but only as a temporary state that will resolve itself once an authority finds the answer.

With additional work, the next move is to the stage of *relativism*, where students make an about-face and abandon their faith in the authority's ability to identify the truth. Ambiguity becomes a fact of life, because humans develop the positions chosen and the facts identified as support, and humans can make mistakes. In brief, students become relativists with the realization that there may never be one true interpretation or answer. Cognitively, students see knowledge as relativistic and contextual, but with qualifications. They may reserve dualistic ideas of right and wrong as subordinate principles for special cases in specific contexts. Thus, even in a

relativistic world, they may permit certain instances where facts are truly facts and only one plausible truth exists.

The final stage of cognitive development is *commitment*. At this level students integrate the knowledge they have acquired with their personal experiences and reflection of the issues at hand, the knowledge acquired, and their lived experiences. Individuals in this stage are willing to change their position, if they acquire new information and have time to reflect on the known situation.

This provides a brief summary of Perry's states of cognitive development for undergraduates. As noted at the beginning of this section, students may be at the duality level in one discipline and at the commitment level in another. The same phenomenon can be seen in individuals of all ages. For example, a physician may commit to a specific set of values with respect to medical professionalism (commitment), and at the same time only fly Air Vermont because they strongly believe that other airlines fly unsafe planes (duality). Because individuals can be at different cognitive levels for different areas, it is important to not overgeneralize the cognitive functioning you see in one area to other areas. This is particularly true with respect to issues of diversity and equity. Students raised in families with minimal educational experiences and resources may have been exposed to dualistic thinking their entire life. As a result, in a discussion of political positions, this student may have a solid dualistic level of thinking. At the same time, they may be at the stage of relativism when it comes to the economy.

It is important to note that students do not typically move from one level to the next on their own. That is something for which they typically need a skilled facilitator. This is where you come into the picture. There are evidence-based ways to move students to higher levels of cognitive growth, as described in the next section.

■ ENCOURAGING COGNITIVE GROWTH

Nelson (2000), a leading authority on developing thinking skills, contends that we can facilitate students' progress through these stages by familiarizing them with the uncertainties and the standards of comparison in our disciplines. He and many others (e.g., Allen, 1981, in the sciences) have achieved excellent results by implementing his ideas. (Kloss, 1994, offers a somewhat different approach tailored to literature instructors.)

Exposure to uncertainties in our knowledge bases helps students realize that often there is no one superior truth nor can there be, given the nature of rational knowledge. Here they see that even experts in the field must search for answers. This realization helps lead them out of dualistic thinking and through multiplistic conceptions of knowledge. Once they can understand uncertainty as legitimate and inherent in the nature of knowledge, they can mature into relativists. Instructive examples of such uncertainties include the following: (1) the range of viable interpretations that can be made of certain

works of literature and art, (2) the different conclusions that can be legitimately drawn from the same historical evidence and scientific data, (3) a discipline's history of scientific revolutions and paradigm shifts, (4) unresolved issues on which a discipline is currently conducting research, and (5) historical and scientific unknowns that may or may not ever be resolved.

Our next step is to help students advance beyond relativism to making tentative commitments and progress toward cognitive maturity. To do so, students need to understand that among all the possible answers and interpretations, some may be more valid than others. They must also learn why some are better than others—that is, what criteria exist to discriminate among the options, to distinguish the wheat from the chaff. Disciplines vary on their criteria for evaluating validity. Each has its own metacognitive *model*—that is, a set of accepted conventions about what makes a sound argument and what constitutes appropriate evidence. Most students have trouble acquiring these conventions on their own; they tend to assume that the rules are invariable across fields. Nelson advises us to make our concepts of evidence and our standards for comparison explicit to our students.

By the time students are solidly in the stage of relativism, they are hungry for criteria on which to rank options and base choices, so they should be highly receptive to a discipline's evaluative framework. To encourage students to reach commitment, we can provide writing and discussion opportunities for them to deduce and examine what their initial commitments imply in other contexts. They may apply their currently preferred framework to a new or different ethical case, historical event, social phenomenon, political issue, scientific problem, or piece of literature. They may even apply it to a real situation in their own lives. Through this process, they begin to realize that a commitment focuses options, closing some doors while opening others.

We should remind students that they are always free to reassess their commitments, modify them, and even make new ones, but with an intellectual and ethical caveat: they should have sound reason to do so, such as new experience or data or a more logical organization of the evidence, not just personal convenience.

Bringing Perry's and Nelson's insights into our courses lays out a genuine challenge for us to consider. Students in any one class may be at different stages, even if they are in the same graduating class. Almost all first-year students fall in the first few positions, but juniors and seniors may be anywhere on the hierarchy. Students may also be at different stages for different parts of the course. It may be wisest, then, to help students at the lower positions catch up with those at the higher ones by explicitly addressing knowledge uncertainties and disciplinary criteria for selecting among perspectives and creating opportunities for students to make and justify choices in your courses.

Keep your students' cognitive growth in mind as you read this book. If you use the outcomes-centered approach to designing a course (see Chapter 2), you could select a certain level of cognitive maturity as a learning outcome for your students.

▇ TEACHING TODAY'S STUDENTS

It is absolutely essential to keep in mind that in each course you will have a wide variety of students. Sitting before you when the semester begins will be first-generation college students, National Merit Scholars, students on the autism spectrum, and students with vastly different lived experiences. You will have students struggling with depression, anxiety, home sickness, attention deficit disorder, cognitive impairment, and schizophrenia. There will be students who start working on a semester-long paper the day it is assigned and others who will start the day before it is due. Some students love working in groups and others will groan in disapproval if you utter the word "group." This is a lot, and the longer you teach, the more you will see. The good news is that there are tools and resources to help you. In

addition, if you work at being a good teacher, you will continue to get better at helping this wide variety of students.

The vast majority of your students will be in the Generation Z cohort (or Gen Z, iGen, or Zoomers). The birth dates being used to define this generation are 1995/1997–2012 (Dimock, 2019). Approximately 35% of Gen Zers know someone who identifies with gender-neutral pronouns (Parker et al., 2019), and using gender-neutral pronouns helps to establish a more inclusive classroom. Millennials were noted as being the most diverse generation ever, and Gen Z is even more diverse (Dimock, 2019). Members of Gen Z are considered the first true digital natives, in that they have not only had internet access their entire lives but also likely do not remember life before the smartphone (Parker & Igielnic, 2020). These students favor educational experiences that blend online and face-to-face teaching, working in groups and independently, and experiential learning (Schroth, 2019).

Gen Z students also lived through the COVID pandemic at an important time in their lives with respect to social development. This will likely have an impact on their social interactions at school and how they view the world. At the writing of this book, it is too early to determine the extent of the impact the pandemic had on Gen Z students' learning, but it is reasonable to assume there will be a lasting impact.

The reason we point out the importance of considering the diversity in your course is that students struggle with many different issues. For example, average graduation rates at 4-year institutions are 74% for Asian students, 64% for White students, 40% for Black students, and 39% for American Indian/Alaska Native Students (National Center for Education Statistics, 2019). Similarly, only 56% of first-generation college students complete a baccalaureate degree, compared to 74% of those students who had a parent go to college (Ives & Castillo-Montoya, 2020). Mental health is another increasingly disconcerting issue for Gen Z students, particularly among some subgroups. For example, 86% of LGBTQIA+ students report experiencing anxiety, 84% suffer from depression, and 75% express concerns about coming out to family (Carrasco, 2021).

Given the struggle many of our students face, particularly in groups that have not been well represented in colleges in the past, it is helpful to keep in mind a quote attributed to Ian McLaren, "Be kind; everyone you meet is fighting a hard battle" (Quote Investigator, n.d.). This does not mean you should have lax standards or allow students to do halfhearted work. The point is that it is important to do your best to create a community, give students an opportunity to work with one another, create a way for students to give you feedback, and make sure your standards are clear. Helping such a diverse group of learners is a challenge, but when you are successful it is an important example of teaching at its best.

MEETING THE CHALLENGE

Being an effective teacher takes a great deal of work. Higher education, as any professional field, is changing all the time. That said, learning was not a strong focus in higher education until the mid-1990s, but then a strong shift began with the publications of Barr & Tagg's (1995) *From Teaching to Learning: A New Paradigm for Undergraduate Education* and Boyer's (1997) book, *Scholarship Reconsidered*, in which he proposed the entire scholarship of teaching and learning (SoTL). As a result, there was an increase in the number of higher education institutions with teaching and learning centers, higher faculty standards for teaching effectiveness, and an explosion of research on how students learn and respond to different instructor behaviors, teaching methods, and instructional settings. Faculty began to receive more credit for doing work on instructional strategies and books, such as the first edition of *Teaching at Its Best*, became important resources.

This book, *Teaching at Its Best* (5th edition), draws on and integrates much of the research on teaching and learning into a practical reference

on the most effective approaches to use for different types of learning outcomes, providing opportunities for faculty members to develop a wider variety of teaching strategies, and a better understanding of how students learn. Overall, this book is designed to help you to be a better teacher. In so doing, you will help even more students to be successful in their studies. The more students we can reach, the fewer students are left behind or fail to reach their potential. Learning new teaching strategies and finding teaching resources is sometimes referred to as "building your teaching toolbox." As you build out your toolbox, you will be moving ever closer to teaching at your best.

REFLECTION QUESTIONS

Reflection Question 1.1: Who will your students likely be next semester? What do you know about the composition of students who are likely to be in your next course (e.g., first-generation, full- or part-time workers, caregivers, cultural backgrounds, etc.)? How can you use this knowledge of other commitments and priorities to meet your students where they are in structuring your course?

Reflection Question 1.2: In the section "How Structure Increases Learning," we discuss systems of patterns that make up any field. These structures may share similarities, but there are also certainly unique aspects. Reflect on your field of expertise and the structures that exist. If you cannot think of any, ask colleagues in your same field if they have ever noticed any specific structure to the discipline, perhaps in reading scholarly articles or textbooks.

Concept Into Practice: In the section "How People Learn," there is a list of 15 findings about how human learning works. Select one from an area you had not thought about previously with respect to teaching. It is important that this is something new for you. After you have selected one, set a timer for 30 minutes. In that time, learn as much as you are able about the topic selected. Reflect on how learning something outside your discipline felt and also how quickly you can learn something new about teaching. As instructors, most of us rarely pursue academics outside our own field, and it's easy to forget how our students feel. Finish by outlining how you will begin to implement the strategy that you selected and learned a bit more about.

CHAPTER 2

Designing Outcomes-Centered Courses

The most important thing about teaching is the extent to which students learn. If students are not learning, where is the value of what we do? Angelo and Cross (1993) noted that "there is no such thing as effective teaching in the absence of learning. Teaching without learning is just talking" (p. 3). Classrooms with ineffective teaching cause students to lose time, money, potential gains in knowledge and cognitive development, and perhaps confidence in themselves or even in the educational system. Less obviously, instructors become frustrated and think poorly of their students when those ineffective instructors inappropriately believe that lack of learning is due to a lack of student motivation. These same instructors may also lose faith in themselves and question their ability as educators, not realizing that anyone can improve their teaching if they work at it. For our mental health, our motivation, student motivation, and positive student learning outcomes, we need a clear idea about what is expected during the educational process and the extent to which students are achieving those outcomes.

Too many faculty members are never shown how to approach course design from a learning perspective. Before 1990, courses focused on teaching and were typically described in terms of content, such as "a comprehensive survey of vertebrate animals including their taxonomy, morphology, evolution, and defining facets of their natural history and behavior" or "an introduction to the process of literary criticism." Course catalogues and many syllabi still contain such descriptions, although an increasing number are including learning outcome statements and therefore have a focus on what students will get out of a course, rather than what will be taught in the course. Another common approach years ago was to organize a course around the course textbook. However, when designing a course based on a textbook, different sections of the same course can look radically difficult when each instructor selects their own text. Another challenge with designing a course on the text is that selecting a new textbook means rethinking all the outcomes. Ultimately, a course designed around course catalog descriptions, syllabi, and textbooks is not focused on students and what they will learn. Focusing on student learning outcomes engages students in the learning process, which we know significantly increases learning.

Because higher education historically anchored on the process of teaching, even now, when the conversation moves to learning, the focus is too often on instruction rather than design. Without a clear understanding of how to put a course together, faculty members think in terms of what they, as faculty, will do, rather than what students will learn. It makes sense that we as faculty members focus on what we are doing, because we want to do it well for our students. But to focus on teaching is misguided, regardless of how much one cares about the students in the class. "To say the purpose of education is to provide instruction is like saying that General Motors' purpose is to operate assembly lines" (Barr & Tagg, 1995, p. 12). At the end of the day, what we really care about is how much our students learn.

To establish a course where you *know* you have maximized learning, teaching at its best starts with designing your courses wisely. The start of course design is the same in every field of study, whether you are teaching an established course for the first time, developing a brand-new course, or revising a course you currently teach. Ask yourself what you desire for your students to know, realize, or be able to do at the end of the course to demonstrate their learning. Learning is a bit like the wind; we can't see it, but we infer that it is there because of the impact it has on things around it. Students may demonstrate learning by writing, discussing, acting, creating a graphic or visual work, conducting an experiment or demonstration, making an oral presentation, designing a website, teaching a lesson, or baking a cake. Whatever the display of learning, you have to be able to perceive it through your senses to appraise the quality of the performance. How else can you determine students' internal state— what they know, realize, or are able to do? This is done through outcomes-centered course design. In the next section, we will explain why we recommend that you use an outcomes-centered course design approach.

WHY OUTCOMES-CENTERED COURSE DESIGN?

As stated in the previous section, we always start the design process by asking ourselves what we want our students to know, realize, or be able to do at the end of the course as a result of our teaching. Because looking at what students have learned comes at the end, we think of this kind of design as starting with the end in mind. This approach echoes Wiggins and McTighe's (2005) backward design strategy, which recommends starting the course design process by articulating what learning you desire your students to know or be able to do at the end of the lecture, unit, or course. Backward design is one of the most popular approaches to course design and the one we typically recommend that faculty members use.

In addition to being beneficial for students, outcomes-centered course design is also a wise choice because it satisfies the accountability requirements of an increasing number of accrediting agencies. These agencies hold institutions and programs accountable for ensuring that students achieve certain learning outcomes, as well as formally assessing students' progress toward that goal. In other words, the agencies require departments and schools to determine what they want their students to be able to do by the time the students graduate and then to produce materials that show the students can do those desired outcomes. Some agencies even take it on themselves to provide the outcomes, demonstrating exactly what abilities and skills the graduates of a certain area should be able to demonstrate. For example, researchers in engineering programs are actively investigating new ways for engineering programs to collect the required outcome data (Hussain et al., 2021).

This chapter focuses primarily on formulating student learning outcomes because outcomes provide the foundation for proper course development, which includes selecting teaching methods and engagement strategies (i.e., brief strategies for clarifying content and giving students practice in thinking about and working with it) that will help students achieve those outcomes (see Chapter 13) and assessment instruments that will measure students' success in performing those outcomes (see Chapters 25 and 26).

■ WRITING OUTCOMES

A learning outcome is a statement of exactly what your students should be able to do after completing your course or at specified points during the course. Some faculty members also set outcomes for individual classes and units of the course. Outcomes are written from a student's point of view—for example, "After studying the processes of photosynthesis and respiration, the student should be able to trace the carbon cycle in a given ecosystem."

Of course, outcomes are promises, and you should make it clear that students have to do their part to make these promises come true. So you might state verbally and in your syllabus something like this: "You will be learning a variety of information, theories, and strategies throughout this course. You can expect to achieve a level of competency for each only if you adhere to course policies, attend classes regularly, complete all assigned work in good faith and on time, and meet all other course expectations of you as a student."

Before you start composing outcomes, find out from your dean or department chair whether an accrediting agency or the program has already mandated outcomes for your course or program. For instance, the National Council for the Accreditation of Teacher Education lists the required outcomes for many education courses. The Accreditation Board for Engineering and Technology provides program outcomes, some of which may be useful and even essential for your course. Some departments engage in *curriculum mapping*, which means listing all courses offered in the department and noting which department-level outcomes are addressed in each course. This makes sure all department-level outcomes are addressed to the extent desired.

If you are free to develop your own outcomes, the first step may be to research the history of the course. Why was it proposed and approved in the first place, and by whom? What special purposes does it serve? What other courses should it prepare students to take? Often new courses emerge to meet the needs of a changing labor market, update curriculum content, ensure accreditation, or give an institution a competitive edge. Knowing the underlying influences can help you orient a course to its intended purposes for student learning (Prégent, 1994).

Second, get to know who your students are so you can aim your course to their needs and level. Refer to the first part of Chapter 1 for the type of student data you will need—all of which should be available from your institution's admissions office, student affairs office, and career center—to find out the academic background, interests, and course expectations of your likely student population. Ask colleagues who have taught the course before what topics, books, teaching methods, activities, and assignments worked and didn't work well for them. The more relevant you can make the material to the target group, the more effective your course will be.

If you cannot gather much information in advance, keep your initial learning outcomes and course design somewhat flexible. On the first day of class, use index cards and icebreakers to learn more about your students and their expectations (see Chapter 7); then adjust the design accordingly.

Technically an outcome has three parts to it, though usually only the first part appears in the outcomes section of a syllabus. Sooner or later, however, you will have to decide the second and third parts as well:

Part 1. A statement of a measurable performance. Learning outcomes center on action verbs (e.g., *define, classify, construct, compute*; see Table 2.1) rather than nebulous verbs reflecting internal states that cannot be observed (such as *know, learn, understand, realize, appreciate*). For example, it would be inappropriate to list:

"At the conclusion of the unit on rocks, students will **understand** the differences between igneous, sedimentary, and metamorphic rocks."

"Understand" is not something you can observe directly. The mistake is corrected in the following example: "At the conclusion of the unit on rocks, students will be able to **list** the differences between igneous, sedimentary and metamorphic rocks." In this second example you can directly observe whether students are able to list the differences or not and from that behavior you can infer that they understand the differences.

Part 2. A statement of conditions for the performance. These conditions define the circumstances under which the students' performance will be assessed. Will they have to list the differences between metamorphic and sedimentary rocks in writing, in an oral presentation, or in a visual medium (drawings, photographs)?

Part 3. Criteria and standards for assessing the performance. By what criteria and standards will you evaluate and ultimately grade a student's performance? What will constitute achieving an outcome at a high level (A work) versus a minimally competent level (C work)? For example: "For an A on essay 3, the student will be able to identify in writing at least three differences between igneous and metamorphic rocks, at least three between igneous and sedimentary rocks, and at least three between metamorphic and sedimentary—for a total of at least nine differences. For a B, the student will be able to identify at least six differences. For a C, the student will be able to identify at least four differences," and so on. Rubrics have such criteria and standards built into them.

When writing outcome statements, it is important to include certain commonly accepted aspects. Your statements of measurable performance should be: specific, measurable, achievable, relevant, and timely. These aspects form the acronym SMART. SMART outcomes have been used extensively for nearly two decades and across all disciplines (Hurt, 2007; Winget & Persky, 2022). When you write an outcome it is important that the outcome pertains to only one area of knowledge, behavior, or activity. If there is more than one, it becomes impossible to separate out the behaviors and decide whether the outcome was fully met, partially met, or some other variation. If you have more than one area of knowledge, behavior, or activity, then write more than one outcome statement. Let's put parts 1, 2, and 3 together to see if we have included all the SMART elements: "At the conclusion of the unit on rocks, students will be able to list the differences between igneous, sedimentary, and metamorphic rocks on the essay portion of a quiz." There are also criteria listed in Part 3 for grades of A, B, and C. This outcome does appear to contain all of the SMART elements:

- *Specific:* Listing differences between three types of rocks is specific.
- *Measurable:* Grading quizzes is a measurable metric.
- *Achievable:* Although the level of students is not noted, it seems reasonable that students are able to achieve this goal.
- *Relevant:* Although the curriculum is not noted, it seems reasonable that knowing the difference between the rocks is relevant to the course and to the unit on rocks.
- *Timely:* It is stated that this outcome will be achieved at the end of the rock unit.

After you have written a few outcomes, you will find them relatively easy to construct. Once you become proficient at writing outcome statements you will be able to quickly write outcomes for essentially every aspect of the course and invaluable for showing that students are learning what you set out for them to learn.

■ TYPES OF OUTCOMES

Virtually every college-level course has *cognitive* outcomes, those pertaining to thinking. However, other types of outcomes may be pertinent to your courses. For example, *psychomotor* skills—the ability to manipulate specific objects correctly and efficiently to accomplish a given purpose—are important in art, architecture, drama, linguistics, some engineering fields, all laboratory sciences, nursing and other health-related fields, and foreign languages. Exhibit 2.1 provides examples of five types of outcomes.

In designing your course, you may decide that you would like a set of different types of outcomes. There are models in place to assist you with such a task. The two primary examples are Fink (2013) and Wiggins and McTighe (2005).

Fink (2013) integrates cognitive, affective, and social outcomes in his model of six *categories of learning*, which are cumulative and interactive. Fink posits that all six of the following categories are essential to create a significant learning experience for our students:

1. *Foundational knowledge.* Students recall and demonstrate understanding of ideas and information, providing the basis for other kinds of learning.
2. *Application.* Students engage in any combination of critical, practical, and creative thinking; acquire key skills; and learn how to manage complex projects, making other kinds of learning useful.
3. *Integration.* Students perceive connections among ideas, disciplines, people, and realms of their lives.
4. *Human dimension.* Students gain a new understanding of themselves or others, often by seeing the human implications of other kinds of learning.
5. *Caring.* Students acquire new interests, feelings, or values about what they are learning, as well as the motivation to learn more about it.
6. *Learning how to learn.* Students learn about the process of their particular learning and learning in general, enabling them to pursue learning more self-consciously, efficiently, and effectively.

Wiggins and McTighe (2005) propose six *facets of understanding* that, like Fink's categories, also blend cognitive, affective, and social outcomes. Although

---

Exhibit 2.1 General Types of Learning Outcomes

Psychomotor—Physical performance; may involve eye-hand coordination. *Examples*: medical/nursing procedures; laboratory techniques; animal handling or grooming; assembling, operating, testing, or repairing machines or vehicles; singing; dancing; playing musical instruments; use of voice, face, and body in public speaking.

Affective—Demonstration of appropriate emotions and affect. *Examples*: demonstrating good bedside manner and empathy with patients; showing trustworthiness and concern for clients, customers, subordinates, or students; showing tolerance for differences; showing dynamism, relaxed confidence, conviction, and audience responsiveness in public speaking.

Social—Appropriate, productive interaction and behavior with other people. *Examples*: cooperation and respect within a team; leadership when needed; assertive (not aggressive, passive, or passive-aggressive) behavior in dealing with conflict; negotiation and mediation skills.

Ethical—Decision-making that takes into account the moral implications and repercussions (effects on other people, animals, environment) of each reasonable option. *Examples*: medical and nursing decisions involving triage, transplants, withholding care, and prolonging life; lawyers' decisions about whether and how to represent a client; managerial decisions involving social, economic, political, or legal trade-offs.

Cognitive—Thinking about facts, terms, concepts, principles, ideas, relationships, patterns, and conclusions. *Examples*: knowledge and remembering; comprehension and translation; application, analysis, synthesis, and creating; evaluation.

used primarily in elementary and secondary education, their framework transfers smoothly to the college level:

1. *Explanation.* The ability to connect ideas, events, and actions to concepts, principles, and generalizations; comparable to *integration* in Fink's framework and *comprehension/understanding* in Bloom's and Anderson and Krathwohl's schema described in the next section.
2. *Interpretation.* The ability to discern the importance or value of the subject matter; comparable to *caring* in Fink's framework.
3. *Application.* The ability to use and adapt knowledge to complex contexts (situations, problems, and the like); contains elements of *application* in Fink's framework and is comparable to *application/applying* in Bloom's and Anderson and Krathwohl's schema.
4. *Perspective taking.* The ability and the willingness to shift perspectives and view an issue or experience critically from multiple points of view; contains elements of the *human dimension* in Fink's framework.
5. *Empathy.* The ability to find value and meaning in the ideas and behavior of others, no matter how alien or puzzling; contains elements of the *human dimension* in Fink's framework.
6. *Self-knowledge.* The ability to self-regulate, practice metacognition, and evaluate one's weaknesses and limitations; similar to *learning how to learn* in Fink's framework.

The "Helpful Frameworks for Designing a Course" section later in this chapter examines how an instructor can create learning experiences that interrelate all of these categories synergistically. For the time being, we will focus on cognitive outcomes, as they are universal in higher education courses.

■ TYPES OF COGNITIVE OUTCOMES

Bloom (1956) developed a useful taxonomy for constructing cognitive outcomes. His framework posits a hierarchy of six cognitive processes, moving from the most concrete, foundational-level process of recalling stored knowledge through several intermediate cognitive modes to the most abstract, highest level of evaluation. (Depending on your field, you may prefer to make application the highest level.) The full set of levels is comprised of:

1. *Knowledge.* The ability to remember and reproduce previously learned material
2. *Comprehension.* The ability to grasp the meaning of material and to restate it in one's own words
3. *Application.* The ability to use learned material in new and concrete situations
4. *Analysis.* The ability to break down material into its component parts so as to understand its organizational structure
5. *Synthesis.* The ability to put pieces of material together to form a new whole
6. *Evaluation.* The ability to judge the value of material for a given purpose

This handy taxonomy continues to be very popular in higher education to this day, but Anderson and Krathwohl (2000) offer a few friendly amendments to it in their newer model. They use more action-oriented gerunds, update the meaning of *knowledge* and *synthesis*, and rank *creating* above *evaluating*:

Remembering	=	Knowledge (lowest)
Understanding	=	Comprehension
Applying	=	Application
Analyzing	=	Analysis
Evaluating	=	Evaluation
Creating	=	Synthesis (highest)

All of these conceptual terms become more concrete in Table 2.1, which lists common student performance verbs for each of Bloom's and Anderson and Krathwohl's cognitive operations. Note that some words (e.g., arrange) may be used at more than one level. This is because the verb may be used in more than one way. For Knowledge/Remembering, "arrange" may mean to put words into categories exactly as they were presented.

Table 2.1   Student Performance Verbs by Level of Cognitive Operation in Bloom's Taxonomy and Anderson and Krathwohl's Taxonomy

1. Knowledge/Remembering		2. Comprehension/Understanding	
Arrange	Omit	Arrange	Paraphrase
Choose	Order	Associate	Outline
Define	Recall	Clarify	Recognize
Duplicate	Recite	Describe	Rephrase
Find	Recognize	Explain	Report
Identify	Relate	Express	Restate
Label	Repeat	Grasp	Review
List	Reproduce	Identify	Select
Match	Select	Indicate	Summarize
Memorize	Spell	Interpret	Translate
Name	Tell	Locate	Visualize

3. Application/Applying		4. Analysis/Analyzing	
Apply	Illustrate	Analyze	Distill
Break down	Interpret	Calculate	Distinguish
Calculate	Make use of	Categorize	Divide
Choose	Manipulate	Classify	Examine
Compute	Operate	Compare	Experiment
Demonstrate	Practice	Contrast	Identify assumptions
Determine	Schedule	Criticize	Induce
Dramatize	Sketch	Deduce	Inspect
Employ	Solve	Derive	Investigate
Give examples	Use	Differentiate	Model
	Utilize	Discriminate	Probe
		Discuss	Question
		Dissect	Simplify
			Test

5/6. Synthesis/Creating		6/5. Evaluation/Evaluating	
Adapt	Imagine	Agree	Dispute
Arrange	Infer	Appraise	Evaluate
Assemble	Integrate	Argue	Judge
Build	Invent	Assess	Justify

(*continued*)

Table 2.1   (Continued)

5/6. Synthesis/Creating		6/5. Evaluation/Evaluating	
Change	Make up	Award	Prioritize
Collect	Manage	Challenge	Persuade
Compose	Modify	Choose	Rank
Conclude	Originate	Conclude	Rate
Construct	Organize	Convince	Recommend
Create	Plan	Criticize	Rule on
Design	Posit	Critique	Score
Develop	Predict	Debate	Select
Discover	Prepare	Decide	Support
Estimate	Produce	Defend	Validate
Extend	Propose	Discount	Value
Formulate	Set up	Discredit	Verify
Forward	Suppose	Disprove	Weight
Generalize	Theorize		

Note: Depending on the use, some verbs may apply to more than one level.

For the level of Comprehension/Understanding, "arrange" may mean to look at concepts and determine how they might be arranged. If this collection fails to meet your needs, Adelman (2015) provides 20 sets of verbs classified by purpose, such as certifying information and materials, performing executive functions, communicating in different ways, and rethinking and reconstructing. Once you select the cognitive operations that you'd like to emphasize in a course, you may find it helpful to refer to this listing while writing your outcomes. Another good reference is Table 2.2, which gives examples of outcomes at each cognitive level in various disciplines.

Bear in mind that the true cognitive level of an outcome depends on the material students are given in a course. If they are handed a formal definition of *iambic pentameter*, then their defining it is a simple recall or comprehension operation. If, however, they are provided only with examples of poems and plays written in iambic pentameter and are asked to abstract a definition from the examples,

they are engaging in the much higher order process of synthesis.

As you check key verbs and draft outcome statements, think about what cognitive operations you are emphasizing. For students to get started in any field, they first must have a firm grasp of cognitive outcomes found on the knowledge/remembering and comprehension/understanding levels. Once students have a foundation, they can proceed to higher levels. For most students, that is when things get interesting. Even introductory courses can engage students in application, analysis, synthesis, and evaluation. One misconception of Bloom's taxonomy is that once a student is at the top, they have reached some kind of conclusion. Instead, it's really just another launching point. After a foundation is built and the student begins to engage in the critical thinking that occurs near the top of the pyramid, new, more complex concepts will appear. That requires building a new foundation for more complex ways to analyze, synthesize, and create.

Table 2.2   Examples of Outcomes Based on Bloom's Taxonomy and Anderson and Krathwohl's Taxonomy

Level	The Student Should Be Able to . . .
Knowledge/Remembering	• Define iambic pentameter. • State Newton's laws of motion. • Identify the major surrealist painters.
Comprehension/ Understanding	• Describe the trends in the graph in one's own words. • Summarize a passage from Socrates' *Apology*. • Properly translate into English passages from Voltaire's *Candide*.
Application/Applying	• Describe an experiment that would test the influence of light and light quality on the Hill reaction of photosynthesis. • Scan a poem for metric foot and rhyme scheme. • Use the Archimedes principle to determine the volume of an irregularly shaped object.
Analysis/Analyzing	• List arguments for and against human cloning. • Determine the variables to be controlled in an experiment. • Discuss the rationale and efficacy of isolationism in the global economy.
Synthesis/Creating	• Write a short story in Hemingway's style. • Compose a logical argument on assisted suicide in opposition to one's personal opinion. • Construct a helium-neon laser.
Evaluation/Evaluating	• Assess the validity of certain conclusions based on the data and statistical analysis. • Critically analyze a novel with evidence to support a critique. • Recommend a portfolio of 20 stock investments based on recent performance and projected value.

Think of the pyramids that represent Bloom's taxonomy stacked one on top of the other. In doing this, it becomes clear there is no limit to what may be accomplished.

Therefore, whatever your course, it is wise to include some higher-order outcomes and increasingly complex terminology to challenge students to higher levels of thinking. Once you draft your outcomes, evaluate them by the rubric shown in Figure 2.1.

■ SEQUENCING OUTCOMES INTO A LEARNING PROCESS

As you design your course, it is important to sequence the learning outcomes, because some outcomes have to precede others. There are concepts students must learn early in the semester so

that more complex tasks can be tackled later in the semester. For instance, if you want your students to be able to develop a research proposal near the end of the course, they will have to be able to do several other things beforehand:

• Frame a research problem or hypothesis.
• Justify its significance.
• Conduct and write up an adequate literature review.
• Devise an appropriate research design.
• Describe the data collection procedures.
• Outline the steps of the analysis (which is premised on some methodological expertise).
• Explain the importance of the expected results.
• Develop a mock budget.

If your course or any prerequisite courses do not include successful completion of foundational

Figure 2.1   Rubric for Evaluating and Revising Student Learning Outcomes

Dimension	Excellent	Common Errors	Needs Revision	Missed the Point
Outcomes are observable, assessable, and measurable.	All of the outcomes are assessable and measurable. Instructor can observe (usually see or hear) and evaluate each learner's performance by clear standards, such as how well, how many, or to what degree.	Some outcomes use verbs that refer to a learner's internal state of mind, such as "know," "understand," or "appreciate," which an instructor cannot observe and assess. Or some outcomes are too general to specify standards for evaluation.	Outcomes fail to describe (1) observable performances that are assessable and measurable and/or (2) what the learners will be able to *do*.	Outcomes list the topics the course will cover or what the instructor will do. Or outcomes use verbs that refer a learner's internal state, which an instructor cannot observe and assess.
Outcomes require high levels of cognition.	Most of the outcomes reflect high levels of cognition – that is, application, analysis, synthesis, or evaluation.	All or almost all the outcomes require low levels of cognition (knowledge and comprehension), such as "recognize," "identify," "define," or "describe."	Not enough outcomes address higher levels of cognition, given the level of the course and the learners.	Outcomes use verbs that describe a low-level r's low-level internal state, such as "know," "understand," or "appreciate."
Outcomes are achievable.	Outcomes are realistic for the course length and credit hours and the level of the learners.	Outcomes are too numerous for the instructor to assess or the learners to achieve.	Outcomes are too advanced for course length/credit hours and/or the learners.	Outcomes don't use action verbs to describe what the learners will be able to *do*.
Outcomes are relevant and meaningful to the learners.	Instructor makes the outcomes relevant and meaningful to the learners and their personal or career goals.	Not all the outcomes and their benefits are relevant and meaningful to the learners and their personal or career goals.	The learners can't make sense out of the outcomes.	Outcomes don't indicate what the learners will be able to *do*.

information or actions, as measured by outcomes, your students will be ill-equipped to write a decent research proposal.

From this perspective, a course is a learning process of advancing through a logical succession of outcomes. This sequencing of outcomes serves as scaffolding for an entire course design and provides increasing levels of complexity.

Ultimate Outcomes

The easiest way to develop this logical succession of student learning outcomes is to formulate your end-of-term, or *ultimate*, outcomes first. These are likely to be the most challenging skills and cognitively advanced learning. No doubt they require high levels of thinking (application, analysis, synthesis, or evaluation) and a combination of skills and abilities that students should have acquired earlier in the course. They probably relate to your discipline's big ideas and enduring understandings (Hansen, 2011). They may even constitute the whole goal of the course. Assessment often takes the form of a major capstone assignment or a comprehensive final, or both.

Mediating Outcomes

From here you work backward, determining what your students will have to be able to do before they can achieve your ultimate outcomes. These abilities are your *mediating* outcomes, and you will probably have quite a few of them, each representing a component or lower-level version of one of your ultimate outcomes. You might want to visualize the working-backward process by picturing a small cluster of trees. Each trunk of a tree represents an *ultimate* learning outcome. The branches from the trunk represent your mediating outcomes, which your students must achieve before attempting the more advanced outcomes, the trunk itself.

Your challenge now is to figure out the most logical and efficient order in which students should acquire these mediating abilities. These outcomes may have a logical internal order of their own. The skill-building logic is probably clearest in cumulative subjects such as mathematics, physics, and engineering. However, many courses, especially those within a loosely organized curriculum, allow instructors a lot of discretionary room in sequencing the mediating outcomes. Textbooks may follow a certain order, but the topical sequencing may be largely arbitrary. In introductory survey courses, literature courses, and even certain science and health science courses, the topics students study and the skills they acquire can be logically organized in different ways. Assessment of mediating outcomes often takes the form of a unit exam, papers comparing and contrasting systems, or a small group project.

Foundational Outcomes

Once you work your way back to the earliest stages of your course, you will reach your *foundational* learning outcomes: those on which the learning process of the course is predicated. These are the leaves on our imaginary grove of trees, and throughout the course there will be many of these outcomes. These will involve one or more of the following:

- Your students will master the most basic skills or the first in a sequence of procedures. At the cognitive level, this means being able to recall and paraphrase elemental facts, principles, processes, and definitions of essential terms and concepts.
- They will identify, question, and abandon the misconceptions about the subject matter that they brought into the course.
- They will identify, question, and abandon their dualistic thinking about the subject matter (a particularly prevalent epistemological misconception) as they come to recognize uncertainties in the field.

These are often the most important learning outcomes we can set for students to successfully accomplish. After all, they can't apply, analyze, synthesize, or evaluate a discipline's knowledge if they cannot speak or write the discipline's language and summarize or paraphrase its basic ideas. If a student is lost in the second week when studying foundational material, the student needs immediate attention or they won't make it through the course. If you organize a course into modules of knowledge that have different sets of basic facts, terms, concepts, or theories, you will probably have foundational outcomes at the start of each module.

Moreover, students cannot accurately map new, valid knowledge onto existing knowledge that is riddled with misconceptions and misinformation. A faulty model will not accommodate the new material you intend for them, and they will not be able to assimilate it, at least not at more than a surface level. One unfortunate byproduct of misinformation and faulty frameworks is dualistic thinking (discussed in Chapter 1). Dualism is an important misconception we should work to discredit before escorting students deeper into our subject matter.

To bring about a major shift in your students' worldview, you must create learning situations that reveal the errors in their mental models and the explanatory superiority of your discipline's model.

To begin to internalize *any* body of knowledge, students must acquire an understanding of what knowledge actually is and isn't. As explained in Chapter 1, knowledge is simply a mental grid that we human beings have created and imposed over a more complex reality to try to understand and manipulate it.

Leveling outcomes (ensuring that outcomes are appropriate for the learner's increasingly advanced grasp of the material, culminating in mastery) is not easy. Do your best to lay out a few ultimate outcomes, with three to four mediating outcomes to support each ultimate outcome. There will also be three to four foundational outcomes to support each mediating outcome.

■ FRAMEWORKS FOR COURSE DESIGN

The following four frameworks are very well established in higher education. They offer suggestions, alone and in combination, for designing courses. You may find one or more of them useful as heuristic devices or even parts of a framework that will stimulate some new ideas for your courses.

Bloom's and Anderson and Krathwohl's Framework

Both Bloom's (1956) and Anderson and Krathwohl's (2000) taxonomies of cognitive operations are hierarchical, from lower order to higher order. They posit that to be able to perform a given level of thinking, learners must be able to perform all the lower-level thinking operations. By extension, a well-designed course should sequence the learning outcomes to lead students up the hierarchy. For most courses the highest levels will be ultimate outcomes, the middle will be mediating outcomes, and the first two levels will be foundational outcomes. This does not mean that foundational outcomes are limited to the beginning of the semester. Any time new foundational material is introduced, it would be appropriate to have a foundational outcome at that time.

It is self-evident that a student has to be able to define certain concepts, state certain principles, and recall certain facts before thinking about them in a more complex way. One point of contention regarding these two hierarchies is the placement of applying/application. Applying should be the top level, not in the middle. The practices of medicine, law, and other professions are all about *applying* knowledge to new, often complicated situations. But before applying knowledge, professionals have to *analyze* the elements of the problematic situation, *evaluate* what knowledge and disciplinary algorithms are most useful and relevant to the situation, and *synthesize* (or *create*) a problem-solving strategy—for example, a legal approach or a medical diagnosis and treatment plan.

Perry's and Baxter Magolda's Framework

The section "The Cognitive Development of Undergraduates" in Chapter 1 summarizes both Perry's (1968) and Baxter Magolda's (1992) parallel frameworks. If you are using one or the other as a course design heuristic, just sequence your learning outcomes to reflect students' progression through the stages or levels. For the primary foundational outcome, which is moving beyond dualism, students could explain the multiple competing interpretations or theories for some disciplinary phenomenon or issue, demonstrating that they realize that authorities don't have all the answers or the one right answer on the matter. To achieve a major mediating outcome (moving through multiplicity and relativism), students would have to analyze and critique these interpretations or theories. For the ultimate outcome (tentative commitment), they would have to embrace one of the interpretations or theories and justify their choice, as well as *qualify* it by explicating the limitations of their chosen viewpoint.

Although this framework may not apply well to an undergraduate science or engineering course, it can work very effectively in high-uncertainty and interpretive disciplines, such as literature, history, the arts, and philosophy. The following example is based on a course taught by Nilson titled Free Will and Determinism. Although it was anchored in philosophy, it featured readings from clinical and behaviorist psychology, sociology, political science, genetics, biochemistry, and sociobiology. These two paragraphs from the syllabus explain the outcomes, starting with the ultimate outcome:

> By the end of this course, you will have developed a well-reasoned, personal position on the role of free will, determinism, compatibilism, fatalism, and spiritual destiny in your own and others' lives. You will be able to express, support, and defend your position orally and in writing while acknowledging its weaknesses and realizing that it can never be validated as "the right answer" and may change over time [Ultimate Outcome: Tentative Commitment]. Hopefully, you will also begin to feel comfortable with the uncertainty and tentativeness of knowledge and with making decisions in spite of it.

> To help you attain these major objectives [outcomes], you will also acquire these supporting abilities: to sift out the various positions on free will and determinism (as well as compatibilism, fatalism, and spiritual destiny) in the assigned literature, along with their implicit premises and "givens," and to express them accurately both orally and in writing [Foundational Outcome: Uncertainty]; to draw sound comparisons and contrasts among them;

to evaluate their strengths, weaknesses, and limitations [Mediating Outcome #1: Uncertainty as Inherent and Legitimate]; and to distinguish among the stronger and the weaker positions [Mediating Outcome #2: Standards for Comparison].

The final paper closely reflected the ultimate outcome, and the first two papers, the two mediating outcomes.

Fink's Framework

Fink's (2013) categories of learning are not designed to sequence outcomes. Although this model is not hierarchical, a few categories must precede others. Foundational knowledge must come before application and integration. The categories of application and integration could also be sequenced, but the order would depend on your discipline, as discussed earlier in this chapter. The remaining categories of human dimension, caring, and learning how to learn have no sequencing expectations. An ideally designed and developed course promotes all six kinds of learning, resulting in a genuinely significant learning experience. The goal is to help students interrelate and engage in them synergistically.

According to Fink, his framework can accommodate courses of all levels and disciplines, whether face-to-face or online, and he provides a comprehensive, step-by-step procedure for applying this model to any course. Here is one generic example. After students acquire some foundational knowledge, have them apply this new knowledge to solve a problem of relevance to them (application) or to resolve a situation where they can see how some phenomenon affects them and others (human dimension). This learning experience should promote their interest in the subject matter (caring). With their interest piqued, they should begin to notice the relationships between the new material and other things they have learned (integration). As they recognize more linkages, they should start drawing additional implications for their own and others' lives (human dimension), as well as other ways to apply the material to improve the quality of life (application). At this point, they should want to learn still more (caring) and realize their need to acquire stronger learning skills (learning how to learn).

This illustration shows that a well-designed course can generate a mutually reinforcing relationship between learning and motivation. Fink also emphasizes course *alignment*—that is, ensuring that the learning activities (teaching methods) and the assessments complement the learning goals (outcomes). (We will revisit his model in Chapter 13.)

Wiggins and McTighe's Framework

Wiggins and McTighe's six facets of understanding (explanation, interpretation, application, perspective taking, empathy, and self-knowledge) overlap so much with Fink's schema, it should be fairly easy to see how each facet can lead to another.

▪ SHOWING STUDENTS THEIR LEARNING PROCESS

Most individuals prefer visuals over text. Our brains are wired to process a lot of visual information, quickly, so it helps students to illustrate your course design. They can see where your course is going in terms of their learning. An *outcomes map* serves this purpose. It is a flowchart of the learning outcomes, starting from your foundational outcomes, progressing through your mediating outcomes, and finally arriving at your ultimate outcomes. Thus, it visually represents the sequence, progression, and accumulation of the skills and abilities that students should be able to demonstrate at various times in the term. It shows how achieving one or more outcomes should enable them to achieve subsequent ones.

Nilson (2007) has written extensively on charting outcomes maps. She furnished for us a couple of examples that she developed. Figure 2.2 is an outcomes map for her Free Will and Determinism course. Following Perry's (1968) framework, it contains just a few outcomes that build up to the ultimate commitment outcome. These outcomes parallel those in the two paragraphs from the syllabus in the previous section. Figure 2.3 is the outcomes map she used for her graduate course, College Teaching. It does not follow any specific course design framework. It has a genuine flowchart look and feel, clearly showing how achieving one outcome equips students to achieve later ones. The students' major assignment is an individual course design and development project, after which they write a statement of teaching philosophy. Nilson made it clear to her students that, of course, she wouldn't be able to assess them on two of the ultimate outcomes—obtaining a teaching position and meeting institutional assessment requirements and goals—but they would leave the course knowing how to achieve these in their fast-approaching future.

Figures 2.2 and 2.3 provide two very different outcomes maps. There are many ways that outcomes maps can vary: the directions in which they flow; their spatial arrangements; their enclosures and connectors; and their use of type sizes, type styles, shadings, and colors. Outcomes maps may or may not follow one of the four course design frameworks presented earlier. They may or may not supply a time schedule such as the week or class number that you expect students to achieve each outcome. However they look, the visual aspect of outcome maps furnishes students with far more information about how their learning will progress through the course than a simple list of outcomes.

▪ OUTCOMES-CENTERED COURSE DEVELOPMENT

Your learning outcomes should direct all the other elements of your course design. This keeps the focus of the course squarely on student learning, which ensures that your course will be well aligned. Your outcomes map is your course skeleton. With that in

Figure 2.2 Outcomes Map for Freshman Seminar, Free Will and Determinism

ULTIMATE LEARNING OUTCOME

To develop and explain in writing a well-reasoned personal position on the role of free will, determinism, compatibilism, and fatalism (including spiritual destiny) in your own and others' lives, and to defend it while acknowledging its weaknesses and limitations (capstone paper 3)

MEDIATING LEARNING OUTCOMES

To assess how research supports or refutes each position (study questions and in-class discussions, weeks 6–12; paper 2 on scientific findings versus clinical reports due week 12)

To assess how one's own life experiences support or refute each position (journaling and in-class discussions, weeks 6–14)

To refute positions from the viewpoints of other positions (simulation/mock trial week 6, based on paper 1)

To apply the positions to interpret and assess a situation (paper 1 on criminal case, due week 6)

FOUNDATIONAL LEARNING OUTCOMES

To express accurately, both orally and in writing, the free willist, determinist, compatibilist, and fatalist positions, along with their assumptions and justifications (readings, study questions, in-class writing exercises, in-class discussions, weeks 1–5)

place, you start developing your course into a more detailed plan, filling it out by putting muscle and connective tissue on the bone structure.

Course Content

With well-developed outcomes, you will have guidance on what you teach. Identify the content that will help your students achieve the learning outcomes for the course. If the content does not help reach an outcome, delete that content. If you specialize in the content area, narrowing it down will challenge you. In such cases, it is helpful to have a colleague without this specialized knowledge assist you in your selections. Be brutal in eliminating extraneous topics. Instructors, especially new ones, tend to pack too much material into a course. It is better to teach a few topics well than to barely cover a lot of topics. In matching content to outcomes,

you will end up with a content map that looks a lot like the outcomes map.

Students' First Exposure to New Material

If your students' first exposure to new material is assigned readings, then choose books, articles, and websites in line with your learning outcomes and content. It is very helpful if you are able to find a textbook that reflects your disciplinary approach and has content that supports learning for the outcomes you have developed. It brings most of the information together, which is helpful to you and your students. You can also supplement the book with additional readings, videos, blogs, or any other source of material.

Setting up a flipped classroom is another option. In such a course, your students' first exposure may take the form of videos or podcasts that

Figure 2.3   Outcomes Map for Graduate Course, College Teaching

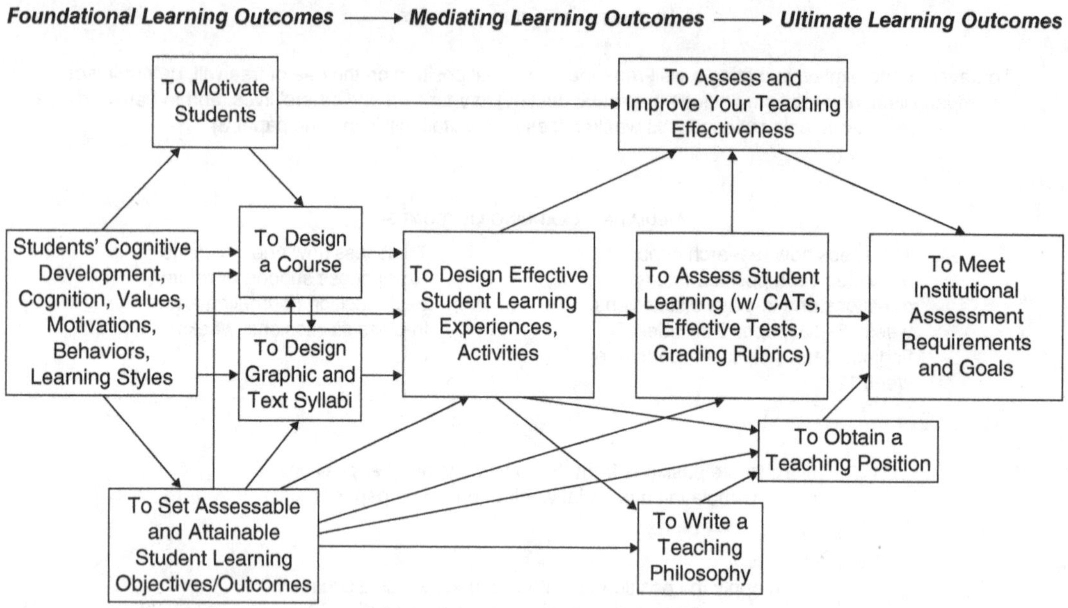

Foundational Learning Outcomes ⟶ *Mediating Learning Outcomes* ⟶ *Ultimate Learning Outcomes*

you have created of your lectures or found on the web (see Chapter 4). Again, everything you ask students to read, watch, or listen to should serve the purpose of helping your students achieve the learning outcomes for the course.

It is one thing to assign readings, videos, or podcasts; it's another thing entirely to get students to read, view, or listen to them attentively and understand them by the time they are due. If you have found students' homework compliance or comprehension to be a problem, you are in excellent company (refer to Chapter 21 for solutions).

Teaching Strategies

The first step when it comes to teaching strategies is to *think* about teaching strategies. It is surprising how many faculty members do not even think about the many options for teaching course content. They carefully craft the content, then walk into the classroom or log in to their class and just *teach*. That will never result in teaching at its best, and at times turns into teaching at its worst. You now know that we establish outcomes and then find teaching strategies that will help students to achieve

those outcomes. Chapter 13 is devoted to helping you make the best decisions—that is, selecting the most effective methods for helping your students achieve your outcomes.

Indeed, your outcomes can and should guide your choice of teaching strategies and activities down to the individual class level. If you want your students to be able to write a certain type of analysis by a certain week of the term, then structure in-class activities and assignments to give them practice in writing that type of analysis. If you want them to research and argue a point of view in class, select activities and group work to give them practice in research, rhetoric, and oral presentation. Always think about learning while you are teaching.

Assessments

Remembering that assessments should mirror outcomes, look to your ultimate outcomes for questions and tasks for your final exam, final paper assignment, or capstone project. After all, these outcomes delineate what you want your students to be able to do by the end of the course. Then move backward through your course and devise assignments and tests that ask students to perform your mediating and foundational outcomes. Once you've written sound outcomes, you've at least outlined your assessments. Chapters 25 and 26 offer good advice about constructing these instruments and assessing student performance on them.

■ THE BIG PICTURE

Once you have a sound course design, you will see many aspects of your course fall into place. For example, your syllabus almost writes itself. You will also be able to do something many faculty members don't even think about: state the three or four outcomes you want for your students when they finish the course. Chapter 5 presents a concise checklist of all the information that can and usually should be included in this important course document.

The next chapter draws on the course design principles presented in this one to explain how to integrate critical thinking into a course. Research tells us that to foster critical thinking in our students, we have to make it an explicit goal in a discipline-based course and build assessable critical thinking outcomes, learning experiences, and assessments into the course.

■ REFLECTION QUESTIONS

Reflection Question 2.1: After reading this chapter, how would you talk to your students on the first day of class about what kind of instructor you will be?

Reflection Question 2.2: Several frameworks are presented in this chapter (Bloom, Fink, Perry, Wiggins). Which feels like it would be the best for you to try when laying out your course design?

Concept Into Practice: Pick one important course topic, and write three connected outcomes, starting with an ultimate, down to a mediating, and ending on foundational. Refer back to the SMART acronym as you are constructing them. When done, check Figure 2.1 to validate your newly created outcomes.

CHAPTER 3

Including Critical Thinking Into a Course Design

In a survey of what employers are looking for in college graduates, the first three items clustered on the list are problem-solving, analytical, and quantitative skills (Koncz & Gray, 2022). These are all aspects of being a critical thinker, and employers consistently look for those skills when hiring college graduates. For students, developing strong critical thinking skills as part of their studies seems like a given. Unfortunately, teaching critical thinking is more challenging than most realize, and it is not something students typically pick up on their own. Across multiple years, students can solve problems, write papers, and take tests, but without purposeful planning, the likelihood of students spontaneously becoming strong critical thinkers while in college is slim.

In order for our courses to help students develop critical thinking, we must explicitly incorporate critical thinking outcomes, learning experiences, and assessments into our course design (Abrami et al., 2008). This is why we devoted an entire chapter to critical thinking and also why

it appears so early in this book. Just as we cannot assume that students acquire critical thinking skills as they move through our content, we cannot teach critical thinking to students unless they have some foundation of content knowledge. Students need at least a modicum of knowledge within a field of study before they can begin to critically examine assumptions, data, arguments, or conclusions (Willingham, 2007). Some faculty members say they do not teach foundational skills, but rather focus on critical thinking skills. It doesn't work that way. If students do not have foundational skills, what are they going to think critically about?

Unfortunately, the literature does not offer an easy, straightforward prescription on teaching critical thinking. It is fragmented into several different perspectives on what critical thinking is and what is required to engage in it. This helps explain why surveys reveal that few university faculty members know how to teach critical thinking—and why many cannot define it or agree on a definition (Paul & Elder, 2013b; Paul et al., 2013). Sadly, a review of critical thinking in business education by Calma and Davies (2020) demonstrated no clear agreement as to what critical thinking means, leading the authors to conclude that "a definition of critical thinking as it applies in business education would be a useful starting point" (p. 13).

Furthermore, the literature includes little empirical testing of teaching techniques that consistently develop critical thinking skills. Soufi and See (2019) conducted an international, systematic review of studies pertaining to teaching critical thinking skills. They found that although many articles claimed certain teaching approaches were effective, no approach contained strong support. The best evidence is for direct instruction of critical thinking skills, although even that finding was inconclusive. The authors of the review claimed that research regarding the best way to teach critical thinking skills is "still rather immature" (p. 140). What the critical thinking literature does provide, however, are questions and tasks that give students direct practice in critical thinking, and we will look at several sets of those here.

■ THE MANY FACES OF CRITICAL THINKING

Some scholars avoid the critical thinking literature altogether and turn to existing cognitive models. For instance, Bloom's (1956) higher-order cognitive operations noted in Chapter 1 can be cast as critical thinking skills. Other scholars look to Perry's (1968) stages of undergraduate cognitive development, which we also noted in Chapter 1, although these do not easily transfer to everyday life applications. The next five frameworks were developed specifically to teach and assess critical thinking. If these are of interest to you, we encourage you to use the references provided to read about these excellent frameworks in more detail.

Brookfield (2017) is a strong advocate of discussion as essential to teaching critical thinking, and he notes nuances in the process of facilitating discussions that develops critical thinking skills. Teaching

critical thinking is much more than having students engage in class discussions or putting students into small groups and having them work together to figure out how to solve a problem. Brookfield (2012) presents four distinct traditions of critical thinking: (1) *analytic philosophy*, which encompasses logic, logical fallacies, argument analysis, and inductive, deductive, analogical, and inferential reasoning; (2) *natural sciences*, characterized by the hypothetical-deductive method and principle of falsifiability; (3) *pragmatism*, which evaluates theories and beliefs according to their practical application; and (4) *critical theory*, which reveals the hidden dynamics of power and ideological manipulation. As you will see in the frameworks that follow, just about every leading approach to critical thinking embraces analytic philosophy and the natural scientific method, although you do not always see pragmatism or critical theory.

Facione (2013) developed the popular California Critical Thinking Skills Test, which assesses thinking skills identified by a large group of philosophers called the Delphi panel (because the group used the Delphi method). Facione (2011a, 2011b) noted and defined the following cognitive skills as core to critical thinking: analysis, inference, evaluation, interpretation, explanation, and self-regulation. He also noted that identifying core cognitive skills is not enough; the way the individual approaches life is also important. In this area he identified the following dispositions of critical thinkers: systematic, inquisitive, judicious, truth-seeking, confident in reasoning, open-minded, and analytical. This perspective falls squarely within the analytic philosophy and natural sciences traditions.

Reflecting the same two traditions, Halpern (2014) proposed a taxonomy of five critical thinking skills: (1) verbal reasoning (identifying weaknesses in persuasive techniques), (2) argument analysis, (3) scientific reasoning (the logic of hypothesis testing), (4) statistical reasoning about likelihood and probability, and (5) decision-making and problem-solving.

Paul and Elder (2013c), the founding leaders of the Foundation for Critical Thinking, posited eight "universal intellectual standards" by which to evaluate critical thinking around a problem, issue, or situation: clarity, accuracy, precision, relevance, depth, breadth, logic, and fairness (e.g., no conflict of interest). Again, analytic philosophy and scientific reasoning underlie these standards. Paul and Elder's perspective includes a great deal more and will receive more elaboration later. Their website, http://www.criticalthinking.org, offers a wealth of free resources on the teaching and learning of critical thinking for faculty members and students at all educational levels.

Finally, Wolcott (2006) also provides a comprehensive website on her step-based, developmental framework (http://www.wolcottlynch.com). Using this framework, the learner's charge is to move students up the "steps for better thinking." Students start at "step 0," where the "performance pattern" is that of the "Confused Fact-Finder." At this stage, comparable to Perry's dualistic stage, students merely repeat whatever information they have read or heard and seek one correct answer to a question or solution to a problem. Once they can move beyond facts and identify a problem or issue, define what information is relevant to it, and accept the uncertainties surrounding it, they arrive at step 1, the "Biased Jumper." Although they understand that no one correct answer may exist, they still view their learning task as choosing one answer or solution and gathering evidence to support it. At step 2, students begin to see their own biases and explore other points of view. Fitting the pattern of a "Perpetual Analyzer," they can identify the assumptions and logic of these alternatives, but for them, the goal is to take a detached, noncommittal, relativistic position toward all the options. Students become the "Pragmatic Performer" at step 3. Confronted with a question or problem, they realize that some options are better than others. They evaluate and compare them on relevant criteria in search of the best answer or solution—that is, the one with the strongest evidence and most solid reasoning. Most of us would likely be happy to guide our students to this lofty performance pattern, but Wolcott's model proposes one more: the "Strategic Re-Visioner." At this final step 4, students view any best answer or solution as

provisional and remain open to better ones as they create new knowledge and recast the question or problem. This perspective mirrors something Albert Einstein once said that has been condensed into the following popular quote: "We can't solve problems by using the same kind of thinking we used when we created them." This paves the way for innovative leaps in thinking and problem-solving. Only Wolcott's framework ventures beyond analytic philosophy and scientific reasoning to add creativity to critical thinking, which paves the way for innovative leaps in thinking and problem-solving.

COMMON GROUND

What understandings and principles can we take from all these perspectives? Let's start with a definition that we can distill from all of those proposed. Critical thinking entails an interpretation and analysis, then an evaluation or judgment about a claim that may or may not be valid, complete, or provide the best possible information. A *claim* may be a belief, value, assumption, problem definition, interpretation, generalization, analysis, viewpoint, position, hypothesis, prediction, solution, inference, decision, justification, or conclusion. Why question a claim? Perhaps the evidence is uncertain or ambiguous. Or the person or organization making the claim may have an interest in one side or another, or the data or the reasoning from the data are suspect. The issue may engender disagreement, debate, or controversy, and therefore other respectable competing claims. Then again, the problem may be fuzzy and ill-defined, or the process for testing the claim unclear or not standardized. No doubt, logic or scientific reasoning will guide the analytic and evaluative thinking processes.

A point of agreement among all these perspectives is that critical thinking is difficult and takes effort. Human nature leads us to recognize patterns and generalize from those patterns in an effort to simplify reality (Zakrajsek, 2022). After all, a straightforward, predictable environment quells fear and stress, permits us some measure of control, and facilitates survival. Patterns and repetition also reduce mental effort, which is, well, less effort. Why question our simplifications unless they fail us? We feel the same about our beliefs, values, allegiances, and habits of mind—probably more so to the extent that we cherish them and build our identities around them. Challenging them can cause acute discomfort. Therefore, critical thinking takes time to overcome our natural resistance to doing it and change our habits of mind.

As instructors, we can increase our students' willingness to explore different ways of thinking and believing. If we can help students see the costs and fallacies of their current mindsets—how some kinds of thinking lead to poor decisions and faulty conclusions—we may be able to help them develop a desire to think critically. We can also show students that with practice, their skill will increase and mental effort will ease, just as any complex and challenging task (e.g., driving a car) become less challenging with practice and repetition.

This brings us to another common ground among the different perspectives: they all posit that critical thinking extends beyond the cognitive domain and encompasses dispositions, attitudes, character traits, and mental health issues. According to Halpern (1999, 2014), a critical thinker must be willing to put effort and persistence into complex tasks; resist impulsiveness and consciously plan and follow through a line of thinking; remain open-minded and flexible; and admit error when necessary and change current thinking strategies for better ones. Paul and Elder (2013d) cite the intellectual traits (or virtues) of intellectual humility, integrity, courage, perseverance, and curiosity; fair-mindedness; and confidence in reason (as opposed to competing sources of knowledge such as revelation, tradition, and authority). Facione et al. (2000) propose the dispositions previously noted and also a long list of *affective dispositions*, among them broad inquisitiveness, trust in reasoned inquiry, honesty in acknowledging one's own biases, understanding of other people's viewpoints, prudence in suspending and modifying judgments, and diligence in seeking relevant information. Linda Nilson's contribution

to the critical thinking literature was pointing out how psychological defense mechanisms (*psychological fallacies*) such as denial, externalization, projection, rationalization, and repression interfere with critical thinking (Nilson, 2021).

Most of the scholars—Halpern (1999, 2014), Facione (2013), and Paul and Elder (2013d)—also contend that critical thinking requires metacognition or self-regulation, which is the habit of monitoring, evaluating, and correcting one's thinking. Only then can students articulate and transfer the thinking skills they are learning to new issues and situations. For instance, students should be able to describe and assess the reasoning process by which they arrived at a certain position or conclusion, including how they gathered and appraised the evidence. They should also be able to explain why they discarded competing positions and conclusions and deemed one to be the best.

With this common ground in mind, let's turn to possible critical thinking learning outcomes for your courses. Then we can examine some of the tasks and questions that can give students practice in the type of thinking that will help them achieve those outcomes.

■ CRITICAL THINKING OUTCOMES FOR YOUR STUDENTS

What you expect your students to be able to do by the end of your course depends in large part on your discipline, especially your *type* of discipline. Following you will find many learning outcomes listed to get you started about the possibilities in your course.

Any course in a discipline that takes a scientific approach to its enterprise, such as the natural, social, and applied sciences, should have some critical thinking outcomes related to the scientific method. These skills, some adapted from the ETS Proficiency Profile (2022), are candidates to consider:

- Interpret and display quantitative relationships in graphs, tables, charts, and other graphics.
- Analyze situations or data to identify problems.

- Identify and summarize the problem, question, or position at issue.
- Categorize problems by the appropriate algorithms to solve them.
- Integrate information or data to solve a problem.
- Assess alternative solutions and implement the optimal ones.
- Explain how new information or data can change the definition of a problem or its optimal solution.
- Evaluate hypotheses for consistency with established facts.
- Develop and justify one's own hypotheses, interpretations, or positions.
- Identify the limitations of one's own hypotheses, interpretations, or positions.
- Identify, analyze, and evaluate key assumptions and the influence of context.
- Design and carry out an experiment to test a given hypothesis.
- Evaluate the appropriateness of procedures for investigating a question of causation.
- Evaluate data for consistency with established facts, hypotheses, or methods.
- Separate factual information from inferences.
- Separate relevant from irrelevant information.
- Identify alternative positions or interpretations of the data or observations.
- Evaluate competing causal explanations.
- Explain the limitations of correlational data.
- Evaluate evidence and identify both reasonable and inappropriate conclusions.
- Identify and evaluate implications.
- Identify new information or data that might support or contradict a hypothesis.

Courses in the technical and problem-solving disciplines might be designed around the outcomes just listed that include the words *problem* or *solution*. However, the criteria for judging the best problem definition or conclusion would include more practical considerations such as cost, time, and client preferences.

In the humanities and some areas of the social sciences, courses focus on arguments anchored in texts, documentary data, logic, and key observations. Their outcomes of choice might include some or all of these:

- Determine the relevance of information for evaluating an argument or conclusion.
- Separate facts from opinions and inferences.
- Locate and use relevant primary and secondary sources to conduct research.
- Analyze explanations for historical and contemporary issues, trends, and problems (Nuhfer et al., 2014).
- Develop explanations for historical and contemporary issues, trends, and problems (Nuhfer et al., 2014).
- Recognize flaws, inconsistencies, and logical fallacies in an argument.
- Evaluate competing interpretations, explanations, evidence, and conclusions.
- Communicate complex ideas effectively.

Finally, courses in the arts have their own distinctive learning outcomes—for example:

- Identify and analyze alternative artistic interpretations of a work.
- Determine how well an artistic interpretation is supported by evidence contained in a work.
- Recognize the salient features or themes in works of art.
- Evaluate works of art according to commonly agreed-on criteria.
- Compare and contrast different works of art to provide evidence of change or growth through history, across cultures, across locations, or in a particular artist.
- Distinguish between objective and subjective analysis and criticism (Nuhfer et al., 2014).
- Create a piece of art and explain its significance.

Given that metacognition must accompany critical thinking, a course with a critical thinking emphasis should have some self-regulated learning outcomes for students as well. Here are a few suggestions (Nilson, 2013a):

- Identify the main points in readings and lectures.
- Set goals for one's performance on exams and assignments.
- Prepare more effectively for exams.
- Consciously observe and evaluate one's own thinking and emotional reactions while doing course activities and assignments (reading, listening, organizing, writing, designing, and the like).
- Assess one's improvement in critical thinking skills.
- Explain the usefulness of critical thinking skills beyond the course.
- Describe how one has changed beliefs, values, attitudes, habits of mind, worldviews, and behaviors as a result of the course.

Teaching self-regulated learning generally means (1) explaining to students what it is and how it benefits learners and (2) leading activities and making assignments that engage students in self-regulated learning practices. Specifically, students reflect on the meaning of the material and on their strategies for learning, studying for a test, or doing an assignment: How did they define and plan the task? What skills did they use while doing the tasks? What problems did they run into, and how did they solve them? How did they arrive at their response or solution? What learning value did this task have for them? What would they do differently the next time? How did their thinking on the topic change, and why (Nilson, 2013a)?

■ GIVING STUDENTS PRACTICE IN CRITICAL THINKING

The kinds of tasks you assign and questions you ask your students will depend on the student learning outcomes in your course. Both in and out of class, give students practice, followed by feedback, in thinking about the content using the skills you have targeted. To teach critical thinking, it is important to ask students to explain how they came to their answer, solution, or conclusion. Giving students this kind of direct practice is your primary strategy for teaching critical thinking skills that last.

Halpern's Tasks

Halpern (2014) suggests teaching students critical thinking skills. Halpern and Sternberg (2020) additionally argue that a primary goal is to teach students to transfer critical thinking skills from a variety of areas of knowledge and contexts, using activities such as:

- Identify and assess assumptions in an argument.
- Identify problems in a situation.
- Explain the connection between new knowledge and prior knowledge.
- Formally plan a strategy to achieve a goal, to include ordering and prioritizing tasks and ranking problems by seriousness and urgency.
- Give and evaluate reasons to support or reject a conclusion.
- Assess degrees of probability and uncertainty.
- Place isolated data into a wider framework or context.
- Recast text-based information into a graphical form.
- Synthesize information from multiple sources.
- Reason through alternatives to select the best option.

Facione's Questions

Facione (2011b) advises that teaching critical thinking starts with what you do in and out of the classroom with your students. It is important to model the appropriate dispositions, attitudes, character traits, and critical thinking skills in the teaching process (Seesholtz & Polk, 2009). In addition, you should encourage their curiosity, questions, and skepticism about claims you make. And you should routinely ask them to explain and justify the claims they make.

Facione et al. (2021) provide a list of questions and tasks you can use to teach students the nature of critical thinking and give them practice in doing it.

- *Interpretation.* What does this mean? How should we understand this? How can we make sense of this? How should we categorize this? Given the context, what was intended by doing this?
- *Analysis.* What do you conclude? Why do you conclude this? Why do you think that? What are your reasons? What are the arguments on both sides? What must we assume to accept that conclusion? Can these two apparently conflicting conclusions be reconciled? If so, how?
- *Inference.* What does this evidence imply? What do these data imply? If we accept/reject this assumption/claim, what are the consequences for us going forward? What unintended consequences may there be? At this point, what conclusions can we draw? What options can we eliminate? What additional information/data do we need? What options have we not yet considered? How do these change our thinking?
- *Evaluation.* How does this claim stack up against the evidence? What reasons might we have to distrust the person making the claim? How sound is the reasoning? Do you see any flaws in the argument? How confident can we be in our conclusion at this point?
- *Explanation.* What exactly did this study/research find? How was the analysis conducted? Why do you favor this answer/solution? How was this decision made?

Facione (2013) also includes a series of self-regulation questions, a topic we have already touched on and will revisit in Chapter 19.

Paul and Elder's Model

Paul and Elder (2013a, 2013c) also provide questions to ask students to hold them accountable for meeting the eight standards for critical thinking—questions that we hope students will internalize to ask themselves. Each standard is independent of the others and important in its own right. Paul and Elder call clarity the *gateway standard* because we cannot evaluate a statement until we can understand what it is saying.

1. *Clarity.* Can you elaborate on that point? Can you phrase it in more specific terms and give an example? For example, the question, "How can we solve our energy problem?" fails to define exactly what the problem is. It needs a sharper focus, something that defines an agent and problem parameters, as this question does: "What can power companies do to reduce energy consumption by businesses and households?"
2. *Accuracy.* How can you validate the accuracy of this statement/evidence?
3. *Precision.* Can you be more specific? Can you give more details?
4. *Relevance.* How does that information/variable bear on the issue? For instance, the price of crude oil is not connected to what power companies can do to reduce energy consumption.
5. *Depth.* How does your conclusion address the complexities and most important aspects of the problem? How well does it take feasibility, trade-offs, and options into account? Just telling people to save energy by driving their cars less does not deal with their need for transportation when no other viable alternatives are available.
6. *Breadth.* What is another viewpoint on the problem? How does the other side see the issue?
7. *Logic.* How does this follow from the evidence or previous statements? How can both this and that be true when they lead to such different conclusions?
8. *Fairness.* Do you have a vested interest in one conclusion or another? Do you have any relevant biases? Are you representing the other viewpoints honestly and impartially?

Paul and Elder (2013a) provide two templates to guide students' analyses of different kinds of texts: one for articles, essays, or chapters, and another for textbooks. They also furnish a third template for evaluating an author's reasoning. Each template poses eight questions that ask students to identify the following elements: the main purpose of the text (author); the key question it (the author) addresses; the most important information or evidence it (the author) offers to support the conclusions; the main conclusions or inferences it (the author) draws; the key idea(s) in its (the author's) line of reasoning; the main assumptions (often unstated and taken for granted) behind its (the author's) line of reasoning; the logical implications or consequences, whether stated or not, of its (the author's) line of reasoning; and its (the author's) main point of view.

The third template consists of evaluative questions for each part of the text the students identify. With respect to the author's purpose, is it well stated and justifiable? With respect to the key question, is it clear, unbiased, respectful of the complexities at issue, and relevant to the purpose? Is the most important information accurate, relevant, essential to the issue, and respectful of the complexities at issue? Are the key ideas clear and justifiably used? Are the assumptions questionable, or does the author address any problems inherent in them? Do the conclusions and inferences logically follow from the information given? Does the author consider alternative points of view or lines of reasoning and respond to objections they may raise? Is the author aware of the implications and consequences of her position? These templates show students the process of critical thinking—identifying, analyzing, and evaluating key points—as applied to common academic reading assignments.

Within Paul and Elder's tradition, Nosich (2012) recommends having students go through this four-step procedure, which he calls *SEE-I*, to clarify an issue, claim, or concept:

1. **S**tate briefly and concisely what needs to be clarified.
2. **E**laborate it in your own words with a fuller explanation.
3. **E**xemplify it with a good example.
4. **I**llustrate it visually with a graphic, such as a concept map, diagram, or drawing, or illustrate it verbally with a metaphor, simile, or analogy.

Wolcott's Task Prompts

Wolcott (2006) offers sets of task prompts for giving students step-by-step practice in ascending the ladder of critical thinking. To get them beyond the "Confused Fact-Finder," you must ask students to do more than merely parrot back information; they need practice identifying problems, finding the information relevant to each problem, and determining the reasons that one approach or solution is neither clear nor certain. The goal is to help students see multiple sides of an issue. This may involve having students collect evidence to make a case

---

Applying Nosich's (2012) *SEE-I* to the Concept of *Bias*

1. Bias, whether explicit or implicit, is the tendency to make a certain judgment or favor a certain position without good reason.
2. Bias is based on preconceptions or distorted views about some aspect of the world. Because our lived experiences cannot include all possible experiences, we all have some form of bias. This makes it impossible for a person to look at evidence dispassionately and come to an impartial conclusion. This leads to prejudices, favoritism, and injustices that we may never perceive.
3. An example of bias is racism.
4. Bias is like wearing blinders. It keeps you from seeing the complete and objective picture of the world.

Although we can never be rid of bias, the more we recognize and understand it, the more we can work to minimize any resulting effects.

for more than one particular approach or solution. Questions you may pose to your students include:

- Why is there disagreement about this problem or issue?
- What are the different points of view on the problem or issue?
- What is uncertain about this problem or issue or the evidence for one side or another?
- Why does this uncertainty exist?
- Why can't the outcome of an approach or solution be predicted with certainty?
- What are all the possible approaches or solutions?
- What evidence supports each approach or solution?

From here students should progress to the "Biased Jumper" performance pattern. Although they grasp the notion that more than one approach or solution exists, they mistakenly believe that they should simply choose one and amass support for it. Your next task is to help students acknowledge and recognize their biases and entertain additional assumptions, interpretations, solutions, or conclusions. At this level, the questions to present to students are more complex:

- How good is the evidence/data in favor of one position (approach or solution) or another?
- How good is the evidence/data supporting a given approach or solution from other points of view?
- What are the strengths and weaknesses of the various pieces of evidence or data?
- What are the assumptions, interpretations, and potential biases behind each approach or solution?
- How do the different arguments compare and contrast?
- What are your own biases on the issue? How do your own experiences and preferences lead you toward or away from different approaches or solutions?
- How can you organize the information differently to help you think more thoroughly and complexly about the issue?

Guiding students through this broader way of thinking should advance them to the pattern of a "Perpetual Analyzer." At this stage, they understand the alternative positions and the reasoning behind them, but their objectivity and relativism paralyze them and they are unable to take a stance. To get them past this on-the-fence attitude, you must ask them questions that help them set priorities, compare their options, and arrive at conclusions:

- What trade-offs does each approach or solution entail? What are your priorities in determining the quality of various approaches or solutions? Which issues or interests are more important and less important in solving the problem, and why?
- How can you select and justify a particular approach or solution?
- How can you defend it against the arguments that support other reasonable approaches or solutions?
- How might changes in priorities lead to other "best" approaches or solutions?
- What does a given audience need to know in order to understand why you selected the approach or solution that you did?
- How should you develop your report/presentation to best communicate your selected approach or solution to your audience?
- Given a different audience or setting, what information and reasoning should you highlight to best communicate your approach or solution?

When students can give intelligent answers to the questions with the pattern of a "Perpetual Analyzer," they mature into the "Pragmatic Performer" pattern. But they may think that their well-reasoned choice settles the matter forever. At this point, you should help them critically examine their approach or solution and acknowledge its flaws and limitations and then encourage them to continue to seek a better option as conditions, information, or their own definition of the problem changes. Posing these questions will help your students emotionally detach from their approach or solution and stay open to revisiting and possibly revising their choice:

- What are the limitations of your chosen approach or solution? What priorities does it fail to serve?
- What are its implications?
- What feasible changes in conditions or new information might motivate you to question your choice?
- Under given conditions ("what if?"), how would you modify your definition of the problem and your chosen approach or solution?
- How can you monitor these conditions and obtain new information relevant to the problem and your approach or solution to it?

Having addressed these issues thoroughly, students attain the highest and most sophisticated performance pattern, the "Strategic Re-Visioner." They can define and justify their priorities; analyze and evaluate alternative approaches and solutions to a problem in view of these priorities; commit themselves, however provisionally, to the best choices; and reexamine these choices over time as conditions change and new information emerges. They can also communicate their thinking processes to others.

The Best Methods for Practice

In conducting an extensive meta-analysis to determine the most effective strategies for teaching critical thinking, Abrami et al. (2015) recommend two methods:

1. Whole-class and group discussions in which the instructor poses questions and presents tasks that require critical thinking. Such discussions may follow readings, videos, simulations, games, role plays, cases, and the like.
2. Opportunities for students to wrestle with and solve authentic or situated problems, such as those related to making life decisions and real-world problems they are likely to face in the future.

Chapter 15 offers proven discussion and questioning techniques and Chapters 16 (experiential learning), 18 (the case method), and 20 (STEM education) are all about using real-world and situated problems to foster student learning.

After students complete any critical thinking task or respond to a question, ask them to recount how they thought through the task or came up with their answer. How did they arrive at their interpretation, position, solution, conclusion, or evaluation? This is just like asking students to show their work on a math problem, only here the work is their critical thinking.

◼ THE GOAL: CRITICAL THINKING IN EVERYDAY LIFE

We teach critical thinking in the context of academic material, but the real benefits for students of learning and practicing critical thinking skills lie far beyond the classroom. Like writing, speaking, and quantitative reasoning, critical thinking is a life skill that pays off in many everyday settings. It should guide a person's consumer, political, financial, occupational, ethical, medical, and legal decisions (Browne & Keeley, 2010; Facione et. al, 2021; Nisbett, 1993; Nosich, 2012; Paul & Elder, 2013b). It can even help one make better personal choices, such as who to trust, who to commit to, and how to discipline children. Yes, all life decisions have a strong emotional component, but it helps to be able to distinguish a rational case from an emotional plea for taking action. News commentators, politicians, advertisers, and various authorities throw fallacious arguments at us every day, and most people fall for them. Television news and entertainment channels compete for viewers by advertising increasingly outlandish information and constant banners of "breaking news."

Our students need to know that critical thinking is a real-world skill that is well worth transferring. Aside from the day-to-day benefits of having critical thinking skills, they must navigate large and looming complex world issues: pandemics, global climate change, gender equality, poverty reduction,

The Socratic Method

Socrates didn't use the term *critical thinking* to describe his questioning method, but his goal was clearly to foster critical thinking among his fellow Athenians at any cost, including his life.

In an instructional context, open the dialogue on a given topic by posing one planned question that requires a student to take a position or point of view. After they articulate their stance, you construct a question that raises a weakness of or exception to that position, to which they respond with a defense or a qualification of their original position, or they assume a new position. In turn, you respond with another question that reveals a possible weakness of or exception to the defense, the qualified position, or the new position, and the student responds as before. And so the dialogue continues. This line of inquiry promotes rational thinking, self-examination, persistence, and pattern recognition, all integral facets of critical thinking.

It is important to note that the Socratic method can be a difficult teaching strategy.

First, because it relies on a one-on-one interaction, it's difficult to scale in today's classroom. Questioning one student too long can make the rest of the class tune out or cause discomfort to the student. Only when you are facing several students who share the same position can you direct the same questions to different students. Because of its scalability problem, the Socratic method in its pure form works best as a tutoring strategy and not a questioning technique in a discussion (see Chapter 15). Certainly, you and fellow classmates should challenge a student's position in a discussion, but the challenges shouldn't evolve into a sustained dialogue with only one student.

Second, the method depends on your ability to craft questions on the spot in response to what a student says. You might not feel comfortable with such a spontaneous, unstructured format. However, with experience, you will be able to anticipate the blind alleys and misdirections students take on specific topics and develop a general discussion plan.

Finally, some students take offense to an instructor hammering them with negative questions, so this process works best when you explain what you are going to do (at least the first time). It is also helpful to be mindful of the tone. You might lighten the tone if responses become tense.

and so on (Brown, 2021). The best and brightest thinkers today were students not that long ago. We stand by what we wrote in the opening paragraph of this chapter: Without purposeful planning, students becoming critical thinkers while in college is left to chance, and we cannot leave something so important to chance.

◼ REFLECTION QUESTIONS

Reflection Question 3.1: How would you respond to a student who asked you to define critical thinking and explain why they should put energy into building critical thinking skills?

Reflection Question 3.2: Halpern, Facione, Paul and Elder, and Wolcott's critical thinking models are provided in this chapter. Which model best resonates with you and why?

Concept Into Practice: Using the "Critical Thinking Outcomes for Your Students" as a jumping-off point, write out seven learning outcomes that will help students to develop critical thinking skills in your course (one ultimate; two mediating; and for each mediating outcome, write two foundational outcomes).

CHAPTER 4

Deciding What Technology to Use

Teaching at its best means considering every tool at our disposal to give our students the richest possible educational experience. Using technology to enhance student learning continues to accelerate and it is likely to continue to do so. Before the pandemic, students reported that 66% of their instructors used technology to engage them in the learning process (Gierdowski, 2019). Then came the COVID-19 pandemic. Classes were moved out of the classroom for safety and all instructors, across the world, had to pivot to emergency remote instruction. During that time, essentially every faculty member who was teaching face-to-face courses had to learn how to implement technologies that could be used in remote instruction. There is no doubt that as students move back to the classrooms, some faculty members will abandon the tech solutions they were forced to use. However, it is likely many will continue looking for technology that will enhance learning, provide more equitable educational opportunities, and make their jobs easier.

This chapter exists because of how crucial technology now is in higher education. We knew there were inequities in the educational system prior to the challenges with COVID-19. During the pandemic, we found out the inequities were worse than we had realized. Educational technologies, aside from enhancing student learning, can be used to address some of those inequities. Students and faculty members expect and are interested in technology in the classroom. This chapter is not designed to tell you what tools to use, but rather to help you decide on the tools that are right for you.

CHOOSING TECHNOLOGIES INTELLIGENTLY

Our fascination with gadgets can make us forget the lower-tech ways of accomplishing the same objective just as well and perhaps better. The very first thing we suggest you ask yourself when you are interested in some technology is whether you can teach well without it. For example, some faculty members express interest in Poll Everywhere for an onsite course to determine how students will respond to a given issue. Is it possible to simply ask students to raise their hand? If the technology doesn't add to student engagement, don't use it. For questions where you simply want students to see how their response fits among peers, hand-raising is likely fine and there is no reason to introduce technology. However, it might be that you want to be able to ask a question in class, have the responses be anonymous, and condense student reactions into a bar chart so that you can discuss the responses. Hand-raising will not allow you to do all that, so in such a case polling software is a good idea. We should always choose technologies because they most effectively help our students achieve learning outcomes, not because others use the technology, the technology looks interesting, or because the technology is popular and we want to look cool.

These are challenging times for educational technology use in the classrooms. The COVID-19 pandemic forced faculty members and institutions to make huge shifts toward creative technology solutions. Unfortunately, the pandemic also resulted in a massive fiscal challenge, with average IT budget cuts of 10% impacting nearly two-thirds of all higher education institutions (Grajek, 2020).

Fortunately, nearly every student has access to some personal device that allows technological access to the classroom, and 81% of students agreed that instructors use technology effectively for course instruction (Brooks & Gierdowski, 2021). Despite institutional cuts, there are currently more opportunities than ever to use technology to advance learning. The challenge, and the reason for this chapter, is to figure out how to do that effectively.

As long as we have sound pedagogical reasons, many high-tech tools do offer benefits and conveniences (Alexander et al., 2019; Kelly & Zakrajsek, 2020; Major et al., 2021;). The technology should:

- *Facilitate student learning* when it would not be feasible or safe to do so in person. Through digital simulations students can perform lab experiments and procedures that would be too dangerous or too expensive to do in reality, such as surgeries, hazardous chemical procedures, and molecular biology experiments. Digital and physical objects can exist in mixed reality to allow for previously unimaginable virtual simulations and interactions, like looking at chemical elements, an atomic structure, a physics motion demonstration, physiological interactions, or historical events like the sinking of the *Titanic*.

- *Increase student engagement, participation, interaction, and activity.* VoiceThread, for instance, allows instructors and students to enjoy online audio discussions asynchronously. Participants can append documents, images, videos, and audio files, to which they can add narrations or comments.

- *Increases equity.* Does the technology make learning possible for individuals who would struggle otherwise to participate? Removing challenges due to transportation, reliable childcare, mobility restrictions, recordings for those who are working, and reduced social anxiety are just a few ways technology might provide new opportunities for learners to be more engaged in the learning process.

- *Allow content creation* (e.g., making videos with smartphones and posting on the learning management system [LMS] for students to introduce themselves prior to the first day of class).

- *Allow practice at retrieval and spaced practice*, as well as "micro" bursts of learning. With technology, students can do these at their own pace and focus on their specific study needs. The technology (app, program, or platform) determines when appropriate time has passed to repeat trials.

- *Reinforce acquisition of the technological literacy* that their future occupations will require. Technology has increased in essentially every occupation at every level.

- *Encompass artificial intelligence* and ability to personalize learning experiences. For example, chatbots can work with students 24/7 on basic clarifications and allow you time for more in-depth student connections. Push notifications can remind students of work and provide tips for challenging tasks.

- *Enhance productivity* by reducing the time spent on routine record keeping and communication (e.g., grading, attendance records, and routine announcements or feedback can be easily managed by your course LMS).
- *Facilitate collaboration among students,* in class or throughout the world. Using tools like Google Suites (e.g., Docs, Slides, Jamboard), discussion boards, wikis, blogs, and Zoom, students can exchange files and web resources, provide peer feedback, and edit projects online at any time.
- *Avoid creating new problems*, such as distractions and temptations that lure students off-task, increase their cognitive load, interfere with the basic mental processes of their learning, or increase financial or cognitive burden.

In this chapter we will not provide detailed information regarding how to use educational technology to teach an exclusively online course. An excellent resource for such material is *Online Teaching at Its Best* by Nilson and Goodson (2018). This chapter will also not focus on long lists of educational instructional technologies. There are hundreds of these lists at the writing of this book. Some will disappear within months, and new technology solutions will be developed. Plus, the chapter would balloon if we presented information on effective use of programs such as photo-sharing websites, photo-editing software, virtual reality, Zoom or FaceTime, apps, Google tools, ePortfolios, and mapping mash-ups. This chapter will focus on concepts and directions to consider in order to give you ideas about what you might need, and from there you will be able to find details for the technology that best suits your needs.

■ MODELS FOR IMPLEMENTING TECHNOLOGY

The number of ways in which you can implement technology into your course is mind-boggling and more extensive all the time. There are literally hundreds of ways to use technology to augment lectures, engage students, and assess learning in face-to-face class, synchronous online, and asynchronous online courses (Major et al., 2021). Following are two established methods to think about integrating technology into your course.

TPACK

The Technological Pedagogical Content Knowledge framework (TPACK) was developed by Mishra and Koehler (2006) and is one of the leading theories of educational technology and educational technology integration. The popularity of this framework is evident in that 233 articles that use some form of survey instrument to measure TPACK use it in a higher education course (Scott, 2021). To implement technology into the classroom, it is helpful to consider the interrelationship between three critical elements: content knowledge, pedagogy, and ability to use technology. Content knowledge is subject matter expertise, including knowledge of your field, concepts used, type of evidence collected, and frameworks within your discipline. This is what you would teach completely independent of any technology.

The second element, pedagogy, pertains to your knowledge of teaching strategies, practices, and processes you engage in as an instructor. Independent of technology, this is how you would teach your course. The concept of considering pedagogy and content knowledge, the first two elements noted, was put forth by Shulman (1986). In 2006, Mishra and Koehler added the third element of technological knowledge, your knowledge of and ability to use technology tools and related resources. Overall, this is your ability to use technology, independent of your teaching.

This framework proposes that successful, effective integration of technology into the classroom can only be achieved when all three elements are considered together. According to TPACK, use of effective educational technology to enhance learning comes at the intersection of how the technology works, the pedagogical practices necessary, and the content that forms the learning outcome.

SAMR

TPACK provides a framework for the conditions under which technology may be successfully implemented, not a strategy for the implementation. Technology is not just for online teaching. Onsite courses can also benefit from proper integration of technology. One way to think about technology integration is according to the Substitution, Augmentation, Modification, and Redefinition (SAMR) model (Puentedura, n.d.; Terada, 2020). The model offers the following four approaches for adding technology to a previously technology-free activity and accompanying changes in outcomes:

1. *Substitution*: Swap technology for previous method with no functional improvement (e.g., PowerPoints instead of blackboard notes; Microsoft Track Changes instead of handwritten notes).
2. *Augmentation*: Swap technology for previous method with functional improvement (e.g., students use Padlet to include images and URLs to respond to a prompt instead of sticky notes on walls; VoiceThread notes for essay feedback instead of handwritten notes).
3. *Modification*: Swap technology for previous method with functional improvement, and redesign lesson and learning outcomes (e.g., students use Jamboard for an interinstitutional gallery walk, where each board is contributed by students from a different school, instead of a gallery walk in a single classroom where students respond to a prompt using posters on a wall).
4. *Redefinition*: Swap technology for previous method to achieve something impossible without the technology tool (e.g., use virtual reality for students to experience the eye of a tornado instead of reading about it in a textbook).

The SAMR model was designed to encourage the instructor to think about how technology specifically augments learning. This model is also a "ladder system" to move up in complexity from substitution to redefinition.

■ LECTURE-RELATED SOFTWARE

It is likely that everyone who teaches is familiar with presentation software such as PowerPoint, Prezi, and Keynote. These programs allow the average faculty member to create text integrated with images, animations, online resources, and video clips, all in full color, as well as sound. You can highlight the text or zoom in on the part of the image you are explaining. If you want to engage students directly with the slides, you can project your presentation onto a whiteboard and have students write on the board based on what is projected from the slide. This is particularly useful when teaching mathematics, engineering, and the physical sciences. If your institution has the space and the money, it can redesign a classroom with tables and chairs to sit four to six students with a screen placed on the wall next to each table. The instructor can project slides onto the student groups' screens and access these screens to project one group's work onto all the screens. You can also use PowerPoint to create voice-over prerecorded lessons (Norman, 2021).

As with most things, moderation is key. Some instructors overuse slides to display text-heavy information they are lecturing about, and this behavior increases student boredom during a lecture (Mann & Robinson, 2009). Here are the most effective uses of slides:

- List of learning outcomes or an outline for the class
- Directions or questions for lecture break activities (see Chapter 14 for many options)
- Animations, video clips, and links to instructional websites
- Diagrams, flowcharts, pictures, photos, drawings, and other graphics

- Equations, formulas, and the like that are particularly challenging
- Material that you project onto a Smartboard so you can write or draw on it

Presentation software is typically a complement to your lecture. As it is important to keep students engaged, it is best to interject active learning strategies to help students to solidify learned material. It is also helpful to sprinkle reflection and discussion questions, short cases, or problems in the PowerPoint slide deck to give students practice in application. Many have found it helpful to strategically place concept-oriented multiple-choice questions into the presentation software to assess students' understanding (Crouch & Mazur, 2001). Fortunately, clickers are designed to interface with PowerPoint (see Chapter 14). Students may find Prezi to be a more engaging presentation software, depending on how you teach and the content to be learned. Used well, Prezi offers a more organic alternative to standard slides, as it is not designed to be linear like PowerPoint and Keynote. You can provide a big-picture view of how the parts of the lectures (topics, concepts, principles, examples, and the like) interrelate (assuming that they actually do), the way a graphic syllabus does (see Chapter 5), and systematically move from part to part as you wish or as students request. When using Prezi, be careful zooming in and out, and give students advance warning that you are doing so. The motion of Prezi can make some learners queasy, particularly those who sit close to the screen.

Regardless of the presentation software being used, when presenting a slide that is primarily text, focus on only one concept per slide and use only key words, keeping the information to an absolute minimum. It is important to give students a chance to read the slides before you begin talking, so you aren't talking while students are reading. The templates should help you arrange your information in a logical and pleasing way. Avoid reading the slides to students, unless you want to emphasize a particular point as a key concept or a portion of a quote.

Reading slides is rarely well received and is considered one of the most egregious technological missteps (Young, 2004). In addition, keep the classroom as light as possible to see the presentation only to the extent necessary. If you are showing very detailed information, the room may need to be dark. If you are showing text and rough images, the room can be well lit and still allow students to see the information. Keeping the lights up will help students to stay awake and to stay more engaged.

One more rule applies to presentation software: avoid jarring color combinations, backgrounds, icons, slide transitions and builds, and special effects. Keep the same colors and backgrounds throughout a presentation unless you have a specific reason for changing the background. For example, you might use a light gray background for information slides, a light blue background for active learning directions, and a light green for applications of the material learned. Colors can be used to signal specific types of information. When choosing colors, be mindful of color contrast so that those with visual challenges will be able to read the slides. One way to test slides is to go to a room with a lot of light and project a slide with text. If you are not able to read the text from the back of the room with the lights on, the contrast may be challenging for someone with vision challenges, even with the room lights down.

Some think flashy-colored slides will stimulate your students to stay awake. That won't work. You keep students awake and engaged with your presentation. In instruction, the fewer the glitzy distractions and the simpler the visuals the better. Nevertheless, students appreciate your adding some design elements to your slides (Clark, 2008). When students create slide presentations, advise them to follow the same design guidelines but still incorporate multimedia vitality and richness. These presentations can be viewed at any time by you or your class and then be revised and preserved in a student's ePortfolio.

Advances in technology are going to soon revolutionize what can be done at the front of the room or on a stage of a large lecture hall. Amazing technology already exists that has been shown to improve student learning outcomes (DiNatale et al., 2020; Golden, 2017). The new technology simply needs to get to a point where it is available and affordable on a large scale. As an example, The Weather Channel is showing how to explain weather using immersive mixed reality (see https://www.youtube.com/watch?v=ZSpEMbab5kM). This includes an impressive display of what being in the path of a tornado would be like (https://www.youtube.com/watch?v=69nUZmQ2w8A&t=337s). You can search "Weather Channel immersive mixed reality" and include whatever natural disaster interests you, such as hurricanes, flash floods, firestorms, and melting glaciers. Once you watch a few of these short videos, you will immediately see the potential in higher education, both to show such videos for the information they contain and to use them directly where students are able to participate. In medical education, mixed reality is now used to show students a virtual patient that appears to stand next to the lecturer.

With technology advancing at the current rate, it is impossible to say how lectures will be augmented in just a few years. However, we can confidently predict that it will be crucial to continue choosing teaching strategies based on student learning outcomes. If you do, the learning environment will help students reach desired outcomes, rather than simply being an exciting use of holograms, mixed/virtual reality, and whatever comes next.

■ THE LEARNING MANAGEMENT SYSTEM

A learning management system (LMS) is a package of instructionally useful software for course administration, file exchange, communication, collaboration, tracking, and reporting (e.g., Blackboard, Moodle, Sakai, Schoology, and Canvas). Some of the tools are designed to streamline the instructor's duties, such as an online syllabus template, a spell-checker, automatic test grading, and a grade book

linked to a spreadsheet program. Other features facilitate and expand opportunities for communication and interaction with and among students, extending the classroom beyond its walls and scheduled meeting times.

Usually an institution decides which LMS will be used by the entire campus, but you can expect yours to have these features (some of which merit elaboration in the subsections that follow): an announcements page; templates for the syllabus, course calendar, pop-up glossary, class roster, student surveys, and student websites; space for posting course materials (text, graphics, multimedia), such as the syllabus, handouts, assigned readings, lecture notes, presentations, and directions for assignments; space for links to library reserve materials; a dropbox for homework assignments and take-home tests; online testing tools (timed, untimed, and multiple-tries option) with automatic grading of closed-ended items; automatic test feedback to students on closed-ended items; an Excel-compatible grade book; email, with a mass mailing option for the instructor; class and team discussion boards, chat rooms, blog space (individual too), and wikis; and online help and search. Blogs and wikis could also be considered social media components.

Space to Post Course Material

Students appreciate the one-stop convenience of obtaining all the course materials whenever and wherever they want (Lang, 2008; Young, 2004). Be sure to consider the timing of posting materials. For example, if you post materials at 9:00 a.m., students in class who work full time are not likely to see that information until well after 5:00 p.m. If you modify materials after posting, be sure to specify that in class or send an email (or other notification) to the class, because students may not notice the change. Of course, even if students are told not to share information, if you post an answer key for homework or exams it likely renders those questions unusable in the future as some students will take images of the answers and make them available to students in a future class.

You can also use this space to post recorded lectures, which is particularly helpful for students who may struggle with chronic illness or other scheduling issues. However, be aware that students may use these recordings in lieu of coming to class unless you make the live class somehow more valuable than the videos you post (Young, 2004; also see Chapter 14). Recorded lectures can also be a jumping-off point for flipped classroom activities, freeing up valuable in-class time for active learning rather than lectures.

Online Preclass Quizzes

Easily administered from an LMS, regular online quizzes can serve as an incentive for students to keep up with the readings, videos, and podcasts, as an inquiry-based diagnostic tool to assess your students' understanding and plan class around clearing up their misconceptions and mistakes, and as a method to support the effectiveness of spaced practice on learning (Evans et al., 2021). The latter use is called *just-in-time-teaching* (JiTT). Research attests that this method raises students' level of preparation for class, participation, engagement, and achievement (Bowen, 2012; Pape-Lindstrom et al., 2018) as long as the quizzes figure substantially into the final grade (Sullivan et al., 2008). Students seem to know the positive effects of online quizzes on their motivation, engagement, and learning, and they have long endorsed them as a wise use of instructional technology (Young, 2004).

Class Email

LMS systems make it very easy to email everyone in the course. You can send housekeeping messages, reminders, study questions, assignments, tips on doing the readings, and connections between the course material and current events. One-to-one email with your students can be helpful. Your students can ask you questions confidentially, saving class time that might otherwise go to individual student questions and concerns, and it makes it easier on students with respect to traveling to your office.

A word of warning: some students may expect quick responses to their emails. Make it clear to the students at the beginning of the semester what they can expect from you in terms of response time. Keep in mind that different faculty members have different response-time policies. A student may have multiple instructors who indicate they will reply to all emails within 8 hours; you certainly do not need to choose to do that, but students need to know what you will do. It is reasonable to let students know that you will reply within 24 hours, except on the weekend, when they may receive a response Monday morning. It is no longer typical practice to not reply to students for several days. That said, if you require a bit more time, just let students know so they understand what to expect.

Discussion Forums and Chat Rooms

Discussion boards are frequently used in asynchronous online courses to enhance critical thinking skills and writing. These boards can also be used in face-to-face courses to augment class discussions. One pervasive challenge with respect to discussion boards is high-level participation. Generate better participation by explaining to students the value and purpose of the discussions, and let students know your expectations for participation, by identifying a way to structure the discussion and the peer moderator role assignment (Aloni & Harrington, 2018; Ghadirian et al., 2019). Although some faculty members find chat rooms as busywork spaces or off-topic chatter spaces, many continue to find chat rooms function to build online communities of practice (Gallard et al., 2021). Google Docs, wikis, blogs, and streams are more commonly used today for small-group collaboration. If you prefer, or your institution requires, LMS discussion boards as part of your course, to provide explanations and models of high-quality and low-quality contributions, and consider having student peers evaluate each other's posts to promote engagement. Be sure to make your presence known as well with occasional instructor contributions.

Blogs

Too much exceptional work in higher education is graded and then never seen again. A blog offers an opportunity to make real-world use of student work. When surveyed, 600 students who had participated in blogging for educational purposes stated they felt blogging enhanced their learning (Garcia et al., 2019). Posts are easy to make, and only the owner can change them. The blogs built into most LMSs allow students to design the site; invite commentators; and post images, audio files, and videos. As they are quasi-public (open to the class and specific individuals granted permission), many students do some of their most conscientious writing on them and enjoy adding multimedia to their posts. Individual blogs are particularly well-suited to journaling. However, students seem more willing to advocate positions and propose explanations on blogs and to connect course material to their personal experience and intellectual growth in private journals (Foster, 2015). You can also use the class blog as a discussion forum and require that students make a specified number of posts on particular topics. However, blogs do not offer topical threading. If you find your LMS blog wanting, try a commercial host (e.g., Blogger, Livejournal, Squarespace, or WordPress), but be aware that the free sites are stripped down and may display advertising.

If you're going to use blogs, it is best to integrate them into other aspects of the course and give students an incentive to post regularly, just as with a discussion forum. You can also have students read and comment on each other's blogs. Although you need to check posts, you need not grade every post and every comment. You can, for example, have students write a self-assessment of their posts around midterm, comparing theirs to the best ones they have read in the class. This exercise tends to improve the quality of posts in the second half of the course. Then at the end of the term, you can ask students to select and submit their best three posts for a grade (Lang, 2008).

The blogs of other entities can also be a source of up-to-date reading material. You and your students can sign up to receive updates of the blogs of political and cultural leaders, scientists, corporations, non-profit organizations, action groups, and social forums. (They usually offer syndication, which means they use a really simple syndication [RSS] feed to reach subscribers by email.)

Higdon and Topaz (2009) adapted individual blogs to JiTT (see Chapter 17). They have their students post their answers to two questions on the readings—the first about the most difficult part of the material and the second about the most interesting part, the material's connection to prior knowledge, or its relevance to their intellectual or career interests. Students submit their responses the night before class and email the link to the blog's RSS feed to the instructor, who (for convenience) aggregates the posts onto a wiki (see the next section). The instructor scans and grades the responses, looking for common difficulties and themes, then adapts the upcoming class to clear the bottlenecks. According to Higdon and Topaz, JiTT blogging enhances students' conceptual understanding, increases their out-of-class time on task, fosters their metacognitive reflection on the material, and improves their ability to transfer knowledge to real-world applications.

Wikis

A wiki is an ever-evolving, collaboratively developed website that allows users to add, remove, edit, revise, update, and make comments on the content. In addition to text, it can accommodate images, video, audio files, and links. Its purpose is to build increasingly higher-quality collective knowledge, so it is ideal for collaborative writing, research, and portfolio assignments, as well as other projects that require sharing, reflection, and evaluation. This is another opportunity for students' efforts to contribute to material available for everyone. All the versions of and changes to the document are recorded and attributed, so users (including the instructor) can easily find out who made what change when and, if expected in the comments, why. Thus, wikis build in accountability.

LMSs offer wiki space that is restricted to students and invited guests, but you can find dozens of other hosts at http://c2.com/cgi/wiki?WikiFarms. You can allocate wikis across individual students, teams, and the entire class, along with read-only or edit rights to each one. You may want your students to read but not modify each other's wikis. With edit rights to every class wiki, you can also provide students with formative feedback as their product develops. Although wikis are user friendly and intuitive, you may want to orient your students to them with video tutorials at sites such as www.youtube.com/watch?v=-dnL00TdmLY. In fact, you might post wiki instructions on the class wiki and ask students to add tips (Allwardt, 2009).

Use of wikis has been shown to motivate students to complete assignments and search online material at a deeper level, and also to enhance class community (Huang, 2019). Cho and Lim (2017) noted that when using wikis, prereading should be set up to relate well to wiki learning activities, wiki guidelines should be used to help students to develop a clear purpose, wiki activities should be scenario based and open ended so students can more easily apply material from their assigned readings to the wiki, feedback and examples are helpful, and students should be provided with opportunities to become familiar with how to post and edit wiki material.

University of Michigan business professor Scott Moore (2009) has made extensive course use of class wikis for lecture notes and test questions. For each class, he assigns one student the task of taking notes on the class wiki and encourages other members of the class to make corrections and additions. He also invites students to make up and post objective test items (with answers), which others can then improve or elaborate on. Students can check and study from the items any time they want, and Moore puts about half the items on actual tests. His class wiki is very active.

Not all wikis garner such interest. Some students back away from discussing difficult topics or critiquing the work of their peers, so you may have to require and monitor regular participation, specify appropriate dimensions for critiquing, and promote and reward serious discussion and constructive criticism (Allwardt, 2009). As with every student discussion tool, you have to be involved with it to make it a success.

THE FLIPPED CLASSROOM

In the purest form of the flipped classroom, you assign as homework your recorded lectures on video or in podcasts, then post them on the LMS or your course website or send them to your class through an RSS feed. The homework can also be print or other media you have produced. In a less pure version, you may assign online videos, podcasts, or print material made by someone else or recordings of campus events, such as speeches, debates, radio shows, interviews, ceremonies, and performances that not all your students can attend live. The recorded materials offer your students the convenience of listening or viewing almost any time and for as many times as they wish. In the loosest use of the term *flipped classroom*, it simply means that students get their first exposure to new material outside class (Walvoord & Anderson, 2010).

In every version of the flipped classroom, students have their first exposure to the material before class and then, while in class, the students do some kind of work such as application problems, problem-solving, concept mapping, case analyses, simulations, writing, designing, website-building assignments, and the like (Berrett, 2012).

If you decide to make videos or podcasts of your lectures, be aware that recording and editing them takes time, and you can't just record and post a 50-minute classroom-delivered lecture as many students would likely opt to not watch it. You have to cut your presentations into short segments of 15, 10, 5, or 2 minutes (depending on engagement level of the content and the way in which it is presented), each segment on a single concept. Being concise and logically organized is critical, so you should write a script that includes examples and stories that clarify the concept and eliminate all extraneous verbiage. When using slides, focus on showing visuals and trim the text down to the bare takeaways (Moore, 2013). You should also incorporate transitions between the recorded segments, tying one segment's topic to that of the previous and the next recording. As new knowledge emerges in your field, you may have to re-record the relevant segments the next time you teach the course.

Ask your campus computer specialists about the best locations for recording and the available technology—for example, Audacity or GarageBand for podcasts, and Camtasia, Echo 360, or LectureScribe (available free at https://people.cs.clemson.edu/~bcdean/lscribe and ideal for recording your whiteboard work) for videos. Zoom, Teams, or any other videoconferencing software can also be used to record minilectures. Many instructors make these recordings in their office; others make them in an empty classroom.

If you assign more professionally made online videos and podcasts on certain topics, here are some free sources, the first one for podcasts and the rest for videos, but some of these may be too long for your students in their current form:

- iTunes: https://itunes.apple.com/us/genre/podcasts/id26?mt=2 thousands of podcasts of varying length on hundreds of subjects
- Annenberg Media: www.learner.org specializing in the arts, literature, language, history, math, social and natural sciences
- Artbabble: www.artbabble.org/partner/national-gallery-art-washington specializing in art and architecture
- Khan Academy: www.khanacademy.org over 10,000 videos in math and science, but videos also in economics, medicine, arts, and test preparation
- Mindgate Media: http://mindgatemedia.com/ondemand films for teaching and learning
- MITOpenCourseware: http://ocw.mit.edu/index.htm lectures and materials from over 2,200 courses

- OpenYale: http://oyc.yale.edu lectures and materials from selected introductory courses
- TED Talks: www.ted.com over 3,500 highly polished lectures of about 20 minutes or less (You can see a TEDx talk by Todd Zakrajsek, at https://www.youtube.com/watch?v=tYg3sLcyLB8)
- TEDEd: http://ed.ted.com TED talks with short lessons ("flips")
- Videolectures: http://videolectures.netfull-length faculty lectures on many subjects
- YouTube: www.youtube.com; www.youtube.com/edu; and Utubersity: http://utubersidad.com/en lessons, lectures, sports, media broadcasts, interviews, and performances (musical, dance, opera, drama, and comedy)

You will find many more websites as well as learning object repositories in the "Web Resources" section later in this chapter, and all of these represent just a sample.

Your students probably won't know what to watch or listen for in your video and podcast assignments and may not do this homework without a compliance incentive in place. Therefore, treat these assignments as you would any reading assignment and provide students with study questions, a scavenger hunt assignment, or some other homework that ensures and shows evidence of at least basic comprehension.

The flipped classroom is a form of blended learning, and we know that blended learning, when done well, significantly improves student learning over that in face-to-face or online courses (Glazer, 2011). Multiple meta-analyses have shown the effectiveness of the flipped classroom ranges from very weak to very strong (Hew et al., 2021). Your implementation matters.

We recommend checking your department to see if others have successfully flipped their courses and seeking guidance from them. There are also several very good books and articles with detailed information pertaining to how to run an effective flipped classroom (e.g., Guo, 2019; Talbert, 2015). Consider the following basic elements of a well-designed flipped class:

1. Out-of-class material is well-developed (videos are scripted, example-heavy, and aimed at "one student" rather than the whole class; print material is published or publishable; slides are visual heavy, rather than text-heavy [Moore, 2013]), short (less than 10 minutes), and valuable for students.
   a. If you are making your own videos, ask your campus computer specialists about resources, or visit https://people.computing.clemson.edu/~bcdean/lscribe for resources.
   b. If you would like to post professionally made resources, consider https://itunes.apple.com/us/genre/podcasts/id26?mt=2—thousands for podcasts or Annenberg Media (the arts, literature, language, history, math, social and natural sciences, www.learner.org), Khan Academy (STEM fields, www.khanacademy.org—over), or Videolectures (faculty lectures on many subjects, http://videolectures.net—full-length), or YouTube, to name just a few.
2. For the materials made available to students prior to class, provide a few tips to give hints or assistance, particularly for challenging material. It does not take long and is helpful, particularly for first-generation and marginalized students.
3. Ensure students have done the prep work before coming to class. Include a compliance incentive like a scavenger hunt while preparing or a quiz or discussion at the start of class to review content. If students are not prepared, the flipped approach simply will not work.
4. Begin class with a quick summary of whatever outside material you assigned. Do not actually teach the content of the material; think of it like a trailer for a movie.
5. Sharpen your facilitation skills. Facilitating engaged learning or working through problems, which is what you will be doing with your class time, is a different instructional approach than lecturing. If you are a skilled lecturer but have not previously facilitated learning environments, start small and build up to a full flipped approach.
6. Have a clear plan for what will be done during class time. "Have a discussion" is not a plan. As always, identify student learning outcomes for the class period.
7. Talk to your students about why you are using this approach and the value they will receive from this.
8. End class in a way that shows students what was learned (e.g., you provide a summary, students review achievement of outcomes, etc.). In a flipped classroom, if you don't "signpost" what was learned, some students will feel the class was a waste of time.

These are some of the key elements of a flipped class approach. If you have colleagues who indicate that they tried flipping their class and it didn't work, it is likely they did not consider one or more of the preceding points.

▪ SOCIAL MEDIA

Many documented cases testify that social media has been an effective complement to online courses (Featherly, 2014). However, the results are somewhat mixed in classroom-based courses.

Social Networking Tools: Facebook

A Facebook page allows you to set up your own social network comprising you, the students in one of your courses, and anyone else you allow. For educational purposes, this network creates a form of learning community, a method to share recourse, opportunities to collaborate, and as a method for communication. Of course, its value depends on the meaningful participation of all students, which an instructor needs to motivate. According to one study, Facebook, Twitter, and Skype have proven effective in helping entering first-generation students integrate into the college environment (Hottell et al., 2014). Although other social networking sites exist, we focus here on Facebook, because at the time of this edition of the book most students know how to use it and do spend time there. In addition, although Facebook numbers are dropping, Toker and Baturay (2019) found that 71% of students use

Facebook for socialization, 71% for studying, and 72% for daily activities. In addition, you can set up collaborative groups, distribute information and media, promote learning resources, and reinforce the sense of community in your course. Students can post links, images, videos, music, and other media. Set up a group specifically for the course and only interact with students in that space. Do not "friend" students on their, or your, personal accounts.

A Facebook course site has two drawbacks. Although it can serve the purpose of an LMS in some capacities, it lacks the templates and most of the features of an LMS. In addition, some students resent using it or Twitter for class purposes because they consider these social media strictly for personal socializing (Cardon, 2014; Marshall, 2015).

Twitter

Twitter is a simple utility for short messages (up to 280 characters) called *tweets*. If your students do not have a Twitter account, it is very easy to set up a new account (they are free) at http://twitter.com. If you are interested in Twitter, but have not used it much as a faculty member in a course you are teaching, or at all, there are helpful guides to get you started (e.g., Cheplygina et al., 2020). Consider the following strategies:

- Just get started. It is easy to get rolling. Tweet stuff, especially retweeting established users for those new to Twitter.
- Look for higher education–tagged entities.
- Learn and follow Twitter etiquette, such as giving credit to things you learn from others (much like giving publication credit when writing).
- Find good and informative people to follow and recognize there are trolls and nasty people. If necessary, block the mean ones.
- Use Twitter and conferences to interface for networking. Tweet that you will be at a conference and find individuals who are also attending.
- Open up a bit and share some personal information at a level comfortable to you. Twitter is not

Facebook. It is generally used for professional things, but you will see photos of pets, and personal accomplishments.

When you use Twitter in class, provide students with some instructions and model substantial tweets. With Twitter, using a hashtag, you can quickly send students the tweeting topics to address, brief announcements ("No class today due to snow"), test and due-date reminders, and links to current events or new developments relevant to your course. Students can communicate with you and their peers as well. Students can set up collaborations using a group hashtag. In addition, you can identify a hashtag related to the course and have students tweet using that hashtag, thereby joining a live conversation outside of the course.

Twitter in education has experienced significant growth over the past few years, particularly in medicine, social sciences, and computer science (Bicen & Haidov, 2021). A few faculty members have experimented with Twitter as a back channel during class, which means students are tweeting class-related questions and comments on the course hashtag site during class. These faculty members claim that this back channel engages students and reduces the social distance between them. Students can also privately tweet questions you can answer later. However, students can't pay attention in class while composing tweets, and the exchanges can roam off topic (Young, 2009). Some students give into the temptation to go to nonclass sites as well.

Some instructors have used Twitter successfully for homework in a range of disciplines (Lang, 2014). In Koh's (2015) film course, students tweet their interpretations of the films they watch, both in class and out of class, allowing her to gain insight into their reactions and give feedback. Many films have slow moments that permit tweeting without losing information. Ferris (2015) requires his information technology students to regularly post tweets that illustrate the use of statistics as evidence by businesses, survey researchers, and scientists, thereby providing his students many more statistical examples than he or the textbook possibly could. In an experimental study in a first-year seminar for pre-health-professional majors (Junco et al., 2010), the students using Twitter for academic and co-curricular discussions showed higher engagement and achievement. However, the treatment group also had additional readings, several reflective writing assignments, and much more extensive faculty support and encouragement, so we can't know how much Twitter was responsible for the favorable results.

MOBILE LEARNING IN CLASS

There are many ways to use smartphones in class, such as having students conduct research, read the news, convert currencies, do language translations, create videos, take quizzes, make use of apps for learning, and respond to polls. Even with the many options, most instructors have yet integrated mobile devices into pedagogy (Morris & Sarapin, 2020). Vahedi et al. (2021) found that only 11% of students report being in classes where instructors integrated the use of smartphones into the course, yet 97% of those believed that the integration was beneficial to their learning.

Unfortunately, students have found many nonacademic ways to use their mobile devices. If we are to motivate and promote our students' learning, we have a responsibility to direct and focus our students' attention so they can attend to, process, encode, and store our material. Morris and Sarapin (2020) noted that 76% of the faculty members in their survey instituted a mobile phone policy as a direct result of student behavior. Just having a policy, however, does not appear to be enough, as 50% of students use their phones for nonacademic purposes even when policies are in place. When we also consider the number of classes with no-mobile-use policy, several studies, have found large percentages of students using their cell phones during class for nonclass purposes, such as texting, surfing social media sites, tweeting, game playing, web surfing, and shopping (Junco & Cotton, 2012; Kuznekoff

& Titsworth, 2013; McCoy, 2016; Pew Research Center, 2021; Tindell & Bohlander, 2012). We know from how people learn that their misdirected attempts to multitask reduce their learning, focus, academic engagement, and grades.

Why can cell phones disrupt learning? Learning is a highly focused process that multitasking and other distractions undermine every stage of, from attending to new information to rehearsing it for transfer into long-term memory. No matter what students may believe, research has long shown that multitasking between two verbal tasks, such as texting and listening to a lecture, or reading and texting comes at a significant cost with respect to learning (Jamet et al., 2020; Loukopoulos et al., 2009). Working with complex new material demands heavy encoding and all our mental resources: visual, auditory, verbal, and processing. Failures anywhere along the learning process result in information being missed or forgotten, and cell phone activities can cause these failures. Texting, tweeting, reading and posting to Facebook, playing games, web surfing, shopping, and the like make learning impossible.

If you still want your students to use their mobile devices in class, they may be able to control themselves better and pay more attention if you follow Cardon's (2014) advice to give them a short break in the middle of the class period to check their devices. Actually, this kind of break would likely be helpful even if mobile devices were not being used.

Outside class, more frequent visits to Facebook and other distracting internet sites while doing homework and at other times are also associated with lower GPAs and fewer hours studying per week (Kirschner & Karpinski, 2010; Patterson, 2015).

LAPTOPS IN CLASS

There are many uses for laptops in the classroom, but caution should be exercised as laptops pose many of the same distractions and learning pitfalls as cell phones (Bugeja, 2007; Flanigan & Titsworth, 2020;

Yoon et al., 2021). In one study, students were on renegade sites about 42% of the time in class, and their grades varied inversely with the proportion of time they spent on such sites (Kraushaar & Novak, 2010). Many universities, law schools, and business schools that mandated laptops in class some years ago aborted their initiatives because faculty members got fed up with too many students wandering off to non-course-related sites. However, very few of these institutions set up training programs and incentives for faculty members to teach with laptops and manage student use. This is unfortunate, since they have been shown to be effective. J. Fischman (2009) noted that when students were shown that those surfing on their laptops scored lower than those who did not, surfing behavior decreased and their scores increased.

Laptops are powerful in-class learning tools when used properly to achieve student learning outcomes. Laptops can allow students to engage in many worthwhile in-class activities: running experiments, collecting and graphing field data, analyzing survey data, posting analyses of musical compositions, preparing multimedia educational materials, conducting engineering and computer science labs, and editing papers for publication—all in your presence so you can help and give feedback (Nilson & Weaver, 2005).

Laptops are also frequently used to take notes. Interestingly, a widely referenced study concluded that taking notes in class by hand was superior to using a computer to take notes (Mueller & Oppenheimer, 2014), but attempts to replicate the results showed no significant difference between taking notes by hand versus typing (Morehead et al., 2019). It appears the primary factor is the extent to which students summarize and record notes (more often done with handwritten notes) as opposed to recording nearly everything presented in class (more often done with laptops). Teaching students to summarize with laptops removed the difference between taking notes by hand and by computer. That said, students are easily distracted while taking notes, so the issue is complex (Flanigan & Titsworth, 2020).

Another consideration is the rapidly growing use of etextbooks by students. Costs of textbooks has grown rapidly with printed textbooks commonly costing $300 to $500 each. As a result, students are more frequently renting etextbooks. Once study showed that when cost of ebooks are lower than print, 89% of the students selected ebooks (Su, 2021). Campuses are also pushing for ebooks as it is easier to maintain inventory and students can get access to the book immediately. This is important, because if students are using ebooks they may desire or even need to have their laptop open with their book open to the material being presented.

Here are additional ways to manage students' in-class laptop use (Nilson & Weaver, 2005; North Carolina State University Physics Education R&D Group, 2015):

- Have students work on their laptop assignments in triads, as they do in SCALE-UP classrooms (students work in groups of three on active learning tasks, keeping each other accountable, while the teacher or some other faculty member circulates). Students are not interested in watching their peers surf, email, play, shop, and the like, and studies support that this set-up reduces failure rates and improves students' problem-solving skills, conceptual understanding, and attitudes toward the material.
- Set tight time limits for these activities.
- Hold students accountable for accomplishing specific objectives by requiring reporting out or written reports.
- Circulate around the classroom to check students' monitors.
- To test students on their laptops, write exams using secure testing software, such as Respondus Lockdown Browser, and have students download the accompanying software that prevents them from leaving the test site.
- Laptop use in the classroom is a highly debated issue. You will have to decide where you land on this debate, allowing, of course, for institutional policies.

WEB RESOURCES

The web contains a wealth of free resources that you may want your students to read, view, hear, critique, analyze, play, or respond to as an assignment, in-class activity, or research source. You can easily link to these resources from your LMS, class Facebook page, or other course websites without violating copyright. Because this electronic space is so vast, your campus library or instructional technology center may offer web search workshops that can save you hours, even days, of roaming around on a browser. Good search engines and your colleagues can also direct you to worthy sites, or you can post your request for recommended sites on one of your discipline's teaching-focused listservs. The sites that follow are examples of great resources that are available and can also be a launching-off point for ideas of other areas in which to search.

Teaching and Learning Tools

Among the web's resources are an amazing array of free digital teaching and learning resources, many of which fall under the category of learning objects (see the "Learning Objects" section later):

- Vanderbilt University Center for Teaching has an extensive list of well-developed teaching guides (https://cft.vanderbilt.edu)
- Clemson University's Office of Teaching Effectiveness and Innovation has an extensive list of resources: http://www.clemson.edu/otei/resource-page.html
- The University of North Carolina at Chapel Hill has resources identified based on your career stage (early, mid, or senior): https://cfe.unc.edu
- Realistic demonstrations, animated or on video (e.g., cellular processes at www.cellsalive.com for biology, bioengineering, and the health professions)
- Performances (musical, dramatic, dance, and sport)
- Virtual science laboratories for hazardous or costly procedures and experiments (e.g., the Chemistry Collective at www.chemcollective.org; see Chapter 20 for more)
- Case studies (e.g., https://guides.library.ubc.ca/businesscases/free)
- Simulations in many disciplines (e.g., political science: https://activelearningps.com/simulation-index)
- Drills and exercises for remediation, practice, or review (e.g., mathematics, reading, and foreign languages)
- High-resolution photos, including many options for diversity so you can use images that reflect the students in your course. These sites have photos that are freely available (as of the time of this writing) to use in presentations: unsplash.com; Pixabay.com; Pexels.com

The Eberly Center for Teaching Excellence at Carnegie Mellon University has an innovative site called "Solve a Teaching Problem" with a branching program to provide for you specific resources based on the issues you are facing: https://www.cmu.edu/teaching/solveproblem/index.html

Collections for Multimedia Research

Here are some extensive cross-disciplinary collections of well-established, research-worthy multimedia sites that you can safely send your students to:

- Calisphere at www.calisphere.universityofcalifornia.edu: a huge collection of websites, scholarly materials, images, electronic books, data, and statistics
- Open Learning Initiative at http://oli.cmu.edu: access to over two dozen online courses and course materials in a wide range of academic fields
- CSERDA Metadata Catalog at www.shodor.org/refdesk/Catalog: a searchable repository of web-based teaching materials for mathematics, computer science, and the sciences
- Internet Archive (aka the WayBack Machine) at https://archive.org: a collection of millions of websites, software, and digitized cultural artifacts

(images, audio files, animations); also courses, study guides, assignments, books, and recorded lectures under "Education"

- MERLOT (Multimedia Educational Resource for Learning and Online Teaching) at www .merlot.org: tens of thousands of annotated links to free learning materials, most peer reviewed, including entire courses, databases, presentations, and collections
- National Science Foundation Internet Library at https://nsdl.oercommons.org: rich and technologically sophisticated instructional materials for the sciences, engineering, mathematics, public health, economics, and other fields
- Online Books Page at www.digital.library.upenn .edu/books: free access to over two million books
- New York Public Library Digital Collections at www.nypl.org/collections: a vast collection of culturally significant images, audio files, videos, print and audio books, articles, maps, DVDs, menus, and research-worthy databases and archives
- Smithsonian Institution at www.si.edu: virtual access to the world's largest museum (actually over a dozen museums), nine research centers, and the National Zoo

Learning Objects

These are self-contained, reusable, digital lessons on specific topics, the best of which are animated, interactive, and truly multimedia. Some can provide eye-catching demonstrations to spark up your minilectures, while others can make valuable in-class laptop activities as well as out-of-class assignments. As they provide lessons, students can learn on their own and at their own pace by playing or running them any number of times. Both faculty members and students perceive learning objects to be powerful teaching and learning tools (Goodsett, 2020; Ip et al., 2001; Shank, 2014), and one study reports that they most benefit students who need the most help (Biktimirov & Nilson, 2007).

Learning objects are housed in open learning object repositories, many of them searchable by discipline. In some cases, you must join an online community, but this entails no cost. One of the repositories in this list even provides annotated links to additional repositories:

- MERLOT (Multimedia Educational Resource for Learning and Online Teaching) at www .merlot.org: tens of thousands of interactive case studies, simulations, games, and animations for every discipline
- OER (Open Educational Resources) Commons at www.oercommons.org: over 50,000 materials, many interactive and animated, for college level and above (much more for K–12) for every discipline
- JORUM at www.jorum.ac.uk: close to 20,000 materials, many interactive and animated, for college-level and continuing education, almost all unique to this site
- Wisconsin Online Resource Center at www .wisc-online.com: thousands of animations, games, and interactive exercises for many content areas, as well as for cognitive, communication, and social skills
- Shodor Interactivate at www.shodor.org/ interactivate: dozens of interactive lessons and exercises for the mathematics, statistics, and some sciences

■ THE FUTURE OF EDUCATIONAL TECHNOLOGY

Think back to 1980, when personal computers hit the market. In 1983, the internet debuted to the general population. Fast forward to 2006, when Facebook went live; 2007, the iPhone debuted; 2008, Apple launched the App Store; and in 2011 and 2014, Siri and Alexa entered the chat. Technology is moving faster and reaching milestones we could not have predicted even a few short years ago. As noted in this chapter, immersive mixed realities, 3D-printed art projects, and artificial intelligence algorithms for medical diagnoses are our reality with amazing developments on the horizon.

Today's high-tech tools and software will be obsolete in a few years, having been superseded by another version, product, or utility that takes us to new opportunities. One safe prediction (for at least the foreseeable future) is that teachers will be needed. Despite extensive increases in digital training aids, the U.S. Bureau of Labor Statistics notes that the fitness/trainer sector will increase faster than the average for all sectors (U.S. Bureau of Labor Statistics, 2022). Positions for postsecondary teachers are expected to grow 12% from 2020–2030. We are like cognitive coaches.

Faculty members, like everyone else, have different approaches to technology. Some pioneers live on the "bleeding edge," testing technology so new that it might not work at all, resulting in large expense with no value. Some are on the slightly safer leading edge, followed by those who are interested, tolerant, or reluctant. These different individuals have all existed on campuses for many years. It is likely, with the speed of technology changes and the impact of the changes, that it will be challenging to be reluctant to make any change. That said, our position was firmly stated in Chapter 2 and we will restate it regularly, but perhaps no more importantly than here: Develop meaningful student learning outcomes. Whenever you adopt any technology, it should help students to meet or exceed those outcomes.

■ REFLECTION QUESTIONS

Reflection Question 4.1: How do you feel about technology? To what extent can it help education and where might it cause us difficulties with respect to our goals of helping students meet learning outcomes?

Reflection Question 4.2: How might you get your students involved in technology changes you could make in your courses? This is more than a class discussion. Reflect on this a bit and think about how they could get involved in a way that they would enjoy and you would be helping them to meet learning outcomes.

Concept Into Practice: Reread the SAMR section of this chapter. Search for additional information online, identify one technology, and then describe how you could use that technology to substitute, augment, modify, and redefine something you currently do. If you are really motivated, put that into practice.

CHAPTER 5

Building a More Complete Syllabus

According to the Oxford Learner's Dictionary (2022), a syllabus is "a list of the topics, books, etc. that students should study in a particular subject at school or college." That was true when the word *syllabus* first appeared in the mid-17th century, but now a course syllabus is so much more. It isn't just that the syllabus is drastically different than it was in the mid-17th century. The typical higher education syllabus is very different now than it was at the beginning of this century, about 20 years ago. The syllabus of today contains a list of topics and resources that will be studied. It is also the students' introduction to the overall subject matter, a motivational document to encourage them to do well, the first step in building a community, a welcome with an expectation of inclusion, indications of expected standards of behavior, a reminder of campus resources, the anticipated tone of the course learning environment, and their first impression of *you*. Many syllabi now include nearly every aspect of the course, such as a schedule of class assignments, readings, and activities; insight into the material; rubrics; grade distribution (or how grades will be assigned if the instructor takes an ungrading

approach); and a description of your approach to teaching. When done well, a syllabus is not just a road map for the student to get through the course, but rather a travelogue to pique students' interest in the expedition and its leader. When it comes to teaching at your best, the syllabus is typically your first interaction with the students you will be working with for the next several months. It is a very important introduction to you and your course.

■ HOW EXTENSIVE? WHAT TONE?

A syllabus is composed of the interests of three groups: students in the course, the faculty member teaching the course, and the university. Students typically desire information specifically about the aspects of the course that impact their grades (e.g., exam dates, extra credit opportunities, when/how often assignments are due, late work policies, makeup exam policy, and consequences for missing class) and the environment in which they will be learning. Faculty members want to provide information that students need to be successful in the course, to let students know expected behavior in building and maintaining a learning community, and encourage students to continue to learn more after the course concludes. In addition to the items students focus on, faculty members will also often include ultimate outcomes, a schedule of reading assignments, instructions for group projects, information about readings, expectations for student participation and mutual respect in the classroom, how to contact the faculty member, office hours, and how to address the faculty member. From the university perspective, the syllabus provides a list of learning outcomes, policy statements about academic integrity, information regarding disability accommodations, awareness of Title IX, and other campus resources that are available.

A comprehensive syllabus now easily runs 5 to 10 pages, with some very lengthy syllabi at 50 pages or more. Many faculty members have concluded, often through hard experience, that they need to include detailed policies, rubrics, directions, personal communications, and so on. This type of syllabus can become so long that it deserves and requires a title page and table of contents. Research is mixed on student preference for length of the syllabus. Harrington and Gabert-Quillen (2015) found that students generally prefer a longer syllabus with all the information included rather than some of the information and a note that more will follow as needed.

Proponents of shorter syllabi posit that many faculty members and institutions have overdone the policies and sanctions and have inadvertently created a legalistic, rule-bound document that assumes students must be threatened or bribed to behave courteously in class, submit their work on time, take tests when scheduled, manifest academic integrity, and the like (Schuman, 2014). They say some have reacted fearfully to highly sensitive, grade-anxious students and have adopted the self-protective ethos of the corporatized university (Schuman, 2014). Supporters of shorter syllabi assert that students respond better to a document that is seen as a reference and contains only information that is needed

(Lightner & Benander, 2018), some advocating for a single piece of paper, front and back (Deans, 2019), which is consistent with Schuman's (2014) suggestion of putting lengthy policies and rules in an appendix away from the important information about the course content, schedule, and assignment basics.

In addition to length, the tone of the syllabus is also very important. Studies show that students prefer a learning-focused syllabus that states strong student learning outcomes and a positive, motivating tone over a traditional content- and policy-focused syllabus (Wheeler et al., 2019). Students indicate that a learning-focused syllabus implied that they would be more involved in the course, would sit through fewer lectures, would learn more, and that the instructor would help them to be successful. Wilson and Ryan (2013) found that students rated instructors of learning-centered syllabi as more engaged, more caring, and offering higher professor–student support.

Intentional and visible caring and support, including in the syllabi, are more important than ever. Even before the COVID-19 pandemic, mental illness services were overwhelmed, and after the onset of the pandemic, perceived stress and anxiety among college students skyrocketed (Hoyt et al., 2021). Syllabi that have supportive tones (e.g., positive language, "we will" statements, rationale for assignments, enthusiasm for the course) and particularly a "reach out" statement, making reaching out for assistance easier for students (Gurung & Galardi, 2021), are known as "warm" syllabi. The reach-out information stated that all students encounter setbacks, provided a crisis hotline number, and normalized needing and asking for help.

As the instructor, you decide the tone (warmer or colder) and focus (learning or content) of your syllabus. However, realize that warmer syllabi need not have easier standards or looser policies than colder syllabi. A warmer syllabus just lets students know you are rooting for them, whereas a cooler syllabus often sounds like you don't care what happens to them in the course. A warm syllabus is not saying you are their friend or their parent; it just provides a sense of camaraderie and care along with your high academic standards. The most important thing is for you to recognize the tone you are setting and to ensure the tone is what you desire. The syllabus should communicate your desire to create a community of learners right from the start of the semester, however that may look (Harrington & Thomas, 2018). The syllabus, in beginning the creation of a community, will often include the learning outcomes, the schedule of topics and assignments, mutual expectations, respectful classroom conduct, and the structure of the course (Gannon, 2018; Habanek, 2005). Ask for feedback from your colleagues or look at examples of syllabi online if you're unsure where you are on this spectrum or where you want to be.

This debate on the length and structure of the syllabus will certainly continue. However, some basic information deserves consideration in every syllabus. The next section suggests essential information to put in a syllabus and models to fill in the rest, along with suggestions to forge a warm, trusting relationship with your class.

▪ ESSENTIAL SYLLABUS ITEMS

Here is an annotated list of items that you should probably put in your course syllabi. They represent what your students really want to know: your policies, assignments, and grading methods (Doolittle & Siudzinski, 2010; Harrington & Thomas, 2018). The length of each can be a few words to a long paragraph, depending on content you feel is necessary to include

- *Basic course information*: the course number and title; days, hours, and location of class meetings for classroom-based courses, and days and times for any online synchronous meetings; credit hours; required or recommended prerequisites for enrollment, including the instructor's permission; any out-of-class requirements, such as attending a performance; required laboratories or recitation or discussion sections, with the same information as given for the course; and the titles and location of any online course materials, exercises, assignments, exams, and supplementary materials that are on the web (give the URL) or in your LMS (specify the folder).

- *Information about yourself*: your full name and title, the way you wish to be addressed, your office hours, office location (if you have one), office phone number, email address, and home page URL (if you have one). Invite your students to take advantage of your face-to-face office hours. Explain that office hours are the times set aside to meet with students, as some first-generation college students believe "office hours" refer to when faculty members are working in their offices and unavailable. You might update the term to *student hours* to help address this misconception. Offer online office hour meetings through Zoom, FaceTime, or Microsoft Teams. This is the standard for online teaching, but can also be helpful for face-to-face classes if students live off campus or have caretaking or transportation challenges. If you decide to give students your home, cell phone number, or set up WhatsApp (or Kik, Snapchat or something similar), consider limiting calls to certain days and reasonable hours, and give communication hours for email as well.

- *The same information about other course personnel*, such as teaching assistants (TAs), technicians, and other assistants, as you gave for yourself. You might encourage section or lab TAs to develop their own brief syllabi.

- *A briefly annotated list of reading materials*, such as assigned books (including edition and cost—reminding students they can buy or rent), journal articles, class packets, and web materials with full citations, price, location (bookstore, library, reserve status, URL, or LMS folder), identification as required or recommended, and your reasons for selecting them. If you do not plan to give regular assignments from the text, consider making it a recommended supplementary source, particularly as some textbooks can cost several hundred dollars. Also check for open educational resources for textbooks. If commercially prepared notes are available, indicate their learning value.

- *Any other materials required for the course,* including cost estimates and where to find them for a good price. For example, some science labs require students to have a personal stock of cleaning supplies and safety equipment. Art and photography classes usually expect students to furnish their own equipment, supplies, and expendable materials. If special types of calculators, computers, or software are called for, these too deserve mention. If the materials won't be used immediately, specify when in the term they will be. Some students, typically from underrepresented groups, are on very tight budgets. Assign items only when essential for learning.

- *A course description*, which may be as brief as a few lines describing the content. However, you might want to elaborate on the organization or flow of the course and your rationale for it. If past experience has shown that students have particular misconceptions, address those briefly.

- *Your student learning outcomes for the course.* These should not be just your ultimate outcomes (what students should be able to do or do better at the end of the course) but also your major mediating and foundational outcomes. Chapter 2 gives guidance on developing solid, assessable learning outcomes; designing a course around them; and charting an outcomes map to show students your plan for their learning process. In fact, outcomes maps better orient your students than a list. However, you don't want students to interpret your outcomes as binding promises to them, and you know your students have to apply themselves to achieve these outcomes, so consider adding this caveat or disclaimer: (1) Students may vary in their competency levels on these outcomes, and (2) they can expect to achieve these outcomes *only*

if they honor course policies, attend class regularly, complete assigned work on time, and participate in class discussions and activities.

- *A list of graded course requirements and breakdown of your grading scale*, such as the number and point values of in-class activities, homework assignments, peer-group evaluations, class participation, discussion, electronic communication, tests, papers, and projects, and so on. If you expect students to participate in class discussions, describe appropriate participation. If you intend to grade class participation, be sure you have some sort of written record to back up this part of the grade. Note that graded participation can be stressful for shy and anxious students (Norlock, 2016). Consider giving students an opportunity to email you their in-class thoughts and grade those just as you would speaking up in class. If you plan to give unannounced quizzes to monitor comprehension, let it be known from the beginning. State if the lowest-scoring work can be thrown out. Finally, explain the grading system you will use (criterion referenced, a curve, or something else; see Chapter 26), along with percentage breakdowns (such as 91–100 = A, 81–90 = B, and so on). Describe any anticipated in-class activities, homework assignments, tests, and quizzes (how much essay versus objective items; see Chapter 25). Note clearly the manner in which grades may be challenged. You might be wise to explain why you are assessing the way you are and how your assessments map onto the learning outcomes. Rationales are an excellent way to warm your syllabus without lowering standards.

- *How major assignments (e.g., papers, projects, recordings, oral presentations) will be evaluated*: with an atomistic key, a holistic rubric, or an analytical rubric (see Chapter 26). Although not required, it is helpful to provide the grading rubric. Explain your policies regarding revisions and extra credit. Also consider having opportunities for extra credit end at least one week before the final so students are not working on extra credit when they should be studying or completing term papers. One other challenge you will want to address are grade protests. It tends to work well to require that students submit all grading inquiries in writing, tying their justification to specific pages in the readings or dated class periods, within 48 hours of the grade being received.

- *Your policies on attendance and tardiness.* If you take off points for lack of attendance or tardiness, you should state *academic reasons* for your requirements (e.g., you conduct learning activities, or that you lecture on important materials not in the readings). Comeford (2022) implemented an attendance policy for an introductory course and an upper-division course and found that with an attendance policy, the introductory course students attended at a significantly higher rate and earned a significantly higher final exam score. However, the upper-division course demonstrated no change in either attendance or final exam score, suggesting that an attendance policy may be more helpful in early college years, but less so later as students better understand the value of attending and the consequences if a class session is missed. Some colleges and universities require faculty members to report students who are excessively absent so that they may contact those students to see if there is a deeper issue. As a result, you may have to keep attendance even if you don't intend to grade on it. To be sure, check with your department about academic regulations at your institution. Instructors usually excuse absences for documented medical reasons, court obligations, a family death, field trips required for another course, scheduled participation in an organized sport, and sometimes commitments scheduled well in advance.

- *Your policies on missed or late exams and assignments.* Students may have good reasons for missing a deadline or a test, as they do for some absences, and documentation can help support that. State whether students can drop one quiz or grade during the term or schedule a makeup, or if their grade on another exam, like the final, will substitute for the grade on the missed one. If you assess penalties for late work, describe them precisely to prevent any later disputes. Check the academic regulations in your institution's course catalogue so your penalties don't exceed what is allowed.

- *A statement of your and your institution's policies on academic dishonesty, as well as how they apply in your course.* Your institution's policies are boilerplate statements that all but first-semester students have seen and heard before, so they might very well belong in an appendix. Your personal stance on academic integrity, however, may deserve a more prominent place. Cheating and plagiarism are all too common on today's college campuses, as Chapter 12 documents. Unless you make a strong statement about your intolerance of them, your students may assume that you are naive or will look the other way. This statement should include the procedures you will follow in prosecuting violations and the sanctions a student may suffer. (It is very important that you check with the institution so that your policy is not stricter than the institution allows.) If your institution has an honor code, state that you will strictly adhere to and enforce it. Also address academic honesty policies with respect to group activities and products in your course. If you don't detail your rules, your students may inadvertently violate your and your institution's policies.

- *A statement of your institution's policies on ADA (Americans with Disabilities Act) accommodations.* Your institution may require you to insert a boilerplate statement somewhere in your syllabus. But you should know some of the accommodations you may have to make. Providing a documented accommodation is not an option, it is a requirement, whether you agree with it or not. At the same time, never provide a student an accommodation if they have no documentation, as such a move can have legal implications down the road. In the traditional classroom, most accommodations are quite simple—for instance, giving students extra time or an isolated place to take an exam or welcoming an American Sign Language (ASL) expert in your classroom. Your institution probably has a disability services office that furnishes quiet exam locations, ASL specialists, and even books on tape. In fact, your responsibilities involve typically little more than cooperating with that office. That said, at times providing the accommodations can be taxing. Remember that the goal of accommodations is to give the student an opportunity to learn, no more, no less. Some students are also rather terse when it comes to requesting accommodations. This can be frustrating for you, but keep in mind their tone is likely a result of years of frustrations.

Your accommodations role grows as you move more material online, however. If you record your lectures, for instance, provide closed captioning and perhaps a transcript. Transcription software like Dragon will often create transcripts automatically. An increasing number of educational technology solutions, such as YouTube and Zoom, automatically provide closed captioning. If you create a website, provide users with navigational help in finding content and ensure that the pages can be read with a screen reader. All prerecorded audio material, such as podcasts, must be captioned, have a text alternative, or display an ASL-signed version. Prerecorded video and images must have an audio track or description. In other words, all material must be available in *multi*media. Many of these accommodations represent teaching at its best for all your students. Other ADA accessibility guidelines lay out technical requirements for audio control, color, contrast, text size control, and text layout. All of the web-content guidelines are at http://www.w3.org/TR/WCAG20, but you should be able to get help from your campus disability services staff, information technologists, and instructional designers.

- *Policies on classroom decorum and academic discourse.* Such policies may seem controlling, but some students are not familiar with the classroom culture or the effects that their behavior can have on other students as well as on you. It is your job to create a learning environment that is as free as possible from distractions, annoyances, name-calling, personal attacks, and other demonstrations of disrespect. Zero in on only the most significant behavioral issues, which will vary by campus and class, and avoid long lists of don'ts. Phrase conduct codes in positive terms when possible. Explain the benefits of paying attention and engaging in civil discussion along with the consequences for violating the codes (see Chapter 11).

- *Proper safety procedures and conduct for laboratories.* Although you would hope that students would have the common sense to apply good safety habits to their work, you cannot assume that these habits are intuitive. Specify strict rules for lab dress (including shoes) and procedures. Let students know if you impose penalties for safety violations. These procedures and policies may merit a separate lab syllabus or handbook.

- *Relevant campus support services for students and their locations* for assistance in mastering course software, doing computer assignments, writing papers or lab reports, learning study skills, and solving homework problems. The appendix identifies such resources on the typical campus. Remember there is a great deal of assistance available for your students throughout the campus. You are not expected to deliver everything your students need on your own.

- *A week-by-week or class-by-class course schedule* with as much of the following information as possible: topics to be covered; in-class activities and formats (lecture, guest speaker, class discussion, group work, demonstration, case study, field trip, role play, simulation, game, debate, panel discussion, video, computer exercise, review session, and so on); dates of announced quizzes and exams; and due dates of all reading assignments and all other homework. Be sure to accommodate holidays and breaks for a variety of faiths and religions.

- *A concluding legal caveat or disclaimer.* During the semester, your course schedule may get thrown off for any number of reasons: snowstorms, floods, a pandemic, hurricanes, firestorms, your own health issues, or discovering that your students are ill-prepared for the material you have planned for them. Disruptions slow down the course and force you to diverge from your syllabus. Students may think they are not getting their money's worth if you fail to get through your syllabus by the end of the course. In our litigious society, they may even file a grievance or threaten to sue if you fail to follow the syllabus schedule. In fact, the courts have not recognized the syllabus as a legally binding contract on an instructor because the students' registration for the course constitutes voluntary acceptance of the terms of the course and the instructor maintains creative control over the content and methods of instruction (Rumore, 2016). Still, you'd be smart to add this caveat/disclaimer regarding changes to the course at the end of the syllabus. This way you make your right to use your own discretion explicit. Although this disclaimer mentions policies, it is best to avoid changing those unless they work in the students' favor.

The above schedule, policies, procedures, and assignments in this course are subject to change in the event of extenuating circumstances, by mutual agreement, and/or to ensure better student learning.

If at all possible, keep exam dates as planned. Some students build work schedules and schedule childcare providers well in advance for study time and exam time. While some students will loudly cheer if an exam date is pushed back, for others the date change has immediate scheduling challenges.

- *Copyright.* An increasing number of faculty members are putting copyright notices on all of their documents, including their syllabi, to avoid students selling, uploading, and otherwise distributing your materials without your permission.
- *Check for campus boilerplate required statements*, and ask your department chair or some other knowl-

edgeable person where you can find prewritten statements that either must be, or are suggested to be, included in the syllabus.

These additional syllabus items are not essential but have merit:

- *Curricular requirements your course satisfies*, such as general education; writing-, speaking-, or ethics-across-the-curriculum; various majors; and any other graduation requirements of your institution or program.
- *Background information about yourself*, such as your degrees, universities you have attended, other institutions where you have taught or conducted research, and your areas of research or special interest in your field. After all, you likely ask your students for some personal and academic information. In addition, most students are keenly interested in you as a professional and a person and appreciate knowing something about you. A little sharing about yourself can also help build their sense of personal loyalty to you.
- *Your teaching philosophy.* This could easily be adapted from cover letters or previous job applications. It can express your commitment to education, your hopes and objectives for your students, your knowledge of how people learn, your view of the mutual rights and obligations between instructors and students, the rapport with students you aim to develop, and your preferred teaching and assessment methods.

■ THE GRAPHIC SYLLABUS

A graphic syllabus, like an outcomes map, is a visual tool to communicate your course to your students more effectively. Specifically, it is a flowchart, graphic organizer, or diagram of the sequencing and organization of your course's major topics through the term. It may also notate the calendar schedule of the topics, the major activities and assignments, and the tests. Kaur (2021) provided identically formatted infographic syllabi with relevant content to a first-year seminar, a 300-level elective liberal arts course, and a 400-level minor elector course. Students in all three courses liked the graphic syllabus, noting it was easy to read, memorable, and engaging. The students also noted that this type of syllabus made them feel less anxious about the course, more comfortable about the requirements of the course, and they spent more time reading it than they do a traditional text-based syllabus. It is important to note that however much information a graphic syllabus contains, it can't include everything that a regular text syllabus should; it is meant to be a supplement, not a replacement. The following material is meant to be an overview and introduction to the graphic syllabus. If you are interested in more detailed information, Nilson's (2007) guides are excellent resources.

Perhaps an example is the best way to understand the concept. Figure 5.1 displays the graphic syllabus of Nilson's undergraduate Social Stratification course from UCLA some years ago. It is fairly simple and unadorned, but it helped the students see the complex interrelationships among the weekly topics. For instance, it makes clear that the first 3 weeks address theory, and the rest of the course focuses on empirical research. It illustrates that one of the two major theories has spawned research on two types of inequality (which support *this* theory), whereas the other major theory has generated research on two other types of inequality (which support *that* theory). During the last few weeks on how social stratification persists, the graphic shows that one explanation derives only from one major theory and its research, while the second one integrates both major theories and their findings, as well as psychology. The flow of course topics takes on a logic and internal cohesion that a list cannot capture. Note that the graphic syllabus flows in only one direction, as a course does through time. A final warning: *Don't* make the syllabus too complex, cluttered, or detailed. Its intent is to *clarify*. And *do* refer to it during the course as you would to a map during a trip.

Aside from clarifying complex relationships among topics, a graphic syllabus offers many other learning benefits. It gives students an additional level of understanding of the course material by providing the big picture of your course content: the structure of the knowledge as an integrated whole and a cohesive system of interpreting phenomena. With a knowledge structure already in hand, students are better able to process and retain the material. In addition, a graphic syllabus reveals why you organized the course the way you did. No doubt you put substantial time and mental effort into your course design and topical organization, but students, who have no background in the field, can't possibly follow your sophisticated logic. They don't know what many of the words mean or how one concept or topic may relate to another. In a graphic, you can show such relationships using spatial arrangements and arrows.

Additional advantages accrue from a graphic syllabus by virtue of its being a visual representation. Students are more likely to comprehend and remember materials they receive both verbally and visually. In addition, visuals require less working memory and fewer cognitive transformations. Visuals even cue the associated textual information, which means that simply recalling the shape of the visual can help a student remember the words within it. Moreover, graphics communicate better than text across cultural and language barriers, so they help us meet the learning needs of a diverse student population.

One final benefit of designing a graphic syllabus is for you. In addition to being a creative outlet, a graphic syllabus can help you identify any snags in your course organization, such as topics that are chronologically misplaced or missing or that don't fit at all.

ENSURING YOUR STUDENTS READ YOUR SYLLABUS

A solid syllabus says good things about you to your class. Among them, it says that you understand students, how they dislike surprises and last-minute

Figure 5.1   Graphic Syllabus of Social Stratification Course

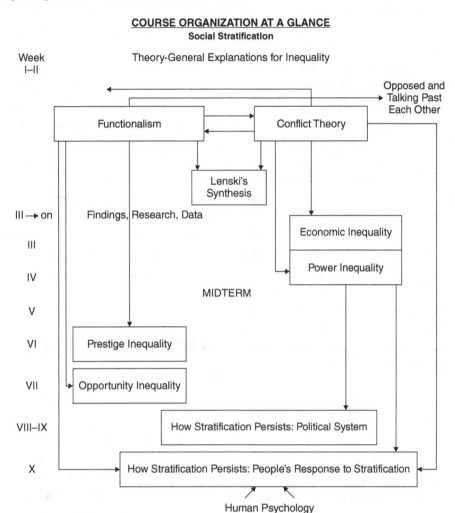

assignments, and how they appreciate an organized, explicit course structure around which they can plan their semester. It says that you respect them, as well as the subject matter of the course.

Even so, you can't expect all students to study your carefully constructed document. Some instructors field student questions that are answered in the syllabus all term. Although they should not be expected to remember every aspect of the course, they should remember that a lot of course information is located in one document. Reading the syllabus out loud during your first class meeting rarely suffices, and besides, your time on the first class period is better spent building community and

modeling what class sessions will look like. Here are six more effective options to encourage students to attend to the information in the syllabus.

First, if your syllabus is just a few pages, have your students read it in class; then break into small groups to do one of several possible syllabus activities. For instance, they can discuss the document and answer each other's questions about it. Or you can structure their discussion around some question, such as: "Compared to the other courses you've taken in college, do you expect this one to be more or less difficult [or require more or less time], and why?" Ballard (2007) has her students make a list of questions that they should never ask her, since the answers are in the syllabus. You can even turn the syllabus into a game by sending the groups on a scavenger hunt for certain critical information. Provide some small prize (e.g., candy or a piece of fruit) for each member in the quickest and most thorough group.

Second, assign the syllabus as homework, answer questions about it the second day of class, and then have each student sign a statement including verbiage such as: "I have thoroughly read the course syllabus and understand its contents. I understand the course requirements and the grading and attendance policies stated in the syllabus" (T. D. I. Campbell, personal communication, September 27, 2001).

Schuman (2014) takes a *third* approach: the Easter egg approach. In computer games, an Easter egg is a hidden artifact, secreted away for a gamer to find. It adds interest to the game. The same can be done for a syllabus. Schuman (2014) inserts, at the end of the document, a brief assignment to email her with a question, which she grades pass (for doing it) or fail. She said about half of her students fail an assignment they didn't even know about, but she does accept late submissions. Other instructors offer extra credit for finding an egg. They can be obvious or well hidden.

A *fourth* alternative is to assign the syllabus as homework and give a quiz on it the second day of class (Gannon, 2018). The test items need not be all factual questions on the number of tests, the point value of assignments, and the like. You can ask interesting and thought-provoking short-answer and short-essay questions, such as: Which of the student learning outcomes for this course are most important to you personally, and why? What are two challenges, based on information in the syllabus, that you anticipate encountering in this course, and what strategies will you use to overcome them? Answers to these questions will give you insight into your students' aspirations, interests, insecurities, and self-assessments.

A *fifth* option is to put students into groups of four and ask them to look through the syllabus and see if there is anything they feel is missing or information in the syllabus that they feel needs a bit more explanation. Have the groups report out on their findings. This helps show students that it is always valuable to get feedback.

One *final* option is to distribute your syllabus the first day and cover the critical components (prerequisites, contact information, ADA accommodations, etc.) immediately, and then continue to refer to components of the syllabus as those aspects arise in the course (Deans, 2019; Gannon, 2018). By referring to the syllabus repeatedly, you are modeling for students that it is a good reference for whatever issues or questions arise in the course. This is just-in-time learning at its purest, and you are almost guaranteed an interested audience.

ADDING A CREATIVE ELEMENT

Whatever items you incorporate into your syllabus, it need not be a sterile desert of text. Of course, you can design a graphic syllabus to accompany it, but you can also add photos, drawings, clip art, word art, and other graphic features to break up and spark up the text. In addition, you can fashion certain sections of the syllabus, such as the course description and schedule of topics, activities, and assignments, around a metaphor—perhaps an itinerary of a term-long adventure, a program of a concert or conference, or even the menu of a multi-course meal. Students appreciate creative touches like these in an otherwise dry document, and such whimsical enhancements can become your personal trademark.

REFLECTION QUESTIONS

Reflection Question 5.1: What are the five most essential items in your syllabus? Where are those five items located? How will students know that they are some of the most important items in that document?

Reflection Question 5.2: How do you encourage your students to read the syllabus? Is there something that could be done weekly to get students to read the syllabus without making it feel like it is a weekly chore?

Concept Into Practice: Ask three different people to read your syllabus. Give them up to a week and ask each to respond to the following question: "Based only on the syllabus, if you were a student, how would you feel about this course and me as an instructor?" Even if all the feedback is positive, try to identify one thing you can improve based on their responses for the upcoming or next semester.

CHAPTER 6

Following Copyright Guidelines

As you prepare to teach a course—classroom, online, or hybrid—you will likely want to include work by people beyond the required books and electronic materials assigned as part of the course. You may find images from a web search to include in a PowerPoint supporting your minilecture, play background music for a student science exhibit, or show a 15-minute clip from a movie for students to critically review. If you do any of these things, and most faculty members do, you have just entered the through-the-looking-glass world of "fair use," "educational purposes," "creative commons," "copyright," and other such Cheshire Cat categories that make most of us wonder what we can use in classes.

Before we hit send to email students a copy of a published article, post a document on a course website or LMS, or even consider showing a video in class, it is good practice to ask yourself whether the creator of the work would be fine with us using it with or without attribution. In this perpetually confusing landscape, the only legally correct answer to any query you make will almost certainly be "probably," "unlikely," or "it depends." For example,

suppose you want to show a video in your class. If it is not permissible to show the video in a public space, the question becomes, "Is a classroom/online course a public place?" Even experts disagree, and the courts have not yet settled the issue. As Mark Twain is credited with saying, "Only one thing is impossible for God: To find any sense in any copyright law on the planet."

In the absence of simple, clear rules that are easily available, it is little wonder that we tend to pick up copyright law by word of mouth. The problem is that individuals typically state what they believe. They often do so with confidence and, as a result, spread myths and misconceptions. These individuals are not acting maliciously, they just don't know what they don't know, and at times can be very confident about it (Kruger & Dunning, 1999).

The legal ambiguities only feed our fears of what might happen to us if we were actually caught or arrested by the copyright enforcers (whoever they may be) for violating their rules, even unknowingly. The laws, guidelines, and enforcement policies are not well publicized in the academic world and may surprise you. Many of the rules are highly technical, make questionable sense, and are difficult to absorb and remember. Rules governing newer technologies also change as lawsuits are resolved and the U.S. Copyright Office issues new regulations and exemptions, some of which have expiration dates.

All the legal information in this chapter comes ultimately from Title 17 of the United States Code, which includes the Copyright Act of 1976 and its subsequent amendments—literally dozens of them, including the Conference on Fair Use (CONFU, 1995–1997), the Digital Millennium Copyright Act of 1998 (DMCA), and the Technology Harmonization and Education Act of 2002 (TEACH Act). The DMCA and the TEACH Act were amendments of the Copyright Act of 1976 and set the guidelines for multimedia use and online and distance learning, some of which have an ambiguous legal status. This chapter focuses on the fair use exemptions that are granted for educational purposes.

Laws, statutes, and guidelines are written to obfuscate, so credit is due those who have interpreted and translated them into plain English; they have served as invaluable factual sources for this chapter: Davidson (2008), Nemire (2007), Orlans (1999), Stim (2019), and the University of Minnesota Libraries (2015). Librarians are always providers of great information and this topic is no different. Many libraries post information that helps us to interpret these laws (e.g., Missouri S&T Library and Learning Resources at https://libguides.mst.edu/c.php?g=395171&p=2685087). We present this information as a guideline and with no guarantees. If you are in doubt, check with the expert on your campus before making your decision as to how best to proceed.

■ WHERE COPYRIGHT DOES AND DOES NOT APPLY

Copyright law does not protect facts, ideas, discoveries, inventions, words, phrases, symbols, designs that identify a source of goods, or some U.S. government publications (you must check on each one). This doesn't mean we don't cite the sources of our facts, other people's ideas, or certain key phrases, for example. We just need not ask permission or purchase a license to use them. Many inventions are protected by patent law, another realm of intellectual property.

Copyright law does, however, protect creative works, whether literary (fiction and nonfiction), musical (including lyrics), dramatic (including accompanying music), choreographic, sculptural, pictorial, graphic, architectural, audiovisual (including motion pictures), or sound recorded.

■ COMMON COPYRIGHT MISCONCEPTIONS

There are several popular misconceptions around copyright. First, merely giving credit to the author of a work is not a way around or substitute for copyright law compliance. All a citation exempts you from is plagiarism. Second, the work may be protected even in the absence of a copyright notice. Although most works have a notice, those published on or after March 1, 1989, are protected even without one. Third, changing someone else's copyrighted work here and there will not make it legally yours. In fact, such action may make you doubly liable: for infringement of copyright *and* of the copyright holder's right of modification.

Finally, flattering or showcasing a work is not likely to allay the copyright owner's objections to your free use of the work. This is especially true of multimedia works; their producers view licenses as a source of income. Freelance writers, music publishers, and musical performers have successfully sued major large organizations like the *New York Times* for the unauthorized publication or distribution of their work on online computer services (Peiser, 2018).

■ FREE USE: FAIR USE, FACTS, AND PUBLIC DOMAIN

Free use means no license or written permission from the copyright holder is required to copy, distribute, or electronically disseminate the work. However, whether a given case qualifies depends on three rather gray criteria: (1) your use is *fair use*, (2) the material you wish to use is factual or an idea, and (3) the work you wish to use is in the public domain.

In general, fair use means use for noncommercial purposes and specifically for purposes of teaching, scholarship, research, criticism, comment, parody, and news reporting. The courts are most likely to find fair use where the copied work is a factual as opposed to a creative work. However, no legal guidelines are available to distinguish factual material or an idea from something else; determinations are made on a case-by-case basis. Another consideration is whether the new work poses market or readership competition for the copyrighted work.

The amount and the significance of the protected work used also figure into the determination of fair use. Use of a tiny amount of the work typically does not raise concerns unless it is substantial in terms of importance, such as the heart of the copied work. For instance, a magazine article that used 300 words from a 200,000-word autobiography written by President Gerald Ford was found to infringe the copyright on the autobiography (Hager, 1985). Even though the copied material was only a tiny portion of the autobiography, it included some of the most powerful passages in the work.

Public domain is a clearer legal concept but is sometimes redefined. A work that was published in the United States is now in the public domain if: (1) it was published on or before 1923, (2) 95 years have elapsed since its publication date if it was published between 1923 and 1977, or (3) 70 years have elapsed since the author's death if it was published after 1977. However, if a work was published between 1923 and 1963 and the copyright owner did not renew the copyright after the 28-year term that once applied, the work has come into public domain. Corporate works published after 1977 enter the public domain 95 years after publication.

The fair use exemption does not permit unlimited copying and distribution. The "privilege" is highly restricted by guidelines with legal force, though they are often ambiguous and arcane, and they do not cover all situations. They were negotiated among educators, authors, and publishers. Of course, no copyright exemption excuses you from citing and crediting your sources.

■ PRINTED TEXT

Although you may find it restrictive, the realm of print media is the one that most liberally allows fair use. It is, of course, the oldest realm.

Single Copying

As an instructor, you may make a single copy, including a transparency or slide, of the following for teaching purposes without obtaining prior permission: a chapter of a book; an article from a periodical or newspaper; a short story, essay, or poem; and a diagram, graph, chart, drawing, cartoon, or picture from a book, periodical, or newspaper.

Multiple Copying

You may make multiple copies—specifically, one copy per student in a course—without first obtaining permission if the work meets the criteria of brevity, spontaneity, and cumulative effect and if each copy contains a copyright notice. At this time, as long as electronic work meets the criteria for copyright, the Copyright Ordinance gives the digital work the same protection as paper copies.

The guidelines define the brevity criterion in this way: (1) an entire poem printed on no more than two pages or an excerpt from a longer poem, not to exceed 250 words copied in either case; (2) an entire article, story, or essay of fewer than 2,500 words or an excerpt of fewer than 1,000 words or less than 10% of the work, whichever is less, but in either event, a minimum of 500 words to be copied; and (3) one chart, graph, diagram, drawing, cartoon, or picture per book or periodical issue. Multiple copying meets the spontaneity criterion when you do not have a reasonable length of time to request and receive permission to copy. What a "reasonable length of time" may be is not specified, but it is not a year. If something is found in August and used in September to kick off your fall semester, it likely meets the spontaneity criterion. It would likely not meet the criterion if is used again in January to kick off the spring semester.

The cumulative effect is considered acceptably small (permission not required) when your copying is for only one course and you do not make multiple copies in more than nine instances per term per course. Furthermore, you may not make multiple copies of more than one short poem, article, story, essay, or two excerpts from the same author or more than three from the same collective work or periodical volume in one term.

If you want to copy and distribute entire or multiple works in a way that would violate the preceding rules, you must first obtain permission.

Copying Short Works

Short works such as children's books are often fewer than 2,500 words, and you may not copy them as a whole. All you may reproduce without permission is an excerpt of no more than two published pages containing not more than 10% of the total words in the text.

Additional "Privileges" and Prohibitions

You are allowed to incorporate text into your multimedia teaching presentations, as can your students into their multimedia projects.

Notwithstanding the previous guidelines, your intentions and the specific work also come into play. You may not make copies under these conditions to create, replace, or substitute for anthologies, compilations, or collective works; to substitute for replacement or purchase of consumable works such as workbooks, exercises, standardized tests, or answer sheets or of the same item term after term; or if you charge students beyond the copying cost or on direction of a higher authority. In addition, you may make copies for your students in only nine instances per term.

IMAGES

The guidelines in this section apply only to photographs and illustrations not in the public domain, which never require permission to use. However, if the one you want to use is part of a copyrighted collection, you should obtain permission for use from the copyright holder.

You may use entire single images but no more than five by a single artist or photographer. If you are taking images from a collection, you may use no more than 15 images or 10% of those in the collection, whichever is fewer.

If an image is not designated for sale or license, you may digitize and use it if you obtain prior permission and limit access (password-protect) to enrolled students and other instructors of the course. Furthermore, your students may download, print out, and transmit it for personal academic use, including course assignments and portfolios, for up to 2 years. You may also use the image at a professional conference.

An alternative to obtaining permission to show copyrighted visual materials is to take and display photographs of them. This option is legal for fair use as long as the quality of the photographic reproductions is lower than that of commercial reproductions, such as professionally produced slides and prints—in other words, as long as the amateur photographs can't compete in the same market (University of Minnesota Libraries, 2015).

Academic art librarians know where to locate specific pictorial, graphic, artistic, and architectural works and what the restrictions for their use may be. The library may already have permission or a license to display certain works. You can find unrestricted fair use materials (no license or permission required) at the Creative Commons (www.creativecommons.org) and also websites with free use of millions of high-quality digital images such as Unsplash.com and Pixabay.com.

IN-CLASS PERFORMANCES

Assuming your institution is accredited, you and your students can freely show videos, play music, recite poetry, read and perform plays, and project slides in a classroom setting. You can show performances from YouTube and other websites in a live class. None of these actions requires permission. Copying sheet music, however, is restricted to out-of-print music and performances "in an emergency."

It is more and more challenging to know what you can and cannot show in the classroom. For example, showing a non-Netflix produced movie in class using your Netflix account is a license issue, not a copyright issue, but still an issue. Netflix does not allow screening of programs in educational settings, with the exception of certain documentaries and other programs on a special page provided for educators. The information can be found at: https://help.netflix.com/en/node/57695. It is unclear as to whether you can stream from other services to play movies or parts of programs to your students in class. Goodspeed (2021) asserts that it is permissible, as long as the programs are educationally related.

The best policy before streaming or showing is to check. Check with your campus, especially librarians, to see if there is a policy in place. Ensure that what you are showing in class has educational value. Check the provider you intend to use to see if they have a policy against what you are doing. Given fair use, if you are showing an educational program in a nonprofit educational setting, you likely are in compliance for copyright. The check with the provider is to ensure you are not creating a licensing problem.

The streaming industry, like the previous generation multimedia firms, is very frustrated. Piracy from streaming illegally costs nearly $30 billion per year (Rowe, 2022). Movie studios have built the home DVD industry into a multibillion-dollar business, in part by rigidly enforcing the distinction between instruction and entertainment.

RECORDING BROADCAST PROGRAMMING

The rules are ambiguous about whether you can record a television program off-the-air at home and then show it in class. If it is a commercial program, some experts consider this illegal, while others recommend that you demonstrate compliance with the spirit of the law by following the guidelines in this section. These guidelines specify what educational institutions (campus media units) can record off-the-air for educational purposes without obtaining a permission or a license from the copyright holder.

Broadcast Programming (Major National and Local Stations)

These guidelines apply only to off-the-air recording by nonprofit educational institutions, which are responsible for ensuring compliance:

- Programs may be kept for only 45 calendar days after the recording date. After this time, they must be deleted.
- The recording may be shown to students only during the first 10 class days after the recording date and may be repeated only once for reinforcement.
- Off-the-air recordings may be made only at the request of an individual instructor and not in anticipation of an instructor's request. The same instructor can request that the program be recorded only once.
- Duplicate copies may be made if several instructors request the recording of the same program.

- After the first 10 classes allowed for showing, the recording may be used only for evaluation, such as for a test.
- Off-the-air recordings may not be edited or combined with other recordings to create a new work or an anthology.
- All recording, including copies, must contain a copyright notice when broadcast.

Public Television

The Public Broadcasting Service, the Public Television Library, the Great Plains National Instructional Television Library, and the Agency for Instructional Television have somewhat less restrictive rules for off-the-air recording for educational purposes:

- Recordings may be made by instructors or students in accredited, nonprofit educational institutions.
- Recordings may be used only for instruction in a classroom, lab, or auditorium but are not restricted to one classroom or one instructor.
- The use of recordings is restricted to one institution and may not be shared outside it.
- Length of allowed retention varies.

Cable Channel Programs

Cable channels require you to ask permission to show any of its programming, even for fair use purposes, but instructors may be allowed to keep their recordings for much longer. The rules vary by program.

■ ONLINE MATERIALS

LMSs and electronic reserves have replaced course packets and hard copy library reserves, and millions of courses are delivered in part or entirely online. As with print, online content must be accessible only to the students enrolled in the class and only for

that term. But because these materials are digitized, the fair use laws governing them are somewhat different, often murky, and more restrictive than those governing course packets.

For starters, the readings on e-reserve should not comprise more than a small amount of all the assigned reading for the course. As specified in the DMCA of 1998, copyright-protected digital materials also include a wide range of content you might not expect: print and electronic books, analog and digital musical recordings, websites, works embedded in websites, print and email messages and attachments, and possibly even databases. In addition, the Technology Harmonization and Education Act of 2002 requires you to add a legal notice in your syllabus that online materials "may" be copyright protected.

Most legal and library authorities argue that you or your institution's library must obtain permission to post any copyrighted digital course content, even when it is available elsewhere on the internet, is being used in a course for the first time, or is supplemental, unless you get your general counsel's approval to skip obtaining permission. That said, some university lawyers contend that fair use protection makes permissions unnecessary (Foster, 2008). Libraries, however, tend to err on the conservative side and routinely obtain permission.

Probably your easiest alternative is providing your class with links to materials that are already available online through your institution's library, which has a license or permission to make the materials available. But what if you want to link to sites not in your library? Here again, the law is cloudy. Some say as long as you are linking directly to the material it does not violate copyright as there is no creation of additional copies of the work (Missouri University S&T Library, 2022). Another safe bet is to use vendor-provided digital content that is sold along with many textbooks (e.g., password-protected websites). Because the cost includes the copyright license, no restrictions apply to its educational use.

The legal area surrounding copyright and fair use of electronic materials is the most volatile, as well as the most restrictive. Recall that in traditional face-to-face classrooms, you and your students can listen to music, read poems aloud, perform plays, display slides, view websites, or stream excerpts of programs, all without prior permission, as long as the purpose is educational. Between 1997 and 2002, you and your students could not do any of these things electronically under fair use protection. The CONFU guidelines required you to obtain a license. Finally, Congress closed this odd legal gap in mid-2002 when it passed the TEACH Act without debate. As the rules stand now, you may, without prior permission, download images from the internet for your teaching, and students may do so for their projects. You may do the same for sound and video files, but subject to severe length limitations: videos to 3 minutes or 10%, whichever is shorter, and music to 10% of the composition, up to a maximum of 30 seconds. The same length limits apply if you or your students take excerpts from a lawfully purchased or rented streamed program. Permission is required only when you or a student wants to exceed these length limits or to post or repost any of the files online.

Don't even think about trying to get permission to put an entire commercially produced motion picture or musical on electronic reserve or online. This would require an exorbitant license.

Electronic copyright law is unsettled, ambiguous, and subject to challenge from both commercial and educational interests. For example, in March 2016, the fair-use status of e-reserves was "mostly" upheld by a U.S. District Court in a lawsuit three academic publishers brought against Georgia State University. It is "mostly" because the decision turned on revenue data, which are not public. So e-reserves remain in foggy territory. Stay tuned to the academic news media to keep abreast of the latest legal developments and clarifications. Another good idea is to make materials available in ways that avoid potential trouble. For example, refer your students to URLs rather than incorporating internet-based text, images, and performances into your online course materials. Also make the most of any vendor-provided digital content that may accompany your textbooks.

Although it is not likely to impact an educational setting, in 2021 the Protecting Lawful Streaming Act (PLSA) was signed into law. The PLSA closed a gap in copyright law that made it possible for large-scale for-profit entities to stream movies, sporting events, music, and television programs. There were already laws on the books that made it a felony to illegally download and distribute content. This act does the same for streaming. This act is primarily aimed at illegal streaming services, which currently have an estimated nine million subscribers.

OBTAINING PERMISSION OR A LICENSE

Perhaps you wish to reproduce, display, or play a work or a portion of a work that exceeds the length limits or otherwise violates the preceding guidelines. Or perhaps your campus library or copy center cannot obtain the necessary permissions or licenses in time for you or your students to use the work. You and your students may follow these procedures to obtain them on your own.

Request in writing (email is okay) the permission of the copyright holder (which is not necessarily the author or creator) to reprint, display, or post online, identifying the exact portion of the work, the number of copies you wish to make and distribute or the planned location on the internet, the expected readership or viewership, and the purpose or planned use of the work (e.g., instruction in a given course for a specific term at a given institution). A permission granted for classroom use applies only to one course during one term. Or you can contact the Copyright

Clearance Center at www.copyright.com. It offers an electronic service that usually obtains your permission within a few days.

You can also request a license from the copyright holder in writing, giving the same precise information as mentioned earlier. Licenses are often required to show a work or portion of a work or to include some nontrivial portion of it in your own scholarship or multimedia production. Licenses always entail fees, but they may be negotiable.

HOW COPYRIGHT VIOLATIONS ARE ACTUALLY HANDLED

What if you forgot to put a long, important journal article on e-reserve, and you decide to make copies of the whole thing and hand them out to your students in class? What penalties might you face? The laws state that you face a judgment of up to $100,000 for each willful infringement, and ignorance of the law is not a defense. What may work is a convincing argument that you were acting in good faith, believing on reasonable grounds that your case qualified as fair use. Your institution will probably defend you if you follow its fair use policies.

However, the law doesn't always operate by the law. In the educational arena, institutions, not individuals, are usually sued, and very few of these have been over the past several decades. Obviously colleges, universities, school systems, and private K–12 schools have much deeper pockets than their teaching staff, so copyright enforcers send them threatening letters every once in a while to remind them of the law and potential penalties. Sometimes a threat is based on a tip that violations have occurred. In such cases, the alleged violator, whether an institution or individual, typically receives a cease-and-desist order. It is wise to follow the order of such a letter.

Historically, the most aggressive copyright enforcer has been the Software Publishers Association, which patrols software pirating (installation or reproduction without site licenses). But even it confines its efforts to organizations and stays out of people's home offices.

FOR FURTHER AND FUTURE REFERENCE

These resources provide further detail on copyright protections, restrictions, and exemptions, as well as the latest changes in the laws and guidelines.

Media-Specific Information

- For images: https://www.copyrightlaws.com/legally-using-images
- For online videos: https://cmsimpact.org/wp-content/uploads/2016/01/online_best_practices_in_fair_use.pdf
- For documentary films: https://cmsimpact.org/wp-content/uploads/2016/01/Documentary-Filmmakers.pdf
- For poetry: https://cmsimpact.org/wp-content/uploads/2016/01/fairusepoetrybooklet_single pg_3.pdf
- For dance-related material: https://cmsimpact.org/wp-content/uploads/2016/01/DHC_fair_use_statement.pdf
- For open courseware: https://cmsimpact.org/wp-content/uploads/2016/01/10-305-OCW-Oct29.pdf
- For film or media: https://guides.libraries.indiana.edu/c.php?g=158548&p=1176292
- For teaching media literacy: http://mediaeducationlab.com/sites/mediaeducationlab.com/files/CodeofBestPracticesinFairUse_0.pdf
- For publishing in communication studies: https://cmsimpact.org/wp-content/uploads/2016/01/WEB_ICA_CODE.pdf

General Copyright Information

- American Association of University Professors (AAUP) Copyright, Distance Education, and

Intellectual Property: https://www.aaup.org/issues/intellectual-property/resources-copyright-distance-education-and-intellectual-property
- Copyright Clearance Center Campus Guide to Copyright Compliance for Academic Institutions: https://www.copyright.com/blog/copyright-and-licensing-around-the-world
- Cornell University Copyright Information Center: https://www.cornell.edu/copyright.cfm
- Hall Davidson Copyright Resources: https://www.davidson.edu/offices-and-services/technology-innovation/it-guidelines-policies/copyright-compliance-laws-and-acts/copyright-policy-resources
- Indiana University Information Policy Office: https://www.iu.edu/copyright/index.html
- 2014 METRO Annual Conference: http://librarian.net/talks/metro
- Stanford University Libraries Copyright and Fair Use: http://fairuse.stanford.edu
- U.S. Copyright Office: www.copyright.gov; 101 Independence Avenue S.E., Washington, DC 20559–6000; (202)707–3000 or 1(877)476–0778 (toll free); circulars and forms are available free at www.copyright.gov/circs
- University of Minnesota Libraries Copyright Information and Education: www.lib.umn.edu/copyright
- University of Texas System Crash Course in Copyright: http://copyright.lib.utexas.edu

Creative Commons Information

Creative Commons (creativecommons.org) originated in 2002 to allow those creating work to share it with others and retain the level of rights they desired. They offer free and easy-to-use online copyright licenses, so if you want to create a Creative Commons copyright license it is very easy to do. This may be for a video you made, an educational framework you created, or a photo you have taken. This is a very popular approach, with over 2 billion licenses to date.

Creative Commons has six license types to choose from.

- CC BY – Reusers can distribute, remix, adapt, and build on material in any medium or format; allows for commercial use, but must give creator attribution
- CC BY-SA – Same as CC BY, but if building upon original material, modified product must be licensed under identical terms
- CC BY-NC – Same as CC BY, but only for noncommercial purposes
- CC BY-NC-SA – Same as CC BY-SA, but only for noncommercial purposes
- CC BY-ND – Copy and distribute in any medium or format in unadapted form only and attribution must be given to creator
- CC BY-NC-ND – Same as CC BY-ND, but only for noncommercial purposes
- CC0 – This is a public dedication tool. The work is copyrighted, but there are no restrictions in how it is used and it may be used without attribution.

For more details, see: https://creativecommons.org/about/cclicenses

Copyright Tools, Charts, Checklists, and Calculators

- Columbia University Libraries: http://copyright.columbia.edu/copyright/files/2009/10/fairuse checklist.pdf
- Stanford University Libraries: http://fairuse.stanford.edu/charts-and-tools
- University of Minnesota Libraries: https://www.lib.umn.edu/services/copyright

■ REFLECTION QUESTIONS

Reflection Question 6.1: What did you learn about copyright guidelines that surprised you or was unexpected?

Reflection Question 6.2: What questions do you still have about copyright that impacts your class?

Where could you find information about the questions you have? Knowing what resources are available to answer these questions is invaluable.

Concept Into Practice: It really isn't onerous to do things the correct way with respect to copyright. Check out Unsplash.com, Pixabay.com, and Creative Commons images for photos that are free to use. Find a few photos that could be used in an upcoming class or presentation. Keep an eye out for the occasional photo in their selection that does require a purchase.

THE HUMAN SIDE OF TEACHING

CHAPTER 7

Establishing a Positive Learning Community

Creating a safe, stimulating, learner-centered classroom environment helps students in many ways. Students in such environments are more likely to achieve the learning outcomes of the course, develop higher-order thinking skills, participate in class activities, behave appropriately in class, be motivated to learn, and be satisfied with the course (Cornelius-White, 2007; Granitz et al., 2009; Richmond et al., 2019). These benefits accrue in online courses too (Kaufmann & Vallade, 2020; Lundberg & Sheridan, 2015). Relatedly, having a positive rapport with you enhances students' attitudes toward you and the course, increases their motivation and participation, augments their perceived learning as well as their actual cognitive and affective learning, and raises both their grades and your student ratings (Allen et al., 2006; Cuseo, 2018; Frisby & Martin, 2010; Meyers, 2009; Schriver & Kulynych, 2021; Wilson & Ryan, 2013).

The primary responsibility for creating an effective classroom environment lies with you. Convey to your students that you designed the course to foster their learning and care very much about not only their learning the material but also their developing as individuals. Teaching is much more than presenting content and giving exams. Motivating students to learn and caring about them as humans is an important part of the job (Fink, 2021). This does not mean that you are to be their friend, parent, or that you have to entertain them in the classroom. But it does mean that you will listen to them, honor their voices, seek and respond to their questions and feedback, adapt to their individual and cultural differences, encourage their participation and best thinking, relate to them with honesty and empathy, and convey your enthusiasm about teaching them. Furthermore, teaching at its best means encouraging students to speak up, experiment, take risks, and make mistakes in a safe environment. All of this is expected for any student who shows respect to you and their fellow classmates (Webb & Barrett, 2014). For all this to happen takes hard work and planning, and that starts with planning a welcoming classroom.

◼ PLANNING A WELCOMING CLASSROOM

Getting the course off on a good start begins with a carefully thought-out course syllabus. That serves as the foundation to your course, and it is important enough that all of Chapter 5 was devoted to that one document. A well-written, carefully considered, learning-centered syllabus demonstrates your desire to bring out the best in students and motivate them to do their best work.

Get as much of your learning management system (LMS) loaded as you can before the first day of the course and check everything carefully to ensure what you want is where you want it. Read through your ultimate, mediating, and foundational student learning outcomes. As noted in Chapter 2, everything done in your course supports helping the students to achieve those outcomes. Along with course materials, carefully prepare for your first class session. You don't get a second chance to make a good first impression, and there is a lot to do to be ready for the first class period of the semester. Anyone who says they "wing it" on the first day is wasting an amazing opportunity. Consider dividing your selections into "essential" and "desirable as time remains."

About one week before classes begin, consider the following tasks to make a strong, positive impression of yourself and your course:

- Send a simple, introductory email to your students through your LMS letting them know you are looking forward to starting and sharing how they can best reach out to you.
- Make a short, recorded introduction. Consider creating a 5–7-minute video explaining a bit about why you enjoy the course and what past students have said about your course. This can easily be done on Zoom/Teams or a site such as Flipgrid (flipgrid.com).
- *Don't* assign students work that is to be done for the first day, even if it is something for fun.

Those who sign up at the last minute won't have the opportunity to prepare and as a result may feel out of place.
- Have students post introductory videos of themselves, if it's a small class in the LMS or on a site such as Flipgrid.com.
- Find exactly where various student support centers are located (e.g., counseling center, student health services, disability student services, the testing center, etc.). It undermines your caring approach if someone asks you where such a service is located and you don't know.

A day or two before your first class, tend to some classroom details:

- Inspect the room to ensure that all the technology that you will need is there, in working order, and that you know how to access and operate it.
  ◦ Check the mic. Does it take batteries? If so, get spares. Plan to use the mic, especially in large rooms, so the students at the back are not struggling to hear and those in the front don't feel like you are shouting.
  ◦ Are dry erase markers and erasers present? If they are not there or aren't working, don't stress about it. Buy some and keep them with you. Consider $10 (or $20, if you want the larger pack of fun colors) money well spent for your students' success.
- Check the lights, the clock (if any), and the heating and air-conditioning system as well. If anything is missing or awry, ask your department office professional to pass on that information to the person who is in charge of fixing such things.
- Orient yourself to the overall classroom. Stand at the front of the room and imagine the seats filled with your students. Think about how you will facilitate active learning exercises and call on students. To what extent will you move about the room? Walk around the room and get comfortable with the space. Lang (2019) points out that this helps reduce the first-day jitters.

Think about the potential diversity of your students: first-generation students, students from other countries, and other populations that might have a different perspective of the class. Plan for and consider researching some cultural differences, especially if your institution is proudly multicultural. For example, it is common in some countries or for those who are shy to have silence, for thinking, between people's statements or to not look at you when they are talking. Try to not misinterpret a cultural norm for confusion or uncertainty. Body language, gestures, common phrases, and even interpersonal distance will all differ among cultures, but do remember many students, regardless of background, will be nervous on that first day. You may be as well, which is fine. There are faculty members who teach for decades who note that they still get nervous for some class periods.

Plan to dress a little more formally for your first day of class than you normally would. A touch of formality conveys professionalism and seriousness. It also gives instructors who are female, young, or physically small an aura of authority and a psychological edge that help separate them from their students (Johnston, 2005; Oliver et al., 2021).

Keep the 30 minutes prior to your class free so that you don't have to rush to class, particularly on the first day. This also gives you time to start preparing yourself—specifically, your body and your voice. You want to project a successful instructor persona to your class—relaxed confidence, goodwill, and an in-command, no-nonsense presence. This will inspire your students' respect for your authority, their confidence in you, their goodwill in return, and their willingness to honor your rules and policies. You also want to convey enthusiasm and controlled passion for the content of the course so you can get their attention and keep them engaged for the entire class. If you don't feel naturally relaxed, confident, and in command, we have provided some information for you in Chapter 11 under "Preventing Incivility." You can make these behaviors come more easily and naturally by practicing a few vocal and physical exercises shortly before class.

A WELCOMING FIRST DAY OF CLASS

First impressions are lasting ones. The first day of class can set the classroom environment for the entire term. Plan to arrive at the room 15–20 minutes before your first class session. That will ensure you are there in time. If there is another class in that room you will get the opportunity to wait in the hall with your students and chat a bit. This will help students see that you are friendly and caring.

Plan a short PowerPoint to introduce key aspects of the course and then post the slides on your course LMS after class to make sure everyone gets a chance to revisit the information if needed. Project a welcome slide with your name and course title as students enter the room, maybe as you greet students prior to the start of class. This reassures students that they are in the right room.

For you, the first day may be cause for anxiety as well as excitement. It may represent innovations and experiments in course content, organization, and design; teaching methods; and assessment methods—not to mention all those new student faces. Overall, it is helpful to use that first class period to help students get to know one another and begin to build community (e.g., icebreakers), review the highlights of the syllabus with a friendly tone, explain the how's and why's of the course, and perhaps to begin to teach content. Certainly, simply reading the syllabus aloud is not considered an effective way to begin the course. But be reassured that the suggestions here are safe and useful, although social icebreakers may be challenging or impossible to manage in a large class.

Think carefully about the expectations and behaviors you want to establish in your classroom for the semester. Lay out these expectations, and lead the kind of class activities that model the level and type of student engagement you have in mind for the rest of the course. For example, if you hope for considerable discussion, engage your students in discussion, perhaps about their expectations of the course or their current conceptions of the subject matter. If you intend to have a number of in-class writing exercises, start with a short one during that first class. If you plan on group work, prepare a small-group activity for the first day.

Model the behavior and professionalism you want from your students. Posting a syllabus ahead of time tells your class that you are careful, well organized, and conscientious about teaching. If you expect them to be prompt, start class right on time. Arrive in the classroom early, and set a welcoming tone by chatting with students informally as they arrive. Make students feel comfortable with you as a person as well as an instructor, but don't confuse your roles; remember the difference between being friendly and being friends.

Exchanging Information

There is a lot of information to exchange on the first day of the semester: your information with students, their information with you, information among peers, and course information. The next several activities need not come in the order presented, but they are strongly recommended for setting an open, safe, and participatory tone for the rest of the term.

Student Information Index Cards

Get to know your students by passing out blank index cards and asking them to write down the following information for you: their full name (with phonetic spelling), what they preferred to be called, their year in school, their major, and a bit about what they know about the course topic. Additional information such as hometown, outside interests, and career aspirations may help you relate class material to your students on a more personal level. Consider also asking them to write out what they

expect from this course and why they are taking it (again, aside from requirements), or what topics they would like to see addressed. You may be able to orient the material toward some of their interests and advise those with erroneous expectations to take a more suitable course.

Your Background

Because you're asking students about themselves, it's only fair to share something about yourself. Students are often interested in learning a bit about you. Divulge only what you are comfortable with, and it need not be much. Give students a summary of your educational and professional background. Share some information about your own research and interests, what attracted you to your discipline, and why you enjoy the content.

Course Information

First, say a few words to promote the course and the material. What big questions will your course address? Why is the material so interesting, relevant, useful, and important? How will your students benefit from learning it? The enthusiasm you show for the course and content is contagious (Burgess et al., 2018). Mark on your copy of the syllabus any points you want to elaborate, clarify, and emphasize. Rather than reading through the whole document, consider choosing one of the options noted in Chapter 5 in the section "Ensuring Your Students Read Your Syllabus."

Following are several considerations for the first day:

1. Mention your office hours and urge students to seek your help outside class. There are several ways to encourage students to visit you for your office hours (Cuseo, 2018). Have 10-minute appointment slots and ask each student to sign up for one. You could also set up quick chats on Zoom/Teams. Make sure students know office hours means times you are there for them, not times you are working in your office.

2. Explain the teaching and assessment strategies you will rely on the most, along with why you've chosen them. Emphasize the learning benefits they have over other reasonable options, especially if your methods are innovative or collaborative. Your explanation will not only reassure students of your professionalism and commitment to their learning but also reduce their resistance to unusual formats.

3. State your expectations of students and their responsibilities for preparing for class and participating. For example, if your course calls for considerable discussion, emphasize the importance of their doing the reading, your rules for calling on them, and your criteria for assessing their contributions. You may want to reserve cold-calling as an option, but to keep the classroom atmosphere safe, honor a few rules. Explain why you are using it—for example, to help ensure they do the reading. Do it regularly, do it fairly (shuffle cards with students' names on it or use an app, such as wheelofnames.com, that randomly selects students), address students by name, permit them to pass on responding, and gently correct wrong answers or let their fellow students do so.

4. Plan to give and enforce rules of classroom decorum. Students expect you to maintain an orderly, civil classroom. If you don't, your teaching effectiveness and your student ratings will suffer, right along with their learning. In fact, many students were never socialized to arrive to class on time, stay seated the whole period, speak only when sanctioned by the instructor, or show respect to both the instructor and their peers. The first or second day of class is the optimal time to set up a code of conduct for the term, and the students who come motivated to learn will appreciate this.

5. Leave some course policies open for your students to decide. This gives them the opportunity to buy into the policies, take responsibility for the success of the course, and invest in their own outcomes (Weimer, 2013). The policies governing classroom conduct and discussions of controversial subjects are ideal candidates. Students can also be allowed to set deadlines for papers, identify how they wish to have feedback on papers, determine point distributions across assignments, and facilitate class discussions (Dobrow et al., 2011; Vander Schee, 2009).

6. Offer your students some advice on how to make the most of class activities by taking notes on summaries of what was learned during active learning tasks. To help students get the most out of minilectures, give students some pointers on some good note-taking strategies. We have provided some suggestions in Chapter 14.

7. Share some helpful reading and study skills and problem-solving strategies appropriate to your subject matter. Better yet, integrate some self-regulated learning activities into your classes, assignments, and test debriefings. Chapter 19 provides an array of options, and you'll find a few for the first day later in this chapter in the section "Subject Matter Icebreakers."

8. Give students an opportunity to identify issues they would like you to consider. Give groups (four to five students) 10 minutes to skim the syllabus to find these points. You may or may not implement what they suggest, but thank the students for their focus and suggestions and let them know within a few days what you have decided. For those you implement, let them know you will use their ideas. For things you won't implement, respectfully explain why. In doing this activity in the past, some of the items from students have been: "If we offer a response to a question in a class discussion, and we are wrong, please don't criticize us for getting it wrong?"; "If it turns out you won't be able to make it to class, could you please email the class to let us know?"; "Could you give us a worksheet with the main concepts that will be on the test?; "If people are having a conversation in class loud enough to distract others, could you ask them to stop?"

Overall, students may have many questions on the first day of class. Although you cannot possibly anticipate all the questions that students will have, following are some likely ones that you should be prepared to field about your testing and grading procedures:

1. What will your tests be like?
2. What types of questions will be on the test?
3. Will you give out review sheets?
4. Will you hold review sessions? In-person or virtual?
5. How will you evaluate papers and other written assignments?
6. How many A's, B's, C's, and so on do you usually give?
7. Is it possible for all students in class to get a good grade?
8. Will extra credit be offered?
9. What is the policy for late papers and makeup exams?

Reciprocal Interview

In this two-way interview, which takes about 50 minutes in small classes, you and your students exchange course-related information (Case et al., 2008). You distribute a handout that asks questions like these:

1. What do you hope to gain from this course?
2. How can I help you reach these goals?
3. What concerns do you have about this course?
4. What resources and background in the subject matter do you bring to it?
5. What student conduct rules should we set up to foster the course's success?
6. What aspects of a class or an instructor impede your learning?

Students write their answers to these questions as individuals for the first 5 minutes and discuss them in groups for the next 10 minutes. Then each group spokesperson reports these responses aloud to the class (15 or so minutes, depending on class size). For the second part of the exercise, your handout should also suggest questions to pose to you about your course goals, your expectations of students,

and your views on grading. (Students can ask other questions as well.) First as individuals, then back in their groups, students select and develop questions for you, which requires about 10 minutes. Then each group spokesperson reads these questions aloud, which you answer over the next 10 minutes.

This activity establishes a comfortable class environment, fosters a sense of community, communicates your openness and commitment to student success, and serves as a social icebreaker (Case et al., 2008). First-generation students and students from underrepresented groups especially appreciate it. If you plan on a lot of group work and class discussion during the term, this exercise will prepare students to participate.

Social Icebreakers: Getting to Know You

If your class size allows it, try to incorporate one or two icebreaker activities on the first day. There are two types: the social or getting-to-know-you variety, which gets students acquainted with each other, and subject matter icebreakers, which motivate students to start thinking about the material. Either icebreaker, if done well, is helpful in beginning to build classroom community during that first class period. There are many more icebreakers for both onsite and virtual situations (e.g., Crothers, 2020; Mack & Udland, 2017) beyond these examples, and you can adapt anything you find to meet the needs of your class. With a quick web search, there are many additional options that may be found quickly.

Simple Self-Introductions

Have students take turns introducing themselves to the class by giving their name, major, their reason for taking the course (once again, aside from fulfilling some requirement), and perhaps something about themselves that they are proud of having done or become. Many variations of this activity ask individuals to reveal a secret about themselves. If a student has a secret, revealing it to perfect strangers on the first day of class is likely to cause more concern than build community.

Class Survey

Ask students to raise their hands in response to some general questions. If students prefer to not raise their hands for a given question or two, that is fine. Questions can be wide-ranging: How many students are from [various regions of the country]? First-year, sophomores, juniors, seniors? How many have a job off campus? How many are married? How many have children? How many like golf? Reading? How many have traveled abroad? To Europe? To Asia? Then you may venture into opinion questions, perhaps some relevant to the course material. Students soon start to form a broad picture of their class and see what they have in common. You may also have students ask questions of the group, provided you make it clear that the questions must be kept appropriate and should not be too personal. They will find it far easier to interact with classmates who share their interests and backgrounds.

Personal Scavenger Hunt

For this more structured activity, give students a list of requirements and tell them to move about the classroom seeking fellow students who meet each one. No one may use a given student for more than one requirement. Some possible requirements are "has been to Europe," "prefers cats to dogs," "has a birthday in the same month you do," "can speak two or more languages fluently," and "cries at movies." You won't know who has done which things, but that is fine. Think of items that you would expect 10–60% of the students have done. This is an ideal place to add some items that may match international students. For example, "have lived on at least two different continents." The "found" students sign their name next to the requirement they meet. You could offer a small prize of a piece of candy or fruit and a small amount of extra-credit for everyone who completes their sheet. This gives students a *reason* for doing the task.

What's in a Name?

If the class is under 30 students, it may work best to do the exercise as a whole class. If it is a large class, have students work in groups of four to six. Have students say their name and then where the name came from. If it has a derivation or if they are named for a family member or other special reason, note that. Choosing a name, for an infant or as an adult, is a big deal. This will also help you to learn your students' names.

Subject Matter Icebreakers

This second type of icebreaker stimulates your students' interest in the subject matter and informs you about what they know, think they know, and know they don't know about it. Some of these can also help you identify or confirm their faulty models and misconceptions about the subject matter. Several additional subject matter icebreakers can be found from an internet search.

Diagnostic Activities

Several classroom assessment techniques, developed by Angelo and Cross (1993), activate your students' prior knowledge and help you assess what they know or think they know about your subject matter, such as the Background Knowledge Probe and Focused Listing. A quick web search of "classroom assessment techniques" will give you many possibilities for consideration. Another option is the knowledge survey, in which you assemble an "exam" from your major learning outcomes, assignment tasks, and test questions and problems from previous offerings of the course. But rather than ask students for the answers, you ask them to rate how confident they are that they could answer the question correctly, perform the task competently, or solve the problem (Nuhfer & Knipp, 2003; Wirth & Perkins, 2008).

Problem Posting

Ask students to think about and jot down problems they expect to encounter with the course or issues they think the course should address. Then record their responses on the board or a slide (McKeachie, 2002). Make sure that the whole class has a chance to contribute, even if you have to coax the quiet members. To build trust, avoid appearing judgmental, and check the accuracy of your understanding by restating the students' comments and requesting their confirmation. Finally, identify the problems and issues the course will address, giving students something to look forward to, and identify which ones it will not address and why. You might use problem posting again before you broach a particularly difficult topic.

This exercise accomplishes several purposes. First, it whets students' appetites for the material. Second, it opens lines of communication between you and your students, as well as among students. Third, it lends validity to their issues and assures them they're not alone. Finally, it reaffirms that you are approachable and interested in listening to their concerns.

Commonsense Inventory

Another way to break students into the subject matter and underline its relevance is to have them judge an inventory of 5 to 15 commonsense statements directly related to the material in your course as true or false. The trick is to ensure that many of these statements run counter to popular beliefs or prejudices—for example, "Suicide is more likely among women than men." "Over half of all marriages occur between persons who live within 20 blocks of each other." You might break the class into small groups to discuss and debate their answers or to reach a consensus around the statements. Then have a spokesperson from each group explain and defend its position. After these presentations, you can give the correct answers, which may spark more debate, or take the cliff-hanger approach and let the class wait for them to unfold during the term.

Drawing the First Class to a Close

At the end of this first class and after you answer all your students' questions, ask students to write down and hand in their responses to general questions like these: What is the most important thing you learned during this first day? How did your expectations of this course change? What questions or concerns do you still have about the course or the subject matter? Such an exercise shows your interest in their learning and their reactions to you and your course. Also ask them if they have any suggestions on what you might do differently next semester, because you are always learning new ways to effectively engage students on the first day of class. This will model for students that we can always get better with good feedback.

It is very important to make productive use of the entire first class period. Don't treat it as a throwaway day or dismiss students early. Only if you treat class time like the precious commodity that it is will your students do so as well. If you conduct some of the activities in this chapter, the time will be more than adequately filled and productively spent. Not only will your students enjoy an introduction to the course and its subject matter, but they will also have a chance to get acquainted with you and their classmates, the first step to developing a sense of community in your classroom. They will also get a solid sense of how you teach.

■ LEARNING STUDENTS' NAMES

Most students, especially at smaller and private colleges and universities, expect their instructors to learn and use their name; this conveys that you care about them. Students expect less personal treatment in large classes of over 100 students, in which case learning their names will make you a legend. If the course is 30 students or fewer, and you set the class up well, you may well be able to learn all their names that first class period. If your course is large (>100 students), learn as many as possible. Chat with students before each class, and set a goal to remember at least five new names each class period. Remember that students tend to sit in the same areas. If you can learn names of students who tend to sit in the front, middle left and right, and the back, you can call on students in different areas of the room. That will give the class the impression that you know most of their names. Try it and see the reaction when you say something like, "Let's get a response from someone toward the back, what do you think, Quinn?"

The best way to remember names is to use them. If you have trouble remembering names, it is important to try to get rid of that feeling. If every time you are introduced to someone your inner thoughts are, "I am terrible at learning names," then you are spending your cognitive energy thinking about the challenge of learning names rather than learning them. It is challenging for everyone to learn names at first, but some people make a point to practice and become better. We can all improve. Following are some strategies to assist you:

1. Make a seating chart. When the first class starts, tell students you have assigned seating for the first 3 weeks of the course. Students may not prefer a seating chart, but they will tolerate it graciously if you say the reason is to learn their names. Seating them in alphabetical order will probably make learning their names easiest for you, and it ensures that proximity-based small groups will be randomly mixed. In addition, it will facilitate your taking attendance (just look for the empty chairs).
2. Let students sit where they want, but ask them to maintain those seats for about 3 weeks. Make a seating chart that first day, and practice visualizing your classroom and populating that space with the images of your students and their names (Foer, 2011).
3. Use LMS photos to help practice remembering names.
4. Take roll in every class. While learning names, you can also use the roll to call on students more or less randomly, as long as you tell your class what you'll be doing. Or you may use the index cards to call on students. Just shuffle them as you would a deck of cards every so often.
5. Make table tents for their desks. Distribute them at the start of each class, and collect them at the end of each session. This is also a subtle way to take attendance.
6. Use your phone to record each student saying their name. Before you do this, check to ensure there is no policy against recording students in class and explain to the students that this recording is *only* to be used for you to learn their names. Also let them opt out if they prefer by raising their hand, which will allow you to skip over them. As you go around the room to record, ask students to say their name clearly, and then you repeat their name. Make one recording of the entire class. Now you have a record of correct pronunciations and an audiovisual reference as you work to learn your students' names.

MAINTAINING A WELCOMING ENVIRONMENT

As with any other relationship, establishing good rapport and a welcoming environment will need steady reinforcement and nurturing. First, practice social immediacies, which is a fancy way of saying to be kind, thoughtful, respectful, and amiable. Use your students' names whenever possible. If you pass them on the sidewalk or in the hall, greet them with a cheery hello, as you would a colleague. If you can, arrive 10 minutes before class, set up your technology, and then chat informally with some of your students as they come in, learning a few additional names each class period. Be happy to see them. Ask them what they did over the weekend or whether they attended a major campus event. Ask them whether they work and what they do. Ask them about their family. Take an interest in their lives beyond the classroom. Listen to your students; try not to interrupt or rush them. Respond to their email as soon as possible. Let them know you look forward to speaking with them during your office/student hours. Encourage them to have high aspirations and to do their best. Help them to see abilities in themselves that they don't yet see. Show that you enjoy talking to them and hearing about their accomplishments. Like everyone else you interact with on a regular basis, they want you to like, respect, and care about them (Brookfield, 2017; Webb & Barrett, 2014).

Second, solicit your students' feedback about how the class is going on a fairly regular basis. Your campus teaching and learning or faculty development center probably interviews classes on request, or you can ask students anonymously for their opinion on your own. For specifics, see the "During-the-Term Student Feedback on Teaching" section in Chapter 23.

Third, keep students apprised of their grades on assignments, quizzes, and exams. Your LMS makes this easy for you, but do remind your students that their scores are available and be sure they know how to access them. Watch for sudden drops in grades and if possible, speak to your student and ask them if they are okay. A referral to the health or counseling center may be a consideration.

Finally, use rubrics to grade all the work that students construct themselves—that is, write, present, draw, design, develop, solve, act out, cook, or compose—and share those rubrics with your students when you make the assignments. Many students regard grading as a mysterious process. After all, they don't have our professional judgment, and if they did, they wouldn't need us! Besides, they have a right to know the criteria on which we will assess them, and we choose these criteria from any number of alternatives.

In the end, establishing and maintaining a welcoming and productive learning environment for all your students simply boils down to following the Golden Rule, to treat others as you would like to be treated. That is at the core of teaching at its best.

■ REFLECTION QUESTIONS

Reflection Question 7.1: Think back across your academic history as a student. Identify a course that was special to you—one that you remember better than the rest in terms of it being a really good experience. What made that course such a great experience? Do you see those elements in your own teaching? That is, are you creating the environment that approximates what you experienced as a student?

Reflection Question 7.2: What do you see as the most important aspects of creating an inclusive learning environment for your students? What does an inclusive environment do to facilitate learning?

Concept Into Practice: Learning names, much like any other kind of learning, takes both a strategy and effort. Outline a strategy that you will use for this or a future semester to learn as many names as possible. Be sure to set some learning outcome statements for this effort, along with criteria for success.

CHAPTER 8

Becoming an Increasingly Inclusive Teacher

Teaching is often talked about as if all learners are the same. We speak of setting outcomes, identifying teaching strategies, and assessing student learning. When we focus on teaching, the classroom full of students is thought of as a cluster, and we teach to the group. If we teach as we best learned as students, which many faculty members do, then our assumption is that students will all do fine in the course if they put in the work. Although that is true of any student who learns best the way the faculty member who is teaching the course, what about the students who do not best learn the way the person teaching the course is teaching?

Each of the students in our courses have specific, unique lived experiences, which means they each have a one-of-a-kind fingerprint of knowledge, opinions, preferences, and behaviors. Given the variety of learners in our courses, it is challenging to work to meet the needs of all learners. It is certainly more challenging than defaulting to methods and strategies that best worked for you when you were a student and then teaching the class as if all learners were the same. Inclusive teaching opens possibilities

for students who are like you and those who are unlike you, and those students who are struggling and those who are excelling. The teachers who are truly teaching at their best facilitate the learning of each individual student.

Inclusivity is not solely an issue of race and ethnicity, although those are both certainly part of inclusive teaching. Inclusivity pertains to all characteristics and all people: race; ethnicity; gender; political affiliation; socioeconomic status; ideology; employment status; neurodivergence, first-generation college student status; transportation issues; food and/or housing uncertainties; and chronic, acute, or invisible physical and psychological conditions. There are many ways in which we can think of diversity of learners, and until recently education has not seriously considered those differences. Education for too long has been tailored for a very specific kind of learner: fast-talking, risk-taking extroverts. Changing this focus may sound overwhelming, but as with all teaching challenges, there are resources. It will take a concerted effort, a growth mindset, and an acceptance from the beginning that you will make mistakes. As Stephen Brookfield regularly notes, there are two ways to do work in the area of diversity, equity, and inclusion: Imperfectly, and not at all (Brookfield, 2020).

Notice that in this chapter, student learning outcomes are thought of as a set of specific characteristics or life experiences of a given student. Work in this area also assumes that all students deserve an opportunity to be successful. It is not enough to allow an individual through the door; we need to provide an environment where they can excel. Anyone enrolling in a course, given that they have met the prerequisites for the course and have a modicum of motivation, should have an opportunity to be successful. This encompasses teaching in a way that gives every student a fair chance to understand, learn, remember, and demonstrate. It goes beyond simply objectively scoring papers or evaluating participation. It means looking carefully at examples used to illustrate concepts, the language used to frame discussions, the images used on PowerPoint slides, and how learners are encouraged. It also means keeping in mind that whatever we do, we should do it with an equity lens. This is true even for actions that are unplanned and urgent, such as emergency remote teaching during a pandemic (Aguliera & Nightengale, 2020). This all takes work, but giving *everyone* an opportunity to thrive in our classrooms and at our institutions—there is no better work.

■ INCLUSIVE CLIMATE IN THE CLASSROOM

If you consistently use only one teaching strategy throughout the course, you will meet the needs of only one type of student, or maybe a few, if you're lucky. For example, lecturing all the time will work for students who have a good foundation of knowledge, are highly motivated to learn, and can maintain focus for long periods of time. However, if periodic think-pair-shares are introduced, students who need a mental break from the lecture *and* those who benefit from sharing and talking through their understandings are now included. The larger your teaching toolbox, the more different types of student learners you will reach. There are many exceptional resources, and more are being published all the time.

How you relate to these students has a powerful impact on their performance and retention (Arif et al., 2021; Guo & Jamal, 2007; Jones, 2004). You are also a role model to all your students of what equity and inclusion look like in action. Following are 18 ways to create a more inclusive classroom climate, some of which were inspired by Addy et al. (2021), Brookfield and Hess (2021), Garibay (2015), Hogan and Sathy (2022), and Tools for Inclusive Teaching (2021).

1. *Teach with empathy.* As the population of marginalized students increases, the lived experiences and current situations of students will become more diverse. Empathetic teaching does not mean lowering standards, but it does mean creating learning environments that can accommodate a range of needs. Give yourself space to better understand and learn from different perspectives. Allow students time for personal stories and sharing of family values and customs. Also keep in mind that some students are dealing with many pressures: job or jobs, children, ill parents, childcare, reliable transportation, and other factors. There are times a term paper may be a day late. That might not be all that bad.

2. *Create an inclusive tone in your syllabus.* Use inclusive language. Speak of working together. Use "I" and "we" constructions, and avoid saying "you." This lets the students know you want them to succeed.

3. *Build more structure into the course.* Classrooms differ in the level of structure on any given day. A course with lectures each class period, a midterm, a final exam, and term paper is a course with next to no structure. However, a course with required

attendance, formative quizzes each class period, active learning strategies, intermittent goals for large assignments, and in-class study time is a course with a great deal of control. Research shows that traditional college students (e.g., White, heterosexual, affluent, parents who attended college) typically do well regardless of level of structure. However, students from underrepresented groups, first-generation students, and anyone who has historically struggled in college do significantly better when structure mechanisms are implemented (e.g., daily quiz). Eddy and Hogan (2014) found that adding structure can decrease the difference between Black students and White students by half, and structure can eliminate differences between first-generation students and those who had parents who attended college.

4. *Include diversity/inclusivity/support statements in the syllabus.* The syllabus is students' first introduction to the classroom and the extent to which they will be included (Fuentes et al., 2020). Providing a diversity or inclusivity statement demonstrates clearly that inclusive teaching is an important consideration, and mandated at many colleges. Diversity and inclusion statements also clearly signal that you aim for the course to be an environment in which the goal is for all students to have the best opportunity to learn. If your institution or department does not have a diversity statement, consider searching the internet for appropriate inclusivity statements to use as a model.

5. *Point out campus resources in the syllabus.* When you specifically direct students to resources and use a tone of support, students are more likely to use those resources (Gurung & Galardi, 2021). Check with the office of diversity and inclusion on your campus for suggestions about which resources might best be included.

6. *Warm syllabi can still be rigorous.* It is all about your tone. Syllabi can reflect a rigorous academic environment while still being human and understanding (Denton & Veloso, 2018).

7. *Implement introductions on the first day of class.* If the size of the class allows, encourage students to briefly introduce themselves and share something about themselves that they are comfortable with others knowing. You can also provide a bit of information to personalize you. You need not, and probably should not, share a great deal of information, just enough to show that you care about the material, and you are an expert in the field but continue to learn. Although it may seem positive, many students do not find it helpful to state that you will learn just as much from them as they will learn from you. Certainly, you should expect to learn a lot from your students, but you are the expert who has been paid to facilitate learning in the class. They should learn a bit more.

8. *Provide safe feedback channels.* Methods for students to provide anonymous feedback regarding any microaggressions, inappropriate comments, or even examples that are biased or consistently ignore or marginalize a particular group show that you are serious about creating an inclusive environment. Let students know that you may not be able to immediately act on all comments, but the comments will all be read, given serious consideration, and implemented when possible. You can also ask questions through this anonymous information system about how you might improve your students' experience (e.g., How might I better encourage open and candid discussions in class? What makes participating in class challenging or easy for you?).

9. *Learn students' names and use them.* Names are deeply meaningful to most individuals (Kim, 2021). When possible, learn the names of your students. If the class is too large to learn all names, learn as many as you can. The more often you can call students by name, during discussion or even as they get settled before class starts, the more inclusive your classroom environment will be.

10. *Treat each student as an individual.* Recognize that everyone has their own lived experiences and

everyone has challenges. Aside from that, we know little about each person until we actually get to know them. Do your best to treat everyone the same, praise students equally for equal-quality responses, and expect the same level of work from everyone (e.g., do not grade a female student's paper easier because you perceive that women struggle more in math). Don't lower standards for students from underrepresented groups but do make additional opportunities available to everyone to achieve equity. Lowering standards may feel like it is helping, but if information is not being learned at the level of peers, cutting students a break on level of quality now may well hurt them in future courses.

There will be differences in how individuals interact with one another. For example, many international students stand physically closer to others than do Americans, many Asian American women are taught to avoid eye contact, and many Asian Americans and Native Americans have learned to listen quietly rather than speak. There are times when you may think a student does not know an answer when the reason they did not speak is due to how they would typically respond in their own culture. It may also be that individuals simply need a bit more time. Sathy and Moore (2020) found that letting students work at their own pace in a statistics course resulted in significant increases in student engagement, interest, and academic gains.

11. *Use inclusive discussion prompts and examples.* How you frame a question or the set-up for a discussion is important in establishing the level of respect expected in the discussion. Use warm and inclusive language whenever possible. This can be done and still address challenging issues (Brookfield & Preskill, 2016). Where possible, use examples that go against stereotypes and biases. For example, if you create an example with a Marine, an accountant, or a surgeon, use a female name in the example. If the example pertains to a nurse, a teacher, or an administrative assistant, use a male name in the example.

12. *Model inclusive language.* Use of gender-neutral pronouns can reduce bias (Tavits & Pérez, 2019). APA and MLA now both encourage the use of gender-neutral pronouns, including plural pronouns (e.g., they, them) in reference to individuals. Chicago writing style discourages the use of singular *they*, but the blanket prohibition on such use has been lifted. If you use inclusive language, students will begin to pick up the verbiage. At the beginning of the semester, explain that you will be using inclusive language and students should give their best efforts as well (e.g., use *significant other* rather than *husband/wife*; *caring adults* rather than *mom* or *dad*; *hey, team* or *hey, folks* rather than *hey, guys*). It does take a while for some of us to get an ear for this, but once you start using more inclusive language, you will hear the difference.

If there are individuals with names you cannot pronounce, ask those students to pronounce their name, and then work to get it as correct as you can right there. If the student says that it isn't important, you can indicate that it is to you. It is also appropriate to let all students know that if there is a name that they would prefer to be called in class, to let you know.

13. *Recognize student fears.* Students come from a variety of backgrounds and may be worried about their academic readiness for college, unfamiliarity with unspoken cultural expectations, financial constraints, and even food/housing insecurities. The stakes are high, and the stress is immense. Acknowledge their efforts and successes and offer resources as appropriate.

14. *Remind students that everyone struggles.* Students who feel that they do not belong or that the classroom climate is not inclusive will fret over challenges with papers, exams, and perhaps even class participation. If they look around and it appears they are the only one struggling, they may give up and quit. Let the class know periodically that everyone struggles and that

when struggles happen there are free resources on campus. Perhaps note that if an assignment or material feels overwhelming, students should come and see you.

15. *Address classroom conflict immediately.* Setting good ground rules focused on respect for one another and building a positive classroom community is very helpful. Before launching a potentially controversial discussion, remind students what a civil intellectual discourse comprises. With your students' participation, set ground rules for civil discussion in class, and intervene if any students act disrespectfully to others. If any of those rules are violated, an immediate response is necessary. Waiting until after class implies to classmates that the inappropriate behavior was tolerated, acceptable, or perhaps even encouraged. Ideally, before the semester begins, think through what types of situations may occur that would need to be addressed and perhaps even speak with a colleague about potential responses. When addressing a violation, remain calm and think of the situation as a growth opportunity for the student who violated the rule. Speak at a steady, calming pace; model desired behavior and inclusive language; and avoid aggressive phrasings. For example, if a student interrupts in class, instead of saying, "Stop interrupting," you could say, "Once Rikki concludes the point being made, you can reply at that time."

16. *Cold call with a warm tone.* "Cold-calling" means asking a student a question or to respond to a prompt when the student had not offered to respond. Many students find cold-calling very stressful. For inclusive classrooms, try warming up your cold calls. For example, ask a question, tell students that they have 30 seconds to think about their responses, and that you will then call on a student at random. You could even give 2 or 3 minutes for students to discuss with classmates or look up an answer in their books. Don't assume that students who aren't volunteering or who clam up when called on

aren't participating or don't know the answer. They might be introverted, insecure about their English, on the autism spectrum, or any number of other considerations (Zakrajsek, 2017). Warming up cold calls means you aren't restricted to those who volunteer (which may well be the same three to five students) but you are making participation less intimidating.

17. *Warm the chilly climate.* For over 40 years, data has consistently shown that women are treated in subtle ways in the classroom that creates an environment in which they are less likely to participate in classroom discussions than men. This phenomenon is referred to as the *chilly climate* (Hall & Sandler, 1982). Even recently, Lee and Mccabe (2020) found that men were 9 times more likely than women to dominate a class discussion and that men are 15 times more likely to interrupt women than women are to interrupt men. Find some way to ensure students are called on equally (e.g., draw from a stack of name cards) and monitor interruptions to ensure all students have a voice.

18. *Offer to help students.* Note that you will assist as you are able. Ask your students to email you or come by your office during office hours if there is anything they feel you could do in class to make their life easier, such as facing the class when you are talking. Recall that if this is an accommodation or something that requires specialized skill (e.g., psychologist) put them in touch with the proper office.

■ DIVERSE PERSPECTIVES

We each have our own perspectives based on our lived experiences, including what we learned from those we interacted with as we grew. These experiences become our cultural reference points. Those who grew up in similar circumstances tend to have similar (but not identical) perspectives. Once you have a well-established perspective, it is easy to forget that it even exists. If we don't consciously work at understanding other perspectives, we see the world without realizing that it is from our reference point. For example, a customer who gets "bad service" at a store rarely considers that the store may be understaffed or the associate may be distracted by their child who is sick at home or their own chronic health condition. A driver on a freeway typically perceives others as driving too fast or too slow, not themselves, and it's always someone else with an accent, not yourself. Watch as you interact the world, and you'll realize that you most often orient yourself as "the standard." This is a common psychological phenomenon, but one that it behooves us to modulate if we can.

The same is true when a faculty member walks into the classroom. As an instructor, you might perceive that some students talk too fast, or not enough, or have a particular distracting mannerism. A key to being an inclusive educator is to recognize your own perspective and how that impacts your teaching strategies, course materials, and interactions with students. This requires some self-reflection and self-identification, both of which can happen at any time, but ideally will happen during course planning so that structure, exams, and assigned materials can be considered. As you pull together resource material for your course, consider your perspective and experiences versus that of your students. For example, you might have enjoyed *Friends* when it aired in the 1990s, and it recently had a resurgence among Gen Z's when Netflix hosted it. However, it wasn't popular among Black viewers, who ratings show as preferring shows such as *Living Single* (Collins et al., 2003). Always be cautious referencing television shows and movies. It does not take long for students to be too young to have seen something that was popular 20 years ago, and you may also alienate students from groups for whom the show was never popular.

Develop a personal rapport with your African American, Native American, Hispanic, and female students (or male students in a predominantly female major). The goal is to develop rapport with anyone who is a member of an underrepresented group on your campus and in your course. Their style of thinking and dealing with the world tends to be relational and interpersonal, which means intuitive, cooperative, holistic, subjective, relationship focused, motivated by personal loyalty, and oriented to socially relevant topics (Anderson & Adams, 1992; Baxter Magolda, 1992). This style contrasts with the analytical, which values analysis, objectivity, logic, reason, structure, sequence, the abstract, debate, challenge, competition, and economic practicality. The analytical approach is prevalent among European American and Asian American males and in the academy in general (Anderson & Adams, 1992). How closely and easily you relate to your diverse and female students will strongly affect their motivation to learn, their trust in your intentions for them, and their overall satisfaction with college (Allen et al., 1991; Gonsalves, 2002; Grant-Thompson & Atkinson, 1997; Kobrak, 1992).

In other words, to ensure diverse perspectives, student participation is invaluable. Use the list of 18 ways to build an inclusive classroom to build community and focus on including the slow-talkers, introverts, students of color, first-generation students, female-identifying students, and myriad others for whom higher education was not originally built but who are far and away the majority. Offer pauses for reflection during class; encourage feedback during class, office hours, or in a discussion board; and remind students that everyone is here to learn and improve.

REPRESENTATION IN COURSE CONTENT

As you prepare your course content, be sure you use inclusive images in PowerPoints or in offered resources (e.g., websites, video clips). It is certainly acceptable to have photos of White males; but the images should not all be of White males.

The images in Figure 8.1 are examples of images that can be used so that students from underrepresented or marginalized groups can see themselves in professional roles. Similarly, incorporate gender-neutral names that represent a variety of

Figure 8.1   Images of Scientists

Source (left to right): Image by Ernesto Eslava from Pixabay; photo by National Cancer Institute on Unsplash; photo by Humberto Chavex on Unsplash.

cultural backgrounds. Regardless of class makeup, it's critical that representation reflect more than just the majority. Story problems should be about more than Sam and Chris filling up their gas tank—introduce students to Olga and José who are bicycling to reduce their carbon footprint, or Alya and Zion who are examining exponential growth of viral load. If you are uncertain about where to find a variety of names for examples, you might search the internet for baby names based on different backgrounds.

There are many ways to present information and ask questions. Simply be aware of your materials and who is being favored by the way questions are traditionally asked. Instead of asking physics students to calculate the release point for a pilot to drop a bomb, the question could just as easily be about dropping aid packages into remote villages. Story problems often focus on buying things (particularly women doing the shopping) or playing sports (particularly men being athletes) and actually talk about malls and calculating the area covered by parking lots, reinforcing gender stereotypes and questionable environmental practices (Bright, 2016). Bright (2016) also noted that textbooks are filled with examples that aren't as relevant to college students, such as a second- to fourth-grade textbook with problems about investing money, purchasing a luxury sportscar, or planning a trip to Paris.

There is no way to create a story problem, have topics for term papers, or even set up multiple-choice questions without some reference to gender,

ethnicity, capitalism, American concepts, or any number of other areas. But we can look at the questions critically and ask whether what is being asked of students is representative of those at the college and also whether the stories negatively portray anyone. Keep in mind that students can be of assistance. Set up a way for students to submit anonymous (if they choose) feedback on any questions or prompts that they feel you could consider changing. Note that this is simply an opportunity for students to comment on instructional materials, not an edict that you change every part of your course.

◼ MITIGATE INEQUITIES IN AND OUT OF THE CLASSROOM

Throughout a course, even if everyone is doing their best to create an inclusive environment, there will be errors. Catching these errors and correcting them as quickly as possible will help ensure that all students have an opportunity to learn and to be successful. Following are a few examples of potential inequities that have been frequently noted in higher education.

Gender Differences

As noted previously, research has constantly shown differences between the contributions of males and females in class. We know males interrupt more and are more likely to dominate conversations (Lee & Mccabe, 2020). With this information, you can watch classroom discussions closely for equity of expression. Give women an opportunity to talk; be prepared to politely interrupt long classroom monologues or have conversations outside of class with long-winded male classmates. Research from multiple countries on 5,300 student interactions across 2 years noted that women ask fewer questions than do men in large classes (Ballen et al., 2018). Women also ask fewer questions during conference talks and academic seminars. As class size approaches 150 students, female participation decreases by 50%. However, in smaller classes or in small groups, women ask *more* questions than men. If you note this phenomenon in your large courses, you can search for ways to encourage women to ask and answer more questions, or perhaps use small-group work more often to balance questions by gender.

Underrepresented Groups and Stereotype Threat

If a student is being dismissed or excluded because they are underrepresented within a given group, it is helpful to draw the excluded person into the conversation. This may be a male in a nursing or education program, a female in an engineering program, a woman wearing a hijab or burka, a student of color in a predominantly White school, or a returning student in a classroom of traditional-aged students. Aside from being excluded from conversations, any of these individuals could be experiencing stereotype threat. Stereotype threat occurs when a member of a minoritized group feels that their personal poor performance would reflect poorly on their entire group, thereby putting additional stress on that individual and resulting in poorer performance. Stereotype threat was first described by Claude Steele in reference to Black students at predominantly White educational institutions (Steele & Aronson, 1995). Steele noted that the stress of being a representative of an underrepresented group typically lowers test scores. Researchers have noted that if the individual believes the test is for formative purposes only, the test takers from the minoritized group often scores as well as the majority group members. However, if the test taker is told the test is diagnostic, then the minoritized student

frequently earns a significantly lower score. The phenomenon of stereotype threat has now been shown to impact individuals including test scores of Native Americans in predominantly White schools (Jaramillo et al., 2016), women in math courses (Spencer at al., 1999), students with lower socioeconomic status (Croizet et al., 2001), and social interactions for individuals on the autism spectrum (Botha et al., 2020).

Faculty Responses

As faculty members, we can also work to ensure that our words do not create inequities or reduce our efforts at an inclusive environment. When responding to questions, it is important to avoid words or phrases that make the student feel like their contribution is being minimized, or even dismissed. For example, imagine that a student provides a response and you appear nonresponsive and then look around the room and say, "Who else has a contribution?" That could seem dismissive of the student's contribution. Instead, give a quick word of affirmation, or, if the answer is wrong, you might thank the student for giving it a try and then ask the question of the class in another way. Keep the tone warm and supportive. The goal in having students respond is to reinforce learning and model for all the students in the class how to think about the problem or issue. The goal should never be about embarrassing students by sarcasm, pointing out rudely why their response is incorrect, or catching them distracted by a device and asking a question you know they can't answer. If you observe behavior you do not approve of, either point out at that time that the behavior is inappropriate or, if possible, speak with the student outside of class.

Lack of Resources

Students may also be constrained by resources and lack reliable high-speed internet, transportation, funds, and so on. If this is the case, let students know of resources on campus. Perhaps an exam review could be done through Zoom or some other app to help mitigate transportation or internet concerns. This can also benefit students who must work (as you could record the session) or those with children (who would not need to hire a sitter). Ask your colleagues and get creative.

Group Representation

Don't ask students to represent their gender, race, ethnicity, age, or any other category. It is totally inappropriate to think that because of an accent, skin color, gender, or a physical challenge that the person is in a position to speak to what others who seem like them would do, say, or think. Imagine how you might respond if a person outside of higher education, while at a dinner party, said, "Hey, you are a college professor, right? I have always wanted to know, what do college profs like better, research or teaching?" It is totally appropriate to ask broadly if anyone in the class has experience with a given issue. However, if you are asking about rap music by a Black artist and there is one Black student in the classroom, to ask that student what they think is feeding into an inappropriate stereotype. It may well be that the Black student in your class listens primarily to classical music and three different White students all listen to the rap music artist to which you are referring.

This brings up the issue of inappropriate biases and assumptions of which we need to be mindful. Don't feel bad that they weren't caught sooner; be glad that you are less likely to make that error in the future. The human brain is wired to make and maintain assumptions to keep us safe (e.g., our brakes will work, there will be food at the grocery store) (Davachi & DuBrow, 2015). However, some assumptions are not valid, and with a bit of work those can be rooted out. Following are some common assumptions that are simply not true.

1. *Individuals who speak quickly are more knowledgeable than those who speak slowly.* There are plenty of examples of people saying a lot of nothing fast and also individuals who think for a bit and then say the most amazing thing.
2. *Individuals who look similar have similar views on a subject.* There certainly will be some similarities among individuals who look similar. That is fairly obvious. What is not obvious are the vast differences. Irrespective of the color of one's skin, team name on the jersey, posture in the back row, or particular gender, individuals have a wide variety of life experiences. Those life experiences impact perceptions, interests, motivation, and a host of other areas far more than superficial similarities.
3. *Certain groups are more argumentative or hostile than others.* This starts for individuals at a young age. Black children are consistently seen as being angrier than White children (Cooke & Halberstadt, 2021). There are argumentative and hostile individuals within any group, but we should never assume everyone within a group is hostile or argumentative. It is unfortunate that some groups are perceived this way, even before the members of the group speak. Many factors make assumptions based on group categorization complex. For example, Livingston et al. (2012) found that research has shown consistently that Black males and White women who show dominance and assertiveness face a backlash that White males do not face. It was also noted that Black females do not face the same backlash as White females. Indeed, their assertiveness is treated more like that of White males (Livingston et al., 2012). Treat everyone as an individual. You have likely already found out in life that sometimes the nicest-looking person turns out to be a terror and an individual who looks grumpy and mean is incredibly helpful.
4. *Students doing poorly in class are not motivated enough to seek out assistance.* You have likely noticed that there are many times that the students who need the most help are those who avoid seeking it. As faculty members, we lament the situation and are frustrated that students seem to not even try to get the help they need. Research has shown that help-seeking behavior is based on many possible factors, and lack of motivation or willingness to put in the work are only two possible reasons out of at least 17 (Black & Allen, 2019; Karabenick & Dembo, 2011). Sometimes students do poorly

in a course because they don't know how to get help or are afraid, not that they don't want to try.

5. *Students from underrepresented groups are less academically prepared.* Don't avoid giving timely, constructive feedback to diverse students about their work out of fear of injuring their self-esteem or being accused of racism. Students from underrepresented groups indeed may interpret your criticisms as racially motivated disrespect, so you should bring up this possibility yourself and explicitly ask them rather than sweeping the issue under the rug. Do your best to let all students understand your criticisms and recommendations are for improvement (Gonsalves, 2002). Don't give inordinate attention to diverse students or make so much of their successes that your behavior implies you didn't expect them to succeed.

6. *Students take advantage of accommodations such as extended time to take tests.* There may well be students who take advantage, but that is certainly not true of most who are eligible for accommodations. Some don't know that they are eligible, some are given accommodations but do not use them for fear of stigma by their classmates or instructors, some believe that using an accommodation is unfair, and some are fearful of disclosing a disability in the first place (Slaughter et al., 2020).

7. *Stereotypes, biases, and assumptions are not a big deal.* The list of stereotypes is nearly endless regarding students who are women, men, Black, Latinx, transgender, homosexual, older (returning), traditional age, Chinese, Muslim, Canadian, science majors, theater majors, from New York (or California, Texas, or any other state), like rap music, like country music, wear bright colored clothes, sit in the front of the room, and on and on. Of course, one could be a combination of just about any of these categories noted. This is a serious issue. Biases and stereotypes impact how individuals approach one another and even how statements are interpreted. Another issue is that those in the group who are stigmatized with stereotypes begin to believe them. That can have serious consequences. If girls consistently hear that they are not good at science and math (which by every measure is not true), they begin to believe it, and that belief impacts their math and science proficiency, which can impact whether they choose a STEM major as young women (Starr & Simpkins, 2021). If you build a strong classroom climate for inclusion, one valuable activity is to take class time and have students ask each other about stereotypes.

■ TEACHING SO EVERYONE LEARNS

By creating an inclusive learning environment so everyone has the opportunity to learn, you can teach at your best and provide the best for your students. Most importantly, constantly check your thoughts and behaviors. Uncover and rectify implicit biases, microaggressions, and examples that may be biased against some students. If you have not done this before, it may feel quite uncomfortable when you start. It is a challenging thing to do. One aspect that makes this challenging is that you cannot create a perfect environment for each student. That would be incredibly challenging if you had only one student, but once you have 2, 50, 100, or several hundred, any choice you make will affect each student differently. You will not be able to make the course ideal for everyone, but you can strive to make it as good as possible for most.

Ask a colleague who is engaged in teaching inclusively to look over your syllabus. Even when trying diligently, it is easy to miss something that another pair of eyes can catch. It is helpful to sit in on classes of colleagues if they are willing to have you there. Take good notes, as this is one of the best ways to really see a course as a student sees it. You can also give feedback to the faculty member who allowed you to sit in on the course, but only if feedback is requested. Otherwise, simply thank the person for the opportunity. You may also ask colleagues to sit in your class. Explain that you are interested in the effectiveness of your teaching strategy, but also whether the class was warm, welcoming, and the extent to which you and your students engaged in inclusive behaviors. Finally, as part of the visit, schedule a 30-minute follow-up on the day you taught (if possible) to discuss what your colleague observed.

Use a wide range of strategies to meet as many students' needs as you can. For example, research has long shown that having students work in small groups increases success for everyone and closes achievement gaps for minoritized groups. Several decades ago, Uri Treisman (1986) noted that Black/ African American students at Berkeley were receiving grades of Ds, Fs, and withdrew at twice the rate of other students despite the fact that they were bright and motivated students. However, when students started working in small groups in addition to lectures, Black students were scoring right along with other students and closed the achievement gaps (Fullilove & Treisman, 1990; Treisman, 2013). This has been reaffirmed by a metanalysis that found not only does *any* engaged learning narrow achievement gaps, but that *more* engaged learning closes gaps even more (Theobald et al., 2020). Of course, if we use small groups in our classes, it is important to teach students *how* to work in small groups (Zakrajsek, 2022). When you do ask students to work together, make your expectations clear. Students who are more results oriented, those on the autism spectrum, and those who are nervous talking to others will all appreciate having a better idea of what is to be done or if the groups are meant to be more informal.

The more strategies you learn, the more students you can reach. Don't forget metacognition, either: If you teach students about the strategies you are using to help them learn, *that* will help them to learn. Discuss why it is important to take time and think during a discussion. Reassure them that answers need not happen within a few seconds of hearing a question. Although silence feels awkward at first, students come to appreciate the time to gather their thoughts, whether it's just a busy day or they are mustering their courage to speak or

translating into a primary language. Regularly insert 10, 15, or even 30 seconds of silence before anyone can respond. In other words, with just a bit of silence you are making the classroom environment more inclusive.

Another strategy is to use low-stakes quizzes, tests, and assignments. This is particularly helpful for students who are nervous, first-generation college students who do not know what to expect, and students with lower self-efficacy.

A final recommendation for inclusive teaching pertains to your office hours. Office hours are important for a number of reasons, but most importantly they give students a chance to meet you and get a better sense of you as a person. It is a great opportunity to let students know you are on their side and want them to be successful. You can find out more about why students are taking your course and their academic plans, and they have an excellent opportunity to learn study strategies and tips to be successful in your course. Note that some students misunderstand what is meant by "office hours," and might even think that it when you are working and should not be disturbed (Nadworny, 2019). Arizona State University (2015) made a satirical video highlighting the confusion around office hours: https://www.youtube.com/watch?v=yQq1-_ujXrM. The video is funny, but rings true for many students. Talking to a faculty member is routine to you and your students who are close to people who have graduated from college, but that is by no means a universal experience. Many individuals are intimidated by the idea of talking to a college professor one-on-one: students who are first-generation, international, from households with lower socioeconomic status, from minoritized or underrepresented groups, shy, susceptible to panic attacks, or struggling in the course. To help these individuals, explain the types of things you talk to students about during office hours, let students know they can come by with another person from class or a friend, and reassure them that it is fine to come by for only a few minutes. You could also hold office hours in a dorm lobby, the library, in the school food court, or any place on campus more comfortable for students.

Keep in mind that almost anything you do to make the classroom and learning more inclusive for some students will make it a better learning experience for all students.

■ UNIVERSAL DESIGN FOR LEARNING

Inclusive teaching means providing educational opportunities to as many individuals as possible, regardless of the barriers they face. This does not happen on its own. Minimizing barriers takes concerted effort. Although there is still much to be done, a great deal of work has been accomplished in this area worldwide, under names like *inclusive design*, *accessible design*, *barrier-free design*, *cooperative design*, or *design for all*. The framework that appears to be dominating is universal design (Persson et al., 2015). The overarching goal is the same, regardless of the design name or framework used: take into consideration the needs of a wide range of individuals and include in the design process the opportunity for as many individuals as possible to successfully navigate or interact with the content (e.g., buildings, equipment, areas designed as a conveyance for individuals, websites, syllabi, etc.). This does not mean that everything has to be designed for everyone. It does mean that we should be taking into consideration multiple perspectives and be proactive in being as inclusive as possible. The overall goal is not to design for individuals with challenges, but rather to design so that those challenges are no longer relevant. For example, automatic doors provide easy entrance to the building whether you are in a wheelchair, pushing a stroller, or walking while carrying a box of binders. Automatic doors make mobility challenges irrelevant with respect to entering a building. Another example is an untimed test. If you tell students they can work on the exam as long as they need, then there is no reason for an accommodation for more time.

There are many resources on universal design for learning (UDL) for faculty members who wish to create more inclusive classrooms. Students receive accommodations based on challenges and limitations, such as slower cognitive processing time, attention deficit disorder, mobility challenges, visual challenges, and hearing challenges. These accommodations allow all students the same chance of success. Using UDL, it is possible to assist students by making these challenges irrelevant. Of course, approved accommodations must remain available where appropriate. The Center for Applied Special Technology (CAST) has worked for many years to provide guidance regarding designing learning environments to reduce barriers so that all learners have the opportunity to be successful (CAST, 2022). Their UDL Guideline tool is helpful when implementing UDL. This tool provides concrete examples that can be used in any discipline and offers multiple ways students may be engaged in the learning process, multiple ways for students to demonstrate learning, and multiple means of action and expression. As you look through the information, do not try to implement everything. Identify a good starting point and try a few suggestions to see what works for you and your students. As you build out your universal design toolbox you will reach more and more students, and, by doing so, you will create an increasingly inclusive course.

■ BUILDING OUT INCLUSIVE TEACHING SKILLS

Inclusivity is, unfortunately, a relatively new concept. Harvard University admitted its first female student in 1936. Southern Oregon University did not graduate its first female ROTC-trained infantry officer until the fall of 2019. The first Black student admitted at the University of North Carolina–Chapel Hill was in 1951 (as a result of a court order), and Clemson University opened its first LGBTQ residential community in 2021. We have been working at inclusion for several decades, but in many cases it is just now starting to make serious advances, and there remains a long way to go. There is no playbook on exactly how to decrease inequities and create inclusive communities. We must embrace a growth mindset and realize that at times we will make mistakes, but that with open communication and steadfast efforts, we are making a difference. As with anything else, the more you work at inclusion, the easier it will become. In relatively short order, you will move closer and closer to implicit inclusion.

As you watch for ways to meet the needs of a diverse group of students, you will see the needs more easily. As you slowly begin to dismantle barriers, you will see that the barriers have been present in education all along—but now you are noticing them. Now you can help your students overcome those unnoticed and unchanged aspects of education that haven't been helpful to anyone and allow everyone the same chance to thrive. Once you see students who used to struggle start to thrive, you will notice those barriers all the time. The same barriers that were there all along, unnoticed and unchanged—that is, until you started to change them. What you do in the classroom can make an important difference in the success rate of students in marginalized groups.

REFLECTION QUESTIONS

Reflection Question 8.1: Many biases, some implicit and some explicit, permeate our institutions and affect virtually all aspects of teaching, learning, and assessment. Identify three biases that you feel have a significant impact at your institution. What impact do you feel those biases have on your students? How might the biases be addressed?

Reflection Question 8.2: Reflect on your perspective when it comes to higher education and learning. What are a few of your behaviors and beliefs that impact how you interact with your students and your colleagues? What student behaviors do you find most foreign to you at present? What do you think those students think of your behaviors? How might individuals in your course come to better understand perspectives of others?

Concept Into Practice: Look through your teaching materials, such as PowerPoint slides, essay questions, term paper prompts, course textbook, or other major assignments. Consider ways to make those course elements more inclusive. For some aspects of the course, students may be able to help identify ways to make course materials more inclusive.

CHAPTER 9

Enhancing Student Motivation

Motivation is a force that "initiates, guides, and maintains goal-directed behaviors" (Lertladaluck et al., 2020, para. 3). When we seek to understand a person's motivation, we are essentially asking "why." Once we understand *why* a person does what they do, we are in a much better position to know how to shape their behavior. This is important because it allows you to help students reach their desired outcomes. There is a big difference between wanting to do something and doing it. That is demonstrated mid-January each year, when most individuals realize that without a better understanding of how motivation works, most New Year's resolutions are quickly just a memory.

When it comes to motivation, three components determine whether and to what extent a goal is reached: activation, persistence, and intensity (Simpson & Balsam, 2016). *Activation* is the mental process of deciding to engage in a course of action, such as deciding to read this chapter to learn more about what motivates students. *Persistence* is continuing to put effort into a course of action, such as picking up this book each evening to read the next chapter. *Intensity* is how much energy is devoted to a course of action, such as turning off extraneous noise and making notes to yourself of what strategies you'd like to use as you read this chapter (high intensity), rather than reading poolside (low intensity).

Understanding motivation is a key aspect of teaching at its best. Motivation is necessary for students to learn, attend class, study for exams, implement what was learned in "the real world," and a host of other goal-directed behavior. If a person is not motivated in some way, there is no resulting behavior.

▪ INTRINSIC AND EXTRINSIC MOTIVATION

Most of us in higher education want students to learn for the sake of learning. This would be considered *intrinsic* motivation. We say something is intrinsic when it is essential, a natural part of something, or coming from within. If, when we teach, we inspire curiosity in our students so that they research the topic on their own or read an extra chapter because they are interested in the topic, they are intrinsically (by their own internal state) motivated. A person is typically more intrinsically motivated as they become more knowledgeable about the content. We consider intrinsic motivation to be ideal because it results in behaviors in the absence of external reinforcements. This is a key to lifelong learning. As experts, we have a great deal of intrinsic motivation; we can see the nuances and patterns buried in the content, and it is fascinating. However, early in the learning process, much of education is learning foundational material. Like drills in basketball and scales in music, learning foundational content is not typically of great interest and therefore it is rarely intrinsically motivating. For such situations, there needs to be an external source of motivation.

Extrinsic motivators come from outside a system and encourage an action independent of any inherent interest. When students want to know how many points a quiz is worth or whether they will get any points for attending class, they are inquiring about extrinsic motivators. Among the most powerful extrinsic motivators are the expectations of significant others, such as parents, spouses, employers, and teachers. Many of today's younger students pursue a college major because of its earning potential. For them, high achievement in the form of top grades may mean entrance into a professional or business school and ultimately a high-paying occupation, all extrinsic motivations.

We can affect extrinsic motivation through grades, points, and praise, but the challenge is that one day students will leave our university and we want them to continue to learn. To do that, it is important to instill intrinsic motivation (Hobson, 2002; Levin, 2001; Svinicki, 2004).

The vast body of research on the relationships among intrinsic motivation, extrinsic motivation, and student performance comes to no clear conclusions. Some individuals have made a strong argument that extrinsic motivation decreases intrinsic motivation (Deci et al., 1999; Kohn, 2018). For example, one argument is that assigning good grades in exchange for studying (extrinsic motivation) decreases a natural interest in learning (intrinsic motivation). This position has been used to promote "ungrading," a movement against grading where points are not earned for doing work (Beatriz, 2021; Gorichanaz, 2022). Ungrading can be beneficial for some students and is currently gaining attention.

The research into motivation is quite complex. For most faculty members, we recommend providing as little external motivation as necessary to get students to do the work, and at the same time emphasizing and instilling intrinsic motivation to the greatest extent possible. Using your interest in the topic as a foundation, show students the value in what they are learning.

■ STUDENTS' PERCEPTIONS OF MOTIVATORS IN THEIR COURSES

A couple of studies have solicited college students' opinions of what makes them want to learn, so we have some idea of what students *think* motivates them. Hobson (2002) identified and ranked the most powerful positive and negative motivators for students. In order of descending importance, the positive motivators are the instructor's positive attitudes and behaviors, a cohesive course structure, a student's prior interest in the material, the relevance of the course content, and the appropriateness of the performance measures. The two most potent demotivators are an instructor's negative attitudes and behaviors and a disorganized course structure. Further down on the list are a poor learning environment, boring or irrelevant course content, and a student's prior disinterest in the material. More recently, Kember (2016) identified that factors affecting motivation are always on a continuum from demotivating to motivating. For example, materials could range from abstract to relevant; teaching styles could range from didactic to engaged learning; acquiring new information could range from rote learning to learning for understanding; and exams could require simple memorization to authentic assessment activities. Interpersonally, teachers could fall anywhere from not relating to students at all to nurturing close, professional relationships.

Kember's (2016) work is exciting, as we have control over the factors noted. We also have control over the factors noted by Hobson (2002), with the exception of the student's prior interest in the material and even that can be creatively reframed. For example, students regularly groan at the concept of *group work,* but they are often open to *peer-supported collaborative work.*

PERCEIVED VALUE OF COLLEGE AND ITS IMPACT ON MOTIVATION

Motivation at the course level tells us nothing about the more general picture of why students go to college in the first place. Most of them take an instrumental view of college, seeing it as a means to an end. For example, 73.3% of the entering college freshmen in 2013 selected "to be able to make more money" as a "very important" reason for attending college; 77.1% selected "to get training for a specific career"; and a whopping 86.3% chose "to be able to get a better job" (Eagan et al., 2013, p. 35), and these reasons have gained currency over the past 40 years (Pryor et al., 2007). Although students' largely extrinsic reasons for attending college foster their desire for the certificate or diploma, it does not cultivate a thirst for knowledge. Still, these freshmen cited intrinsic reasons as "very important" as well: 81.6% "to learn about things that interest me," 69.6% "to gain a general education and appreciation of ideas" and 45.9% "to make me a more cultured person." But extrinsic reasons still predominate.

Unfortunately, the relationships between intrinsic and extrinsic motivation can be quite complex. Many faculty members complain that today's students are "not motivated." Everyone is motivated to some extent. It may be that students are simply not interested in the topics their classes are addressing, or they may not think they will need the material in the future, or they may want to learn the material but *not to work* to learn it. Students tend

not to know much about what learning for depth and retention requires. Because they are learners, they need to know, and if we don't tell them, who will? In addition, many of them seem not to understand that learning requires more time, effort, focus, and perseverance than they think it should. Instead of lamenting that students are not motivated, it is important to consider that if one knows more about motivation, it is likely to be helpful in enhancing student motivation toward learning.

THEORIES OF MOTIVATION

Presented here are several theories of academic motivation, particularly crucial and challenging at this time in students' lives on the global stage (Hattie et al., 2020). These models work best when two or more are applied together. These motivational theories should give you an idea about what motivates your students, and then, following these theories, we provide 50 concrete strategies to enhance students' motivation.

Reinforcement Theory

The basic foundation of reinforcement theory is that humans engage in a behavior and if that behavior is reinforced, they are more likely to engage in that behavior again. If the behavior is punished, they are less likely to engage in that behavior again (Skinner, 1974). A student who attends class and learns something valuable is reinforced for going-to-class behavior and is likely to attend again (reinforced for going to class). If a student studies for an exam and scores a high grade, they are likely to study again in the future (reinforced for studying). If going to class produces nothing of value, the behavior of attending class will decrease (punished for going to class). If an instructor makes fun of a student who answers a question in class, that student may not volunteer to answer a question again (punished for responding). Reinforcement does not always entail receiving something. It can also be the removal of something negative, also known as negative reinforcement. For example, if I ask my daughter every night if she's started her paper, she may get frustrated and write the paper just to get me to stop asking. Removal of the unpleasant stimulus (asking repeatedly) to cause something to happen (writing the paper) is a negative reinforcement.

A fascinating and important aspect of reinforcement theory is that the reinforcement does not necessarily need to occur every time the behavior occurs. This is called intermittent reinforcement (Nevin, 2012). Reinforcement typically works best if there is a continuous reinforcement as you start to pick up a behavior, and then rewards are given intermittently, but often enough to continue making the behavior worthwhile. A prime example is playing a video game. The game starts off easy, and the player is successful at nearly every challenge (continuous reinforcement). However, as the game gets more difficult, the player fails more and more but keeps playing as they are still reinforced, just not every time (intermittent reinforcement). As long as there is some progress (intermittent reinforcement), the player will keep trying.

Academics is much like a video game. It is often helpful to set students up for near continuous success early in the semester (e.g., softball questions in class, quiz questions lower on Bloom's taxonomy). Across time, the continuous reinforcement shifts to intermittent reinforcement, which is also highly resistant to extinction. That means students will persevere even if they don't get every answer correct on the test or even points every time they participate. However, they must perceive that the reinforcement is at an acceptable level. Overly challenging exams or harshly graded papers can be demotivating to many students.

Goal Setting

According to goal-setting theory (Locke & Latham, 1990), setting a goal increases students' motivation to attain it. Certainly, mastering some definable body of material and earning a good grade qualify as possible goals for students. This motivation in turn increases the energy, work, persistence, and thought they will give toward achieving it.

For this process to work, a few conditions must hold. First, students must believe that they have freely chosen the goal, and they might not always think they have in what they perceive to be required courses. Second, they have to see the goal as specific and measurable, as an assessment or a grade typically is. Third, they must get feedback about their progress toward the goal, and they almost always do in classes. Finally, students must size up the goal as challenging but achievable. Difficulty does not necessarily discourage; in fact, the higher the difficulty, the more effort a student will put toward the goal.

Goal-setting theory caught on in business and industry, which is why you often hear terms like *sales goals, service goals, training goals, strategic goals*, and the like. It became one of the most widely implemented and tested theories of organization behavior of the past 50 years (Redmond & Perrin, 2014). Does it work with students? Yes, but only to the extent that they regard their goals as freely chosen and not imposed by the program or institution. Some students look at the courses in their major and any general education course, even if they have a choice of 300 of them, as required and therefore not freely chosen. However, you can incorporate choices into your courses, such as different ways to satisfy course requirements and choices among assignments, topics, media used, and the like. Giving students options cultivates that sense of free will.

Goal Orientation

Students who work primarily for good grades have what is called a *performance goal* orientation. They aim to display higher competency than others and to avoid making mistakes and failing in front of others. Given the stakes, they tend to eschew risk-taking. For them, learning often exerts stress on their self-esteem and induces insecurity. By contrast, students who work out of a desire to learn have a *learning goal* orientation. Because they don't care about what others may think of their performance, they willingly take risks, make mistakes, and seek feedback so they can improve. As instructors, we want to foster this type of goal orientation because it engenders deeper learning and retention of our material than does the former.

Using this model, we can encourage learning over performance goals by doing what we can to create a safe and secure classroom environment (see Chapter 7), reduce students' stress over tests and assignments, deemphasize grades and competition, allow alternative ways to satisfy course requirements, reward risk-taking and persistence, and role-model a learning goal orientation (Svinicki, 2004).

Expectancy Theory

Vroom's (1964) valence, instrumentality, and expectancy (VIE) theory was developed to quantify one's motivation based on what information is available at the time a decision is made. The motivational force, which determines whether an individual engages in a behavior, is the product of the following three assessments by an individual.

1. Valence: The extent to which the outcome is desired or not desired. An individual may be as motivated to not have an outcome (negative valence) as they are to have an outcome (positive valence). For example, getting a good grade for medical school applications is a high positive valence, and avoiding being benched during a varsity basketball game is a high negative valence.
2. Expectancy: The belief that the effort expended will result in achieving a goal. For example, a student who believes that with effort expended they will be able to learn the course material has high expectancy. They believe that studying will result in learning (high expectancy). If a student feels they just don't understand the material or that they always forget things after studying, they would also not believe that exerting energy studying would lead to learning (low expectancy).
3. Instrumentality: The belief that achieving a goal will result in a desired outcome. For example,

does the student believe that learning the material will result in a good grade on the exam (high instrumentality). Students might also believe that even if they learn the material they will not earn a good test score because either they are poor test takers or the faculty member writes tricky tests (low instrumentality).

To determine motivation, a person simply multiplies the valence (V: −1 to +1) by the instrumentality (I: 0.0–1.0) by the expectancy (E: 0.0–1.0). It is important to note that the three elements are multiplied: If any one of the elements is zero, then there is no motivation. According to this model, you can enhance student motivation to learn by helping them see the importance of the material and earning good grades on papers and exams (high valence), teaching them how to learn (expectancy), and having a clear course grading policy so students can easily see what is needed to get a desired grade (instrumentality). Any secrecy or perceived inequity quickly zeroes out motivation.

Many other specific suggestions for enhancing students' sense of agency and capability, and therefore their expectancy to achieve, are offered among the 50 strategies in the next section.

Self-Determination Theory

This theory posits a set of built-in human needs that can motivate students to action and achievement (Deci & Ryan, 2002). Like everyone else, students have an innate need to grow, develop, and attain fulfillment as a person. In order to grow and be fulfilled, they must believe they have these three qualities:

1. *Competence*, which requires that they master new knowledge and skills and live through new experiences
2. *Relatedness*, meaning feeling attached to others, valued by them, and integrated into a social group
3. *Autonomy*, that is, the sense that they can freely choose and are in control of their own goals, outcomes, and behaviors

Therefore, conditions that help students satisfy these needs should foster motivation. Students develop their competency when they perceive that they are acquiring relevant, interesting skills and knowledge. Faculty members need to explain the hidden value of learning tasks that are not obviously interesting, useful, and worth the effort to complete. Students feel more socially connected when someone they respect, such as their instructor, praises their response, piece of work, or contribution. However, they prize their attachments to and approval of their peers just as much, if not more. So, we should set up at least a few group activities or assignments (see Chapter 10) and cultivate a sense of classroom community (see Chapter 7). Finally, students have a stronger sense of volition and control when they can make choices about their assignments, when the instructor pays attention to their feedback, and when they have some input into the course design and topical emphases. You will notice that student choice keeps coming up as a motivating factor.

Attribution Theory

Attribution theory was important in bringing learning theory to motivation (Dweck, 2018). When we observe someone doing something, there is no way to know for certain their motivation, or reason, for engaging in the behavior. Even if an individual states their reason, they might (knowingly or unknowingly) not be telling the truth. The challenge is that we must have a sense of causes of behavior to bring order to our world and allow society to function. As a result, we make attributions, particularly if something negative or unexpected occurs (Weiner, 2018).

The attributions we make are impacted by three factors (Weiner, 2018):

1. *Locus of control,* whether an individual sees the cause as internal or external, such as believing an A is a result of studying (internal locus) versus an easy test or a lucky guess (external locus).
2. *Stability*, or the extent to which behavior is consistent. For example, if a faculty member consistently offers positive feedback when students participate, regardless of right answer, their behavior is stable and consistent. If they sometimes make sarcastic comments and sometimes praise answers, the faculty member's behavior is unstable and unpredictable. We tend to attribute deviations from a norm to an external locus.
3. *Controllability*, or the extent to which the individual has control over the situation in which they find themselves. Imagine the difference between a student who falls asleep in class because they stayed up till 3 a.m. playing *Animal Crossing* versus working two jobs to support their studies and their family. In both cases, the behavior is the same, and frustrating in class, but one situation seems to have more controllability than the other.

According to attribution theory, we are motivated by our perceptions. Nothing about the reality changes. If students see their ability to do well on a group project as internal (they have the ability), stable (they tend to organize groups and work well as a team), and controllable (they know if they work hard the outcome will be positive), then there is high motivation to work on this project. Imagine the same project where the attributions are the opposite: their success is based on luck (external), sometimes group members do their work and sometimes they do not (unstable), and there is nothing the faculty member will do if the group falls apart and team members don't do their share (uncontrollable). This situation would result in much less effort expended.

Social Belonging

Relatedness seems to be an important factor in student success and retention that has generated enough research to justify its own subsection here. In fact, Chambliss and Takacs (2014) make a strong empirical case that personal relationships play a critical role in determining how academically successful students are or even whether they finish college.

Just a small handful of good friends and one or two faculty members who inspire or take an interest in them can make all the difference in their motivation and learning. The effects of social support prove particularly strong among ethnic minorities and first-generation students (Cox, 2011; Dennis et al., 2005; Jackson et al., 2003). Moreover, students must be able to perceive this support for the persistence benefits to accrue, so it must be quite explicit (Dennis et al., 2005). Therefore, you should say to a promising but struggling student, "I believe in you. I *know* you can do it."

You may have more importance in your students' lives than you know. Chickering and Gamson (1987) considered frequent in-class and out-of-class contact with a faculty member the single most powerful motivator of undergraduates' academic commitment. How warm and caring Native American students thought their professors were predicted their college persistence and retention (Jackson et al., 2003). Umbach and Wawrzynski (2005) studied the effects of faculty behavior on learning and engagement on more than 42,000 students at 137 colleges and universities and reported that instructor interaction, experiential learning, active and collaborative teaching strategies, and a focus on higher-order thinking all led to greater student engagement and learning. Even in large lecture classes, which hinder faculty-student interaction, just talking with students in small groups can help. Student-to-student relationships also increase students' academic motivation as long as the friendships do not foster alcohol use, which depresses motivation (Li et al., 2013).

■ FIFTY STRATEGIES TO MOTIVATE STUDENTS

There is a strong connection between teaching and student motivation to learn (Kember, 2016). If you are not interested in the content, why would students be motivated to learn that material? If your course is not well-designed, students will not understand why they should learn the content. If teaching strategies are not carefully chosen and explained, students will be unsure how to engage with the material. Finally, the assignments and tests must be well integrated and explained or students may fail to see value in learning the content at all. Across all four of these areas, the overarching theme comes down to "better teaching generates more rewarding learning experiences, which beget more motivation to learn." That is, you motivate students using the same methods and formats that you do to teach them effectively. To motivate students at their highest levels, it is imperative to engage in teaching at its best. We hope the following 50 strategies provide ideas for you to adopt and adapt to your specific class (Ambrose et al., 2010; Biggs, 2003; Bjork & Bjork, 2011; Chambliss & Takacs, 2014; Cox, 2011; Davis, 2009; Dweck, 2007; Gabriel, 2008; Hobson, 2002; Levin, 2001; Major et al., 2021; McGuire, 2015; Persellin & Daniels, 2014; Svinicki, 2004; Theall & Franklin, 1999; Zakrajsek, 2022).

Your Persona

1. *Teach with enthusiasm and energy.* Strive for vocal variety and constant eye contact. Vary your speaking pace, and add dramatic pauses after major points. Gesture and move around the class. Be expressive. To your students, your dynamism signifies your passion for the material and for teaching it. As a display of your motivation, it motivates them.

2. *Explain your reasons for being so interested in the material*, and make it relevant to your students' concerns. Show how your field fits into the big picture and how it contributes to society. In so doing, you also become a role model for student interest and involvement.

3. *Get to know your students.* If you collected information about your students on the first day of class, weave that information throughout the semester. This information will help you tailor the material to their interests. First-generation and nontraditional students may be hesitant to

approach you, so this technique is particularly helpful to make sure they are included (Cox, 2011).

4. *Let your students get to know you.* Make yourself more human by sharing a little personal information about yourself.

5. *Learn and use your students' names and help them learn one another's names.* You can help by having social icebreakers at the beginning of the term and using their names yourself, especially when you refer to students' previous comments. Name badges and tents serve everyone in the class (see Chapter 7).

6. *Foster good lines of communication in both directions.* Convey your expectations and assessments, but also invite your students' feedback in the form of classroom assessment exercises and midterm assessment of your teaching (see Chapter 23).

7. *Use humor where appropriate.* A joke or humorous anecdote lightens the mood and has the synapse-building benefits of emotional intensity (see Chapter 1). Just be sensitive to context, setting, and audience.

8. *Maintain classroom order and civility* to earn your students' respect, as well as create a positive learning environment (see Chapter 11).

Your Course and Subject Matter

9. *Design and develop your course with care,* and explain its organization and your rationale for it to your students (see Chapter 2).

10. *Allow students some voice* in determining the course content, policies, conduct rules, and assignments. If they have contributed, they will feel more invested and responsible for their learning.

11. *Build in readings and activities that will move students beyond their simplistic dualistic beliefs about your field* (see Chapters 1 through 3). The constricted, naive view of learning as memorizing definitions and facts isn't very motivating, even if the challenge can seem a bit frightening at first.

12. *Highlight the occupational potential of your subject matter.* Inform students about the jobs and careers that are available in your discipline, what attractions they hold, and how your course prepares students for these opportunities. Whenever possible, link new knowledge to its usefulness in some occupation.

13. For numerous ways to *motivate students to do the readings and other homework on time,* see Chapter 21. When students come prepared, you can fill class time with engaging and intrinsically motivating activities.

14. *Create a safe learning environment* in which errors and failure are seen as normal and valuable learning opportunities.

Your Teaching

15. *Explain to your class why you have chosen* the teaching methods, readings, assignments, in-class activities, policies, and assessment strategies that you are using. Students don't assume that everything you do is for their own good.

16. *Help students practice transferring skills* that they have learned in other courses into yours and vice versa.

17. *Explain the value and personal meaning of your material and learning activities.* Connect them to students' futures and the real world to make them meaningful and worthwhile.

18. *Use examples, anecdotes, and realistic case studies freely, and provide students with models of major homework assignments.* Many students learn inductively, experientially, and concretely.

19. *Ensure that students review the material at least two or three times in different modes* (see Chapter 22).

20. *Teach by inquiry when possible.* Students find it satisfying and intrinsically motivating to reason through a problem and discover underlying principles on their own (see Chapter 17).

21. *Use a variety of student-active teaching formats and methods,* such as discussion, debates, press conferences, symposia, role-playing, simulations, academic games, project-based learning, the case

method, problem-solving, and others, all covered in later chapters. Schedule short exercises and learning checks every 10 to 20 minutes during your lectures (see Chapter 14). These activities directly engage students in the material and give them opportunities to achieve a level of mastery for achievement's sake.

22. *Share strategies and tips for students to learn your material*, including reading, studying, problem-solving strategies, and metacognitive strategies, and self-regulated learning practices (see Chapter 19). Most of your students greatly underestimate the work that learning and thinking involve.

23. *Use group learning formats.* They are student active and add the motivational factor of social belonging. Just be sure to set up and manage the groups properly (see Chapter 10).

24. *Bring the arts into your teaching to stir student emotions.* This is a standard culture-learning strategy in the foreign languages, but it has far broader application. In mathematics courses, you can show the utility of concepts and equations in visual design and musical composition. In history, anthropology, literature, and comparative politics courses, you can acquaint students with the art of the historical age or the place. If possible, you can have them read Indigenous literature and listen to Indigenous music.

25. *Make the material accessible.* Explain it in common language, avoiding jargon where possible, and make it accessible to students with disabilities.

26. *Hold students to high expectations.* Don't just tell them to do their best. Refuse to accept shoddy work. Give it back to them ungraded, and tell them you know they can do better on the assignment. Be sure to make your expectations clear.

27. *Invite guest presenters in class.* Have industry leaders, authors, or other knowledgeable individuals attend class or participate through videoconferencing such as Zoom/Teams.

Your Assignments and Tests

28. *Reinforce the idea that all students can improve their cognitive and other abilities with practice* and are in control of their academic fates. In other words, build up their sense of self-efficacy, their belief in an internal locus of control, and a growth mindset. Credit their successes to their effort and focus, not inborn talent or luck (Dweck, 2007).

29. *Give students opportunities for success early in the term.*

30. *Give frequent positive feedback early in the course* to encourage students to believe that they can do well.

31. *Provide many and varied opportunities for graded assessment* so that no single assessment counts too much toward the final grade. Test early and often.

32. *Give students practice tests* with the same types of items that will appear on the actual test.

33. *Provide review sheets that tell students what cognitive operations they will have to perform with key concepts on the tests.* In other words, write out the learning outcomes you will be testing them on.

34. Although students must acquire some facts and terminology to master the basics of any discipline, *focus your tests and assignments on their conceptual understanding and ability to apply the material*, and prepare them for the task accordingly. Facts are only tools with which to construct broader concepts and are thus means to a goal, not goals in themselves.

35. *Assign tasks that build in challenge and some desirable difficulty*—not too easy but not overwhelming (see Chapter 1).

36. *Set realistic performance goals, and help students achieve them by encouraging them to set their own reasonable goals.* Striving to exceed a personal best is a mighty motivator.

37. *Allow students options for demonstrating their learning*, such as choices in the topics and media of projects and other major assignments.

38. *Design authentic, useful assignments and activities*—those that give students practice in their future occupational and citizenship activities.

39. *Give assignments that have students reflect on their progress.* For example, have students write a learning analysis of their first test in which they appraise how they studied and how they can improve their studying (see Chapter 19).

40. *Evaluate student-constructed work by using an explicit rubric* (a specific set of criteria with descriptions of performance standards) that students can study and ask questions about before they tackle an assignment (see Chapter 26). A well-written rubric makes your expectations clearer.

41. *Be fair.* Make tests consonant with your learning outcomes, topical emphases, and previous quizzes and assignments. Tests should be a means of showing students what they have mastered, not what they haven't.

42. *Give students prompt and constant feedback* on their performance, as well as early feedback on stages and drafts of major assignments.

43. *Accentuate the positive in grading.* Be sure to praise good work and be constructive in criticism and suggestions for improvement. Acknowledge improvements made. Confine negative comments to the particular performance, not the performer.

44. *Let students assess themselves.* Of course, you must explicitly teach them how to do this first, and accurate self-assessment is a challenging skill to master.

45. *Inform students about your previous students who have succeeded* in graduate school, professional school, or careers. You needn't name names.

46. *Give students second chances.* Test early and often. Let students drop the lowest quiz or test score. Let them write explanations for their multiple-choice and true/false item answers. Provide chances for them to earn back some of their lost points.

47. *Use criterion-referenced grading* instead of norm-referenced grading (see Chapter 26). The former system gives all the students in a class the opportunity to earn high grades.

48. *Use specifications (specs) grading* for some of your assignments or your entire course. Specs grading means assigning grades according to how well students fulfill certain work requirements, as specified in the syllabus or an appendix to it. To get higher grades, students have to successfully complete either more work that shows evidence of more learning or more challenging work that shows evidence of more advanced learning. Under these conditions, students are often more motivated to learn because they have a greater sense of choice of assignments, self-determination, and responsibility for their grade, as well as less fear about creative risk-taking and grade anxiety (see Chapter 26).

49. *Give extra credit or bonus points only to students who have successfully completed their regular assigned work.* For example, Golding (2008) increased her class attendance and on-time homework turn-ins by giving students bonus problems to work on at the beginning of class in exchange for their assigned homework problems. The same rule can apply to giving students the chance to earn back lost points.

50. *Role-model a learning orientation and encourage it* over a performance orientation. Explain the value of mistakes in learning and retaining the material. Deemphasize grades and competition, and focus on the relevance and utility of the content and skills.

This last recommendation is among the most important, especially among students who have seen repeatedly that grades are the focus in educational systems. Modeling learning over doing well on a test will be challenging for some. Ideally, learning and performance are closely related.

■ NO MAGIC BULLETS

As you implement some of these 50 strategies, you will motivate many of your students. If you implement all of them, you will motivate *almost all* of your students. Keep in mind you might not be able to motivate a student, no matter what you do. The ultimate decision to engage in any behavior resides with the individual. You can enhance motivation, but you cannot make a student do anything. In addition, a few will resist your efforts due to their problems with relating to authority, committing themselves to a goal, deferring gratification, and other issues. But don't let those few eclipse your success with many. Celebrate those you inspire.

■ REFLECTION QUESTIONS

Reflection Question 9.1: Think for a moment about what really motivated you as an undergraduate in college. Why did you go to college? What kept you going when you hit rough spots? Now think about your students. What do you think motivated them to attend college? What keeps them going during rough spots? There is a high probability that you are not like your students. You went on to become a college faculty member and most of your students will not. How can you adjust to best motivate your students?

Reflection Question 9.2: Consider the theories of motivation noted in the chapter, allowing that they are brief summaries and that more information is available in the literature. Which theories (select two or three) best line up with your approach to motivating your students? Explain how what you do fits within the framework of the theory.

Concept Into Practice: There are four sections within the 50 strategies to motivate students: your persona, your course and subject matter, your teaching, and your assignments and tests. Identify one strategy from each category. Across several weeks, put those four strategies into practice. Note the extent to which each was successful, and what could make it even better.

CHAPTER 10

Managing Productive Groups

Discussed in more detail in Chapter 14, in the mid to late 1990s there was a seismic shift in higher education as we moved from teaching to learning (Barr & Tagg, 1995; King, 1993); a shift from students sitting in their rows and listening throughout the class period to them working together. They might work together for a few minutes, at times for a class period, and at other times for the entire semester. In higher education, some quickly realized the incredible benefits that working in groups could have for our students. Research emerged supporting the value of active learning and having students work in small groups (e.g., Hake, 1998). There was research and strategies at this same time about how to teach students to work well in small groups (e.g., Johnson & Johnson, 1992; Smith, 1994). Adoption of active learning strategies has moved forward, although at a measured pace. Unfortunately, teaching students how to work well in those groups has proceeded even slower. In this chapter, we will share current research and our own decades of experience in how to promote the best outcomes for your students to engage in active learning by working in groups.

■ A GROUP BY ANY OTHER NAME

Through much of the 1990s, the term *cooperative learning* referred to a structured teaching method where small student groups work together on a common task (Millis & Cottell, 1998). About this same time, *collaborative learning* emerged as a term favored in the sciences and engineering. Following Mazur's (1997) lead, the terms *peer instruction* and *peer tutoring* appeared when referring to student pairs or small groups in class explaining their answers to multiple-choice items to one another. The label *collaborative* has largely replaced *cooperative* across the disciplines. However, not everyone sees these terms as referring to the same thing. Some view *cooperative* learning groups as more structured than *collaborative* ones (e.g., Davidson & Major, 2014).

However, there is an even more structured version of group work known as *team-based learning*, which builds in mutual, positive interdependence and individual accountability more than any other version of working in groups. To ensure preparation for class, students take team as well as individual tests, and both may count equally toward their grades

(Michaelsen et al., 2004; Sibley & Ostafichuk, 2014; Sweet & Michaelsen, 2012). There is also a wide range of small group activities that can take anywhere from a few minutes to an entire class period (Barkley & Major, 2022; Major et al., 2021). Groups can be given clear instructions (structured) or nebulous directions (ill-defined). The final product can be a specific outcome or totally uncertain. There are many configurations to which the single term *group work* has been given. This leads to challenges. Suppose a student had a bad experience doing group work that was set up by an instructor as a semester-long, ill-defined, team-based learning format, for a project that had no set outcome, and no guidance for the process. Even though you plan to have students work in groups for 3 weeks on a structured task, where students create product ideas using a team-based learning approach, and there are weekly check-ins to see how groups are doing, the students in your course hear "group work" and immediately recall the terrible time they last were forced to work in groups. It does not seem to matter that these two experiences are very different from one another.

This is why saying the words "group work" on the first day of the semester often leads to groans and general student uneasiness. As with the example just given, most students have had at least one negative group work experience in their academic career and they don't realize that *group work* encompasses a wide variety of teaching strategies, with a wide variety of nuances, taught by instructors with a wide variety of teaching experience. If you are using group learning, it is a good idea to stay away from the term *group work* if at all possible. Use a specific term that will help to both head off preconceived notions and expand your students' knowledge of the wide types of group work possible. You might say, "In this class we will work in well-defined small teams to create new ways to think about mental illness. The tasks will be well structured, and I will check in with each team regularly. I am excited about this as the thoughts you arrive at will at times be the first time I have ever heard such ideas, and I have been studying this field

for a very long time. That is the power of good team collaboration." That will result in fewer groans and get students more excited about the semester than saying that they will work in groups to look at perceptions of mental illness.

◼ THE CASE FOR GROUP LEARNING

The evidence supporting the effectiveness of group over individual learning is overwhelming. One of the first literature reviews on this topic was completed by Johnson et al. (1991), who reported that most of the hundreds of studies published to that point found cooperative learning to be superior to competitive and individual approaches to teaching, and the other studies found no detrimental effects to using groups. In a meta-analysis of 225 studies, Freeman et al. (2014) noted that "students in a traditional lecture course are 1.5 times more likely to fail than students in courses with active learning" (p. 8410). In a meta-analysis in which authors compared courses taught by the same instructor using traditional lecture versus classrooms that involved any intensity of active learning, results indicated that the inclusion of active learning not only led to greater learning gains, it also resulted in a 33% reduction in the achievement gap between students from minoritized groups versus nonminoritized groups in STEM courses (Theobald et al., 2020).

With such strong evidence that including group work into classroom teaching is effective, one might expect faculty members to quickly adapt to this form of teaching. However, group learning had a slow start in higher education. Faculty members hadn't learned that way, which means they had no model for how to teach in that manner. Facilitating groups is very different than delivering a lecture. In addition, as faculty members had typically experienced no trouble learning individually, it was hard for them to understand why their students would. Faculty members also had to relinquish the control and the center stage of the classroom, not a satisfying prospect for comfortable, committed lecturers.

Besides, using groups in learning as a teaching method hailed from the K–12 world.

The research on the positive effects of group learning was well established long ago across several variables—achievement/productivity (learning), positive attitudes and ethics, the quality of interpersonal relationships, and psychological health—and group work enhances all of them for students at all educational levels and of all backgrounds (Johnson & Johnson, 1989, 1994; Johnson et al., 1991, 2014; Pascarella & Terenzini, 2005; Romero, 2009; Springer et al., 1999). Light (1990, 1992) reported similar results for out-of-class study groups in the Harvard Assessment Seminars. According to Hattie's (2009) mega-meta-analysis of over 800 meta-analyses on the effects of various teaching and learning strategies on student achievement, group work has an effect size of .59—that is, a one standard deviation increase in group learning experiences leads to just under three-fifths of a standard deviation increase in learning. Current research continues to show the positive outcomes of having students work in groups. Sometimes the positive outcomes of actual increased learning have occurred even when students indicate that they feel they learn more from lecture than from working in groups (Deslauriers et al., 2019).

■ CAUTIONS ABOUT GROUP LEARNING

A few caveats are in order. Study groups may not always enhance learning. Arum and Roksa (2011) found that groups didn't enhance learning unless they were organized and monitored by a campus learning-assistance unit. An additional challenge is that weaker students in a group may freeload off the stronger ones, as stronger students so desperately want to get an A in the course that they often take over and do all the work. Another concern is students' lack of maturity and understanding of group member responsibilities. Although most young students have been learning in groups all through school, we should not expect them to

monitor and sanction each other for poor team behavior. Students often hesitate to evaluate each other's group contributions and performance honestly. Frequently they cover up for social loafers and refuse to sanction them, showing more loyalty to their peers than to learning. Students didn't always do this; early studies found that group members punished their dysfunctional peers (Jalajas & Sutton, 1984; Murrell, 1984). But now students expect *you* as the instructor to know about the freeloaders and administer justice by giving different individual grades on the group product, even if you have explained that their grades will depend solely on quality of the group product (Jassawalla et al., 2008). Their expectations no doubt reflect their many years in K–12 group work, where teachers handed down the rules of engagement and intervened when violations occurred, so they come to college ill prepared and ill trained for adult-level team dynamics. In higher education, it is our responsibility to teach them to bear collective responsibilities (Jassawalla et al., 2008).

Unfortunately, your students may know very little about group dynamics, making it important for you to teach them some basic principles. It does not take much time to teach students foundational aspects of working well in groups, such as communication patterns, division of labor, setting meeting times, and how to handle those who do not do their share of work before anyone fails to do their share of work (Zakrajsek, 2022).

Simply putting students into groups will not likely result in students learning group work skills (Hogan & Young, 2021). To give your students a crash course in group dynamics as well as the wisdom and the tools to collaborate successfully, refer them to Kennedy and Nilson's (2008) free online book, *Successful Strategies for Teams* (https://ctl.utexas .edu/sites/default/files/TeamworkHandbook-KennedyandNilson.pdf). It is written simply and is colorfully illustrated for undergraduates.

Setting up and managing group learning may be the most challenging method you ever use, so start small. Begin with in-class ad hoc groups (also called informal groups; see the next section) doing a small-scale, pretested technique, like those in the "Tried-and-True In-Class Group Activities" section later, perhaps in an optional help or review session. It may not work perfectly (any strategy can fall short the first time tried). Identify what did not go as planned and continue to improve your system each semester. In addition, sell group work to your class by explaining that decades of research document its superior effectiveness.

■ MANAGING AND TROUBLESHOOTING IN-CLASS AD HOC GROUPS

Ad hoc groups, used within class periods, present fewer management challenges than formal, long-term, project-based groups and entail virtually no setup because students work with one to three peers sitting close to them in the classroom. Many classroom activities rely on ad hoc groups unless you have formal, long-term groups sit together in class. Still, the success of these groups depends on your following these guidelines:

1. *Give groups a specific, structured task with an end product* (problem solution, a list of ideas, or a group test answer sheet) to prevent any confusion. Also let groups know that they should decide who will report out before they start their work. You can get the structure of the activity to students as a paper handout, email to the group through your LMS, or use a collaboration space such as Padlet.

2. *Before groups begin working, let them know how you will bring the activity to a close.* For example, inform students that you will signal when time is up by raising your hand. They should then stop talking and raise their hands as soon as they see yours up. This technique enables you to silence a large lecture hall in seconds.

3. *Make the task more challenging than what you would give an individual student.* It should go beyond what students have learned and require group synergy to complete.

4. *Give the task a tight time limit to keep groups focused*—just enough time for an on-task group to finish. Bring a timer or stopwatch with you to class.

5. *For reporting out*, let the class know you will start with a few volunteers and then cold-call on a few additional groups. Keep the reporting out as brief and light as possible to keep stress down.

6. *Walk around the room and monitor* what is being discussed. This will give you hints as to which group to call on for good responses, to know when groups are nearing completion, and to get distracted students back on task.

7. *Change the composition of the groups two or more times during the term.* Having students get to know each other will help build community. You might have a seating chart, which you can use for taking attendance and learning names, and rearranging seating.

Tried-and-True In-Class Group Activities

Following are just a few proven, safe group activities from Barkley et al. (2014) and Major et al. (2021) and from our two careers of running in-class ad hoc groups. These two books and a quick search online will easily provide in excess of 100 additional options to engage students in small groups. Many of these activities also work well as classroom assessment techniques (see Chapter 23).

Think-Pair-Share

Give students a question or problem, and ask them to think quietly of an answer or solution. Have them discuss their responses with their neighbor and then share them with the class. You can also set the requirement that they come to a consensus or submit one piece of written work as a pair. Set a time limit of 1 or 2 minutes for the pair exchange. You can extend this format by having each pair in agreement join another pair in agreement to come to a consensus together. For variations on the think-pair-share visit https://www.scholarlyteacher.com/teachingtips.

Webquest

Have students work in groups of two to four to search the web to find answers to a question or prompt provided to them. Point out to students how different their responses are, even though everyone had the same prompt.

Observation Teams Discussion

Students observe some situation related to learning outcomes for the course. The observation could be a short film, a TED talk, or a YouTube clip. After viewing the situation, the group describes the important aspects of what they saw and discusses the meaning of the interaction viewed.

Jigsaw

Each member of a *base group* is assigned a minitopic to research. Students then meet in *expert groups* with others assigned the same minitopic to discuss and refine their understanding. The base groups reform, and members teach their minitopics to their teammates.

Structured/Academic Controversy

Pairs within a group of four are assigned opposing sides of an issue. Each pair researches its assigned position, and the group discusses the issue with the goal of exposing as much information as possible about the subject. Pairs can then switch sides and continue the discussion (see Chapter 16).

Numbered Heads Together

Assign a number to each member of a team of four. Pose a thought question or problem, and allow a few minutes for discussion. Call out a number, designating only students with that number to act as the group spokesperson. This exercise promotes individual accountability.

Talking Chips

This method guarantees equal participation in discussion groups. Each group member receives the same number of poker chips (or any other markers, such as index cards, pencils, or pens). Each time a member wishes to speak, he tosses a chip into the center of the table. Once individuals have used up their chips, they can no longer speak. The discussion proceeds until all members have exhausted their chips. Then they reclaim their chips and begin another round.

Anonymous Cards

Each student is given an index card. Provide a prompt that corresponds to the information in the course for that day (e.g., "What are the major contributing factors to inflation?" "Name the three most important bones in the body that allow humans to walk," or "What is the most important issue in the next presidential election?") Students first respond to the prompt. Students then move about the room quickly, exchange cards with at least five different classmates, and then return to their seats. This scrambles the cards but retains all the responses from the students in the room. From this point, there are several options. Groups could discuss the responses on the cards, sort them into piles based on some criteria, or identify one card and then form a group response to what is written on that card.

■ SETTING UP, MANAGING, AND TROUBLESHOOTING FORMAL, PROJECT-BASED GROUPS

For semester-long project-based groups to be successful, your task is a bit more challenging. You must build certain features into the structure of the groups by the way you assemble them, design tasks, manage activities, and determine grades. The cooperative learning scholars have worked many years on this type of group and have noted the following essential features (Felder & Brent, 2001; Johnson et al., 1991; Johnson & Johnson, 1994; Millis, 1990; Millis & Cottell, 1998).

Positive Interdependence

For a long-term, project-based group to function effectively, each group member must feel a sense of personal responsibility for the success of their teammates. In addition, their success must depend at least in part on the group's success. In brief, members must feel they need one another to complete the task at the desired level of quality. To develop this element, you can do one or more of the following:

- Assign a group product on which all members sign off and are given a group grade. It is a good idea to also separately grade individual contributions to ensure accountability.
- Give group as well as individual quizzes and tests that count toward each member's individual grade. You might have individuals take a quiz, and then the group takes the same quiz. Individual scores are an average of the individual quiz and group quiz results.
- On individual tests, give group members bonus points if they all score above a given level.
- Assign each member a different part of the total task (task interdependence), along with unique information for that task that other group members do not have.
- Randomly select students to speak for their group in class, ensuring everyone in the group understands the work being done (give warning that this will be done).
- Require that all members edit one another's work using Word's Track Changes tool, a wiki, Google Docs, or some other shared editing space.
- Assign group members different roles. Common roles are recorder, spokesperson, researcher, summarizer, checker/corrector, skeptic, organizer/manager, observer, writer, timekeeper, conflict resolver, and runner/liaison to other groups or the instructor. Less-known ones are coordinator, driver (of the group's operating style), finisher (lends a sense of urgency to the task), implementer (of group decisions), supporter (harmonizer), monitor-evaluator, originator (of ideas), and resource investigator (Belbin, 2004). For online groups, roles such as data gatherer, data manager, and multimedia specialist may be more appropriate (Barkley et al., 2014).

Individual Accountability

All members must be held responsible for their own learning as well as for the learning of other group members. At the same time, no member should feel that they are giving more (or less) than an equal share of effort to the group task. In other words, no freeloaders, social loafers, dominators, hogs, or hitchhikers are allowed. You can build in this element in several ways, some of which overlap with those already mentioned:

- Base final grades predominantly on individual quizzes, tests, papers, and other assignments.
- Count the team grades only for students who pass the individual quizzes, tests, and written assignments.
- Assign group members different roles (see the previous subsection for possible roles).
- Assign group members primary responsibility for different parts of the team project and grade them on their part (e.g., one member develops the bibliography, another conducts the research, and another does the write-up).
- Add an individual assignment in which students reflect on the process of completing their designated portion of the group work (Huang, 2014).
- Give groups time in class as soon as you form them for members to discuss, develop, and agree on a contract detailing their policies and expectations, including when and where they will hold out-of-class meetings, how they will divide the labor and responsibilities, how they will evaluate each other, when the sections of the project will be due (unless you set these dates), and how they will address members who skip meetings, fail to prepare, refuse to contribute, don't share resources, or fail to complete assignments on time. These documents reduce group problems and keep students more honest and responsible (Barkley et al., 2014; Oakley et al., 2004). It is a good idea to read all contracts and suggest changes if necessary.

- Allow teams to petition you to fire a noncontributing member (after a verbal and a written warning) and have them put this in the contract. This mimics post-graduation jobs.
- If a member finds themselves among a group of students who refuse to do their work, allow an overburdened member to resign from the group and seek membership on another team. This is similar to an employee on a dysfunctional project securing a new team or a new job.
- Base a portion (5–30%) of the project grade on peer performance evaluations, and break the project into stages to help ensure that students write honest evaluations after each stage.

This last strategy deserves elaboration. At the end of a unit of work or perhaps monthly, have members assign each of their teammates a letter grade for their group contributions, estimate the percentage of the work they contributed, or allocate a limited number of points across their teammates. If you use percentages or points, you may want to set up a system in which students do not assign any points to themselves. Have each member list contributions of each other member, and then assign a grade to the contributions. Make it clear to students that listing a contribution that did not occur is falsifying a report and will result in a zero for the person completing the evaluation. Having students justify grades with contribution reports serves two important purposes. First, a group member cannot simply give another member a high grade if there is not work to back up the grade. Second, this process provides cover for a student who might feel pressured to give a student a high grade when that student has not done assigned work. Keep in mind that each group member is grading all other group members. That means for a student to get an undeserved high grade, the student in question would need to convince all other group members to lie about what they did, with the penalty that everyone who does lie receives a zero.

Of course, students must have criteria on which to grade their peers on being a good team member, such as attendance, preparation, promptness, leadership, quality of contributions, quantity of contributions, and social skills. You can have students brainstorm criteria in a whole-class discussion, have the groups develop their own criteria to incorporate into their group contract, or you can provide them. If you choose the last option, you should include these five criteria—contributing to the team's work, communicating effectively, striving for a high-quality product, doing one's share of the work, and making every effort to solve team problems and resolve conflicts—because students value these behaviors the most in their teammates (Crutchfield & Klamon, 2014). In any case, the peer portion of the final grade should reflect the amount and importance of group work in the course—at least 5–20% but no more than 30%.

Appropriate Group Composition, Size, and Duration

According to the research, groups that are heterogeneous in terms of ability, race, gender, and other characteristics help students develop social skills, understand and get along with those of differing social backgrounds, and learn the material better (Heller & Hollabaugh, 1992; Johnson & Johnson, 1994; Millis, 1990; Millis & Cottell, 1998). Depending on your course, it is typically most helpful to maximize heterogeneity on a variable relevant to the work to be done. For example, if you want groups to develop programs on academic success, it could be helpful to have heterogeneity based on age, ethnicity, and major to get different perspectives regarding what is needed to help students succeed.

The research also suggests it is not a good idea to let students form their own groups, except for quick, short-task, ad hoc groups. Students forming their own groups may reinforce existing cliques and homogeneity, encourage discussion of extracurricular topics, bias peer performance evaluations, and create problems if friends or dating students have a falling out in their personal lives which will be hard to keep separate from the group tasks.

Optimal group size varies with the open-endedness of the task. Many quick in-class activities work well with two students, as that provides the maximum number of students who can talk at one time in the classroom. A triad seems to be optimal for mathematical and scientific problem-solving tasks that allow alternative means to one correct answer (Heller & Hollabaugh, 1992). Triads work well when the task might be too challenging for two. Four or five is best for tasks with several possible good answers or solutions. If the group is learning a new skill, and instructors need to correct errors during skills practice, the optimal group size is six (Nabecker et al., 2021). Typically, the maximum effective group size is seven members, which works well for complex challenges and when you desire more diversity in each group (Sibley & Ostafichuk, 2014).

Time to Meet

If possible, allocate some class time for teams to meet, particularly early in the project. It is challenging to get any group together, whether students or faculty members. Recognize that everyone is busy and this is not easy, but it is possible. Encourage students to meet through a virtual platform such as Google Chat, Zoom, Microsoft Teams, or BlueJeans Meetings. Meeting virtually is more inclusive as it does not require students to get childcare, have reliable transportation, or travel to areas where they may not feel safe. That said, it does require internet connection. Encourage students to call in if they don't have reliable internet. It is helpful if meetings can be recorded, for future reference and for anyone who may not be able to meet at a given time. Finally, encourage students to set up several meeting times well in advance of when the project is due, including one extra one at the end that they can cancel if they don't need it.

Genuine Challenge

A group task is best when it makes students *learn* something, not just *do* something. It should go beyond the course material, be a harder task than you'd assign to students working alone, and push the group for synergy and higher-order thinking processes (application, analysis, synthesis, evaluation). In addition, it should be complex enough to have multiple respectable answers or multiple means to the best answer. This set-up rule for group work is too often forgotten. Students learn more in groups not only because they discuss the material and teach each other but also because they should be tackling a more challenging task than they otherwise would and they see there are more viable perspectives than just their own (and sometimes those other ideas are amazing).

Explicit Attention to Collaborative Social Skills

Working together effectively in long-term, stable groups requires good team-member behaviors—not only those that students think to put in their contract but also listening actively, taking turns talking, not interrupting, encouraging others, cooperating, being open-minded, giving constructive feedback, tactfully defending one's views, compromising, and showing respect for others. Young students in particular need occasions for reflection and feedback on their social and communication skills. They have to acquire the courage to express criticism constructively to their peers. Unfortunately, some instructors shy away from overseeing group processing sessions largely because they don't know how to run one. But it's really quite easy.

Processing best begins with students' assessing themselves as teammates, referring to the contract and answering questions such as these (Kustra & Potter, 2008):

- How many of my group's meetings did I attend?
- How well prepared was I for each meeting?
- How consistently did I complete whatever task I was assigned to do?
- How well did I listen to others in my group? How open was I to their ideas?

- Did I ever interrupt them or get angry with them?
- When I disagreed with one or more teammates, was I tactful and sensitive to their reactions? Did I try to find common ground or otherwise resolve the conflict? Did I propose or agree to a compromise?
- How much did I comment productively on my teammates' ideas, including giving them praise and encouragement?
- How well did I play my assigned roles?
- How consistently did I share my knowledge and resources with my group?

Students should present their self-assessments orally or in writing within their groups. Then their teammates should provide feedback, couching it in the same terms as a response to the self-assessment. Counsel students to make their feedback helpful, not hurtful, to their teammates; this is not the time to unload. In addition, they should supply positive as well as negative evaluations. Furthermore, they should describe specific behaviors, not judge the person, and ask whether he understands the feedback, recalls the behaviors mentioned, or has questions. Following this procedure, students are more likely to take the feedback seriously and accept it (Kustra & Potter, 2008).

After the individual self-assessments and feedback, the students should address some questions within their groups while a recorder takes notes:

- How well have we included and encouraged all our members in our discussions?
- How evenly have we shared the work?
- How well have we handled conflict?
- How could we accomplish our tasks more effectively and enhance their quality?
- How could we function as a group more smoothly?

The recorder should save these notes and read them aloud at the next group processing session. Then the group members can assess how much they have improved (Kustra & Potter, 2008).

Criterion-Referenced Grading

Chapter 26 examines different grading systems, but in group learning, each student should have an opportunity to earn an A. An absolute grading scale like criterion-referenced grading gives all students an equal chance to achieve. Grading on a curve (i.e., norm-referenced grading) undercuts the spirit of cooperation and the prospect of group success on which group learning relies.

■ TEAM-BASED LEARNING

Team-based learning is a way of designing and running a course that relies on in-class group learning almost exclusively. It requires you to structure or restructure a course in a very specific way. Larry Michaelson was the central architect of *team-based learning* when he began to use it in his business courses in the 1970s, and it quickly became popular in medical education. It has since become a popular teaching strategy throughout higher education and the world (Chen et al., 2018). It works well for any academic discipline or subject matter as long as you incorporate the following four essential elements, all of which team-based learning enthusiasts have tested for their effectiveness (Michaelsen et al., 2004; Sibley & Ostafichuk, 2014; Sweet & Michaelsen, 2012):

1. *Heterogeneous, term-long teams of five to seven members.* As the instructor, you should create teams yourself; never let students form their own.
2. *The Readiness Assurance Process (RAP) at the beginning of each topical module* (1 to 1½ hours). Designed to ensure that students prepare for class, this process begins with assigning readings, video, or podcasts that students will need to complete to do the in-class problem-solving and application activities. The next two stages, which open the class that starts the module, are an individual multiple-choice test on the assigned material, followed by the same test taken by the teams. The score is often the average of the individual

score and the team score. The test is referred to as the Team Readiness Assessment Test (TRAT). Both TRATs must be graded immediately, either by Immediate Feedback Assessment Technique (IF-AT) scratch-off cards or the digital version of the TRAT. Information can be found at https://cognalearn.com. Teams invariably score higher than its members do in the individual tests. Teams that disagree with an answer can go through the Appeal Process, which requires them to write a formal justification for their opinion. In the last stage, you judge the validity of any appeals and clarify any points of confusion. This double-testing procedure greatly improves students' retention of the content over individual tests (Cortright et al., 2003).

3. *Challenging, structured problem solving and application activities* (2–5 hours). To develop these activities, follow the 4S framework (note the S in each stage):

   a. Make the problems *significant*, complex, and open to different perspectives. They may have more than one correct answer.

   b. Give all teams the *same* problems to work on at the same times. While they are working, you move from team to team to track student progress and clear up any confusion, but allow students to struggle with the problem on their own.

   c. Require each team to come to consensus on a *single, specific* choice among the possible answers or on a very short answer, such as one or two words, a number, or a location on a graphic. Teams have to prepare to defend their choice.

   d. Have all teams reveal their answer *simultaneously* using "voting cards" (with A, B, C, D, and E on them), sticky notes, pushpins, or a small whiteboard. Then cold-call on specific students to justify their team's answer, rotating the task around the team so that over time all members have the experience of being spokesperson. Differences of opinion are bound to launch a lively discussion.

As you can see, team-based learning inherently runs like a flipped classroom.

4. *Individual accountability for class preparation, including accountability to teammates*. Students are loathe to let down their teammates during the TRAT and in-class activities, and they are later evaluated by their peers for part of their grade. Thus, freeloaders are much rarer than in other forms of project-based group work.

Course grading strategies vary, and some instructors don't calculate the in-class problem-solving and application activities into the final grade at all. Here is one model:

Individual readiness assurance tests	10%
Team readiness assurance tests	10%
Peer performance evaluations	5%
Individual homework assignments	20%
Midterm (individual)	20%
Final (individual)	35%

Team-based learning does not devote time to a discussion of good team-member behavior or group processing. Such behavior is considered intuitive, and teams must resolve any internal conflicts and inequities on their own without instructor intervention (which may include firing the offending member). After all, the work world is not interested in a team's interactional problems and preferences.

When designing a team-based learning course, you still start with your student learning outcomes and design TRATs, problem-solving and application activities, and other homework assignments and tests to support and assess student performance on these outcomes. But you may also want to incorporate social outcomes and even aim to shift students' mental models of people, learning, responsibility, and collaboration. Planning such a course requires a good chunk of time. One upside is that you won't need to prepare and deliver lectures. Besides, research documents that students learn as much or more in a team-based learning course than they do in courses using other instructional methods (Kubitz, 2014).

A comprehensive online resource on implementing team-based learning can be found at: www.teambasedlearning.org.

PREPARING STUDENTS FOR LIFE

Younger college students are intent on learning what they will need to succeed in the real world they are about to enter, whereas older ones want to know how they can function more effectively in it at a higher level. Group work—team-based learning, in particular—helps them meet their goals. Course-related groups imitate those in the workplace just so far, however, because the latter generally have managers who monitor how well the members meet their responsibilities; freeloading and other team misbehavior can have profound career consequences. Still, collaboration is the way the world works because well-functioning teams generate more innovative and creative ideas and devise better solutions to problems than do individuals with a competitive ethos. Teaching at its best requires that we prepare students to become high-functioning team members as both leaders and followers. This means we must implement group learning with care, teaching students to

assume collective responsibility and share a collaborative ethos.

REFLECTION QUESTIONS

Reflection Question 11.1: When you were a student, how did you feel about group work? What did you enjoy or dislike? Have those feelings changed? That is, how do you currently feel about working as part of a team versus doing work on your own?

Reflection Question 11.2: What are the outcomes you desire when you use short ad hoc groups in class? If it is to give a break from a lecture, why not just tell the students they have a 5-minute break? What is accomplished by doing ad hoc groups?

Concept Into Practice: Identify how you will use groups in your course, either through ad hoc active learning groups or more structured groups, such as project-based groups, team-based learning, or some other semester-long group assignment. Before you start, take 15 minutes of class time and ask students to work in groups of four to identify what they like and do not like about working in groups. You can then use that information to make your group work assignments more effective.

CHAPTER 11

Preventing and Responding to Classroom Incivility

Student incivility was already a growing problem in higher education, and then the COVID-19 pandemic made it even more challenging (Abraham et al., 2022; Wright & Hill, 2015). Colleges are increasingly including sections directly addressing civility in their policies section of their college catalogues. These statements often include language pertaining to bullying, equity, inclusion, positive dialogues, and treating one another with respect. This list of challenges in higher education is only a sampling of the many aspects of civility throughout higher education.

Even if your institution has a policy on the books, it will still be up to you to identify issues; sanction disciplinary problems; and maintain a controlled, orderly environment that is conducive to learning. Because you may need to make a decision quickly if a disruption occurs in the classroom, it is important to know the options you have given a variety of situations before the semester begins. Most institutions no longer let faculty members

determine the punishment for cheating on exams, plagiarism, and inappropriate collaborative work. There are processes in place. Again, find out the process at your institution, and do not take another faculty member's word for this unless they are an expert in this area. The consequences are just too high to be wrong on this.

Knowing preventive measures and constructive responses to disruption can greatly serve your relationship with your students because even minor incivilities can mar the atmosphere, break your concentration, and get under your skin. Losing your temper is not an option nor is it teaching at your best, and the action will almost certainly be recorded and posted online. Effectively controlling your classes may be one of the most important things you can do as a new faculty member. Boice (2000) found the ability of junior faculty members to maintain classroom civility to be the best single predictor of their persistence and success in an academic career.

■ WHAT IS INCIVILITY?

In higher education, *incivility* encompasses classroom, online, and even out-of-class behaviors that we perceive to be disrespectful or disruptive to the learning process. These behaviors may be poor self-regulation, an attempt to annoy us and other students, show hostility toward us and other students, waste class time, or impede the learning of everyone. Following are some specific behaviors that qualify as incivil (Abraham et al., 2022; Boice, 2000; Race & Pickford, 2007; Royce, 2000; Thomason, 2014):

- Talking to other students at inappropriate times
- Arriving late to class and leaving early
- Wasting discussion board or class time by being unprepared to contribute, dominating discussion, repeating questions, or asking argumentative or loaded questions
- Speaking or writing to the instructor or another student disrespectfully or discourteously
- Noisily eating or chewing gum in class
- Groaning, sighing, and rolling eyes in a rude manner
- Making sarcastic remarks or gestures in class
- Taunting or belittling the instructor or another student
- Sleeping in class
- Arriving in class under the influence of drugs or alcohol
- Ignoring a direct question
- Using a computer or cell phone inappropriately
- Letting a cell phone go off in class
- Dressing inappropriately, such as wearing to class T-shirts with vulgar slogans, too little clothing, or pajamas (classes in dorms)
- Reading or doing course work for another course
- Leaving trash on a desk or table in the classroom
- Cheating on a quiz, exam, or project
- Bullying
- Demanding a makeup exam, extension, grade change, or special favor of the instructor
- Challenging the instructor's knowledge or credibility in class
- Making harassing, hostile, or vulgar comments or physical gestures
- Making statements that are microaggressions
- Sending the instructor or another student an inappropriate email
- Threatening the instructor or another student with physical harm
- Plagiarism
- Inappropriate or unapproved student collaboration

Incivility ranges from mildly disruptive to dangerous behavior. Every faculty member we know who has taught for more than a few years has experienced some form of incivility. It is not a matter of if, but rather when. The best way to address incivility is to be ready for it. Do not go looking for incivilities, but do read though the list and have at least an idea of what you would do if any of the items on this list were to happen in one of your classes.

It is also important to know the policy at your campus on classroom uncivil behavior so you know how to react the moment an issue occurs. There may be an office or an honor court to refer students to, or you may have the authority to administratively drop the student from your class. It is not wise to guess, and don't take the word from someone who thinks they know.

■ WHY THE INCIVILITIES?

Individuals who have been faculty members for many decades will speak of the times when "students knew their role." They were quieter in class, deferential, and "respectful" to their professors and their peers. Yes, there were always a few who would act up, but not many and the intensity would typically be considered relatively mild at present. Then the 1990s arrived and shifted the educational paradigm. The concept was to build up childrens', and then college students', self-esteem with the thought that those with high self-esteem would be self-assured and as a result be better learners and performers.

This resulted in what many used to call the *self-esteem movement* and *the trophy generation*, and at the time it was the dominant thought (Baumeister & Vohs, 2018). The particular challenge was that after years of children being told they were brilliant and fantastic no matter what, when told in a college course that their responses were not right all the time, the students were angry at faculty members. So angry that at times, parents came in with students to talk about the issue. That movement was just taking off in the early 1990s. In 1993 King wrote the now relatively famous article "From Sage on the Stage to Guide on the Side" (King, 1993).

Just two years later, a new paradigm was being advocated in higher education, with a thesis of moving from a focus on teaching to a focus on learning (Barr & Tagg, 1995). That helped emphasize King's (1993) point that we didn't need experts lecturing, but rather facilitators that would guide student conversations. In this middle of all of this, Kohn (1993, 2018) wrote a fantastic book warning readers of focusing on self-esteem. The subtitle of Kohn's (1993) book is *The Trouble with Gold Stars, Incentive Plans, A's, Praise, and Other Bribes.*

We know active learning is extremely beneficial to learning, that students should not be made to feel bad about themselves, and that focusing on student learning outcomes is important—as faculty members we *do* need to come down from the stage at times. However, when the narrative shifts for a whole generation, the dynamic in the classroom shifts as well. When faculty members are not held in high esteem, it becomes easier to criticize, challenge, and be defiant in a college classroom, something that a few decades earlier would have been regarded very differently. In addition to parenting style changes, our access to information changed dramatically in 2007 with the introduction of the iPhone and in 2012 with the introduction of Facebook. Everyone had a platform for sharing, watching, and, unfortunately, bullying. These social and technological paradigm shifts laid a solid foundation for in-class and online incivilities, but there are certainly other influences. Both the academy and Western society in general have changed in ways that have exacerbated behavioral and disciplinary problems:

- Increasing diversity has brought together many students who don't share Western-centric academic values, norms, and communication styles.
- Class sizes, especially low-level required classes, have increased, making students feel anonymous, invisible, and unaccountable for their behavior.
- The K–12 system has done little to enforce discipline, uphold academic rigor, or nurture a love of learning.
- Parents, like K–12 teachers, were told to build children's self-esteem, indulge them, and be cautious of punishment (Kristensen, 2007).
- College enrollment had been on a slow but steady decline for several years, and then accelerated during the COVID pandemic (Knox & Weissman, 2022), so administrators now expel only the most serious offensive behaviors.
- Contingent faculty members, those outside of tenure track, teach more than 50% of the courses in colleges and universities. Because these instructors must get high student ratings to have a chance at keeping their jobs, they cannot afford to enforce much discipline or rigor.
- More young students still live at home and mature more slowly (Kristensen, 2007).
- Mass media portrays uncivil disagreement as normal (Kristensen, 2007).
- Young students and their parents take a consumer attitude toward college, and the students feel entitled to do what they choose in class or online and still get good grades; after all, they think, they bought those grades (Singleton-Jackson et al., 2010).
- Relatedly, many students don't have much respect for faculty members at present (Mayo, 2019). According to the 2018 Global Teacher Status Index, the United States ranked 16th out of 35 countries with respect to how we regard our teachers relative to other jobs (Strauss, 2018).

China and Malaysia were at the top, with teachers seen as being on the same level as physicians.
- Many Americans have lost trust in and respect for authority in general.
- Western culture has become increasingly informal in most forms of self-expression, including dress, language, and behavior.
- Students in the United States and throughout the world are struggling with stress and mental illness at levels never seen before (Ochnik et al., 2021; Suyo-Vega et al., 2022).

In spite of these broad social and cultural changes, most students still expect you to establish and maintain an orderly, civil classroom. They too are bothered by their peers' annoying behaviors and expect you to quell such distractions (Boice, 2000; Young, 2003).

Unfortunately, you will acquire practice at managing classroom incivilities. Although no strategy is absolutely foolproof, the next section is designed to give you some ideas. Three things to keep in mind are: (1) Just like everything else you will do as a faculty member, you will get better as you go. (2) Address issues as soon as possible. Challenges never get easier later. (3) Although there will be a few challenging students, for most faculty members, a vast majority of your students will be respectful and interested in learning.

PREVENTING INCIVILITY

Students who engage in uncivil classroom behavior are extremely distracting and potentially dangerous, but they are by far the minority of the students. Research also consistently shows that as the intensity of the incivility increases, the number of cases decreases (Alberts et al., 2010; Boice, 1996). Setting standards and expectations with students is a helpful process (Myers et al., 2016). It helps students to better understand which behaviors will not be tolerated and why. In addition, by having a class agreement as to what is acceptable, any student

who does engage in incivility is much less likely to attract others to participate. Work with students to establish a classroom community that includes citizenship behaviors of involvement, courtesy, classroom connectedness, instructor rapport, and cognitive interest.

Although we should always treat students with respect, it is possible to be too lenient and unintentionally project an image of weakness. Some students will feel free to take advantage of your apparent vulnerability, giving them the courage to be more forceful with their position. You also don't want to project the opposite image—a cold, distant, condescending professor, possibly with a cynical attitude; a sarcastic sense of humor; an uncaring heart; or a mean, critical streak. If so, many students will feel justified in returning your seemingly bad attitude in kind. Either way, you are likely to encounter a disproportionate amount of student incivility. As with so many things, the answer lies somewhere in the middle (Boice, 2000). It is certainly possible to be a helpful and caring faculty member who has firm boundaries and expectations for behavior.

Part of the performance dimension of teaching involves projecting a certain persona to your students (Carroll, 2003a, 2003b), so why not consciously fashion one that will command their respect, and inspire their trust and loyalty, exuding relaxed confidence, goodwill, and an in-command, no-nonsense attitude? Some of you live your life this way, whereas others may find it a bit more challenging. Whether you carry this aura naturally or have to work at it, there are concrete behaviors, some verbal and some nonverbal, that you may find helpful.

Command Class Attention

Keeping students on task, interested, and learning is challenging, but can be learned and regularly improved. The same can be said for managing a classroom with a minimal level of distraction. Following is a simple listing of powerful behaviors for commanding class attention (adapted from Toastmasters International speech manuals and related materials):

1. *Effective use of voice.* Volume adjusted to be audible for the room and audience; words enunciated clearly; rich, resonant voice quality, projected from the chest and diaphragm; vocal variety (changes in intonation to complement the content and for emphasis); volume variety (either extreme for emphasis); varied and appropriate speaking pace (never hurried and dramatically slower for more important content); and pausing briefly for emphasis before and after major points.

2. *Effective use of body.* Solid, natural stance; natural movement around the lectern or stage and out toward the audience (for emphasis and to complement the content); abundant gestures to complement the content (especially broad ones before large audiences); word dramatization (e.g., momentarily acting out *timid, angry, anxious, huge*); varied facial expressions (more dramatic in a large room), including smiles where appropriate; only occasional glances, if any, at notes; steady eye contact with the audience (at least 3 seconds per audience sector or quadrant is recommended).

3. *Effective use of visual aids and props.* Smooth transitions to and handling of visual aids; uses of visual aids or props that clarify or dramatize a point.

4. *Emotions to project.* Relaxed confidence and conviction; enthusiasm, excitement, passion, a sense of drama, curiosity; sincerity, concern, honesty, openness, warmth, goodwill, caring, a sense of humor.

5. *Minimization or elimination of distracting behaviors.* Um, uh, you know, like, sort of, kind of, and-and, that-that; mispronunciations; false sentence starts; midsentence switches to the start of a new sentence; volume fade-outs at end of sentences; pacing, swaying, or other repetitive movements; leaning on the lectern, against the wall, against the chalkboard; and lengthy checks of notes.

6. *Unneeded apologies.* It is appropriate to apologize for starting late or running over on time. Avoid apologizing for work you feel you should have done ahead of time. For example, if you forget a section of material, unless it is critical for understanding, don't apologize, just go to the next thing in the class session. If a figure is too small to read on a presentation slide, fix it prior to class or delete it. If you get to class and something is not as you would like it, work through it. For example, you could say, "I know you can't see the detail on this graph. I just wanted to show you how the trend changed across three years."

7. *Not speaking for too long.* As you will read in Chapter 14, most students will need a pause every 15 minutes or so to digest your information, sooner for dense material or information for which students likely have limited prior knowledge. Pose a question, open the floor for questions, or use a student-active break (see Chapter 14). When students are losing focus while you are presenting, if you don't shift your students' attention to a learning activity, they will shift their attention to a nonlearning activity.

Although this combination of skills may seem like a lot, you likely have learned most of them already and may need to focus on only a few. For now, the most important skill you should check is your eye contact with your students, a powerful form of crowd engagement, and control. Make sure to purposely look at the entire room. Many faculty tend to focus on "the T zone," across the first few rows and down the middle. Eye contact also personalizes your comments, encourages students to return your attentiveness to them in kind, and enables you to read their faces to gauge their interest and understanding.

Another key skill is to monitor your voice. Its tonal variety and pace reflect your level of engagement in the material and your enjoyment of teaching. A voice can sound monotone to an audience because the person speaks at the same pitch or at the same pace for long periods of time. If you find yourself droning this way through a dry section of your lecture, try consciously to modulate your voice and vary your speaking pace to keep student interest.

If you tend to get nervous before teaching, take three or four slow, deep breaths from your diaphragm and push out all the old air before inhaling again. This breathing is also good for your vocal resonance and projection as well as your brain, since oxygen increases cognitive functioning. Arrive at the classroom early and talk to students who have also arrived early. That will warm you up and give you an opportunity to learn a few more names or to learn something about students you can later use to maintain interest. Transform your nervous energy into enthusiasm. Practice a power stance before you leave your office. This can create a sense of confidence and assurance. A few physical exercises before class can help you feel larger, more animated, and more dynamic.

Balance Authority and Approachability

Research demonstrates that different faculty members report incivilities differently (Abraham et al., 2022). Older White males report the lowest levels of incivility, while women, younger faculty, and faculty of color tend to have higher reports. Being caring or helpful, intolerant of incivility, and clear with expectations seem to help decrease instances of incivility. You can continue to be caring and helpful to students and still address any incivilities directly and firmly. Actually, it is helpful to most students in the class if you are firm and direct with anyone who engages in disruptive behavior.

If needed, there are strategies you can use that will add an air of authority to your persona and help you take stronger control of your classes:

- Stand up rather than sit in front of your class, move around the room, and use broad gestures. The dramatic effect is designed to make you appear larger than life.
- Try to deepen your voice slightly and project it further by speaking from your diaphragm.

Also avoid ending a declarative sentence with a questioning rise in pitch.
- Try slowing your rate of speech just a bit, particularly if you are a fast talker. This is particularly helpful if you are stressed or angry as rate of speech typically increases in such situations. This means slowing your voice may be just bringing your rate back to a typical rate for you. This is particularly helpful if a student engages in a disruptive behavior. It will help de-escalate the situation. Try practicing this when you are in nonacademic situations and having a tense conversation with someone.
- Favor more formal dress to convey that you are serious and business minded, especially if you are a woman (Johnston, 2005).
- Add an air of formality and dignity to your classroom. For instance, address students by their last names, and ask that they address you by your title (Dr. or Professor) and last name.
- Refer in class to your own scholarship where appropriate. This establishes you as an authority on the subject and elevates you in your students' eyes.
- Prepare for incivilities. There are some incivilities that occur frequently enough that you can anticipate you will see them at some point. Practicing ahead of time can help take a bit of the affect and anxiety out of the situation. A few of the more common possible situations include, side conversations loud enough for others to hear, talking on a phone during class, walking in late and disrupting class, disagreeing with a point you made and then escalating the exchange, challenging a grade during class, and making a derogatory comment about you or your teaching strategy loud enough for other students to hear.

Some instructors try too hard to prevent incivilities and create the opposite problem of intimidating students. They can do so by too perfectly matching the somewhat chilly professorial stereotype with coming off as domineering. From your students' viewpoint, you may fall in this category if you are male and are some combination of very tall, physically large, deep-voiced, serious, reserved, or have an aggressive or curt social style. The following behaviors can warm up your persona, making you seem more approachable and likable:

- Assume a more relaxed posture in the classroom. Sit down or perch casually on the corner of a desk.
- Speak more softly (but audibly) in class.
- Interact with the class on a regular basis, perhaps by tossing out questions to answer or problems to solve.
- Dress down slightly; for example, wear a loosened tie and a sports jacket, a two-piece suit rather than a three-piece suit, or no jacket or suit coat at all.
- Chat casually with students before and after class so they can see you as friendly, warm, and personable. Address students by their first names. (If you are a TA, consider asking them to call you by your first name.) Consciously practice social immediacies (see the next section).
- Smile when appropriate.
- If you are a TA or a faculty member still taking courses, mention that you too are a student, so you can identify with the academic demands they are facing.

As you likely noticed, some of the suggestions in this list are the opposite of the previous list. We each have physical and psychological characteristics that make us who we are and influence how we interact with others. The same is true in the classroom. Some faculty members have a way of being that projects confidence and caring. Students will want to talk to those faculty members and wait in the hall for a turn to do so. Some faculty members have a face that is shaped in such a way that they look angry. Students will find such individuals harder to approach. Some of us are timid, some outgoing, some naturally loud, and others talk softly. Talk to colleagues for advice with respect to how people perceive you and how you can best project

the right image in the course. The goal is for you to be your authentic self, and for students to understand that you care about their success, but you expect them to do the work they are asked to do and to treat one another with respect.

Show That You Care

Wherever your persona falls on the authority-approachability continuum, you can help reduce the probability of class incivilities and conflict by practicing social immediacies—that is, conveying both verbally and nonverbally that you care about your students as learners and as people. Like everyone else in the world, students want to be liked and respected. You can verbally express, for example, concern for their learning and future success, high expectations for them, interest in their activities outside class, empathy with their learning challenges and stress, and your availability to help them outside class. You can also learn and use their names. Nonverbally, you can communicate your respect for and interest in them by making regular eye contact, speaking with energy and enthusiasm, standing with an open body posture, and smiling frequently. It is important to really listen to students when they speak. Try not to think about what you will say before they even finish speaking. When students raise a problem in the course, you can clarify your course objectives and schedule and enlist students to help resolve the issue.

All of these instructor behaviors, along with teaching interactively, are associated with more civil student conduct and greater student attentiveness in class (Abraham et al., 2022; Meyers et al., 2006; Wilson & Taylor, 2001).

Set Ground Rules

Students typically respond well to rules if they are reasonable and clearly stated. As a faculty member, it is easy to forget that different faculty members can have vastly different ground rules regarding such foundational considerations as absences, in-class participation, or extra credit. It is important to let students know what you expect in your course and equally important to not expect them to know without being told. There are very few standards across all courses, including what constitutes incivility.

Therefore, announce on the first day exactly what behaviors you expect and what behaviors you will not tolerate in your course, and why. Your most convincing reason, and one that is research based, is that such behaviors annoy the other students in the class (Boice, 2000). This conveys your goodwill. You might reiterate this reason when handling a noisy disruption.

Some conduct rules also belong in your syllabus. Focus on the most common incivilities you encounter, such as side conversations, unauthorized cell phone use, and disrespecting classmates. Just don't make the list too long. Overall, it is best to state rules in a positive way—for example, "Students are expected to hand in assignments on time," rather than, "Students will be penalized for late assignments." Either way, you must specify and enforce the consequences for violating the rules. The same applies to online incivilities, such as trolling and attacking fellow students for their opinions. You can find college-level netiquette guidelines at:

- http://edtech2.boisestate.edu/frankm/573/ netiquette.html
- https://tilt.colostate.edu/TipsAndGuides/Tip/ 128

Some classroom instructors (onsite, and adaptable to online) have reduced incivilities by having their students collectively draw up a classroom-conduct contract, or a set of rules for behavior to which they will agree. On the first day of class, lead a discussion on the student behaviors that genuinely bother the members of the class. You can add one or two behaviors to the list or start with your expectations and let students add suggestions to that list. Then from the notes you take, write up a contract or agreement for all students to sign at the next class meeting in which they promise not to engage in the disruptive behaviors listed.

Model Desired Behavior

Sometimes classroom incivility starts with the instructor's behavior toward the students, such as being rude, sarcastic, condescending, indifferent, insensitive, or inflexible. Your efforts to model good manners do not guarantee that students will do the same, but the best way to get respect is to give respect. Students will consider your standards and requirements fairer if your behavior reflects them. For instance, if you value punctuality, come to class early and be ready to start class on time. If you want assignments turned in on time, return papers promptly. If you expect students to come to your office hours, it is important to be in your office during office hours.

Through the years there have been many reports of faculty behavior that students find offensive (Stork & Hartley, 2009). These behaviors include intimidating students, not helping students when assignments are unclear, hitting on students, embarrassing students, talking about a student who is not present, keeping the class past the end time, punishing the entire class because of being unhappy with the behavior of one or two students, using a student's work as a negative example, acting superior, speaking poorly of another professor, and cutting students off during a discussion. While not offensive, talking to the board, straying from the syllabus, or talking fast are often considered insensitive or rude, which may later encourage incivility in the class. One activity that works well on the first-day-of-class discussion is to have students work in groups of four or five for about 5 minutes and then suggest behaviors they don't want *us* to do.

We show students respect when we explain why we have chosen the readings, teaching methods, class activities, and assignments that we have without their having to ask. They are unlikely to assume that we do what we do for their own good or because of our knowledge of how people learn, so we need to convince them. We can tell them how many other inferior textbooks we reviewed, how much research stands behind the effectiveness of our methods, and how well our assignments will prepare them for their future careers. We might even summarize our teaching philosophy or post it on the LMS for students to read if they choose (see Chapter 27 on writing one).

A final way to show respect for students is to hold them to high expectations, explain to them that you know they can do it, and then congratulate them when they reach tough goals.

■ RESPONDING WISELY TO INCIVILITY

When you encounter a classroom incivility in your classroom, stay calm and in control. Take a breath and visualize a peaceful scene—or anything else to keep you from losing your temper. No matter how much an offensive student tries to bait you, you lose credibility if you lower yourself to their level. Several students will also likely begin recording on their phones as soon as the interaction starts, and regardless of how much you are in the right, it won't look good on social media. By keeping your composure, you will also more likely win the sympathy and support of the other students. Viewing an incivility as a teaching moment may help you stay cool. Consider how your class as a whole might learn something from this. Even if the comment or behavior appears to be directed at you, try to move the exchange from you to the students and their learning. If you handle the situation well, students in the class may even start using social pressure to assist you in the matter.

For instance, whenever you sanction a student for mild, garden-variety uncivil behavior, smile through your firmness. A smile conveys not only warmth and approachability but also unflappable cool and relaxed confidence. It says you don't take the misconduct personally, that you are just doing your job to maintain a productive learning environment, and that student misbehavior doesn't get under your skin. With this kind of cool, students sense they can't bait you, so they are much less likely to do so.

Keeping your composure, however, does not mean accepting and tolerating the abuse. It is critical that you do not ignore or otherwise tolerate the behavior, particularly early in the semester. Whenever unacceptable behavior occurs, you must respond immediately. The worst thing you can do is ignore the behavior (Meyers et al., 2006). Students who engage in disruptive behavior never just decide to stop on their own. The longer you let the incivility continue, the more challenging addressing the behavior will become later. Following are specific, appropriate measures you can take in response to disruptive behaviors based on decades of our experience in higher education as well as the work of our colleagues (Boice, 2000; Feldmann, 2001; Gonzalez & Lopez, 2001; Meyers et al., 2006; Race & Pickford, 2007; Thomason, 2014).

Side Conversations in Class

Occasional comments or questions from one student to another are to be expected. However, chronic talkers bother other students and interfere with your train of thought. To stop them, you have several options. The simplest is to pause, allowing their voices to fill the silence. You may also want to accompany your pause with a long stare at the offenders. Staring at them with a smile lets them know they are being disruptive, but you are not escalating the situation. Another option is to walk over to the offender(s) while you continue to teach. If appropriate, refer to the classroom conduct contract that the class authored and signed. If you don't have a contract, pleasantly say something like, "Could you please have that conversation after class? You are making it challenging for your classmates to learn." If the problem happens more than a few times, ask to chat with the students after class.

Sleeping During Class

Students sleeping during class has become an increasingly common challenge. There are many reasons a student may fall asleep in your class, and it is highly likely that it is not about you at all.

Ian Maclaren is credited with the quote "Be kind, for everyone is fighting a hard battle." Students are working more hours than ever before, with low-income students working longer hours than higher-income students. In addition, students who are Black, Latinx, older, and female may well be working even more hours. The number of hours has risen through the years and as of 2018, 81% of part-time students and 43% of full-time students are employed (Remenick & Bergman, 2021).

Regardless of the reason, it is certainly not acceptable to be sleeping in class. It is worth considering why a student may be sleeping, and, according to experts, it is unlikely to be due to disrespect or bad decision-making. You might consider a quick think-pair-share related to your lecture and discreetly wake the student and make sure they are okay. Definitely plan to talk to the student outside of class. In addition to letting them know it is disruptive to sleep during class, ask them if they are doing okay. There may be resources on campus that can help. Many times, students are just trying to do too much.

Arriving Late or Leaving Early

Clearly state your policies on these offenses in your syllabus and on the first day of class, and never reteach material for the tardy. You can insist that students inform you in advance of any special circumstances that will require them to be late to class or necessitate them leaving early. You can even subtract course points for coming late and leaving early as long as you set this policy at the start. Alternatively, you can set aside an area near the door for latecomers and early leavers and not make this a big issue. Finally, to discourage packing up early, you can routinely schedule important class activities at the beginning as well as the end of class.

Chronic offenders of these policies deserve their day in court—that is, talk to them or email them privately about the problem. They may be late because the previous hour's class tends to run late or is a long walk away, or they may have to leave your class a little early to get to their job on time.

Dominating Discussion

If certain students habitually try to monopolize class time, tell them to speak with you after class to clarify their questions and discuss more of the issues. You can also broaden the discussion and call attention away from the disruptive student by extending your wait time after your questions or asking the rest of the class for the answers. If a student is rambling around or off the subject, take control by seizing the chance to interrupt them and paraphrase whatever meaning you can salvage. Then supply an answer and move along. Alternatively, you can defer answering it for the sake of saving class time and advise them to raise it outside class. Note that individuals who are neurodivergent often have difficulty understanding that they are dominating class time and may fail to interpret social cues you may use to try to get them to stop. In such cases, a conversation during office hours is very helpful.

Asking Questions You've Already Answered

Rather than putting down the student ("Where were you when I gave the assignment/stated the equation/etc.?"), just answer the question civilly and quickly, or say that you already answered the question and will repeat the answer only outside class. Another option is to refer that student to the written instructions you've provided and ask exactly which part needs clarification. You could use the question as a form of a classroom assessment test. Say, "I answered that a while back, but this is a good opportunity for me to see if I was clear. Could someone answer this question for me?" If done with the correct tone it does not seem rude, but it does get the point across.

Asking Argumentative or Loaded Questions

A student who tries to entrap you in an argument for the sake of arguing either wants attention or has an authority problem. Acknowledge the input and quickly move on. Lowering yourself to taking the bait jeopardizes your credibility with the class. If another incident occurs, tell the student you will discuss the issue outside class. After class, inform the student in private that you do not appreciate it and will not tolerate such behavior in your classroom. Also mention that it disturbs other students and wastes their class time. Another strategy is to handle questions through a different medium. You can collect written questions in a box and briefly address some of them at the next class meeting. You can also encourage students to email their questions to you or put them on the course website. Although less personal, these options offer a less confrontational format. You may also be able to turn the argumentative or loaded question back on the student:

> STUDENT: You're not really saying . . . ?
>
> INSTRUCTOR: What I'm saying is . . . Now, if you had 15 seconds to respond on a reality TV program, what would you say is your perspective on this topic?

Demanding a Grade Change

Bringing up grade concerns during class time both takes away valuable time for learning content and creates a chorus of similar complaints. Consider clarifying in your syllabus that you will only take grade challenges in writing, within 48 hours of an exam or assignment. Refer students who start to bring up concerns during class to this policy.

If a student still comes to you demanding a grade change, try to neutralize their emotion and give them a chance to calm down. Schedule an appointment in your office to continue the conversation. Then open with a positive, empathetic statement: "I understand your frustration. Let's take a look at your paper [or test] and talk about the grading." Have the student read the answer aloud to help hear any errors. Maintain eye contact and try to agree with them whenever possible. If necessary, explicitly disassociate the grade from their worth as a person. Even if you can't turn the student's opinion around, you can reduce both your own and their anxiety levels by showing yourself to be an ally (at least partially). Finally, try to give them a

graceful way to retreat from the situation. Just don't be intimidated into changing the grade.

It is very rare that an instructor feels physically threatened by a hostile student, and it invariably happens when others are not around. Although verbal hostility usually calls for a private approach, the physical version requires quite the opposite: try to move yourself and the student into as public a place as possible, even if just the hallway. A colleague or student may call campus security on your behalf.

Using a Computer or Cell Phone in Class for Nonclass Purposes

If your students are using a computer in class, you can't monitor their screens unless you teach from the back of the room, and you may or may not be able to roam around to see what they are doing. But you can take measures to focus students on an in-class computer task. Keep them extra busy by giving them minimal time to complete it. Also have them work in small groups, each group at one laptop or terminal. Chances are that three or four students won't be able to agree on a renegade site. Finally, hold them accountable for completing the task by requiring report-outs or written reports. Between in-class assignments, have them turn off their computers or close their laptops.

Monitoring and controlling students' cell phone use poses tougher challenges because the devices are much smaller and easier to hide. Between 90% and 92% of college students admit to using their cell phones in class for nonclass purposes, such as texting, checking Facebook, tweeting, playing games, web surfing, and the like (McCoy, 2013; Tindell & Bohlander, 2012). Professionals are increasingly recognizing that there are individuals who are obsessive about their smartphones and becoming addicted to them. This obsession has even been given a name, nomophobia, or the fear of being without a mobile device. Predictably, distractive smartphone usage is most common in large classes and long classes and during lectures versus group activities (Berry & Westfall, 2015).

You could ban the use of laptops and cell phones in class, but you have to keep a sharp eye out for offenders and enforce your ban. Your syllabus should warn students that engaging in renegade computer or cell phone activities will bring serious consequences, such as removal from class or a grade reduction (e.g., being marked absent or losing points). According to students, only fairly drastic measures like these work, as public or private reprimands do not (Berry & Westfall, 2015).

If you prefer a more flexible policy, you might give students a short break in the middle of the class period to check their devices (Cardon, 2014), as suggested in Chapter 4, or allow devices out any time except small group activities. This may help students to control themselves better and pay more attention during class. You can also note that smartphones and laptops may not be used in any way that will distract others in class. Increasingly, mobile phones have features, such as the pulldown refresh, that are designed to be addictive. Technology distractions are not likely to decrease.

Whatever system you decide on—and do realize that devices can be at least neutral or sometimes critical for student success—make sure you can enforce what you choose.

Asking for Extensions and Missing Assignment Deadlines

In your syllabus, specify penalties for late work (e.g., docking a portion of the grade), with or without an approved extension. Some instructors feel comfortable strictly enforcing this policy, whereas others prefer to be flexible. Students occasionally have good reasons for not meeting deadlines, but they also occasionally lie. You must assess each extension request and excuse on a case-by-case, student-by-student basis, perhaps allowing a single, documented incident but drawing the line at the second.

A student with a habitual problem deserves a private talk and the full penalties. You might ask other instructors in your department for the names of any chronic cases that they have encountered.

If you can devise systems, such as multiple check-ins for papers and tickets that can be used for an extra day to work on a paper, you will decrease incivilities related to deadlines.

Showing Disrespect in General

If your prevention measures fail, talk to offenders privately and explain that their behavior is affecting their fellow students' ability to learn. Avoid showing or inciting anger by keeping your voice low. Be aware that sometimes students show disrespect to get the attention they believe they can't get through any other means. They want to vent their anger toward authority or express some other deep-seated emotional problem. Leave such cases to the professionals, and refer these students to your institution's psychological or counseling center.

If your warnings fail or you face grievous and repeated displays of disrespect and abuse in class, don't hesitate to order the offenders out of the classroom, at least for that day. Should they refuse to leave, call campus security. After the incident, review it with the students in class so they can serve as witnesses, tell your department chair, and make a written record of the verbal exchange. Although calling security is a last-resort response, it's a good idea to have campus security as a contact in your phone. Taking this tack should end your incivility problems in the class for the rest of the term (Carroll, 2003a).

If the disrespect takes the form of an abusive online post to a discussion board, take a screenshot of the post and then delete the post. As soon as you are able, email or phone the perpetrator to point out the inappropriateness of the post and the consequences of doing this again. A reasonable penalty is blocking the student's posts for the rest of the term, an action that should hurt the offender's grade.

■ SEEKING ASSISTANCE

You are not alone in having to deal with student incivilities. Ask respected colleagues how they handle them. Requesting their advice will not lead them to believe you are an ineffective teacher. Another source of strategies is the student affairs staff. These officers usually understand students and their worlds and how to communicate with them better than many faculty members, and the dean of student affairs should know about even mildly threatening incivilities. Contacting the student affairs office also helps to establish patterns of behavior and note deviations or concerning increases. The student affairs office will also know if a behavior might lead to expulsion from the institution or even arrest.

In addition, refer students with ego, authority, or anger management problems to your institution's psychological or counseling center. Finally, speak outside class with your best-behaved students, enlisting them to help you keep an orderly learning environment. You might ask them to subtly communicate their disapproval of the misconduct during class or talk to the offending students outside class.

■ REFLECTION QUESTIONS

Reflection Question 11.1: Think about your experience in higher education as a faculty member. Describe three experiences with classroom incivilities that you found inappropriate, distracting, or frustrating. For each instance, think about how you handled the disruption. Would you now do the same in a similar situation? If not, how would you now respond?

Reflection Question 11.2: What is your approach to preventing or minimizing the number of classroom incivilities in your course? How, and to what extent, do you currently include students in establishing a learning environment as free from disruption as possible?

Concept Into Practice: An instructor can prevent or minimize classroom disruptions through modeling desired behavior. Explain what behaviors could create a safe, inclusive, and disruption-free learning environment for your students.

CHAPTER 12

Preserving Academic Integrity

Reports of scandalous and unethical behaviors of leaders in business, politics, sports, and even education seem to be occurring regularly. Unfortunately, this normalizes unethical behavior, and the often small price these leaders pay for unethical behavior makes it look profitable. These impressions have been reinforced by several large-scale cheating scandals at well-known universities, some with well-established honor codes. In addition to cheating on exams, plagiarizing papers, and hiring an individual to sit in for the registered student, there are also video images of high-profile actors and business leaders using unethical means to get their children sports scholarships to bypass traditional entrance requirements into prestigious schools, which is bad enough, but it turns out these children didn't even play the sport for which they were admitted on scholarship (Davies, 2021). No wonder those who cheat in college do not feel bad for violating norms and rules in order to get ahead (Lovett-Hooper et al., 2007).

There are a great many definitions and variations of *academic misconduct*. Ultimately, academic misconduct is attempting to acquire, or helping anyone else to acquire, any credit that would count toward the final grade in any college or university course through a means that would be deemed inappropriate by the faculty member teaching that course. This definition has several important components.

1. "Attempting to": Even if an attempt to cheat doesn't work, it's still cheating (e.g., writing definitions on one's arm is still cheating even if the definitions turn out to be wrong and the items on the exam are marked incorrect).
2. "Acquiring or helping anyone else to acquire": If the student helps someone else cheat with no personal gain, it's still cheating (e.g., passing a friend answers).
3. "Any credit that would count toward the final grade": Requesting an extension of 3 days for a major paper due to a family member being ill when there is no such illness (e.g., the extension would ostensibly result in a higher grade, otherwise why request the extension).
4. "In any college or university course": If college credit is received, it does not matter if the course

is in one's major (e.g., in a one-credit physical education course on running if a student fills out a log that running took place when it did not).

5. "Through a means that would be deemed inappropriate": This allows faculty members to determine whether something is cheating *in that context*, even if the behavior wasn't explicitly forbidden or appropriate in another context (e.g., group work is allowed to complete homework assignments, but considered cheating on a take-home exam).

This means, of course, that we need to be as clear as possible to keep students from inadvertently engaging in academic misconduct. For example, students may not consider lying about a grandparent being ill to request a make-up exam to be dishonest, but that is academic misconduct. One option is to share the five preceding points with your students.

■ HOW PREVALENT IS CHEATING?

A jaw-dropping 32% of undergraduates in a recent survey reported cheating on exams (ICAI, 2020). On this same survey, 28% of undergraduates reported working with other students on an assignment when the instructor asked students to work individually. Of course, students don't need to work with other students, as there are several online resources for that. A new verb for college students is "chegging." Adams (2021) wrote an article in *Forbes* noting that at the time the article was written, for $14.95 per month, students can use Chegg's database of over 45 million textbook and exam problems. In this same article Adams (2021) reported that Chegg employs over 70,000 freelance professionals (e.g., experts in STEM disciplines) who are available 24 hours a day, 7 days a week, to answer questions posed by their subscribers, often providing responses in under 15 minutes. Whether "chegging" or not, 90% of college students admit to using the internet to cheat (Berry et al., 2006). Plagiarism is also quite common: 79% of 300 students surveyed

indicated they plagiarized from internet sources, and 42% said they bought a custom written paper (Schaffhauser, 2017). Sadly, 54% of students think cheating is okay, and perhaps even needed to stay competitive (Schaffhauser, 2017). It is interesting to note that students come to college well accustomed to cheating. The ICAI (2020) website notes that 95% of high school students reported some form of cheating, with 64% admitting to cheating on a test and 58% knowingly plagiarizing a paper.

Defining and addressing "cheating" during the COVID-19 pandemic revealed some interesting findings. Universities initially appeared to confirm fears of cheating while testing at home, reporting increases of 50% to 300% more cheating incidences (Daniels et al., 2021; Dey, 2021). Eighty percent of students reported that cheating occurred more frequently in online courses than it did in face-to-face classes (Walsh et al., 2021). Lancaster and Cotarlan (2021) noted a nearly 200% increase in file-sharing websites such as Chegg and Course Hero following the onset of the COVID-19 pandemic. However, it's unclear how much of this "cheating" was intentional versus a side effect of the new environment. Certainly, some students cheated, but there were also cases of confusion. When taking a test at home and told it is an open-resource test, does that include the internet? What about asking a parent? A parent is a resource. Universities concerned about teaching began using software solutions that locked browsers. Others closed exams if the test-taker looked around the room extensively. However, psychology has long known that our eyes move more when we are thinking (Ehrlichman & Micic, 2012), and individuals with ADD are especially likely to look around the room while thinking. Individuals with poor internet connections ran into challenges taking online exams. So many systems were put into place to catch cheaters, and the whole situation was so unprecedented and ambiguous, that more students (truly cheating or not) were caught in the net. It is easier for a computer keeping an eye on a single student to detect "cheating" than it is for a faculty member to catch a cheater in a room full of students (Dey, 2021). A deep discussion also emerged about the ethics of online exam monitoring systems and the serious implications on the basis of equity (Coghlan et al., 2021). This discussion peaked during the COVID-19 pandemic lockdown when all students were sent home, but it is ongoing, and it will likely continue. Note that any system has to be carefully considered in terms of fairness and equity.

Cover your bases, and make it clear to students what constitutes cheating in this new normal and what the consequences will be. Put a copyright notice on all of your exams and assignments, and explain to students that if they upload any of your materials, even a single test question or the instructions for the term paper, they are guilty of posting copywritten material without permission.

■ WHY DO STUDENTS CHEAT?

Some college student demographics and activities are related to the prevalence of cheating. Cheating is more common among student who are younger (traditional age), are international (Grasgreen, 2012), earn lower grades (Hutton, 2006; McCabe et al., 2012), have joined a fraternity or sorority, are very involved in extracurricular activities, or engage in heavy drinking and partying behavior (Grasgreen, 2012; Hutton, 2006; McCabe et al., 2012).

When asked why they cheat, here are some top-ranking reasons:

1. Laziness or the easy way out (McCoy, 2021)
2. Need for better grades (Center for Academic Integrity survey cited in Hutton, 2006); grades too low to get into desired program or obtain desired honors, or scholarship at risk (Grasgreen, 2012; Lang, 2013; Yardley et al., 2009)
3. Pressure to succeed (Center for Academic Integrity survey cited in Hutton, 2006); competitive pressures (Josephson Institute, 2012)
4. Time pressures (Grasgreen, 2012; Yardley et al., 2009)
5. Difficulty of the course, test, or assignment (Yardley et al., 2009)
6. Inadequate preparation for the test or assignment (Yardley et al., 2009)
7. Disinterest in the material (Lang, 2013; McCoy, 2021)
8. Faculty members not enforcing academic integrity and not reporting cheaters, which half admit to doing (McCabe, 2005; McCabe et al., 2012; Nadelson, 2007; Young, 2010)
9. Uncertainty about what constitutes cheating or plagiarism (Burt, 2010)
10. Community-wide ethos of cheating (McCoy, 2021)
11. Instructor "not worthy of honesty" due to unfairness, arbitrary assignments, irrelevant material, focus on grades, or lack of concern about student learning (Anderman et al., 2007; Hutton, 2006; Yardley et al., 2009)

■ DETECTING CHEATING

Students do not realize how easy it is to catch certain acts of academic misconduct. During exams, eyes can easily be seen darting back and forth; heads looking about; and notes, blue books, and cheat sheets making the rounds. A baseball cap pulled low over the eyes is not normally worn that way. Sometimes you can spot a ringer by an unfamiliar face. Other tip-offs are a heavily erased exam, suspicious behavior (e.g., leaving the room during the exam, rustling through one's things, hiding a cell phone in one's lap, repeatedly looking at one's hands and arms), and, of course, a considerable number of identical answers, particularly incorrect ones, across exams. Be mindful, too, if a student exam scores suddenly increase.

Plagiarism may be detected with the use of software or by pasting a sentence into a search engine with quote marks. Watch for papers (1) without references; (2) with references that don't fit the text; (3) with odd, esoteric, or inaccessible references; (4) references written in different styles; (5) on a topic other than the one assigned; (6) with a format different from your requirements; (7) with a cover page typeface different from the text's; (8) with a shifting writing style; (9) heavy on facts not tied together; (10) very similar to another student's paper; or (11) that don't sound like the way a student in question talks or writes (Suarez & Martin, 2001). Also be suspicious if a student who does not typically do work before it is due submits an early draft, a document that won't open, or a paper obviously written for another class. Some of these seem innocuous, such as a file that won't open or the wrong file submitted, but if you don't catch it for several days, the student can apologize and immediately send you the correct file, which may have been worked on for several days after the deadline (they can reset the computer timestamp).

Many first-year and international students do not know what plagiarism is. Not all high schools teach plagiarism, and most international students follow a different set of values and norms, particularly those from what are called *high-power-distance* cultures, which include all of Asia, most of the Middle East, much of Europe and Latin America, and some of Africa. This kind of culture exalts those in authority and requires deference to them (Dimitrov, 2009). Copying their published work pays tribute to their expertise and acknowledges that the student cannot phrase the message as well (Fox, 1994). This attitude does not necessarily reflect theft, but it is in violation of the expectations for your carefully described guidelines.

You can teach students about plagiarism or assign one of several websites that explain what it is, how to avoid it, and how it differs from paraphrasing (e.g., www.virtualsalt.com/antiplag.htm, and https://plagiarism.duke.edu). Some institutions have even created online plagiarism games (e.g., https://www.lycoming.edu/library/plagiarism-game). In an experiment involving 500 students, Dee and Jacob (2012) found that having students take an interactive online tutorial on plagiarism before they turned in a paper reduced their incidence of plagiarism by two-thirds. If possible, have your students put their paper drafts through some plagiarism-detection software, such as Grammarly. It is important to keep in mind, though, that many services are now available that will either write an original paper for a student or make adjustments necessary to avoid plagiarism detection software.

◼ FORTY WAYS TO CATCH A CHEATER OR PREVENT CHEATING

As already noted in this chapter, unfortunately, a lot of students do cheat on exams and plagiarize papers. We are not police, but it is our responsibility to do our best to mitigate unethical behavior. For example, the University of North Carolina at Chapel Hill Honor code includes faculty members' responsibilities, such as taking reasonable steps to reduce the risk of cheating. So, how do we practically take responsibility to reduce the risk of cheating? Start with the section in this chapter that asks "Why Do Students Cheat?" and remove as many of those elements as possible. For example, make assignments less valuable, help students with time management skills, make content more interesting, and instill a class ethos of not cheating. In addition, consider that the web has plenty of sites for how to cheat, including videos of "creative" ways to cheat on tests. Do a quick search on your own and keep up with the most recent trends in cheating. Students love to write about how they get away with cheating. Following you will find a list of 40 ways to make cheating more difficult, heighten students' perceived chances of getting caught and facing dire consequences, and ways to reduce students' motivation to cheat (Budhai, 2020; Darby, 2020; Keyser & Doyle, 2020; Supiano, 2020; Swauger, 2020; Walsh et al., 2021):

1. Motivate your students' interest in your subject, and help them understand its relevance to their careers and the broader world so they will want to learn it.

2. Deemphasize grades as much as you are comfortable with, up to and including ungrading.

3. Define academic dishonesty, cheating, and plagiarism for your students, and give examples and hypothetical cases. Also teach them how to cite sources correctly.

4. State verbally and in writing your own and your institution's policies on academic dishonesty and their applications to each assignment and test you give. Emphasize that you strictly enforce these policies and what penalties violators are risking, including turning all cases over to student affairs (or the appropriate office), if that is your policy. Include these statements in your syllabus.

5. If you do not reuse test questions, post past exams on your course LMS or website for all students to use. This will ensure all students have equal access.

6. Ban the use of cell phones, tablets, laptops, smartwatches, and other electronic devices during tests. Students can use them to store information, photograph the exam for friends, text friends for answers, and search the internet.

7. Allow students to bring one 3×5 index card with anything written on it that they choose. This will make hidden notes less valuable. If a notecard is not allowed, be on the lookout for notes on anything from toes of shoes to the inside label of a drink.

8. Make up different forms of tests, especially multiple-choice tests, by varying the order of the questions. The test tools in LMSs usually can do this for you.

9. If your on-site class with paper exams is so large that you can't recognize all your students, ask students to print and sign their name on the exam. Then check student IDs or driver's licenses against the signatures when students pick up exams.

10. Tell students that if they make it easy for another student to copy from their exam, they, too, are guilty of cheating.

11. If the room permits, space students as far apart as possible and be firm with respect to where they sit. The less a student wishes to sit as assigned the more important it is to do so.

12. If you have an exam for which students fill out blue books, have each student bring one blank book, which they turn in just before the test; then distribute the books randomly. This keeps a student from lightly writing notes in their book that they may erase during the exam.

13. Proctor tests judiciously, enlisting the aid of your TAs and colleagues. Don't work on any other project while proctoring. If you have proctors, tell students only you will answer questions. This will keep responses consistent, and proctors are not distracted.

14. Check for cheat notes in nearby restrooms.

15. When grading tests manually, mark incorrect answers with an X or a slash in ink, draw a line down the answer sheet through the answers, and/or place a mark at the end of each short answer or essay in colored ink.

16. Return exams, papers, and assignments to students in person or electronically so everyone has copies of the questions, not just individuals using websites where course materials can be uploaded by some students and viewed by others.

17. Collect tests after you go over graded tests with students. If the test question forms are separate from the answer sheets, have students put their names on the forms to ensure you can account for all of them.

18. Give explicit collaboration rules for all out-of-class assignments.

19. Change your writing assignments as often as possible to discourage paper recycling.

20. Explain the relevance and purpose of all assignments and in-class activities.

21. Take class time to discuss difficulties in the assignments and how to overcome them.

22. Make specific format requirements, and do not accept papers that do not follow assigned format.

23. Require a certain combination of sources in an assignment: so many from the web, so many from print material in the campus library, so many from videos in the campus collection, and so on.
24. Teach students the types of plagiarism and how and when to cite sources.
25. Guide and monitor students through the process of researching and writing papers and completing projects. Have them turn in work in stages and get to know their work and voice.
26. Require students to turn in a screenshot of the first page of any material they cite or use.
27. Explain to students your rationales behind your assessment instruments and grading standards.
28. Clearly and repeatedly communicate to your students how much you care about them and their success in your course and their lives beyond. In addition to telling them explicitly, tell them implicitly by showing them respect, kindness, and understanding.
29. Set up a discussion forum so students can use each other in class as a resource. Don't give them access to the roster so they can set up a group chat (which you cannot monitor).
30. Give students alternative ways to show their learning (e.g., exam, paper, video, group project).
31. Require students to go to the writing center for assistance outlining a paper and reading the first draft of the paper.
32. Consider online proctoring software, but be mindful of the pitfalls of using such software (e.g., flagging students on the autism spectrum and those with ADD for their eye movements; noise level of parents with small children [Swauger, 2020]).
33. Check the properties of student-submitted documents to see the original author of the file and when it was created.
34. Randomly select a handful of multiple-choice questions on each exam and ask students to explain their rationale for their choice.
35. Require students to sign an integrity statement at the top of each exam and to turn in a provided integrity statement with any papers written.
36. For online tests, show one item at a time and prohibit backtracking.
37. Do not use publisher test bank items verbatim.
38. Break high-stakes exams and assignments into smaller units.
39. Break papers into stages and go over stages with student in short meetings.
40. If your institution has an honor code, point out that schools with honor codes have less cheating, in turn benefitting those who don't cheat.

If you suspect any form of academic dishonesty, take swift, decisive action. Getting away with cheating will embolden the person doing the cheating and if that person tells others it will change the culture of the classroom. Also realize that a student who cheats in your class likely cheats in others. Know your institution's policies and the person to whom to report the violation. Do this before you catch anyone cheating so you know immediately how to respond. Ask your dean or chair, or refer to your institution's faculty handbook, student handbook, or course catalogue. Ask senior colleagues how much de facto discretion you have and should take. Usually an instructor's ad hoc penalties are more lenient than institutional ones and don't go on a student's record.

■ HONOR CODES

Campuses with a well-established and traditional honor code have historically had a lower incidence of cheating, by as much as 50%, as compared to campuses that do not (Schwartz et al., 2013; Tatum, 2022; Tatum et al., 2018).

With honor codes, students are responsible for policing one another. In fact, they run the honor system either solely by students (e.g., University of North Carolina at Chapel Hill, Rice, and the University of Virginia) or with student and faculty members both on the hearing board (e.g., James Madison University). Cheating violations usually carry a heavy penalty, such as expulsion. Typically, students pledge their adherence to the honor code in writing on every graded test and assignment, which serves to remind them of the code and reinforce their commitment to it. However, the real reason for the difference in cheating rates lies in campus culture's regard for academic integrity and a traditional honor code (Tatum, 2022).

Research in this area has historically lumped together campuses with traditional honor codes and modified honor codes. "Briefly, we define a traditional honor system as including an honor pledge, dual-responsibility, a requirement to report oneself and others, a requirement for faculty members to turn over all suspected cases, and a student-run adjudication system." (Tatum et al., 2018, p. 304). Modified honor systems lack one or more of these components. Schwartz et al. (2013) found that colleges with traditional honor systems had the lowest levels of test cheating, followed by modified honor systems. Colleges with no honor systems had the highest level of test cheating, approximately twice the rate of traditional honor systems (45% versus 23%). Tatum et al. (2018) also investigated size of institution and student-faculty ratio size and found no effect due to either of those two variables. When asking about whether students would self-report or report others, Tatum et al. (2018) found no significant difference between modified honor systems and no honor system. The impact of honor systems is clearly complex.

CHANGING STUDENT VALUES

It seems like whatever you look for you are most likely to find. There is no doubt, as the statistics presented in this chapter show, that a lot of cheating is happening in higher education. Our society seems to continually diminish the value of higher education and of being truthful. In many respects, it is challenging to even know what the truth is. Of course, we also know that if one perceives dishonesty is the norm, then it encourages more dishonesty. All that said, we can't bury our heads in the sand and pretend cheating is not a problem. To do so opens the gates and allows cheaters an easy path.

On this topic, there is no easy way forward. This chapter presents a good deal of information about academic misconduct, but if cheating has not happened to you, you will find that when you catch it, it is seriously unpleasant. Cheating is like a punch in the stomach. If you care about your job and your students (and if you are reading this book, we believe you do), it will make you sad and angry, particularly if it is one of your favorite students. All experienced faculty members have had it happen. It will happen to you. And when it happens, you will have a choice to make. You can focus all of your energy on being suspicious and locking down the course. Or, you can focus on the students with integrity and hold those without accountable. Mostly, do your best to keep the heart of a teacher and remember that those who build communities and relationships epitomize teaching at its best. Be one of those teachers.

REFLECTION QUESTIONS

Reflection Question 12.1: What do you see as one of the biggest reasons students cheat on exams and papers? In what ways is that reflected in our society? When it comes to academic integrity, do you see the path forward as more promising or more challenging?

Reflection Question 12.2: How much time and energy do you think a faculty member should allocate to the issue of integrity? Should we focus on the disciplinary content and processes of our field and let students decide themselves whether to have integrity or not? Or should we do our best to model and instill integrity to the greatest extent possible? Maybe the answer lies somewhere in the middle?

Concept Into Practice: Find out the policies on your campus with respect to academic integrity and cheating. Even if you have been teaching for several years in your current department, unless you have already had the conversations, chat with colleagues about how they approach academic integrity as a concept and what they do when they catch students cheating. The goal here is to better prepare yourself.

PART 3

TRIED-AND-TRUE TEACHING METHODS

CHAPTER 13

Matching Teaching Methods with Learning Outcomes

Your selection of teaching methods is critical to your students' learning. Derek Bok (2006) argues that it is even more important than the content you select, and he bemoans that faculty members' discussions too often neglect the topic of pedagogy. He points out the discouraging research finding that the average student cannot remember most of the factual content of a lecture within 15 minutes after it ends, but lessons learned through more active learning methods can leave students changed forever. In Bok's (2006) own words:

> In contrast, interests, values, and cognitive skills are all likely to last longer, as are concepts and knowledge that students have acquired not by passively reading or listening to lectures but through their own mental effort . . . The residue of knowledge and the habits of mind students take away from college are likely to be determined less by *which* courses they take than by *how* they are taught and *how well* they are taught. (pp. 48–49)

Let's turn to the critical issue of how you will teach your courses. This chapter extends the *course design* process in Chapter 2 into *course development*: selecting the best teaching methods for enabling students to achieve learning outcomes. If your outcomes map is your skeleton, your methods are the muscles on the bones. Fortunately, some of your fellow faculty members have devised and conducted research on numerous teaching innovations over the past few decades, so you have plenty of worthy options to choose from. Both Part Three of this book, which opens with this chapter, and Part Four focus on a wide range of well-researched methods that we know can generate powerful learning experiences, assuming they are implemented properly and for appropriate purposes. Chapters 13 through 18 lay out ground rules for setting up and managing them correctly, and this chapter gives an overview of which methods to use when, with the *when* depending on your learning outcomes.

As Figure 13.1 shows, your student learning outcomes provide the foundation for every aspect of your course, and you should align all the other

Figure 13.1   The Logic of Aligned Course and Curriculum Design

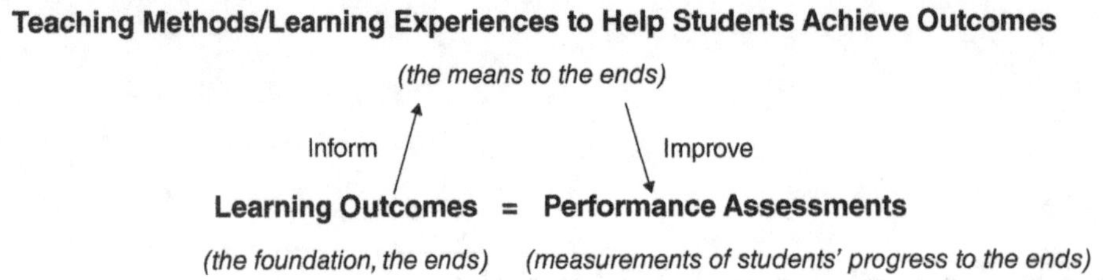

Teaching Methods/Learning Experiences to Help Students Achieve Outcomes

(the means to the ends)

Inform ↗   ↘ Improve

Learning Outcomes = **Performance Assessments**

(the foundation, the ends)   *(measurements of students' progress to the ends)*

components with them. Because outcomes are the primary focus of any learning, outcomes inform your choice of teaching methods (how you teach or facilitate), which encompass all the learning experiences you give your students in the form of assignments and activities (active listening is an activity), whether as homework or in class. The most appropriate means of instruction will afford your students content, practice, and feedback, in the areas specified in your learning outcomes. The way in which you have your students practice should imitate the way you plan to assess student performances for a grade: by multiple-choice items, a case analysis, a literary analysis, a lab demonstration of proper use of equipment, a creative multimedia project, a concept map, a diagram, a solution to a real-world problem, solutions to mathematical word problems, and so on. If it does, it should improve your students' performance on your assessment instruments. Note the equals sign in Figure 13.1 between outcomes and assessment. If you want your students to be able to do X, Y, and Z, let them practice X, Y, and Z, and then assess their progress by having them demonstrate proficiency in X, Y, and Z.

If your outcomes go beyond students' recognizing and regurgitating correct facts, terms, equations, and algorithms—and they should go beyond these knowledge-level cognitive operations—you should be familiar with multiple means to help your students achieve your ends. As eminent psychologist Abraham Maslow (1966) once said, "It is tempting, if the only tool you have is a hammer, to treat everything as if it were a nail" (p. 15). For nearly 1,000 years, lectures have been the primary method of instruction (Brockliss, 1996). Starting in the mid-1990s, a shift began that demonstrated that added engaged learning strategies to the lecture greatly improved learning outcomes. Suddenly, we had more tools than the pedagogical hammer of the lecture (Major et al., 2021). Learning new strategies is often referred to as *building a teaching toolbox*. As an instructor, one of your most critical tasks is to choose the best tool for the job—or, more accurately, choose the best tools for the job, as you can usually identify several means to reach your ends.

■ TYPES OF TOOLS

When it comes to teaching, everyone has a base. What is your go-to tool that never lets you down and can be used across a variety of settings? Once you have identified that foundational tool, begin to build out your toolbox. If you remain a growth-minded faculty member, you will never stop adding new tools. Across your career you will see that continually learning new tools is not a burden. Quite the contrary, it is what will keep teaching exciting for you. A complete teaching toolbox contains three types of tools to select from: course formats, major teaching methods, and teaching moves.

Course Formats

Course formats frame the class period, the overall view of what will be done and how it will be done. It may be lecture meetings only, lecture meetings with discussion sections, lecture meetings with laboratories, lecture meetings with skill activity sessions, discussion meetings with some lecture, discussion meetings with skill activity sessions, skill activity sessions alone, or a seminar. In a seminar, as opposed to a discussion section, students prepare their contributions in advance, whether research presentations, arguments, points of view, or interpretations. In a skill-activity section, students have the chance to practice something, so it may be scheduled in a room other than a regular classroom, such as a computer lab, a language lab, a studio, a stage, a music room, or a clinic with medical equipment or a simulated human body. It may take place outside or off-campus, perhaps in a botanical garden, a forest, a hospital, a museum, or a music hall.

We don't know the relative learning impact of different formats, but we do know quite a bit about the effects of closely related variables: the degree of in-class student activity (or lack thereof; see Chapter 1) and class size. Hoyt and Perera (2000) identified not the actual impact of formats but the success that faculty members perceive formats having for certain learning objectives. These objectives were somewhat different from the outcomes presented in Chapter 2 for course design. In Hoyt and Perera's study, they ranged from "substantive knowledge" (of facts, principles and theories, and applications) to much higher-order abilities such as general cognitive and academic skills (communication and critical thinking), lifelong learning skills (research and interest), personal development (broad liberal knowledge and values development), and other skills and competencies (team skills and creativity). Hoyt and Perera found that faculty members consider lecture/discussion, lecture/lab, and lecture/skill activity pretty ineffective—"average" at best—in equipping students to meet these objectives. (Lecture/lab achieved a high average on factual knowledge, as did lecture/discussion on values development.) Discussion/lecture did better on general cognitive and academic skills and personal development (liberal knowledge). Skill activity alone earned high ratings on developing students' communication skills, creative capacities, and liberal knowledge, but average on the other objectives. The only formats that

faculty members saw as highly effective on almost all the objectives were discussion/skill activity and seminar. Not surprisingly, both have a great deal of student activity and small-size classes.

You may not think you have control over your formats, but you may be able to negotiate a change. Introductory courses are typically lecture based, perhaps with discussion, lab, or skill activity sections, while freshman seminars are set up as seminars or discussion sessions. Courses in the major may be anchored in the lecture, discussion, skill activity, or seminar format. If you believe that a different format from the one currently attached to your course would strengthen student learning, make a case to your department chair. Point out that you have learning outcomes that your students are unlikely to achieve because, for all practical purposes, the current format prohibits implementing the effective teaching methods and moves. You have nothing to lose by asking, and you and your students have a great deal to gain.

The next two sections address which teaching methods and moves are most effective for various learning outcomes.

Major Teaching Methods

The tools in this category comprise major methods—that is, multiweek assignments or in-class activities that require considerable time. We may schedule one on a regular or semiregular basis during a course or devote one or more class periods to it. For instance, we rarely have just one discussion or one small-group activity during a term-long course. If we do plan just one, it probably won't work very well because it will violate students' expectations. If we choose to give interactive lectures, we probably give many of them. If we use the case method to teach, we probably assign and debrief at least several cases during the term. We may have just one simulation, one substantial project-based learning assignment, or one service-learning project, but each of these is likely to require students to put in hours of class time or homework.

Before turning to the outcomes each method serves well, let us review the basic definitions of these methods. Most of them have their own chapter or a section of a chapter in Parts Three, Four, or Five of this book.

- *Lecture*: Instructor presenting material and answering student questions that arise (Chapter 14)
- *Interactive lecture*: Lecture mixed with student activities (such as answering a multiple-choice objective item, solving a problem, comparing and filling in lecture notes, debriefing a minicase, doing a think-pair-share exercise, or a small-group discussion) (Chapter 14)
- *Recitation*: Students answering knowledge and comprehension questions (Chapter 15)
- *Directed discussion*: Class discussion that follows a more or less orderly set of questions that the instructor has crafted to lead students to certain realizations or conclusions or to help them meet a specific learning outcome (Chapter 15)
- *Writing and speaking exercises*: Any of many informal assignments and activities, usually in-class and ungraded, to help students learn material, clarify their thinking, or make progress on a formal assignment (Chapter 22)
- *Classroom assessment techniques*: Informal assignments and activities, usually in-class and ungraded, to inform the instructor how well students are mastering new material just presented or read; often overlap with writing and speaking exercises (Chapter 23)
- *Group work/learning*: Students doing a learning activity or creating a product in small groups of two to six in or out of class; must be carefully managed by the instructor (Chapter 10)
- *Student-peer feedback*: Students giving one another feedback on a written or an orally presented product, usually a written draft or practice speech (Chapter 23)
- *Cookbook science labs*: Pairs or triads of students conducting a traditional, often predictable experiment following prescribed, cookbook-like procedures (Chapter 20 recommends and illustrates more effective inquiry-based labs)
- *Just-in-time-teaching*: Instructor adjusts class activities and lectures to respond to the misconceptions revealed by students' electronic responses to conceptual questions; an extension of electronic daily quizzes to motivate students to do the readings (Chapters 17 and 21)
- *Case method*: Students applying course knowledge to devise one or more solutions or resolutions to problems or dilemmas presented in a realistic story or situation; an individual, small-group, or whole-class activity (Chapter 18)
- *Inquiry-based or inquiry-guided learning*: Students learning or applying material in order to meet a challenge, such as to answer a question, conduct an experiment, or interpret data (Chapter 17)
- *Project-based learning*: Students (as individuals or in groups) applying course knowledge to produce something, such as a report (written or oral), process or product design, research or program proposal, or computer code; often paired with group work (Chapter 17)
- *Role-plays*: Students acting out instructor-assigned roles, improvising the script, in a realistic and problematic social or interpersonal situation, such as Reacting to the Past (Chapter 16)
- *Simulations*: Students playing out, face-to-face or on a computer, a hypothetical social situation that abstracts key elements from reality (Chapter 16)
- *Service-learning*: Students learning from the experience of performing community service and systematically reflecting on it (Chapter 16)
- *Fieldwork and clinicals*: Students learning how to conduct research and make sound professional judgments in real-world situations

The outcomes we will consider should sound familiar. As you will recall from Chapters 1 and 2, the first six on this list come from Bloom (1956) and Anderson and Krathwohl (2000), the seventh from Perry (1968), and the last from Nelson (2000):

1. *Knowledge/remembering*: To memorize or recognize facts, terms, principles, or algorithms
2. *Comprehension/understanding*: To translate, restate in one's own words
3. *Application/applying*: To use, apply, make useful
4. *Analysis/analyzing*: To identify and examine components, compare and contrast, identify assumptions, deduce implications
5. *Synthesis/creating*: To make connections, identify new relationships, design something new (new to students)
6. *Evaluation/evaluating*: To make a judgment, assess validity, select and defend
7. *Cognitive development*: To progress from dualism to multiplicity to relativism to a tentative commitment to the most worthy perspective available; to come to understand the nature of knowledge as inherently uncertain but subject to definite standards of comparison
8. *Shift in mental models*: To replace a faulty understanding of a phenomenon with the discipline's more valid mental model

Table 13.1 provides suggestions for bringing these outcomes and the major methods together in answering the question, "Which methods for which outcomes?" Two caveats are in order. First, this table represents the general findings of a large body of literature on the methods listed. The references are embedded in the chapters and chapter sections on each method. Second, the efficacy of the interactive lecture, directed discussion, and group work depends entirely on the tasks you have students do or the questions you have them discuss. For identifying productive tasks and questions for your outcomes, see Chapters 14 and 15 (as well as Exhibit 13.1, which lists short in-class assignments and activities that help students master each of Bloom's cognitive operations).

Davis and Arend (2013) propose another model, shown in Table 13.2, relating methods to outcomes, but with different categories of outcomes. They also identify the origins and theories behind the appropriate methods.

The overlap between the models in Tables 13.1 and 13.2 is considerable. For instance, Davis and Arend identify "presentations" and "explanations" as appropriate methods for acquiring knowledge, which roughly equate to lectures, interactive lectures, and recitation in Table 13.1. Their "decision-making" and "practicing professional judgment" rely mostly on analysis and evaluation. However, Table 13.1 encompasses only cognitive outcomes, whereas Davis and Arend give some attention to psychomotor ("building skills") and affective ("exploring attitudes, feelings, and perspectives") outcomes as well. In fact, the only disagreement between the two models pertains to how many methods experiential learning encompasses. In this book, *experiential* includes what they categorize as "virtual realities" (see Chapter 16).

Teaching Moves

Teaching moves are the ways you explain and elaborate on material, the learning-to-learn strategies you share with your class, the short in-class activities and exercises students do, and the questions you ask them to contemplate. The practice you give them should resemble the ways you plan to assess their learning. If you plan to assess whether or not someone can change a tire, the best option for their learning and practice is actually changing a tire, not looking at photos of tire-changing steps or only through being told how to change a tire.

Compared to major methods, these mini-methods entail much less time and commitment. You may use a dozen or more of them in a given class period—one to help students recall the readings, the next to clarify a knotty point, another to explain new material, yet another for a lecture break in which students apply the material, and so on. If one doesn't seem to work well, you can immediately

Table 13.1 Teaching Methods Found to Be Effective for Helping Students Achieve Different Learning Outcomes

	Knowledge	Comprehension	Application	Analysis	Synthesis	Evaluation	Cognitive Development	Shift in Models
Lecture	X	X						
Interactive lecture	X	X	a	a	a	a	a	
Recitation	X	X						
Directed discussion		X	a	a	a	a	a	a
Writing/ speaking exercises		X	X	X	X	X		
Classroom assessment techniques	X	X	X	X		X		
Group work or learning		X	a	a	a	a	a	
Student-peer feedback		X		X		X		
Cookbook science labs		X	X					
Just-in-time-teaching	X	X						X
Case method			X	X	X	X	X	
Inquiry based or inquiry guided	X[b]	X	X	X	X	X	X	X
Problem-based learning	X[b]		X	X	X	X	X	
Project-based learning	X[b]	X	X	X	X	X	X	
Role-plays and simulations		X	X	X		X		X
Service-learning			X	X	X	X		X
Fieldwork/ clinicals	X		X	X	X	X	X	X

Note: An X indicates this method can help students achieve this learning outcome if the method is properly implemented to serve this outcome. Poor implementation or implementation for other ends may work against students' achieving the outcome.
[a]Depends on the lecture-break tasks, the discussion questions, or the group tasks assigned.
[b]The knowledge acquired may be narrowly focused on the problem or project.

Table 13.2 Davis and Arend's (2013) Model of Learning Outcomes, Ways of Learning, and Teaching Methods

Intended Learning Outcomes: What Students Learn	Ways of Learning: Origins and Theory	Common Methods: What the Teacher Provides
Building skills Physical and procedural skills where accuracy, precision, and efficiency are important	*Behavioral learning* Behavioral psychology, operant conditioning	Tasks and procedures Practice exercises
Acquiring knowledge Basic information, concepts, and terminology in a discipline or field of study	*Cognitive learning* Cognitive psychology, attention, information processing, memory	Presentations Explanations
Developing critical, creative, and dialogical thinking Improved thinking and reasoning processes	*Learning through inquiry* Logic, critical, and creative-thinking theory, classical philosophy	Question-driven inquiries Discussions
Cultivating problem-solving and decision-making abilities Mental strategies for finding solutions and making choices	*Learning with mental models* Gestalt psychology, problem solving, and decision theory	Problems Case studies Labs Projects
Exploring attitudes, feelings, and perspectives Awareness of attitudes, biases, and other perspectives; ability to collaborate	*Learning through groups and teams* Human communication theory; group counseling theory	Group activities Team projects
Practicing professional judgment Sound judgment and appropriate professional action in complex, context-dependent situations	*Learning through virtual realities* Psychodrama, sociodrama, gaming theory	Role-playing Simulations Dramatic scenarios Games
Reflecting on experience Self-discovery and personal growth from real-world experience	*Experiential learning* Experiential learning, cognitive neuroscience, constructivism	Internships Service-learning Study abroad

Source: From Davis, J. R., & Arend, B. D. (2013). *Facilitating seven ways of learning: A resource for more purposeful, effective, and enjoyable college teaching*. Stylus, p. 38. Reprinted with permission from the publisher.

try another. When a teaching move involves the students in an activity, not only do they get practice, but you obtain immediate feedback on their misconceptions, misunderstandings, and mastery. In turn, you can give them or they can give each other immediate feedback. Thus, many of these moves serve to assess as well as teach.

Exhibit 13.1 lists effective teaching moves by the learning outcome they serve. Some of them specify what you can do or say in class to familiarize your students with different ways of thinking about

and working with the material. The rest are activities and exercises for your students to give them practice and your feedback on their learning. The existing literature addresses these minimethods only in terms of their relationship to Bloom's cognitive operations (Goodson, 2005). But these operations do represent key learning outcomes and easily map onto Anderson and Krathwohl's (2000). This list is not exhaustive, but it is a rich heuristic device that may inspire you to devise additional teaching moves to serve your purposes.

Exhibit 13.1   Effective Teaching Moves for Six Learning Outcomes (Bloom's Cognitive Operations)

KNOWLEDGE

For You to Do

- Suggest prior knowledge to which students can link new and future information and knowledge.
- Chunk knowledge into coherent groups, categories, or themes.
- Share devices to improve memory such as mnemonic patterns, maps, charts, comparisons, groupings, highlighting of key words or first letters, visual images, and rhymes.
- Point out parts, main ideas, patterns, and relationships within sets of facts or information.

For Students to Do

- Practice recalling and restating information.
- Practice recognizing or identifying information.
- Practice recalling and reproducing information.
- Practice restating concept definitions and principles.

Comprehension

For You to Do

- Outline new or upcoming material in simple form.
- Concept-map or mind-map new or upcoming material.
- Explain with concrete examples, metaphors, questions, or visual representations.

For Students to Do

- Restate or paraphrase and summarize information or knowledge.
- Describe or explain phenomena or concepts using words different from those used in the initial teaching.
- Identify the correct meaning of concepts or terms.
- Add details or explanations to basic content.
- Relate new to previously learned content.
- Construct visual representations of main ideas (mind or concept maps, tables, flowcharts, graphs, diagrams, or pictures).

Application

For You to Do

- Give multiple examples of a phenomenon that are meaningful to students.
- Define the procedures for use, including the rules, principles, and steps.
- Provide the vocabulary and concepts related to procedures.
- Explain steps as they are applied.
- Define the contexts, problems, situations, or goals for which given procedures are appropriate.

- Explain the reasons that procedures work for different types of situations or goals.
- Ensure students' readiness by diagnosing and strengthening their command of related concepts, rules, and decision-making skills.
- Begin with simple, highly structured problems and gradually move to more complex, less structured ones.
- Use questions to guide student thinking about problem components, goals, and issues.
- Give students guidance in observing and gathering information, asking appropriate questions, and generating solutions.

For Students to Do

- Generate new examples and nonexamples.
- Paraphrase the procedures, principles, rules, and steps for using or applying the material.
- Practice applying the material to problems or situations to gain speed, consistency, and ease in following the problem-solving steps.
- Practice choosing the types of problem-solving strategies for different situations.
- Solve simple, structured problems and then complex, unstructured ones.
- Practice recognizing the correct use of procedures, principles, rules, and steps with routine problems, then complex ones.
- Demonstrate the correct use of procedures, principles, rules, and steps with routine problems, then complex ones.

Analysis
For You to Do

- Point out the important and the unimportant features or ideas.
- Point out examples and nonexamples of a concept, highlighting similarities and differences.
- Give a wide range of examples, increasing their complexity over time.
- Emphasize the relationships among concepts.
- Explain different types of thinking strategies, including how to think open-mindedly, responsibly, and accurately.
- Emphasize persistence when answers are not apparent.
- Encourage students to self-evaluate and reflect on their learning.
- Ask questions that make students explain why they are doing what they are doing.
- Explain and model how to conduct systematic inquiry, detect flaws and fallacies in thinking, and adjust patterns of thinking.

For Students to Do

- Classify concepts, examples, or phenomena into correct categories.
- Use types of thinking strategies to analyze and evaluate their own thinking.
- Practice choosing the best type of thinking strategy to use in different real-world situations and explaining why their choice is superior.
- Detect and identify flaws and fallacies in thinking.

- Identify and explain instances of open- and closed-mindedness.
- Identify and explain instances of responsible versus irresponsible and accurate versus inaccurate applications of thinking strategies.
- Answer questions that require persistence in discovering and analyzing data or information.

Synthesis
For You to Do

- Promote careful observation, analysis, description, and definition.
- Explain the process and methods of scientific inquiry.
- Explain and provide examples of how to identify a research problem, speculate about causes, formulate testable hypotheses, and identify and interpret results and consequences.
- Model inquiry and discovery processes.
- Show students examples of creativity to solve problems.
- Encourage students to take novel approaches to situations and problems.
- Explain phenomena using metaphors and analogies.
- Give students examples of reframing a problem—turning it upside down or inside out or changing perceptions about it.
- Pose questions and problems with multiple good answers or solutions.
- Give students opportunities for ungraded creative performance and behavior.

For Students to Do

- Explain their experiences with inquiry activities and the results.
- Resolve a situation or solve a problem that requires speculation, inquiry, and hypothesis formation.
- Resolve a situation or solve a problem requiring a novel approach.
- Design a research study to resolve conflicting findings.
- Write the conclusions section of a research study.
- Develop products or solutions to fit within particular functions and resources.
- Manipulate concrete data to solve challenging thinking situations.
- Practice reframing a problem—turning it upside down or inside out, or changing perceptions about it.
- Explain phenomena using metaphors and analogies.

Evaluation
For You to Do

- Create conflict or perplexity by posing paradoxes, dilemmas, or other situations to challenge students' concepts, beliefs, ideas, and attitudes.
- Explain how to recognize and generate proof, logic, argument, and criteria for judgments.
- Explain the consequences of choices, actions, or behaviors.
- Provide relevant human or social models that portray the desired choices, actions, or behaviors.
- Explain with examples how factors such as culture, experience, desires, interests, and passions, as well as systematic thinking, influence choice and interpretations.

For Students to Do

- Evaluate the validity of given information, results, or conclusions.
- Draw inferences from observations, and make predictions from limited information.
- Explain how they form new judgments and how and why their current judgments differ from their previous ones.
- Identify factors that influence choice and interpretations, such as culture, experience, desires, interests, and passions, as well as systematic thinking.
- Detect mistakes, false analogies, relevant versus irrelevant issues, contradictions, and faulty predictions.
- Critique a research study.
- Choose among possible behaviors, perspectives, or approaches, and provide justifications for these choices.

Note: Partially adapted from Goodson (2005) with permission.

A TOOL FOR ORGANIZING YOUR COURSE

Fink and Fink (2009) provide a useful tool for putting all the elements of your course together and ensuring they are well aligned (see Table 13.3). The "learning goals" are equivalent to learning outcomes and the "learning activities" to teaching methods and moves. The examples given represent material from an anthropology or sociology course. Fink and Fink (2009) offer additional examples from a variety of courses.

Once you have formulated your learning outcomes, you can refer to Tables 13.1 and 13.2 as well as Exhibit 13.1 to decide on and design your most effective learning activities. We will get to assessment

Table 13.3   Fink and Fink's Three-Column Tool for Developing a Well-Aligned Course

Learning Goals	Assessment Activities	Learning Activities
1. Describe the differences in social stratification systems among bands, tribes, chiefdoms, and states.	Daily quizzes Multiple-choice and multiple true/false questions on tests	Readings Interactive lectures
2. Apply knowledge of social stratification systems to predict what the system looks like in given societies.	Written homework assignments around case studies of societies Stimulus-based multiple-choice questions on tests	Break activities during interactive lectures Discussions around cases studies
3. Evaluate the effects of a person's status in a social stratification system on his or her self-esteem, mental and physical health, and material aspirations.	Reflective written homework assignments Essay questions on tests	Readings Break activities during interactive lectures Discussions Reflective writing

in Part Five, and Chapters 25 and 26 will help you choose and implement the most appropriate activities for your outcomes.

HAS OUR KNOWLEDGE CHANGED OUR TEACHING?

As we accumulate knowledge on the effectiveness of different teaching formats, methods, and moves for various learning outcomes, we run out of excuses for relying on traditional lecture both for effectiveness and for equity (Freeman et al., 2014). This is particularly true when data shows that including active learning strategies results in large achievement gap reductions for minoritized populations (Ballen et al., 2017; Eddy & Hogan, 2014; Theobald et al., 2020). In 2006, Bok didn't mince words accusing faculty members of avoiding pedagogical debates for their own self-protection from change:

> It is relatively easy to move courses around by changing curricular requirements. It is quite another matter to decide what methods of pedagogy should be altered. Reforms of the latter kind require much more effort. . . . To avoid such difficulties, faculty have taken the principle of academic freedom and stretched it well beyond its original meaning to gain immunity from interference with how their courses should be taught. . . . Teaching methods have become the personal prerogative of the instructor rather than a subject appropriate for collective deliberation. The result is to shield from faculty review one of the most important ingredients in undergraduate education. (p. 49)

He implies that those who continue to dodge the clear evidence in favor of including student-centered methods shouldn't be completely free to choose their pedagogy. Maybe they should only be allowed to choose from a limited range of methods and moves known to be effective. This idea isn't absurd. Departments, institutions, and regional and professional accreditation agencies already mandate learning outcomes, so why shouldn't they or some other unit mandate methods?

Fortunately, faculty members are heading off the threat of external regulation by choosing better teaching strategies on their own. In a 2013–2014 survey, almost 83% of faculty members responding said they use discussion in all or most of their undergraduate courses, up from about 70% in 1989–1990. In this same time period, fewer reported using lecture in all or most of their courses: just under 51% versus about 56%. In addition, more indicated using cooperative learning, group projects, and peer feedback on students' work in 2013–2014 than they did in 1989–1990 (Eagan et al., 2014). Researchers are identifying barriers to moving toward more evidence-based teaching strategies, such as "time constraints," which is by far the most frequent challenge noted (Shadle et al., 2017).

Call this modest progress, but it is change, and it has taken place against some student resistance. Although most students enjoy active learning strategies, some do not (Amador et al., 2006; Tharayil et al., 2018). In fact, a few of the best teaching methods for helping students acquire high-level thinking skills (e.g., problem-based learning) can lower an instructor's student ratings. There are many reasons students prefer the lecture over active learning, perhaps mostly because it is a system that is familiar to them. The good news is that resistance can be overcome by a variety of techniques that faculty members are finding to be effective (Nguyen et al., 2021; Tharayil et al., 2018).

Some students protest that these methods require too much work, lack sufficient structure, demand more independence than they can or want to manage, or cause undue grade anxiety because they are being asked to do things they've never done before. Some complain that they have to teach themselves too much and that the instructors aren't doing their jobs. At the same time, colleges and universities are striving to serve and retain students. In this crunch, which should take higher priority:

student satisfaction or student learning? This is a values matter that only institutions can resolve for themselves. But we can help ourselves tremendously by explaining to our students why we choose certain teaching methods and moves over others. When we refer to the research standing behind our selections, we reaffirm to our students our commitment to do our best by them by following that research and engaging in teaching at its best.

■ REFLECTION QUESTIONS

Reflection Question 13.1: What is currently your preferred teaching method, and why? Before you say because it was the way you were taught, think a bit more carefully about the different ways you were taught. There is typically something else at play regarding why you teach as you do.

Reflection Question 13.2: What do you find to be the biggest barrier to trying new teaching formats? Is there a way to reduce that barrier?

Concept Into Practice: Look through the teaching moves listed in Exhibit 13.1. Identify five moves that you don't currently use but would benefit one of your courses. Integrate those strategies over the coming weeks or in the upcoming semester. Also, find five moves that students could do and create an assignment or task that requires them to use those five moves (it is not expected that these be done all at once).

CHAPTER 14

Lecturing for Student Learning

The lecture has been around for close to 1,000 years, often closely resembling in delivery what it looked like nearly a millennium ago. Our world outside the classroom, however, has changed a great deal. With respect to teaching, until about 500 years ago, the spoken word was about the only way to transmit knowledge to those who needed to learn it. It did work, but it was not terribly efficient. If one knowledgeable person informs five people, each with a quill and scroll or a really good memory, that information does spread, but at a slow pace. Information exchange went through its first real transformation when Gutenberg got his press going in 1493. Individuals no longer needed to seek out a knowledgeable person; they could get a copy of a book and have the information right in their hands. As books became accessible, there were those who questioned if it would mean the end of the lecture: "Lectures were once useful, but now when all can read, and books are so numerous, lectures are unnecessary" (Boswell, 1904/1791, p. 401). Yet, people kept lecturing and learners flocked to hear them.

In the late 1980s, another transformation in education was occurring. The internet was taking off, which meant not only that individuals could get information faster than when it was in print but that it was possible to easily communicate and share information with other knowledgeable people. Publications began to appear suggesting that we should move from lecturing to experiential learning (Van Eynde & Spencer, 1988). Yet, people kept on lecturing.

In 1992, the first smartphone was invented. Many individuals could look information up as soon as they had a question, on a device they held in their hands and nearly anywhere they were. Online learning exploded and technology just kept getting better. In 2021, artificial intelligence was being fine-tuned that could customize and adapt content based on the learners' facial expressions, gestures, and posture (Kulikowski, 2021). And, you guessed it, lecture is still an important part of the college landscape. There will continue to be calls for the end of lecture, but as we point out in this chapter, lecture still has its place as an effective teaching strategy, when done correctly.

IT ISN'T LECTURE VERSUS ACTIVE LEARNING

There is a well-publicized ongoing battle between the lecture and active learning. Articles abound with titles like "Is Lecturing Always Unethical?" (Handelsman, 2011) and "Lectures Are Not Just Boring, They're Ineffective, Too, Study Finds" (Bajak, 2014). Pick up nearly any higher education publication and you'll find articles praising active learning and making claims that lectures are unethical, boring, and ineffective. The problem is that research isn't actually making these claims.

The active learning versus lecture debate really got rolling in the 1990s. The American Association of Higher Education had a conference in 1996 with the overall theme of "Taking Learning Seriously," Barr and Tagg (1995) published an article urging higher education to move from teaching to learning, and King's (1993) now famous phrase "from sage on the stage to guide on the side" entered the lexicon. These works set up a strong push to stop focusing on teaching (i.e., lecturing) and instead focus on learning (i.e., students working in groups).

The statement "active learning is more effective than lecturing" came from this movement and is likely the best-known phrase in all of education. Most individuals fail to stop and think critically about that statement and how the research would be done to collect the data to support that statement. If we wish to compare active learning to lecture, there would need to be many all-lecture courses and many all-active/engaged learning courses. However, when we look closer at the methodology of the studies in this area, we discover that although there are many class sessions that are "all lecture," it is much more challenging to find "all-active-learning" classrooms. So, the researchers and those comparing the studies (Freeman et al., 2014; Hake, 1998) set a criterion whereby there could be some lecture in the active learning group of studies and those would all be in the category of active learning. This begs the question, how much lecture could be in a classroom and still have researchers count it as "active learning"? Freeman et al. (2014) coded active learning as "intensities ranging from 10% to 100% of class time." Think about that. This study, a phenomenally important, heavily cited meta-analysis, classified a session as active learning if there were 5 minutes of an in-class worksheet or a clicker question in a 50-minute class session. That means this is not lecture versus active learning; it is all-lecture learning versus lecture plus active learning (Zakrajsek, 2018).

That means the major research findings to date have not been that active learning is more effective than lecture, but rather that adding active and engaged strategies to the lecture is more effective than classes that are all lecture. This also means that the data do not indicate that lectures are bad or don't work. Lectures lose some effectiveness if you lecture all of the time or lecture poorly. That said, the research does not say lectures are bad (Zakrajsek, 2018).

Lectures can be very effective, both in conveying information, but also as a method to set up an effective active-learning activity. That may be one reason that the lecture, around for nearly 1,000 years, remains the single most used teaching strategy (Smith & Valentine, 2012).

WHEN LECTURES WORK AND OTHER LECTURE CONSIDERATIONS

The lecture is simply too large of a concept to say that it is either effective or it is not. How would you respond to the question, Are books effective? Are movies effective? Is food healthy? There are just too many variables; an overall evaluation is not possible. Fortunately, the research *is* clear that although lecturing for entire class periods is generally not effective, adding active learning in addition to a lecture *is* effective (Freeman et al., 2014; Hake, 1998; Miller et al., 2015).

When Lecture Works Well

There are certainly times that lectures work well or are even preferred (e.g., TED Talks, political speeches). There are those who claim that one cannot learn from lectures because they are passive, one-way communication. Stories, if uninterrupted are passive, one-way communication. Books, movies, TED talks, television programs are all one-way communication. It is certainly possible to learn from movies and books. Stories and tales have been used for centuries to pass information from generation to generation. All those mediums could be lectures, if the information were edited and handed to a faculty member. There is no doubt that lectures can be powerful given the right conditions.

Knowing when to use the lecture is a skill you will develop as you gain more experience as an instructor. Drawing from Barkley and Major (2018), Harrington and Zakrajsek (2017), Major et al. (2021), and Svinicki and McKeachie (2013), the lecture works well when:

- Students need to understand core facts and knowledge quickly.
- The lecturer is very interested in the material.
- It would be dangerous to provide information in any other way (e.g., volatile compounds in a lab, or parents explaining to children why they should not play in the street).
- You want to model a problem-solving approach or a kind of higher-order thinking before asking your students to try it themselves.
- You want to give your students material not available in print or as a recording, such as a brief summary of background knowledge, the very latest findings, your own related research, or other material too advanced for students to understand on their own.
- You want to present a particular organization of the material that clarifies the structure of the reading, the course, or the field, or use a particular type of lecture (e.g., Socratic lecture or problem-based lecture).

- You want to add your personal viewpoint on the subject matter.
- You want to pique your students' curiosity and motivation to learn if your style is very expressive.
- You would like to give students brief segments of information through recordings, such as for a flipped classroom. Lecture length is appropriate for the material (e.g., fewer than 10 minutes for technical and dense information; 30 to 45 minutes for general overviews)
- You wish to bring in other points of view by having more than one lecturer.
- You have a short amount of time to convey a lot of information.
- You introduce new material, rather than material students (should have) read for homework

Student Attention-Span Limits

Nearly every time the topic of lectures comes up, it isn't too long before someone mentions attention spans. Collecting good data on attention spans has always been challenging. For example, Wilson and Korn (2007) conducted a literature review and noted methodological problems with the research on students' attention span and claimed that at the time we knew little that is reliable about the topic. Still, researchers have long noted very consistent patterns (Bligh, 2000; Bonwell & Eison 1991; Middendorf & Kalish, 1996): a lecture begins with a 5-minute settling-in period during which students are fairly attentive. This attentiveness extends another 5 to 10 minutes, and then at about 15 minutes into the lecture the students (as a group) have taken in about as much information as they can at that time or they are struggling to hold attention to the lecturer. Focus and note-taking increasingly drops after that first 15 minutes and until the last several minutes of the period, when they revive in anticipation of the end of class. The time about 10 to 15 minutes into the class period is the perfect time to change up teaching strategies. If you add an active learning strategy into your course at that 10- to 15-minute mark, you will be doing exactly what the research says is effective. You won't have stopped lecturing in the course; instead you will have switched to a series of minilectures, each followed by an active learning strategy. This is a strategy Crouch and Mazur (2001) repeatedly showed was extremely effective.

Posting Presentation Slides

It is common for students to ask instructors to post slides on the LMS before or after a live lecture. Many students claim that they benefit from downloading the lecture slides before class so they can listen more intently and write fewer of their own notes. Some contend that reading the notes and slides reinforces hearing them (Clark, 2008). Posting slides ahead of time is helpful for some, but makes learning more challenging for others. How deeply are students processing a lecture when they are just following along with prepackaged material? If they are not taking notes, they are not judging what is more or less important, translating the material into their own words, or distilling it down to an abbreviated version. In addition, with the slides in hand, the pressure to pay attention decreases. Not surprisingly, then, slides and handouts that duplicate the lecture presentation seem not to increase student learning or improve exam performance (Kinchin, 2006; Noppe, 2007). Also, unless you make every class more valuable than the documents you post, your live attendance and even participation are likely to drop (Young, 2004).

Therefore, think about what you wish to accomplish when you post your notes. If you do decide to post prior to class, the best document to post in advance is a *skeletal outline* of your lecture. Although you can create it in a presentation program, using a word-processed document is even better. Allow plenty of white space between major topics, and advise your students to print out the document and bring it to class for notetaking or, if laptops are allowed, they work on the Word file. It can also be while listening to your recorded lecture. It will enable them to follow your organization. In fact, skeletal notes are an effective

learning aid that works particularly well with lectures. Because skeletal notes improve note-taking, students perform better on tests, suggesting they learn more (Cornelius & Owen-DeSchryver, 2008; Miyatsu et al., 2018).

■ PREPARING AN EFFECTIVE LECTURE

Bligh (2000) lays out several organizational models for lectures, but they share the common ground summarized here.

Class Outcomes

First, determine your student learning outcomes for the class period or recording. What precisely do you want your students to learn to do? How will you express your outcomes to the class? If a lecture serves only one or two of the multiple objectives you have for the class, then it should fill only part of the period.

Overview

Whenever possible, limit a lecture or recording to one major topic. Some students find it difficult to pick up a lecture from one period to the next, and some need to see the big picture before any of the details and examples will make sense to them. Also lay out a time-content schedule, bearing in mind the two most common lecturing errors: trying to include too much material and delivering the material too fast. While you're lecturing, you will have to proceed slowly enough, including pausing after major points, for students to take notes. If anything, underbudget content.

To start planning your lecture, subdivide the major topic into 15- to 20-minute chunks. If you will lecture live, plan active learning strategies of 2 to 10 minutes between these chunks. Don't let class size deter you. Most of the break activities in this chapter can be—and have been—conducted in large lectures of hundreds of students as well as smaller classes. Finally, allow 2 to 5 minutes for a recap activity at the end.

Let us turn to the internal organization of your lecture. The skeleton for any lecture is the introduction, the body (and how it is organized), and the conclusion (McKeachie, 2002).

Introduction

For a class-long lecture, the ideal introduction has three parts, the order of which is really an aesthetic decision: (1) a statement that frames the lecture in the context of the course outcomes, (2) a statement reviewing and transitioning from the material covered in the previous class period, and (3) an attention grabber for the beginning of the class and the beginning of any new chunk of material. Effective attention grabbers include an intriguing question the lecture material will answer; a story or parable that illustrates the new subject matter of the day; a reel, YouTube clip, or some other social media; a reference to a current event or movie, a case or a problem that requires the lecture's information to solve; or a strong generalization that contradicts common thought. The idea is to draw in the class with surprise, familiarity, curiosity, or suspense. If you are not sure where to get good online clips, you can make an assignment for students to work together to find video clips. Just make them due one week before that material is to be covered in class and ask the students if they are okay with you using their clip and their names to open that block of material.

Body

The body is your presentation and explication of new material. It is within this section that you subdivide the major topic into minilectures, each of which should revolve around only one major point. There is no best logic to follow in organizing a minilecture except to keep it simple. You can choose from an array of options: deduction (theory to phenomena/examples); induction (phenomena/examples to theory); hypothesis testing (theory and literature to hypothesis to evidence); problem to solution; cause to effect; concept to application; familiar to unfamiliar; debate to resolution; a chronology of events (a story or process)—to name just some common possibilities.

Organizational Outline

Make whatever organization you select explicit to students. For instance, tell the class, "I am going to describe some common manifestations of dysfunctional family behavior and then give you a definition and general principles that apply to the phenomenon." In addition, furnish students with a skeletal outline of each lecture that they can print out and use to take notes. At the very least, provide a general outline of the main points of your lecture on the board or a slide to help students follow your logical flow.

Finally, try to integrate as many of these learning aids as you can:

- *Visuals.* As you plan the material, think about how you can convey or repackage it visually—in pictures, photographs, slides, graphic metaphors, diagrams, graphs, or concept or mind maps (spatial arrangements of concepts or stages linked by lines or arrows). Prepare these graphics for presentation to the class. Such visual aids facilitate almost everyone's learning (see Chapter 22).
- *Examples.* Think about illustrating abstract concepts and relationships with examples. Ideally these examples should be striking, vivid, current, common in everyday life, and related to students' experiences (past, present, or future). Making them humorous also helps students remember them.
- *Restatements.* Consider how you can restate each important point in two or three different ways—in scholarly terms, lay formal language, and informal language. Restatements not only demystify the material, making it more comprehensible, but they also build students' vocabulary and encourage their own paraphrasing of the material.

Conclusion

For learning purposes, the conclusion should be a 2- to 3-minute recap of the most important points in your lecture. It is too important to be rushed after the bell. As you recount the material through your recap, leave a few minutes to ask students some questions and allow them to ask questions when needed. It will help the recap if you tell students at the beginning of the class that there will be a recap at the end, so they should circle anything they feel is important and should be in the recap. The prospect of having to retrieve the material helps keep all students on their toes. The recap activity may take the form of an oral summary presented by one or more students, a free-recall writing exercise, or a quiz.

Whether graded or ungraded, a quiz at the end of the class period is a particularly effective means to ensure students retain more lecture content. Recall lecture's infamous forgetting curve: 38% of the material gone within minutes, 55% in 3–4 days, and 76% in 8 weeks. Now recall from Chapter 1 that people learn less by reviewing material and more from being tested or testing themselves on it, because the latter activities involve greater cognitive processing and practice retrieving (Brown et al., 2014; Dunlosky et al., 2013; Karpicke & Blunt, 2011; Roediger & Karpicke, 2006; Rohrer & Pashler, 2010; Winne & Nesbit, 2010).

Your Lecture Notes

Your lecture notes should be easy to read at a glance and as sketchy as you can handle. After all, you know the material, so all you need is a map showing your next conceptual destination. Therefore, consider laying out the lecture graphically in flowcharts, concept maps, tree diagrams, Venn diagrams, or network models, including any visual aids you plan to put on the board. Some instructors like to color-code their notes for quick visual reference. If a graphic organization does not appeal to you, make an outline of your lecture but be sure it contains only headings. In any case, write big and leave a lot of white space. Confine the words in your notes to key concepts and phrases, transitions to make explicit to the class, and directions to yourself (e.g., *board, pause, slide, survey class, ask class question, break activity 2—voltage problem*). The habit to avoid is writing out sentences (except direct quotes). When individuals get stressed, which can happen to anyone, during a lecture or presentation it is too easy to slip into a mode of reading the notes, which never goes well with students.

■ DELIVERING AN EFFECTIVE LECTURE

Delivering a lecture is a lot like giving a performance. Some individuals enjoy speaking to a group and draw energy from the experience, (extroverts) whereas other individuals manage the lecture period well but are exhausted afterwards (introverts). Regardless of your current level of comfort and ability, everyone can get better with practice and it takes practice to regularly find yourself teaching at your best. We should also not assume that those who are good on the stage are extroverted individuals. Glenn Close, Tom Hanks, Harrison Ford, and many other high-profile actors and actresses are reportedly very introverted, and they are all quite good on a stage. Because lecturing is a performance art, you may find it helpful to speak with a colleague in the theater department for suggestions. If done well, a lecture can be highly motivational. An expressive, enthusiastic instructor can ignite students' interest in the material. Do work at this skill because a reserved, boring presenter can easily douse students' interest. The platform skills that convey energy, dynamism, and charisma can be isolated (they are listed in Chapter 11) and learned. Public speaking courses and clubs help people develop and practice eye contact, effective verbal pacing and pausing, vocal quality and variety, facial expressions, gestures and movements, lectern and microphone use, visual aid display, and other skills to help you to become an effective presenter. Those who start out weak in these skills but work on them diligently can achieve impressive results within a year.

Don't dismiss such presentation techniques as mere acting. They have a powerful impact on students' motivation and learning, which can also have a positive impact on students' ratings. It's important to note that regardless of how good you are at lectures, students will learn more if you pair your minilectures with engagement strategies.

■ COMBINING LECTURE WITH ENGAGEMENT: THE INTERACTIVE LECTURE

Research on cognitive learning supports that after 10–15 minutes of lecture, most students need to do something with that new information or it will be lost. An active learning break is also a great, proactive opportunity to make sure that students aren't lost. During these sessions, students should be in some way interacting with the material (and often one another) for brief, controlled periods of time. Some individuals call these "lecture breaks," but they are not breaks so much as times to solidify the information (Harrington & Zakrajsek, 2017). With the appropriate activities, you can help your students achieve the highest-level cognitive outcomes. Ideally the active learning strategies should give them the opportunity to practice performing your learning outcomes or working with the lecture content you just gave. How well they complete the activity task should illustrate their level of understanding and give you next steps. After all, you shouldn't move onto the next chunk of material unless most of your students comprehend the current chunk.

To keep the activities focused and controlled, carefully time-control them. Inform your students that they will have X (a number you provide) number of minutes to complete the assigned activity. Set a timer and stop the activity when time is up. Not everyone has to finish. With practice, and when

students understand you will hold them to the time, they will get more efficient. Also, circulate around the classroom to get a sense of where students are on the task, keep them on task, and answer any procedural questions.

If you select the right activity, it will work well in any size class. For example, in larger classes, having students work with their neighbors (in ad hoc pairs or triads) is quicker and easier than having them get into preorganized small groups unless you arrange for group members to sit together during every class.

Expect the classroom to get noisy. Learning, especially when going well, is often loud. After their activity time is up, you can bring even the largest class to silence within seconds by taking this tip from cooperative learning researchers. Let your students know that you will raise your hand when the time is up. Tell your students that as soon as they see any hand up, they should stop talking and raise their hand. Using this technique at teaching conferences, we have seen a room of a thousand participants, deep into an active learning exercise, become quiet within 10 seconds.

Example Active Learning Strategies

Following are some commonly used teaching strategies, along with the number of minutes each typically takes. They come mainly from Angelo and Cross (1993), Barkley and Major (2022), Cuseo (2002), Harrington and Zakrajsek (2017), Major et al. (2021), and informal collegial exchanges. The first set is comprised of individual active learning strategies, where the student is actively engaged in independent work, followed by a class discussion. The second set involve group-based activities (groups of two or more students), where groups typically come to an answer or resolution and then some groups share. Sharing, individually or in groups, may be volunteer, your calling on members, or random assignments. Let these examples serve as your inspiration to conceive and experiment with your own innovations.

Individual Active-Learning Strategies

The following strategies are designed for students to be actively involved with the material without collaborating with other students. This allows students to engage with the material that enhances learning.

Solve-a-Problem. After a minilecture, students compare answers with a neighbor to see if they arrived at the same answer. Time: 1–3 minutes for problem-solving, depending on the problem's complexity, plus 1–2 minutes for surveying responses.

Periodic Free-Recall. Students put away their lecture notes and write down the most important one, two, or three points of your minilecture, as well as any questions they have. The first two times you do this, give specific instructions. After that, just telling about a free recall activity will do. Again, this activity makes students review and mentally process your minilecture content. Time: 3 minutes, plus 1–2 minutes to answer students' questions.

Active Listening Checks. Lovett (2008) built on the periodic free-recall activity, adding that students hand in their three most important points, and then you reveal what you intended as most important. Lovett (2008), the researcher who devised this activity, uses it to improve her students' listening and note-taking skills. From the first time she did this in class to the third time, the percentage of students who correctly identified her three most important points rose from 45% to 75%. Time: 2–3 minutes.

Reflection/Reaction Paragraph. Students individually write out their affective reaction to the minilecture content (or video or demonstration). Ask a few volunteers to share. Time: 3–4 minutes.

Correct the Error. Using immediate minilecture content, students correct an error that you have intentionally made in a statement, equation, or visual. The error may be an illogical or inaccurate statement, premise, inference, prediction, or implication.

Grouped Active Learning Strategies

The following strategies are designed for students to work collaborating with other students. This allows students to engage with others in class to learn other perspectives, to get clarity when needed, and the opportunity to explain concepts and check with others to see if those explanations are sounding correct.

Think(Write)-Pair-Share. In this very common activity, give a prompt and enforce that students are to think or write for 1 minute in response to the prompt. Students then turn to a neighbor and share with each other for 2 minutes. For the final step, pairs of students share with the class. There are many variations on this strategy. Time: 6 minutes.

Practice Test Item. Put a multiple-choice item, preferably a conceptual or application type, related to your minilecture on the board or a slide, and give four response options. Ask students to share if they selected a, b, c, or d. You can also ask students to rate their confidence level in their answer by using fingers to rate confidence from 1 (very low) to 5 (very high). Then give them a minute to convince their neighbor of their answer, and survey their responses a second time. This activity makes students apply and discuss your minilecture content while it's fresh in their minds, and it immediately informs you of how well they have understood the material. You can then clarify misconceptions before proceeding to new material. Time: 3 minutes, plus 1–3 minutes to debrief and answer questions.

Support a Statement. Provide the class with a statement from your minilecture. Have students work in groups of three or four to garner support for a statement you present: conclusion, inference, theory, opinion, or description. In addition to your minilecture, sources of support may be the readings or evidence they generate on their own.

Listen, Recall, and Ask: Then Pair, Compare, and Answer. Students only listen to your minilecture, no note-taking allowed. Then they open their notebooks and write down all the major points they can recall, as well as any questions they have. Instruct students to leave generous space between the major points they write down. Finally, they pair off with their neighbor and compare lecture notes, filling in what they may have missed and answering one another's questions. Again, this activity makes students test themselves, and practice retrieval of your lecture content. Time: 3–4 minutes for individual note writing plus 2–4 minutes for pair fill-ins and question answering.

Quick Case Study. Students debrief a short case study (1–4 paragraphs, ideally short enough to be displayed on a slide; addressed further in Chapter 18) that requires them to apply your minilecture content to a realistic, problematic situation. You might ask specific questions for students to answer or use the standard debriefing formula: What is the problem? What is the remedy? What is the prevention? Students can work individually or, better yet, in pairs or groups of up to six. Time: 3–5 minutes, depending on the case length and complexity, plus 5–10 minutes for class exchange and discussion.

You will find still more options for lecture breaks in Chapter 10 (on group learning), Chapter 19 (on teaching students how to learn), Chapter 24 (on feedback), and resources such as the book, *Teaching for Learning: 101 Intentionally Designed Educational Activities to Put Your Students on the Path to Success* (Major et al., 2021).

Surveying Student Responses

When you develop a lecture activity around a multiple-choice item—or, for that matter, a true-false item—follow up by surveying your students' responses before and after they discuss their answers with their neighbors. The fact that students commit to an answer makes them more interested in finding out what the correct response is, and the results furnish you with valuable feedback on their understanding.

You can collect those responses in several ways. First, you can ask for a show of hands for each response. Although this option is very simple, it has its weaknesses. In a large class, you can't know for sure whether everyone is participating, and as you don't have time to count all the hands, you may get only a vague measure of the distribution of responses. You have no record of these responses either. One additional problem is that responses are not anonymous, so students may mindlessly change their answers just to follow the crowd.

Second, you can distribute four or five cards as small as 5-by-8 inches (you can use heavy cover stock) of different colors to each student, where each color signifies an answer—for example, red for a, blue for b, yellow for c, and green for d. Then have students put up the color of card that signifies their response choice. With this alternative, you can get a somewhat better idea of your participation rate and response distribution, especially if you have students put the stock directly in front of their faces. If you see a face, you can coax the student to make a choice. With students' faces covered by their choices, the answers become more anonymous as well. The only problem is that you have no record of the responses.

Third, you can use clickers, more formally known as personal or classroom response systems, or their online equivalent, such as Poll Everywhere or Socrative with students' mobile devices. You could also use Kahoot! and turn the responding into a game. Check with your department and institutional technology to find out if your campus has a campus-wide site license in the event that your choice charges for use. With clickers, students simply push a button indicating their response or type in their answer, and a receiver connected to your computer picks up the signals and immediately tallies all the answers, displaying them in a histogram or word cloud on your monitor. You then have the option of revealing these results to the class.

Of course, you have to learn the technology, but you can tell exactly who isn't participating (and coax them to respond) and exactly how the responses distribute, and you can archive the survey results. The process is completely anonymous to the class, so only you know how each student is responding. This also means you can take a confidential survey on sensitive attitudinal or behavioral topics. If you think students may be concerned about your knowing their individual responses, you can turn off your receiver's identification function and tell them that you have done so.

With the polling software, students similarly click on or type in their answers, and you get an appropriate distribution graphic on the web or on a presentation slide. You can take anonymous or respondent-identified polls and also archive the results. Bear in mind, however, the warning in Chapter 4 about letting students use their mobile phones in class. They might click in their answer and immediately switch to their preferred social media experience.

The research on the impact of active learning strategies mixed with minilectures—posing a multiple-choice question and surveying student responses before and after a short pair discussion—has been conducted on student response systems. Compared to a traditional lecture, incorporating clicker breaks enhances student learning substantially, often by an entire letter grade on tests (Gauci et al., 2009; Mazur Group, 2008; Reay et al., 2008; more references at Bruff, 2016). The good news is that lower-tech survey methods, such as least colored cards, can produce learning gains just as impressive as clickers (Lasry, 2008). The payoff comes from the active learning activity itself, not the technology. Therefore, the vast majority of the learning-relevant research involving clickers applies to hand-raising and colored cards as well.

The literature reports that having students respond regularly in class using clickers or some other student response system increases class attendance, broadens class participation to literally the entire class, multiplies the chances for both student-to-student and student-to-faculty interaction, affords students regular practice in

higher-order thinking, teaches them to critically examine and defend their thinking, provides formative assessment of learning, provides instant feedback to students and the instructor on their understanding and short-term retention, heightens students' attention and alertness in class (even early and late in the day), enhances their engagement in the material, and develops their metacognition, allowing for mindful and self-regulated learning (Bergtrom, 2006; Crouch & Mazur, 2001; Deal, 2007; Mazur Group, 2008; Radosevich et al., 2008; more references at Bruff, 2016). You can also use this technique to assess students' prior knowledge and launch discussion.

Clickers also offer additional opportunities to take attendance instantly; grade student participation based on correct and incorrect responses; play academic games; and give objective-item quizzes. Although some faculty members use clickers for quizzes and high-stakes exams, this is not the purpose they were meant to serve, and it's a risky proposition. They are best used for learning and formative feedback.

Of course, potential benefits depend on the questions, which best require higher-order thinking and problem-solving skills. For example, they may ask students to choose an example of a principle. They may survey an opinion, pose an ethical dilemma, have students classify a concept, or challenge them to make a prediction. If clickers collect the responses anonymously, the questions can address controversial or personal matters, such as students' opinions on hot-button issues or private experiences that illustrate a theory, principle, or finding (Bruff, 2009).

As this lecture break technique started in large physics class, the STEM fields (science, technology, engineering, and mathematics) already have large online collections of well-tested questions and other resources for using clickers (e.g., www.cwsei .ubc.ca/resources/clickers.htm#questions). Other resources for a wider array of disciplines are available at Bruff (2016) and http://cft.vanderbilt.edu/docs/classroom-response-system-clickers-bibliography.

■ TEACHING STUDENTS TO TAKE GOOD NOTES

Because an important part of learning from lectures is taking notes, this last section of this chapter is devoted to helping ensure students are getting the best educational experience possible, which includes taking notes in class. The good news is that students do see the value of taking notes in lecture courses. This is evident in the number of students who report taking notes. Most students (86.8%) report putting a lot of effort into taking notes in their classes (Witherby & Tauber, 2019). Notes are primarily taken by hand (85.1%), with only about 19% of students taking notes using a laptop. When presentation slides are given to students, Witherby & Tauber (2019) found that only 15.3% of the students reported taking no notes.

An issue that needs to be taken into consideration when it comes to note-taking is to ensure students understand the value of notes and methods to take good notes. Much like working in groups and studying, students are rarely taught to take notes prior to coming to college. The good news is that it will not take you much time to make a significant difference in the note-taking ability of your students.

Teaching Note-Taking

After selling students on note-taking, acquaint them with some note-taking systems (Bligh, 2000; Chen, 2019; Ellis, 2006; Major et al., 2021). Show them how to make a formal outline with first-level headings, second-level headings, and so on. (Points of equal importance or generality should start at the same distance from the left margin.) Tell them about the Cornell system: drawing a line down each page one-third in from the left, taking lecture notes on the right two-thirds of the page, and reserving the left one-third for reviewing activities, such as condensing the notes and rewriting the most critical content. Display or hand out your own lecture notes just once or twice early in the term to provide students a model of how they should be taking

notes. You might also teach your students how to reorganize their notes into concept maps, mind maps, graphic organizers, matrices, and diagrams so they can take advantage of the learning and memory benefits of visual representation. As an engaged learning strategy, teach students note-taking pairs, where two students work together by comparing notes at pauses during the lecture. Finally, teach students the value of organizing notes after class, preferably immediately after class, and augmenting notes in any area not understood. No one strategy is equally effective for everyone, so advise students to try out at least a couple.

In addition, explain to your students that the real art of taking notes is putting the information into their own words. They should avoid mindless transcription, which has been shown to have limited value (Dunlosky et al., 2013). Students should avoid writing complete sentences unless the specific wording is crucial. Advise them to take notes sparingly in longhand, dropping all unnecessary words and recording only the words and symbols needed to recall the idea they signify later. There was a much-discussed study pertaining to note-taking by hand versus on a laptop (Mueller & Oppenheimer, 2014). The experiment demonstrated that students who took notes by hand learned more than did those who took notes by computer. The results have not held up to replication (Morehead et al., 2019). A potential rationale for the finding comes from cognitive psychology that putting information into your own words leads to better recall of the information. It appears that students who take notes by computer are more likely to key in everything said, whereas those taking notes by the slower method of handwriting had to distill the major issue and record that. Share with your students that it is always best to distill what they are hearing to the most important element and to write general ideas rather than everything said.

Finally, share with your class some proven note-taking pointers, such as those listed in Exhibit 14.1 (Bligh, 2000; Ellis, 2006; Kiewra, 2005; Mueller & Oppenheimer, 2014; Svinicki, 2014).

Exhibit 14.1   Fifteen Tips for Taking Good Class Notes*

1. Arrive early to class. Review your notes from the previous class and the assigned readings. Ask your instructor to clarify anything that doesn't make sense from the notes taken in the prior class session.

2. Avoid cramming your notes or writing too small. Strive for easy readability. Leave a generous left margin for rewriting important words and abbreviated key content later.

3. Occasionally glance back over the last few lines of notes you have taken, and clarify any illegible letters, words, or symbols.

4. Make key words, important relationships, and conclusions stand out. Underline, highlight, box, or circle them, or rewrite them in the left margin.

5. Organize your notes according to your instructor's introductory, transitional, and concluding words and phrases, such as "the following three factors," "the most important consideration," "in addition to," "however," "on the other hand," "nevertheless," "by contrast," and "in conclusion." These phrases signal the structure of the lecture: cause and effect, relationships, comparisons and contrasts, exceptions, examples, shifts in topics, debates and controversies, and general conclusions.

6. Identify the most important points by watching for certain instructor cues: repetition, pauses, a slower speaking pace, a drop in pitch, a rise in interest or intensity, writing something on the board, showing a slide, a dramatic pause, and writing on the board.

7. Pay close attention to your instructor's body language, gestures, and facial expressions as well as vocal changes and movements around the room. Your instructor's subtlest actions punctuate and add meaning to the substance of the lecture.

8. Whenever possible, draw a picture, concept map, or diagram to organize and abbreviate the relationships in the lecture material. You may want to do this after a lecture. Almost everyone can recall a visual more easily than a written description.

9. Develop and use your own shorthand, such as abbreviations and symbols for common or key words—for instance, *btn* for "between," + for "and," *b/c* for "because," *rel* for "relationship," *df* or = for "definition," *cnd* for "condition," *nec* for "necessary" or "necessitates," *hyp* for "hypothesis," Δ for "change," *T4* for "therefore," + for "more," − for "less," ↑ for "increasing," ↓ for "decreasing;" → for "causes," ← for "is caused by," and two opposing arrows for "conflicts with."

10. Take notes quickly and at opportune times. Use your instructor's pauses, extended examples, repetitions, and lighter moments to record notes. Try to not be writing one thing when you need to be listening closely to another.

11. To help speed your note-taking, try different pens until you find an instrument that glides smoothly and rapidly for you.

12. If your instructor tends to speak or to move from point to point too quickly, politely ask them to slow down. You are probably the most courageous student of many others who cannot keep up either.

13. If you lose focus and miss part of a lecture, leave a space and ask a classmate, a TA, or your instructor to help you fill in the blank.

14. Separate your own comments and reactions from your lecture notes.

15. Review, edit, clarify, and elaborate your notes within 24 hours of the lecture, review the notes within 48 hours again, and again three weeks later, even if for just a few minutes. While reviewing, recite, extract, and rewrite the key concepts and relationships. The knowledge will become yours forever.

*Most of these tips also apply to taking notes on readings, videos, and podcasts.

MAKING THE LECTURE EFFECTIVE

A well-crafted lecture can be a student-centered and student-active learning experience. You can enliven minilectures with stimulating active learning activities, graphics, video clips, demonstrations, animations, and the like. Keep in mind that you are the expert in the course, and this material is easily retrieved when you need to use the information and it is also relatively easily applied to new situations. Finally, it is easy to learn new information when you have structures and ways to let the previous information help you. None of this is true for the novice. As a result, we have to help our student in their work to take good notes in our courses.

You can do a lot to help students take good lecture notes; these strategies have already been detailed in this chapter. Still, they are worth highlighting here. For starters, you can organize your lectures clearly and simply, giving each an introduction, a body, and a conclusion, and make the organization explicit in class. You can deliver your content using nonverbal cues (vocal variety, gestures, movement) to signal the most important points. You can chunk the content into minilectures, each making one major point, with student-active breaks between them. You can also schedule lecture breaks and end-of-class review activities that allow students to review, fill in, and revise their notes, individually or in pairs,

Furthermore, you can facilitate note-taking by teaching students to be better note-takers. Explain how the Cornell methods and skeletal outline notes work. Practice note-taking activities that give students practice in active listening, conceptual thinking, problem-solving, knowledge application, reflection, and retrieval of material—skills that encourage and enable academic success and lifelong learning. The skills they learn in your course will help them to learn more in your course. In addition, these skills are needed in nearly every course, and later in meetings at most jobs. Therefore, you are not just teaching a skill that will help them in your course. You are teaching them a skill that potentially will help them for life.

REFLECTION QUESTIONS

Reflection Question 14.1: This chapter supports the concept that lectures are more effective when paired with active learning strategies, rather than active learning is more effective than lectures. What is your position regarding these two claims? Is the material in the chapter convincing, or is more information needed? Explain.

Reflection Question 14.2: Should faculty members teach students how to take notes? Explain why we should or should not take time to teach students these skills.

Concept Into Practice: Identify one active learning strategy, either from this chapter or another source, that could augment one of your lectures. Make sure that the activity pairs well with your current class strategies and, most importantly, that it helps students achieve a learning outcome.

CHAPTER 15

Leading Effective Discussions

I n education, all discussions include talking, but not all talking is an *academic discussion*. Discussion is a productive exchange of viewpoints, a collective exploration of issues involving higher-order thinking. For it to bear fruit and not turn into a free-association, free-for-all bull session, or an argument, you as the instructor must chart its course and content, steer it in the right direction, and keep hot air from blowing it off course. Using the backward design approach, you don't need to know exactly what will be said, but you should have an idea about what you hope to have accomplished by the end of the course. Following the discussion, in what way will your students be different? One of the positive aspects of the discussion teaching method is that you can plan the general course, but nobody knows for sure how you will get there. Even after teaching for many years, you never know when something wonderful and unexpected will happen in a discussion. Your challenge is to strike that delicate balance between structure and flow.

■ WHEN TO CHOOSE DISCUSSION

Well planned and well managed, discussion can help your students achieve a wide variety of learning outcomes. In addition to our extended use of discussion through the years, many researchers have studied the impact of discussions in higher education and have uncovered many benefits to the discussion as a way of teaching (Brookfield & Preskill, 2005, 2016; Dallimore et al., 2008; Gilmore & Schall, 1996; Herman & Nilson, 2018; Howard, 2015; Kustra & Potter, 2008):

- Examining and possibly changing attitudes, beliefs, values, and behaviors
- Exploring unfamiliar ideas open-mindedly
- Deep, conceptual learning
- Active listening
- Exposure to diverse perspectives
- Critical thinking
- Problem-solving

- Communicating orally
- Synthesizing and integrating ideas
- Transferring knowledge to new situations
- Retaining the material
- Enhanced interest in the subject matter
- Developing inclusive language skills

The problem-solving skills that discussion fosters apply not only to math problems but also to all other kinds of solution-oriented tasks, whether they call for one correct answer, one best answer, or divergent thinking, or convergent thinking. Such tasks include resolving ethical dilemmas; designing a research project; explaining deviations from expected results; writing a computer program; solving a case study; evaluating various positions on an issue; analyzing a piece of literature; and developing approaches to tackling real-world social, political, economic, technological, and environmental problems. Because discussion models democratic values, it often promotes civic engagement and good citizenship (Brookfield & Preskill, 2005; Siegel-Stechler, 2021). You may also choose to use discussions along with lectures. This is done often enough that one type of lecture is called the *discussion lecture* (Barkley & Major, 2018; Harrington & Zakrajsek, 2017; Major et al. 2021). With this approach you weave lectures among the prompts used to stimulate discussion.

■ SETTING THE STAGE FOR DISCUSSION AT THE START OF YOUR COURSE

One of the first decisions you must make is to what extent you expect all students to speak up in class discussions. Think carefully about *why* you want students to speak up, and make it clear to the students that speaking up is for their benefit, too. Consider the following:

- What mechanism you will put in place to help students participate (e.g., warm calling, texting)?

- What teaching strategies will you use (snowball, circle of voices)?
- Should each student speak during each class period?
- Can you keep quiet while offering ways for students to stay engaged?

Once you decide how much and how students should be required to speak, it is helpful to think through the community you will build and active learning strategies you will use to get there. The more students feel part of a community, the easier it will be for them to participate in a discussion. Strategies might include:

- Think-Pair-Share and Polling: Allow a bit more time and low-pressure, smaller group or even anonymous participations before talking with the whole class.
- One-Minute Pause: Ask everyone to think about a prompt for one minute without discussion. Then at the one-minute mark (or whatever time you deem), ask for student volunteers to offer a response.
- Alternate Communication Styles: Some students have a very difficult time speaking in front of the entire class or cultural restraints against doing so, especially in a predominantly White setting (Walls & Hall, 2017). Consider allowing everyone to email what they would have said in class, and fold those comments into the next discussion
- Keep Focus: Some students have learned that they only need to look attentive in class while relying on talkative peers to keep the discussion going (Howard, 2015).

Deciding to have a discussion as an integral class activity, even if not a primary one, should be done with thought and planning. If set up well, you can support students, help them to develop skills as strong classroom speakers, and learn a great deal in the process. There are a few things that are consistently helpful. First, start out with a discussion on the first day of class. You can even discuss the syllabus. That will set the tone and let students know you are serious about the discussion method. Second, let students know the primary ground rule: everyone's participation is expected, their words will be given respectful consideration, and there will be ways for everyone to participate. Third, let students know that discussion will play a key role in your course, explaining your reasons for using discussion—for instance, how the research supports its effectiveness in helping them achieve your learning outcomes. Fourth, ensure class discussions relate to other parts of the course, such as readings, written assignments, and tests. The goal is to have an integrated course, not a course that has discussion added as a strategy. When you can, build homework, quizzes, and tests around both the readings and the discussions about them. Point out these connections to students.

Finally, explain the true nature of discussion as the expression of different, legitimate points of view. Respectful disagreement enriches the learning experience. In fact, college is all about hearing, trying on, and appraising different perspectives. Students should listen actively, respectfully, and carefully to every opinion put on the table, evaluate the evidence for and against that claim, and be prepared with evidence to defend their own positions. Overall, it is critical that they understand that their contributions are truly valuable.

"Education is the ability to listen to almost anything without losing your temper or your self-confidence."
—Robert Frost

ENCOURAGING PARTICIPATION

If you decide that all students should participate in class discussions in some way, the next challenge is to actually get participation. If you can get broad and active participation, most of the other problems that can appear in a discussion—domination by one or two students, topical tangents, silent sectors of the room—simply disappear. The recommendations in this chapter are designed to help ensure that all your students will come to a discussion prepared, comfortable, and willing to contribute.

Giving All Students the Opportunity to Participate

There is a deep bias in education when it comes to answering questions and participating in class discussions. Students who are fast-talking, risk-taking extroverts receive the most attention (Zakrajsek, 2021). Hands shoot up or voices start talking over each other right away. Indeed, tension in the class begins to build after only 3 to 4 seconds without a response. For most of us, waiting 4 seconds for an answer feels like an eternity, but for questions that require thought, that is not much time at all. The students must hear the question for the first time, think about how they might respond to the question, and then determine how to begin their response. Indeed, if a person takes only 3 to 4 seconds to initiate that response, we doubt whether it is a well-thought-out response.

Some students *can* formulate a response quickly and raise their hand, eager to share, but they are by far the minority. Some of the quieter students in the class may well be introverts, but not all quiet students are introverts (Zakrajsek, 2017). There are many reasons students may not regularly participate in the classroom, and there are different strategies to make it more possible for them to participate. A nonexhaustive list of reasons includes: shyness, English as second language, previously embarrassed responding in a class discussion, peer pressure to not participate, intimidating nonverbal cues from faculty members, lack of knowledge/understanding of the material, a disinterest in the course, a generalized fear of failure. What if instead of asking, "How can we *make* all students participate" we ask, "How can we *help* all students participate"? Consider the following strategies:

- Allow 30 seconds for thinking before anyone can respond.
- Pair students to talk for a minute or two and then ask for responses from pairs.
- Students can tweet their responses with a unique hashtag for the class and then respond to the tweets.
- Use in-class polling such as Poll Everywhere and Socrative.
- Students can work in small groups on a problem and then respond.
- Ask a question at the end of class, and students email short responses, which become a focus for discussion next class.
- Work on nonverbal cues when asking questions.
- Use affirmations for good answers and be sincere in noting attempts when incorrect.
- Use a short quiz or other method to induce students to come to class having read assigned material.
- Announce in class that anyone uncomfortable speaking out in class should come by your office to find a way for them to participate.

Techniques such as walking around the room to increase pressure, cold-calling, and other techniques designed to encourage students to participate in a class discussion can certainly be used and are very effective when done well. That said, in an inclusive classroom it is imperative that we consider how challenging it may be for a student to say anything in front of 30, 50, 100, or hundreds of colleagues. We are used to it, but it is terrifying for some.

Making Participation Part of the Course Grade

You may or may not wish to include the quality and quantity of class participation in your final grading scheme. Doing so will likely increase the number of your students coming to class prepared to participate (Dallimore et al., 2006). It is important to ensure your system is clear in your syllabus and discuss it with your students as part of your first-day presentation. Clearly note the different ways students may participate in discussions. Also explain your conception of adequate quality and quantity. To help articulate your standards, put the phrase "class participation grading rubric" in a search engine and peruse the examples your colleagues use.

Keeping track of who participates and the quality of their participation is no small matter. You may have students display a colorful sticky note on the front of their desk for each of their contributions, or you may have index cards with students' names. There are many systems. Find one that you feel will work for you, and make it clear on the first day of the semester. To head off uneven participation, especially the problem of a couple of dominant students, you can limit the number of contributions each student can make in each class before everyone has spoken. You could give students a participation point for each of their first two comments but no more points for any subsequent ones (Lang, 2008).

Consider the class level, size, and your ability to assign points fairly across students when deciding the weight to give participation in the final grade. First-year students may feel comfortable with 20% of the course grade based on class participation in discussions in a class of 20 to 25 students but may find it unreasonably stressful in a class of 45 to 50 students. More advanced students should be able to handle a higher percentage weight even in a larger class. You might have students vote on the percentage (give them options) and follow the majority rule.

Keep in mind as you develop a participation component to your course that some students will find it much easier than others to participate in class. Some students, upon reading that participation is 10% of the grade, will immediately assume those points are gone and look through the rest of the syllabus to see if they can pass the course. Before immediately jumping to the opinion that discussion or not participating in a class discussion is their choice, be mindful that some are terrified to speak out. Imagine you signed up for a course and found out a small portion of the grade was contingent on you doing something that terrified you. It is reasonable to expect everyone to contribute. With consideration you can likely identify a variety of ways to make that happen.

Setting Ground Rules for Participation

How do you foresee conducting class discussions? One important decision is whether you will call on raised hands or cold-call students by random selection, such as shuffling and drawing index cards with their names or by choosing students who haven't spoken recently.

The first method keeps the class relaxed but participants in such situations tend to be a few verbal individuals monopolizing the floor and most students playing passive wallflowers. You may even wind up inadvertently reinforcing social inequities unless you make special efforts to draw out and validate your underrepresented students. The second method, cold-calling by random selection, obviously ensures broad participation and motivates preparation. Researchers have found that when the rate of cold-calling is high in the course, more students voluntarily answered questions (Dallimore et al., 2012). Another option is a combination. You might first ask for a few volunteers and then later in the class period cold-call on students. The volunteers serve as a model for how to answer questions or bring up points of discussion. In addition, students may well realize that it is better to volunteer early in the class period and answer something they want to answer rather than being called on to answer a question they may not know later in the class session.

With the variety of methods to allow students to participate, cold-calling may never be necessary. That said, if you do employ that technique, it is best to set an escape hatch, perhaps by permitting students to pass on answering a question. It is demoralizing to the class and counterproductive to the discussion to badger, belittle, or otherwise put a person on the spot for not having a comment when you demand it. Although it's possible they are not prepared, that is not the only reason a person might refuse to participate. They may simply agree with other recent remarks, have no questions at the time, be having a bad day and not feel like talking, or they may be petrified to say anything at that moment. To cover these possibilities, inform your class that you will occasionally accept responses such as, "I don't want to talk right now," "Will you please call on me later?" or provide them a hand gesture that indicates they prefer not to respond at that time.

You should make it clear, however, that you will not tolerate certain negative behaviors: purposefully steering the discussion off-track; trying to degenerate it into a comedy act; instigating an inappropriate debate; personally attacking a fellow student; displaying one's temper; asking wheedling, argumentative, or loaded questions; or engaging in more general uncivil classroom behaviors. It is often helpful to lead a class discussion on what the rules of civility should be during discussions (Kustra & Potter, 2008). Ask the students to recount the best and the worst discussions in their educational experience. How did people treat each other? What behaviors induced the silence, anger, or fear of others? From this point, the class can generate their own ground rules, and you can supplement them as necessary.

One final rule to be sure students understand is that "the only stupid question is the one not asked." Some students are downright terrified by the prospect of looking stupid or foolish to you or their peers. They appreciate being told that you will welcome all questions and ensure that they are answered. Assure them that if a premise or aspect of what is asked is wrong it will be corrected, but it will be done politely and respectfully, the same as should be done in any exchange.

SKILLFUL DISCUSSION MANAGEMENT

There is nothing more important than to keep firmly in mind that you are the discussion *facilitator*. Some faculty members say, "This isn't *my* class, we are all equal in this class." It is helpful to get students involved, but as the instructor of record, you are responsible for the course. You are still the one assigning grades, selecting topics, and facilitating learning experiences so that each and every student gets the best experience possible. You can certainly share the space and the learning, but you are the expert, and it is your responsibility to help them to learn, and their responsibility that they themselves learn.

Some believe that those facilitating discussions simply walk into a classroom and students will want to talk. Facilitating class discussions that bring about higher-order thinking that transfers to other situations is complex and typically has a carefully calculated beginning structure. After identifying good source material for the students to read, developing good discussion prompts, creating a quiz or holding students in some way accountable for coming to class prepared, and determining a general structure with alternatives for the class session—you are ready to facilitate. The process of facilitating can begin before class. Arriving a little early and casually chatting with students as they arrive allows you the opportunity to get a sense of their mood and can loosen them up for dialogue. If there is a minilecture prior to starting the discussion, you will need to be ready for the transition. If the entire class period is discussion, then you are set to start the discussion and add to it when necessary. Once the discussion takes off, your role largely involves directing traffic. That does not mean you are passive. Good facilitators are keeping an eye on all students, helping those who wish to speak but can't find a place to enter the conversation, noting those who feel slighted by a comment, or nudging discussions back on track with a well-placed remark. Facilitating a discussion can be exhausting, but when students come up with insights based on the readings you assigned, especially if the energy drives a quiet student to participate, discussion can be one of the most exciting ways to teach.

Facilitating discussions means you may take on one of any number of roles, depending on the circumstances. You may briefly assume the role of: coach, moderator, host, listener, observer, information provider, presenter, counselor, recorder, monitor, instigator, navigator, translator, peacemaker, and summarizer. During contentious exchanges, you may even find yourself playing referee. Congratulate yourself when students start speaking to each other directly rather than through you. Your goal is to make yourself superfluous. The next several sections list ways to achieve that goal with the greatest amount of student participation possible.

Ready the Class and Ignite the Exchange

Students come to class with all manner of things on their mind, and the subject matter of your course may not rank among them. So before launching into a discussion, warm up the class to the topic of the day (Brookfield & Preskill, 2005; Jones, 2008). To start out:

- Put up a written outline/road map for the discussion/class period.
- Ask students to summarize the previous class discussion(s).
- Ask a few recall questions on the readings.
- Ask for students' emotional reactions to the readings.
- Refer to a well-known current event or an experience from your previous class, such as a video, demonstration, or role play.
- Pose a highly controversial question.
- Assign students to write a response to a prompt.
- Have students brainstorm what they already know about a topic or what outcomes they anticipate of a situation or an experiment.
- Take the role of counterpointer and argue in favor of a position that you know that some students will argue against. While you're

assuming the role, wear something or have a signal so students know when you are playing the "devil's advocate" role.

Lower Social Barriers and Reduce Shyness

We may find it easy to speak in front of a class, but some students rarely engage in that behavior. Here are some ways to make speaking out in class less stressful for them:

- Arrange seats in a circle.
- Have short icebreakers across multiple days early in semester.
- Have students fill out index cards the first day, letting them share any information they'd like about their student and personal lives.
- Call students by name.
- Help students learn their classmates' names; use name tags or tents.
- Casually chat with students before and after class.
- Get to know students through office hour appointments. (Frequently pass around a sign-up sheet.)
- Refer back to the previous contributions of students (by name) during discussions.
- Frequently break your class into small groups to solve problems and answer complex questions.
- Extend students' participation by having them post to a class blog, wiki, discussion board, or chat.
- Have students jot down answers and reactions to complex questions before calling on anyone.
- See quiet students outside of class and ask how it might be more comfortable for them to participate in the discussions.

Motivate Students to Prepare

You must take some measures to ensure that students have something to contribute or most will not do the assigned work:

- Include meaningful discussion participation in the course grade (10–30% or as bonus points).
- Distribute study guide questions on the readings.
- Give a quiz over the material (alert students there will be a quiz).
- Have a random-selection "calling-on" policy. This technique works especially well when you provide study questions on the readings in advance.
- Use some of the many reading compliance strategies in Chapter 21, such as requiring students to take reading notes, write answers to study guide questions, or submit written questions on readings; or giving daily quizzes on the readings; or setting up in-class games or simulations that require doing the readings to do well.
- Allow students to use their reading notes, answers to study questions, and the like to answer the discussion questions.

Motivate Students to Pay Attention

Too many students tune out of discussions because they fail to see the value of their peers' thoughts. Here are some ways to keep their attention on task:

- Advise students on how and why to takes notes on discussions.
- Write the major points made on the board.
- Include the content of discussions in assignments and exams (and say you will do this).
- Ask students to comment on and react to one another's contributions.
- In small-group discussions, randomly select a few groups to summarize their progress, answers, conclusions, and so on, and within each group randomly select the spokesperson.
- Regularly select a student to summarize the discussion at the end of class; then invite other students to add major points.
- Let students know each class will end with a short writing assignment—that is, ask students to write down (1) the most important things they learned during the class and (2) any questions or points they found the most confusing. Collect these to ensure students do them. They may be

graded or ungraded and may be handed back or not. You can also sample a few to see how students experienced the class and even use some as prompts for the next discussion.

Moderate to Maintain Momentum

As the facilitator, your goal is to say as little as possible once the discussion is rolling. If needed, you can be a resource, but your goal is to shift the spotlight from you to your students every chance you get. Methods to help you do that include:

- Before commenting on an answer yourself, ask other students to react to their peers' contributions.
- Ask students to address comments directly to one another.
- Ask students to help you clarify points.
- If the class is splitting into camps on an issue, set up a spontaneous debate, allowing students to change their mind as it progresses. For a twist, have each side argue in favor of the opposition.
- Step in, preferably with a thoughtful follow-up question, only if no student supplies the needed clarification, correction, or knowledge or if the discussion strays off track.
- Be sure a topic is settled before moving on. Ask if anyone has something to add or qualify.
- Ask a student to summarize the main points made during the discussion of the topic. Then move on, making a logical transition to the next topic.
- If a student begins to get verbally aggressive toward another student, moderate the conversation. Students often do not want you to "save them," but, rather, they want you to control the situation so that is does not get out of hand and keep the focus on the conversation, not the person.

What if traffic comes to a screeching halt and no one says a word after a generous wait time?

Be prepared, as this has happened to everyone at times. Perhaps ask students why they are silent. It may be your question was ambiguous or too complex, or you used words your students didn't understand, or they misunderstood your meaning.

Respond Honestly to Student Responses

Give approval, verbal or nonverbal, to all student contributions by nodding, looking interested or accepting, or recording the response on the board. But provide verbal feedback suitable to the response. Students want to know how correct and complete their own and their classmates' answers are, but they want you to deliver your judgment in a diplomatic, encouraging way. Here are some verbal response options you may wish to use:

- *When the answer is correct*, praise according to what it deserves.
- *When the answer is correct but is only one of several correct possibilities*, ask another student to extend or add to it. Or frame a question that is an extension of the answer. Avoid premature closure.
- *When the answer is incomplete*, follow up with a question that directs the student to include more—for example, "How might you modify your answer if you took into account the _____ aspect?"
- *When the answer is unclear*, try to rephrase it, and ask the student if this is what she means.
- *When the answer is wrong or seems to be wrong*, follow up with one or more gently delivered Socratic questions designed to lead the student to discover their error—for example, "Yes, but if you come to that conclusion, don't you also have to assume _____?" (See the box on the Socratic method near the end of Chapter 3.)
- Avoid identifying and correcting errors yourself for as long as possible. It is best if students catch and correct incorrect discussion contributions.

◼ QUESTIONING TECHNIQUES

Questions are the heart of a discussion, and framing thoughtful ones is a key teaching skill and has been for millennia. Socrates honed it to such a fine art that an entire method of questioning is attributed to him. Not just any type of question can launch and carry a discussion. Questions that demand only recall and rephrasing serve recitation well, but not discussion. Other types of questions serve no purpose whatsoever—in particular, a string of questions an instructor may nervously fire off to fill an awkward silence and vague questions that may sound open but are actually too confusing or unfocused for anyone to know how to answer. For example, this one calls for logical acrobatics: "Who else knows what else doesn't fall into this category?" This one is too global: "What about the breakdown of the family?" Students resist taking the risk required to attack such questions. Two common questions that represent well-meaning attempts to help rarely work the way intended: "Does everyone understand this?" and, "Any questions?" If there are 5 minutes left in a class period and you ask, "Are there any questions?" you might as well ask, "Does anyone have something they would like to say that will keep the entire class from leaving early today?" Instead, you could say, "We have 5 minutes left before we go. If anyone has any questions, feel free to ask them now. Otherwise, we can continue to talk for a few minutes about (insert here something you have been talking about that interests you)."

Constructing questions that ignite and sustain discussion involves much more than turning around a couple of words in a sentence and adding a question mark. Well-crafted questions take thought and creativity in order to evoke the same from students. Let's look at a couple of question typologies that offer additional ideas for developing multiple, varying points of view on an issue. Note that all of these question types require higher-order thinking.

McKeachie's Discussion Questions

McKeachie (2002) suggests four types of fruitful, challenging questions, which vaguely overlap with Bloom's cognitive operations of analysis, synthesis, and evaluations:

1. *Comparative questions:* These ask students to compare and contrast different theories, research studies, literary works, and so on. Indirectly, they help students identify the important dimensions for comparison.
2. *Evaluative questions:* This type extends comparisons to judgments of the relative validity, effectiveness, or strength of what is being compared.
3. *Connective and cause-and-effect questions:* These challenge students to link facts, concepts, relationships, authors, theories, and the like that are not explicitly integrated in assigned materials and might not appear to be related. These questions are particularly useful in cross-disciplinary courses. They can also ask students to draw and reflect on their personal experiences, connecting these to theories and research findings. When students realize these links, the material becomes more meaningful to them.
4. *Critical questions:* This type invites students to examine the validity of a particular argument, research claim, or interpretation. Such questions foster careful, active reading. If the class has trouble getting started, you can initiate the discussion by presenting an equally plausible alternative argument. Asking for comments on what a student has just said is also a critical question. Used in this context, it fosters good listening skills.

Brookfield and Preskill's "Momentum" Questions

Brookfield and Preskill (2005) propose seven types of questions that serve the express purpose of sustaining the momentum of a discussion. These questions are designed to make students probe into issues more deeply, reconsider positions in novel and more critical ways, and stay intellectually stimulated:

1. *Questions requesting more evidence:* As the name states, such a question asks a student to defend their position, especially when the evidence for the position is questionable or another student challenges it as unsupported. Pose such a question in a matter-of-fact way as a simple request for more information—data, facts, passages from the text—so as not to alienate the student.

2. *Clarification questions:* This type invites the student to rephrase or elaborate on their ideas to make them more understandable to the rest of the class. You can request an example, an application, or a fuller explanation.

3. *Cause-and-effect questions:* These questions coax students to consider the possible causal relationship between variables or events and, thereby, formulate hypotheses. You can use them to challenge a conventional wisdom or introduce the scientific method.

4. *Hypothetical questions:* These are "what-if" inquiries that require students to think creatively to make up plausible scenarios to explore how changing the circumstances or parameters of a situation might alter the results. They can induce imaginative thinking and even send a discussion off on fanciful tangents, but students still have to use their prior knowledge and experience to come up with supportable extrapolations. Hypothetical questions can extend cause-and-effect questions. If, for example, the class established the impact of education on income, you could pose this hypothetical scenario to help students define the limits of the relationship: "What if everyone in the society got a bachelor's degree? Does that mean that everyone would make a similarly high income?"

5. *Open questions:* These questions invite risk-taking and creativity in problem-solving and have the greatest potential for expanding students' intellectual and affective horizons. No matter how they are phrased, they are truly open only if you welcome all well-meaning responses and aren't fishing for a preferred answer. You can accept the weaker contributions as opportunities for the students to build and expand on them and follow up with clarification questions, requests for more evidence, cause-and-effect questions, and hypothetical questions.

6. *Linking or extension questions:* A high-quality discussion depends on students actively listening to one another's contributions. Linking or extension questions encourage this by asking students to think about the relationships between their responses and those of their classmates.

7. *Summary and synthesis questions:* To enhance the learning value of discussion, you should close with a few wrap-up questions that ask students to summarize or synthesize the important ideas shared during the exchange. Students have to review and reflect on the discussion, identifying and articulating the intellectual highlights. These questions can take a variety of forms. They can ask outright for the one or two most important ideas that emerged or for some key concept that best encapsulates the exchange. Or they can ask what points the discussion clarified, what issues remain unresolved, or what topics should be addressed next time to advance the group's understanding.

■ ORGANIZING DISCUSSION QUESTIONS

The most engaging discussions are not just a list of loosely connected questions. Rather, they have a direction and a destination. They comprise a purposeful sequence of questions that guide students through a more or less orderly process of thinking about a topic more deeply.

Working Backward from End-of-Class Outcomes

Backward design can be applied to designing a discussion session as well as an entire course. First, jot down your ultimate outcomes for the class period: the one, two, or three things you want your students to be able to do (classify, explain, analyze, assess, and so on) by the end of class. For each performance, create one or two key questions that will assess the students' facility. Then for each key question, develop another two or three questions that logically proceed and will prepare the students to answer the key questions intelligently. In other words, work backward from the key questions you want your students to answer well at the end through the questions that will lead them to that facility.

When class begins, launch the discussion with one of the last questions you framed. You can lend structure to the discussion by displaying all your questions (key assessment ones last) on the board or a slide or in a handout with note-taking space below each question. Still, unless you have framed too many questions, you can afford to be flexible. You can allow the discussion to wander a bit, then easily redirect it back to your list of questions.

The next section on Bloom's hierarchy of questions suggests a logical sequencing scheme for the working-backward strategy.

Guiding Students Up Bloom's Hierarchy of Questions

You can view Bloom's (1956) taxonomy of questions as a hierarchical ladder of cognitive levels for leading your students from knowledge, the lowest thinking level, to evaluation, the highest. This schema was set out in Chapter 2, where we applied it to developing learning outcomes. The lists of verbs associated with each cognitive operation are just as useful here for framing questions, so refer back to Table 2.1.

To structure a discussion as a process of inquiry, you might start off with knowledge (recitation) questions on the highlights of the previous class or the reading assignment. A factual recall exercise serves as a mental warm-up for the students and gives those who come in unprepared the chance to pick up a few major points and follow along, if not participate later. As you can see in Table 15.1, knowledge questions often ask *who*, *what*, *where*, and *when*, as well as *how* and *why*, when students have already read or been told the correct answer. Avoid questions that call for one- or two-word answers; aim for multisentence responses. But do not spend more than a few minutes on this level, especially if you depend on raised hands to call on students. The interesting discussions, for both you and the students, lie further up the cognitive ladder.

Rapidly move the discussion up the hierarchy through comprehension so you can find out whether your students correctly understand the material and can put it in their own words. Draw on the questions in Table 15.1. At this juncture, you can identify and correct any misconceptions they have about the subject matter that might get in the way of their deeper learning. If they do comprehend the material, they should be able to answer application questions, think of appropriate examples, and use the material to solve problems. If they can do this, they should be ready to progress to analysis of the material: distilling its elements; drawing comparisons and contrasts; identifying assumptions, evidence, causes, effects, and implications; and reasoning through explanations and arguments.

Once students have explored the material, they are prepared to step outside its confines and attempt synthesis. As illustrated in Table 15.1, this type of question calls for integrating elements of the material in new and creative ways: drawing new conclusions and generalizations; composing or designing a new model, theory, or approach; or combining elements from different sources. When students can synthesize material, they have mastered it well enough to address evaluation questions. They now can make informed judgments about its strengths and shortcomings; its costs and benefits; and its ethical, aesthetic, or practical merit.

Table 15.1 Examples of Questions at Each Cognitive Level of Bloom's Taxonomy/Hierarchy

Cognitive Level	Questions
Knowledge	• Who did _____ to _____? • What do you recall about _____? • What does the term _____ mean? • When did _____ take place? Where did it take place? • How does the process work? (Describe it.)
Comprehension	• In your own words, what does the term _____ mean? • How would you explain _____ in nontechnical terms? • Can you show us what you mean? • What do think the author/researcher is saying? • Can you summarize the key points of _____?
Application	• What would be an example of _____? • How would you solve this problem? • What approach would you use? • How would you apply _____ in this situation? • What would be a challenge to applying _____?
Analysis	• How are _____ and _____ alike? How are they different? • What are the different parts of _____? • What evidence does the author/researcher offer? • What assumptions are behind the argument? • What inferences can you draw about _____?
Synthesis	• What conclusions can you come to about _____? • What generalizations can you make about _____? • How would you adapt (change) the design (plan) for _____? • How can you resolve the differences (paradox, apparent conflict)? • What new model could accommodate these disparate findings?
Evaluation	• What would you choose, and why? • What are the relevant data, and why? • Why do you approve or disapprove? • Why do you think the conclusions are valid or invalid? • How would you rank (rate, prioritize) the _____?

Structured as a hierarchy, Bloom's taxonomy helps rein in students from leaping into issues they aren't yet prepared to tackle. Often they are all too eager to jump to judging content without thoroughly understanding and examining it first. In addition, if you teach the taxonomy to your students, they acquire a whole new metacognitive perspective on thinking processes and levels. If you label the level of your questions, you maximize your chances of obtaining the level of answers you are seeking. Students also quickly learn to classify and better frame their own questions.

The taxonomy should be used flexibly, however. Some discussion tasks, such as debriefing a case, may call for an inextricable combination of application, analysis, synthesis, and evaluation. Moreover, a comprehension question in one course may be an analysis task in another. How any question is classified depends on what the students have previously received as "knowledge" from you and the readings you assign.

TURNING THE TABLES

Teaching at its best does not mean that you must always be the person leading the discussion and posing the questions. If you model and teach good discussion facilitation and questioning techniques, you can have your students lead discussions and develop and organize the questions. The quality of these questions tells you how diligently your students are reading and reflecting on those readings.

REFLECTION QUESTIONS

Reflection Question 15.1: What do you see as the balance between pushing students to participate in discussions versus providing a variety of ways to help draw students into the conversation? Imagine you have five students who never participate in discussions. Given the information in this chapter, how might you address such a situation?

Reflection Question 15.2: What are the primary considerations when developing discussion questions for a class session? What types of questions do you see as being best to bring about the most learning for students?

Concept Into Practice: Identify a discussion you intend to have in one of your classes or a discussion you could have. Using backward design, set up a series of questions that could be asked. Start with one key question you could ask at the end of the discussion period to illustrate an ultimate outcome. From there, create two questions that could be asked about one-half of the way through the discussion. Finally, identify two questions that could be used to get the discussion started.

CHAPTER 16

Coordinating Experiential Learning Experiences

Much of education involves artificially constructed educational experiences that play off from real-life experiences. Lectures can be an efficient way to transmit information to students, but placing a group of students in rows of desks to listen to an expert explain a concept is an artificially constructed learning environment. We would never encounter that kind of learning environment in nature. The same can be said of much of active learning, with discussions and scenarios designed for students to learn, but not directly tied to the way humans typically learn. In this chapter, we look at a few of the more popular teaching strategies that involve putting students into situations that simulate or approximate real-life situations. This type of learning is in some ways experiential learning, although for the purpose of this book, we define what we are discussing as *realistic learning*.

The process of learning through an experience is heavily rooted in education. John Dewey (1859–1952), Carl Rogers (1902–1987), bell hooks (1952–2021), and David Kolb (b. 1939) are just a few of the many who have well established the concept of

engagement in educational activities that put students into seemingly real-life situations. Research finds time and again that teaching methods that use real-life participatory learning experiences, such as role-playing, simulations, games, and service-learning, ensure higher student motivation, more learning at higher cognitive levels, greater appreciation of the subject matter and its utility, and longer retention of the material than does the traditional lecture (Berry, 2008; Bowen, 2012; Carnes, 2014; Cerra et al., 2022; Raupach et al., 2021; Vlachopoulos & Makri, 2017). These methods also meet a wider range of instructional goals than do methods that are less active. In this chapter, we begin with moderately engaging strategies that require minimal adaptation and move to the more powerful instructional strategies, which generally require more time and energy on your part.

ROLE-PLAYING

Role-playing provides an opportunity for students to learn in a true-to-life, problematic social or interpersonal situation that they act out, improvising the script. The situation must incorporate potential conflict between the roles and some need for the players to reach a resolution (Halpern & Associates, 1994). When one player is not supposed to know the full story about another player's intentions, problem, or goals, you should provide written descriptions for each role for the players to review in private. You also must decide what information to give to the rest of the class and the role you would like them to play. The class might serve as a jury, be asked to note how the individuals interacted, or look for subtle meanings of the words chosen by the role-players. Following the enactment, lead a debriefing discussion with an opportunity for reflection. You should ask the players how they felt in their role at crucial junctures and what intentions and interests motivated their actions, and ask the rest of the students what behavioral patterns they observed and how these behaviors reflected concepts and principles addressed in the course.

Although role-playing relies on make-believe, those same roles provide real-life learning through realistic scenarios in the classroom in which students identify with the roles they play and observe. This technique is used successfully in both therapy and instruction, especially in the humanities, social sciences, counseling, clinical psychology, and nursing. It has also long been used in education.

Here are some examples of role plays to inspire your own ideas:

- A professional (doctor, lawyer, or clergy, for example) and client disagree over an approach the professional is taking to address the client's problem.
- Worker representatives try to convince executives not to close an unprofitable plant.
- Co-owners of a quickly growing small business must hire a manager, but one owner wants to hire an older experienced applicant with a ton of related experience and the other owner wants to hire a young applicant with little management experience but who appears to be a rising star.

- An instructor has to decide what to do in response to one or more students complaining about a grade, a course policy, an assignment, or their team's dysfunctional dynamics.
- A politician experiences ethical conflict between partisan and administrative roles or between ideological stance and the need for campaign funds.
- A couple or family argues over money, (un)employment, discipline of the children, authority, autonomy, communication, moving, in-laws, domestic violence, or alcohol or drug use. This scenario may spotlight the roles of social worker, physician, clergy, law enforcer, lawyer, or therapist.
- For a foreign language course, a role play may be any situation a person may face traveling in that country.
- If you teach literature, consider casting students in the roles of the characters and letting them play out a hypothetical scene that extends the piece of literature.
- In other fields, search out case studies that you can adapt to role-playing. There are many options for any field. You could also have students pair off or get into groups of the appropriate size and have multiple role plays happening at the same time.

Regardless of how you engage students in a role play, it is important to have them reflect at the end. This could be done through a discussion or written assignment, focusing on what they learned by playing the role or about others' roles, what they would do differently next time, and what they learned about the situation. Students will learn through the role play, but they will potentially learn much more through reflecting on the role play.

Reacting to the Past

In the mid-1990s, Barnard College history professor Mark C. Carnes started conducting his classes around a game he called *Reacting to the Past*. This is a form of role play, but instead of improvising a contemporary situation or an isolated incident from the past, Reacting to the Past is a more complex and decidedly rich look at an historical occurrence. When done well, this includes many students in the role play and can have the realism of a simulation. Students assume the identity of historical figures and write papers and make oral presentations that reflect their figure's beliefs, values, and ideas. In addition, they strategize ways to win the game. Winning entails persuading uncommitted parties to one's side while operating within the given historical and social context. Therefore, Socrates may be acquitted, Louis XVI may retain power after the French Revolution, and a plague in London may be prevented in 1854. A student game book supplies all the essential historical background and rules information, as well as primary source readings. Students learn history because the game accurately incorporates the cultural, sociological, economic, political, and technological contexts of the period and place under study. However, even though they learn the actual history, they can play history differently than the actual figures did and generate different historical outcomes.

As the instructor, you have your own manual and role as game master. You have to dedicate a sufficient number of class periods, most commonly from 8 to 12, for the game and set it up. But then students pretty much run the game on their own. In fact, Reacting to the Past is famous for motivating tremendous engagement, effort, and research on their part.

Reacting to the Past has spawned a cottage industry of conferences and workshops (see http://reacting.barnard.edu) and Reacting games. Twenty-one games have been published by W. W. Norton & Company (listed at http://reacting.barnard.edu/games), with even more under review (listed at http://reacting.barnard.edu/games/under_review), and hundreds more have been developed and used by faculty members at over 300 North American institutions (listed at https://docs.google.com/spreadsheet/pub?key=0AslHquj5C_74dHZoX3MycjBzbzdtam80WWxJS0JMYUE&output=html) Carnes (2014) draws on these resources as he outlines the history of Reacting to the Past and amasses

evidence of its teaching effectiveness. Watson and Hagood (2018) published an edited book of the impact of Reacting to the Past with 10 chapters written by 26 college and university faulty members. If you want to incorporate Reacting to the Past into your course, these two books are excellent resources.

Student Presentation Role Plays

Employers place a high premium on communication skills, with hiring managers and executives indicating that new college graduates need good communication skills when looking for jobs (Finley, 2021). One interesting way to enhance these skills is for students to engage in role plays that include building speaking skills.

Variations on a Debate

Every field has topics amenable to a two-sided (at least), fact-based argument. A debate format can be as simple as statements of the affirmative and the negative, plus rebuttals, each with a strict time limit. But the following variations foster deeper student learning and critical thinking. To obtain the best results, you may have to teach your students rhetorical structure, the basic rules of evidence, and common logical fallacies before having them debate.

In a *change-your-mind debate*, designate different sides of the classroom as "for the affirmative" or "for the negative," with the middle as "uncertain/undecided/neutral." Before the debate, students sit in the area representing their current position and can change their seating location during the debate as their opinions sway. After the debate, lead a debriefing and reflection discussion focusing on the opinion changers ("What changed your mind?") and the undecided students, who are likely to provide the most objective analysis of both the debate and the issue at hand.

In *point-counterpoint* (Silberman, 1994), divide your class into groups—as many groups as there are positions on an issue—and tell each group to come up with arguments in favor of its assigned position. Select one student to launch the debate by presenting one argument for their group's stance; then call on each group in turn to give a different argument or counterargument. Conclude with a class discussion comparing the various positions.

Yet another variant is *structured controversy* or *academic controversy*, in which two pairs in a group of four students formally debate each other on an issue, then switch sides, and finally synthesize a joint position (Johnson et al., 1991). Done properly, this activity requires that students conduct considerable outside research and write a final report.

When students have to research and debate a position counter to their own, their minds open to both their own biases and the other side of the issue; sometimes they even change to that of the other side. In addition, they realize the key role of understanding in civil discourse (Budesheim & Lundquist, 2000; Chrisler, 2013; Trujillo-Jenks & Rosen, 2015). One challenge in using the debate format is that only a few students participate, leaving many students who may become disinterested in the process. To counter this, you might employ speed rounds in any of the debate options already listed. During a speed round, the instructor goes back and forth between the two sides, and any student may participate by raising their hand and speaking for a predetermined time, such as 15 seconds. Once a student has contributed, they may not participate again until all on their side have participated (Treme, 2018). This not only involves all students, but the students must also listen to what is being said so they know if the point they are about to make is appropriate and has not been made previously.

Panel Discussion, Symposium, and Town Meeting

In a *panel discussion*, four or five students briefly present different points of view on a topic, usually representing authorities or historical figures—for example, Freud, Jung, Adler, Skinner, and Rogers in a psychology course; Franklin, Jefferson, Burr, Madison, and Washington in an early American history course; or Swift, Wordsworth, Coleridge, Burns, and Fielding in an 18th-century English literature

course. Then the class addresses thoughtful questions and challenges, preferably prepared in advance, to the various panel members.

The *symposium* is a similar format, often used in advanced seminars, in which individual students or teams present their independently conducted research papers that express their own ideas. The rest of the class asks probing questions and offers constructive criticism, which is especially useful if students revise their work. In addition, you may assign one or two discussants to interrelate and critique the papers for each class period. Discussants should have at least a couple of days to review the symposium products in advance.

You can also make the entire class into a panel by calling a *town meeting* on a multisided issue or complex case (Silberman, 1994). After doing some outside research on the issue or situation, students prepare to voice their views within a time limit you set, following the format of each speaker calling on the next speaker.

▪ SERIOUS GAMES AND SIMULATIONS

Most students enjoy low-stakes competitions and find "winning" to be enjoyable. Games and simulations can bring the course material to life and emotionally engage an entire class as few other methods can. In a systematic review of games and simulations in higher education, Vlachopoulos and Makri (2017) reviewed data from 99 studies from all over the world with a total of 20,406 participants. Although there were some challenges with respect to identifying common terminology, the review showcased many positive aspects of gaming on student motivation and learning. The point of academic games and simulations is to have fun and learn, not to show anyone is better than anyone else or have the focus on high-stakes prizes. The games and simulations in this section are restricted to in-class activities, but there are a number of online games and simulations that may also be employed.

Serious Games

Many academic games are modeled on traditional games, such as *Bingo* and *Go Fish*, and classic television game shows, such as *Jeopardy, Family Feud, Wheel of Fortune, Password,* and *Who Wants to Be a Millionaire?* Recently some faculty members have adapted *Survivor* to subjects as disparate as physiology (Howard et al., 2002) and music theory (Berry, 2008). The questions and answers come from the course material and can easily capture knowledge, comprehension, and application levels of thinking, if not higher. Games provide an effective and painless, even fun, review format (Kaupins, 2005; Moy et al., 2000), and in this context, students can sometimes submit the questions and even run the game.

Games can also supply a format for almost every class period. After opening her music theory classes with a minilecture, Berry (2008) assigns groups of students a challenge for that day. The group members tally their individual and group scores, although the groups don't vote off the lowest-scoring member.

"Serious games" became popular in the early 2000s and continue to increase in popularity (Sipiyaruk et al., 2017; Zhonggen, 2019). The term *serious* simply means that the game is designed for some purpose other than entertainment. In educational settings, serious games are instructional and lead to many positive learning outcomes (Moro et al., 2020). If you teach biology, medicine, or nursing, you can find examples of free serious games at http://www.nobelprize.org/educational. A good source of educational games, particularly those available online, is Bowen (2012) and is located at http://teachingnaked.com/games. Another helpful website that lists 50 different sites for serious educational games is located at: https://www.onlinecolleges.net/50-great-sites-for-serious-educational-games.

Simulations

By abstracting key elements from reality, simulations allow students to live out the hypotheses and implications of theories, giving them intense emotional, cognitive, and behavioral experiences that they would otherwise never have. This method developed a strong faculty and student following during the 1970s and the early 1980s around a growing market of simulations of societies, formal organizations, corporations, markets, urban areas, cultures, world politics, and other complex macrosocial realms. These were strictly face-to-face enactments of hypothetical social situations, unmediated by computers, some requiring many hours and an array of supporting materials. One early simulation that is free to use and has endured is Barnga (https://sites.lsa.umich.edu/inclusive-teaching/barnga) that encourages those participating to consider cross-cultural assumptions and communication. It includes an 18-minute recording of how to facilitate a Barnga activity in your course.

Among these early simulations was a variant called a *frame simulation*. It offers instructors different scenarios or settings to choose from or to develop on their own. Some are now on interactive computer sites and still serve an important instructional purpose. For example, students can play the *Prisoner's Dilemma* under various conditions and payoff rules that illustrate different psychological and sociological principles (https://serendipstudio.org/oneworld). Another frame simulation, structured like a mock trial, comes with a free suite of actual cases relevant to several disciplines (https://store.streetlaw.org/mock-trials). In fact, frame simulations can revolve around any decision-making body: a court, a board of directors, a review board, a legislature, or an administrative agency (Hertel & Millis, 2002).

Computers ushered in an expanded selection of products available on the web or in software packages. They range from individual tutorial programs (computer-assisted instruction) to full-blown multimedia simulations. Among the latter are history and political science simulations on the Civil War and World War I at http://www.historysimulation.com. Many more options in the social sciences are available at http://teachinghistory.org/teaching-materials/ask-a-master-teacher/23691.

The field of business may have the most simulations, and they tend to be marketed under straightforward titles such as *Airline, Corporation, Supply Chain, Manager, Marketer, Human Resource Management, Collective Bargaining Simulated,* and *Entrepreneur*. Several companies produce and sell computerized business simulations (e.g., http://goventureceo.com, http://www.bsg-online.com, http://www.capsim.com), as does Harvard Business School Publishing (https://hbsp.harvard.edu/simulations).

The sciences and engineering also have simulations, enhanced by animation and interactivity. Among these are hundreds of virtual laboratories allowing students to conduct experiments and manipulate parameters in ways that would be too dangerous or too costly in real life. In hydraulics, for instance, students can solve complex canalization problems by varying the delivery, inflow, outflow, and power of various pumps. In electrical engineering, they can manipulate the performance of an electrical network and study overloading, breaks, and the like. You will find the URLs for free simulations listed in Chapter 20. In the health sciences, faculty members can program SimMan and other medical software to simulate specific diagnostic situations. To obtain data for diagnosing the symptoms, students can even ask questions of the hypothetical patient and get answers, as well as run hypothetical tests.

Simulations are not just for young students. They are mainstays of adult education and job training. The military runs battle simulations, hospitals and emergency response agencies hold disaster preparedness simulations, and companies use simulations to teach their employees new skills. Try a search for simulations in areas related to your course content. With the number of new simulations appearing, it is very possible there is a simulation you can use.

Running Games and Simulations

A game or simulation and its debriefing take a good deal of class time—at least an hour for the very simplest. In addition, to grab your students' full attention, you should assess them on the quality of their strategy. Here is the conventional wisdom for running simulations. First and foremost, be prepared. Read the instructor's manual or directions at least twice at a leisurely pace well in advance. Mark the directions you will give students at each stage of the game or simulation. In general, it's best not to give all the instructions at the beginning because too much information will confuse students. List your preclass set-up tasks. Know the sequence of events and the schedule of distributing artifacts and materials, but don't hesitate to refer to the manual. Finally, to grab your students' full attention, you should inform them that you will assess them on the quality of their strategy.

Most facilitators run games and simulations at too slow a pace. The challenge is to keep the experience moving, even if the tempo puts pressure on the students. They need a long enough time to realize the constraints, costs, and benefits of their decision-making options, but not necessarily long enough to answer every question that arises, come to a full consensus, or feel completely comfortable with their decisions. After all, a game, and especially a simulation, must imitate life as much as possible. (For more detailed advice, see Hertel & Millis, 2002.)

Debriefing Serious Games and Simulations

The debriefing process is an essential component of a simulation or a serious game. It disengages students from the emotional aspects of the experience and settles them back into the classroom reality, allowing them to transform what they experienced into meaningful learning. They should be able to identify the disciplinary concepts and principles illustrated in the simulation and game and assess their own decision-making abilities. In addition, a debriefing brings out the disparate perceptions, feelings, and experiences each player had (Hertel & Millis, 2002).

So important is the debriefing that you should prepare the questions in advance, progressing through three phases (Hertel & Millis, 2002). First, ask students to recount their experience and their feelings about it. A successful simulation or game may evoke some pretty strong emotions, both negative and positive. Second, have them explain their actions within the context of their roles, specifically their intentions and motivations behind their decisions. If different roles had different information, students may reveal what they knew and didn't know, what their goals were, and what strategy they had for attaining them. Finally, return students to their true role as learners with questions about the connection between their simulated experiences and the concepts, principles, theories, and hypotheses they have studied in your course. Help them translate the concrete into the abstract and derive generalizations related to the subject matter.

If you desire to assess the effectiveness of the simulation or game, an analysis of 31 research papers resulted in an evaluation framework with four phases of running simulations: preparation, introduction, interaction, and conclusion (Faizan et al., 2019).

■ SERVICE-LEARNING: MOVING LEARNING OUT OF THE CLASSROOM

Service-learning is a method by which students meet a community need, realize student learning outcomes for the course, and reflect on their experiences. According to instructors and "graduates," service-learning is almost uniformly a positive, life-changing experience for students—the kind they never forget. It teaches not just in the abstract but also in a concrete, real-world context. Most faculty members also find it effective in meeting course objectives in a meaningful way. Because the experience often stimulates emotions, it helps students progress toward achieving certain affective, social, and ethical learning outcomes, as well as higher-order cognitive outcomes. In addition, the emotions themselves strongly enhance learning and memory (see Chapter 1).

Service-learning is a powerful teaching strategy. However, because of the effort needed to use a service-learning approach, only about 7% of faculty members teach service-learning courses (Campus Compact, 2012). Service-learning has been studied extensively for its positive effects on students. Research conducted some years ago found that it enhances the following (Astin et al., 2000; Coquyt, 2020; Eyler & Giles, 1999):

- Students' personal development (sense of identity and efficacy, spiritual and moral growth)
- Students' social and interpersonal development (leadership, communication, ability to work with others)
- Students' cultural and racial understanding
- Students' sense of civic responsibility, citizenship skills, and societal effectiveness
- Students' commitment to service in their career choice and future voluntary activities
- Students' relationships with faculty members
- Students' satisfaction with college and likelihood of graduation
- Relations between the institution and the community
- In many studies, students' academic learning and abilities on some dimensions: writing skills, the ability to apply knowledge to the real world, complexity of understanding, problem analysis, critical thinking, and cognitive development (but no clear effect on grades, grade point average, or later standardized test scores)

Another national study (Gray et al., 1999) found more mixed effects. On the positive side, students in service-learning courses were indeed more satisfied with their courses than were students in non-service-learning courses. In the same comparison, students perceived that their service-learning experience slightly enhanced their civic engagement, their interpersonal skills, and their understanding of people of different backgrounds from their own. However, they reported no effect on their academic skills (writing, analytical, quantitative, or knowledge) or their professional skills (confidence in their choice of major and career, expectation of graduation, or career preparation). In fact, students who opted out of service-learning felt that they *did* advance their academic and professional skills.

In a small-scale study, students who opted for a service-learning experience in a rehabilitation services course scored no higher on the objective tests of medical facts and procedures, but they did perform better on the case studies requiring an assessment of the services being given than the students who didn't (Mpofu, 2007).

According to a meta-analysis of the best-designed studies, service-learning has a moderate, statistically significant impact on students' understanding of the course material, their ability to transfer course content and skills to different settings, and their capacity to reframe complex social issues, which requires critical thinking (Novak et al., 2007). In summary, then, service-learning provides some modest academic benefits, as well as some social and affective ones.

How positive the service-learning experience is depends on several factors. The single most powerful determinant is a student's degree of interest in the subject matter before the experience. Therefore, service-learning is best reserved for upper-level courses in a major (Astin et al., 2000). Other known influences are under the instructor's control: how much students can share and discuss their experiences in class; how much training they have for the experience; how many hours per week they perform service; how well tied the experience is to the course content; and how much written and oral reflection students are asked to do, especially in tying the experience back to the course content (Astin et al., 2000; Gray et al., 1999, 2000; Zlotkowski, 1998). Situations with fewer than 20 hours of service dulls the approach's impact (Gray et al., 2000).

Implementing Service-Learning

Is service-learning right for your courses? First, examine your learning outcomes. This method merits consideration if you have outcomes that are affective, ethical, or social beyond working effectively in a group, or if your cognitive outcomes are served by students' practicing on an outside clientele. If either of these is true, try to identify community needs that truly complement your subject matter. For example, if you teach children's literature and want your students to be able to critique works from a child's point of view, then their reading books to children makes sense. If you teach public relations, having your students conduct a PR campaign for a local nonprofit organization clearly benefits their learning. If you teach public health or community nursing, your students can better master the subject matter if they plan and implement a community health or health education effort. If you teach political science, consider a civic engagement project in which your students learn how to navigate the politics at the various levels of government by conducting partnership projects in your course (Redlawsk et al., 2009).

Second, be aware of the ethical questions that some engagement experiences raise, even though requiring them is legal. If the experience involves working for social change, is it appropriate to require students to do this, no matter how they feel about the changes aimed for? Should they have to give service even if their current politics and ethics don't warrant it? Will they be placed in physical danger? To ensure you are in line with department and college guidelines, check with your department chair any time you require your students to complete any course-related work off campus.

Third, consider your time constraints and commitment. Service-learning requires more planning and coordination than most other methods, especially your first foray into this area, and you should start laying the groundwork at least a few months in advance. Before you contact any agency, consult with the community and civic engagement office. It already has ties with local organizations and can recommend appropriate clients that need and want students' help. This unit may also save you time by contacting potential clients. If your campus doesn't have an engagement or volunteer office, start contacting local agencies, such as schools, medical and mental health facilities, social service agencies, and the local United Way. If you are working in a small community without those services, check with local faith-based organization, as these grass-roots organizations are typically keenly aware of where there is need in the community. Then schedule a face-to-face meeting with the key contact person to find out about the organization's needs and expectations and to explain your own ideas for your course. Ensure that the agency will orient and supervise your students. Alternatively, have students find their own agency and work out the project details.

Then start making course design decisions. Will the service-learning be required, optional, or extra credit? Will you offer an alternative assignment? How many hours will be required? How much will it count toward students' final grades? What will be the requirements of the service-learning experience? How will you assess and grade it? How will you link the service to the course content? When will you have students discuss their experiences? What writing tasks will you assign for reflection? (It is best to have multiple reflection assignments.) How will you grade these reflection assignments? This information will be needed for your syllabus. What previous course components will be eliminated to make time for engagement activities?

Finally, make the necessary logistical arrangements: getting help with liability issues from your institution's risk management office (e.g., release forms); creating student teams if appropriate (highly advisable to mitigate any physical danger); helping students and the agency coordinate schedules; ensuring students are oriented and supervised at the agency; arranging for student transportation, even if just car pools; and devising a system to monitor students' hours of service.

Two journals and several books offer additional guidance for instructors and a wealth of ideas for solid engagement projects, including exemplars:

- *Journal of Higher Education Outreach and Engagement*, an open access journal available at http://openjournals.libs.uga.edu/index.php/jheoe

- *Michigan Journal of Community Service-Learning*, issues available for purchase at https://ginsberg.umich.edu/mijournal
- Campus Compact. (2003). *Introduction to Service-Learning Toolkit: Readings and Resources for Faculty* (2nd ed.). Author. Strong on learning theory, teaching strategies, and practical advice in implementing the method.
- Clayton, P. H., Bringle, R. G., & Hatcher, J. A. (Eds.). (2013). *Research on Service-Learning: Conceptual Frameworks and Assessment, Vol. 2A: Students and Faculty*. Stylus. Contains rich research on both students and faculty.
- Duke University template regarding how to write a service-learning syllabus: https://servicelearning.duke.edu/sites/servicelearning.duke.edu/files/documents/constructing-sl-syllabi.original.pdf
- Zlotkowski, E. (Ed.). (1998). *Successful Service-Learning Programs: New Models of Excellence in Higher Education*. Jossey-Bass. Detailed descriptions of strong service-learning courses.

In addition, you can go to YouTube, put "service-learning" into the search box, and watch dozens of examples of the method in action, along with many different suggestions on how to implement service-learning into your courses.

Service-Learning and Volunteerism

The concepts of *service-learning* and *volunteerism* are often confused. Both are important to the community and can be impactful for the participating student. That said, there are differences between the two approaches. Service-learning does involve meeting a community need, but also has the essential components of meeting the learning outcomes of the course and having the students engage in reflection. In volunteering, students help the organization and meet a need, for which a teacher may award extra credit, but aside from documenting the time spent working and perhaps a paper explaining what was completed, there is no other tie to the course itself.

It is important to note that if credit is given to students for volunteering, the work being done should in no way benefit you as the instructor of the course. Additionally, be careful that the behavior for which the student is given credit does not cause more harm than benefit. Shelters in college towns are often overrun with animals that are turned in at the end of the academic year, and unfortunately, some of those are students who received credit for adopting the pet at the beginning of the semester. Finally, work being done for credit should not interfere with students learning course content. There is little advantage to having a student secure extra credit points for working at a soup kitchen if the student would be better served studying for exams during those hours.

■ MAXIMIZING THE VALUE OF STRUCTURED PARTICIPATORY LEARNING EXPERIENCES

Debriefing and reflection following any academic real-life experience is a valuable educational activity. This is true after role plays, academic games, simulations, and service-learning experiences. Substantial role-plays, games, simulations, and engagement activities deserve some kind of written reflection to give students the time and emotional distance they need to glean additional insights. In fact, service-learning without reflection is merely service.

Do supply students with direction to ensure their thinking doesn't dissolve into a stream of consciousness. Guide students toward developing their metacognitive and meta-emotional awareness and control—that is, their self-regulated learning skills (Nilson, 2013a). So what questions might you ask them to answer? After a role play, game, or simulation, any of these probes may be appropriate:

- What were your goals, and how did they change during the experience?
- How did you change your strategies during the experience? How did you use feedback from the simulation or game and other players?

- How did your emotions change during the experience? How did you overcome discouragement, fatigue, and any other emotional barrier?
- If students solved a problem: How did you arrive at your best solution? What was your reasoning in defining the problem, deciding what principles and concepts to apply to it, developing alternative solutions, assessing their relative worth, and determining the best one?
- Evaluate your goal achievement, strategies, problem-solving decisions, and overall performance.
- Why was this experience valuable? What did it teach you? What skills did it develop? How did it help you progress toward achieving any of the course learning outcomes?

After a service-learning experience, pose questions like these:

- What are the links between your experience and the outcomes and content of the course?
- What feedback did you receive from the people and the agency you served, and how did you use it?
- What academic and personal value did the experience have for you? What did you learn from it? What intellectual and personal strengths and weaknesses did it reveal in you?
- What skills did you gain or improve? When do you think these skills will prove useful in the future?
- How would you assess the value of your contribution?
- What would you do differently if you could?

Creating educational opportunities for students to engage in learning that simulates any form of real-life experience can be a valuable experience. Such an experience allows students to see how their learning informs real-life experiences, how experiences can help solidify learning, and how reflecting on such experiences can impact future experiences. If you decide to adopt this form of teaching strategy, it will take you additional time. That said, the impact on the students and your enjoyment in the outcomes, based on those who have done this previously, is likely to be significant.

REFLECTION QUESTIONS

Reflection Question 16.1: Why might role-playing create a more significant learning experience than would talking about the topic and content of that which is being role-played? What is the advantage of assuming the role versus talking about such a role?

Reflection Question 16.2: How might service-learning impact moral development in a course in which you teach? What would be necessary with respect to the student participation in order for this moral development to happen?

Concept Into Practice: Search the web for a simulation related to some aspect of a course in which you teach. If nothing is found, expand the search to content closely related to what you teach. How might the simulation be included in your course structure?

CHAPTER 17

Teaching with Inquiry-Guided Methods

I n many ways, inquiry is at the root of a primary goal of higher education: We want our students to become independent, lifelong learners. For this to happen, students need to learn how to answer questions; identify good questions to ask; effectively assess their progress; and, when feasible, advance a position by developing models and concepts. Inquiry-guided learning is an excellent instructional approach that helps students achieve these desired educational outcomes.

In 1998, the influential Boyer Commission on Educating Undergraduates in the Research University wrote a blueprint for educating undergraduates. The commission offered 10 recommendations with the goal of reinventing undergraduate education, with the second recommendation being that institutions in higher education should "(2) construct an inquiry-based freshman year" (Boyer Commission on Educating Undergraduates in the Research University, 1998). Their inquiry-based suggestion, also known as inquiry-guided learning, was quickly adopted by many institutions within the United States and abroad. Although *inquiry-guided learning* as a term had mass appeal, it has been challenging to define and standardize as an instructional approach. It may also be called *inquiry-based learning, inquiry learning, guided inquiry, guided discovery,* and *Process Oriented Guided Inquiry Learning (POGIL)* and has a range of slightly different definitions. The root of the challenge is that inquiry-guided learning is not a single strategy, but rather an approach that encompasses many teaching strategies. As such, it is not easy to name or specifically describe (Lee, 2012).

DEFINITIONS OF INQUIRY-GUIDED LEARNING

Inquiry-guided learning, whatever minor variation being used, involves giving students a challenge, such as a question, a hypothesis, or simply data to interpret, and they learn whatever they must to meet that challenge, which may or may not go beyond the course material (Prince & Felder, 2007). The students may also develop questions as part of the process, although it is not strictly necessary. The inquiry may have a very narrow scope—for instance, one question that a segment of the lecture raises—or a very broad one entailing a major term project based on outside research. Prince and Felder also consider inquiry-guided learning an umbrella for several major methods—the case method, problem-based learning, discovery learning, project-based learning, and just-in-time-teaching (JiTT)—all of which they call *inductive teaching*. The case method and solving challenging STEM problems merit their own chapters in this book (see Chapters 18 and 20), as they are complex, well-researched, and widely used across the disciplines. The remaining approaches require less explanation and are treated within this chapter. These methods all launch the learning process with a realistic, problematic situation and require that students do research and assemble facts, data, and concepts to resolve the given problem or situation. Giving students challenging problems in the STEM disciplines also qualifies as inductive teaching.

THE EFFECTIVENESS OF INQUIRY-GUIDED LEARNING

Inquiry-guided learning's inductive nature makes it a powerful learning method. It typically involves acquisition and comprehension of knowledge, analysis of data, evaluation of evidence, application of findings to a situation or problem, and synthesis of one or more resolutions. In short, it requires that students engage in multiple modes of higher-order thinking. In addition, it introduces *desirable difficulties* into the learning process, which, as we noted in Chapter 1, promote deep learning and long-term retention of the material (Bjork, 1994, 2013; Bjork & Bjork, 2011).

Compared to lecture-based instruction, inquiry-guided learning does an excellent job of fostering students' academic achievement and improving their critical thinking, reflective learning, problem-solving, and laboratory skills (Archer-Kuhn et al., 2020; McCreary et al., 2006; Oliver-Hoyo & Allen, 2005; Oliver-Hoyo et al., 2004).

Engagement in inquiry-guided activities is also related to a student's perceived gains in science and technology understanding, intellectual development, and vocational preparation (Hu et al., 2008; Justice

et al., 2007; Pascarella & Terenzini, 2005). A meta-analysis of 46 comparisons from journal articles published between 1998 and 2017, with 12,585 students represented, showed a positive effect on students' academic achievement (Chen & Yang, 2019). To be fair, however, it does have a negative effect on perceived gains in general education and personal development, and its positive impacts are not as strong for low-performing students as they are for high-performing students (Hu et al., 2008).

THE NEED FOR STUDENT GUIDANCE

Like every other teaching method, the benefits of inquiry-guided learning depend on its implementation. To be effective, students must have sufficient guidance and scaffolding through the inquiry process—that is, explicit directions about what to do and how to do it, assuming they are dealing with new material. Hudspith and Jenkins (2001) noted that this process could take two terms to do well, whereas others assert that inquiry-guided learning can be done effectively within a single semester and could even be a supplement to another teaching strategy to address a targeted content area (Lee, 2011). Regardless of how inquiry is incorporated into the course, an overwhelming amount of research documents the need for sufficient guidance and scaffolding, as well as the failure of minimally guided, problem-centered instruction, commonly called *discovery learning* or *open discovery* (Aulls, 2002; Kirschner et al., 2006; Klahr & Nigam, 2004; Mayer, 2004; Moreno, 2004; National Survey of Student Engagement, 2007). The challenge with discovery learning is that in practice, without guidance of any kind, students are unlikely to discover a field's basic principles in a semester by following the investigative techniques of professional researchers. However, the stronger the students' background knowledge in the subject matter, the less guidance they need (Kirschner et al., 2006), so an instructor can, and often should, withdraw scaffolding as they acquire more knowledge (Hmelo-Silver et al., 2007). As students begin thinking more like experts, they are better able to identify key characteristics of a problem as well as the procedures and algorithms to solve it, thereby drawing on "internal guidance" (Kirschner et al., 2006). Acquiring this knowledge base may require somewhat more conventional learning strategies.

The literature endorses two forms of guidance, or scaffolding, both of which make up for a weak or incomplete command of basic knowledge. The first form is *worked examples*, which serve as models of problem-solving schemata for students. They illustrate the procedures and logic for approaching and working through problems (Chi et al., 1982). When students can follow a model, they have enough working memory available for processing these procedures and the reasoning behind them. Without worked examples, they have to divert much of their working memory to searching their long-term memory for possible strategies (Kirschner et al., 2006). Numerous studies from the 1980s and 1990s show that students learn more when they can study worked examples before tackling comparable problems on their own (Kirschner et al., 2006).

The second form of guidance is *process worksheets*. These lay out a proven sequence of problem-solving steps for students to follow, sometimes with hints and heuristics. With this structure, students don't rush headlong into problems. They must first identify the useful information they do and don't have, classify the problem, visualize it (in mathematics, the physical sciences, and engineering), and perform whatever other steps are prescribed for reasoning through the type of problem. As a result, students display improved task performance (Nadolski et al., 2005).

It is quite easy to vary the amount of guidance and challenge for students (Lee, 2011). To increase guidance, you can do more modeling, use journal articles as models, add guiding questions, share heuristics, provide assessment rubrics, assign readings, or minilecture on background knowledge or relevant inquiry skills, such as hypothesis development or data analysis. To augment challenge, you can introduce irrelevant information, expand the scope of the inquiry, withhold helpful information, and suggest multiple perspectives. Experience will teach you where the optimal balance lies (Lee, 2011).

OBJECTS OF INQUIRY

What might students inquire about? For most courses, it is helpful to supply the object of their inquiry. The following are categories of objects that apply to many disciplines, as well as possible questions to pursue (Hudspith & Jenkins, 2001):

- *A phenomenon*: Does it exist? If so, to what magnitude? What are its causes? What are its effects? Examples: black holes, transgender students participating in primary school sports, dual coding, election fraud, plate tectonics, near-death experiences, a change in the violent crime rate.
- *The absence of an expected phenomenon*: What prevents (prevented) it from happening? Examples: what prevents acceptance of evolutionary theory in the curricula of many K–12 school systems, bipartisan support of U.S. Supreme Court nominees, a foreign nation's economic collapse.
- *A perceived relationship*: Does it exist? To what extent? To what extent is it causal or spurious? Examples: the links between education and income, religiosity and political affiliation, global warming and human activity, diet and cancer, capital punishment and violent crime rates.
- *A controversy*: What underlies it? Examples: Why do physicians disagree about the role the mind plays in healing? Should masks be required during a pandemic? Why do some people believe that tax cuts on dividends and interest stimulate the economy and others do not? What are the criteria for determining which paintings are important pieces of work?
- *A theory*: How well does it explain and predict a phenomenon? How is it related to one or more other theories? Examples: evolutionary biology,

the "great man" theory of history, the big bang theory, functionalism/pluralism versus conflict theory/elitism.

- *A complex concept*: What is its meaning? How well grounded is it in fact or observation? Examples: opioid addiction, dark matter, genetic marker, constructivism, cultural drift.
- *A process*: How does it work? Examples: How does lupus undermine the immune system? How does economic development lower birthrates? How does the U.S. Census Bureau determine what to ask and how to ask it on the census questionnaire? How do people make decisions about purchasing a house?
- *A solution to a problem*: How can a given problem be solved? Examples: How can we reduce the incidence of school shootings? How can we determine the reasons behind the demise of the Neanderthals? How can we respond more effectively to the next pandemic given what we learned during COVID-19? How can we reverse the trend of increasing economic inequality?
- *A course of action*: How sound or desirable is it? Examples: producing genetically engineered foods, setting the legal drinking age at 21, allowing secure voting drop boxes throughout a large city, instituting charter schools to spur improvement in the public school system, allowing private corporations to oversee healthcare, charging young undocumented immigrants in-state college tuition.

■ MODES OF INQUIRY

Another way of getting your mind around inquiry-guided activities, especially if you teach in the sciences, engineering, or technical fields, is to consider various modes of inquiry (Arons, 1993). Students can tackle tasks such as these:

- Observe phenomena qualitatively and interpret what they perceive, trying to identify patterns.
- Formulate concepts out of their observations.

- Develop and test models that reflect their observations and concepts.
- Examine and use a new piece of equipment to make measurements, analyze the data, and present the results.
- Use everyday items to create sculptures and predict who might have the best response to the pieces.
- Distinguish explicitly between what they have observed and what they are inferring in interpreting the results of observations and experiments.
- Answer probing questions about a given research study, such as, "How do we know . . . ?" "Why do we think . . . ?" and "How strong is the evidence for . . . ?"
- Ask and answer "What will happen if . . . ?" questions (called *hypothetical-deductive reasoning*) about an experiment or other type of research study. If possible, students can follow up by proposing hypotheses and testing them in an experiment that they themselves design.

Although often targeted toward physical and biological sciences, these modes can be adapted for any area in higher education. In fact, inquiry-guided learning works very well in the arts and humanities. Perhaps the most varied examples of this method's implementation appear in Lee's (2004) edited volume, which showcases the teaching scholarship of North Carolina State University faculty members. In addition to inquiry-based courses in food science, microbiology, physics, paper science and engineering, forestry, and psychology, you can read about such courses in history, design, music appreciation, French culture and civilization, and Spanish language. In history, for example, students do what historians do: find, evaluate, and analyze primary sources and then develop logical arguments supporting particular historical interpretations with evidence from their research (Slatta, 2004). In Spanish for Engineers, students research how the Spanish culture, in history and today, influences and informs technology (Kennedy & Navey-Davis, 2004). In music appreciation, they investigate the scientific aspects of music (sound, acoustics, hearing, and recording technology), as well as the artistic (musical expression, interpretation, meaning, and value). Although the former aspects allow experimentation and testing, the latter, lacking universally agreed-on standards, permit students to develop and defend their own reasoned judgments (Kramer & Arnold, 2004). Across the disciplines, students have the opportunity to learn inductively and critically think their way to their own conclusions.

TYPES OF INQUIRY-BASED LEARNING

The following section contains information regarding three common types of inquiry-based learning: just-in-time teaching (JiTT), project-based learning, and problem-based learning.

JiTT

Students receive conceptual questions on reading assignments, usually multiple choice, shortly before each class through the LMS. (Because this material has not yet been discussed in class, JiTT is considered inductive.) The instructor then designs or adjusts their plan for the upcoming class based on students' answers. The goal is to address and challenge students' misconceptions on the subject matter before they become further ingrained and inhibit learning of new material.

The research on this method attests to its learning effectiveness. Novak et al. (1999) credited it with reducing attrition by 40% and raising students' normalized gains on the Force Concept Inventory by 35–40% in physics courses that were previously lecture based. A study on a large introductory biology course found comparable and additional benefits to JiTT: higher normalized pretest-posttest gains and lower attrition, plus improved student preparation, study habits, and class participation (Marrs & Novak, 2004). Research in general chemistry and organic chemistry courses also documented higher

student achievement and engagement due to JiTT (Slunt & Giancarlo, 2004). Williams Ware et al. (2021) successfully employed JiTT in nursing skills labs focused on teaching cardiac rhythms.

Some instructors are wary of trying JiTT because they have to prepare conceptual questions on all the readings. However, these items are the same type as those used in the interactive lecture, and some disciplines, especially the sciences, already have dedicated websites with many conceptual multiple-choice questions for collegial use (see Chapter 14).

Project-Based Learning

Project-based learning (PBL) was developed by William Kilpatrick and explained in a short narrative book (Kilpatrick, 1929). For most of higher education we present content to students, develop ways for them to practice, and then we assess their learning. Project-based learning turns this around and adds an element of what students may encounter in their lived experiences. Students, often in teams, are given a project or design their own project. This might be a piece of equipment, a product or architectural design, a computer code, a strategy for containing a virus in a small town, an artistic or literary work, a website, a scientific poster, or a research paper. A key to project-based learning is that students collect, analyze, and present real data.

Positive results have been noted through research on project-based learning, including investigations into affective outcomes, cognitive outcomes, and behavioral outcomes (Guo et al., 2020). Compared to more conventional methods, project-based learning contributes to students' conceptual understanding, problem-solving skills, attitudes about learning, and self-regulation. Students engaged in project-based learning perform the same or better than those using traditional learning on content-focused tests (Mills & Treagust, 2003; Thomas, 2000). In a meta-analysis including research that spanned 20 years and represented 12,585 students, Chen and Yang (2019) found a medium-to-large mean weighted effect size of .71 for student achievement when project-based learning was used, as compared to traditional instruction. Graduate students in education who choose their own projects have reported significant improvements in their communication, creativity, problem-solving, self-direction, and sense of responsibility (Wurdinger & Qureshi, 2015).

There are two essential elements of projects. First is the question selected, which will guide learning activities and the organization of the groups' project. The second element is the artifact(s) resulting from the project, or the solution of students as determined by the activities used to propel the driving question.

In a review of the literature, Kokotsaki et al. (2016) summarized the work of project-based learning experts and identified six elements that are considered essential if you adopt a project-based learning approach.

1. Student Support: Students must be guided in the areas of time management, working in groups, and use of technology resources. Group sizes for project-based learning range from two to six.
2. Teacher Support: As with any teaching strategy, senior management support is critical, as is ongoing professional development and networking with others engaged in project-based learning.
3. Effective Group Work: Students need to be taught strategies to work well in groups (see Chapter 10).
4. Balanced Instructional Methods: Lectures can be used to provide a base of knowledge and skills after which students can engage in independent work. Providing the necessary background material in readings, homework problems, and minilectures, although somewhat intensive to set up, are essential for project-based learning (Duda, 2014).

5. Assessment: The emphasis should be on reflection, self, and peer evaluation. Planning for assessment means regularly identifying progress being made with respect to this form of learning.
6. Student Choice and Autonomy: In developing their projects, students should feel ownership and control over their learning.

The actual classroom management of using project-based and problem-based learning is similar to case-based learning, which is detailed in Chapter 18. Project-based learning has been successfully used in higher education for decades. If this teaching strategy is of interest to you, it would be wise to seek out a colleague who has used this approach previously or check with your campus center for teaching and learning. If these options are not available, there are many resources in the literature detailing the value of project-based learning and ways to get started, such as: https://www.youtube.com/watch?v=vc0S5fdwng0 and the Worchester Polytechnic Institute's Center for Project-Based Learning, at https://wp.wpi.edu/projectbasedlearning.

Problem-Based Learning

Problem-based learning (also referred to as PBL) is a subset of project-based learning. When you see PBL, clarify whether the reference is to project-based learning or problem-based learning. Whereas project-based learning results in a product, problem-based learning is focused on learning through solving a problem (Blumenfeld et al., 1991). Problem-based learning was first developed at Case Western University in the 1950s and simultaneously emerged at McMaster University in the late 1960s. During the 1970s, problem-based learning spread to several dozen North American medical schools (Jonas et al., 1989; Kaufman, 1985; Kaufman et al., 1989;

Kirschner et al., 2006). By the 2000s, PBL was being used throughout the United States in a wide variety of disciplines.

Problem-based learning problems tend to be messy and fuzzy by design, requiring that students search for information outside what the course material alone can provide. Students must do their own research, which usually makes the problem-solving process a sizable project best conducted by teams of at least four (Duch et al., 2001). PBL tends to leave students more or less on their own to research their problem and devise solutions to it, but the following series of steps are a helpful and virtually necessary framework (Amador et al., 2006; Edens, 2000):

1. Team members review the problem, which is typically ill structured, and clarify the meaning of terms they do not understand.
2. They analyze and define the problem (at times with guidance you provide).
3. They identify and organize the knowledge they already have to solve the problem. This may also mean identifying and ignoring extraneous information given in the problem.
4. They identify the new knowledge they need to acquire to solve the problem—the *learning issues.*
5. They organize and rank-order the learning issues and set objectives for outside research. (You may or may not provide references.)
6. They divide the work among themselves.
7. They conduct the assigned research individually by agreed-on deadlines.
8. They continue to meet to share research findings and conduct additional research as needed.
9. They merge their newly acquired and previous knowledge into what they consider to be the best possible solution. (This step qualifies PBL as a constructivist method.)
10. They write up or orally present their solution.

Once the instructor guides students through the basic procedures, the teams should work as independently as possible. Each devises its own internal organization and decision-making rules for evaluating alternative formulations of and solutions to the problem. Members integrate course materials with outside library, internet, interview, survey, documentary, or field research. Depending on the problem, the assessable product may take any of several possible forms: a lengthy memo, a report, a scholarly manuscript, a budget, a plan of action, or an oral presentation to the class or a hypothetical decision-making body. As with project-based learning, assessment may be done via reflection, self, and peer evaluation. In addition, solutions may also be assessed if a rubric is developed ahead of time and shared with students.

Problem-based learning is not used as frequently as it was a decade or more ago, so up-to-date, well-tested PBL scenarios can be a challenge to find. However, quite a few are available in the sciences and business and several in the social sciences and medicine. The best source across the disciplines is https://www.itue.udel.edu/resources/pbl-resources. This site also has some articles on teaching with PBL.

Problem-based learning is based on the well-tested principle of students learning by actively doing (see Chapter 1), and they typically get to practice a variety of higher-order and social skills: recording, scheduling, conducting meetings, discussing, prioritizing, organizing, planning, researching, applying, analyzing, integrating, evaluating, making decisions, compromising, cooperating, persuading, negotiating, and resolving conflict. Beyond these basics, you decide and determine what your students will learn to do and what additional knowledge they will acquire by their research in your choice or design of a problem.

According to the research, problem-based learning is especially effective in developing the following abilities in students (Albanese & Dast, 2014; Dochy et al., 2003; Edens, 2000; Hintz, 2005; Hung et al., 2003; Major & Palmer, 2001; Mierson & Parikh, 2000; Prince, 2004; Prince & Felder, 2006; Strobel & van Barneveld, 2009; Svensson et al., 2021):

- Teamwork
- Project management and leadership
- Oral and often written communication
- Emotional intelligence
- Tolerance for uncertainty
- Critical thinking and analysis
- Conceptual understanding and deep learning
- High-level strategies for understanding and self-directed study
- Application (transfer) of content knowledge
- Clinical performance (health fields)
- Application of metacognitive strategies
- Research and information-seeking skills
- Retention of knowledge
- Decision-making
- Problem-solving (of course), including knowledge transfer, often across disciplines

In addition, problem-based learning activates prior knowledge and imparts new knowledge in the context in which it will later be used. In this way, it builds in enough redundancy to ensure the knowledge is well understood and retained. If the problem mirrors situations that students will encounter in their future occupations, PBL develops career realism as well as skills.

If you want to compose your own PBL problem, follow these steps (adapted from D. Johnston in Biggs, 2003, and Mastascusa et al., 2011):

1. Identify the concepts, knowledge, and skills required to propose a good solution.
2. Write out your student learning outcomes for the PBL project.
3. Find a real problem that fits your learning outcomes and that your students may encounter in their careers or civic lives.
4. Write your problem as you would a case: in the present tense, with specific data and a practitioner role or multiple roles that students can assume. Embellish the problem with unnecessary information, dramatic detail, character development, and the like.
5. Consider omitting some information that you know students can either estimate or find out in the course of their research.
6. Consider structuring your problem as an extended rollout type, letting realism be your guide.
7. Define the deliverable—for example, a decision, a lengthy memo, a manuscript, a report, a budget, a plan of action, or a persuasive presentation—and develop a rubric for assessing student products. Be sure the deliverable integrates decisions that students have to make.

After testing and refining your problem in your course, you can even publish it if you also write a facilitator's guide. Include in the guide the information in the preceding steps, and add content background for facilitators and suggested resources for students.

■ UPCOMING INQUIRY-GUIDED METHODS

Inquiry-guided learning is a powerful, deliberately ambiguous, active learning technique that supports students in becoming lifelong independent learners. Research consistently shows that students like inquiry-guided learning, as it gives them an opportunity to address more real-world issues. Faculty members like this approach for the same reason. The case study approach is one of the most researched and employed strategies of inquiry-guided learning, and for that reason the entirety of Chapter 18 is devoted to the case study method. This approach belongs in anyone's teaching at its best toolbox. In addition, you will see the inquiry-guided methods of SCALE-UP and POGIL in Chapter 20, when we turn our attention to STEM education.

■ REFLECTION QUESTIONS

Reflection Question 17.1: To what extent have you used (or seen) some form of inquiry-guided strategies incorporated with other teaching strategies in the classroom, online or face-to-face?

Reflection Question 17.2: What objects of inquiry are particularly important in your subject area? Why?

Concept into Practice: Complete a web search to find either a project or a problem that would fit with the content in a course you are teaching, or going to teach. Outline briefly the theme of the project or problem, the learning outcome for the course that it would address, and a rough outline of how you would implement this inquiry-guided learning component in your course. NOTE: If you already use an inquiry-guided method of learning, try an area of inquiry-guided learning you have not done so that you may check out a new area.

CHAPTER 18

Creating Engaging Cases

The case method is an inquiry-guided approach designed to help students learn how to solve open-ended, high-uncertainty problems that have multiple respectable solutions—some better than others, to be sure. The case method was first used heavily in law, medicine, and business. The use of cases has spread across the college curriculum and is appropriate to any discipline with real-world application. Chapter 20 suggests ways to construct tutorials and laboratories to teach students the process of scientific problem-solving.

It is important to understand that the case method for teaching is fundamentally different from the case study approach used by researchers to investigate an issue by studying a single person or incident. The case method of teaching exposes students to problematic, real-world situations and challenges them to apply course knowledge to analyze the issues and formulate workable solutions. Teaching through case studies works well in courses with 20–30 students, but has also been used in large-enrollment courses (Tayce et al., 2019).

Cases are based on real or realistic stories that present problems or dilemmas that are quite well structured but lack an obvious or clear resolution.

Cases are usually text-based, but some are available dramatized on video. Those in web-based learning objects may add the dramatic realism of interactivity. If canned cases do not suit your instructional purposes, you can write your own at no cost but your time. Anyone with a bit of storytelling flair should find case writing an entertaining activity. To guide you in writing or selecting cases, this chapter identifies the qualities of a good case and describes the many types of cases.

THE EFFECTIVENESS OF THE CASE METHOD

Aside from the fact that students enjoy the case method, good cases are rich educational tools for a host of reasons. Cases:

- Require students' active engagement in and use of the material (Nohria, 2021; Sharkey et al., 2007).
- Accustom students to solving problems within uncertain, risk-laden environments, thus promoting cognitive development from the dualistic

mode of thinking to informed judgments about the best approaches and solutions to difficult problems (Fasko, 2003).

- Foster higher-level critical thinking and cognitive skills such as application, analysis, synthesis, and evaluation, all of which come into play in the process of thinking through and developing solutions to a case (Burgess et al., 2021; Dinan, 2002; Habron & Dann, 2002; Yadav et al., 2014).
- Raise awareness of the ethical side of decisions and biases we each brings to situations (Lundeberg et al., 2002; Nohria, 2021).
- Demand both inductive and deductive thinking, compensating for higher education's usual focus on the latter (Schröter & Röber, 2021).
- Serve as excellent writing assignments, paper topics, and essay questions, as well as springboards for discussion, review, and team activities.
- Promote collaboration and self-confidence (Nohria, 2021).
- Increase class attendance (Kaur et al., 2020).
- Improve the students' perceptions of and confidence in their learning, as well as faculty members' attitudes about teaching (Lundeberg & Yadav, 2006a, 2006b; Sharkey et al., 2007).
- Enhance students' achievement of their learning outcomes in their instructors' eyes (Lundeberg & Yadav, 2006a, 2006b; Rybarczyk et al., 2007).

On the student-involvement continuum from didactic methods (lecture) on the low end to experiential methods (such as role plays, simulations, and service-learning) on the high end, the case method falls somewhere in the middle, depending on the case. The more it resembles a simulation, the more experiential the learning is.

THE SUBJECT MATTER AND WEBSITES FOR CASES

The case method accommodates any discipline or subfield that has a context for application or use. This is why professional schools have adopted it as a central instructional method. Business and law did so decades ago; in fact, Harvard Business School built a whole curriculum and publishing company around it. Medicine, nursing, clinical psychology, educational administration, and pastoral studies followed, as have many engineering and science fields, and music history (Chiaramonte, 1994), philosophy (ethics), economics (macro, legal aspects), political science (policy analysis, public administration, constitutional law), sociology (social problems, criminology, organizations), experimental and organizational psychology, biology (resource management, ecology, paleontology), mathematics, and research methods (study design and implementation to test a given hypothesis).

Following are examples of tested cases, a few for purchase, but the vast majority may be used for free. Check your discipline for cases that have already been written and tested:

- For all sciences (over 500 cases, all peer reviewed): https://www.nsta.org/case-studies
- For biology, especially molecular (almost 40 cases): http://www.caseitproject.org
- For ethics in engineering (over 40 cases): https://www.depts.ttu.edu/murdoughcenter/products/cases.php
- For ethics in engineering (over 100 cases): https://ethics.tamu.edu/nsf-report
- For statistics (26 cases): https://www.causeweb.org/cause/resources/library/r1286
- For a variety of disciplines from all over the world: https://www.thecasecentre.org/buy/products/freeCases

If you teach physics or mathematics, you can find many dozens of *context-rich problems*, which are essentially minicases, at https://groups.spa.umn.edu/physed/Research/CRP/on-lineArchive/ola.php and learn to write your own at http://groups.physics.umn.edu/physed/Research/CRP/crcreate.html.

An excellent source of advice and strategies for teaching with the case method can be found at: http://serc.carleton.edu/sp/library/cases/index.html.

A Chemistry, Geology, or Environmental Engineering Case

As an environmental chemist with the Environmental Protection Agency, you are charged with directing the remediation of a residential area with lead levels in the soil of 700–900 ppm. Your funding for this project is limited. Your advisory team is bitterly divided between two strategies: physical removal of the lead-contaminated soil and phytoremediation.

These sources offer relevant cases in medicine, nursing, the allied health fields, and public health:

- For epidemiology and public health (8 cases for purchase): http://www.cdc.gov/epicasestudies
- For pathology (over 850 cases): http://path.upmc.edu/cases.html
- For the health fields on allergies (8 cases): https://allianceallergy.com/case-studies

Even faculty and TA development has embraced the method. It uses cases portraying problems that instructors may encounter with classes and individual students—for example, challenges to authority, hostile reactions to sensitive material, accusations of discrimination, grading and academic honesty disputes, and difficulties implementing new teaching and assessment techniques.

■ TYPES OF CASES

A good case may range from brief to very long. *Bullet cases* make one teaching point in just two or three sentences. They serve as good small-group discussion topics and short essay questions. *Minicases* are a tightly focused paragraph or two; if dramatized in a minute or two, they are called *vignettes*. They generate more discussion and analysis than do bullet cases. You can easily modify either type by confining the possible solutions to four or five reasonable options, much like a multiple-choice question. Then students must identify and justify their selection of the best solution. At the other extreme are cases like those that Harvard Business School publishes, which range from a couple of pages to over 40 pages.

Most cases, and virtually all bullet cases and minicases, represent a one-time snapshot of a situation. Depending on their length, cases are typically designed to occupy students for 15 to 20 minutes, a class period or two, or a single homework assignment. Longer cases can either elaborate the specifics in a snapshot or tell an unfolding story in segments over real or condensed time, in which case they are *continuous cases*. Because real-life situations usually evolve over time, this structure adds realism. For instance, some faculty development cases describe

A Faculty Development Case

Three weeks after midterms, Hadley stops by your office on Monday afternoon. You had noticed that Hadley missed class the past two weeks for a total of four class periods, also missing a one-page response paper that was due last Thursday. Hadley is asking if there is any way to make up the missed assignment and maybe take a makeup exam on Friday instead of the scheduled test on Wednesday in two days. Hadley explained the absence over the past two weeks was due to a flare-up of depression with extreme fatigue that was so bad it was next to impossible just to get out of bed to go to the bathroom. Prior to missing the last 2 weeks, Hadley had no absences and a 91% average in the course.

A Minicase for Physics or Mathematics

You are a consultant for a semiprofessional baseball league. There have been discussions about creating higher-scoring games, but not too high. The goal is to have teams score about 10 runs per game. What aspects of the game can change to increase the number of hits?—for example, the bases, pitcher's mound, and size of fields (i.e., distances of fence from home plate).

an instructor's shifting relationship with a class over a term, with each minichapter presenting different issues to consider. Some medical and nursing cases follow the progression of a disease or a pregnancy in a hypothetical patient.

A final type, the *sequential-interactive case*, tells a continuing story that shifts directions according to student decisions, much the way a *choose-your-own-adventure* book works. It leads students through a process of narrowing down their solutions or decisions by providing additional information *as the students request it*. Approaching the experiential realism of a simulation, this type of case casts students in the key decision-making role throughout, requiring that at least their minds act it out. Here is a step-by-step outline of how you can structure such a case across subject matter, with the medical or clinical variant in parentheses:

1. Students study a case giving limited information on the nature or root cause of a problem. First, they brainstorm all interpretations or causes (diagnoses) and their solutions (treatment plans). Then they rank-order the interpretations or causes (diagnoses) according to the ease and feasibility for verifying or eliminating them (ease and safety of testing).
2. Students request specific additional information, beginning with what they have ranked as the easiest and most feasible to obtain (easiest and safest to test) to help them narrow down the possible interpretations or causes (diagnoses).
3. You provide the information as they request it. (You should have additional information on hand for any likely request that may be made.)

4. Students again rank-order the possible interpretations or causes (diagnoses) in light of the new information and repeat step 2.
5. You repeat step 3.
6. Students select the most likely one or two interpretations or causes (diagnoses) and their solutions (treatment plans).

Depending on the subject matter and the problem, you may also want to include the ease and feasibility of implementing a solution (treatment plan) as a rank-ordering criterion. After all, if students identify widespread poverty as the root cause of a problem, they may not be able to develop a workable, action-oriented solution. Alternatively, you may wish to focus attention on the relative importance or likelihood of a cause. The case method is extremely flexible.

■ WHAT MAKES A GOOD CASE, AND HOW TO WRITE YOUR OWN

Make it clear to students what your role will be during the case discussion. Are you a resource or are you to be treated as an invisible observer? You might also consider creating your own facilitator's guide, listing outcomes, resources, main points, and other items for easy reference as the class works through the case and questions or comments arise.

Prior to writing (or choosing) a case, consider your learners and who they are. In Chapter 1 we included a section on the importance of knowing your students. We will use cases to illustrate one more example of why that is important. In building or selecting a case it is important to keep in mind what skills, knowledge, practices your students have or need to develop (Montrosse-Moorhead et al., 2022). It is also helpful to keep in mind the cultural relevance by selecting cases that resonate with the learner with respect to their culture and background. Finally, the current situation of the learner is an important consideration—where do they live, are they in a high- or low-population area, and what interests your learners?

A good case may be written in the second or third person and in the present or past tense, and it may be almost any length. What is important is that it have the following qualities.

1. *Scope.* If you are new to teaching with cases, start with lower complexity and time-bound scenarios. You can always build out as you (and your students) become more comfortable with the format.
2. *Realism.* Real or hypothetical, a case should depict a currently relevant situation with which students can empathize or identify. Realism is further enhanced by technical detail, character development, historical context, the inclusion of irrelevant as well as relevant information, and extension over time or a decision-making process (see the next section). If using a real case, be sure to change names and any other identifiers as appropriate.
3. *Opportunities for synthesis.* Cases should require students to draw on accumulated knowledge of the subject matter to analyze the problems and formulate solutions. Without some review built into the situations, students may forget to apply the basics in real decision-making situations in their careers.
4. *Uncertainty.* Although some solutions will be better than others, a case should offer room for multiple solutions and valid debate. Several solutions may be viable, but you may have students select just one course of action or rank-order their options and justify their decisions. The uncertainty surrounding the solutions may be due to

uncertainty in the knowledge base (a trait of all bodies of knowledge), information missing in the case (as is often true in reality), or the genuine validity of different approaches to the problem.
5. *Risk.* The decisions students make must have some importance, even if it is only hypothetical—for example, a character's employment, health, or life; an organization's survival or success; a country's welfare; the outcome of a legal case; social justice; or public security. Something valuable must be at stake.
6. *Technology.* The case may involve some technology as part of the case. Cases may also be set up such that individuals work in a collaborative space (e.g., Padlet, Jamboard), whether in an online, or onsite course.
7. *Assessment.* Identify how you will assess student learning and the effectiveness of using the case method. Keep in mind backward design as a framework to decide what is important and meeting student learning outcomes as the real value of using cases (Schröter & Röber, 2021).

Inspiration for good cases can come from a wide variety of sources. Once you get used to looking for material to serve as a focus of a case, you will see viable material everywhere (Herreid, 2019). Sources for your cases include:

- News, journal, or magazine articles
- Product descriptions or advertisements
- Provocative statements by experts or leaders
- Testimonials and complaints by patients or users
- Excerpts from memos, letters, primary sources, ethnographies, laws, or public policies
- Cartoons
- Data sources, such as spreadsheets, graphs, charts, clinicals, and public records
- Flyers posted in public places
- Social media feeds
- Your own professional or personal experience

After you have selected the subject matter, identified the type of case you wish to present, and written the case, it is a good idea to confirm that the case will actually help students achieve your overall learning outcomes for the course. Cases should not be used because they are interesting or because students enjoy working on them, although those are undoubtedly benefits of using the case method. Cases should be used only if they are educationally valuable and a good use of time. It is extremely helpful to have a colleague look everything over before you launch your case, particularly if you have a colleague who frequently uses cases. Thank your colleague for whatever advice is provided and adapt as necessary. If no one in your department uses cases, check to see if someone in the college of business might be willing to take 15 minutes to talk to you about your case. Once your case has been reviewed and approved as a valuable learning opportunity, it is time to get it into the hands of your students.

■ FACILITATING CASES

On the Harvard Business School website, one of the pioneers of case-method teaching described this teaching approach as "the art of managing uncertainty" (Christensen Center, n.d., para. 1). By design, this approach brings with it a good deal of uncertainty as it provides neither a prescriptive route nor a single correct solution. As such, it is best used by faculty members with a very strong grasp of the content and typically a bit of teaching experience.

Facilitating the case method is very different from teaching strategies that are more scripted. For example, the lecture is a predictable educational experience, as you deliver information in one direction or respond to questions that typically closely align with the material being presented. Even other active learning strategies, such as the think-pair-share or student response questions, often have expected results or a specific way of going about the activity. The case method, on the other hand, as noted at the beginning of this chapter, has no designated route that students must take; indeed, it's unknown where

they will end up. That makes facilitating cases more challenging and, as one gains teaching experience, brings more interest and excitement into the course (Schröter & Röber, 2021).

Preparing for and Introducing the Case

With an appropriate case and discussion questions, the first decision is how to open the case activity. One possibility is to give students some background information prior to the class period in which the case is revealed. Students may be assigned information to find or issues to investigate to prepare for the case. You may also assign a reading or other material for students to complete that is due the day of the case. Let students know if you are going to give a quiz to check that they did the work. A "pop" quiz catches those who didn't do the work, but it doesn't motivate students to prepare if students didn't expect the quiz.

Prior to having students start the case, you may choose to do any of the following either individually or in combination:

- Give students a short multiple-choice quiz that you told them would occur to hold them accountable for preparing as assigned.
- Remind students that everyone in the group is expected to participate and encourage students to support one another.
- Reinforce that the goal is to come up with a conclusion supported by the group, not to see which person has the best ideas or solutions.
- Deliver a minilecture just prior to the case to provide key information.
- Give a worksheet with key details of the case to consider.
- Provide a worksheet of questions that are to be answered as the case is worked.
- Inform groups that they are to come up with two conclusions, a primary conclusion and a secondary conclusion (to reaffirm that there are no single correct responses).
- Note the time they have to complete the case and at which point you will give time warnings.

Monitoring Progress

Decide ahead of time what your role will be as the cases are being worked. You may play the role of a supervisor, a client, or a lawyer, or any other role that may provide information if requested. If you do participate, ensure your role is a minor role and consider how much time it will take you to respond to groups. You don't want to create a backlog of groups waiting to ask you for something, as they will likely not be doing anything while waiting. You might decide that you are available only for clarifying what something in the case means. It is also perfectly acceptable to simply tell the groups that once the cases start, they may not ask you anything until it is time to stop working the cases.

Debriefing

For cases to function well as homework assignments, paper topics, essay exam questions, or discussion springboards, you will need to guide students through a productive debriefing. That is, challenge them with good questions about the case—questions that engage them in application, analysis, and synthesis of the material, plus critical evaluation of their proposed interpretations and solutions.

The simplest formula for debriefing a case is problems-remedies-prevention, that is: "What are the problems?" "What are the solutions?" and, if applicable, "How could these problems have been prevented?" The structure for sequential-interactive cases often follows this basic formula.

You can launch a case discussion with the entire class (see Chapter 15) or have students discuss a case in groups (see Chapter 10). Using groups offers still more options:

- All groups can work on the same case with the proviso that each group reach a consensus on its answers (otherwise majority rules). This format works well only with cases that can generate widely different interpretations.
- All groups can work on the same case, but with each group addressing different questions.

- After a general class discussion identifying the problems in the case, one group addresses solutions and the other half preventions.
- Each group works on a different case and presents a descriptive summary and debriefing to the rest of the class.

A few logistical considerations will help make the debriefing successful. First and foremost, remember that the students have been asked to work a case that *has no correct answer*. Listen carefully to what they are saying. It is very easy to start to formulate a response and even to interrupt students to "correct" the issues they are presenting. That will stifle future discussions and discourage creative approaches as they will simply wait for you to explain what should have been done. Overall, try to refrain from dominating the discussion and telling students what they could have done. Give credit and credence to their work and let them know when they have come up with creative solutions, even if the solution is not viable. Excellent outcomes can result by adapting a process that led to an incorrect finding in another situation.

As a group is reporting out, try to engage other groups by asking what they think of the conclusion or what aspect impressed them the most. Having one group report out for several minutes, followed by a comment of "Very good, let's move to the next group" is not engaging for anyone in the class. You might also ask a few students to serve as note-takers for the report out. Finally, discuss the highlights of what was learned and how the case method drew out and solidified information that would not have happened through a lecture. This is a helpful wrap-up activity for any teaching method that is new to your students. If you point out how the teaching method used enhanced learning and review what was learned, students will be more receptive to these strategies in the future.

Cases are used extensively in medical education and they have many tips for those curious about using cases. Following are a few examples from Coggins et al. (2021):

- Identify your criteria for reporting out. Frame it so that you are ready for a productive session.
- Let students know why debriefing is important. Students too often see the case as the learning and forget that much can be learned during the debriefing.
- Focus on what was learned, and be sure students know that suggestions or critiques of their work by you or others is to enhance the learning of everyone. We should never expect to be perfect when learning.
- Establish processes and a tone for reporting out that is consistent with the culture and community of the room.
- Point out that hindsight bias means that once you have the data from a situation, many people think they would have done something better. When watching sports, it is always easy to know what the play should have been once the play is over.
- Always be working on your facilitation skills. You can get increasingly better at debriefing cases, which will increase the value for your students.

A POSTSCRIPT FOR PIONEERS

If the case method is rarely, if ever, used in your field but you can see a place for it in your course, trying it poses very little risk. It is a tried-and-true method in many fields, and course evaluations show that students find it both highly instructive and enjoy-

able. Just make sure you are using a high-quality case and questions. You might show drafts of your own creations to colleagues before using them in class. Remember too that you will undoubtedly continue to improve your cases over time.

REFLECTION QUESTIONS

Reflection Question 18.1: Could students help to write cases? What would be the value of having students participate in case writing? From their perspective, what might they find interesting and with what would they struggle?

Reflection Question 18.2: What do you see as your strengths and challenges in facilitating a class session using the case method? If you taught using a case, what other teaching methods, if any, might you combine with the case? Why?

Concept Into Practice: Select any topic in a course for which you do not currently have a case. Write one case that could be used in your course. Use the guidance of the section in this chapter on "What Makes a Good Case, and How to Write Your Own." Be sure to identify the learning object being met, the subject, the type of case, and the basics of how you would facilitate the case. Once it is complete, explain it to a colleague and request feedback. Then, if appropriate, use the case you wrote in your course.

PART 4

TOOLS AND TECHNIQUES TO FACILITATE LEARNING

CHAPTER 19

Helping Students Learn How to Learn

umans are born wired to learn, but we are not born *knowing how* to learn. Overall, we do manage to learn a great deal: how to walk, the date of our friends' birthdays, how to read, and how to teach. We are learning all the time. If you are awake, you are processing information. But doing something does not mean you know how it is done. Even if you do it a lot. I use my computer for hours every day, but I have no idea how my pushing squares on a keyboard results in the text I see on a screen. Learning is like that. We, and our students, do it all the time without knowing how it works.

Processing structured, chunks of information in a classroom is very different from everyday learning, and despite the fact that all students must interface with and make meaning from this new knowledge, *we never teach them how*. K–12 teachers may expose students to some mnemonic devices, such as the acronym HOMES for the names of the Great Lakes, and a few study and test-taking tips that students may or may not apply on their own such as flashcards and reading assigned materials. But teachers don't explain how the mind processes new information, how to facilitate and deepen that

processing, and how to strengthen memory for what has been learned. If students don't learn how to learn on their own and if we don't teach them, then they likely never will. Imagine how much more students could learn if they knew more about how the learning process works. In this chapter we will share just a few key aspects of learning that you can share with your students. These are not strategies solely for students who struggle academically. They are strategies for everyone.

■ LEARNING AS AN "INSIDE JOB"

As an instructor, the first thing we must all come to terms with is that you cannot make anyone learn. They must do that for themselves. That said, how you present information will have a large impact on how they learn, and if you teach some aspects of learning, you will have an even larger impact. The best thing about teaching students how to learn is that once they get started they will start to see possibilities on their own. That is like a boost to lifelong learning. You just need to get them started.

It all starts with the senses. All new information comes in through the senses: sight, sound, touch, odor, or taste. If the learner attends to sensory information (e.g., listens to the words their professor is saying, or looks at a figure in the textbook), it moves to working memory. If sensory information is received, but not processed in any way (e.g., scanning a textbook page without reading the content), it is lost within a few seconds. One helpful tip to give students is to check every few minutes to ensure they are still concentrating while reading. Also, if their concentration is on their phones or social media, the lecture content isn't being processed by their sensory system. They might be present, but they are not learning.

When attended to, information moves from sensory memory into working memory and can be held there as long as the learner is actively attending to the material. If related prior knowledge can be pulled from long-term memory, the prior knowledge is attached to the new information and then encoded and stored as a new memory. This process is called elaboration, as the learner has elaborated on the new information. If the information is not encoded or attached to prior knowledge, it is lost, typically in less than 30 seconds. That newly encoded information from earlier in the day kind of hangs around until the person sleeps. The new memory is consolidated during sleep. Once consolidated it will stay with you for a while. If a person is sleep deprived, they may temporarily learn new information, but it will not be consolidated and therefore lost. Information consolidated in long-term memory may be retained for years, but only if the newly consolidated information is regularly retrieved and updated. Information that is not retrieved and used, even briefly, can be lost. Every time information is retrieved, it is strengthened. If you retrieve something just to strengthen it, that is called retrieval practice. That is the best way to learn something new (Agarwal et al., 2021).

Figure 19.1 shows a memory model that was first proposed by Atkinson and Shiffrin (1968), and later adapted by Baddeley and Hitch, who added working memory in 1974 (Baddeley, 2012). The field of learning and memory has become more

Figure 19.1   Model of Learning and Memory Processes

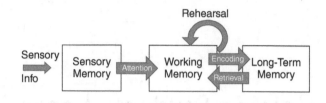

complex since that time, but this model is still helpful in understanding the foundations of learning and memory.

The entire process of learning and memory is all controlled by the learner. Our job as educators is to make it easier for students to lead themselves through the learning process. First and foremost, we can tell them about these steps in learning. We can also inspire their interest in the material by displaying our passion for it and explaining its relevance to the world and their own lives. We can catch their attention with intriguing class openers, humor, eye contact, vocal variety, physical movement, expressiveness, our reasons for our choice of teaching methods and assignments, and interesting activities for them to do in class. We can minimize distractions by discouraging unsanctioned uses of technology and other disruptive classroom behaviors. We can jump-start students' elaborative rehearsal and encoding of new material by pausing frequently for them to reflect on it, discuss it, write about it, or apply it to a problem. And we can give them retrieval practice by quizzing them, leading recitations, having them do a free-recall exercise, or having them discuss the material in small groups. But ultimately students have to choose to maintain their attention, continue the rehearsing and encoding, and practice retrieving on their own to recall the material during the next test, for the final exam, and beyond. Participation in class-time activities will help, but it alone cannot complete the learning process.

Deep, long-lasting learning is self-aware, which is an internal state of mind. In other words, deep learners are aware of their learning. First, they think about their learning goals. If they read a book chapter, do they want to be able to recognize, reproduce, apply, or critique the important information? Then they choose a strategy for accomplishing this goal—perhaps note-taking, jotting down answers to study questions, visually representing the material, occasionally self-quizzing, reviewing, or writing a summary. As they are following their plan, they check in on their learning every so often to assess how well it's going. What can they recall? How is the information organized? What are the main points or themes? If the strategy doesn't seem to be working well, they replace it with a more promising one. Finally, they check learning at the end. How well did they meet their goals? What did they learn about their learning?

This process, called *self-regulated learning* (SRL), is the conscious planning, monitoring, and evaluating of one's learning with the intention of maximizing it (Nilson, 2013a). Most students do not practice it, first, because a person can go a lifetime and not realize that process is there. Second, most do not practice this because they don't know the extent to which they can enhance their learning through this process. SRL proceeds through three stages:

1. Planning a strategy before the learning or performance task, which includes conducting a task analysis
2. Monitoring one's learning during the task
3. Evaluating one's learning after the task

In addition, the process takes place in three dimensions:

1. The *metacognitive*, which constitutes metacognition, often defined as "thinking about one's thinking" or "knowing what you know"
2. The *meta-emotional*, which involves monitoring and directing one's emotions to ensure sufficient motivation, justified confidence, open-mindedness to challenging ideas, and perseverance
3. The *environmental*, which entails finding and setting up the best physical conditions for one's learning

At this juncture, we can distinguish between SRL and metacognition. Metacognition is mainly cognitive (Flavell, 1976; McGuire, 2015; Zakrajsek, 2022), although some scholars (e.g., Hostetter & Savion, 2013) include a few emotional and environmental elements (motivation, study context) in their definition of the former. SRL encompasses metacognition and more.

THE LEARNER'S QUESTIONS

If we cross the three processes of SRL by its three dimensions, we get Table 19.1 with nine cells of questions that the savvy learner will ask themselves in the process of learning something.

The learner might not ask themselves all the questions every time they start a task because they may already know the answers. For example, they may know what kind of task it is because they've done it successfully hundreds of times before, and probably also know the best strategy to use. Presumably they heard about various approaches over the years, experimented with them, and identified those that work most effectively. But they will still have to monitor their progress, understanding, focus, reactions, and mental connections and evaluate their learning at the end. Emotionally, they may never have to question their confidence in their ability to do the task well, but they still have to examine and monitor their motivation and interest in the material, check for affective resistance to the content, and assess their emotional response to their metacognitive evaluation of their learning. Similarly, they may be quite familiar with their optimal learning environment, but they still need to monitor themselves for mental fatigue, time their breaks, and resist distractions.

THE EVIDENCE FOR SRL

Perhaps the strongest evidence that SRL enhances student achievement and performance comes from Hattie's (2009) mega-meta-analysis of more than 800 meta-analyses on the effects of different teaching and learning methods and teacher competencies

Table 19.1 Questions That Self-Regulated Learners Ask Themselves

	Metacognitive	Meta-emotional	Environmental
Planning before a learning or performance task (task analysis)	• What kind of a task is this? • What is my goal? How will I know I have reached it? • What do I already know about the topic? • What additional information, if any, will I need? • What strategies should I use: actively listening, taking notes, outlining, visually representing the material, occasionally self-quizzing, reviewing, or writing a summary? • What strengths can I bring to the task? • What are my weaknesses, and how can I make up for them?	• How interested and motivated am I to do the task, and how can I increase my interest and motivation if they are low? • What's the value or relevance of what I'll be learning? • How confident am I in my ability to learn this material? If not very, how can I increase my belief in my ability to learn it without becoming overconfident? What similar tasks can I recall doing well in the past?	• What is the best environment for the task that I can create? • Am I in a good physical place and position to do this task? • Is the temperature right for me? How about the background sounds? • Have I had enough sleep? • Have I had the right amount of coffee today? • Have I put potential distractions far away? • How much time and what resources will I need? Are these resources handy?
Monitoring during a learning or performance task	• Am I sure I know what I am doing? • Does my approach to the task make sense? • Am I making good progress toward my goal? • How well are my strategies working? • What changes in approach or strategies should I make, if any? • How focused am I? Am I getting tired? If so, how can I keep myself focused and alert? • What material is the most important? • What material am I having trouble understanding? • How does what I am learning relate to what I already know? • How is my thinking on the topic changing?	• If my interest and motivation are sagging, how is what I'm learning relevant to my experience or my future? • What material is challenging my preconceptions about the subject? Am I resisting it? • Am I starting to get discouraged or give up? Am I thinking I'm just no good at this subject? How can I change this negative thinking? What similar tasks can I recall doing well in the past?	• Should I try another environment to see if it works better? • How about another physical position? • How are the temperature and background sounds working out? • Am I staying away from distractions? If not, I have to get farther away from them. • Do I need a short break to refresh my mind and body?

	Metacognitive	Meta-emotional	Environmental
Evaluating after a learning or performance task	• Did I achieve my goal or master what I set out to learn? • What were the most important points I learned? • Can I see and organize the interrelationships among them? • What am I still having trouble understanding? • What questions do I have to ask my instructor? • How has my thinking on the topic changed? • Which approaches and strategies worked well, and which didn't? • What do I need to do differently next time I take on a similar task?	• How am I reacting emotionally to my evaluation of my learning? (Being pleased reinforces a learner's motivation and other positive emotions they generate about the material and their ability to learn it. Being disappointed may lead either to improving learning strategies or defensively withdrawing their energy from task. This last reaction in turn undermines the positive emotions needed to begin the next learning or performance task.)	• How well did I avoid distractions and stay on task? • If not that well, how can I avoid distractions more effectively in the future? • Do I need to experiment more with different physical factors to find the best working environment and break schedule for myself?

Source: Some questions are adapted from Schraw (1998) and Tanner (2012).

on student learning and achievement at all educational levels. Although he found that all the causal factors have some positive impact, some are much more powerful than others.

Hattie looked specifically at the effect size of the various methods and teacher skills. Among the strongest factors was the teacher's clarity in communicating, with an effect size of .75. This number means that when clarity increases by 1 standard deviation, student learning/achievement increases by three-fourths of a standard deviation. Getting feedback had a slightly weaker effect size of .73; spaced (as opposed to mass) practice .71; and metacognitive strategies, which are only the cognitive aspect of SRL, .69. This last effect size was measurably larger than those of mastery learning, group work, computer-assisted instruction, time on task, and test-taking strategies. McGuire (2015) recounts many cases of failing students who became B, and even A, students, just by using the metacognitive strategies she taught them in a very short amount

of time. Often just a few minutes is enough to make an enormous difference in their lives.

We find more evidence in a series of research studies conducted in developmental courses at the New York City College of Technology, also known as City Tech (Zimmerman et al., 2011). The first study measured the effects of SRL activities and assignments in a semester-long developmental mathematics course enrolling 140 students in six sections. In the randomized experimental design, three of the sections received traditional instruction and served as the control group, and the other three incorporated SRL activities and served as the treatment group. In all the sections, faculty members administered the same 15- to 20-minute quizzes with four or five problems every two or three class periods, as well as the same major exams and final exam.

However, at the beginning of the course, the instructors of the SRL sections explained to their classes how errors offer learning opportunities, and they modeled and provided practice in error detection and strategy adaptation. In addition, they asked students to not only show all their work in their problem solutions but also rate their confidence in their ability to solve each problem, first before they tried to solve it and again after solving it, so over-confident students learned to correct their inflated self-assessments. On the quizzes, students also had the chance to earn back lost points by completing a self-reflection form for each missed or incomplete problem for which they wrote an analysis of their error and re-solved a similar problem.

The results, shown in Figure 19.2, were statistically significant and unequivocal. Sixty-eight percent of the students in the SRL treatment-group sections passed the course, versus 49% of those in the control-group sections. In addition, 64% of the former students passed the gateway test in math required for admission into credit-bearing courses, versus only 39% of the control-group students.

Following the same randomized experimental design and treatment structure, the study was replicated with students enrolled in sections of an intensive five-week developmental math course offered in the summer. As Figure 19.3 shows, 84% of the students in the SRL sections passed the course versus 63% of the control-group students. The following fall semester, 60% of the former students successfully completed a credit-bearing math course versus only 34% of the latter.

Figure 19.2 Percentages of City Tech Students Passing the Course and Gateway Exam in Traditional Versus SRL Sections of Developmental Math

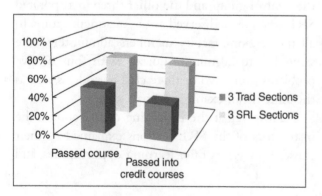

Figure 19.3 Percentages of City Tech Students Passing the Summer Course and a For-Credit Fall-Semester Math Course in the Traditional Versus SRL Sections of Developmental Math

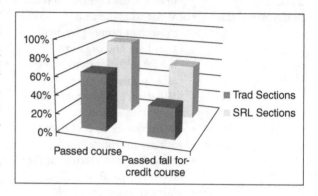

The City Tech developmental writing faculty members decided to follow Zimmerman et al.'s lead and conducted a similar study with the students taking a five-week intensive writing course offered in the summer. Again, some sections were infused with SRL activities and assignments and the others served as the control group, but they otherwise had the same lessons, quizzes, and exams. The quizzes and exams asked students to do writing tasks such as paraphrasing or summarizing a passage of text. But in the SRL sections, students received revision sheets after their quizzes were returned, and they could redo any writing task that they didn't do correctly. They also answered questions about where they erred in the quiz, how they prepared for it, and how they would prepare better next time.

The strategy of having students identify and correct their errors worked just as effectively in writing as in math. As Figure 19.4 shows, 72% of the treatment-group students passed the gateway exam in writing, whereas only 52% of the control-group students did. The following fall semester, 65% of the former students successfully completed a credit-bearing writing course, compared to only 32% of the latter students.

You can find the results of more experimental studies on the effects of SRL at the SRL Program website (http://www.selfregulatedlearning .blogspot.com). This additional research includes students enrolled in a variety of courses at a number of two-year, four-year, and secondary institutions.

Figure 19.4   Percentages of City Tech Students Passing the Gateway Exam and a For-Credit Fall-Semester Writing Course in the Traditional Versus SRL Sections of Developmental Writing

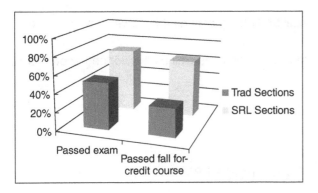

Every study reported that students performed much better in classes and following classes that incorporated SRL activities and assignments.

ACTIVITIES AND ASSIGNMENTS FOR EVERY OCCASION

At this point, you may be asking how you can enhance your courses with SRL components. This section will acquaint you with a sample of SRL activities and assignments. You'll find dozens more in Nilson (2013a). Some of these focus on planning (e.g., goal setting), others on monitoring, and still others on evaluation. Several are intended for the beginning and the end of a course. Those that take place during a lecture are sometimes called *lecture wrappers*; those designed to accompany readings, *reading wrappers*; those piggybacked on assignments, *assignment wrappers* or *meta-assignments*; and those associated with quizzes or exams, *exam wrappers*. If they generate homework to hand in, the reading wrappers also serve to enhance reading compliance and comprehension (see Chapter 21).

Students don't mind these additional tasks because they are short, low stress, low stakes, and useful for learning about themselves and improving their grades. You won't mind them either, because you don't have to grade the in-class activities and you can grade most of the assignments as pass/fail, credit/no credit at a glance. If the assignment is worth 5 points, students will earn all 5 points if their work meets all the specifications that you set for the assignment—for example, all the questions are answered, the problem is attempted in good faith, the short essay addresses the topic and is at least 150 words long—or no points at all if it doesn't. This standard motivates students to read the directions and take the assignment seriously.

Following are SRL activities or assignments and the course components they are designed for. The first box presents four paired activities or assignments to bookend a course.

Course Bookends: Paired Activities for the Beginning and End of a Course

Beginning of the Course	End of the Course
Informal essay: How I Earned an A in This Course (Zander & Zander, 2000)	Informal essay: How I Earned an A in This Course—or Not
Reflections on the nature of the course material (Kraft, 2008; Suskie, 2009)	Repeat reflections and compare.
Take-a-stance-and-justify essays on course material	Correct first essays and rewrite them using course content; usable as the final exam (J. M. Coggeshall, personal correspondence, 2010–2011).
Knowledge survey (student confidence survey) on course learning outcomes and related knowledge and skills (Nuhfer & Knipp, 2003; Wirth & Perkins, 2008)	Repeat knowledge survey and compare.

For Live Lectures: Periodic Free-Recall

1. Students listen to a 10- to 20-minute minilecture, then close their notebooks when the instructor pauses.
2. They write down all the important points they can recall and any questions they have, leaving space between the points.
3. They pair up to compare, fill in, and fine-tune their free-recall notes, as well as answer one another's questions.
   (Bonwell & Eison, 1991)

For Live Lectures: Active Listening Checks

1. Students listen to a 10- to 20-minute minilecture, paying special attention for the three most important points (they may take notes).
2. The instructor pauses, and they write down the three most important points and turn these in.
3. The instructor reveals the three most important points.
4. Students assess their listening skills.
   (Lovett, 2008)

For Reading, Videos, or Podcasts: Minute Papers

- What is the most useful or valuable thing you learned?
- What is the most important point or central concept?
- What idea or fact surprised you?
- What stands out in your mind?
- What helped or hindered your understanding?
- How does the content connect or conflict with your prior knowledge, beliefs, or values?
  (Chew, quoted in Lang, 2012; Wirth, n.d.)

For Live Lectures, Readings, Videos, or Podcasts: Reflective Writing

- What are the most important concepts or principles you just heard/read, and what don't you understand clearly?
- What comparisons and connections can you make between what you just heard/read and your prior learning, preconceptions, existing framework of knowledge, or other courses?
- How did you react emotionally to what you just heard/read? Explain how the material reinforced, challenged, or modified your attitudes, values, or beliefs.
  (Araujo, quoted in Schell, 2012; Kalman, 2007; Mezeske, 2009; Wirth, n.d.)

For Readings, Videos, or Podcasts: Read, Recall, Review

1. Read (or watch or listen). Then put away the book and any notes.
2. Recall all you can, and write it down (to turn in for homework).
3. Review the reading for what you misunderstood or forgot, and write down these points (also to turn in for homework).

(McDaniel et al., 2009; Roediger & Butler, 2010; Roediger & Karpicke, 2006)

For Live Lectures, Readings, Videos, or Podcasts: Visual Representations of the Content

See Chapter 22, the section "Examples of Visuals for Learning."

For Math-Based Homework Problems

- "Think aloud": Student pairs talk through solving a few homework problems in class and guide each other through the process (Whimbey & Lochhead, 1999).
- For each problem solved incorrectly or not at all, students write an error analysis or a description of the correct strategy and solve the same or a similar problem (Zimmerman et al., 2011).

For Papers and Projects: Reflective Writing

- Describe the research (or writing) process you went through while completing this assignment, including what steps you took, what strategies you followed, what problems you encountered, and how you overcame them.
- Describe your reasoning to define the problem, decide what principles and concepts to apply, develop alternative solutions, and identify one solution as the best possible.
- Write a paraphrase of instructor feedback.
- Identify your goals and strategies for your revision.
- Explain the value of this assignment to you. What knowledge did you gain? What skills did you gain or improve? When do you think this knowledge or these skills will be useful in the future?
- How will you do a better job on a similar assignment next time?
- What advice on this assignment do you have for the students who will take this course the next time it is given? How should they best prepare? What strategies do you recommend? What problems and pitfalls can you warn them about? What are they likely to gain from doing the assignment?

(Jensen, 2011; MacDonald, 2013; Mezeske, 2009; Suskie, 2009)

For Experiential Learning (Service-Learning/Community Engagement, Fieldwork, Simulation, Game, or Role Play): Reflective Writing

- Connect specific aspects of your experience to the learning outcomes, key concepts, key principles, and other content of the course.
- Explain and evaluate your goals, strategies, decisions, and responses to other players. How and why did these change during the experience?
- Evaluate how well you achieved your goals, how effective your strategies were, and how well you performed overall.
(Brown & Rose, 2008; Nilson, 2013a; Suskie, 2009; Tai-Seale, 2001)

For Graded Exams: Reflective Questions

1. Compare your expected and actual performance.
2. How do you feel about your grade?
3. How many hours did you study, and was this enough time?
4. How did you study? What exactly did you do to prepare for this exam?
5. Where and why did you lose points? Do you see any patterns?
6. Set your performance goal for the next exam and design a study game plan. What will you do differently?
(Barkley, 2009)

For Graded Exams: Test Autopsy

Error analysis form; reflective questions may be added

Question Profile			Reason Answer Was Incorrect			
Question Missed	Points Lost	Type of Question	Carelessness	Unfamiliar Material	Misinterpreted Question	Did Not Finish

(Academic Success Center, Iowa State University, 2011; Achacoso, 2004)

Self-Correcting Exams

Students take a multiple-choice exam in class, submit their answers on a form, and have until the next class meeting to use all their course resources to correct any wrong answers. They receive two points for each correct answer on the original test and one point for every wrong answer they correct (Gruhn & Cheng, 2014).

■ SOURCES FOR TEACHING YOUR STUDENTS HOW TO LEARN

You can teach your students how to learn by sharing the information on learning in this book, especially Chapters 1, 4, 22, and this one. Or if you don't have the time or feel comfortable doing that, you can assign any of several readily available readings about learning, all written for students:

- "Learning (Your First Job)," by Robert Leamnson (2002) at http://www.udel.edu/CIS/106/iaydin/07F/misc/firstJob.pdf (12 pages of wise advice on the effort that studying and learning involve).
- *The New Science of Learning: How to Learn in Harmony with Your Brain* (3rd ed.), by Todd Zakrajsek (2022). Stylus (265 pages; an easy-to-read learner's manual for the mind).
- *Teach Yourself How to Learn*, by Saundra Yancy McGuire (2018). Stylus (176 pages; easy to read with many case studies of students who taught themselves to learn).

The messages in these readings will probably be news to your students and should easily spark discussion, so leave some class time for it.

■ REFLECTION QUESTIONS

Reflection Question 19.1: What strategies did you find most helpful for learning as an undergraduate? What areas do you wish you had more guidance in with respect to learning?

Reflection Question 19.2: Look over the nine cells pertaining to self-regulated learners and three dimensions of metacognition. To what extent would you or do you find it valuable to ask yourself these questions for your current work?

Concept Into Practice: Find five things in this chapter that you feel would be most important to teach your students to give them better strategies to teach themselves how to learn. Prepare the information in a way that will best convey the information to the students. (Note that the preparation is itself a metacognitive activity that will help you understand the material.)

CHAPTER 20

Enhancing Student Success in STEM Disciplines

Every society needs citizens with expertise in science, technology, engineering, and math (STEM). These individuals erect buildings, build bridges, stabilize economies, create new cell phones, predict weather, discover vaccines, cure diseases, develop faster airplanes, and build more fuel-efficient cars. If you look around you right now, almost everything your eye lands on is something that those from STEM disciplines had a hand in creating. The fields of interest for this chapter are science, technology, engineering, and math, fields together referred to as STEM.

Unfortunately, the United States struggles to educate and graduate individuals in STEM disciplines, starting early in our educational system. In the international Trends in International Mathematics and Science Study (*TIMMS 2019 U.S. Highlights Web Report*, 2019), eighth graders in the United States ranked 16th in math, behind countries such as Lithuania, Ireland, China, Russia, Korea, and Japan. Our eighth graders scored a bit better in science, but still an embarrassing 14th place. These disconcerting rankings began dropping long ago and

have remained in this area for several years. In 2018, the National Science and Technology Council, at the direction of the president of the United States, reported that our students are simply not being well prepared for demanding STEM majors (Vought, 2019); in fact, only 20% of college-bound high school students are academically prepared for STEM degrees. At present, the United States graduates only 10% of the world's students with STEM degrees, even as demand from U.S. employers continues to increase.

Who *is* acquiring these high-paying degrees, then? Vought (2019) reported that "underrepresented racial and ethnic groups make up 27% of the population but comprise only 11% of the STEM workforce" (p. 3). The numbers are also poor for American veterans and individuals with disabilities. Women account for only 30% of the STEM workforce, even though they make up half of the population. This is disconcerting, as boys and girls in early education score similarly in math, yet girls exhibit lower math confidence than boys as early as first grade, even when the girls have higher scores

(Ganley, 2018; Ganley & Lubienski, 2016). With lower confidence, an individual is less likely to choose a math-related major, even if it is desired. We must find a way for students from underrepresented groups to succeed in STEM fields.

Since the founding of the nation, science, technology, engineering, and mathematics have been a source of inspirational discoveries and transformative technological advances, helping the United States develop the world's most competitive economy, and preserving peace through strength. The pace of innovation is accelerating globally, and with it the competition for scientific and technical talent. Now more than ever the innovation capacity of the United States—and its prosperity and security—depends on an effective and inclusive STEM educational ecosystem (Vought, 2019).

Successfully completing a STEM degree certainly requires effort on the students' part. But to make their effort effective, it is our responsibility to engage in teaching at its best. It is also important to note that this chapter is equally important for faculty members who do not teach in the STEM disciplines. The information and strategies in this chapter apply to any discipline, and if our students are to be successful, it is important that we help all students in all disciplines to build their confidence.

■ WHY WE ARE LIKELY LOSING STEM MAJORS

For many years there was an effort to encourage individuals from underrepresented groups to enroll in STEM programs. That has worked, as enrollment numbers have been on the rise for many years (Chen, 2013). The new challenge is that STEM graduation rates have declined (National Science Foundation, 2016).

Many studies report much lower STEM graduation rates for underrepresented minority (URM) students compared to majority students. URM students and majority students enter STEM disciplines at the approximately the same rate, relative to their percentage of the national population. However,

there are large differences in graduation rates. The Higher Education Research Institute (2010) found that of the students who enrolled in college intending to major in a STEM field, graduation rates were 24.5% for White students; 32.4% for Asian American Students; 15.9% for Latino students; 13.2% of Black students; and 14% for Native American students. The two most significant factors for these differences were a) whether students took STEM courses in high school and b) student GPA in high school. URM students tended to take STEM classes less often, resulting in lower STEM graduation rates (Eagan et al., 2010). However, summer bridge courses or other "extra term" offerings can help reduce this gap. Kendricks et al. (2013) found that mentoring in college also had a significant impact on graduation rates for URM students.

Although the STEM fields engage in the discovery and identification of facts, they are not just mountains of factoids, although undergraduate science education often gives that impression. One reason lies with the overreliance on lecture, often the instructor's technique of choice because it maximizes the amount of factual information that can be conveyed. Lectures certainly have their place, and the minilecture can be powerful; however, research going back to Fullilove and Treisman (1990) demonstrates that adding active learning strategies to a classroom improves the grades of all students, particularly Black students. Eddy and Hogan (2014) found that increasing active learning strategies resulted in students feeling more community in the classroom and that the course had greater value, both of which are also factors in URM students dropping out of STEM majors. It is worthwhile to note that the courses in this study had enrollment of approximately 400 students, meaning these strategies can be used in courses of essentially any size of enrollment. In a large meta-analysis of over 50,000, Theobald et al. (2020) noted that the disparities between majority and URM students disappeared when active learning is being employed at least 67% of the time.

We also need to consider preparedness of students. Everyone who has ever taught has navigated the challenges of students who enroll in a course without the prerequisite set of skills, whether due to poor preparation in high school or missing previous courses. Although difficult in any discipline, foundational knowledge from prerequisite courses in the sciences and engineering is critical. That said, there are creative ways to allow individuals who are less prepared to be successful. Instead of criticizing these individuals for not having strong backgrounds, we can make adjustments to meet our students where they are and get them where they want to be, and where we want them to be. As just one example, Harvey Mudd College made their introductory computer science course more accessible to students without previous coding experience (DiMenna, 2019). They offered separate sections, with the same content, for those with and those without coding experience. Instructors had noticed that those with coding experience would dominate conversations, making those without coding experience lose confidence and drop the course. In particular, female students tended to arrive with less programming experience than their male counterparts and dropped out at higher rates than men. After splitting sections based on experience, students with less experience learned in a more positive environment, and female computer science graduate rates increased from 10% of class in 2010 to 56% in 2018. Again, the sections were taught the same, it was only the environment that changed. This shows that there are ways to address challenges pertaining to prerequisite knowledge without lowering standards with respect to content. This example is important because it takes creative thinking, but we simply must find ways to correct the tremendous biases that are keeping an inordinate number of women out of STEM disciplines, a trend going back decades (Lockhart, 2020, 2021; Savaria & Monteiro, 2017).

To impact graduation rates of URM students, we need only find the right programs. The "weed out" mentality is an old concept and must be replaced with innovative programs that help all students to succeed while keeping standards high. The students have the motivation. In many cases, it is our systems that cause them to fail. Interventions to help students from underrepresented groups include programs to boost second-year GPA, which has been shown to be a solid predictor of STEM degree completion. This suggests programs like summer academic boot camps, tutors, and similar programs help raise second-year GPAs (Premraj et al., 2021). In addition, as noted previously, teaching strategies that include active and engaged learning can greatly increase grades for all students, and decrease discrepancies for URM students.

Another final issue is that students in STEM disciplines often resist active and engaged teaching and learning strategies, even though the data is overwhelming that adding active learning to lectures enhances learning (Deslauriers et al., 2019; Finelli et al., 2018; Shekhar et al., 2020; Tharayil et al., 2018). There are several reasons students tend to resist active learning in STEM courses. Some of the top reasons noted include:

- *Perception of low value.* Students perceive that learning would be faster and better with a lecture rather than active learning.
- *Takes too much time.* Often when active learning strategies are used in class, students must come prepared. If students don't typically prepare, the preparation is seen as extra time.
- *Not being familiar with active learning.* Knowing how and why active learning works enhances both learning and later recall of information.
- *Students have not developed teamwork skills,* making the collaborative work less effective than it might otherwise be.

▓ IMPROVING STUDENT LEARNING IN STEM COURSES: GENERAL ADVICE

It is imperative that we teach in ways that prepare the next generation of learners and leaders for the increasingly complex challenges that we will all face. This will certainly require the foundational principles for teaching at its best. To address these challenges, the U.S. Department of Education's "Partnership for 21st Century Learning" identified the skills our students need to meet the demands of the 21 century. These skills include teamwork, leadership, problem-solving, and critical thinking (McGunagle & Zizka, 2020). This moves the focus of teaching to strategies designed to make sense of information, although content remains important as well. The goal is to teach students how to gather, evaluate, and use information to make decisions. To incorporate these skills into the teaching and learning landscape, many educational experts turned to STEM education as a learning system that integrates the disciplines of science, technology, engineering, and mathematics.

There is also an increasing inclusion of the arts into STEM, notated as *STEAM*. This term recognizes a "dynamic synergy between visual arts and the natural sciences" (Buczynski et al., 2012, p. 29). In this nexus of art and science, the five universal constructs for success in the 21st century are adaptability, complex communication skills, nonroutine problem-solving, self-management, and systems-level thinking. Also included in the STEAM ethos are five art strategies that support science learning: depiction, projection, reformatting, mimicry, and metaphor/analogy (Marshall, 2010). There is a growing position that it is impossible to learn scientific concepts without visualizations. For example, you must depict a double-helix to discuss DNA. That is why education is increasingly turning to STEAM as a model for learning (Danielson et al., 2022).

In addition to the universal constructs for success and the strategies for incorporation of art, there are additional fundamental issues that are important to consider. First, instructors have to address misconceptions about the subject matter that students bring into the classroom. If you don't already know your students' faulty mental models, you can discover them by giving a diagnostic exam the first week, asking students to explain a certain phenomenon, having them apply concepts to a realistic problem, or having them draw a concept map or flowchart of some basic material or process (Mastascusa et al., 2011). Expect misconceptions to appear in the sciences because the layperson's intuitive understandings of natural phenomena are often wrong. If incorrect thinking is not addressed, students will return to their prior incorrect thinking.

Second, students need help filling in the paradigm—that is, acquiring the discipline's hierarchical mental structure of knowledge (Hanson, 2006; Wieman, 2007). They are not likely to see this hierarchical organization unless we tell them about it explicitly, and a concept map can help (see Chapter 22). After all, it took us years to develop our own frameworks; it's doubtful anyone told us about it when we were in school. Why not alleviate our students' struggle and quicken their learning by showing them how experts structure their vast knowledge?

Third, look at new ways to address the heavy cognitive load that students face in STEM courses. We can show students how to recognize patterns across concepts, principles, and problems and how to chunk knowledge into categories based on such patterns (Zakrajsek, 2022). Researchers are also looking at ways to bring self-regulation and cognitive load together to increase learning (Nückles et al., 2020. Their program includes metacognitive processing and using journal writing to motivate self-regulated learning (metacognition and self-regulated learning are presented in Chapter 19).

Fourth, help students learn to transfer their knowledge to new situations, which won't likely happen unless we have a strategy to teach them. The case method is useful here (Chapter 18). First, we lead students through two or three contrasting cases that are structured around the same underlying concepts and principles—for example, flow rate and pressure interdependence, or rain forests as illustrated in temperate and tropical climates. Then we present a problem or question that coaxes students to identify the commonalities across the cases and construct a general abstract model based on the commonalities (Mastascusa et al., 2011).

One final principle to facilitate science education—in fact, learning in any discipline—is to encourage metacognition. That is, students need to acquire the expert's habit of monitoring their own thinking, of honestly assessing how deeply they understand the material (Hanson, 2006; Mastascusa et al., 2011; Wieman, 2007). The next chapter revisits metacognition as a dimension of self-regulated learning and offers a number of ways to foster it in our students.

IMPROVING STUDENT LEARNING IN STEM COURSES: SPECIFIC STRATEGIES

An enormous amount of research on STEM education all leads to the same conclusion: adding cross-disciplinary, inquiry-guided, problem-focused, collaborative, alternative teaching strategies to a course is much more effective than traditional full-class length lectures. Students who learn by these newer approaches leave their individual STEM courses with better skills in higher-order thinking, problem-solving, and experimental design (e.g., Beichner et al., 2007; Duda, 2014; Freeman et al., 2014; Giuliodori et al., 2006; Haak et al., 2011; Hanson, 2006; Hodges, 2015; McCreary et al., 2006; Prince & Felder, 2007; Schroeder et al., 2007; Theobald et al., 2020; Wieman, 2014; Yadav et al., 2014) and stronger conceptual understanding of the content (Crouch & Mazur, 2001; Hanson, 2006; Hodges, 2015; Wieman, 2014; Yadav et al., 2014). Furthermore, these gains come with no loss in content coverage or mastery (Duda, 2014), whether the class is small or large (Eddy & Hogan, 2014).

These alternative strategies may be relatively small, inexpensive changes, such as giving 10- to 12-minute minilectures with conceptual multiple-choice questions at the end of each minilecture. Students answer the questions on their own, and then turn to a neighbor to discuss their choice for one minute before you pick up with the next

minilecture (Crouch & Mazur, 2001; Eddy & Hogan, 2014; Freeman et al., 2014; Haak et al., 2011; Hodges, 2015; Wieman, 2007). The change may also be as complex as a complete course redesign, such as combining lecture, recitation, and laboratory into a tutorial or workshop format (Beichner et al., 2007; Breslow, 2010; Deslauriers et al., 2011; Duda, 2014; Hodges, 2015).

Making Modest Changes to the Lecture

If you are going to make changes, it is best to start small. Let's start with the modest changes you can make in your STEM courses within a lecture format:

- *Interspersing conceptual multiple-choice questions* and having individual students and then groups choose the right answer (see Chapters 4 and 16).
- *Integrating case studies and problem-based learning scenarios*, which abound in the sciences, as in-class activities or homework (Yadav et al., 2014; see Chapters 17 and 18).
- *Incorporating just-in-time teaching (JiTT)*. Research finds that this reduces attrition, raises standardized test scores, and improves student preparation (Marrs & Novak, 2004; see Chapter 17).
- *Doing experimental demonstrations* during lecture, whether live (not requiring data collection) or online interactive simulations that double as virtual labs (Wieman, 2007; see the URLs later for sources). Students become involved when they not only watch but also discuss what they have observed and interpret the results. In the course of the discussion, you explain the concepts and principles illustrated and the real-life applications.
- *Modeling expert reasoning*—in particular, project-solving strategies, but perhaps more self-consciously and explicitly than you have before. Recall from Chapter 17 that novice learners grappling with new material need guidance and scaffolding through the inquiry process. The research recommends two forms of guidance. One form, *worked examples*, provides students with a problem-solving model. Following

a logical set of procedures frees up enough of the learners' working memory to let them process the reasoning behind the procedures. We know from numerous studies that students learn more when they can study worked examples before trying to solve comparable problems on their own (Kirschner et al., 2006). To accomplish this goal, model the cognitive processes involved and explicitly describe the steps and flow of your thinking. Students then grasp the techniques for solving problems and appreciate what these techniques can do for them.

- *Teaching the steps of inquiry-guided learning.* The second form of inquiry guidance that benefits novice learners is *process worksheets*—an optimal sequence of problem-solving steps for students to follow, supplemented by hints and rules of thumbs when available. This reasoning structure improves students' problem-solving performance by making them carefully examine and recast problems in conceptual terms, thus preventing them from rushing headlong into misdirected calculations (Nadolski et al., 2005). The literature endorses teaching students a tried-and-true stepwise method for tackling and solving problems adaptable to any quantitatively based discipline (Kalman, 2007). During your interactive lecture (see Chapters 14 and 17), you can build in problem-solving opportunities and have students follow and display this method in this exercise and again in their homework. The following five-step procedure helps students to translate the problem into different representations, each more abstract and more mathematically detailed than the last:

Step 1: Visualize the problem. Sketch or diagram the main parts of the problem. Identify the known and unknown quantities and other constraints. Restate the question in different terms to make it more understandable.

Step 2: Describe in writing the principles and concepts at work in the problem. Then translate the diagram into symbolic terms, and symbolically represent the target variable.

Step 3: Plan a solution. Identify the equations necessary to solve the problem, and work backward from the target variable to see if enough information is available to arrive at a solution.

Step 4: Execute the plan. Plug in the appropriate numerical values for the variables, and compute a solution.

Step 5: Check and evaluate your solution. Is the solution complete? Are the proper units used? Is the sign correct? Is the magnitude of the answer reasonable?

Some students may profit from incorporating a few more steps: reading the problem at least twice, preferably aloud, before trying to restate it (Step 1); thinking about the relationships among the different pieces of information given before describing the relevant principles and concepts (Step 2); if the complexity of the numbers in the problem is getting in the way, substituting simpler numbers before planning the solution (Step 3); and pausing while computing (Step 4) to review their intuitive understanding of each concept (Pauk, 2001).

Supplementing the Lecture

Experience has taught us that making substantial course modifications, such as turning classes into a studio or workshop experience where carefully assembled student groups solve complex, realistic problems, probably requires departmental action (Breslow, 2010; Wieman et al., 2010). If you are teaching a lecture course with recitation sessions, you may be able to make those sessions inquiry guided, problem focused, interactive, and collaborative by modeling them on McDermott and Shaffer's (2002, 2011–2012) physics. In this format, student groups answer conceptual questions on a worksheet while the instructor and TAs rotate around the groups asking questions to test learning and stimulate reflection. On occasion, students work with a few simple laboratory items, but the activity is usually paper and pencil (or on a laptop). Compared to traditional recitation sessions, the tutorials/ workshops (or *suites*) significantly increase students' learning gains and raise course completion rates (Preszler, 2009). These improvements in learning, performance, and retention extend across all types of students but are greater for females and, with respect to grades, URM students (Preszler, 2009). In lieu of worksheets, you can bring context-rich cases (see Chapter 18) into these sessions.

Two additional encompassing transformations in science and engineering education go under the acronyms of POGIL (Process Oriented Guided Inquiry Learning) and SCALE-UP (Student-Centered Active Learning Environment for Undergraduate Programs). Although the instructor may lecture during some class meetings or give minilectures at the beginning of most class meetings, both innovations replace a great deal of lecture with hands-on, small-group activities, such as answering critical thinking questions, developing concepts, or inquiry-guided problem-solving. As SCALE-UP places three students around one laptop, these triads may also engage in computer-based simulations or hypothesis-testing labs. These activities are known as *tangibles* and *ponderables* (Beichner et al., 2007). While the students are working, the instructor and TAs circulate around the class posing questions. Near the end of the class, at least some of the groups make oral reports, and all turn in written reports or completed worksheets (Beichner et al., 2007; Hanson, 2006).

Both POGIL, which started in chemistry courses, and SCALE-UP, which was introduced in physics, have proved highly successful in promoting student learning. Compared to traditional lecturing, and in one case, interactive lecturing, POGIL has been found to increase student interest in the subject matter, raise student ratings of the instructor and the course, improve learning skills and test performance, and reduce the drop-fail-withdraw (D-F-W) rate to statistically significant degrees. Faculty members do fear that when focus shifts to process-oriented guided learning, students fail to learn content. Walker and Warfa (2017) conducted a meta-analysis of 21 studies involving 7,876 students. The researchers found that students in POGIL-type classes scored roughly 0.3 standard deviations higher than students in lecture-based courses. This is not a large increase, but it is an increase, demonstrating that achievement outcomes need not suffer. More importantly, Walker and Warfa found that POGIL reduced the risk of failing a course by 38%. Other researchers have noted that students prefer POGIL to traditional lecturing and deem the activities challenging and valuable for their learning (Lewis & Lewis, 2005; Rodriguez et al., 2020).

SCALE-UP has achieved similar significant results. Students display deeper conceptual understanding, better problem-solving skills, higher test scores, and more favorable attitudes toward the discipline (Beichner et al., 2007; Felege & Ralph, 2019; Oliver-Hoyo & Beichner, 2004). (However, according to Breslow [2010], the SCALE-UP-based TEAL Initiative at MIT initially encountered strong student pushback and even some from faculty members.)

Not surprisingly, POGIL and SCALE-UP have spread to other disciplines. For the sciences, engineering, and mathematics, you can find plenty of online inquiry-guided activities. Start with the websites listed in the "Online Resources in STEM Education" section later in this chapter.

SCALE-UP requires some serious investments in new facilities. Short of constructing new buildings, to create spaces more conducive to students working regularly in small groups, institutions are tearing out some of their lecture halls and replacing them with large, one-level, computer-smart classrooms and large round tables, each with nine movable chairs and electrical outlets. In addition, either the students or the institution must purchase laptops— one for each student triad (Beichner et al., 2007). Note that class size need not necessarily decrease; large lecture classes can also pivot. A quick web search of "large active learning classrooms" returned a few examples of large classrooms designed for active learning: University of Minnesota–171 students; Ohio University–135 students; University of Wyoming–200 students; UC-Irvine–400 students.

If your campus is looking at redesigning a classroom or creating classrooms in a new building, it may be possible to assist those making decisions on how to best structure a learning environment. A few key concepts are (Aalderink, 2019):

1. Start with student learning in mind, rather than your teaching.
2. Consider how teaching will mesh with student learning to create powerful pedagogical opportunities.
3. Consider current and developing technology possibilities and whether the room will start with all of the latest technologies or have space to build out upcoming possibilities.
4. Ensure there are plans to train educators how to use the space well.
5. Secure institution-wide support.
6. Consider ways to build cross-institutional cooperation.

Making Problems More Real and Challenging

STEAM education aims to solve problems that focus on one discipline, such as math, but draw in the other disciplines within STEM and consider how information will be conveyed through use of art. Ideally, students will be working on real-world problems, which furnish more interesting, meaningful, and challenging contexts for students to apply and hone their skills. Heller and Hollabaugh (1992) devised the idea of *context-rich problems* in physics as part of their approach to promote good problem-solving skills. As mentioned in Chapter 17, these problems are short cases about real objects and realistic events, more like those that students encounter in the real world, making the work interesting and relevant. They thus incorporate the motivation to understand the problem, perform the calculations, and find a solution (e.g., planning a skateboard stunt, deciding whether to fight a traffic ticket). These problems also have these additional characteristics:

- They may not refer specifically to the unknown variable.

- They may include irrelevant information not needed to solve the problem, which is common in real-life scenarios.
- They may require students to supply missing information from common knowledge or educated guessing.
- They do not specifically mention the reasonable assumptions that may be necessary to reach a workable solution.

If you teach physics, you can find a collection of context-rich problems at https://groups.spa.umn.edu/physed/Research/CRP/on-lineArchive/ola.php. If your courses include introductory engineering, you can learn to write your own such problems at http://groups.physics.umn.edu/physed/Research/CRP/crcreate.html.

Context-rich problems are designed to be difficult—too difficult for most students to generate satisfactory answers working on their own—emphasizing the importance of working in groups or teams. Group learning spreads the thinking and reasoning load over several students and gets them discussing the concepts and principles behind a problem and the possible strategies for solving it. Ultimately students must choose the type of problem and approach to reaching a solution from among the alternatives suggested, which weans them away from the mechanical application of algorithms and builds their individual problem-solving skills.

■ GETTING REAL IN THE LAB

Real, everyday science often involves solving problems in a laboratory, even if the data are collected and partially analyzed in the field. Science education should imitate the reality of scientific methodology in the lab—that is, devising hypothesis-testing strategies and procedures using reasoning and trial-and-error to meet the experimental objectives with valid and reliable findings. Too many institutions continue to have traditional lab learning approaches and manuals that are outmoded, ineffective, and ripe for replacement with inquiry-guided labs.

Starting the Lab

When the lab is disembodied from concepts, it lacks meaning and relevance, so it is critical that the labs be lined up with and stay aligned with the *lecture* portion of the course. In addition, it is very helpful to students to place the lab in the bigger scientific picture before proceeding into the actual activities. Explaining the objectives of the lab and the major concepts to be learned provides important additional educational value.

Begin a lab by asking students to review the previous week's material. You might have them do a 2-minute free-write to activate their memory (see Chapter 22). After you ask a couple of students to read their responses aloud, tie this particular lab to the course's progression of topics and labs, sketching as cohesive a big picture as possible. Then introduce the day's objectives or principles and ask the students to explain the hypotheses to be tested or questions to be answered.

Designing the Lab

In many science and engineering courses across the continent, laboratories long ago began revamping learning spaces to incorporate SCALE-UP and other active learning strategies (Felder & Brent, 2001; Hodges, 2015; Howard & Miskowski, 2005; Odom, 2002; Reddish, 2003). Labs:

- Reflect the *inquiry-guided learning* model—that is, labs have students learn or apply material to meet some kind of a challenge, such as answering questions, solving problems, conducting an experiment, or interpreting data. In one way or another, students conduct real scientific investigations, identifying and solving problems the way scientists actually do, only with the instructor's guidance. Students develop their own strategy to test a hypothesis or find answers, along with the procedures to carry it out. The lab manual provides neither, and the lab results are not predictable.
- Focus on developing students' *critical thinking, decision-making, and complex reasoning skills,*

including inductive thinking, by giving students opportunities to practice them. Students devise one or more explanations for unexpected results and include them in their lab reports.

- Foster genuine *teamwork and collaboration.* As the labs are novel and challenging, students mutually need each other, as they would in a professional setting. In many cases, each person has an individual grade based on work they do for the lab and a group grade based on the combined efforts. In addition to sharing their discoveries, results, and conclusions, students may even exchange their lab reports for peer review (Odom, 2002).
- Feature *modern technology,* such as industry equipment in current use and updated software (e.g., spreadsheet, database, statistical, and mathematical) for analyzing the data and displaying the results. As a result of the remote instruction forced during the COVID pandemic, universities also reimagined the concept of virtual labs. As a result, students are learning skills as they navigate in-person and virtual labs interchangeably. New lab concepts give students remote access to industry-level resources and equipment. Remote access to learning labs means students can complete lab assignments as part of their study abroad programs (Morad, 2022). This is likely just a sign of labs to come as technology advances.

Odom (2002) offers an excellent inquiry-based lab example in physics, in which students spend 2 weeks developing their own procedures to determine properties of a pendulum and *g*, the acceleration due to the earth's gravity. The results of these programs have been very positive. Students actually discuss and even argue about the best plan of attack, and they divide the labor on their own. Compared to students in courses with traditional cookbook labs, they hand in higher-quality lab reports, do significantly better on tests, have higher final grades, give the course higher evaluations, and enjoy the labs more (Felder & Brent, 2001; Hodges, 2015; Howard & Miskowski, 2005). In addition, they make greater improvements in scientific reasoning (Benford & Lawson, 2001), as well as other higher-order thinking skills, such as data analysis and interpretation (Howard & Miskowski, 2005). They retain the lab material longer as well (Lord & Orkwiszewski, 2006; Luckie et al., 2004). In some labs, the C students show the greatest gains in achievement. In addition, students are more motivated and more engaged, they perceive they are learning more in the course and the labs, and they assess their team functioning more favorably (Kimmel, 2002).

■ ONLINE RESOURCES FOR STEM EDUCATION

A rich variety of POGIL, SCALE-UP, tutorial/workshop activities, and inquiry-guided labs are available online as virtual labs, field trips, problem scenarios, and simulations for all the STEM fields. Following are a few examples of what is available:

Physics

http://phet.colorado.edu
http://web.mit.edu/8.02t/www/802TEAL3D

Chemistry

http://www.chemcollective.org/find.phphttp://onlinelabs.in/chemistry

Biology

http://onlinelabs.in/biology

Human Anatomy

http://onlinelabs.in/anatomy

Geography

https://www.nationalgeographic.org/society/education-resources

Geology

http://onlinelabs.in/geology

Engineering

https://www.engineering.com/story/top-10-online-resources-for-stem

Statistics

http://www.math.uah.edu/stat http://onlinestatbook.com/rvls.html

Multidisciplinary Sites

https://pogil.org/educators/resources
https://serc.carleton.edu/sp/library/pogil/index.html
http://www.merlot.org
http://virtuallaboratory.colorado.edu
http://www.shodor.org/interactivate
https://www.nsf.gov/news/classroom/index.jsp

■ WHY STEM EDUCATION IS SO IMPORTANT

The data consistently show that we continue to fall behind other countries in scientific literacy and quantitative reasoning at all grade levels. As a secondary concern, the rate of new STEM-related job openings in the United States is growing at a rate faster than we can produce graduates to fill those jobs. Many of the jobs are filled by international employees. This is not good for a nation.

If these reasons to improve STEM education aren't pressing enough, then consider the broader place of these disciplines, especially the sciences, in our country. In a truly enlightened, democratic society, people must be scientifically and quantitatively literate—not only conversant in but also comfortable with these fields. Everyone who teaches in these disciplines plays a crucial role in fostering a society that is well-informed enough to govern itself intelligently and to advance scientific knowledge. Self-government requires not only a well-informed populace but also one that can solve its own increasingly complex problems. Problem-solving of every type—open-ended and closed-ended, qualitative and quantitative, high-uncertainty and formulaic—is STEM's stock-in-trade. This fact alone makes it an essential component of higher education. But we have to ensure that students learn how problem-solving and knowledge building really proceed in a trial-and-error, collaborative manner that demands complex reasoning, strategic thinking, and inventiveness.

A final note for those of you who do not teach in a STEM area, yet still read the material as suggested at the beginning of the chapter: You are also critical in the advancement of hard sciences. First, defend the value of scientists and scientific discoveries. There are those who will say science can't be trusted or even that we don't need scientists. Yet, even the most fervent of those individuals will pay attention to a catastrophic weather forecast (science), seek out medical care if very ill (science), drive a car (science), or enjoy air conditioning on a globally climate-changed very hot day (science *and* science). Second, when students explain to you that they are struggling in biology, physics, chemistry, math, or any other STEM area, encourage them to remain growth-minded. Nobody is "born" to do this; these are learned skills that take time and are important.

Let them know that we all struggle from time to time, but with work it is amazing what can be done. Careless statements from a faculty member such as, "I never liked chemistry," or "I can't do math either" may be all a tired or frustrated student needs to hear to make the decision to drop their STEM major. When a student is struggling, perhaps remind them of a quote from Nelson Mandela, "I never lose. I either win or I learn."

■ REFLECTION QUESTIONS

Reflection Question 20.1: What do you see as core issues causing a loss of STEM majors at your institution? Are these preventable issues? What would need to be done to increase retention of those majors?

Reflection Question 20.2: What do you see as being primarily different in teaching STEAM courses as compared to courses in other areas of the overall university offerings? In thinking about this question, consider both the students and the typical instructional approach.

Concept Into Practice: Whether you teach in a STEAM area or not, think about how you would help a struggling student in a STEM major. For sake of this exercise, assume they are a first-year student who is receiving grades of Cs in all of their courses and is frustrated because they graduated with an A average in high school.

CHAPTER 21

Ensuring Students Prepare for Class

One of the most frequent and persistent teaching challenges faculty members face is getting students to come to class prepared. You can't lead a discussion or other engaging activities if students haven't prepared, whether by reading the book chapter, completing online materials, watching assigned videos, or listening to podcasts. It is also a challenge when students do complete homework, but only superficially. Completing prework on material before engaging with it in class is critical for building a focused base of knowledge. Having this base to draw on means that your active and engaged in-class learning strategies will be effective, but it also supports the concept of lifelong learning. The first exposure students have to course material should be on their own outside of class, and they should be prepared to advance the discussion in class. Students will be frustrated that they are asked to work on course material on their own first, but research supports this as an important part of learning, and struggling a bit is helpful as well (Bjork & Bjork, 2020; Walvoord & Anderson, 2010). As this chapter will show, there are ways to encourage students to come to class prepared. For example, Moravec et al. (2010) moved a portion of the course material to an online resource and provided a small incentive for students to complete a worksheet on the material prior to class. This was done specifically to create time for active learning strategies. Results showed that students who learned the material listed as class preparation learned that content significantly better than material that was first learned in class. In addition, the researchers found no difference between providing textual or video-based material.

However, finding a way to encourage all of your students to prepare properly is not easy. In 1981, about 80% of students did preclass readings (measured by pop quizzes), but by 1997 that number had dropped to 20% (Burchfield & Sappington, 2000). In 2022, instructors are reporting record levels of students not doing homework. A great number of students are struggling in many ways, hugely impacted by the COVID-19 pandemic, prompting some educators to cut back on homework or stop giving it altogether. Some high school teachers are even rethinking the entire concept of homework (Lempres, 2022), with a focus more on student wellness. However, at the college level, some homework greatly facilitates what can be done in class and the amount and depth that can be learned in a semester. The question is how this potential shift in homework at the secondary level will affect our incoming postsecondary students and how our own teaching strategies can meet them and still being effective.

In this chapter, we will discuss why students don't prepare and how to both encourage and hold them accountable for preparation. This is a challenging area, even for seasoned faculty members. That said, when you are engaged in teaching at its best, there are strategies and considerations that will help you to help your students. If they come to class prepared, they will get as much as possible from their educational experience.

■ WHY STUDENTS DON'T PREPARE

We are living in an increasingly complex world with many distractions. Some students will do preparation work, regardless; some will not, and feel terrible; and some don't see the point in the work at all. Be sensitive to different situations and offer different strategies to help students tune out distractions and come prepared.

No Perceived Need to Prepare

Past behavior is always a good indication of future behavior. Unfortunately, this is not good news when it comes to students coming to college right out of high school. The Brookings Institute sampled approximately 2,500 full-time high school students (Hansen & Quintero, 2017) and found that students averaged less than one hour per day on homework, even though teachers claim they gave what should have amounted to about 3.5 hours per day. This means that although students were told they needed to do homework, they consistently received the message that it was not true. When students arrive in our classes and we explain that they will need to do outside work and prepare for class, they likely will respond to that message

the same as the way they have responded to it in the past. It may be helpful to assign some work early in the semester and immediately hold them accountable for the work to demonstrate that what worked in high school will not work in college.

Basing their expectations of the present on the past, many students believe that they shouldn't have to work any harder in college than they did in high school, and they see themselves as intelligent enough to slide through their college courses. Clearly, they consider reading tangential to their learning (Brost & Bradley, 2006).

This attitude is further reinforced when faculty members insist that students must prepare for class, and then go ahead and lecture over the assigned reading, podcast, video, and so on. The idea of assigning work is that students have a better understanding of the material, and we don't lecture over it again. Instead, we can use the first few minutes of class to take questions about the reading or clarify sticking points. You may also spend just a minute or two and point out some major aspects of the chapter that will come into play in this class period. Otherwise, we should be leading activities on the material, specifically making students practice it, apply it, examine it, and work with it. These activities ensure better learning and retention of the readings and hold students accountable for doing them and maintain their interest. Students are very smart and will figure out quickly if they need to do the assigned work in your class to come prepared.

Poor Reading and Writing Abilities

Although much of class preparation includes watching videos and listening to podcasts, readings are still the mainstay of higher education. Unfortunately, roughly half of the high school graduates in the United States do not have the reading skills that college-level work requires (Kuh et al., 2005). This is particularly true of first-generation college students who lack an understanding of what their literacy levels should be entering college (Wahleithner, 2020). One problem that gets in the way of students' reading comprehension and speed is their inability to focus for more than a few minutes (Blue, 2003). Students often do not realize that reading is a mind activity, not an eye activity, and a very engrossing one that demands concentrated, sustained attention.

It's a circular challenge. Students don't practice reading much, at least not textbooks. On a weekly basis, they dedicate almost 9 hours to reading on the internet, chiefly social media such as Facebook, Instagram, and Twitter, and a little over 4 hours to extracurricular reading, such as the news, graphic novels, and nonacademic books. But they give only 7.7 hours to academic reading (Huang et al., 2013). They complain that reading textbooks is tedious and time-consuming, and some admit they do it only if they have to for an exam. Mintz (2022) noted that only 11% of adults with a bachelor's or some other advanced academic degree have read or listened to a book in the past year. With limited reading experience, students also lack a sophisticated vocabulary, which slows their reading speed, impedes their comprehension, and discourages them from further reading. This in turn makes it challenging to build a sophisticated vocabulary, which slows reading speed.

As of the writing of this book, COVID-19 has had an unknown, but clearly detrimental, impact on literacy. Schools have been disrupted for 2 years, and waves of variants continue to cause challenges. School closures have been particularly damaging for those with low-socioeconomic status and those in underrepresented populations (Goldstein, 2022).

Cannot Afford Books and Resources

Full-time students pay an average of $1,226 for textbooks and other class resources per academic year (Hanson, 2022). This is a large sum of money for college students, reflected in the statistic that 11% of students report skipping meals in order to afford course materials and books, and 67% of students said they didn't buy at least some required resources because of the cost. Annual cost of college textbooks also tends to be higher for 2-year institutions as

compared to four-year institutions (Hanson, 2022). Students know these practices will impact their grade, but they simply don't have the funds for resources. The best they can do is take the reduced grade for not turning in homework and work hard to get a passing grade. The open-access book project is changing this by offering free textbooks. They may not be ideal, but for some courses, it might mean students are able to prepare for class as they have the resource (i.e., book) to do so (https://www.oercommons.org/hubs/open-textbooks).

Competing Activities

It is important to keep in mind that students do not have only our assignment to complete. Imagine that on Tuesday afternoon you assign a student a chapter to read and accompanying worksheet to complete before the next class on Thursday afternoon. That student might have a biology paper due Wednesday, a psychology exam on Friday, and a video to watch with accompanying report for economics on Thursday morning. This same student may well need to work 4 hours Tuesday night and 4 hours Wednesday night for their job. Twenty-five percent of full-time undergraduates and 66% of part-time undergraduates work 20 hours per week or more (National Center for Education Statistics, 2022).

In addition to their work, many students have family, friends, and community service obligations. Individuals should also have a bit of time when they are not working, so we should factor in an hour or two per evening for students to, well, not work. Although some students will spend more time than they should engaging in extracurricular activities, there are certainly mental health considerations that make playing in a basketball game or going for a hike or even logging in to Dota a healthy option. We must remember that our courses have stiff competition for students' time.

It all comes down to time. Students do need to do the work to prepare for our courses, but we need to be mindful of the amount we are asking them to do. If a student feels overwhelmed by homework they may well shut down. Periodically, ask a few students before class how much time their homework and course preparation are taking.

No Perceived Value to Preparing

Another reason students fail to prepare for class is that there is no payoff for doing the requested work. If students are at college to gain an education and enhance their intellectual abilities, preparing for class is obviously a good use of time. However, students are increasingly emphasizing the practical aspect of higher education. These students view college as a means to an end—the end being a high-paying job that can support their consumer habits. According to a 2021 report, the extent to which Americans agree that colleges and universities have a positive impact on the United States is 58%, which is a reportedly a 10% drop from just 1 year prior (Daugherty, 2022). In that same report, 76% of the respondents indicated that higher education is a good return on investment. This is consistent with a trend that has been occurring for many years. Higher education is less about learning and growing, and is increasingly something individuals do because it is needed to get something they want (more money through a better job).

As Kohn (2018) notes, when one thing is set up as being contingent on something else, humans typically devalue and dislike the item that is the roadblock. Therefore, with the perspective that individuals must earn a college degree to reach the job they desire, college becomes a barrier to getting the job. To earn a college degree students must learn (learning becomes the barrier to getting the degree). Likewise, for some individuals, preparing for class is one of the first of a string of barriers that is getting in the way of what they want. For such people, because preparing for class is a barrier, if there is a way around it, there is no loss to them. This means if I can pass the class without preparing for class, or even buying the textbook for the course, there is no loss if my ultimate objective is to only to make money. If my outcome is to learn and to make money, then for learning, preparing for class is no longer a barrier.

Additional Reasons Students Don't Prepare for Class

We have provided several reasons why students may come to class unprepared. Following are a few more to consider as you reflect on students in your class. Students may:

- Not understand how to complete the homework
- Find assignments boring (monotone videos, dry text)
- Find assignments are not aligned with the course.
- Be navigating physical challenges (e.g., can't sit long periods, eyes hurt, nervous if not moving, adjusting to a medication change).
- Be navigating mental challenges (e.g., periodic depression, ADHD, etc.)
- Not have the book because only a few chapters are used from it

There are many possibilities beyond those we list here. Don't become overwhelmed. Just like anything else, start out with the basics, and as your skills grow you can expand. Perhaps the most important thing to keep in mind is that if you don't incorporate the assigned work into the class, students will figure out quickly you just want them to work more, not that they need to do the work to enhance their learning. Show them how that happens.

◾ HOW WE CAN EQUIP AND INDUCE STUDENTS TO COME PREPARED

There are several things you can do to teach your students how to prepare for class. First, assume your students will prepare for class as assigned and focus on those who do. As humans we are drawn to the negative cases. You can go to a busy store and co-exist well with hundreds of people and then you see one person try to cut in line. Immediately, your perception is, "People are so rude here. I don't like coming to this store." In situations like this, it is easy to forget the vast majority of people working well together. Try not to focus on those who didn't do the work. That will change your demeanor in class and tilt the classroom community in a direction you may not desire.

Make the default assumption that students are trying their best. If a student comes to class unprepared a few classes in a row, ask them off to the side if they are okay. By doing that you set a tone that students are doing the prep work and if you are not, there must be something wrong with your situation. Work to hold the class up to that level. Coming from a place of positivity helps achieve that goal. Instead of, "Where is everybody? I guess they didn't do the reading and are playing hooky," try, "Alright, let's get going. I hope you enjoyed (or learned a lot from) the reading, because today we're going to . . ." Coming from a default assumption that students are trying also means sharing with them strategies for success like how to read a textbook, watch a video, or listen to a podcast with purpose, or take good notes. If students already know about these strategies, a refresher is always helpful. If they are not aware that the strategies exist, you may unobtrusively help those who aren't prepared because they were not able to do the work, but are too embarrassed to talk to you about it.

Teach Students Proven Reading Methods

The simplest proven reading method, at least for factual and problem-solving material, is what is sometimes called active recall or the 3R (read-recite-review) strategy (McDaniel et al., 2009; Roediger & Karpicke, 2006). Students read a section of text, then close the book and recite aloud or write down as much as they can remember, and finally reread the section looking for what they missed or misunderstood. In other words, they reinforce their reading by reproducing the material and practicing retrieval with self-testing. In terms of student performance on multiple-choice and problem-solving tests, this technique works as effectively as note-taking in

less time and better than rereading the text multiple times (McDaniel et al., 2009; Roediger & Karpicke, 2006).

Although this technique has been studied on reading, the general learning principle is the *testing effect*, which states that being tested or self-testing provides retrieval practice, and this recalling of information facilitates remembering the material later (Roediger & Butler, 2010; Roediger & Karpicke, 2006; Rohrer et al., 2010; see Chapter 1). It will also work well when viewing and listening to media.

There are other strategies similar to the 3Rs. For example, SQ3R stands for survey-question-read-recall-review, and PQR3 is short for preview-question-read-recite-review. Just about all of them advise students to do the following:

1. Scan the reading to get a sense of what it's about, how it's organized, and where it's going, noting the titles, subtitles, graphics, bold and italicized words, conclusion, and summaries.
2. Review the purpose for reading. Because few students approach their reading with a purpose, we have to give them one or teach them how to devise their own purpose (see the next section).
3. Read with purpose to find what you are looking for, while thinking about what you are reading and paraphrasing what you are finding (most effectively in written notes).
4. Review the main points of the reading. We may have to induce students to complete this step by giving them a structured review assignment (see the "Require Students to Review" section later).

If you think about these steps, you may realize that you've been following them for years. They work for faculty members as much as they work for students. For example, when you pick up a research article, you don't usually read it straight through from the first word to the last. Rather, you read the abstract, thumb through the pages to glance at the tables and figures, then scan the conclusion, and perhaps work your way back to the results or methods. The last thing you may read is the literature review, which normally comes right after the abstract. This is the way an expert approaches a piece of academic reading, which is quite different from the way one reads a magazine article or a novel. Our students have not yet learned to make the distinctions.

Teach Students How to Do the Homework

It may be helpful to guide students through the homework assignments designed to help them to prepare for class. Depending on the class and the students, students may be unsure about what to do. Raimondi et al. (2020) tried multiple iterations to encourage students to come to class prepared and found guiding the students to be the most successful. On the first day of the semester, students were given a sample homework assignment, directions to complete it, and placed in groups to do the work. Students could help each other, and the faculty member could be consulted as needed. The researchers also provided students with completed homework assignments and an assignment template to guide them through the correct steps. Using a guided approach, students were better able to prepare for each class session.

Give Students a Purpose for Their Reading, Viewing, and Listening

Having a purpose for reading is the hallmark of the expert reader. When you pick up a scholarly article or book, you're usually looking for something relevant to your research, a course you teach, or a long-term interest. One of the reasons that you scan it first is to see if you have a purpose for reading it. If you find you do, your scan informs you where to focus. By contrast, students approach their readings with little or no purpose except to get it over with. They may not have a preexisting interest in the material, and they probably don't know what they are supposed to look for, which is why they complain that they can't tell what is and isn't important. We don't help them any by telling them that all the material is important.

We must give our students a purpose—that is, things to look for or a strategy for devising their own purpose—for the readings, videos, and podcasts we assign. If you cannot clearly see the purpose, it would be best if you could come up with another assignment for students to prepare for class. Possible purposes include seeking answers to questions, and the best questions are our own study questions—what Maurer and Longfield (2013) call "reading guides." Developing our own questions allows us to direct our students' attention to what we deem important and worth gaining in the assignments. In addition, we can ask students to apply, analyze, synthesize, and evaluate the material, getting them to deeply process it and think both practically and critically about it. For a point-of-view nonfiction piece of work, we can provide students with several generic thinking questions that ensure solid comprehension and analysis:

- What is the author's position or claim?
- What are the main arguments given in support of this position or claim?
- What evidence or data does the author furnish to support his or her position or claim?
- Evaluate the author's case, identifying any questionable evidence or data, missing information, or flaws in logical or analysis.

If you are using project-solving, case-based, or problem-solving learning, note the purpose may be solving the assigned problems. Advise students to review the questions or problems before they read, watch, or listen so they will be primed to be on the lookout for the answers or the solution strategies.

To guarantee that students process the content with the purpose we have in mind, it may be necessary for students to write out their answers or solutions and turn them in as daily graded homework or in a journal we collect and grade occasionally.

Require Students to Review

Although all the study skills and reading skills books and websites recommend taking this final step of review, students usually don't do it. We may have to push them by assigning a written homework exercise that makes them consolidate and integrate the new knowledge they have gained in the readings, videos, and podcasts. The simplest review assignment for students is to write out the main points and put them together into a one- or two-sentence summary. Another review strategy, one that requires less writing but more thinking, is to have students draw a graphic of the material, such as a concept map, mind map, concept circle diagram, flowchart, or whatever else is appropriate. In a graphic, students must construct their understanding of the organization of the concepts and principles. If their understanding is valid, the product gives them a mental structure with which to retain and elaborate on the knowledge. If your students haven't done this in other classes, teach them how by modeling the method in class; then having them work in small groups to map, diagram, or chart some material a few times; and finally assigning the task as individual homework. Chapter 22 explains a variety of graphic aids to learning and ways to teach them to students.

A third type of assignment, *reflective writing*, relies on freewriting about the readings, in response to open-ended thinking questions (Wirth, n.d.) or section by section (Kalman, 2007). In the latter, students read a section or two of the assigned chapter while highlighting, jotting down marginalia, or doing whatever else helps their comprehension. Then for roughly two-thirds of a page, they free-write about the section—not summarizing it but writing about what it means and then about what they don't understand. By this process, they generate questions to ask in class. In reflective writing, students are reviewing not just the material but also their understanding of it, and this should work equally well with videos and podcasts.

Assign Realistic Workloads

When assigning readings, keep in mind that you have expertise in the area you are teaching. That means an article that may take you 10 minutes to read may take your students over an hour. Experts often forget that we have internalized a large disciplinary vocabulary that is a foreign language to students. We have also learned a variety of cognitive shortcuts that make our reading much easier. For us, a single term may recall an entire mental structure of concepts, principles, assumptions, and implications that enriches our understanding of the sentence and foreshadows the next sentence. The unending flow of meaning allows us to move through the text quickly with unwavering focus. Even our brightest students stumble over new-to-them technical vocabulary and bring shallow, if any, associations to their academic readings. And they can't possibly appreciate their value or our reasons for selecting them.

As noted in Chapter 4, assigned videos and podcasts should be relatively short, typically 5–10 minutes to allow processing. Videos may be as short as 2–3 minutes and still be extremely valuable. True, we can assign several of them at a time, but we have to be careful. We have to be even more careful not to overload with reading assignments, given our students' reading challenges. Less can be more because students are more likely to complete shorter ones than longer ones (Hobson, 2004). Ultimately, the evidence suggests that we should require only the most essential readings, those most crucial to our learning outcomes.

It is also helpful to ensure our readings are aimed at the students' level—particularly because many may have reading challenges (Hobson, 2004). Even if we teach them how to read the material, they will need practice before they become fluent at it. A few readability indexes are available on the web at https://www.webfx.com/tools/read-able. Just copy and paste some text into the calculator, and you obtain both an age-level and a reading-ease score. This will give you a good indication about whether your assigned readings are at the proper level. This is important, as reading time estimates vary significantly, based on the level of the text. To determine about how long it will take students to read assigned work, you can use the Course Workload Estimator developed by the Rice University Center for Teaching Excellence: https://www.cte.rice.edu/workload. This online tool will assist in maintaining realistic workload assignments for your students. The website also has helpful information regarding reading speeds based on page density, text difficulty, and reading purpose. Based on these variables, it is important to note that assigned readings from a textbook with many new concepts where students are to engage in the content through working problems, drawing inferences and evaluating what is being read may take around 12 minutes per page. That means a student may well spend 2 hours working their way through just 10 pages.

Sell the Readings, Videos, and Podcasts

To an extent, we can motivate some students to do the assignments by promoting them. We can explain their purpose, relevance, and our reasons for choosing them over other options. In the syllabus, we can emphasize how central they are to the course and learning outcomes. Each day or week, we can preview and promote the next assignment, noting what questions it will answer and what value it will hold for their immediate learning and later lives and careers. We can also place it in the context of the next class, later assignments, upcoming in-class activities, and the larger course and curriculum (Hobson, 2004).

Let's not underestimate the potential impact of such efforts. Students cite their personal desire to learn as their single strongest motivator for doing the readings, far above wanting to participate in discussion or feeling obligated (Bradley, 2007). Chances are we can influence their desire with a short, persuasive pitch. If you are not certain that it will work well in your class, then the next section pertaining to tools to hold students accountable will be extremely valuable for you. The information can be read in a few minutes and will almost certainly help you increase the proportion of students preparing for class.

Websites Designed to Help Students to Successfully Prepare for Class

The following sites can be very helpful for students learning to learn. It may be helpful for you to skim the sites for what you consider the best ideas and share them with your students in an effort to help them to prepare for each class.

- http://www.collegeatlas.org/college-study-guides.html
- http://www.how-to-study.com/pqr.htm
- http://www.mindtools.com/rdstratg.html
- https://ucc.vt.edu/academic_support/study_skills_information.html http://studygs.net

◼ FOUR TOOLS FOR HOLDING STUDENTS ACCOUNTABLE

The following four suggestions have elements drawn from a large number of sources. You may use them in any combination. As with any course planning, using backward design will be helpful. Think about what you intend for your desired outcome. Wanting students to come prepared is important, but keep in mind what you want your students to do during the class period; the focus is having the students do the preclass work meaningfully. You could differentiate between "good work" and "just writing things down" with a 3-point scale (0 = not done, 1 = completed, 2 = good work). To encourage students to complete assignments, scores can be part of the final grade in the course. Something in the area of 5–10% is common (Kalman, 2007; Sullivan et al., 2008). Perhaps the most important thing, as noted previously, is not to lecture over the material students are supposed to be completing.

Homework

Some research finds that required written homework for submission motivates students to prepare for class more regularly and carefully than does any schedule of quizzes, even if it is not always graded (Carney et al., 2008). In fact, Hoeft (2012) found that her daily, graded journal assignments on the readings more than doubled the percentage of reading-compliant students (from 46 to 95%), and Eddy and Hogan (2014) reported similar results. With some forms of homework, you may want to remind your students to use their homework to refer to and take notes on in class. The options for homework on the readings, videos, or podcasts are almost limitless:

- Notes on the topic, or an abstract or summary (Barrineau, 2001; Kalman, 2007; Kalman & Kalman, 1996; Peirce, 2006)
- An outline or graphic (Peirce, 2006)
- One or more questions on the content written on cards or posted electronically (Martin, 2000). You may even ask for specific types of questions (multiple choice, true-false, essay, and so on) for possible use in future tests.
- Answers to study, reading-response, journaling, or end-of-chapter questions (Carney et al., 2008; Eddy & Hogan, 2014; Hoeft, 2012; Peirce, 2006). Questions that make students reflect on the personal relevance of the material also enhance their perceptions of their ability to participate productively in class discussions (Carney et al., 2008; Onodipe et al., 2020)
- Solutions to problems
- Any type of outside material that illustrates an important point in the readings or an application of them—for example, a magazine or news article, a printed advertisement, a photograph, a website, or an object
- Many faculty members are finding ways to use gamification to encourage students to complete homework (Kulhanek et al., 2021)

For content comprehension, quizzes may surpass homework. Hoeft (2012) found that her students, when reading for answers to her journal questions, merely skimmed material, and as a result only 42% of them demonstrated basic comprehension.

Quizzes

Frequent, regular quizzes are proven accountability tools (Carney et al., 2008; Heiner, 2014; Hoeft, 2012; Lin, 2014; Thompson, 2002), and they induce homework compliance more effectively than randomly administered (chance or pop) quizzes (Carney et al., 2008). They also enhance student performance on major exams and increase class attendance (Lin, 2014; Pape-Lindstrom et al., 2018). With daily quizzes, Hoeft (2012) reported a 74% reading compliance rate, which is low compared to other studies, and a 53% basic comprehension rate among the compliant, which surpassed answering journal questions.

You can administer accountability quizzes in class or online shortly before class. Either way, they should focus on the major points and concepts, not details, and the items should be easy for you to grade quickly—either multiple choice or short essay. One study found short essay questions more effective than multiple-choice items in helping students gauge their own learning (Sullivan et al., 2008). Remember that you can grade the answers as simply acceptable/not acceptable (credit/no credit) based on whether they address the question and meet the required length.

Just-in-time teaching, an inquiry-based method described in Chapter 17, is a type of daily quiz on the readings or other assignment. Students submit their answers online to conceptual multiple-choice items 30 to 60 minutes before each class, giving you just enough time to adjust your lesson plan to clarify any comprehension problems they had. We know this method raises students' level of preparation for class, participation in class, engagement, and achievement (Marrs & Novak, 2004) as long as it appreciably figures into the final grade (Sullivan et al., 2008).

With in-class quizzes, you can dictate the questions or display them on a slide. You can also have students make up the questions as homework submitted earlier. Finally, you can follow the individual quiz with a group quiz where students have the chance to discuss the material (see the "Team-Based Learning" section in Chapter 10).

In-Class Activities

Such activities include problem-solving and written exercises. Students can solve provided problems or design new ones for future tests. Written exercises may be a one-minute paper, a reading response mini-essay, a summary, or any of a wide assortment of short writing assignments described in Chapters 19 and 22 and classroom assessment activities suggested in Chapter 23. They can even be graphics, such as a map, diagram, or flowchart of the material (see Chapter 22).

To encourage high-quality work, you might allow students to use whatever they create as their in-class products during future tests. One summary exercise that is particularly effective at motivating students to seriously study the readings, videos, or podcasts is a *mind dump*. You allow students 5 or 10 minutes to write down everything they can remember from their studying. Then you collect these recollections and return them to their authors at the beginning of tests. Although students may have little time to hunt through them during tests, they will feel less anxious and no doubt will have better mastery of the material just for having written about it.

Individual accountability is critical for reading compliance, but some of these exercises are adaptable to groups. In fact, the more challenging ones, such as writing higher-order multiple-choice items for future tests, may benefit from the synergy of multiple minds. You can find many more structured group activities in Chapter 10.

You will need to keep individual students and groups on task and accountable. You can have them sign and hand in their exercises or problem solutions. If valid answers emerged during class, you don't have to correct or write feedback on them. Just check off that they completed the task. Or randomly call on several students or groups to read their answer, explain their solution, or display their graphic. If the exercise or problem has one right answer and not everyone comes up with it, don't correct those with wrong answers. Let students with different results debate them.

Recitation

As explained in Chapter 14, recitation is students' recalling and reproducing, either verbatim or in their own words, material they are supposed to have already learned from assigned readings, videos, podcasts, or live lectures—that is, performing knowledge/remembering and comprehension/understanding cognitive operations. It's then easy to move into higher-order discussion questions. In classic recitation, you pose recall questions and randomly cold-call on students. Keeping in mind that cold-calling is a controversial topic, there are ways to do it that both bring about the advantages of this strategy and mitigate some of the potential harm (Waugh & Andrews, 2020). Cold-calling can both encourage more students to participate in class and increase the diversity of those heard. A major outcome is that it holds the students accountable for the material they were to prepare for class that day.

One way to warm the cold call, yet hold the student accountable, is to have students pair and talk about a concept after the question has been read, but prior to calling on someone. You need only give one minute for classmates to pair up and talk in groups of two or three. There are many ways to adapt cold-calling situations that are a bit kinder to those who struggle with speaking out in class (Zakrajsek, 2017). Keep in mind that if you randomly cold-call on individual students through the class period, there will be students with elevated heart rates not paying attention to anything that is being taught because they are afraid of messing up if they are called on. Those individuals did the work, but if you call on them, they likely will not be able to answer and then feel even more anxiety. One option is to have students form intact groups that stay together for a period of time, such as a month. The cold-calling, using a random method, is directed at the groups. One instructor noted that students were more likely to come prepared so as to not let their group members down. When called on, anyone in the group can answer and anyone else in the group can assist. This strategy has been successfully used in classes with hundreds of students (Waugh & Andrews, 2020).

MANAGING YOUR WORKLOAD

You may be concerned that accountability tools will generate too heavy a workload. Consider how much time the tools actually demand and what other tasks they can eliminate. Yes, you will have to find or create short homework assignments, quiz items, recitation questions, or in-class exercises and activities, and you will have to grade them in some fashion. However:

- Your students can make up questions and problems for you, whether for quizzes, tests, in-class activities, or recitation.
- Grading can be quick and effortless (Kalman, 2007; Thompson, 2002). With written homework, short essay quizzes, and submitted in-class activities, you need only check the work for completeness or a good-faith effort, and you can grade recitation on the fly in class.
- You can give fewer major tests and assignments, saving yourself considerable preparation and grading time.
- You can require and collect all written homework, but you only have to grade some of it some of the time (Carney et al., 2008).
- You need not prepare lectures.

Encouraging and helping students to prepare for class is also an equity and inclusion issue. Eddy & Hogan (2014) found that adding structure to class is helpful for all students, but even more helpful for Black students and first-generation college students. Being ready for class is highly valuable in terms of what you can teach. Consider how much more your students will learn and how deeply you can take them into the material if they prepare for class. Imagine the discussions and other activities you could lead! There is a time-savings position here. Students who are doing well in class, write better papers, and score better on exams require less of our time.

REFLECTION QUESTIONS

Reflection Question 21.1: Were you the type of student who regularly prepared for class? Did you prepare more extensively for some classes than others? Overall, what factors caused you to prepare or not? For this reflection, if you didn't prepare and it was because you didn't have enough time, is there anything in hindsight that you could have done differently?

Reflection Question 21.2: What is your preference for holding students accountable for preparing for class? What might your choice say about who you are as an instructor?

Concept Into Practice: Based on the information in this chapter, identify one new thing you can implement that will increase the number of students who show up to your class prepared. Think about how you can build out from your strengths. Think of something that aligns with who you are as a teacher and will help you build your teaching toolbox and help students at the same time.

CHAPTER 22

Integrating Styles and Modes of Learning

Humans use physiological mechanisms, called modes, to encode sensory information into memory for later use. The primary modes are vision, hearing, and touch. We *hear* recordings of music, we *see* paintings by masters, and we *feel* the dirt and petals as we plant flowers. When it comes to learning, the mode by which something is processed is very important and provides cues with which we can later recall that information. For example, you may recognize a song after only a few notes; if you and a close friend listened to that song together many times, you may recognize the song and also immediately think about your friend. That is the power of learning through modes.

Although modes are external and objective, learning styles are internal and vary based on the individual and circumstance. Learning styles are ways in which individuals *prefer* to gather, think about, organize, and store information. Styles may be directly related to a mode. For example, if a person prefers to learn by looking at things, they have a more visual learning style. An individual who prefers to think about things may be said to have a reflective learning style, whereas an extrovert may

thrive when learning with others. Given that *styles* can mean many different things, it is challenging to firmly state what it means to have a style of learning, but as it is an intrinsic component of learning, it warrants discussion.

In this chapter we look at several modes of learning, as well as the styles by which people prefer to learn. The field is not nearly as straightforward as many believe, and the complex research presented here supports that.

▪ LEARNING STYLES

A learning style is how a person prefers to process information, including how it is gathered, thought about, and combined with prior information to create a new memory for learning. Learning styles appear to have been originally based on the work of Carl Jung (1964), one of the first in psychology to propose that individuals fall into specific types, regardless of life circumstances. Jung asserted that you are born preferring a learning style, and your type is typically stable throughout life. One of the categories he described was how one interacts with the world. He called the two interaction types extraversion and introversion. The theories of Jung served as a foundation for the Myers-Briggs Type Indicator test, a personality index that began in the 1940s and continues to be widely popular today.

Learning styles became popular because individuals typically want to better understand themselves, and learning styles tests neatly put people into distinct categories. Research showing that individuals do not actually cluster into groups and remain there, actually measured by tests such as the Myers-Briggs itself (Druckman & Porter, 1991), does not seem to discourage individuals from being ardent followers of learning styles theory. Quite the contrary, in fact. Coffield et al. (2004) surveyed the literature and identified 71 learning styles models, with 13 of the models having a major following of individuals.

Learning styles models remain prominent in schools due largely to the belief that each learner is unique, and if an instructor is just able to identify a student's learning style, the curriculum can be tailored to them. This sounds fantastic; who wouldn't want a customized learning experience? That said, this isn't really a practical approach, and as it turns out, there are a set of universal learning principles that work for all learners (Zakrajsek, 2022). Individuals do have preferences, based on inherent characteristics (e.g., more outgoing, more shy) and experiences (e.g., often went to museums as a child and developed visual processing acuity; worked with a parent on rebuilding cars as a hobby and developed kinesthetic skills). The more we practice a style, the better we will become at learning that way. This may even occur subconsciously, leading people to believe that their preference is truly innate and immutable. Taking learning styles inventories that reinforce people's learned *preferences* and present them as *requirements* has unfortunately reinforced this misunderstanding, leading to the myth of meshing (Pashler et al., 2009). Learning styles inventories can certainly help instructors tailor their plans to their students' preferences, but inventories shouldn't be confused with diagnostic tools. The research just isn't there.

■ LEARNING STYLES MYTH

This widespread belief that it is good educational practice to teach students in a way consistent with their dominant learning style is called *meshing*. The problem is that although there are literally thousands of articles written about teaching to a given learning style, there is simply no evidence that meshing results in better learning (Husman & O'Loughlin, 2018; Knoll et al., 2017). The learning-style myth is often referred to as the myth that will not die (Coffield et al., 2004; Kirschner & van Merriënboer, 2013; Papadatou-Pastou et al., 2020; Riener & Willingham, 2010; Willingham, 2005). For more information on this position, simply search the web for "learning style myth."

Nancekivell et al. (2020) noted that approximately half of those who believe meshing, particularly in early childhood education, also believe that learning styles are "easily detectable and measurable in the brain, determined at birth, heritable, and predictive of life outcomes" (p. 233). Aside from this being false, when young children are taught in their perceived "required" learning style, those children are less likely to develop a broader range of information processing strategies as they are not getting the chance to practice them.

It turns out that when verbal and visual learners are given tasks that require them to process things both visually and verbally, they don't do better on the task that matches their style of learning. That is, *processing information according to your preferred style, even though it feels like it is better, does not result in better learning than when you process in a different style* (Willingham, 2018). The major disconnect with meshing is that some types of problems are simply better solved in a particular way. For example, there is no advantage to a learner with a kinesthetic preference trying to think kinesthetically when differentiating a Monet painting from a van

Gogh painting. In such a situation, it is best to use visual parts of the brain to solve the challenge visually. Similarly, it is not ideal for a person to be either totally reflective or totally intuitive, but rather to use the style of thinking that would best solve that type of problem.

Although there is widespread criticism of teaching to a given learning style and universal agreement among cognitive psychologists and cognitive neuroscientists that meshing does not provide an advantage to students, learning styles continue to persist. Indeed, government-distributed test-preparation material for teacher certification exams includes research that has debunked meshing (Furey, 2020). The most frustrating part of this is that since the 1970s research has consistently failed to find any advantage to meshing. Furey (2020) also noted that 67% of teacher-preparation programs still require students to include learning styles in lesson-planning assignments. In addition, 59% of teacher education textbooks advise taking students' learning styles into account.

One could argue that it doesn't hurt to teach meshing, or provide instruction that matches a student's preferred learning style. Unfortunately, there is not an unlimited amount of time in the classroom, especially for something that simply does not have support. If you are going to teach students how to play a clarinet, kinesthetic instruction makes the most sense. Give students clarinets and have them practice. One would not give students learning styles inventories and then provide photos of how to play different notes on the clarinet to visual learners and lecture on how to play different notes to auditory learners. The same could be said for most instruction. Instead of taking time to restrict teaching to particular learning styles, it is much better to simply teach all students in multiple ways, which has been shown by research to promote learning (Mayer, 2002). There is simply not enough time in class to either encourage students to pursue learning in a preferred, but ineffective way, or take class time and resources to be a less effective, fractured instructor.

Of the 71 learning style models noted by Coffield et al. (2004), several are multimillion-dollar commercial entities. Be cautious of any model that provides "evidence" that their model "works." It might, but to have credibility, it should be independently studied and supported by cognitive psychologists and cognitive neuroscientists, and that's rare, if it truly exists at all. Remember Furey's (2020) comment: "Year after year, the proof eludes us—even with the cheeky promise of a $5,000 cash prize for anyone who can demonstrate a positive effect of incorporating learning styles into an educational intervention" (para. 5).

■ MODES OF LEARNING

Over the past several decades, cognitive psychological research consistently shows that people learn new material best when they receive it multiple times through multiple senses and in multiple modes (or modalities), which are learning channels in different parts of their brain (Feldon, 2010; Kress et al., 2006; Mayer, 2005, 2009; Metiri Group, 2008; Nancekivell et al., 2021; Vekiri, 2002). Scholars dispute the number and types of modes, but all agree that the more modes learners activate, the more learning that occurs. As Feldon (2010) explains it, each modality has "limited bandwidth" (p. 19), so it is best to distribute new information across several modes. Therefore, all students should read, listen, talk, write, see, draw, act/experience, and ultimately think new material into their system. They should go through new material in at least two or three different modes, and it's our job to arrange the learning experiences to ensure they do so.

Again, we should teach using most appropriate modes for the content (Willingham, 2005a)—for example, visuals for inherently visual material (art and art history, cartography, geology, biology, physics); reading and listening for poetry and literature; listening, seeing, and acting (experience) for drama; and seeing and experiencing for physical procedures. Learning relatively recent history can draw on almost every mode. In fact, just about every kind of knowledge can and should be conveyed in more than one mode as each mode provides its own retrieval cues when it is time to remember the learned information.

The Reading Mode

Reading is typically students' first exposure to new material, but unfortunately, many of today's students lack good reading comprehension skills. If you can point out to your students that there are ways for anyone to improve their reading, you will impact the rest of their lives. There are many active learning strategies to help students to better process material in the reading mode, such as prereading, guided reading, contextualizing, summarizing, and postreading (Major et al., 2021). Chapters 19 and 21 and "The Writing Mode" section later in this chapter offer additional ways to improve skills and make the most of the reading mode, including pairing or following reading with an activity in the writing, speaking, or visual mode (see later). Prepared visuals complement readings especially well for comprehension purposes, as long as both are in close proximity to each other (Mayer, 2005, 2009; Metiri Group, 2008).

The Listening Mode

Listening can be a powerful way to learn new material. The challenge occurs when students confuse listening with simply hearing or being within earshot, just as they may confuse reading with running their eyes over a page. Both listening and reading presume focusing *attention* on the words—specifically, interpreting their meaning, making decisions about the importance of the message, translating the message into written shorthand symbols, relating it to what one already knows, and perhaps dialoguing with or questioning it. This deep processing constitutes elaborative rehearsal and eventual encoding of the message into long-term memory.

Students are typically not taught how to listen actively, but we can teach them. Refer back to the self-regulated learning activities in Chapter 19 that are designed for live lectures, podcasts, and videos: periodic free recall (Bonwell & Eison, 1991); active listening checks (Lovett, 2008); minute papers (Chew, quoted in Lang, 2012; Wirth, n.d.); reflective writing (Araujo, quoted in Schell, 2012; Kalman, 2007; Mezeske, 2009; Wirth, n.d.); and Read (or listen), Recall, Review (Major et al., 2021; McDaniel et al., 2009; Roediger & Butler, 2010). These exercises, especially periodic free-recall and active listening checks, give students the chance to test the effectiveness of their listening and, if necessary, practice listening more intently. If recorded, they can review by replaying the recording to find out what they may have missed.

Listening also has a benefit over reading: it is at least sometimes easier for the brain to process material delivered orally than in written form. For instance, listening to a narrative that accompanies visual material (a graph, video, or animation) carries a lower cognitive load than does reading about the visual material (Mayer, 2005, 2009; Metiri Group, 2008).

The Speaking Mode

Speaking is inherently more active than listening in that when speaking a person must think through what they want to say and how to put it into words. Speaking is also a powerful learning technique, because speaking requires the speaker to recall the information, and practicing at recall is an effective learning strategy (Gurung & Burns, 2018). Even the *possibility* of speaking in response to someone else's words typically makes one's listening more active. This is why students learn so effectively from discussion. They learn even more when the exchange takes place in a small group where they can enjoy plenty of opportunities to speak and respond to others.

Chapter 19 presents two SRL activities that rely on pairs using the speaking mode: periodic free recall, in which students help each other reconstruct a lecture (Bonwell & Eison, 1991), and think-aloud, in which they help each other talk through solutions to math-based problems (Whimbey & Lochhead, 1999). Speaking makes sharp and explicit ideas and strategies that would otherwise lie fuzzy and unformed and would probably be forgotten.

The Experiential Mode

Of course, real experience can be a powerful way to learn, but so can acting out a role in a realistic situation, as acting affords a vicarious, empathy-based experience. Strategies such as role plays and Reacting to the Past are effective experiential modes that can be done in the classroom with a wide variety of topics (Major et al., 2021; Watson & Hagood, 2018). Either way, experience still requires focused and systematic reflection, preferably using the modes of discussion and writing, to generate actual learning. Chapter 16 details experiential learning and accompanying reflection questions (also see Chapter 19).

The Writing Mode

Writing is not just a medium of communication but a powerful method for thinking and learning in several ways (Bean, 2011; Walvoord, 2014). First, writing about content helps students learn it better and retain it longer—whatever the subject and whether the exercise involves note-taking, outlining, summarizing, recording focused thought, composing short answers, or writing full-fledged essays. Second, writing makes students think actively about the material, and, depending on your prompt, you can make your students think at higher-order cognitive levels, as well as affectively and ethically. Third, writing exercises can define audiences other than the instructor and therefore develop students' sensitivity to the interests, backgrounds, and vocabularies of different readers. A fourth benefit of writing is as a classroom assessment to find out quickly how learning is progressing for students, while you're still focusing on a particular topic. This way you can diagnose and clarify points of confusion before you

give the next exam and move on to other topics (Angelo & Cross, 1993). Reading such short, informal writing assignments takes no more time than any other type of class preparation. Finally, many writing exercises give students the chance to learn about themselves—their feelings, values, cognitive processes, and learning strengths and weaknesses. This is why so many of the self-regulated learning activities and assignments (described in Chapter 19) involve writing.

Following are two examples of strategies that activate the writing mode. For 15 additional evidence-based strategies, including Graffiti Boards, Sentence Passage Spring Boards, Wikipedia Article, and Field Notes, see Major et al. (2021).

Free-Writing

Students write about a predetermined topic for a brief, specified number of minutes (1–3) as fast as they can think and put words on paper. The objective is to activate prior knowledge or generate ideas by free association, disregarding grammar, spelling, punctuation, and the like. Free-writing serves as effective in-class warm-up exercises. It can help students recall the previous class meeting and encourages them to keep up with assigned reading. Here are some possible free-writing topics:

- Have students write down all the important points they can remember from the previous discussion.
- Have them summarize the most important points from the assigned readings (or from the day's lecture or class activities).
- Write three key words on the board from the previous class (or assigned reading) and ask students to explain their importance.
- Have students define a concept in their own words, explain the parts of a complex concept, give real-life examples of a concept, or compare concepts from today's class with those from the previous class.
- Write a seed sentence on the board—that is, a major hypothesis, conclusion, or provocative

statement related to class or readings—and have them write their reactions.

- Have them apply a principle to their own experience.
- Have them free-write answers to test review questions to prepare for a tightly timed essay test.

Of course, free-writing needn't be private. Students can share them with one another, in which case the activity is called *inkshedding* (Hunt, 2004). They can trade and comment on one another's free-writing. Their purpose is not to evaluate the other's writing but to understand it. After such an exercise, the class is ready for discussion.

Free-writing can also be assigned as homework, as Kalman (2007) does to ensure his students prepare for class and process the readings (see Chapter 21). After students read a section or two of a chapter, they begin free-writing about what they just read and what they don't understand. Then they go on to the next section and free-write again. At the end of the assigned chapter or unit, they write three sentences, one on each of three key concepts they have identified in the readings. Students usually write three or more pages of notes and reflection.

The one-minute paper, discussed in Chapters 15 and 23, is a type of free-writing designed to close a learning experience, such as a minilecture, in-class activity, or reading. It helps students absorb, digest, elaborate, and internalize new material, moving it into long-term memory. It also makes them think about the material, especially what they didn't understand, which is precisely what you need to know before wrapping up a topic.

Journals

Students summarize what they are learning or how they are reacting, cognitively and emotionally, to the lectures, discussions, readings, laboratories, homework problems, or other written assignments. Ideally, students write journal entries regularly at the end of each lecture, discussion, or lab or as a meta-assignment. Journals help learners keep up with the course, as well as read and listen actively. Writing

such as this also induces students to think about the material and what they are learning. Some instructors require just one weekly journal-writing session, either in class or as homework, on any or all aspects of a course. Students should have a special notebook, blog, wiki, or word-processing file solely for their journals.

Here are some possible probes:

- What is new to you about this material, and what did you already know?
- Does any point contradict what you already knew or believed?
- What patterns of reasoning (or data) does the speaker/author offer as evidence?
- How convincing do you find the speaker's/author's reasoning or data?
- Is there any line of reasoning that you do not follow?
- Is this reasoning familiar to you from other courses?
- What don't you understand?
- What questions remain in your mind?

You should collect and check off journals regularly or intermittently, but you need not grade them. If you do, don't weigh them very much toward the final grade. But do write comments in them to develop a personal dialogue with each student. If you want to try journaling, consult Stevens and Cooper (2009) for more ideas and guidelines.

The Visual Mode

The brain processes visual information in as little as one-tenth of a second (Semetko & Scammell, 2012). Pure visual images, unfettered by text, convey information directly, efficiently, and quickly. Visuals, then, can serve our instructional purposes very effectively. They come in many forms—flowcharts, diagrams, graphs, tables, matrices, pictures, drawings, figures, even animations—offering countless options for depicting course material. They can be created and displayed on a computer, but they can be just as powerful when hand-drawn. We can provide them to help students learn and to become accustomed to using visuals, so they can go on to develop graphic representations of their own understanding of the subject matter. As the next section details, these visual schemas can give students the scaffolding they need to better understand and remember the learning process you have planned for them and your course content.

The evidence that graphics of all kinds facilitate comprehension, transfer, and retention of course material has generated a large body of research and several sizable literature reviews (e.g., Vekiri, 2002). Many of the studies center around specific visual tools, such as concept maps and mind maps, which are summarized in the next section. Whatever the type, visuals cue the text, helping students remember the indicated relationships and the contents inside the boxes, circles, or cells. You may even remember recalling material during a test by picturing the page of the textbook where the material was located and reading it in your mind's eye.

Other research focuses on multimedia learning. For instance, adding a visual to either text or auditory material enhances retention and facilitates later retrieval (Fadel, 2008; Mayer, 2005; Medina, 2008). In fact, according to Ginns's (2005) meta-analysis, pairing graphics with spoken text enhances student learning significantly more than combining graphics with printed text. However, auditory information alone has little staying power. People can retrieve only 10% of auditory input after 3 days, but if that material is complemented with a visual, the retrieval rate soars to 65% (Kalyuga, 2000; Mayer & Gallini, 1990). This strong effect reflects the fact that our brains process visual, text, and auditory material through independent channels, which means that each medium reinforces the learning of the other (Fadel, 2008).

Visuals, alone or in concert with other modes, foster deeper learning because they show the relationships among concepts (Medina, 2008; Vekiri, 2002). More generally, Marzano (2003) documents that "nonlinguistic representations" of material, which include graphics, images, metaphors, and art forms, have an effect size on learning of .75, meaning that students exposed to them score 0.75 standard deviations higher on tests than students not so exposed. This effect size is comparable to that of collaborative learning and reinforcement and feedback. Hattie's (2009) meta-analysis of meta-analyses obtains a lower effect size of .57, but it is only for concept maps. This figure, too, approximates that for cooperative learning. One more benefit of graphics—this one particularly important in the global village we now inhabit—is that they communicate across cultures. Many of the conventions used in visuals, such as spatial proximity among closely related elements and the use of arrows to indicate direction or movement, seem to be universal, anchored in the basic human processes of visual perception (Tversky, 1995, 2001).

Two theories in cognitive psychology, the visual argument theory and cognitive theory, explain why visuals are so effective. They are discussed in the following sections.

The Visual Argument Theory
According to this theory, visuals work so effectively because they convey information more efficiently than text—that is, visual information requires less working memory and fewer cognitive transformations to process and draw inferences from (Fawcett et al., 2012; Hockley, 2008; Robinson & Molina, 2002). In other words, it is less taxing on the mind to derive meaning from graphics than from words. In addition, a good graphic does a much better job than text of (1) inducing learners to attend to the conceptual relationships rather than just memorize terms; (2) enabling them to recognize patterns among concepts; (3) helping them elaborate their cognitive schemata by inferring new, complex relationships; and (4) helping them integrate new knowledge into their existing cognitive structures (Hyerle, 1996; Robinson & Kiewra, 1995; Robinson et al., 1998).

Simply showing learners a picture of this organization teaches them a great deal about the nature of knowledge—for one, that it is not a list of loosely linked ideas but a tightly structured web of interrelated categories and principles. In addition, the mind need not interpret or infer the conceptual interrelationships because they are transparently displayed in the spatial arrangements, the shapes of the enclosures, the types of lines, the directions of the arrows, the colors, and any other graphic features the designer may use to distinguish causal links and direction, strength of relationship, level of generality, and the like.

McMaster University professor Dale Roy (cited in Gedalof, 1998) demonstrated the superior efficacy of graphics on a faculty audience, a group highly skilled in processing text. He asked participants to prepare a brief oral presentation, which included developing one text-based page to present and one visual representation. After the participants delivered their minilesson, the rest of the audience reconstructed it from memory. The faculty members were consistently able to reproduce almost all the visual material but no more than half of the text-based presentation.

Cognitive Theory: The Big Picture

Chapter 1 has already addressed the critical importance of learners' seeing the organized big picture of knowledge, which includes recognizing patterns in how the world works. It is having this big picture of our field that makes us experts. In our mind's eye, this structure resembles a complex web of patterns that our colleagues have identified and verbalized. This pattern consists of highly organized information that enables us to easily assimilate new information into the existing pattern with the ability to store, retrieve, and use information from a vast collection of concepts, facts, data, and principles (Zakrajsek, 2022). We developed this schema over many years of intensive study—probably the hard way without the help of conceptual maps.

Without such a valid and robust mental structure, our students are disciplinary novices. They bring to our courses little background knowledge, no filing system for new knowledge, and often faulty models and misconceptions about the subject matter (Svinicki, 2004). After all, the mind is so wired to seek patterns that it can make mistakes in its quest. Students are unfamiliar with the hierarchy of concepts and principles, cannot discern patterns and generalizations, and lack the algorithms that facilitate applying knowledge to solving conceptual problems (DeJong & Ferguson-Hessler, 1996; Kozma et al., 1996). As a result, they wander through a knowledge base picking up pieces of it on a superficial level, memorizing isolated facts and terms, and using trial-and-error to solve problems and answer questions (Glaser, 1991). What they need to advance beyond novice is an empirically grounded big picture of the hierarchical structure of the body of knowledge—one convincing enough to override their misconceptions, as well as accurate and comprehensive enough to accommodate new knowledge and multiple conceptual networks (Baume & Baume, 2008). This is their entrée into expert thinking and a framework for deep, meaningful learning. In fact, students can't really learn and get beyond memorizing without it. The mind depends on organization; it acquires and stores new knowledge only if it perceives its organization and logical place within the mental structure of prior knowledge (Hanson, 2006; Svinicki, 2004; Wieman, 2007; Zull, 2002, 2011).

As the chances are very slim that students will independently build such cognitive schemata in a semester or two of casual study, we would be wise to furnish them with relevant structures of our discipline, with valid, ready-made frameworks for filing this content (Kozma et al., 1996). They need to internalize this scaffolding, especially at the introductory level, where they have little prior knowledge of the subject matter on which to map new knowledge, before we elaborate it with details, conditions, and qualifications (Carlile & Jordan, 2005; Zull, 2002, 2011). In addition, we should help students become aware of any faulty mental models they may harbor and guide them in reconciling these with more accurate cognitive structures. Specifically, we can give them practice in reinterpreting their prior observations and experiences. Otherwise, if all we impart are masses of content, they will graduate mentally unchanged and uneducated, with only memory traces of their college years.

Because mental structures of knowledge are so crucial to students' learning, we need to convey them in the most transparent and efficient way possible. We know that the cognitive models of experts like ourselves look like hierarchical networks of complexly interrelated concepts and principles (Hanson, 2006; Wieman, 2007). Many types of visuals are similarly structured to display component parts in hierarchical or weblike arrangements. Therefore, well-crafted graphics should do an excellent job of depicting disciplinary schemata. The next section examines three types that are suitable to the task.

◼ EXAMPLES OF VISUALS FOR LEARNING

Ausubel (1968) coined the term *advance organizer* decades ago to apply to any graphic that offered an opening overview of a lesson, whether a flowchart, diagram, chart, table, matrix, web, map, figure, or something else. In this section we focus on the major types of graphics that spatially display the relationships among ideas and concepts. Such visuals can serve as an advance organizer; a constructivist assignment for student groups or individuals; or a planning and memory aid for managing projects, solving problems, running meetings, organizing papers and presentations, integrating and summarizing material, and even writing creative works (Svinicki, 2004; Wycoff, 1991). In other words, we can use graphics to not only help students acquire and retain knowledge but also teach them tools that will facilitate their work in college and beyond and engage the creativity of the visual-holistic side of the brain. In addition, having students draw their own graphics can make excellent homework assignments—for example, summarizing their understanding of the readings or reviewing for tests—as well as challenging group activities during class and even test questions. The products can

help you diagnose students' misconceptions and assess their conceptual, analytical, and synthesis skills without your having to read essays.

Following are three examples of strategies that activate the visual mode for learning. For 11 additional evidence-based strategies, including main idea detail charts, matrices, and cause and effect chains, see Major et al. (2021).

Concept Maps

In cognitive psychology, a concept is a human-defined pattern or common ground across a category of objects, events, or properties. For instance, concepts that represent objects include *force, light, food, population, weather, pressure*, and *energy*. Examples of those describing events are *rain, photosynthesis, osmosis, conversion, fission*, and *marriage*. Among those designating properties are *taste, density, life-giving, volume*, and *texture*. A concept map graphically displays the hierarchical organization of several (up to 20 or so) concepts, from the most inclusive/general/broad/abstract concept at the top to the most exclusive/specific/narrow/concrete concepts at the bottom. Therefore, it frequently looks like a network or spider web, typically pyramidal in overall shape, in which the lines link concepts or ideas to one another. Research has consistently shown that drawing concept maps enhances student learning. Looking across a wide variety of studies, a meta-analysis of studies demonstrated the effectiveness of students studying and constructing concept maps on learning across 142 studies involving nearly 12,000 students (Schroeder et al., 2018).

You can teach your students how to draw a concept map by having them follow these steps (Wandersee, 2002b):

1. Identify key concepts, perhaps 12 to 20, from the readings, your last lecture, or another source.
2. Write each concept on a small index card or sticky note.
3. Identify the main topic or concept, and place it at top center. This is called the *superordinate* concept. It is either the most inclusive, general,

broad, or abstract or the first stage in a process or sequence.

4. Rank-order or cluster all the remaining ideas, called *subordinate* concepts, from the most inclusive, general, broad, or abstract, placing these higher up and closer to the main concept, to the most exclusive, specific, narrow, or concrete, placing these lower down. In the case of a process or sequence, order the concepts chronologically. The object is to structure the concepts and their interrelations correctly.

5. Arrange the concepts in a linkable hierarchy.

6. Draw the entire hierarchy on a piece of paper with enclosures around the concepts and linking lines that are labeled to specify the relationship. The linked concepts together with the labeled link are called a *proposition*. Because the map's presumed direction is downward, arrows are not necessary.

7. Check for cross-links (connections going across the branches); draw these links as dotted lines, and label them.

In addition, several universities have created and posted training videos on YouTube (recommended in Persellin & Daniels, 2014):

- https://www.youtube.com/watch?v=eYtoZRmWLBc
- http://www.youtube.com/watch?v=Gm1owf0uGFM
- http://www.youtube.com/watch?v=P0DBS-YbRc0&list=TLacCperJK3vA

Figure 22.1 elaborates the very simple map in which "population" is the superordinate concept, extending it by seven additional concepts arranged on three levels. Where a concept falls in the hierarchy depends on the lesson. In one map, a concept may be superordinate and in another subordinate. As Figure 22.2 illustrates, "photosynthesis" may be on the lowest (fourth) level in a concept map that starts with "energy," ranking below "light" and "life-giving," but "photosynthesis" can also be a superordinate concept, in which case "light" may be subordinate.

Concept maps are quite easy to write instructions for and to assess, which is why they make good gradable assignments and tests. The key evaluative dimensions are:

- The number of concepts included, unless you provide them
- The number of valid propositions (links between concepts)
- The number of valid levels in the hierarchy
- The number of valid cross-links
- The number of valid examples

Therefore, you can instruct students to draw a map with a given number of concepts interrelated with a given number of links, spanning a given number of hierarchical levels, with a given number of cross-links and examples. Novak and Gowin (1984), who devised what is the leading scoring model for concept maps, recommends giving 1 point for each valid link, 5 points for each valid level, 10 points for each valid cross-link, and 1 point for each valid example. Quicker still is a computer-based technique that scores maps by the number of links and the geometrical distances between concepts (Taricani & Clariana, 2006).

Many researchers have found that concept maps facilitate students' mastery of content and development of cognitive skills. In fact, concept maps have proven their value in some of the most challenging subjects, such as accounting (Leauby & Brazina, 1998), applied statistics (Schau & Mattern, 1997), biology (Kinchin, 2000, 2001), chemistry (Regis & Albertazzi, 1996), conceptual astronomy (Zeilik et al., 1997), geoscience (Rebich & Gauthier, 2005), marine ecology (Beaudry & Wilson, 2010), mathematics (Brinkmann, 2003), medicine (Hoffman et al., 2002; McGaghie et al., 2000; West et al., 2000), and nursing (Baugh & Mellott, 1998; King & Shell, 2002), among others. In Zeilik et al.'s (1997) experimental study, the astronomy students who developed concept

Figure 22.1   Concept Map of "Population" with a Total of Nine Concepts

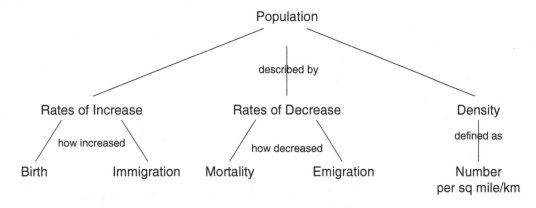

Figure 22.2   Two Simple Concept Maps Illustrating How Concepts in One Map Can Change Levels in Another Map

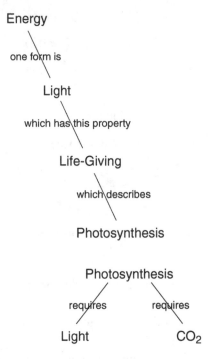

maps scored higher than the control group on three kinds of conceptual examinations: one measuring the ability to relate concepts, another of multiple-choice items designed to identify faulty models, and a third fill-in-the-blank concept map. Among the skills that concept maps are known to enhance are postsecondary reading comprehension (Katayama, 1997; Robinson & Kiewra, 1995), writing (Beaudry & Wilson, 2010), critical thinking (King & Shell, 2002; Nixon-Cobb, 2005), and problem-solving (Kalman, 2007).

Of course, the effectiveness of concept maps, like every other teaching tool, depends on how they are used. Instructors have often maximized their interactive, constructivist potential by having students develop them along with the instructor or in peer groups, as well as individually. When students draw the maps, they are actively constructing their own knowledge (Kinchin, 2000, 2001), clarifying and organizing it (Hoffman et al., 2002; McGaghie et al., 2000), reinforcing their understanding of the material, and integrating it with prior knowledge (Plotnick, 2001). In addition, they are making explicit to both the instructor and themselves any misconceptions they may have and the progress they are making in correctly and complexly structuring the subject material (Vojtek & Vojtek, 2000).

Venn Diagrams

Venn diagrams illustrate the relationships among concepts in terms of the distances and the overlaps among circles and the relative sizes of the circles. When drawn by the instructor, they can disentangle complex conceptual interrelationships for the students and serve as a memorable image. Of course, students can create their own to clarify their understanding of conceptual interconnections, in which case they should also draw their diagram and write an accompanying sentence or two to explain its meaning (Wandersee, 2002a).

Here are some basic guidelines for creating these diagrams (Wandersee, 2002a):

- The relative sizes of the circles reflect the relative importance, quantities, variable values, or level of generality of the concepts.
- A smaller circle drawn within a larger one indicates that the latter concept encompasses the former.
- Partially overlapping circles mean that one concept includes some instances of the other concept.
- Superimposed circles show that the concepts are equivalent and share all the same instances.
- Completely separate circles denote unrelated or independent concepts.
- Broken circles convey that the conceptual boundaries are not well understood.
- Adding color enhances the diagram, especially when the colors of overlapping areas accurately reflect the combination of the circle colors.
- Detail in a diagram can be shown by projecting out a new diagram of an enlarged section of the original diagram (called *telescoping*).

The video at https://www.youtube.com/watch?v=YAjxRUGS0Gc gives a good tutorial of the full potential of complex Venn diagrams. The Venn diagram showcased in Figure 22.3 is another excellent example that illustrates the complicated relationships among different classifications of explicit, first-order, ordinary differential equations (ODEs). Its creator, Daniel D. Warner, professor of mathematical sciences at Clemson University, designed it for his sophomore course for engineering and science majors on differential equations and his calculus course for life science majors. He gives it to his students along with the assignment of constructing an example of an ODE that is exclusive to each portion of the diagram. (Possible correct answers are in brackets, where a, b, r, N, and Ta are constants.) Because the diagram has eight portions, the solution involves eight different ODEs (D. D. Warner, personal communication, April 8, 16, 2009).

Figure 22.3 Concept Circle Diagram (Venn Diagram) for the Classification of Explicit, First-Order, Ordinary Differential Equations

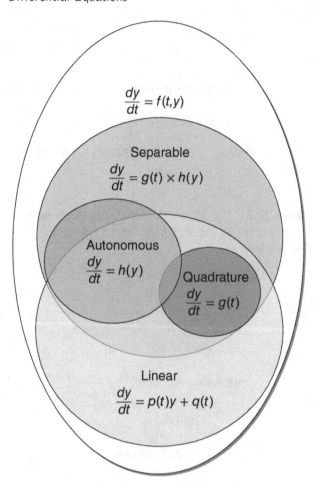

Source: Created by Daniel D. Warner. Reprinted with his permission.

1. General and neither separable nor linear [$dy/dt = $ a + b cos(t) exp(y)]
2. Separable and neither autonomous nor linear [$dy/dt = $ a cos(t) sin(y)]
3. Linear and not separable [$dy/dt = $ a − y/(b − t), a mixing model, or $dy/dt = $ −m g t − b y, like an object falling with air resistance]
4. Autonomous and not linear [$dy/dt = $ r(1 − y/N) y, logistic growth]
5. Autonomous and linear but not quadrature [$dy/dt = $ r y, Malthusian growth, or $dy/dt = $ r (Ta − y), Newton's law of cooling]
6. Quadrature and not autonomous [$dy/dt = $ r t + a, variable velocity, constant acceleration]

7. Linear and separable but neither autonomous nor quadrature [$dy/dt = (t + a)(y - b)$]
8. Autonomous and quadrature (a very small set, but not empty) [$dy/dt = r$, constant velocity].

Infographics

Infographics are graphic representations of information intended to convey meaning quickly. The graphics aspect takes advantage of the speed at which individuals can process visually, particularly picking up patterns, along with brief textual content to give the image deeper meaning. Graphic representations of data have been around for hundreds of years, but exploded in popularity with the publication of Edward Tufte's (1983) book, *Visual Explanations, The Visual Display of Quantitative Information*. By the year 2000, computer applications made it easy for anyone to create engaging infographics. In 2002, the Norwegian music duo Röyksopp even created a music video made up entirely of infographics (see https://www.youtube.com/watch?v=aIYSsnrmmug).

Infographics are being used in a number of ways throughout education. Baglama et al. (2017) used infographics to successfully assist students struggling with the mathematical challenge of dyscalculia. Faculty members also use infographics to help students explain experiments, communicate findings, and share knowledge (Scott et al., 2017). Infographics work well to facilitate learning in many ways, including increased engagement, recall of information, collaboration skills, critical thinking, information literacy, and communication skills (Jaleniauskiene & Kasperiuniene, 2022).

■ COMBINING MODES

Students should receive new material multiple times but not by repeating the same learning activities. Just rereading a text again and again, for example, is an inefficient use of time (McDaniel et al., 2009; Roediger & Butler, 2010; Roediger & Karpicke, 2006) and, sadly, our students' default strategy. Rather, students need to process the same material through different parts of their brain. It's pretty easy to provide these opportunities, and you may already be doing it. Let's say you assign a reading and give a short essay quiz the day it's due. Then you have students separate into groups to discuss what they wrote. You have already led them through the material in three different modes. Or maybe you assign a podcast of your lecture and give students study questions on it to answer in writing as homework. Then in class you ask some recitation and discussion questions, or break students into groups to draw a concept map of the video, or have them do a role-play or short simulation based on the video. Again, you have furnished a solid set of multimodal learning experiences.

Not just any combination of modes works effectively. For instance, students are bored and frustrated when they are assigned a reading, then the instructor lectures on the reading, and the presentation slides outline the reading and the lecture (Cardon, 2014). All three renditions are verbal, and two involve reading, so students will rationally choose their favorite (or least taxing) medium to get the material. They correctly anticipate that going through the same material several times in one mode or two very similar modes will do them little good, and they aren't likely to process the material deeply or retain it. In other words, to keep our students' interest and facilitate their learning, we must avoid redundancy in the repetition we provide.

■ REFLECTION QUESTIONS

Reflection Question 22.1: What do you think makes meshing learning styles such a challenging myth to debunk? How would you speak with someone who still believes that students should ideally be taught solely in their specific learning style?

Reflection Question 22.2: What three modes of learning have you found to best work for you? In what situations?

Concept Into Practice: Create an infographic pertaining to some aspect of your course material. Present this infographic to your students with the assignment for them to make a similar infographic on their own.

CHAPTER 23

Improving Student Performance with Feedback

Feedback is one of the most powerful teaching and learning methods available. In his meta-analysis of 800 meta-analyses, Hattie (2009) found that feedback has an impressive average effect size of .73 on student achievement. In a smaller meta-analysis, he and Timperley (2007) reported a similar average effect size of .79. Feedback has been found time and again to be extremely important to learning, provided the feedback is offered in a way that can be used by the learner.

Feedback to students can come from the instructor, peers, and the students themselves. The same is true for us as faculty members. To teach at our best and bring about as much student achievement as possible, we need objective feedback regarding student progress and students to suggest how we might enhance their learning. This chapter addresses all these facets of feedback.

FEEDBACK FAILS AND SUGGESTIONS FOR SUCCESS

Some general considerations regarding formative feedback help to make it meaningful for students. Even with the best of intentions, and with the knowledge that feedback is critical to success, feedback is at times a negative experience for students. In this section, we provide some cautions with respect to feedback, followed by some general rules for success.

Why Feedback Fails

Although feedback is designed to help students, they do not always take it well. This has historically been a challenging area to research, but O'Donovan et al. (2021) employed an interesting approach.

The researchers had students bring examples of actual feedback received from their professors, and, with feedback in hand, students were interviewed by student researchers. Students brought in both good and bad examples from the same professors, demonstrating that perceptions of effective and ineffective feedback are based on more than just who students like or don't like.

O'Donovan et al. (2021) reported that student perception of feedback is very complex, considering factors such as length, other instructor communication, student ability, and so on. The research gave some solid suggestions on what students regarded as "bad" feedback. Interestingly, the actual grade received didn't seem to affect the perception of feedback if the preceding positive criteria were met. Feedback was typically rated as "bad" if it was very short (felt cryptic and as if it had been skimmed) or overly long (felt as if the grader was picking at small details). Feedback was also taken poorly if the instructor wasn't otherwise communicative, or the assignment standards or rubric were ambiguous. Feedback was generally negative if the grader failed to recognize the effort put into the writing.

In conducting focus groups with students, Winstone et al. (2017) found some additional factors that create barriers to making use of feedback received. Students noted challenges when they did not understand what the feedback meant and the purpose of the feedback. Faculty members can address these issues by first letting students know if they can use the feedback to submit work or whether the feedback is designed to be used on future work. As for the meaning of feedback, it is helpful for faculty members, as experts, to use language students can easily understand. Sometimes students have trouble knowing how to turn feedback into action. For example, suppose I write on a student paper, "Your work is not well developed." That could mean several different things, particularly to a first-generation college student or student from an underrepresented group who has never heard phrases such as that before.

Feedback That Facilitates Learning

There are two major types of feedback, *summative* and *formative*. *Summative feedback* provides an evaluation of how much the student has learned at the end of an assignment, such as a test grade along with our comments that justify the grade given. The comments can certainly help students do better in the future, but the primary focus, particularly by students, is that evaluative component of how they did. That is what ends up becoming the grade in the course. By contrast, *formative feedback* comprises all the recommendations for improving their work at an early stage, before it receives a grade, with the expectation that they will revise it accordingly. If you attach a grade to such drafts, it should be mainly to motivate student effort during the work's development and should count only for a portion of the work's final grade.

Formative feedback benefits both you and your students in several ways. For you, it yields better final student products, greatly reduces plagiarism, and changes your role from judge to facilitator or coach. For students, it encourages steady writing and work habits, gives them criteria on which to improve their work and their communication skills, and teaches them the professional creation process, which always involves extensive revision.

The research by O'Donovan et al. (2021) gives suggestions on how to provide both formative and summative feedback that students find valuable. For example, some students like more feedback and others prefer less. Perhaps as part of turning in assignments, you could have a box for students to check if they would prefer less detailed feedback. Assignments can be more clearly outlined with opportunities for students to ask clarifying questions. You could also require, for a small percentage of an assignment's final grade, that students must point out what they found most helpful and suggest one way that your feedback could have been more helpful.

Students found the feedback helpful if the assignment matched students' sense of self-efficacy and experience with the subject, if the reason for the grade was transparent, and if the grader had a communicative relationship with the student. Most of the feedback that is rated as positive comes down to communication and community. It is always helpful to build a strong community, do your best to get to know your students, and keep lines of communication open. In general, students appreciate feedback, provided the feedback offers guidance on how to improve and that their work is praised, which can give students more confidence in their skills (Bader et al., 2019).

Many students are also very positive about the opportunity to immediately use the feedback to improve their work, so assignments should have clear goals and allow student self-efficacy at the outset (Lopez-Pastor & Sicilia-Camacho, 2017). This means that as faculty members we must help students accurately assess their abilities (which are often higher than students realize). To do this, there must be processes in place to help students to assess their own learning, perhaps by rubrics and also periodic low-stakes learning assessments. If feedback is designed to help guide student learning, the feedback should focus on the learning process and managing that learning, rather than on any characteristics of the learner. Consider the following strategies to help make feedback functional.

- *Set and enforce deadlines for students to complete a major work in stages.* The stages may be: find a topic, gather resources, develop an outline, submit a draft for peer review, and submit a final draft. Each stage provides an occasion for feedback.
- *Set clear criteria for what each stage must accomplish, what elements it must contain, and what questions it must answer. Grade pass/fail.* Students receive all the points if they meet all the criteria and no points if they miss any. This will ensure that students attend to your requirements and submit high-quality drafts, which they otherwise may not do (Nilson, 2015). Chapter 26 more fully explains this type of grading, called *specifications* (or *specs*) grading because you grade work pass/

fail based on whether it meets the necessary specifications.

- *Ensure students understand that formative feedback focuses on major problems in their work* and that making the suggested changes does not guarantee them an A.
- *Comment more on major writing issues*, such as content, reasoning, and organization, *and less on style and grammar.*
- *Make your comments constructive, improvement directed, and process centered.* Suggest how to correct and improve the work in relation to your predefined criteria. Do praise where deserved, because students often do not hear what they are doing right. Focus on praising the effort and the process students went through to produce the work, not on their intelligence or the product itself, to ensure they keep putting forth the necessary effort (Coffield, 2014; Dweck, 2007; Halvorson, 2014). No one excels by sitting on their laurels.
- Whether you are giving students formative or summative feedback, *make a follow-up assignment in which they must paraphrase or summarize your feedback back to you.* If you are using a rubric, they should include your standards as feedback as well (Dirkx et al., 2021). This way, they have to read all of your feedback carefully and make sense of it. Otherwise, they often ignore or don't try very hard to understand our comments and corrections (Duncan, 2007; Hattie & Timperley, 2007) and rarely ask us to clarify what they don't comprehend. We in turn will find out how our students interpret our comments and corrections and can clarify what they misunderstand. Perhaps the words, abbreviations, and symbols we use are unclear. Only when students attend to and accurately understand our feedback can we expect them to improve their work in their revisions or later assignments.
- *When students revise a piece of work, have them also write out their goals and plans for revision.* They should explain the changes they make in the work in response to the feedback they've received.

- *Provide feedback as promptly as you can*, in time for it to be useful to students. Such feedback, whether formative or summative, will help students do better on the next iteration, but only if it arrives in a timely manner. Assignments need to be scheduled and days blocked off on the calendar for reading work so that feedback can be delivered in a timely manner.

How we provide feedback—that is, our feedback medium—also matters to students. In a recent survey, more than 75% of students said that they find face-to-face feedback "very" or "extremely effective," no doubt because we can best convey our meaning using our whole person and students can ask for clarification on the spot. Feedback is more effective when thought of as a dialogue rather than simply providing information to the student (Nicol, 2010). Almost the same proportion, close to 70%, viewed written or typed comments just as favorably. But only around 33% of students found video- or audio-recorded comments "very" or "extremely effective" (Turnitin, 2014).

Keep in mind that individuals differ in what feedback works best for them. Students who are first-generation college, those from underrepresented groups, and those with imposter syndrome may react more negatively to formative feedback. Unless you specifically explain the intention of this feedback, it may fuel their concern as to whether they belong in college.

With this information about *how* to provide feedback, always consider from *where* feedback is coming. Feedback may be obtained from peers, self, and instructors. Feedback may also be obtained as part of the teaching process through classroom assessment techniques. Finally, our students giving feedback to us is actually also formative feedback for them. Their feedback helps us teach better, which helps them learn better and achieve desired outcomes.

Dweck (2007) famously noted that learners have either a growth mindset or a fixed mindset. Those with a growth mindset believe that a person can get better with effort, versus the fixed mindset belief that our abilities are fairly well established from a very young age. This is particularly important with respect to feedback. Growth-minded individuals desire feedback, as they see the information as a way to improve. Fixed-minded individuals, on the other hand, see feedback as either reinforcing how good they are or a criticism of them as a person. This fundamental response to feedback means that it is important to frame learning as a growth-minded endeavor and emphasize that we should *all* be seeking feedback so that we can grow our skills and become ever stronger (Ramani et al., 2019).

METACOGNITION AS FEEDBACK

A student's ability to assess their work does not develop just by reading our assessments. We have to set self-assessment as a learning outcome and incorporate activities that will teach them and give them practice in how to do it. In addition, we must lay out very clear quality standards for a given assignment (Boud et al., 2013).

As a form of self-assessment, metacognition is the process of knowing what you know, or thinking about what you are thinking about. It is reflection that leads to understanding, which tends to lead to better learning. By better understanding what we do not know, we are able to look for ways to improve. In the section pertaining to self-regulated learning (Chapter 19), metacognitive processes were listed in Table 19.1.

Metacognition has three general components: metacognitive knowledge, metacognitive regulation, and metacognitive experiences. The component most relevant to feedback is *metacognitive regulation*, which is the extent to which one understands their learning experience. Research has demonstrated that those who are more self-aware do better at tasks (McIntosh et al., 2019). In order for metacognitive regulation to improve the learning process, learners need three additional skills. The first skill is planning, or identifying the strategies that will best facilitate the learning process. To select the proper strategies, the learner needs to identify the relevant tasks to accomplish, and assess prior knowledge, consider strengths and weakness, and pinpoint gaps in provided information. As these skills are developed, it becomes easier to appropriately allocate resources.

The next skill is monitoring, which is assessing how things are going. When these skills are developed, the learner can efficiently and accurately analyze what strategies are currently working, at what pace learning is happening, the level of focus needed, and obstructions to the learning process. Have you ever read a journal article and realized at the conclusion that you were planning dinner instead? Your metacognitive process of monitoring was not going well.

The final skill is evaluating, a retrospective analysis of how things transpired. This includes assessing the final product and the resources it took to make it to that point. This will tell students how much they actually learned, if the approach was appropriate, and whether they will need additional resources (e.g., information from the instructor, a visit to the writing center) going forward.

Many examples exist clearly showing that students who actively work at metacognitive regulation see significant improvement on future exams and assignments (Casselman & Atwood, 2017; McGuire, 2015). In Chapter 19 in Table 19.1 you will find an extensive list of questions students can use to develop better metacognitive regulation skills. A different set of questions can be used to monitor evaluating skills, which is a bit more straightforward, since it is an objective analysis based on actual outcomes. Among "The Learner's Questions" in Chapter 19 are self-testing, evaluation queries such as, "What can I recall?" "What were the most important points I learned?" and "Can I see and organize the interrelationships among them?" If students have little or nothing to say in response, they know they haven't learned the material as well as they should.

PEER FEEDBACK

Peer assessment allows students to give and receive feedback among their colleagues. It can be a highly effective practice that supports learning among students and helps them to facilitate self-regulation processes, particularly when students are trained with metacognition in mind (Mercader et al., 2020).

Keep in mind that students may not have much experience with providing feedback or assessment. Model for them how to give good feedback: focus on the issues and not the person, stick to the rubric, be positive and forward-thinking, and provide suggestions where appropriate. Training will help students provide and interpret feedback in a way that is more likely to result in deep learning.

Typically, peer feedback is best restricted to formative feedback and very low-stakes grading. Asking students to assign grades puts students in very awkward situations and may even be against university policy. Consider having students read their classmates' drafts of papers before they are submitted to you. This allows students to get feedback and make foundational changes prior to you grading the work. Overall, providing an opportunity for students to give peer feedback includes them more deeply in the learning process. It gives students an opportunity to see the challenges of providing feedback and increases their self-regulation of learning. The processes of giving and receiving feedback, summarizing major points, clarifying, and noting gaps in content also provide additional learning exposures (Mercader et al., 2020).

CLASSROOM ASSESSMENT TECHNIQUES

As we teach, we need to know if students are actually learning, or just looking in our general direction as we lecture. Students also need to know if they are learning before they take the exam. The metacognitive processes of monitoring and evaluating help all parties realize during class whether and to what extent learning is taking place, before their shortfalls in understanding adversely affect their grades and motivation. Such information can also help you assess, and ultimately enhance, your teaching effectiveness because it may even help you shape and focus your content and teaching strategy the next time your class meets. It can do the same for your students' subsequent learning by directing their attention to the areas they need to study more. In fact, in Hattie's (2009) meta-analysis, furnishing "formative evaluation" to instructors had a remarkable effect size of .90 on student achievement, even larger than the feedback we give to students.

Classroom assessment techniques (CATs) were developed precisely to serve these purposes (Angelo, 1991a). You can use them regularly or intermittently without violating the structure and content of your course and quickly identify trouble spots your class is encountering. Knowing what your students did not process the first time through the material, you can turn around a potentially disappointing situation. This is particularly valuable for vulnerable students in the course. First-generation students and students from underrepresented groups often struggle in and out of class during their first year of college (Havlik et al., 2020). Helping those students to catch challenges with material early in the semester can be essential to their success. CATs formalize and systematize the process, ensuring that you assess your whole class equally. Given their purpose, they are especially appropriate for student-active lecture breaks, but they make stimulating warm-up activities at the beginning of class and good wrap-up exercises at the end of class.

Selecting Appropriate CATs

Different CATs are designed to measure students' progress in different types of learning. So before selecting a CAT, consider which type you wish to assess (Angelo, 1991b). *Declarative learning* is learning *what*—that is, learning the facts and principles of a given field. In terms of Bloom's (1956) taxonomy of cognitive operations (see Chapter 2), declarative learning focuses on knowledge and comprehension at the lower-level end of the scale. *Procedural learning*

is learning how to do something, from the specific tasks of a given discipline to universal skills such as writing, critical thinking, and reasoning. Its emphasis is application. The third type, *conditional learning*, is learning when and where to apply the acquired declarative knowledge and procedural skills. Too often taught only implicitly through examples and modeling, it can be better taught explicitly using the case method, project-based learning, role-playing, simulations, and service-learning (see Chapters 17 and 18). Although conditional learning clearly entails application, it also involves analysis and synthesis. Finally, *reflective learning* is learning why, which engages students in analysis, synthesis, and evaluation. It directs their attention to their beliefs, values, and motives for learning about a particular topic. Without this reflection, higher education is little more than job training.

Some Proven CATs

Chapters 19 and 22 introduced several popular CATs that also serve as self-regulated learning and writing-to-learn exercises, such as the one-minute paper and the one-sentence summary. There are many options for assessing student learning in real time (Angelo & Cross, 1993; Major et al., 2021). A few examples follow.

Background Knowledge Probe

This is essentially a diagnostic pretest to administer on the first day of class or when you begin a new unit of instruction. It can consist of 2 or 3 short-answer or essay questions or 15 to 20 multiple-choice items about students' attitudes and understanding. This CAT can provide information not only on your students' prior knowledge but also on their motivation, beliefs, values, and misconceptions about the subject matter and, if you use open-ended questions, their writing skills. The results also tell you what material to cover and what existing knowledge you can use to map on new knowledge. Finally, probes activate students' prior knowledge, readying them for additional learning.

Anonymous Cards

Provide a prompt that captures an essential concept in the class and either distribute index cards to the class or ask students in advance to bring their own. After providing the prompt, give students a few minutes to write a response on their card without including any identifying information. Once students have finished writing, have students exchange cards with at least five other students (first trade should not be anyone immediately adjacent to them). Once they have traded, have students get into groups of three to five to read and discuss the cards they ended up with. Call on a few groups to report out and augment responses as needed. This will allow you to see what was discussed, and students can tell if what they wrote was in line with the correct response.

Muddiest Point

Ask your students to write down what they perceived as the muddiest point in a lecture, a reading, a video, or a demonstration. Reserve some time at the end of class to ask and answer questions; then collect the students' responses. You can clarify the muddy points during the next class. Struggling students who are not comfortable asking questions publicly find it to be a lifeline. In addition, it enables you to see the material through your students' eyes, reminding you of the many different ways they process information. Finally, knowing that they will have to identify a muddy point induces students to pay closer attention in class. And when the time comes for the CAT, they have to review whatever learning experience they are reflecting on.

Paper or Project Prospectus

A prospectus is a detailed plan for a project or paper—perhaps even a first draft that focuses students on the topic, the purpose, the issues to address, the audience, the organization, and the time, skills, and other resources needed—in fact, whatever guidelines you provide for the final product. First, students need to understand these guidelines—that is, the important facets and likely pitfalls of the assignment. For the prospectus itself, you might compose a list of three to seven questions that students must answer. Advise students not to begin substantive work on their actual assignment until they receive feedback on their prospectus from you and possibly other students. This CAT is a major assignment in itself, so you may want to make it required and grade it, but without counting it heavily toward the final grade. The prospectus accommodates many different types of assignments and teaches crucial, transferable planning and organizational skills. In addition, it gives students early enough feedback to help them produce a better product.

Application Cards

After a lecture segment, demonstration, or video on procedure, principle, or theory, have students write down on a card or piece of paper one or more real-world applications of the material. As you read through them, select the best ones to read to the class at the next meeting. This CAT gives students practice in transferring knowledge to useful applications.

Peer Instruction Concept Test

The "Surveying Student Responses" section of Chapter 14 describes a lecture break activity that quickly gives you feedback on your students' understanding while enhancing their learning: you display a multiple-choice or true/false item on the topic you were just talking about and, using clickers, online polling, or colored cards, survey your students' responses before and after they discuss their answers with their neighbors. Crouch and Mazur (2001) devised and tested this technique under the name of "peer instruction." This process also allows students to get a sense of the type of multiple-choice questions you typically ask prior to a high-stakes exam.

DURING-THE-TERM STUDENT FEEDBACK ON TEACHING

Recall Hattie's (2009) finding that furnishing "formative evaluation" to instructors has a whopping effect size of .90 on student achievement. That formative feedback entails not only classroom assessment but also midterm feedback solicited directly from your students. Most students take the opportunity to give their instructors in-progress feedback more seriously than they do end-of-term evaluations. When the course is over, why should they make thoughtful judgments and remarks when it won't do them any good? The best time to gather students' feedback is early enough in the term for their input to make a difference.

You have the option to gather and analyze your own midterm student feedback. You can collect it anonymously online using the polling tool in your LMS or a polling or survey website; Survey Monkey (www.surveymonkey.com) has course evaluation templates. Or you can have students fill out a paper form or index card in class. You can use items similar to those on your institution's or department's official ratings form or tailor items to your needs. For instance, you can set up a 1-to-5 agree-disagree scale for statements like these: "This class stimulates my interest in the subject matter." "I learn a great deal from answering clicker questions in class." "The daily quizzes help me keep up with the readings."

You can also ask students a set of open-ended questions, such as, "What things are helping you learn in this class? What would help you learn more? What are you doing to learn in this class? What could you do to learn even more?" These are also popular open-ended probes: "To help my learning: Keep doing X. Stop doing Y. Start doing Z." If you try a new teaching technique, ask the students anonymously how it helped or didn't help their learning. Or you can ask about the effectiveness of specific teaching methods, activities, assignments, or readings. Just be sure to focus your students' attention on their learning. Students don't always know when they are and aren't learning, but they will appreciate your interest in their reactions. This process could be done two or three times during the semester, starting around the fourth week of the course.

Alternatively, ask your institution's teaching and learning center (see the Appendix) to collect and analyze student feedback. The typical procedure, often called a *small group instructional diagnosis* (SGID), a *small group analysis* (SGA), or a *class interview*, relies on focus-group methodology. You leave your classroom, and a center staff member explains the procedure to your students, breaks them into groups of three to six, and gives each group one form to complete. The form asks open-ended questions like those earlier in this paragraph or similar ones, such as, "What are your instructor's primary teaching strengths?" and, "What are your instructor's primary teaching weaknesses?" Your students discuss their answers in small groups and generally concur on what they write on the form. The staff member then has the groups share their responses and may even survey student agreement with these responses. A day or so later, they prepare a write-up and meet with you to review the results. Research shows that soliciting early student feedback and having an interpretive consultation with a specialist result in significantly higher student ratings at the end of the term (Finelli et al., 2008), as well as course improvements (Payette & Brown, 2018). Typically, any effort you make to gather midterm student feedback lifts your ratings at least modestly.

You should discuss the results with your class as soon as possible (Davis, 2009). Start out by thanking your students for their honest and thoughtful suggestions. You can pick and choose among the changes your students may request, explaining to them why you are making some of the changes they recommend and not others. In fact, you can address many of their concerns just by providing your reasons for the teaching and assessment decisions you have made. (They may have forgotten the reasons you already gave.) Again, this book supplies plenty of research-based rationales for effective choices.

■ THE POWER OF FEEDBACK

The combination of providing quality feedback to your students and, in turn, soliciting and using it from them can have a greater positive impact on student achievement than just about anything else you can do. True, not all your students will understand and use your feedback or that of their peers all the time, but those who do will benefit immensely. Just build in an assignment to ensure they read and process the feedback they receive.

■ REFLECTION QUESTIONS

Reflection Question 23.1: What has been your experience in giving students feedback designed to help them to improve their learning? What areas do you feel are strongest for you and what areas, based on the chapter, are areas you could improve with respect to giving feedback that students would find positive?

Reflection Question 23.2: To what extent do you engage in metacognitive processes when you are learning? Describe any metacognitive regulation strategies you use. If you do not use any, which strategies would be most valuable for you to develop?

Concept Into Practice: Identify one CAT that you have not used in the past that you would like to incorporate going forward. Describe the technique (you may need to search the internet to find one that suits you), note when you would use it, and reflect on what specifically you hope to learn about your students' learning from that technique.

PART 5

ASSESSMENT AND GRADING

CHAPTER 24

Helping Students to Prepare for Exams

Helping students prepare for exams does not increase grade inflation, nor is it teaching to the test. You are helping them understand how the test will work, the overall content, and the form it will take. Telling students that the test will be 10 multiple-choice questions about U.S. states and their capitals helps students plan how to study. Telling students that there will be a test on capital cities and they should pay particular attention to states that start with "M" is biased and teaching to the test. Helping students to prepare for exams simply allows students to demonstrate what they know and what they can do.

As you write your exams, consider that different types of exams call for different types of study strategies, and most students learn based on how they anticipate being tested (Wergin, 1988). Factual memorization for a recall-oriented objective test requires a different kind of study effort from that for analyses of problems or situations. A multiple-choice test is best prepared for in a way different than how one would prepare for an essay exam. In fact, students perform better on the multiple-choice portion of a test if they know ahead of time that there will be an essay question on the test as well (Drake, 2009). In other words, studying to use higher-order thinking on a test better prepares a learner to perform whatever level of cognitive operation is required. Unfortunately, many students do not realize that their study strategy needs to change based on the type of exam they are taking. You can help them with that. Helping students to know what to expect will let them focus on learning. This chapter is designed to help you help your students to prepare properly.

■ IMPORTANCE OF HELPING STUDENTS TO PREPARE

Think for a moment about the purpose of exams. They are designed to identify the extent to which students have learned what you are attempting to teach them (e.g., critical concepts, a specific procedure, or how to create a new product). An ideal scenario for the testing situation is that a student, who has prepared at a given level, arrives with confidence and no more than a moderate amount of stress. Unfortunately, that scenario is rarer than we would like.

Equity issues contribute to stress and confidence levels relative to exam preparation. For example, students with higher levels of test anxiety and those with less confidence receive lower course grades than their less test-anxious and more confident peers (Hembree, 1988; von der Embse et al., 2018). These findings are particularly salient in STEM areas, where women demonstrate lower scores on higher-stakes exams than do men, even after researchers control for incoming preparation. Interestingly, women do not score lower than men on low-stakes assessments, such as in-class assignments and homework, implying that the stress of the situation is hindering women's performance. As a result of the high-stakes tests, women receive lower grades and are less successful, even though they score similarly to men at the beginning of their programs. Similarly, stereotype threat and its accompanying anxiety have long explained why Black students score lower than White students when the Black students are made aware of their race just prior to taking the test (Croizet et al., 2001; Steele, 1997); it is a result of stress, not lack of knowledge

Another factor impacting exam scores is the extent to which a student is skilled at taking exams or knows what kind of studying is needed to do well on an exam. Some students struggle with understanding what is being asked on the exam, how to word their answers, or how in-depth their answers should be. Other students are test savvy, and much of their scores have nothing to do with what they have learned and everything to do with how well they can dissect exam questions. Many of these factors impact self-efficacy, or the ability of a person to persist when facing a challenge. In particular, van der Zanden et al. (2018) noted that first-generation students perceived themselves as less likely to be successful, lowering their self-efficacy and test performance as a result.

Individuals should not end up with lower grades and even flunk out of programs simply due to the stress of the situation or poor self-efficacy in preparing for or dissecting the test. If we can help students to prepare and increase their self-efficacy, we will be moving a bit closer to more equity in these situations.

TEST PREPARATION MEASURES

Many students, and faculty members fail to notice that, in addition to assessing performance, tests are also instruments of learning. Students study, practice, and review based on the test you give them. Think back to your undergraduate days and reflect on the studying you did for exams. You will likely realize that in many respects, you learned as much, or more, while studying than you did in the classroom. That means that as faculty members we can teach students both as we help them prepare for exams and by the exams we give.

Along with the information in this chapter, a helpful way to assist your students with exam preparation is to look periodically at the list in Chapter 1 of the 15 items in the section "How People Learn." Those are evidence-based strategies that will help any student learn faster and retain information longer. It is also helpful to let students know that learning takes work across time, not crammed all into one session. That means the best time for a student to start to study for the exam is when they start learning. While reading, use reading strategies that facilitate long-term retrieval of the information. While in class, take notes in a way that helps to recall information. At the end of a study session, explain what was learned. The best overall way to think about a test is that you learn as you go, review just before the test one last time, take the test, and then keep on learning. The test is not the end of the sequence for learning, it is a check-in along the way.

Following are some additional, easily implemented ways to help students get ready for tests and learn even more in the process.

Reading and Review Strategies

Throughout this book, strategies are provided for you to help your students prepare for exams. In addition to the list noted in Chapter 1, a few areas that may be particularly helpful are techniques for taking notes on your lectures and class activities (Chapter 14), showing them the value of being a self-regulated learner (Chapter 19), and explaining ways to read academic material effectively (Chapter 21). As you review and reflect through *Teaching at Its Best* you will see dozens of research-based strategies to help your students to read and review course material.

When it comes to exams, just reading class notes over, even multiple times, is not all that helpful. As noted in Chapter 19, the most efficient and effective way to study written material, at least for factual and problem-solving tests, is *active recall* or the *read-recall-review* strategy (Major et al., 2021; McDaniel et al., 2009; Roediger & Karpicke, 2006). Following this method, when reading it is best for students to read a section of their text or notes, cover the material, recite aloud or jot down as much as they can remember, and review the section to find what they missed or misunderstood. In addition to reinforcing their reading by restating and hearing the material, students practice retrieval, which is exactly the skill they will need during the test. If they read a section and then cannot recite to themselves what they just read it is because their brains are thinking of something else, or the material is confusing. In either case, there is little benefit in proceeding. Using this strategy, you will also never again finish reading a chapter in a book, only to realize you were thinking about something else the entire time.

Other exam preparation techniques worth sharing include drawing visual representations of the material in which students organize and integrate the concepts, principles, processes, and similarities and differences among phenomena that your course has recently introduced. This may be done with concept maps, mind maps, concept circle diagrams, flowcharts, cycles, or compare-and-contrast matrices. Students who learn inductively from examples may also benefit from reviewing particularly fitting examples of concepts and processes, explaining why they are such fitting examples, and formulating different ones on their own.

Active Study Strategies

Yes, using active learning strategies in class helps students prepare for exams. Working in groups is consistently associated with higher exam scores, particularly for individuals in underrepresented groups within a course, such as women in an engineering course or a Black student in any class in a predominantly White college (Eddy & Hogan, 2014).

Review Guides

Review guides are a bit like maps, and they are especially helpful for first-year, first-generation, or any other students who do not yet know what college-level assessment involves. You can make a review guide as simple as a list or an outline of important topics that you have emphasized, but this alone only tells students what to memorize.

Students gain much more from a sample test or a list of review questions that mirror your student learning outcomes and represent the variety of item formats that will appear on the test. If you plan to use some factual and terminological multiple-choice questions on the test, then put some examples of those items on the review sheet. If you intend to test analysis and synthesis with an essay question, develop some essay questions that require those same cognitive operations. This method is highly effective, and you can draw appropriate items from previous tests.

Perhaps the best option for students is what is called a *test blueprint* (Suskie, 2009). It can also help you design a test that assesses your students' achievement of your outcomes, so have your syllabus and outcomes map (see Chapters 2 and 5) handy. To make a test blueprint, begin by listing all the major content areas that your test will address; then designate their relative importance by the percentage of the test (or number of points) to be devoted to each area. Within each content area, write down what you want students to be able to do or demonstrate, using action verbs and avoiding internal-states verbs such as *know, understand, realize,* and *appreciate* (see Chapter 2). These statements should reflect your learning outcomes, though probably on a more micro level than in your syllabus or outcomes map. Finally, allocate points or items across these outcome statements according to how central they are in this part of the course. In other words, instead of just listing concepts for students to "know," tell them more specifically that, for instance, they should be able to *recognize* the definitions, purposes, and examples of a list of concepts and be able to *reproduce* a given list of principles. Then let these statements serve as the blueprint for your test questions.

Given the number of organizations that now buy from students even a single question from an exam and then piece together the test, you may need to make new exams each time you teach the course. In such a case, the most equitable scenario is to make your earlier versions available to all your current students. This helps to even the playing field for those who don't have access to your previous tests through membership in those online sites or other sources. These earlier exams make excellent review sheets for students.

Review Sessions

Students typically really like review sessions, but they are not always helpful (Levant & Paolo, 2017). Review sessions are valuable for students to understand the structure of the test, your expectations, and clarify specific sticking points. Overall, reviews work well only if students have already made significant progress in their independent or small-group studying. Therefore, you should make it clear that you will not be summarizing the past few weeks of lectures and readings or dispensing the answers to the review questions. These sessions are designed for students to review material, not learn it.

The most productive way to conduct a review session is to have students ask specific questions on the material. With respect to their questions, always ask the class for answers before giving a response, perhaps even having the entire class participate in brainstorming and refining the answers. If there are no questions from students, have a few ready

you can provide and let small groups develop and orally present their answers. Invite other students to evaluate the group's answers and then offer your own assessment. Finally, it's often ideal to offer a videoconference option for these review sessions. Students with caretaking responsibilities or transportation concerns can attend, and the session can be recorded and made available for anyone who had a conflict at the time of the review.

Help Sessions, Supplemental Instruction, or Course Clinics

This measure takes the review session one step further by establishing weekly meetings of an hour or longer during which you or your TA answers questions. A regularly scheduled meeting motivates students to keep up with the course and not wait until the last minute to cram for a test. It also reduces stress by encouraging them to study without the impending threat of an exam. Supplemental instruction is available at many schools. There may be resources available for your course from your teaching and learning center.

Lessons from Previous Exams

The best preparation for any given exam may be analyzing where one went wrong in similar previous exams, and we should never miss an opportunity to help students learn by their mistakes or realize their control over their academic performance. As described in Chapter 19, Barkley (2009) recommends giving students a list of reflection questions to answer in class or as homework when returning their graded exams. The test autopsy, also introduced in Chapter 19, turns students' attention to the errors they made during previous exams to help them identify their faulty strategies, such as misreading questions and failing to budget their time (Academic Success Center, Iowa State University, Ames, IA, 2011; Achacoso, 2004). Point out that students should focus on strategies to improve on the next exam, rather than individual questions (unless the same questions will be asked again). Memorizing test responses does not help on future tests if the information is to be used in a new way (Picklesimer et al., 2019).

You can also capitalize on students' learning from their mistakes by having them redo tasks that they did not complete or do properly on the exams. If they failed to solve a problem correctly, they can earn back some of the points they lost by laying out the correct strategy and then re-solving the same or a similar problem (Zimmerman et al., 2011).

▨ MEASURES TO ENSURE STUDENTS UNDERSTAND OUR LANGUAGE

Students, especially in their first year, often do poorly on exams because they are not exactly sure what a question, especially an essay question, is asking them to do. They may not know what the verb designating the task means as it pertains to the test. This sometimes explains why some students appear to not follow directions. It may be helpful to provide them with written definitions of common exam verbs, along with review questions or sessions that give them practice in the cognitive operations (Anderson & Krathwohl, 2000; Ellis, 2006; Reiner et al., 2004):

- *Analyze*: Break something down into parts, such as a theory into its components, a process into its stages, or an event into its causes. Analysis involves characterizing the whole, identifying its parts, and showing how the parts interrelate.
- *Assess/criticize/critique/evaluate*: Determine or judge the degree to which something meets or fails to meet certain criteria. If the criteria are not provided in the question, develop them for making judgments.
- *Categorize/classify*: Sort into major, general groups or types that you name or identify.
- *Compare/contrast*: Identify the important similarities and differences between two or more elements in order to reveal something significant about them. Identify similarities if the command is to compare and differences if it is to contrast.

- *Create/devise*: Put together, organize, or reorganize elements to make a new approach, product, process, or solution.
- *Defend/justify*: Give good reasons to support a position, and explain how or why something happened.
- *Define/identify*: Give the key characteristics by which a concept, thing, or event can be understood. Place it in a general class; then distinguish it from other members of that class.
- *Develop*: Create, elaborate on, or make more effective, detailed, or usable.
- *Discuss/examine*: Debate, argue, and evaluate the various sides of an issue.
- *Generate*: Think up, devise, or brainstorm good ideas or alternatives.
- *Infer*: Logically conclude on the basis of what is known.
- *Interpret/explain*: State what you think the author or speaker of a quotation or statement means, and why.
- *Illustrate*: Use a concrete example to explain or clarify the essential attributes of a problem or concept, or clarify a point using a diagram, chart, table, or other graphic.
- *List/enumerate*: Give the essential points one by one, in a logical order if applicable. It may be helpful to number the points.
- *Prove/validate*: Establish that something is true by citing factual evidence or giving clear, logical reasons.
- *Synthesize*: Put together elements in a new way so as to make a novel theory, approach, product, process, or solution.
- *Trace*: Describe the course or progress of a phenomenon, trend, or development.

▨ ANXIETY-REDUCTION MEASURES

Moderate anxiety is normal before an exam and can motivate and energize students to study and to stay sharp for the exam. From their review of the test anxiety literature, Mealy and Host (1993) identified three types of anxious students. Those of the first type lack adequate study skills and are aware of the problem; they are not well prepared for exams and worry about performing poorly. The second group comprises students who have adequate study strategies but become distracted during a test. The third group mistakenly believes that they have adequate study skills but do poorly on exams, then wonder what the problem could be. They place the blame for not doing well on the exam on external causes, such as instructors, "unfair exams," or loud roommates who made it impossible for them to study.

Mealy and Host (1993) also asked students how an instructor can affect their anxiety before, during, and after a test. They received four kinds of responses:

1. The vast majority of students want some kind of review before the test and are less anxious after attending one. They feel more confident if they are sure they have correct information in their notes.
2. Students become stressed when their instructor tells them that the test will be hard. Many do not mind a challenging exam, but they want to hear how they should study, followed by some words of reassurance.
3. Most students get nervous when their instructor walks around the room during a test and looks over their shoulders. Although this may help keep cheating in check, it also raises the anxiety of stress-sensitive students.
4. Many students resent interruptions during a test. Even if you break in to correct or clarify an exam item, it throws off their train of thought.

In summary, taking measures to prepare your students for tests, such as providing quality review sheets and review sessions, along with building their self-confidence and minimizing test interruptions, will help allay their test anxiety. So will these actions:

1. Have your test schedule written in your syllabus, and stick to it as closely as possible.

2. Have in your syllabus a clear grading system and your policies on missed quizzes and tests.
3. Consider dropping your students' lowest test or quiz score from your final grade calculations; anyone can have a bad day or a legitimate reason for missing a class, such as a changed dose of their prescription medicine or a family crisis.
4. Test frequently, reducing the relative weight of each test so that one poor performance will not cost students dearly.
5. Tailor your tests to the time allotted. If it takes you so many minutes to complete one of your tests, figure that it will take your students at least three times as long. Not being able to finish a test discourages students early in the test session, even if you tell them they are not expected to finish it.
6. Teach students relaxation techniques, such as deep breathing, counting to 10, and visualizing a successful test session (Ellis, 2006).

Stress does not have to be, and probably won't be, absent; however, approximately 15% of students have anxiety that is at times debilitating (Thomas et al., 2018). Refer these individuals to your institution's counseling center, as you should for other emotional and psychological problems, or the academic assistance center, or both (see the Appendix).

■ WHAT THE EFFORT IS WORTH

Taking measures to prepare your students for a test is another way to teach them by ensuring that students review, synthesize, and retain the material. Some of these measures can also help you better plan and organize a test so that it assesses exactly what you want to assess. Whatever else you can do to reduce your students' test anxiety allows them to better demonstrate their actual learning and gives you a more valid assessment of their understanding and skills. It is only by seeing their honest achievement that you can appraise how successful your teaching has been.

■ REFLECTION QUESTIONS

Reflection Question 24.1: Students score poorly on tests for a variety of reasons. One is that they are not prepared. Think of five additional reasons they may score poorly on your exams. To what extent would you be able to assist students with each of the items you noted?

Reflection Question 24.2: As experts, we often slip into technical language when writing our exam questions and fail to take into consideration our students' novice knowledge of these terms. How could (or does) this disconnect affect student understanding of exam questions and their success on exams in your course?

Concept Into Practice: Identify one anxiety reduction strategy that you could use in one of your courses. What resources would you need (if any)? Who would most benefit from this strategy (other than "students with anxiety")? When is the first opportunity you would have to put this into practice?

CHAPTER 25

Constructing Student Assessments for Grading

I t is easy to think of exams, papers, and other assignments as being separate from teaching. You teach, and then periodically you devote class time to assessment to determine the extent to which students have learned. That way of thinking is not teaching at its best. Recall that backward design has three interrelated parts. First, create student learning outcomes. Second, determine how you will assess whether the outcomes were met. Third, select a teaching strategy to bring about successful outcomes. The second component, knowing that outcomes have been met via assessment, is a critical part of teaching, and the focus of this chapter.

When you assess student performance for a grade, score, or rating, you are conducting a *summative assessment*. Typically, tests or exams, quizzes, assignments, projects, and some in-class activities fall under this category. For this chapter, we have assembled information regarding the advantages and disadvantages of various types of assessments. You will also find best practices for designing meaningful test items and assignments: first, objective test items, and then test items and assignments

that require students to construct a response. The time and effort invested in writing a good test or assignment are not without reward. One of the greatest joys of teaching is seeing a student who works hard on a block of material score a higher grade than expected. Aligning good outcomes, well-designed tests, and well-delivered teaching is a challenge that, if done well, will change the lives of our students.

GENERAL TESTING GUIDELINES

Summative assessment is serious business to your institution. Accreditation bodies and graduation rates are both meaningful to a college and critical considerations relative to how you assess your students. Students themselves are also concerned with your assessment of them. A low grade may mean the student has to retake the course or even leave the institution. For these reasons and many more, assessing student learning appropriately is important to your student, you, and your institution.

It's All About Outcomes

Outcomes provide a desired destination. How will you know that students have arrived at your desired destination? By assessing their learning. Therefore, before you begin writing a quiz or an exam, think seriously about which outcome(s) you are measuring and what you wish to know. A test can assess just short-term memory skills or the abilities to analyze, synthesize, and evaluate the material (see Chapter 2). Review your learning outcomes, and identify the cognitive level of each. If outcomes focus primarily on knowledge, comprehension, and application, then so should your test questions. Too often, faculty members teach students concepts to learn, and then ask students to give examples in real life of those concepts on exams. Application is a higher cognitive level than is knowing a concept. If you want students to give you examples or apply a concept in some way, then they should be taught how to apply the concepts. Then the test can assess whether they can apply the concept in a new situation or in a new way (Suskie, 2009; Walvoord & Anderson, 2010).

Lessons Learned by Experience and Research

The following recommendations represent much of the conventional wisdom on test construction (NBME, 2020; Ory & Ryan, 1993; Suskie, 2009; Walvoord & Anderson, 2010).

- *Test early and often.* Frequent testing and quizzing yield benefits for you and your students. Early testing furnishes students with feedback they can use to optimize their course performance. Frequent testing reduces the penalties for any single poor performance and reliability of your overall assessment—that is, its stability, repeatability, and internal consistency. Over more test items and occasions, the effects of random errors, such as students' misinterpretations and distractions, tend to weaken. Students get better grades, are less likely to withdraw from the course, and are

more satisfied with the course and instructor (Myers & Myers, 2007).

- *Compose test questions as you create your lesson plan and immediately after you cover the material in the class.* The material and the cognitive levels are fresh when you are pulling together the information for class. Immediately after class is the best time to adjust your test questions based on class events. You can also draw on student contributions and comments. This strategy ensures you have a stock of questions to use when quiz and exam times arrive.

- *Sample content appropriately.* Assessment is always only a sample of content, and how big of a sample depends on the test. First, determine what content will frame the test, then consider the relative importance of the material. There should be more test items from important material. Trivial material should receive very little attention. Avoid asking questions about a footnote, optional reading, or offhand comment to "trick" students or see if they are reading, unless you have explained in advance that some questions will draw on this sort of material.

- *Give detailed instructions for all tests.* At least once before the test, provide test details for students. Specify how much time the test is allotted; how many questions of each type; how many points each item is worth; where to record answers; whether to show work; and whether books, notes, or calculators may be used. Encourage students to ask questions to clarify structure and content. Provide the information in multiple ways, such as saying it in class, emailing a handout to students, and posting the information in the LMS. Don't provide the information once and punish students who miss the information.

- *Start the test with some warm-up questions.* Asking a few easy questions at the beginning gives students some low-stress practice in retrieving the material and builds their confidence. However, don't tell students if you do this. If you do, and they miss the first two "easy questions," it will make the test even more stressful for them.

- *Proofread the test form for errors.* Check for spelling and grammar mistakes, split items (those that begin on one page and continue on the next), inconsistencies and errors in format, missing or ambiguous instructions, and inadequate space for constructed responses. Reread the stem for each alternative to ensure the grammar is correct.
- *Have a colleague review the test for clarity and content.* This is a particularly good idea if you are somewhat inexperienced at teaching or writing test items. The items may seem crystal clear to you, but ambiguous to someone else.
- *After the test, conduct an item analysis of your new objective items.* Check whether the overwhelming majority of your students missed certain questions. If so, these items were written poorly, too difficult, or did not reflect the content covered prior to the exam. Check also for any items that all or almost all the students answered correctly. These items have been historically considered "too easy," but if it is a foundational piece of information everyone should know, it is appropriate that most students would answer correctly. There may be someone on your campus who can assist with item analysis. For a quick resource, see Rao et al. (2016).

■ OBJECTIVE TEST ITEMS

Objective items include completion (fill-in-the-blank); true/false, matching; multiple choice; and multiple true/false, the least known and least used on this list. Famous for measuring knowledge and comprehension, the last three types can also assess most kinds of higher-order thinking very efficiently. When they do, they are called "performance tasks," and we too often gloss over assessing such thinking skills (Chun, 2010). As most objective items are graded by computer, they are frequently used in large classes. However, objective tests cannot measure students' abilities to create, organize, communicate, define problems, or conduct research.

Good objective questions, the unambiguous and discriminating ones, take time and thought to write, so give yourself sufficient time to create a test or quiz. It can easily take professional test writers 15 to 20 minutes to create one good item. It is important to note that test bank items bundled with textbooks are rarely, if ever, composed by professionals. Test banks contain a disproportionate number of trivial, factual knowledge–type questions, as they are the fastest and easiest items to write.

The rest of this section lays out the advantages and disadvantages of each type of objective item and furnishes guidelines for constructing them (NBME, 2020; Rodriguez & Albano, 2017; Rudolph et al., 2019; Suskie, 2009; Waugh & Gronlund, 2012). Each type has its place and using a variety of questions gives you the opportunity to use a format that best matches your intended student learning outcomes.

Completion (Fill-in-the-Blank)

These items measure only how well students have memorized facts, terms, and symbols, but some material is so basic that students have to be able to reproduce it. This type of item is well suited to language learning, as precise representations of words are critical. Completion items are also a good fit for vocabulary in any discipline, provided precision is important. Consider whether you will accept a variety of responses, such as, John Fitzgerald Kennedy, John F. Kennedy, John Kennedy, Jack Kennedy, J. F. Kennedy, Kennedy, J. F. K., and perhaps even *J.F. Kennady*. In such cases, computer-scoring completion items are possible only if you list every possible variation of the correct answer that you will accept as right. One option is to restrict all fill-ins to one word and insist on the correct spelling.

Advantages

- Easy to prepare and grade
- Can assess knowledge, recall, spelling, and vocabulary well
- Eliminates guessing

Disadvantages

- Cannot assess higher levels of cognition
- Highly structured and inflexible; may require an all-or-nothing response
- Not useful as a diagnostic tool
- Difficult to construct so that the desired response is unambiguous
- May be difficult to grade by computer

Construction

- Estimate 30 seconds to 1 minute for students to answer each item.
- Use clear wording to elicit a unique response.
- Avoid grammatical cues; use *a/an* and *is/are*, for instance, to reduce cluing.
- Omit only significant words from the statement.
- Omit words from the middle or end of a statement, not the beginning.
- Make all fill-in lines the same length.
- Place the response lines in a column to the left or right if grading by hand.
- Use language similar to what you and the readings have used to explain the material.

True/False

This type of item encourages guessing because students have a 50-50 chance of selecting the correct answer. It also tends to focus on recall of terms and facts, sometimes trivial ones. You can avoid both limitations by having students correct false statements. But then you cannot use a computer to grade these items; the job will fall to you.

Advantages

- Easy to prepare and grade
- Can test a lot of material in a short time
- Useful as a diagnostic tool if students correct the false statements
- Can tap higher levels of cognition by having students correct the false statements

Disadvantages

- High guessing factor for simple true/false questions
- May be difficult to create unequivocally true or false statements
- Encourages testing of trivial factual knowledge
- Often leads to incorrect responses because the best students may see too many nuances, read in multiple meanings, or conceive of exceptions and get items wrong although they know the material well
- May include verbal clues (e.g., questions with *usually*, *seldom*, and *often* are frequently true, while those with *never, always*, and *every* are commonly false)

Construction

- Estimate 30 seconds to 1 minute for students to answer each item.
- Use statements that are only entirely true or entirely false.
- Focus each statement on a single idea or problem.
- Write positive statements; negative and double-negative statements are confusing.
- Avoid verbal cues to the correct answers (e.g., *usually, seldom, often, never, always*, and *every*).
- Use familiar language that is similar to what you and the readings have used to explain the material.
- Use random technique (coin toss or random number table) to set up true or false items.
- Avoid always making true statements long and false statements short, or vice versa. Students quickly pick up on these patterns.
- Add higher-level cognitive challenge items and have students rewrite false statements to make them true.
- Allow students to write a qualifying statement during the test for a small percentage of the items to explain why they selected T or F. You need to read the qualifying statement only if they get the item wrong.

Matching

One way of looking at matching items is as a set of multiple-choice items that share the same set of response options (Suskie, 2009). The key to composing them is to assemble homogeneous items in the stimulus or question column with homogeneous items in the response or option column, such that every response is plausible for every stimulus. Common matches include theories with their originator; people with their major achievement or work; causes with their effect; terms with their definitions; foreign words with their translation; and pieces of equipment, tools, lab apparatus, or organs with their use or function. If you wish, you can list stimuli with multiple correct responses; just inform students that some items may have more than one answer or specify the number for each stimulus. Check to see whether the testing tool in your LMS can grade multiple-answer matching items.

Matches can also involve visuals, such as concepts or chemicals with their symbol, pictures of objects with their name, or labeled parts in a picture with their function. In fact, if your matching responses are embedded in one large graphic, such as a representation of a cell, a part of human anatomy, an electrical system, or a machine, you can have students describe a process by specifying a sequence of responses.

The examples thus far assess only lower-level thinking, but you can test higher-order cognitive skills by having students match causes with *likely* effects; concepts with *new* examples of them; and *new* hypothetical problems with concepts, tools, or approaches needed to solve them (Suskie, 2009). Of course, new examples or problems need just be new to your students.

Advantages

- Easy to grade
- Can assess knowledge and recall as well as higher levels of cognition
- Relatively unambiguous
- Can test a lot of material in a short time

Disadvantages

- Difficult to construct a common set of stimuli and responses
- High guessing factor
- Not useful as a diagnostic tool

Construction

- Estimate 30 seconds to 1 minute for students to answer each item.
- Keep stimuli and responses short and simple.
- The typical convention is for stimulus on left to be numbered and the response items on the right to have capital letters.
- List the possible responses in some logical order—alphabetical, numerical, or chronological—to reduce student search time.
- Add challenge and reduce process-of-elimination thinking by inserting one or more unmatchable responses or one or more responses that match more than one stimulus. Just be sure to add this statement to the directions: "Some responses may be used more than once and others not at all."
- To add even more challenge, include a few stimuli that require multiple responses or a sequence of responses. Inform your students by adding something like the following statement to the directions: "Some items require multiple responses or a sequence of responses describing a process."
- Limit the list of stimuli and responses to 15 or fewer.
- Keep all stimuli and responses on one page.
- If students write down their response choice, have them use capital letters to avoid ambiguity.

Multiple Choice

Multiple-choice items are by far the most popular type of objective test item in North America (Brown & Abdulnabi, 2017). Educational Testing Services and publishers' test banks rely on them heavily. You would think good ones would be easy to write, but they aren't. A solid, clean multiple-choice question avoids two tricky pitfalls: diverting a knowledgeable student away from the correct response and cluing a poorly prepared student toward the correct response (Suskie, 2009). Faulty phraseology and construction can do either. Test bank items that accompany textbooks usually avoid these flaws, but they do so at the cost of challenging students and assessing their higher-order thinking. To meet these higher standards, you have to search out proven, concept-oriented multiple-choice items or compose your own. If your area is the sciences or mathematics, you should be able to find some high-quality items in the clicker question databases you can access at http://www.cwsei.ubc.ca/resources/clickers.htm#questions. For STEM and other disciplines, check out http://cft.vanderbilt.edu/docs/classroom-response-system-clickers-bibliography and Bruff (2016). You might also search the web using "'clicker questions' + teaching" and look for your discipline. But don't be discouraged from writing your own and teaching your students how to write good ones.

One way to guarantee that your multiple-choice questions will assess higher-order thinking is to compose what are called *interpretive exercises* (Suskie, 2009) or stimulus-based items. These are a series of multiple-choice items based on a new (to the students), realistic stimulus—a table, graph, diagram, flowchart, drawing, photo, map, schematic, equation, data set, description of an experiment, report, statement, quotation, passage, poem, situation, or short case—that students must interpret intelligently to answer the items correctly. The process of interpreting and reasoning from the stimulus normally requires, in addition to knowledge, comprehension, application, analysis, synthesis, or evaluation. If you prefer, you can look at the types of thinking involved as interpretation, inference, problem-solving, generalization, and conclusion drawing.

This type of multiple-choice question frequently appears in professionally written standardized tests, such as the SAT, the Graduate Record Examination (GRE), and the California Critical Thinking Skills Test (CCTST), as well as most licensing exams. Following are two college-level examples, the first of which focuses on an experiment and the second, on a situation or minicase. Correct answers are marked with an asterisk.

Scenario 1: Statistics

A research team is interested in determining whether brief walks three times a day impact individuals' overall mood. A total of 35 women and 25 men participated in the study. Participants were given instructions on how to download an app that would track their walks and transmit the number of walking minutes to the research team. Participants were to walk three times a day for 5 to 7 minutes per walk. Three random times per day their app would buzz. At that time participants were to rate their mood on a scale from 1 (bad mood) to 10 (great mood). They obtained a correlation of .58, with a two-tailed probability of .0057, and the alpha was .10.

1. Which is an example of a properly written research question?
   a. Is there a relationship between brief walks and overall mood?*
   b. Does walking cause a person to be in a better mood?
   c. Do women or men benefit the most from brief walks during the day?
   d. Is a two-tailed probability test appropriate for a study about walking?
2. What is the correct statistical test for this study?
   a. Independent t-test
   b. Spearman rho*
   c. ANOVA
   d. Z-test

3. What is the correct statistical null hypothesis?
   a. There is no correlation between sleep and energy expended.
   b. rho equals +1.0.
   c. *R* equals zero.
   d. rho equals zero.*
4. What conclusions should you draw regarding the null hypothesis?
   a. Reject*
   b. Accept
   c. Cannot determine without more information
5. What conclusions should you draw regarding this study?
   a. Brief walks cause people to be in a better mood
   b. The correlation was curvilinear.
   c. A relationship exists between brief walks and mood.*
   d. Brief walking is not related to mood.

Scenario 2: Biology

One day you see a child watching a wasp drag a paralyzed grasshopper down a small hole in the ground. When asked what he is doing, he replies, "I'm watching that wasp store paralyzed grasshoppers in her nest to feed her offspring."

1. Which of the following is the best description of his reply?
   a. He is not a careful observer.
   b. He is stating a conclusion only partly derived from his observation.*
   c. He is stating a conclusion entirely drawn from his observation.
   d. He is making no assumptions even though he should.
2. Which of the following additional observations would add the most strength to the student's reply in question 1?
   a. Observing the wasp digging a similar hole
   b. Observing the wasp dragging more grasshoppers into the hole
   c. Digging into the hole and observing wasp eggs on the paralyzed grasshopper*
   d. Observing adult wasps emerging from the hole a month later
3. Both of you wait until the wasp leaves the area; then you dig into the hole and observe three paralyzed grasshoppers, each with a white egg on its side. The student states that this evidence supports his reply in question 1. Which of the following assumptions is he making?
   a. The eggs are grasshopper eggs.
   b. The wasp laid the eggs.*
   c. The wasp dug the hole.
   d. The wasp will return with more grasshoppers.

4. You take the white eggs to the biology laboratory. Ten days later, immature wasps hatched from the eggs. The student states that this evidence supports his reply in question 1. Which of the following assumptions was he making?
   a. The wasp dug the hole.
   b. The wasp stung the grasshoppers.
   c. The grasshoppers were dead.
   d. Paralyzed grasshoppers cannot lay eggs.*

Reprinted with permission from the Learning Sciences, University of Texas at Austin, 2015.

Whether you use this type or the standard kind of multiple-choice item, these are the plusses and minuses and the best practices in constructing them:

Advantages

- Easy and quick to grade
- Reduces some of the burden of assessing in large classes
- Can assess knowledge, comprehension, application, analysis, synthesis, and evaluation and do so more efficiently than can constructed response questions
- Useful as a diagnostic tool since students' wrong choices can indicate weaknesses and misconceptions
- Familiar to students

Disadvantages

- Difficult and time-consuming to construct
- Can seem ambiguous to students
- Often tests for recognition rather than recall of information
- Encourages students to find the correct answer by process of elimination

Construction

- Estimate 1–2 minutes for students to answer each question.
- Address one problem or concept per question.

- Strive for clarity and conciseness; avoid wordiness.
- Include in the stem any words that may repeat in the response alternatives.
- Avoid lifting phrases directly from your lecture or the readings and thereby requiring only simple recall.
- Use familiar language that is similar to what you and the readings have used to explain the material.
- Use the words *no, not, never, none*, and *except* sparingly, and make them stand out by italicizing, bolding, or underlining them.
- Write the correct response first, then the distractors.
- Make all responses equally plausible and attractive. Absurd options make guessing easier and can be distracting.
- Make all responses the same length. There is a tendency to make the correct response longer.
- Make all responses grammatically parallel and about the same length.
- Present the options in some logical order—alphabetical, numerical, or chronological—to reduce the possibility of cluing students or falling into a pattern.
- Avoid grammatical cues to correct answers. These can be subtle, but test-wise students look for them.
- Use three to five responses per item, six at most.
- Make sure each item has only one clearly best response, unless you are constructing a "Multiple True/False" test (see next section).

- Incorporate graphics where appropriate.
- If you want to use *none of the above* or *all of the above*, use it liberally, and make it the correct option no more than 50% of the time. These options discriminate the more from the less knowledgeable students; even the "all of the above" option makes an item more challenging to students (Huang et al., 2007).
- Extensive information about good construction and avoiding flaws may be found in the NBME Item-Writing Guide (NBME, 2020).

Stimulus-based multiple-choice items (or interpretive exercises) provide a small section of a document or an illustration, and questions are based on that. These items have a few additional construction guidelines:

- Give students prior practice in interpreting the types of stimuli you put on the test and in performing the cognitive operations each item requires.
- Minimize interlocking items—that is, items that responding to correctly requires having responded correctly to previous items in the series.
- Longer and more complex stimuli should yield a longer series of multiple-choice questions.
- Start looking for good stimuli, and you will find them; they are all around you.
- Be creative with the stimuli and use different kinds.

Multiple True/False

Perhaps the least used, least known, and yet statistically strongest objective test question is the multiple true/false item. This is a combination of the stem of a multiple-choice item and the alternatives of a true/false item. Like a multiple-choice item, it has a stem and a list of responses, and it may (or may not) involve interpreting a stimulus. But students do not select one right response; they decide whether each option is true or false in relation to the stem. Therefore, a multiple true/false item is flexible enough to accommodate multiple correct answers. Here is an example with the true and false responses marked:

When constructing a completion (fill-in-the-blank) test item, it is recommended that you:

T 1. Estimate 30 seconds to 1 minute for students to answer each item.
F 2. Locate the word(s) to fill in at the beginning of the sentence, not in the middle or at the end of it.
F 3. Vary the length of the fill-in lines according to the length of the correct answer.
T 4. Omit only significant words from the sentence to complete.

Note that this single stem, one multiple true/false item, presented four decision points: two distractors and two correct responses. In essence, it created four separate objective items, and it did so efficiently using no more words than for one item. With 10 stems, then, you can easily generate 40 to 50 items, and a test with 50 items is much more reliable than one with only 10. This can be scored as one point for each statement that is correct. Another scoring option is to allocate half a point if the test taker gets at least half of the true/false statement correct and one point if they are all correct. In summary, multiple true/false items are more flexible, efficient, and reliable than multiple-choice and most other objective test items (Lahner et al., 2018).

Multiple true/false items share a great deal with true/false and multiple-choice questions in terms of their advantages, disadvantages, and construction guidelines. However, they have a few of their own:

Advantages

- Superior flexibility, efficiency, and reliability
- Easier and quicker to develop than multiple-choice items
- Adds challenge and eliminates process-of-elimination thinking

Disadvantage

- One faulty stem undercuts the value of multiple items.

Construction

- Take extra care to write clear, concise, unambiguous stems.
- Be sure the distractors are clearly true or false in relation to the stem.
- Consider allowing students to write a rebuttal to their wrong answer for a small percentage of the items.

Short Answer

The short answer test falls right between objective and constructed response. It does require the test taker to construct a response, but in many cases the response is not long enough to allow students to construct or justify a deeply considered response. Sam et al. (2019) used very short answer questions on a pathology exam. This was done because multiple-choice questions are associated with cuing and tend to promote rote learning. Students were given from one to four words to answer the questions. The reliability was very similar to the single-best answer multiple-choice items and got away from the cuing and rote memory noted.

Instructors typically use a short-answer question to test *recall* of information, comprehension, or application of some content.

Advantages

- Easy to construct
- Can assess recall, comprehension, and application

- Requires a command of vocabulary or problem-solving skills
- Very useful as a diagnostic tool
- Encourages instructors to give students individual feedback

Disadvantages

- Time-consuming to grade given the amount of knowledge tested
- Students are rarely taught how to appropriately respond to this type of question

Construction

- Estimate 2 to 5 minutes per item.
- Be very specific and concise in identifying the task that students are to perform. See the advice following for constructing essay questions and writing assignments.
- Use familiar language that is similar to what you and the readings have used to explain the material.
- Indicate whether diagrams or illustrations are required or are acceptable in place of a written answer.
- Require students to show their work for full credit on problems.
- Leave an appropriate amount of space for the answers. Too much space invites students to write too much.
- Create a scoring rubric before you begin to grade these items. If the scoring rubric needs adjusting, regrade any papers scored to that point.

■ CONSTRUCTED-RESPONSE TEST ITEMS AND ASSIGNMENTS

A constructed-response instrument is an interrogatory statement (a question) or an imperative statement (a task description) that an instructor composes to assess student achievement of one or more learning outcomes (Ory & Ryan, 1993).

It is usually an essay item on a test or an assignment. Typically, students write their answers, but complex graphics, such as concept maps, mind maps, matrices, and concept circle diagrams (see Chapter 22), may do the job just as well. For an assignment, you may use more creative media like video productions, musical compositions, artistic performances, visually rich websites, oral presentations, poster presentations, and the like.

Constructed-response instruments, especially essay tests, have been misnamed *subjective* (as opposed to *objective*). This poorly chosen descriptor ignores professional judgment and gives students the mistaken impression that faculty members have no clear standards for evaluating their work. We do have standards, of course, but they often do not boil down to a dualist right or wrong answer. Moreover, each of us may prioritize different criteria on given essay questions and assignments. This is why we should explain our grading criteria and standards to students at the same time we talk about the test or the assignment (see Chapter 26).

Some constructed-response instruments have just one correct answer with limited leeway for phraseology, such as science lab reports and mathematically based problem solutions; Suskie (2009) calls these *restricted response* instruments. Here is an example from a finance exam: "What are the six major capital budgeting techniques? Define them (you need not give their formula). Under what two categories are they normally grouped? Categorize all six techniques." Every introductory finance textbook supplies the answers to these questions. This next set is less clear: "What is the difference between experimental research and survey research? What do they have in common?" If there have been discussions in the course about how different experimental research designs are similar and different, and how a variety of survey research designs are similar and different, but there was never a discussion of compare and contrasting between the two methods, then these questions demand higher-order thinking. Similarly, there may have been some discussion and practice in a course about applying concepts, but for

a constructed-response application question or task you would make use of problems, cases, diagrams, graphs, data sets, and the like that students have not seen before to assess higher-order thinking skills.

If you are testing students on material they have been exposed to previously, you could use a *restricted response* constructed test item, but it is more efficient to use objective items to assess their recall, recognition, and comprehension. *Extended response* constructed responses are best reserved for questions and tasks that have multiple respectable answers and require professional judgment to assess (Suskie, 2009). This is because they take more time and effort to grade than do objective items, even with the time-saving grading methods that Chapter 26 recommends. If students write the product, as they usually do, you must interpret their sometimes rambling thoughts, distracting grammar and spelling, confusing punctuation, and handwriting, and then evaluate content. Therefore, use constructed-response instruments with discretion, such as when the learning outcome you are assessing requires students to generate, as opposed to select, an answer. If your outcome calls only for selection, then you might as well use objective items (Reiner et al., 2004).

Following are advantages, disadvantages, and construction guidelines for constructed response instruments. Those that apply only to essay test items are marked with a †.

Advantages

- Quick and relatively easy to construct
- Encourages students to study in a deeper, more integrated manner †
- Discourages last-minute cramming †
- Can assess all types of higher-order thinking
- Can assess students' abilities to logically compose and present an argument
- Can assess their reasoning skills (you get inside their heads)
- Can assess them authentically, that is, on tasks that they are likely to do in real-world work

- Can encourage creativity and originality
- Gives practice in writing
- Reduces incidence of cheating†
- Students get more individualized feedback
- Varies the type of assessment from objective tests

Disadvantages

- More time-consuming to grade than objective items
- Difficult to standardize grading (but see Chapter 26 for ways to handle the variability)
- Penalizes students who read or work slowly, have poor writing skills, or are nonnative English speakers
- Can mislead students if they do not understand the verbs used in the questions or don't read the entire question carefully
- Encourages grading protests if scoring rubric not used
- Easy to make a question or task too broad for students to zero in on the answer

Construction

- Specify exactly what you want the students to do, following the guidelines in the next section.
- Estimate 15 minutes to 1 hour per essay question.†
- Put on the test your estimate of how much time an answer should require to help students budget their time wisely.†
- Give the point value for each essay.†
- Give several shorter essay questions rather than one or two long ones, particularly early in the semester. This strategy covers more material and spreads the risk.
- Consider giving students a choice among two or more essay questions. Having options lowers their anxiety and lets them show you the best of what they have learned.
- If you let students choose among several questions, limit their choices—for example, select 3 out of 5 questions to answer rather than 3 out of 10.

Making Constructed-Response Instruments Specific Enough

Be specific and concise in describing the task you want students to perform or the answer you expect to the questions you ask. Identify the key points that students should address. Rather than beginning a question with an interrogative word such as *why, how,* or *what*, start with a descriptive verb, such as *explain* (see Chapters 2 and 24 for a list of common test and assignment verbs and their definitions) and state exactly how elaborate the answer should be and, to an extent, how it might best be organized (Reiner et al., 2004)—for instance: "*Describe three ways* that social integration could break down in the modern world, according to Durkheim. Then *assess* how closely *each one* applies to the United States today."

All you have to do is to decide exactly how you would like an excellent answer to read. Then you can transform a vague question like, "What were the causes of the collapse of the Ming dynasty?" into a well-defined, multistage task:

Select *three key* causes of the collapse of the Ming dynasty, and decide which was *most* important, which was *second* in importance, and which was *last* in importance. Write a paragraph on each cause, not only describing its impact on the Ming dynasty, but also supporting why you rank-order it as you do. Explain any interrelationships that exist among the causes.

If the content lends itself, it is also an excellent strategy to situate an essay question or writing assignment in a novel (but not foreign) problem (Reiner et al., 2004). Problem-focused assessment gives students practice in real-world application, and for this reason it is authentic. You can take a theoretical task such as, "How should a manager handle an employee who threatens to quit," and place it in a realistic situation:

> One of the best employees in the marketing department tells their manager that they need an immediate 10% raise. What specific issues should the manager discuss with the employee if the manager wants to keep the employee, but cannot give any raises at this time?

The final example of an essay question or writing assignment that needs and gets a makeover asks students to perform a low-level and vaguely stated task: "Summarize the most important trends in social inequality that we have seen in the United States since the 1960s." The revision assumes that students can perform this low-level task and requires that they analyze and synthesize that knowledge in a new way to address a contemporary real-world paradox:

> Recall the trends in social inequality that we have seen in the United States since the 1960s. Also recall that during this time, (1) the relationship between educational and income attainment has been consistently positive and (2) educational attainment has increased. How then is it possible that the distributions of income and wealth have become more polarized over this time period? Resolve this apparent contradiction, taking into account other major determinants of income, the role of the occupational structure, and the type of economy in the United States.

With direction, organization, and hints in the instructions, you can prepare your class to perform truly high-order cognitive operations. But do remember that you have to give your students prior practice in the types of thinking you ask them to do in graded assessments. If you identify these types of thinking from the start in your learning outcomes, you will be able to select and implement the teaching formats, methods, and moves that will create the learning experiences to give your students the practice they need.

If you want to use an essay question or give a writing assignment that students may view as controversial or value-based, do assure them in advance that you will assess their work strictly on the validity of their arguments, the strength of their evidence, or the quality of their presentation, not the opinion or viewpoint they express. Be sure to incorporate whatever grading dimensions you define in your grading rubric.

Ideas for Good Test Essays and Writing Assignments

For a little inspiration, consider how you might adapt these general ideas for engaging test essays and writing assignments to your course material:

- Discuss the relevance of course material to a life decision.
- Argue against a position you believe in.
- Set the conditions under which a relationship or concept does and does not apply.
- What if _____ [a specific change occurs, time or place shifts, or an assumption is violated]? Would a relationship still hold? How would it be changed?
- Push an idea to its limits, to the point of absurdity.
- Determine whether a problem can or cannot be solved given available information.
- Separate relevant from irrelevant information to solve a problem.

- Break a problem into subproblems.
- Explain a specific complex phenomenon to a 12-year-old.
- Design a study to test a relationship between two variables.
- Suggest reasons that different research studies may obtain different results.
- Design a study to reconcile different results across several studies.
- Imagine you are a _____ with the following problem to solve: _____. Draw on course material to structure an approach to the problem or to propose a solution.
- Design a society, government, private or public organization, or funding agency to accomplish a certain purpose.

■ USING ASSESSMENTS TO MAKE TEACHING ADJUSTMENTS

How your students perform on your summative assessments provides excellent data you can use for your personal self-assessment of your teaching and give you data to help you to make adjustments as needed. Pay close attention to the subject areas in which your students underperformed and try to figure out why.

- Did you deviate from your student learning outcomes as you taught the material?
- Did you assign the relevant readings without a compliance incentive or a comprehension exercise?
- Did you use teaching methods or moves that weren't among the most effective for the material?
- Did you give your students too little practice in the required cognitive operations?
- Did you fail to emphasize the content in class or in your review guide or session?

- Did the content challenge misconceptions, beliefs, or values that your students hold dear?

These are just a few of the reasons that your students may have faltered. You can even ask them directly why their performance fell short of what you expected, and their answers may prove helpful. Diagnosing the difficulty now means that you will reduce or eliminate your disappointment next time and become a better instructor. Growth-minded instructors recognize there are always ways to improve, provided there is good feedback. Student assessments make excellent feedback.

■ REFLECTION QUESTIONS

Reflection Question 25.1: How do you normally approach test construction? Do you have an overall plan to create the assessment, or do you figure out how many of each question type is appropriate, and then start writing questions? If you don't have an assessment plan, what might one look like for your course?

Reflection Question 25.2: Which types of test items do you like the best and which do you like the least? With this in mind, consider whether you offer assessments that meet the needs of the course, or if they are more heavily based on the types of items you prefer.

Concept Into Practice: Select one test you have constructed; take a serious look at the items it contains. Based on this chapter, consider ways that some of the items may be rewritten (e.g., matching rather than short answer, rewriting some of the multiple-choice items, or doing an item analysis). The goal is to identify a specific way your assessments might become stronger in the future.

CHAPTER 26

Grading Student Assessments

Grading is a task that many of us view with dread and disdain, but perhaps that is because few of us were taught how to grade efficiently and effectively. When have you heard a colleague say they were working on becoming a better grader? Believe it or not, grading can be an important part of the teaching and learning process; grades provide students with a sense of how much they have learned and may give you an idea of the effectiveness of your teaching. Grades are also used by future employers, graduate schools, and professional programs to determine the academic standing and perhaps even work ethic of a student. Overall, grades are used throughout higher education, but it has not always been that way. Grading first appeared in the mid-1600s, but as recently as the early 1970s only two-thirds of primary and secondary schools in the United States used letter grades (Schinske & Tanner, 2014). Today grades are ubiquitous, but some have begun to seriously question whether they are actually harmful to students' work in higher education (Blum, 2020; Eyler, 2022; Jaschik, 2009; Kohn, 2018).

GRADING SYSTEMS

Grading is a summative assessment that occurs at the end of a learning process, which may be after a small section of content, a portion of a course, or at the end of the course. Grading typically follows one of two basic standard systems, norm referenced or criterion referenced.

Norm-Referenced Grading

Commonly called *grading on a curve*, this approach assesses each student's performance relative to all other students' performances. Strengths of this system are that the best and worst performances set the parameters within which other performances are judged, so an instructor can give a highly challenging test without unduly lowering his students' grades or an easy test that still differentiates the quality of student performance. Norm-referenced grading also sets the average on the graded work to a C, or with a slight adjustment any class grade point average an instructor considers reasonable. Finally, norm-referenced grading typically has the same number of grades of D and F as it does A and B, so it combats grade inflation.

That said, its relative nature gives it some serious flaws. First, it places students in competition with each other for class ranking so you cannot expect them to work cooperatively together in graded group work. Second, norm-referenced grading statistically assumes a bell-shaped (*normal*) distribution of student scores, a phenomenon that rarely occurs naturally, particularly in small courses and upper-division courses. Third, the grades the system yields are unrelated to any absolute performance standard. So if all students in a class perform poorly, some inadequate performances will receive an A anyway. Conversely, in a high-achieving class, some excellent performances unjustly receive failing grades of F.

Norm-referenced grading has fallen into disfavor for several reasons. For one, higher education has widely embraced group work, and for another, it no longer aims to screen out the low achievers. The retention rate has replaced the attrition rate as an institution's badge of honor. Finally, since the 1990s, education has been solidly based on outcomes (Spady, 1994). The modern thought is that grades are better anchored to a desired outcome (criterion) rather than a distribution of scores that are not related to standards in any way.

Criterion-Referenced Grading

This type of grading standard system requires instructors to set absolute standards of performance (grading criteria) in advance, giving all students sole responsibility for their own grades. Criterion-referenced grading serves the purpose of assessing how well students achieve given learning outcomes. It allows the possibility that all students will attain A's or, conversely, that all students will fail. In addition, it encourages cooperation and collaboration among students. Finally, if criteria are clearly specified and rubrics are used, racial bias in teacher evaluations of students is greatly reduced (Quinn, 2020).

To be sure, criterion-referenced grading has drawbacks. In particular, it is difficult to develop meaningful, valid standards for assigning grades based on absolute knowledge acquisition (Ory & Ryan, 1993). Instructors who are unfamiliar with their student population may have no idea how scores will distribute on any given test or assignment. (As the nightmare goes, all the scores cluster around 95% or all lag below 70.) But with more experience, instructors learn how to design and grade tests and assignments to differentiate performances.

◼ GRADING CONSTRUCTED RESPONSES

Grading answers to constructed-response questions requires considerable thought and strategies to ensure accuracy, consistency, and fairness within reasonable time frames (Hauer et al., 2020; Suskie, 2009; Walvoord & Anderson, 2010; Zimmaro, 2022). Certain practices help ensure those qualities:

1. Removing students' names from their work to reduce grading biases
2. Providing a grading rubric (defined later in the chapter) along with the directions for an assignment or before an essay test, or distributing a detailed grading key when returning student work
3. Supplying samples of exemplary work and helping students understand what makes them excellent, along with the directions for an assignment or before an essay test
4. Allowing students to make revisions after receiving feedback on earlier drafts
5. Commenting as generously as your time allows, including on what the student did right
6. Making specific comments, not a cryptic "What?" or "?"
7. Identifying a few key areas for improvement, especially those emphasized in your grading rubric
8. Directing comments to the performance, not the student
9. Reviewing exams when you return them so that students understand what you wanted and how they can improve their performance

10. Referring all students to your institution's academic assistance center and writing center (see the Appendix)

Because grading constructive responses takes so much time, a good practice that will save you time and focus your students on your most important expectations is to set *gateway criteria*. This is a requirement that students must meet before you grade their work (Walvoord & Anderson, 2010). Gateway criteria may center around mechanics, organization, labeling of graphs and tables, types or number of references, reference style, or any other features that you consider bottom-line signs of a good-faith effort. It is important to be certain students understand that if they miss this criteria you will *not* grade their work. Any work that misses minimum specifically stated criteria will have many serious issues and take you a good deal of time to grade—and will still result in a failing grade. At your discretion, you can accept a revision of the work but dock the grade as a late submission or accept the work only after the student has visited the writing center for assistance.

Beyond having gateway criteria, you can choose from three commonly used grading methods: atomistic, holistic, and analytical grading.

Atomistic Grading

Atomistic grading technique follows a key. To develop a key, first list the components of an ideal response on paper and then allocate point values among the components. As you read a student's work, mentally check off the components on your list or write the number of points earned next to the component on the student's work. You typically give partial credit to an incomplete or partially correct answer. Then, total the point values for the grade. This approach helps inexperienced instructors become accustomed to the quality range of student work and the grading process.

This method is content focused and serves well for grading test items and assignments that require only knowledge or comprehension and have one correct response. It can also be used with criteria that have fairly clear standards of right and wrong: conformity to specified format, organization, quality of data or evidence, logic of reasoning, style (sentence structure, word choice, and tone), and mechanics (grammar, punctuation, and spelling). You can easily keep track of four or five dimensions and, if you wish, give each a different point value or weight—for example, 20 points for content, 15 for organization, 10 for style, and 5 for mechanics, for a total of 50 points. In terms of allocating points on such criteria, this method resembles analytical grading, addressed later in the chapter. If you have general assessment dimensions like these, do explain them and their point values to your class in advance, perhaps when you give the assignment or conduct a review for the test. Your students need to understand the criteria on which you will evaluate their work.

Atomistic grading takes a great deal of time because it requires attention to minute detail and because most instructors feel obligated to explain what is wrong or missing on each student's work. It may be more efficient to show students a copy of the key when returning the test or paper. Although atomistic grading seems highly objective, it still invites grading protests and point mongering, especially for partial credit. In addition, it is difficult to remember precisely how one graded a similarly but not identically flawed response 20 or 30 papers ago. Consistency across multiple graders can also be difficult to maintain. Perhaps a more serious weakness in atomistic grading is its rigidity when applied to essays and assignments that require higher-level thinking and have multiple respectable answers. The key can quickly become unruly if you try to lay out standards for grading every possible acceptable response, and it may not include all such responses.

Holistic Grading

Over the years, this method has been called *global grading* and *single impression scoring*. As the name implies, an instructor grades a student-constructed response on their overall evaluation of its quality. The technique is relatively quick, efficient, reliable, and fair when backed by instructor experience, practice, and familiarity with the student performance range at the institution. In addition, it easily accommodates essays and assignments that demand higher-order thinking and have multiple respectable responses.

With inductive holistic grading, which is suitable for small classes, you read quickly through all the responses or papers, rank each above or below the ones you have already read, from best to worst, and then group them for assigning grades. Finally, you write up descriptions of the quality of each group and give them to students when you return their work. To personalize the feedback, you can add comments to each student's sheet or highlight the most applicable parts of the appropriate description. Although the descriptions are customized to the student products, this schema presents a couple of problems. Because it relies on your comparative evaluations of students' responses and papers, it contains an element of norm-referenced grading (curving). Moreover, students cannot know in advance the dimensions on which you will assess their work.

With deductive holistic grading, which is suitable for any size class, students do know in advance and in some detail how their work will be evaluated. At the same time you compose the writing assignment or essay question, you decide the four or five dimensions on which you will assess the student product. Four or five criteria are a reasonable number to explain to your students and to remember while you are grading. Furthermore, your students cannot do their best on more than a handful of dimensions at one time. We carry around years or decades of experience with which we judge scholarly work. Students do not have this background. Besides, it is unfair to them to critique their novice efforts on the full array of professional dimensions, even if we don't expect high performance. So select just a few as the most important skills for students to demonstrate in any given piece of work, and forget the rest. You can focus on other dimensions in other assignments and essays.

Your relevant assessment criteria will vary according to your discipline, the course level, the nature of your material, and the task you are assigning. Here are just 14 of the possible options:

1. Following directions (particularly salient for first-year students)
2. Accurate statement of facts, figures, definitions, equations, or text material
3. Proper use of technical terminology
4. Demonstration of accurate understanding of the materials and texts
5. Proper references to texts and other sources
6. Organization, conformity to the required organizing framework of format
7. Precision of measurement, quality of data
8. Specification of limits, qualifications to results, and conclusions
9. Clarity of expression or explanations
10. Conciseness, parsimony
11. Strength or tightness of arguments (internal consistency, evidence, and logic)
12. Mechanics (spelling, grammar, and punctuation)
13. Writing style, as suitable to the discipline and assignment
14. Creativity of thought, design, or solution

After choosing the criteria of interest, you then write out descriptions of what the student product will look like at the different levels of quality. If you are assigning letter grades, you will describe the qualities of A, B, C, D, and F work on the dimensions you selected for the assignment or essay. If you are allocating points, you will describe the work for each point or range of points. You might link words to the grades or point ranges, such as *exemplary, competent, developing*, and *unacceptable*. The document you generate is called a *rubric*, defined as an assessment and grading tool that lays out specific expectations for an essay or assignment (writing, speaking, multimedia, and so on) and describes each level of performance quality on selected criteria. In holistic grading, these descriptions take the form of paragraphs in which each sentence typically addresses a different dimension in the rubric.

An example rubric should clarify. Let's say our assignment is to write a classic five-paragraph essay arguing in favor of norm-referenced grading or criterion-referenced grading, drawing on several readings on the topic. Let's assume our rubric focuses on satisfying the assignment (with an emphasis on following the classic five-paragraph essay format), demonstrating an accurate understanding of the readings, backing one's argument with evidence from the readings, and mechanics. The holistic rubric may look like this:

- *A essays* contain *all or almost all* of the following characteristics:
  - Classic five-paragraph essay format
  - Thesis (position) stated in the first paragraph
  - Evidence provided in each of the next three paragraphs
  - Conclusion with a summary or synthesis
  - Appropriate and accurate references to the readings
  - All evidence to support its argument drawn from the readings
  - No more than two spelling, punctuation, or grammatical errors
- *B essays* contain *most or many* of the following characteristics:
  - Classic five-paragraph essay format previously described with no more than one minor deviation
  - Generally accurate and appropriate references to the readings
  - A thin, incomplete, or shaky understanding of the readings in a couple of places
  - All evidence to support its argument drawn from the readings
  - Missing some parts of the readings that would lend more evidence to the argument
  - More than two but fewer than eight spelling, punctuation, or grammatical errors

- *C essays* contain *most or many* of the following characteristics:
  - Significant deviations from the classic five-paragraph essay format described earlier—for example, failing to state a clear position in the first paragraph, mixing arguments across paragraphs, or closing with a new argument or information
  - A spotty or superficial understanding of the readings referred to
  - Missing some parts of the readings that would lend more evidence to the argument
  - Quite a few (eight or more) spelling, punctuation, or grammatical errors, though not enough to make parts of it incomprehensible.
- *D essays* contain *most or many* of the following characteristics:
  - Failure to follow the classic five-paragraph essay format—for example, failing to state a clear position or use the rest of the essay to bring evidence from the readings to support it, or both
  - Little understanding or knowledge of the readings
  - Little or no relevant evidence drawn from the readings
  - Frequent and serious enough errors in spelling, punctuation, and grammar to be distracting or to render the essay incomprehensible in places
- *Failing essays* contain *either* of the following characteristics, or it is not turned in:
  - Failure to address the assignment in topic or format
  - Frequent and serious enough errors in spelling, punctuation, and grammar to render the essay incomprehensible overall

Distribute copies of the rubric to your students along with the assignment directions or review sheet, and explain them with examples. This way, students will know to concentrate on the dimensions that are most important to you, and they will understand the quality of work you expect. To increase the odds that they will pay attention to your scoring rubric, you might ask them to attach the document to the product they hand in and score their own paper using the rubric. You could even give a point or two of additional credit if the student fills out a rubric similar to how you fill it out.

When you grade the essays or papers, you decide which performance description best fits the work and write that grade on the paper or essay. That is really all you have to do, and this can reduce your grading time to a fraction of what atomistic grading requires. The rubric explains the reasons for the grade, although you should write personal comments as time permits.

The literature offers examples of holistic rubrics written in paragraphs for many types of assignments: letters (Montgomery, 2002); portfolios (Stevens & Levi, 2012); integrative essays (Benander, cited in Walvoord & Anderson, 2010); oral presentations, class participation, and journals (Baughin et al., 2002); essay tests and website designs (Brookhart, 1999); and mathematical problem-solving (Baughin et al., 2002; Benander et al., 2000; Montgomery, 2002). As these models demonstrate, it is best not to abbreviate the descriptions of the B, C, and D products because students are likely to focus only on the description of their own grade. However, the description of F work may be briefer because such serious shortcomings often transcend the rubric.

This holistic approach can shortchange students if the rubric provides an overall rationale for each grade without making the grading criteria clear and obvious enough to furnish meaningful feedback. After all, it is quite possible that a student's work contains elements of two, three, or even more performance levels. For example, the work may follow the organizational format perfectly but demonstrate a poor understanding of the readings and contain a moderate number of mechanical errors. In this case, you need a rubric that allows you to mark or highlight the salient descriptors on different performance levels, as in our sample rubric where the criteria are broken out. Of course, you can always write personalized comments on each student's work, but this sacrifices the efficiency and time-saving advantages of holistic grading.

As a result, many instructors favor a synthesized rubric that combines some of the specificity of atomistic grading with the efficiency and professional judgment involved in the deductive holistic method.

Analytical Grading: The Effective Synthesis of Atomistic and Holistic

This grading technique follows the procedures of deductive holistic grading—focusing on four to six assessment criteria, writing descriptions for each performance level, and providing students with the rubric in advance—and shares the advantage of speed and efficiency. But rather than writing an overall description of the student product for each performance level, you write a brief description for each performance level on each criterion and assess the product not overall but independently on each criterion. Then you total or average the points gained across all the criteria to derive an overall point total grade.

This grading method certainly requires you to write more descriptions than does the holistic method—as many as the number of performance levels times the number of criteria—and you may find yourself writing more extensive or specific descriptions. However, these furnish your students with more detailed instructions, expectations, and feedback as well as clearer justification for your assessment. In addition, you can give different weights to your criteria reflecting their relative importance in the piece of work. Just don't make your system too complicated for your students to follow.

Although you can write the descriptions in full sentences and even paragraphs, you can also use more succinct phrases. In addition, you can display the rubric in an easy-to-read matrix or table for clarity, listing the assessment dimensions down the left side of the page to define rows and the levels of performance (usually the possible numbers of points) across the top to create columns. The cells contain your descriptions of the performance quality on each dimension.

For purposes of illustration, let's return to that essay assignment arguing in favor of norm-referenced or criterion-referenced grading and transform the holistic rubric shown previously into an analytical one (Table 26.1). (Only holistic rubrics with well-defined, consistent dimensions easily convert into an analytical version.)

When you use your rubric to grade, first test it out on three or four pieces of student work. Although you are ethically bound not to make substantive changes, you may tweak it if needed. As you read a student product, mark (underline, highlight, check, star, or circle) the applicable phrases in the descriptions on the student's copy of the rubric. This grading method accommodates wide differences in a student's performance across criteria. Then calculate the point total or letter grade from the distribution of your markings and write that in a discrete place on the student's work. Add your personalized comments on the work or the rubric only as your time permits. If you have composed a good rubric, you shouldn't have much more to say. Finally, return the work with the student's copy of the rubric.

With a little experience, you will be able to develop rubrics quickly and at the same time that you design an assignment or write an essay test question. For the latter use, you can prepare a generic rubric that doesn't give away the question. When students can work on an assignment or study for a test with the rubric in front of them, they are less likely to explain away a poor performance with, "I didn't know what he wanted."

You will find more examples of analytical rubrics in matrix/table form than any other kind, and models are available for every grading purpose. Look in the assessment literature (Badia, 2019; Baughin et al., 2002; Montgomery, 2002; Stevens & Levi, 2012; Suskie, 2009; Walvoord & Anderson, 2010) and on dedicated websites, such as RubiStar (http://rubistar.4teachers.org), Teachnology (http://www.teach-nology.com/web_tools/rubrics), iRubric (http://www.rcampus.com/rubricshellc.cfm?mode=gallery&sms=home&srcgoogle&gclid=CNSCsu3PmZMCFQv_sgodPBO_xA), and Tech4Learning (http://myt4l.com/index.php?v=pl&page_ac=view&type=tools&tool=rubricmaker). All these sites feature not just models but also rubric generators, allowing you to create your own for specific assignments.

RubiStar, for example, offers a drop-down menu of appropriate criteria to choose from. When you select a dimension, it displays descriptions of four quality levels, which you can then edit to your needs. RubiStar was designed primarily for and by K–12 teachers, but many of the models and generated rubrics easily adapt to college-level work.

Automated Essay Scoring

Automated essay scoring (AES) of constructed responses, or essays, has been in development since 1966 with a program called Project Essay Grade (Page, 2003). That means for nearly 60 years, researchers have been working on an artificial system that can grade essay responses to test questions and papers with both reliability and validity. Reliability is measured by correlating the AES with human raters who have very high correlations with one another. Essentially, multiple humans set the target score, and then AES is rated based on its ability to correlate highly with that number. AES systems have made extensive progress recently, with some systems demonstrating correlations with human scores of up to .97 (Hussein et al., 2019). AES systems are faster and more reliable than human raters, once the systems have been appropriately programmed, which can be an extensive process. AES systems also eliminate several forms of human bias, such as fatigue, harshness/leniency, stereotyping, rater drift, contrast effects, and halo effect (Kumar & Boulanger, 2020).

AES systems are making significant gains. Algorithms are being fine-tuned to address several challenges, such as students who write more in an effort to score more points. However, at the publication of this edition of *Teaching at Its Best*, AES systems are still less effective at assessing the creativity

Table 26.1 Analytical Grading Rubric for a Hypothetical Essay Assignment

Grade Criteria	A/19–20	B/16–18	C/13–15	D/10–12	F/Below 10
Format	Follows the classic five-paragraph essay format strictly, stating the thesis (position) in the first paragraph, providing evidence in each of the next three paragraphs, and concluding with a summary or synthesis	Follows the classic five-paragraph essay format with no more than one minor deviation	Breaks significantly from the classic five-paragraph essay format—failing to state a clear position in the first paragraph, mixing arguments across paragraphs, or closing with a new argument or information	Does not follow the classic five-paragraph essay format—failing to state a clear position or use the rest of essay to bring evidence from the readings to support it	Fails to address the assignment in topic or format, or frequent errors in spelling, punctuation, and grammar render the essay incomprehensible, or not turned in
Command of readings	Consistently makes appropriate and accurate references to the readings	Generally accurate in referring to readings, but shows a thin, incomplete, or shaky understanding of some readings in a couple of places	Refers to the readings, but demonstrates a spotty or superficial understanding of them	Demonstrates little understanding or knowledge of the readings	
Evidence from readings	Provides all the evidence available in the readings to support its argument	Provides evidence available in the readings, but misses some parts that would lend evidence to the argument	Misses opportunities to use the readings for evidence	Draws little relevant evidence from the readings	
Mechanics	No more than two spelling, punctuation, or grammatical errors	No more than several spelling, punctuation, or grammatical errors	Quite a few spelling, punctuation, or grammatical errors, though not enough to make parts of the essay incomprehensible	Frequent errors in spelling, punctuation, and grammar that are distracting or render the essay incomprehensible in places	

of a written piece of work. That said, at this rate of progress there is no doubt that will also be solved soon. The final challenge will be to develop relatively inexpensive systems so those in education will be able to use them. Machine-scored constructed essays will be a significant move forward for faculty members, allowing them to assign papers and essays in large courses, quickly return grades, and provide detailed feedback. With every gain comes a loss, however, as there is a sense of really knowing a student that comes from reading their work in free-response format.

▇ GRADING LAB REPORTS

Although this is a specialized kind of grading for a specialized kind of writing, the guidelines for grading constructed responses still apply. No doubt, you'll be examining these features: the student's presentation of the problem, the hypothesis, and the results; their analysis of the results; and their ability to follow the scientific method. In lower-level science courses, you can familiarize your students with the proper format and content by providing them with models, perhaps from other courses. You can also have them organize their reports with an outline or flowchart and practice-write the various sections.

Another excellent way to help your students produce good reports is to give them the grading rubric in advance. Rodgers (1995) developed a detailed analytical rubric, presented in an easy-to-read matrix, to grade his students' chemistry lab reports. His rubric has a daunting 21 assessment dimensions, but they fall within four more general criteria—focus, appearance, content, and structure—and have only three levels of point allocations: 2, 4, and 6. For example, under "focus," Rodgers has nine dimensions (1995, p. 21):

1. Shows understanding of the experimental objectives
2. Abstract describes what was done and what the major results were

3. Concise, no unnecessary statements or observations
4. Introduction shows depth
5. Written with an objective, scientific tone
6. Give suggestions for improvement and further study in conclusions
7. Relates the experiment to other known chemical principles
8. Shows detailed understanding of the scientific method
9. Distinguishes between a theory and a proof

Nine dimensions may seem imposing, but many of the cells have only one- or two-word descriptors, such as "very clear," "demonstrated," or "unsophisticated." Even when the descriptor is considerably longer, it is very easy to simply check, circle, or highlight the most appropriate option. At the end, you total the points accumulated across all 21 dimensions by calculating or eyeballing.

Rodgers (1995) recorded how long it took to grade a lab report using his old atomistic method versus his new rubric method. He timed both himself and his trained TAs. The results were quite startling. His previous grading technique required 15 to 20 minutes per report, whereas the new method took only an average of 3 1/2 minutes (for him) and 4 minutes (for his TAs) per report. In other words, rubric grading reduced lab report grading time by 75% to 80%. Rodgers was also pleased with the reliability and overall grading results.

▇ MECHANICS OF WRITING

Addressing the mechanics of writing—spelling, grammar, sentence structure, and punctuation—was once a challenge for instructors. At this time, programs such as Microsoft Word and Google Docs have mechanics built into their programs. Students can also download a free version of Grammarly.com. If these built-in programs are not sufficient, students can work with the writing center on issues pertaining to mechanics. As a result of these resources, both built into programs and available on campus, it is relatively easy for students to turn in papers with respectable spelling, grammar, and punctuation. The only reason a paper would have poor mechanics today is if the student simply does not take the time to correct it. As a result, it's typically effective to let students know that you simply will not read papers that are not mechanically sound.

SPECIFICATIONS (SPECS) GRADING

Specifications (specs) grading was developed on the premise that students can achieve much more than we typically ask of them (Nilson, 2015). Specs grading motivates students to do higher-quality work, even right after the pandemic when overall student motivation was very low (Prof, 2022), and saves you time grading. In addition, most students prefer it to traditional methods. Although you can adopt just pieces of this new system and combine it with features of traditional grading, the greatest benefits derive from the three integrated parts (Nilson, 2015).

First, you grade all assignments and tests satisfactory/unsatisfactory, pass/fail, or full credit/no credit, depending on whether the student work meets the specifications, or specs, that you laid out for it. You can think of the specs as a one-level rubric. However, you set the passing bar at B work or even higher. The specs may be as simple as "completeness"—for instance, all the questions are answered, or all the problems are attempted in good faith, or the work follows the directions and meets a required minimum length. Or the specs may be more complex—for example, a description of a good literature review or the required contents (questions that must be answered) and length of each section of a proposal, a report, or a reflection. You might also recommend how many hours students should put into a given assignment. In any case, you must write the specs very carefully to describe exactly what features in the work you are going to look for. In fact, most of our assignments

already follow a formula. The specs should simply lay out that formula. At your discretion, they can also include on-time submission.

From the students' point of view, they must read and follow the specs because there is too much at stake not to. They can't slide by and depend on partial credit for a slipshod, 11-hour product. We are not asking too much of our students simply to follow directions and put some effort into their work. Other academics (cited in Nilson, 2015) have implemented pass/fail grading of assignments and tests and have reported gratifying results.

Second, you add flexibility and second chances for your students with a virtual token system. For example, students may start the semester with three tokens that they can exchange for a 24-hour extension on an assignment, the chance to revise an unsatisfactory assignment, take a makeup exam, or have an absence or late arrival to class not count against them. You have to keep track of students' tokens as you would points, but you don't have to listen to excuses and requests for special treatment. If you choose, students can also earn tokens by submitting satisfactory work early, doing an additional assignment, or having perfect attendance all term. Of course, students who do what they are supposed to do (submit satisfactory work the first time and on time, attend class, and take their exams when scheduled) will not lose any tokens. Perhaps because of the game-like quality of a system, students prize their tokens and try not to use them, especially if, at the end of the course, you reward the students with the most tokens with a small prize or a gift certificate for a slice of pizza. The token system meshes with any type of grading.

How do you wind up with letter grades at the end of course? If you want to maintain the point system, then you make each passed test or assignment worth so many points (all or nothing), total the points, and convert them to percentages. However, you don't have to use points anymore or haggle with students about points ever again. Rather—and this is the third aspect of specs grading—you base a student's course grade on the *bundle* of assignments and tests completed at a satisfactory level. The bundles for higher grades require some combination of more work (more learning) and more challenging work (more advanced learning)—that is, students have to jump more hurdles or higher hurdles for higher grades—or both. More advanced, challenging work may require higher-order cognitive skills in Bloom's (1956) hierarchy, higher-stage thinking in Perry's (1968) schema of undergraduate development, or higher-step skills in Wolcott's (2006) framework of critical thinking. Or it may involve solving more complex problems.

Ultimately, students have the freedom to choose the grade they want on the basis of their motivation, time available, needs, and commitment. If a student chooses a C because that's all they need in your course, you can respect that. You may be able to schedule the deadlines for the C and D bundles before the end of the term, send those students aiming for a C or D on their way, and then direct your attention to the students engaged in larger bundles of work. However, we should encourage all our students, especially the underprepared and first-generation ones, to vie for the higher grades.

Bundles allow you to associate each grade with the learning outcomes that are achieved by successfully completing a bundle. In our current grading system, a course grade provides no clue as to which outcomes a student has achieved. If our grades did reflect the outcomes achieved, programs wouldn't have to assess students' competencies for accreditation. A simple four-bundle example will clarify:

- For a D, students must successfully complete/pass all the exams and assignments in the easiest and most basic bundle. Doing so requires only knowledge and comprehension (or perhaps the knowledge and skills required by the accrediting agency).
- For a C, students must successfully complete/pass all the work in that basic bundle and a second bundle, somewhat more challenging, that requires application.

- For a B, students must successfully complete/pass all the work in the first and second bundles, plus a third bundle, still more challenging, that requires analysis.
- For an A, students must successfully complete/pass all the work in the first, second, and third bundles, plus a fourth bundle, even more challenging, that requires synthesis (creativity) and evaluation.

Unless all your students aspire to an A, you have less work to grade, especially the kind that consumes your time: the lower-quality attempts at cognitively complex assignments. Because your students chose their final grade, they are more likely to see it as their own responsibility. They should also be motivated to work harder not only because more is at stake but also because they clearly control their own outcome, at least if the specs are clear. This should reduce their grade anxiety and shift their orientation more toward learning than performance (Locke & Latham, 1990; Wigfield & Eccles, 2000).

This very brief introduction to specs grading has probably left you with more questions than answers, and understandably so, because specs grading demands a whole new gestalt on something we've done one way for so long that we can't imagine another way. The answers to your questions and many more details and examples are in Nilson (2015).

■ RETURNING STUDENTS' WORK

Under the provisions of the Buckley Amendment (the Family Educational Rights and Privacy Act), it is illegal to publicly display scores or grades with any identifying information, including any part of students' Social Security numbers. To protect students' privacy, also avoid returning work in class by handing out papers that are in order of the score on the assignment or test. Any grade should be written on an interior page or in some way that others cannot see the grade.

For students to be able to learn from your feedback on a piece of work, return the graded work as quickly as possible. Allow class time for review, questions, problem re-solving exercises, and self-regulated learning exercises (see Chapter 19) so students can learn what they did not the first time. It is best not to proceed to new material until students assure you that they understand what they did wrong. Some instructors give a statistical grading summary showing the distribution of points, the class mean and median, the standard deviation, and the cutoff lines for grades (already built into the criterion-referenced system).

Returning graded work in class can take precious time but need not. You can assign each of your students a number and place their graded work into correspondingly numbered slots in an accordion file (McIntosh, 2010). You can let them pick up their work before or after class or during a break. For a large class, use multiple accordion files. Just let students know that they must go only into their own slot.

Students have trouble seeing their mistakes on their graded work as learning opportunities. They see only the points they missed. But if you give them any kind of credit for fixing errors made, most will eagerly diagnose and correct their errors. Chapter 19 suggests several in-class or homework activities for helping students learn by their mistakes or poor study strategies. The reflective questions and the test autopsy also help students take responsibility for their test performance.

Returning student work brings us to the unpleasant topic of grade disputes. No matter how carefully you grade, a few students will be dissatisfied with their scores. One of the best defenses of the grade you assign is a solid rubric. If a rubric lays out how points are earned, there are very few (if any) subjective point values to discuss. An extremely important rule is to never discuss a grade with a student in a heightened emotional state. One option is to explain that grades do not have to be adjusted immediately and that you give up to 72 hours (or whatever period you prefer) to challenge a grade.

You might require that all grade challenges must be submitted via email with justifications citing specific material in the readings or your lectures. Students who cannot make a case within three days probably do not have one. However you decide to respond to grade challenges, clearly state your policy in your syllabus and stick to it.

One additional note that has the potential to become tricky in class occurs when going over multiple-choice items. If, for example, you note that the answer to question two is B and explain why, students might also claim that alternative C is correct. First, note that multiple-choice questions are designed so that the best alternative should be chosen. Another alternative may be correct. All alternatives may be correct. The question is which is the best answer. However, if students persist, remind them that they have 72 hours and that any item may be challenged in writing via email. You can then give credit to anyone who makes a good claim. If, during class you agree that a given alternative response is acceptable, anyone in class with that alternative will want the points, even if they guessed on that item. Some faculty members will remove an item while going over the test. That can be unfair to students because if they had that item correct and did not have a 100%, their grade will decrease when that item is removed. Stick to a policy of students submitting any grade challenges in writing.

■ UNGRADING

Which do you think students should focus on more, grades or learning? When students receive a paper with detailed feedback and a letter grade, which draws the students' attention? Students are heavily grade focused, with test anxiety cropping up in students as young as 8 years old (Donolato et al., 2020). Despite our best efforts, many faculty members are equally focused on grades over learning, fretting as much or more about bell curves and accreditation requirements as we do about student development.

Given such concerns, many in higher education are seriously questioning why we continue to have so many graded assignments in our courses (Schinske & Tanner, 2014). Some are now proposing a strategy called ungrading (Blum, 2020). Students receive an end-of-course grade, but individual elements are not graded. Grades are determined through self-reflection and metacognition. Students learn to better understand when they are learning and reflect on what they have learned. They still write papers, learn concepts, and have discussions. The difference is that instead of taking an exam and getting a score based on the proportion of correct answers, they reflect on their learning and *assign themselves a grade.* This moves the focus away from grades and memorization to increased curiosity, student engagement, and a deeper understanding of content (Stenson, 2022). Although it may sound like such a class would result in reduced academic standards and everyone giving themselves an "A," that is not what happens. There are safeguards to keep students from simply giving themselves high grades without doing any work, although those safeguards are rarely needed. Some students even rate themselves too low and their grade is raised (Stommel, 2018).

To move to an ungrading, or self-grading, concept is a large commitment. That said, once it is accomplished, you spend much less time grading and more time interacting with students. Many students are nervous with the concept of ungrading when they first encounter it, so it is important to have discussions about grades, what they mean, and why the ungraded approach is being taken. In addition, students often need assistance with better understanding metacognitive processes and self-reflection. If this is of interest to you and yet it seems like a large step, there are ways to first give it a try and to build some confidence about the impact of this kind of pedagogical move. One option to give ungrading a try is to create one or two required assignments that will not receive a score (Miller, 2022). This could be a summary of a paper to be written or a WebQuest of a topic to be covered in the next chapter, but

have students include a short reflection of their performance. Essentially, they should consider how well they felt they did, what surprised them, and what they might do differently the next time they did a similar assignment.

Ungrading is a move to shift the focus of education on the learning and away from the grade. It reduces competitiveness and encourages cooperation. This process encourages students who might otherwise struggle and makes it okay to make mistakes. Overall, it gives students an opportunity to have ownership over their learning.

GRADES SHOULD MAKE SENSE

Regardless of the system you use to assess students, grades should never come as a surprise. Standards of grades are typically based on criteria, rather than on how well another student in the class does on the assignment or exam. When constructed responses such as essay questions or papers are required, rubrics take away the mystery of how you are grading their work. Grading systems such as specifications grading allow student to select the level of work they desire to do and provide a very specific set of work to be done. Even with ungrading, the final grade assigned should make sense. For some faculty members, this is accomplished by describing the system to students and letting them know how they are to select their own grade. In any system you may use, assessment strategies that students understand give them an opportunity to do their best.

REFLECTION QUESTIONS

Reflection Question 26.1: There is no doubt that automated scoring systems will be widely available soon (perhaps while this edition of *Teaching at Its Best* is still in use). What do you see as the primary advantage of automated scoring, in addition to the time it saves you in grading? What do you see as a loss to what you feel is important with respect to teaching and learning?

Reflection Question 26.2: How is specifications grading different from the system you use in your courses? How do you think your students would respond to this type of grading system?

Concept Into Practice: Give ungrading a try. Identify one assignment that you could require in your class that would result in moving students forward with respect to learning in your course. Include a reflective component that includes an honest appraisal of their completed work, what they found challenging about the assignment, and what they might do differently next time. Include also a discussion that the focus is on learning rather than the grade and that the lack of a grade does not mean the assignment or the resulting work by the student is any less important.

CHAPTER 27

Defining and Documenting Teaching Effectiveness

Documenting teaching effectiveness and success is important for career milestones, such as tenure decisions, promotions, annual reviews, or contract renewals. Those applying for an academic position are often asked to provide evidence of teaching effectiveness. In this chapter, we define teaching effectiveness and examine the ways that institutions try to measure it. In particular, we summarize major research findings for the one tool nearly every institution uses, *student evaluations of teaching (SET)*, which, we must keep in mind, are student perceptions of teaching effectiveness, not truly objective measures. We will look at how student ratings relate to student learning, what the ratings actually measure, and how you can improve your student evaluation scores. We then explain and evaluate other approaches to measuring teaching effectiveness: peer evaluation, the teaching philosophy statement, the teaching portfolio, measures of learning in a course, and the Teaching Practices Inventory. We also lay out a comprehensive faculty evaluation system that assesses every aspect of the faculty members' role and helps to support diversity,

equity, and inclusion. Evaluating teaching effectiveness is extremely important, but it turns out to be more complex than most realize. That said, if we strive for teaching at its best, we need to be able to document how we are doing it so we know the extent of our success and where to focus our efforts.

■ WHAT IS TEACHING EFFECTIVENESS?

Virtually every institution of higher learning assesses their faculty on *teaching effectiveness*, but the criterion eludes a clear definition, as it means different things to different people. For example, teaching effectiveness may be an instructor's degree of success in facilitating student learning. This seems clear enough until we try to specify what is meant by *student learning*. Does this mean the knowledge and skills students acquire in our classrooms, the ability to reach advanced cognitive levels and effectively communicate what they have learned? To what extent should the dimensions of development of affective, ethical, social, and psychomotor learning for the student be considered? Should teaching creativity and self-care be part of teaching effectiveness? The only thing that is clear is that this is all very complicated.

Of course, faculty members do not have complete control over the extent to which students learn. Some students may or may not be willing or able to learn the material in a given course, despite the instructor's best efforts (e.g., students enrolled in courses for which they do not have prerequisite skills). Conversely, what about students who enter a course already having a firm understanding of course content? Should the faculty member be given credit for the prior learning students bring to a course?

An effective measure of learning gains (i.e., teaching effectiveness) are independently developed standardized tests tailored to each course and administered at the beginning and end of a semester. Unfortunately, such tests exist for only a few introductory courses (e.g., physics and chemistry), and they capture only the cognitive learning in a fixed period. Measuring teaching effectiveness is complex, so to measure it well or indeed at all requires multiple approaches.

◼ WHAT STUDENT RATINGS DO AND DO NOT MEASURE

SET is designed to tap students' perceptions of and reactions to an instructor and a course. However, student satisfaction with their instructor isn't the same as learning, and the two aren't necessarily related. Students' ratings are often comprised of flawed, homespun items with questionable validity and reliability (Arreola, 2007; Kreitzer & Sweet-Cushman, 2022).

The first published scale of rating teachers dates back to 1915, and student evaluations were used at several U.S. universities in the 1920s (Marsh, 1987). In the 1970s and early 1980s, student ratings (the global items) had a moderately strong positive correlation with student learning, as measured by an external exam—between .44 and .47, according to meta-analyses by Cohen (1981), Feldman (1989), and Marsh (1984). These three meta-analyses supplied the *validity* of student ratings so they could be reasonably used in personnel decisions such as promotion, reappointment, tenure, raises, and teaching awards. The stronger the relationship between student ratings and learning, and the fewer and weaker the biases in ratings, the more valid the ratings. As Cohen (1981) put it:

> It [teaching effectiveness] can be further operationalized as the amount students learn in a particular course . . . . If student ratings are to have any utility in evaluating teaching, they must show at least a moderately strong relationship to this index. (p. 281)

Unfortunately, SET appears to be increasingly demonstrating lower validity and greater levels of bias. Across the years, many types of biases have been documented that lessen the correlation between student rating and true teaching effectiveness. Examples include perceiving lecture as more effective than engaged learning (when performance data for those students show it is not), gender, race, age, charisma, difficulty of the course, class size, physical attractiveness, and the timing of asking students to fill out the evaluations (Deslauriers et al., 2019; Kreitzer & Sweet-Cushman, 2022; Mitchell & Martin, 2018; Nilson, 2012; Stroebe, 2020; Weimer, 2013). As far as course rigor, challenge, and required student effort are concerned, the results are mixed. Some studies find that students' scores on the relevant items correlate negatively with instructor ratings (Clayson, 2009; Steiner et al., 2006; Weinberg et al., 2007). However, others document a positive relationship (Beyers, 2008; Dee, 2007; Martin et al., 2008). It may depend on the institution. One final bias deserves special attention: students' anticipated grade in the course. Students who anticipate a higher grade in the course tend to give higher evaluations, regardless of their actual grade (Ewing, 2012; Nilson, 2012).

The relationship between ratings and learning as reported by Cohen (1981) and Feldman (1989) was recently reanalyzed to take into consideration the impact of small studies with large effects (therefore exaggerating findings) and the absence of studies that found no effect (as "no effect" studies are less often published) (Uttl et al., 2017). When these corrections were made and more recent studies on student evaluation of teaching were included, the correlation between student rating and teaching effectiveness fell to below .1.

Unfortunately, few studies have examined the honesty or factual accuracy of the ratings students provide, but those that have (Clayson & Haley, 2011; Cox et al., 2022; Sproule, 2002) show that student responses on the forms often misrepresent reality. In Clayson and Haley's (2011) survey, about a third of the students confessed to stretching the truth on their rating forms, 56% said they knew peers who had, and 20% admitted to lying in their comments.

Esarey and Valders (2020) proposed a new way to look at SET, employing a model that has been used in industrial/organizational psychology for approximately 80 years (Taylor & Russell, 1939). The model is used to test the impact of a given standardized assessment (in industry a performance appraisal) that is correlated, but not highly, with worker performance when making personnel decisions. It is the best industry can do to determine the accuracy of an evaluation instrument, such as an annual performance evaluation, that is used to make important decisions like raises, promotions, and terminations. In higher education we have a similar evaluation instrument that is used for important decisions. It is the SET.

Based on this industry model, Esarey and Valders (2020) ran simulated comparisons on a distribution of student rating scores. Doing this allowed the researchers to tell us the relative value of a given SET score. Suppose, for example, you have an overall student evaluation score of 4.5 out of 5. Does that mean you are a better teacher than a colleague in another department who received a 4.0 out of 5? Suppose your overall teaching evaluation score is at the 90th percentile. Is that good? Does that number help you demonstrate teaching excellence in your tenure portfolio? Better understanding of the level of accuracy, and inaccuracy, of these numbers is important, given that they are used administratively to compare one faculty member to one another for important decisions of things like who is the better teacher, which helps with decisions related to hiring, teaching awards, tenure, promotion, and reappointment. These are a lot of very important uses for SET scores. After running one million simulations, Esarey and Valders found that one-third of the time, a less-effective instructor received a higher student rating than the more-effective instructor. Obviously, that is not an acceptable level of error when making important personnel decisions.

Esarey and Valders (2020) also compared individual student ratings to a distribution of scores. This also produced disheartening results. If an institution decided to give a teaching award to a faculty member who scored at the 95th percentile for all student rating scores at the institution, due to random error, approximately 18% of this elite group would actually be no better than the median instructor. In other words, even if your institution is full of totally unbiased, honest students and uses a scale highly correlated to teaching effectiveness, giving awards to instructors in the top 5% of instructors would mean nearly one in every five of your high-scoring award winners would, in reality, be average instructors.

Based on these observed limitations, if student ratings are going to continue to be used to make important decisions, that can in the case of tenure and promotion be life changing, several considerations are advised (Benton & Young, 2018). First, it is important to statistically adjust scores to remove as many biases as possible (e.g., age, gender, race, ethnicity, course difficulty). Second, keep in mind that small differences in student ratings are meaningless. A faculty member with an overall average student rating of 3.00 is best not seen as being any different from another faculty member with an average overall rating of 3.10. Use ranges, not exact scores. Finally, and most importantly, use multiple measures when making personnel decisions, and be certain your additional measure is not heavily dependent on student ratings. For example, letters from chairs often speak of a faculty member's outstanding teaching evaluations, which means those scores also bias the chair's evaluation.

Given the psychometric challenges associated with SET, they really should not be used as the only, or even primary, measure of teaching effectiveness. This is particularly true for important personnel and award decisions. That said, if you are a faculty member at an institution that uses these evaluations to document teaching effectiveness, you can't make these measures more valid and less biased, but you can use what you know about teaching at its best to improve your student ratings.

■ HOW TO IMPROVE YOUR STUDENT RATINGS

Given the importance that is often placed on SET, it is well worth looking into ways to increase your numbers. Many of the ways to raise student ratings are actually associated with good teaching, so you may prefer to think of this as improving teaching strategies to make learning more effective and efficient for your students. To improve anything, the first step is to know your current situation. With respect to student ratings, that means looking strategically at the ratings you have received in the past. If you are a new instructor, then start with the first semester you receive evaluations. Regardless of how the student ratings are used at your college, look at them as if they were formative feedback. If you maintain a growth-minded approach to teaching, feedback is very helpful.

For each course, carefully analyze your statistical summary and student comments, looking for patterns and trends. Remember that these forms collect students' *perceptions* of your behavior and effectiveness along with their affective reactions based on how you made them feel. This is different from, but hopefully related to, objective reality. You

may not think you are being condescending, impatient, or disorganized, but if several students note those areas, your behavior is coming across to the students in that way. Again, look for trends; never make changes based on or get overly concerned about a single comment, unless it pertains to racism, sexism, or other important area that may well be experienced by only one or a few, based on the composition of the course (Zakrajsek, 2019). If you teach a course with a small number of students from an underrepresented group, and even a single written evaluation indicates that you make statements that feel like microaggressions, that single comment *should* be taken seriously and result in reflection. However, if one student indicates that the textbook is terrible, or that the engaged learning strategies waste class time, then set those singular comments aside and focus on trends. If you have 30 students in your course, and two students say they dislike the gallery walk exercise and no one else mentions it, probably most of the class liked it. Deleting that exercise in such a case would likely be a mistake.

As you look at your ratings, see if the objective items with counts or medians listed are consistent with the written comments. Consider the factors related to ratings that you can and cannot control. For instance, you cannot change your race, accent, gender, age, rank, the curriculum, the condition of your classroom, or the size of your classes. Nor can you affect your students' prior interest in the subject matter, their academic commitment, or their motivation to take your course. But there are many things you can change. Some of those items are listed in Table 27.1, along with the chapters in this book that contain the relevant information.

Although some of these behaviors have little to do with student learning, at least none of them undermine learning and several of them enhance it—notably, improving your use of class time, being better prepared, being increasingly inclusive, organizing your course more transparently, attracting and maintaining student attention, increasing student choice and control, having students work in groups, giving them quality feedback, and getting feedback

Table 27.1   Changes You Can Make to Improve Your Student Ratings

	Changes You Can Make	Relevant Chapters in This Book
1.	Improve your use of class time, your preparation, the organization of your course (even if it is just making that organization more apparent to students with a graphic syllabus and an outcomes map), and your public speaking skills.	2, 5, and 14
2.	Add warmth, empathy, and caring to your instructor persona by learning students' names, encouraging their success, smiling, and exhibiting a few other simple immediacy behaviors.	7 and 9
3.	Cultivate a sense of community, safety, and comfort in your class.	7, 9, 15, and 10
4.	Teach inclusively; involve as many students as possible in ways in which they are comfortable.	8
5.	Enhance your instructor persona by projecting more enthusiasm, energy, relaxed self-confidence, authority, and in-command leadership—qualities that will stimulate students' interest in the material and maintain their respectful attention; balance authority and approachability.	9, 11, 14, 15, and 21
6.	Give students choices and control when possible.	9
7.	Explain why you teach and assess the way you do, emphasizing the evidence-based learning benefits to students; also explain why you focus on the content that you do, emphasizing its relevance for work and life in general.	9
8.	Vary your teaching and assessment activities and assignments, and avoid doing any one thing for too long.	9 and 22
9.	Help students see how much they are learning by providing plenty of feedback and having them reflect and write about their newly acquired or improved skills.	19 and 23
10.	Solicit feedback (at least some of it anonymous) from students on how well they think they are learning in the class and what can be improved; thank them and fine-tune your course accordingly, or explain why you will not make a requested change.	9, 19, and 23
11.	Explain how important student ratings and comments are to your institution and to you personally.	27

from them. However, some of these do require a bit of your time outside class or during class. One particularly challenging area is grading. Grading more leniently would probably increase your ratings, but in good conscience, we can only advise you to grade similarly to your colleagues and in a way that feels appropriate to you. As the findings are mixed on how course rigor, challenge, and required effort affect ratings, we cannot give definitive advice. It is likely that your evaluations will decrease if you expect significantly more work or grade more harshly than anyone in your department. Do keep in mind, particularly if you are new to a department, that if you feel the entire department has standards that are too lax or overly stringent, it is possible that your standards are the ones on either extreme. There are few times that an absolute standard exists. One way to successfully introduce a bit more rigor is to explain to students the rewards the extra work will bring, what the work will enable your students to do, and how that work will help them grow (Geddes, 2014).

DOCUMENTING YOUR EFFECTIVENESS

Without exception, all scholars interested in student ratings, regardless of what they think about these ratings, recommend that you include other teaching-related data in your reviews as well (Arreola, 2007; Benton & Young, 2018; Seldin et al., 2010). Therefore, although your institution probably requires you to submit your student ratings, you should always provide additional evidence; the reviewers will usually look at whatever you supply. Regardless of the questions on the student evaluations of teaching forms, there are things students are in no position to answer. For example, current students are in no position to judge your course content, whether you are knowledgeable in your discipline, the extent to which you are organized, if you teach at the appropriate level, or the longer-term impact of your teaching. Although submitting the materials described in this section cannot guarantee you a favorable review, they may make the academic reward system more responsive to your teaching achievements (Seldin et al., 2010).

Peer Evaluations of Teaching

Peers have the expertise to advise on and judge your course content, book selections, online resources, class activities, demonstrations, and the technical aspects of instructional design, such as the syllabus and assignments. In fact, a committee of your colleagues should evaluate your course documents, including assignments and exams, as part of every major review. When used for formative purposes, peer observations may provide feedback that can help you improve your teaching, especially your presentation skills.

Although peers can provide valuable perspectives, it is questionable whether peer observations should be included in a review. In some departments, politics can make peer reviews impossible. Another challenge is that the observers rarely have training in conducting an observation, nor are they instructional experts familiar with the wide range of best teaching practices. Some of them may not understand the more innovative methods and activities you are using in your classroom. To help make peer review effective, consider the following suggestions (Fletcher, 2018):

- Develop specific criteria and establish a good evaluation form that everyone will use. Items on the form should be more behavioral (what the instructor did) than subjective (students seemed motivated).
- Meet with the instructor beforehand to discuss teaching philosophy, preferred methods, characteristics of the course and students, and learning outcomes for the course and the specific class session.
- Sessions to be observed should be agreed to in advance.
- Agree that everything about the visitation is kept confidential and shared only as needed. Any information learned or strategies used will not be used by the observer without permission of the instructor.
- The observer should not participate in the class session, and students should be told of the reason for the visit.

Peer review systems have been used in industry for many years. When well-structured, peer evaluations can yield important information.

The Teaching Philosophy

This one- to two-page single-spaced statement is often a required part of an academic job application and faculty review materials, including a teaching portfolio. It does not document your teaching effectiveness as much as it shows you have reflected on your teaching and use presumably effective strategies. Following an essay format with an introduction and conclusion, it is a personal statement written in the first person and incorporating both cognitive and affective elements. It should explain your theory of how learning occurs and how teaching can foster it; the values, goals, or ideals that motivate you to teach; and the specific teaching methods you use, linking them to your learning theory or your motivating values, goals, or ideals, or both (Corrall, 2017; Johnston, 2003; Schönwetter et al., 2002).

If you can identify a key belief that is central to how you teach, you can generate a statement of your teaching philosophy just by answering these questions: What assumptions about teaching, learning, students, education, and the like underlie your key belief? What values, principles, goals, or ideals does it reflect or spring from? What teaching strategies logically flow from it? Your key belief should align with your assumptions, values and goals, and methods.

If you have trouble articulating key beliefs, a theory of teaching and learning, or your motivations for teaching, complete one or both of these free online teaching inventories: the Teaching Goals Inventory at https://tgi.its.uiowa.edu and the Teaching Perspectives Inventory (TPI) at http://www.teachingperspectives.com/tpi. In addition to finding out more about your own teaching identity, you will learn richly descriptive terms for various teaching aims and approaches that you can use in your statement.

If appropriate, two other topics belong in a teaching philosophy. First, you should at least mention any research on teaching you have done, even if you have not published it. If you have published it, refer your reader to the section of your curriculum vitae where you list it. Second, you should explain, if possible, any problematic student evaluations you have received in recent years. As mentioned earlier in this chapter, some students have been known to penalize instructors who stretch students' abilities, emphasize critical thinking, or use student-centered practices. If your evaluations have suffered for any of these reasons and you have continued to teach the way you do because you know it increases student learning, then state this in your philosophy as an illustration of your strong educational principles.

Make your statement inviting. Do not try to cram in more text by covering all the available white space. Leave margins of at least 1 inch all around and use 11- or 12-point type. Write clearly, simply, and with conviction, and use transitions generously to shepherd your readers through the document. Once you have a good draft of your statement, appraise it against the teaching philosophy rubric in Table 27.2, and revise it to meet the specifications and qualities under "Excellent." If it is helpful to see examples of teaching philosophy statements, you may view (but not duplicate) examples from engineering, humanities, natural and physical sciences, and social sciences at: https://crlt.umich.edu/tstrategies/tstpum.

The Teaching Portfolio

This is a collection of materials that you assemble to highlight your major teaching strengths and achievements, comparable to your publications, grants, and scholarly honors in your research record (Seldin et al., 2010). It opens with a statement of around five pages where you furnish basic information about your teaching responsibilities: the courses you teach, your student learning outcomes, your approach to course design, your expectations for student progress, and your assessment strategies. The statement should also annotate and evaluate the content you selected for your portfolio, specifically explaining and justifying your criteria for assessing your teaching effectiveness.

Institutions that use teaching portfolios require different components and organization, so check first with your chair. For example, your institution may want you to integrate your teaching philosophy, 5-year teaching goals, self-evaluation, course updates and improvements, and teaching-related professional activities into your teaching statement. Or it may recommend you write your annotations a certain way. To ensure objectivity and cogency in selecting materials, prepare your portfolio in consultation with a trusted colleague, your department chair, or a teaching and learning center consultant.

Table 27.2   Rubric for Assessing and Revising a Statement of Teaching Philosophy

	Excellent	Needs Some Revision	Needs Considerable Revision	Needs a Complete Rewrite
Content; coverage of essential topics	Thoroughly and thoughtfully presents a theory of teaching and learning; teaching values, goals, and ideals; and compatible teaching methods.	Addresses the three essential topics but does so too briefly or superficially.	Fails to address one of the three essential topics.	Fails to address two of the three essential topics.
Balance of personal and professional	Well balanced; formal in tone but maintains the sense of "I."	Occasionally too informal or too impersonal.	Often lapses into an inappropriate informality or loses the sense of "I."	A personal stream of consciousness or a totally impersonal essay with no sense of "I."
Structure and organization	Essay is coherent with a clear introduction, a strong conclusion, and logical transitions between paragraphs and sentences.	Essay is generally coherent but lacks either a clear introduction or a strong conclusion. Has some logical transitions between paragraphs and sentences.	Essay lacks a coherent structure and organization. Some paragraphs seem out of place, unconnected to the surrounding text. Lacks either a strong introduction or a clear, strong conclusion. Has few logical transitions between paragraphs and sentences.	Essay is incoherent and unstructured. Lacks a clear introduction, a clear conclusion, and logical transitions between paragraphs and sentences.
Writing style and mechanics (grammar, punctuation, spelling, and sentence structure)	Writing is clear, concise, and smooth. It follows the rules of standard written English. Each sentence is connected to the ones before and after. Structure of sentences varies. Very few, if any, mechanical errors.	Writing follows rules of standard written English with few errors in sentence structure and syntax. Sentences are usually connected. Some minor mechanical errors.	Writing violates some rules of standard written English and is sometimes awkward and difficult to understand. Some sentences seem unconnected and out of place. Frequent mechanical errors.	Writing often violates rules of standard written English and is generally awkward and difficult to understand. Sentences are unconnected, monotonously structured, and full of mechanical errors.
Presentation and length	Neatly typed, single-spaced, 11- or 12-point type. Optimal length: one to one and a half pages, possibly two pages if very experienced.	A bit too long or too short.	Somewhat too long or too short.	Sloppy, double-spaced, type too small, cramped, or much too long or too short.

A subset of items from the following list is often found in a portfolio (Seldin et al., 2010):

- Your teaching philosophy
- Your teaching goals for the next 5 years (number of years may vary)
- A brief self-evaluation with your teaching improvement strategies and efforts, including the teaching and learning center services, workshops, and programs you have taken advantage of
- Descriptions of improvements and updates in your course assignments, materials, and activities
- A list of your teaching-related professional activities, such as instructional research (the scholarship of teaching and learning), publications, journal editing and reviewing, conference presentations, and invited teaching workshops. Include abstracts or reprints of your published research and summaries of your unpublished research in an appendix.
- Syllabi and other important course materials
- A list of students you have advised or supervised in research projects
- Teaching awards, honors, and other types of recognition, such as teaching committee appointments
- A recording of one of your class periods
- Student ratings and comments from all your courses

Ask whether your department or institution would like any of these testimonial-type materials to be included:

- Statements from peers or administrators who have observed your teaching
- Statements from colleagues at other institutions who have reviewed submitted materials demonstrating your teaching effectiveness
- Statements from peers who have reviewed your course materials
- Statements from peers on how well you have prepared your students for more advanced courses
- A statement from your chair or supervisor about your past and projected departmental contributions
- Statements from employers about graduates who studied a great deal with you
- Statements from service-learning clients on the impact of your students' projects
- Statements from your advisees and research mentees about how you have influenced them
- Statements and letters, solicited and unsolicited, from former students about your longer-term teaching impact

Finally, your reviewers may be interested in more data from and about your students:

- Student feedback that reflects improvement, perceived learning, or satisfaction—aside from student ratings and comments
- Samples of student work on graded assignments. Do include samples of varying quality with your feedback and your reasons for the grades you assigned.
- Surveys of student knowledge at the beginning and the end of a course
- Improvements in students' attitudes about the subject matter, as documented by final reflection or personal-growth essays or by attitudinal surveys you administer at the beginning and the end of the course
- Students' opinions of their success in achieving your learning outcomes (an extra student-ratings-form item if you can add one)
- A list of your successful mentees in the discipline
- A list of presentations and publications that include students as co-authors
- Information on how you have influenced students' postgraduate and career choices
- Students' scores on standardized tests, especially the sections of national and licensing exams that reflect your courses

You can see examples of high-quality teaching portfolios in Seldin et al. (2010) or at http://cft.van derbilt.edu/guides-sub-pages/teaching-portfolios, https://www.hawkeyecollege.edu/employees/teaching-and-learning-services/teaching-portfolio, and https://www.cmu.edu/teaching/resources/teachingportfolios.

Teaching portfolios, although important collections of career progressions, are tenuous reflections of student learning. Their contents vary, and no doubt faculty members put in whatever makes them look best. In addition, no clear guidelines exist for evaluating them, and they require a great deal of time from both the reviewee and the reviewers.

Measures of Student Learning in a Course

Standardized tests and student portfolios are used to measure student learning on the institutional, school, and program levels, but they do not transfer well to the course level. As mentioned earlier, course-specific standardized tests are very rarely available, and student portfolios are too cumbersome and time-consuming for colleagues and administrators to evaluate. A measure of learning in a course must be easy to determine and reduce to a single number; otherwise administrators will not use them in faculty reviews. If possible, an instrument should also do double-duty as a learning enhancement or major assessment that the instructor would normally give. (A longer version of this section appears in Nilson, 2013b.)

The instruments presented in Table 27.3 can meet these conditions and have all been used to measure learning for one purpose or another. They are classified by when the instructor collects the data—only at the end of the course or at the beginning and the end (pre- and posttest)—and whether the data tap learning directly or indirectly, where *indirectly* means as perceived by students. Recall from the section on student ratings that few students correctly perceive their own learning (Bowman, 2011; Johnson, 2003; Weinberg et al., 2009), although Sera and McPherson (2019) did find that students can get better at self-assessment with practice. In addition, Falchikov and Boud's (1989) meta-analysis of the student self-assessment literature tells us that students tend to rate their abilities more favorably than faculty members do, especially in non-STEM and introductory courses. Therefore, indirect

Table 27.3   Course-Level Measures of Student Learning Classified as End-of-Course Only or Pre- and Posttest and Direct or Indirect Measures

Type	Indirect Measure	Direct Measure
End-of-course only	Perceived Student Assessment of Learning Gains (SALG)	Capstone paper, journal entry, or essay final exam (integrative or targeted)
Pre- and posttest	Knowledge surveys (student self-confidence)	First-week writing (ungraded) and correction exercise as final exam
		First-week essays (ungraded) and value-added essay final exam
		First-week final exam (ungraded) and final exam

Source: Table adapted from Nilson, L. B. (2013a). Measuring student learning to document faculty teaching effectiveness. In J. E. Groccia & L. Cruz (Eds.), *To improve the academy: Vol. 32. Resources for faculty, instructional, and organizational development* (pp. 287–300). Jossey-Bass.

measures of learning are flawed. However, so are direct methods because the typical instruments used to assess learning (our exams and assignments) are not validated (Wieman, 2015).

End-of-Course-Only Indirect Measures

Here you ask students about their *perceived* learning gains. The best-known and most widely used instrument of this kind is the Student Assessment of Learning Gains (SALG) survey at http://www.salgsite.org. Students assess not only their learning gains—general, conceptual, skill, attitudinal, and integrative—but also how much the main course components—class activities, assessments, specific learning methods, laboratories, and resources provided—helped them achieve those gains. Response options vary from "no gains" to "great gains" or from "no help" to "great help" on a 5-point scale. In validity tests of the current instrument, the student scores overall correlated moderately but significantly (r = .41) with student scores on the final exam. For unexplained reasons, the comparable correlations in specific topical areas ranged between .49 and 0.

You can easily adapt the questions to any course in any discipline, and SALG results have been submitted as evidence of student learning in faculty reviews. To obtain a single number, just average the scores on the relevant learning-gains items. The instrument also gives students a chance to reflect on what they have learned, which has value as a self-regulated learning activity.

Pre- and Posttest Direct Measures

For these measures you assess your students' course-related knowledge and skills at the beginning of the course and again at the end using the same or very similar assessment. For example, Griffiths (2010) gives her students an ungraded, in-class writing assignment the first week in her Miscarriage of Justice course. It emphasizes facts, terms, and processes they know little or nothing about. For the final, she places her students in the role of professor to critique and grade their first-week assignments. They correct their earlier errors, poor reasoning, and misconceptions, and then they answer the same questions again drawing on the course material. For another example, anthropology professor John ("Mike") Coggeshall (personal communication, 2010–2011) also gives his students an ungraded, in-class writing assignment the first week of class. He presents seven claims—some true, but mostly commonly believed myths (e.g., that the arrival of the Europeans was responsible for Native Americans developing complex societies)—and asks students to agree or disagree and explain why. For the final exam, he has them critique and rewrite four of their original answers, drawing their evidence from the course and explaining how and why their thinking has changed, if it has. He grades these *value-added* essays on the quality of the evidence students use to justify their end-of-course position, which reflects

his central ultimate learning outcome. For his faculty reviews, he reports the percentage of students who supported their positions with anthropological evidence, and all of his reviewers accept this figure as evidence of student learning.

A final option, one that works well for objective tests, is to give the final exam twice—first as an ungraded diagnostic test at the beginning of the course and later as the final. Give the diagnostic test in class—students will need little time to complete it (and tell them not to guess)—to prevent them from copying it, and don't let students take photos of the test with their phones. If you tell them after they complete the assignment that they took the final exam, they will try to remember all they can and watch for relevant material during the course. If you feel uncomfortable with this arrangement, use a previous final exam as the pretest if you have one that reflects the current content of your course. Also use a previous final exam if you teach online, as you do not want students downloading the current final.

Even though you do not grade the pretest, you do score it so you can calculate your students' learning gains during your course. One way to obtain a meaningful measure of student learning is by calculating the *average normalized gain*, which is that ratio of the *actual* average learning gain (posttest minus pretest) to the *possible* learning gain in the course (100 in the posttest minus the pretest) (Hake, 1998). This tells how much the students learned of all that they *could* have learned in the course:

$$\frac{\left(\text{Average posttest \%} - \text{Average pretest \%}\right)}{\left(100\% - \text{Average pretest \%}\right)} \times 100$$

If students' average score was 20% on the pretest and 75% on the final, the students learned 68.75% of the knowledge and skills that they *could* have learned in the course:

$$\frac{\left(75 - 20\right)}{\left(100 - 20\right)} \times 100 = \frac{55}{80} \times 100 = .6875 \times 100 = 68.75$$

The Teaching Practices Inventory (TPI)

The newest measure of teaching effectiveness is an inventory of teaching practices that research documents as highly effective in promoting student learning. Wieman and Gilbert (2014) developed the science and mathematics inventory and in 2018 developed a natural and social sciences version. It accommodates most face-to-face classes (not seminars, instructional labs, or project-based classes) in most disciplines (perhaps not the humanities) (Wieman, 2015). It was extensively tested on instructors and reviewed by many faculty members and experts. For the most part, the TPI asks instructors to check a box if they use a certain practice in their course (form in Wieman & Gilbert, 2014). The resulting teaching practices fall into eight categories:

1. Course information provided to students
2. Supporting materials provided
3. In-class activities (whole class and small group), demonstrations, simulations, and videos
4. Homework assignments
5. Feedback, testing, and grading policies
6. Other (e.g., diagnostics, new methods, assessments, and student reflections and choice)
7. Training and supervision of teaching assistants (TAs)
8. Collaboration/sharing with other faculty members and use of teaching and learning literature

Although the form takes just 10 minutes to complete, a colleague should review the course documents and observe one or (preferably) more classes to corroborate the instructor's responses. This colleague should receive training in the classroom observation protocol (Smith et al., 2013).

The TPI is an indirect measure that measures the means or methods of good teaching in an attempt to measure the goal of good teaching, which is student learning. It's possible that an instructor who uses good teaching methods can still implement them poorly or fail to relate well to students.

Choosing Among Alternatives

Every method we use to document teaching effectiveness has strengths and weaknesses. As noted multiple times, it is best practice to use more than one method, particularly when the end goal is related to evaluating for promotion, tenure, and reappointment decisions or large teaching awards.

■ A COMPREHENSIVE FACULTY EVALUATION SYSTEM

The key, and the challenge, to instituting any comprehensive faculty evaluation system is forging a departmental (or college) consensus on appropriate faculty activities, their relative value, the relative value of their components, and the relative value of their information sources. The decision-making process is all about publicly articulating values. Arreola's (2007) system, now used in whole or in part at hundreds of North American institutions, includes detailed, step-by-step guidelines for implementing faculty evaluation on a comprehensive scale, starting with these departmental decisions:

Step 1. Determine and list all the faculty activities worth evaluating at your institution: research, teaching, advising, community service, professional service, university service, and so on.

Step 2. Weight the importance of each activity in percentages that add up to 100%.

Step 3. Define each activity as a list of components—that is, observable or documentable products, performances, and achievements. For example, a department may agree to define teaching in terms of content expertise, instructional design skills, instructional delivery skills, impact on student learning, and course management.

Step 4. Operationalize each component—that is, break it down into measurable chunks. For example, a faculty member may break down content expertise into content currency, importance, and balance (more examples later).

Step 5. Weight the components of each role, again in percentages.

Step 6. Determine the best sources of evaluation information—for example, students, department peers, outside peers in specialized areas, the department chair, or someone else.

Step 7. Weight each information source by its appropriate worth. (A spreadsheet can do all the arithmetic required in steps 2, 4, and 6.)

Step 8. Determine how to gather the information from each source, such as by using forms or questionnaires.

Step 9. Select or design the appropriate policies, procedures, protocols, and forms for your system. Model forms are available in Chism (2007) and Arreola (2007).

Once the department sets the parameters and implements the system, each faculty member under review ends up with a composite rating, usually between 1.0 and 4.0 or between 1.0 and 5.0, that represents the collective judgment of that individual's performance in each faculty role (one for research, one for teaching, and so on). These numbers are weighted (as in Step 2) and added to create an overall composite rating, which is then compared against the evaluative standards set by the top-level administration. Therefore, faculty members are not compared against one another but against an absolute standard. In a 1.0-to-4.0 system where 1.0 denotes "unsatisfactory" and 4.0 means "exemplary" or "exceptional," 3.0 may designate the "acceptable" level. This system easily adapts to any review: reappointment, tenure, promotions, raises, and posttenure.

Steps 4 through 8 deserve clarification with an extended example. In Step 4, content expertise

was operationalized as currency, importance, and balance. Let's look at how the other components of teaching effectiveness suggested in Step 3 might be operationalized.

- Instructional Design Skills
  - Comprehensive syllabus
  - Well-organized course
  - Attainable, assessable student learning outcomes
  - Activities and assignments that help students achieve outcomes
  - Assessment instruments that measure students' achievement of outcomes
- Instructional Delivery Skills
  - Well-organized classes (activities, demonstrations, presentations)
  - Sufficient student activity/engagement
  - Enthusiasm, creation of student interest
  - Clear communication (explanations)
  - Good public speaking skills
- Impact on Student Learning
  - Tests and assignments challenging? (student perceptions)
  - Learning outcomes met? (student perceptions)
  - Want to learn more about the subject? (student perceptions)
  - Perceived learning gains (student perceptions)
  - Preparation for later courses
  - Pre- to postcourse learning gains
- Course Management
  - Course paperwork processed on time
  - Books and other course materials available on time
  - Field trips well planned
  - Grades submitted on time
  - Other policies and procedures followed

To continue with this example, these components might be weighted by percentages and the best assessors of the operationalized components determined, as shown here:

Content expertise	15%	Department peers
Instructional design	30%	Students and department peers
Instructional delivery	20%	Students and department peers
Learning impact	30%	Students for "perceived"; department peers and faculty reviewee for "actual"
Course management	5%	Department chair
	100%	

Then the judgments of the assessors would be weighted proportionally and the assessment data specified, as this example shows:

Content expertise	15%	Department peers	1.00	Syllabi reviewed, peer observations
Instructional design	30%	Students	0.50	Student ratings on design items
		Department peers	0.50	Syllabi, activities and assignments, and graded work and tests reviewed
Instructional delivery	20%	Students	0.75	Student ratings on delivery items
		Department peers	0.25	Peer observations
Learning impact	30%	Students	0.25	Perceived learning gains items
		Department peers	0.50	Graded work and tests reviewed; peers' experience with students
		Reviewee	0.25	Pre- to postcourse learning gains
Course management	5%	Department chair	1.00	Chair's records

The final worksheet for evaluating a faculty member's teaching effectiveness might look something like this:

Content expertise	15%	Peers	1.00	$4 \times 0.15 \times 1 = 0.60$
Instructional design	30%	Students	0.50	$3 \times 0.3 \times 0.50 = 0.45$
		Peers	0.50	$3 \times 0.3 \times 0.50 = 0.45$
Instructional delivery	20%	Students	0.75	$3 \times 0.2 \times 0.75 = 0.45$
		Peers	0.25	$2 \times 0.2 \times 0.25 = 0.10$
Learning impact	30%	Students	0.25	$3 \times 0.3 \times 0.25 = 0.23$
		Peers	0.50	$4 \times 0.3 \times 0.50 = 0.60$
		Reviewee	0.25	$4 \times 0.3 \times 0.25 = 0.30$
Course management	5%	Chair	1.00	$2 \times 0.05 \times 1 = 0.10$
Composite rating for teaching				*3.28*

To review, the first column on the far left is the component of the teaching role; the next columns, the percentage weight of that component, then the best assessing parties, and then the proportional weight of the judgment of each assessing party. The next column, which shows numbers from 2 to 4 in bold, designates the rating the faculty member received from each assessing party on the 1.0-to-4.0 scale, where 1.0 denotes "unsatisfactory" and 4.0, "exemplary" or "exceptional." The number is multiplied by the weight of the component, then by the weight of the assessing party. Finally, the numbers in the far right column are summed to obtain the overall composite rating. In this example, the faculty member under review achieves a 3.28, which exceeds the acceptable level of 3.0.

Some academics have complained that such a step-by-step system undermines professional and administrative judgment, but all it really does is eliminate a review party's discretion to say one thing and do another—for example, to claim to value teaching and service but to decide the fate of faculty careers solely on the research record. By demanding integrity and making the review process transparent, such a system can only benefit those who value, practice, and document teaching at its best.

COMPLEX AND ESSENTIAL

It is challenging to document student learning. That makes it extremely difficult to determine how well an individual brings about learning in others. And that is just in the cognitive domain. In addition, learning involves an array of outcomes in areas of affective, social, ethical, and psychomotor—and standardized tests cannot possibly tap them all. Even with all these areas, there is more. Faculty members must manage the interpersonal interactions of a group. It is a lot. We have to rely on subjective qualitative information like a teaching philosophy or teaching portfolio, quantitative measures with known flaws such as measures of learning in a course, student ratings, or the TPI.

What instrument, what assembly of data could possibly capture this elusive, multilayered, multifaceted transaction in which one individual tries to induce other individuals to process new knowledge, acquire new skills, work well together, and change their thinking in the process? It is one of the largest challenges in all of higher education. But it is also critical that we keep striving to create the best system of evaluation possible. Defining what is meant by effective teaching and then evaluating it in a clear and consistent manner is at the heart of diversity, equity, and inclusion for faculty members. It is challenging to guard against the many implicit stereotypes and biases pertaining to race, gender, and age. A well-designed, comprehensive, and transparent faculty evaluation system guides faculty members who are unfamiliar with expected outcomes. This is particularly important when first-generation college students, who are often from underrepresented groups, become faculty members. The evaluation system not only documents performance but also illuminates the path to success. An added bonus is that with clear and consistent documentation, it is glaringly obviously when there is not equity with respect to pay, promotion, reappointment, and teaching awards. Most importantly, a clear evaluation system provides feedback and opportunity for reflection that helps faculty members to be exceptional teachers, and it also allows a system to recognize those who are successful in helping students to be successful in their educational pursuits.

REFLECTION QUESTIONS

Reflection Question 27.1: What are three specific areas in which you think students can legitimately evaluate your teaching effectiveness? In what three areas can students *not* evaluate your effectiveness? Explain.

Reflection Question 27.2: Is it ethical to change behavior with a goal of increasing student ratings of teaching effectiveness? Explain, giving two or three examples.

Concept Into Practice: Draft a teaching philosophy statement. If you already have one, edit it based on what you have learned from this chapter.

Support Resources at Your Institution

Each college and university is a large, multilayered organization—a few rival cities in size and complexity—each with its own unique subculture, norms, and values, official power structures, informal power networks, and infrastructure of services and support units. Even seasoned faculty members in a new institution feel unsettled as they anticipate unfamiliar policies, forms, procedures, expectations, and types of students. Teaching at its best means recognizing when we need help and knowing where to find it. Throughout your campus are experts who can assist your students with just about any issue that arises (Zakrajsek, 2014, 2015). All you need to know is where the expertise is located.

Most colleges and universities offer a wealth of instructional support services and resources—the library and computer services being among the most obvious. But the institutional help available from some individuals and units may not be obvious from their titles or names alone. In some cases, you may not even think to look for such resources. The people and campus offices described in this Appendix are well worth your getting to know. The

referral services they provide can save you countless hours, and the information they furnish can prevent costly, however innocent, mistakes.

▮ FOR FACULTY, STAFF, AND STUDENTS

Colleagues, especially senior ones, are perhaps the most conveniently located and sometimes the most knowledgeable sources of information on discipline-specific issues. Colleagues also know how best to teach certain material, what to expect of students in specific courses, how to motivate students in a given subject, how to locate appropriate guest speakers, how to prepare for tenure and other faculty reviews, how to obtain special services or funding, and what assistance to request from department support staff. Colleagues are also excellent sources of informal feedback on teaching; most will be happy to serve as a classroom observer or reviewer of a recorded class. (Also see the "teaching and learning center" later.) If there is any area in which you feel you feel uncertain, there is a colleague who may well be able to assist. Examples include grading papers (English); giving individual students bad news (clinical psychology); groupwork (business); difficult dialogues (religion); grading presentations (speech communication); and preparing excellent conference presentations (visual arts).

Department chairs can offer broader, departmental perspectives on discipline-specific issues. They are especially well informed on departmental curriculum matters and can advise you on proposals to develop new courses and revise established ones. They may also provide the best counsel on standards and procedures for promotion and tenure. Because they have the opportunity to study the student evaluations of all the courses and sections in the department, they can help interpret your student ratings and written comments as well as suggest ways to improve them. Finally, your department chair may be the best person to help you with classroom logistics—for example, if the classroom you are assigned doesn't meet your class size, ventilation, or technological needs, or if you need a room reserved for special class activities and sessions. In large universities, departments may control a set of classrooms and handle such matters.

The *dean's office* of your college, school, or division can advise you about promotion and tenure matters, student characteristics, curriculum issues, and course design and development from a still broader perspective. Demographic and academic data about the student body will prove particularly valuable in helping you decide on the objectives, outcomes, design, and content for each of your courses. You will also need information about curriculum policies and procedures: What general education or breadth requirements do your courses satisfy? What percentage of students will enroll in a particular course because they are required to take it? How do you propose and get approval for a new course? What components and assignments must a course have to qualify for *honors*, *writing*, or any other special designation?

The *library* is no longer just a place to find books. Having adapted to the technological age in record time, libraries have expanded into one-stop shops for electronic information, as well as print resources, and librarians have evolved into the sentinels of information literacy. They can help you and your students develop papers, providing easy access to an impressive range of academic search engines, indexes, and databases, such as Academic OneFile, LexisNexis, InfoTrac, OneSearch, Ingenta, Web of Science, and EBSCO Host, which allow you to find scholarly publications by subject, author, publication type, and other criteria. These resources can help your students broaden their research horizons beyond Google, and librarians will teach your class how to use them for the assignments you have in mind. Beyond print and electronic resources, libraries also typically maintain a collection of instructionally useful videos, CDs, and DVDs.

A *teaching and learning, faculty development*, or *instructional development center* has become an increasingly common resource on research as well as teaching-oriented campuses. These centers provide an incredibly wide variety of services. Our advice is that if you have a center like this, make it a point to check out their website and drop by in person to see what they have to offer.

A *center for academic computing, information technology*, or *instructional technology* is the most likely unit to handle the faculty members', as well as students' and staff members', computing needs, from setting up email accounts to replacing old terminals. Its major functions are client support in both hardware and software and training workshops in commonly used office, technical, and instructional software. This support usually includes buying the software and licenses and installing the software on request. Almost all campuses have some brand of learning management systems, such as Blackboard and Canvas. These centers also transformed most traditional classrooms into smart classrooms equipped with software-rich computer terminals or laptop stations, LCD projectors, and DVD players. Scheduling, maintaining, and updating these classrooms are a full-time job.

Centers vary in how much instructional design they do for faculty members who are teaching wholly or partly online. On one extreme, some universities expect instructors to learn the necessary software for website design, animation, photo and video digitizing and editing, and so forth in specialized workshops and on their own. On the other extreme are the institutions that employ instructional designers and technologists to do much of the materials development and all the technical work.

A *women's center* typically leads efforts related to women and gender equity. Valuing community, relationships, and connections, such centers typically provide female-identifying–focused lecture series, libraries, support groups, along with many other events and resources. No doubt, it offers legal and policy information about sexual harassment as well as emotional support for those who may have a complaint. However, complaints are probably processed by the "equal opportunity" unit described later.

A *multicultural center; racial/ethnic cultural center; or diversity, equity, and inclusion (DEI) office* is sure to be a rich institutional resource—and an essential one on today's highly diverse campuses. They usually offer symposia and lectures on cultural topics and coordinate multicultural celebrations and commemorations. Many maintain libraries of print materials and videos—most valuable if you are teaching multicultural subjects—and a few sponsor art exhibits and musical performances. They may also provide support services for students of colors.

Of particular value to faculty members and staff members are their cultural awareness programs, including diversity training workshops. These centers can also answer your private questions about the minority student population on your campus and cultural differences among various groups. They will help you resolve any concerns about relating to students of color in the classroom.

An *international center* typically administers study abroad and international internship programs and sets up new ones to meet the demands of a rapidly changing world economy. For example, many universities have recently added programs in China, Southeast Asia, the Middle East, and India. Often in conjunction with an area studies center, this kind of unit may also equip students and faculty members traveling abroad with some basic global competencies, such as information on the social and cultural differences between Americans and natives of the host country. In addition, the center provides acculturation counseling and support for international students and their families, as well as legal advice on visas, work permits, taxes, and so on. On some campuses, the international center is also responsible for ESL (English as a Second Language) or ESOL (English for Speakers of Other Languages) testing and courses.

An *equal opportunity center* may go by any number of names, but you should look for key words such as *opportunity development, affirmative action, access, equality, equity, Title IX Office,* or *civil rights*. Its purpose is to coordinate state and federally mandated programs designed to ensure equal opportunities for minorities, women, individuals with disabilities, and other disadvantaged groups. It also serves as a source of information for students, faculty members, and staff members who may have questions or complaints related to equal opportunity in education, employment, and campus programs and activities. If a complaint is judged valid, it will also advise on grievance procedures.

Sexual harassment falls under the equal opportunity umbrella. Often in collaboration with a women's center (see earlier), an equal opportunity office disseminates information on the legal definition of sexual harassment, the institution's policy regarding it, specific types of harassment behavior, its prevalence, its prevention, procedures for filing a complaint or a grievance, and confidential support and counseling services. The website for the US Department of Education Title IX and Sex Discrimination information can be found at: https://www2.ed.gov/about/offices/list/ocr/docs/tix_dis.html.

A *disabilities services center* issues written certifications of students' learning and physical disabilities for instructors, although they probably do not conduct tests for these disabilities. As required by the

Americans with Disabilities Act (ADA) of 1990, this type of center ensures that people with disabilities have equal access to public programs and services. Therefore, it also recommends the special accommodations, if any, that instructors should make for identified students in their teaching and testing.

Most accommodations are minor (e.g., an isolated test environment, a longer test period), and the center may provide special facilities for them (e.g., proctored testing rooms). In any case, the center will advise you about exactly what accommodations are needed. For the hearing-impaired classroom student, you may have to stand or sit where the student can lip-read. For a visually impaired classroom student, you may have to vocalize or verbally describe any visual materials you present or distribute to the class. Appropriate testing may require you to make a large-print copy of the exam or allow the students use of a reader, scribe, or computer during the test. Note, it is best to provide an accommodation to an individual *only* if it has been officially sanctioned by your institution.

Online learning demands more extensive adaptations, although sometimes the student's own specialized computer hardware and software will take care of access. Still, instructors must be mindful to keep websites uncluttered and to provide captions or transcripts for audio materials and text alternatives for visual materials. Instructional designers can best advise on online course-accessibility issues.

Campus tech stores. The convenience of an on-campus location, student-centered software, on-site technology experts, laptop repair, *and* special discounts? The campus tech store should be your students' first stop any time they need a new program or device during their years of study. Even if students don't plan to use what they buy specifically for school (e.g., a snack, a notebook for personal journaling, a new bag), the student discount still applies.

■ JUST FOR STUDENTS

The centers previously described may serve your own or your students' needs. Let's consider now the units and individuals who specialize in serving students.

Students seeking general academic counsel should be referred to their academic advisers; those requesting information or assistance with respect to a specific course should be sent to the instructor or the department. At times, however, students need help with other problems, some that most instructors are ill-equipped to address. These include learning disabilities, math or test anxiety, severe writing problems, poor study and test-taking skills, weak academic backgrounds, emotional difficulties, and career planning questions. These cases call for a referral to a unit in the next group.

Almost all campuses have a facility designed to help students improve their academic skills. It is often called a *learning, learning skills, learning resources, academic assistance, academic support,* or *academic success center,* and its services typically include individual counseling in academic skills, individual and small group tutoring, and workshops in learning strategies, such as reading skills, study skills, note-taking, test preparation, and test taking. Some tutoring may be geared to specific courses or subject matter that are known to give students trouble, such as calculus, chemistry, physics, biology, economics, and foreign languages. This type of center may also offer ESL testing and courses.

A *writing* or *communication program* may be housed in a learning center or comprise its own stand-alone unit. It is likely to provide individual and small-group tutoring in the mechanics of grammar and punctuation as well as the structure of exam essays, short papers, critical papers, and research papers. It may even schedule formal writing workshops. Staff members are trained not to outline or edit student work, but rather to show students how to master the stages of the writing process on their own. If "communication" is in the title, the unit may also help students improve their public speaking and presentation skills.

A *psychological* or *counseling center* is the place to refer students who manifest any type of psychological or emotional disorder. It gives free individual counseling for psychological, emotional, and sometimes academic problems, and it may coordinate group programs for personal growth, self-improvement, and self-awareness. If it is associated with a medical facility or it has a physician on staff, it may also prescribe drugs and administer shots.

A *career center* helps students identify and achieve their occupational goals. It typically provides assessment tests in skills and interests and resources for career exploration as well as information on internship opportunities and summer jobs. Workshops on job search strategies, résumé preparation, communication and decision-making skills, and job interview techniques may also be available. Some centers hold campus job fairs and help graduates obtain jobs.

International Student Registry Card. If your students haven't purchased an International Student Registry Card (ISIC) yet, encourage them to do so immediately. Depending on the issuing institution, it will cost $4 to 25. This card allows student status to be recognized in more than 130 countries and affords them student discounts on everything from public transport across Europe to museum entrance fees to late-night pizza orders.

Professor office hours. Some students think that office hours are the hours you are working in your office and should not be interrupted. Be certain students know when you are available and the types of things you will assist them with during those times. Also note what you will not do during office hours, such as repeat an entire class session if the student is unable to attend class.

Due to space, not all possible resources have been listed. A few additional places your students may find helpful include: Veterans Office, Campus Ministries, First-Generation Student Center, Wellness and Fitness Center, Private Study Rooms, Computer Labs, Food Pantry, and Safety Programs (walk-safe escorts and free shuttles).

• • •

Our best advice is for you to get into the habit of assuming there is assistance on campus for anything you can imagine. Search the internet, chat with a senior colleague, or even check with the office professional in the provost office. (They know pretty much everything.) If your campus does not have something, there may be web-based information at another institution.

REFERENCES

Aalderink, S. (October 30, 2019). Active learning spaces: Lessons learned in the United States. *Educause Review.* https://er.educause.edu/blogs/2019/10/active-learning-spaces-lessons-learned-in-the-united-states

Abraham, A. E., Busch, C. A., Brownell, S. E., & Cooper, K.M. (2022). Instructor perceptions of student incivility in the online undergraduate science classroom. *Journal of Microbiology & Biology Education, 23*(1), e00271-21. https://doi.org/10.1128/jmbe.00271-21

Abrami, P. C., Bernard, R. M., Borokhovski, E., Wade, A., Surkes, M. A., Tamim, R., & Zhang, D. (2008). Instructional interventions affecting critical thinking skills and dispositions: A stage 1 meta-analysis. *Review of Educational Research, 78*(4), 1102–1134. https://doi.org/10.3102/0034654308326084

Abrami, P. C., Bernard, R. M., Borokhovski, E., Waddington, D. I., Wade, C. A., & Persson, T. (2015). Strategies for teaching students to think critically: A meta-analysis. *Review of Educational Research, 85*(2), 275–314. https://doi.org/10.3102/0034654314551063

Academic Success Center, Iowa State University, (2011). *Exam prep: Test autopsy.* https://www.asc.dso.iastate.edu/files/documents//Exam%20Prep--Test%20Autopsy.pdf

Achacoso, M. V. (2004). Post-test analysis: A tool for developing students' metacognitive awareness and self-regulation. In M. V. Achacoso & M. D. Svinicki (Eds.), *New directions for teaching and learning, No. 100: Alternative strategies for evaluating student learning* (pp. 115–119). Jossey-Bass.

Adams, S. (2021, January 28). This $12 billion company is getting rich off students cheating their way through COVID. *Forbes.* https://www.forbes.com/sites/susanadams/2021/01/28/this-12-billion-company-is-getting-rich-off-students-cheating-their-way-through-covid/?sh=6ef5f064363f

Addy, T. M., Dube, D., Mitchell, K.A., & SoRelle, M. (2021). *What inclusive instructors do: Principles and practices for excellence in college teaching.* Stylus.

Adelman, C. (2015). *To imagine a verb: The language and syntax of learning outcomes statements.* National Institute for Learning Outcomes Assessment, Occasional Paper 24. http://learningoutcomesassessment.org/documents/Occasional_Paper_24.pdf

Agarwal, P. K., Nunes, L. D., & Blunt, J. R. (2021). Retrieval practice consistently benefits student learning: A systematic review of applied research in schools and classrooms. *Educational Psychology Review, 33*(4), 1409–1453. https://doi.org/10.1007/s10648-021-09595-9

Albanese, M. A., & Dast, L. (2014). Problem-based learning: Outcomes evidence from the health professions. *Journal of Excellence in College Teaching, 25*(3&4), 239–252. https://eric.ed.gov/?id=EJ1041364

Alberts, H. C., Hazen, H. D., & Theobald, R. B. (2010). Classroom incivilities: The challenge of interactions

355

between college students and instructors in the U.S. *Journal of Geography in Higher Education, 34*(3), 439–462. https://doi.org/10.1080/03098260903502679

Alexander, B., Ashford-Rowe, K., Barajas-Murphy, N., Dobbin, G., Knott, J., McCormack, M., Pomerantz, J., Seilhamer, R., & Weber, N. (2019). *Educause Horizon Report: 2019 higher education edition.* https://library.educause.edu/~/media/files/library/2019/4/2019horizonreport.pdf

Allen, M., Witt, P. L., & Wheeless, L. R. (2006). The role of teacher immediacy as a motivational factor in student learning: Using a meta-analysis to test a causal model. *Communication Education, 55*(1), 21–31. https://doi.org/10.1080/03634520500343368

Allen, R. D. (1981). Intellectual development and the understanding of science: Applications of William Perry's theory to science teaching. *Journal of College Science Teaching, 10,* 94–97.

Allen, W., Epps, E., & Haniff, N. (1991). *College in Black and White: African American students in predominantly White and historically Black public universities.* SUNY Press.

Allwardt, D. (2009, April). *Using wikis for collaborative writing assignments: Best practices and fair warnings.* Poster session presented at the Third Annual Innovations in Teaching Forum, Western Illinois University, Macomb.

Aloni, M., & Harrington, C. (2018). Research-based practices for improving the effectiveness of asynchronous online discussion boards. *Scholarship of Teaching and Learning in Psychology, 4*(4), 271–289. https://doi.org/10.1037/stl0000121

Amador, J. A., Miles, L., & Peters, C. B. (2006). *The practice of problem-based learning: A guide to implementing PBL in the college classroom.* Jossey-Bass/Anker.

Ambrose, S. A., Bridges, M. W., DiPietro, M., Lovett, M. C., & Norman, M. K. (2010). *How learning works: Seven research-based principles for smart teaching.* Jossey-Bass.

Anderman, L., Freeman, T., & Mueller, C. (2007). The "social" side of social context: Interpersonal and affiliative dimensions of students' experiences and academic dishonesty. In E. Anderman & T. Murdock (Eds.), *Psychology of academic cheating* (pp. 203–228). Elsevier.

Anderson, J. A., & Adams, M. (1992). Acknowledging the learning styles of diverse populations: Implications for instructional design. In L. Border & N. V. N. Chism (Eds.), *New directions for teaching and learning: No. 49. Teaching for diversity* (pp. 19–33). Jossey-Bass.

Anderson, L. W., & Krathwohl, D. R. (2000). *A taxonomy for learning, teaching, and assessment: A revision of Bloom's taxonomy of educational objectives.* Longman.

Angelo, T. A. (1991a). Introduction and overview: From classroom assessment to classroom research. In T. A. Angelo (Ed.), *New directions for teaching and learning: No. 46. Classroom research: Early lessons from success* (pp. 7–15). Jossey-Bass.

Angelo, T. A. (1991b). Ten easy pieces: Assessing higher learning in four dimensions. In T. A. Angelo (Ed.), *New directions for teaching and learning: No. 46. Classroom research: Early lessons from success* (pp. 17–31). Jossey-Bass.

Angelo, T. A., & Cross, K. P. (1993). *Classroom assessment techniques: A handbook for college teachers* (2nd ed.). Jossey-Bass.

Archer-Kuhn, B., Lee, Y., Finnessey, S., & Liu, J. (2020). Inquiry-based learning as a facilitator to student engagement in undergraduate and graduate social work programs. *Teaching & Learning Inquiry, 8*(1), 187–207. https://doi.org/10.20343/teachlearninqu.8.1.13

Arif, S., Massey, M., Klinard, N., Charbonneau, J., Jabre, L., Martins, A. B., Gaitor, D., Kirton, R., Albury, C., & Nanglu, K. (2021). Ten simple rules for supporting historically underrepresented students in science. *PLoS Computational Biology, 17*(9), e1009313. https://doi.org/10.1371/journal.pcbi.1009313

Arizona State University. (2015). *Introducing faculty office hours: Arizona State University (ASU).* YouTube. https://www.youtube.com/watch?v=yQq1-_ujXrM

Arocha, J. F., & Patel, V. L. (1995). Novice diagnostic reasoning in medicine: Accounting of clinical evidence. *Journal of the Learning Sciences, 4,* 355–384. https://www.jstor.org/stable/1466784

Arons, A. B. (1993). Guiding insight and inquiry in the introductory physics lab. *Physics Teacher, 31*(5), 278–282. https://doi.org/10.1119/1.2343763

Arreola, R. A. (2007). *Developing a comprehensive faculty evaluation system: A guide to designing, building, and operating large-scale faculty evaluations systems* (3rd ed.). Jossey-Bass/Anker.

Arum, R., & Roksa, J. (2011). *Academically adrift: Limited learning on college campuses.* University of Chicago Press.

Aslanian, C. B. (2001). *Adult students today.* College Board.

Astin, A. W., Vogelgesang, L. J., Ikeda, E. K., & Yee, J. A. (2000). *How service learning affects students.* Higher Education Research Institute.

Atkinson, R. C., & Shiffrin, R. M. (1968). Human memory: A proposed system and its control processes. In K. W. Spence & J. T. Spence (Eds.)., *The psychology of learning and motivation* (Vol. 2, pp. 89–195). Academic Press. https://doi.org/10.1016/S0079-7421(08)60422-3

Aulls, M. W. (2002). The contributions of co-occurring forms of classroom discourse and academic activities to curriculum events and instruction. *Journal of Educational Psychology, 94*(3), 520–538. https://doi.org/10.1037/0022-0663.94.3.520

Ausubel, D. (1968). *Educational psychology: A cognitive view.* Holt.

Badia, G. (2019). Holistic or analytic rubrics? Grading information literacy instruction. *College & Undergraduate Libraries, 26*(2), 109–116. https://doi.org/10.1080/10691316.2019.1638081

Bader, M., Burner, T., Iversen, S. H., & Varga, Z. (2019). Student perspectives on formative feedback as part of writing portfolios. *Assessment & Evaluation in Higher Education, 44*(7), 1017–1028. https://doi.org/10.1080/02602938.2018.1564811

Baddeley, A. (2012). Working memory: Theories, models, and controversies. *Annual Review of Psychology, 63*(1), 1–29. https://doi.org/10.1146/annurev-psych-120710-100422

Baglama, B., Yucesoy, Y., Uzunboylu, H., & Özcan, D. (2017). Can infographics facilitate the learning of individuals with mathematical learning difficulties? *International Journal of Cognitive Research in Science, Engineering and Education, 5*(2), 119–128. https://doi.org/10.5937/IJCRSEE1702119B

Bajak, A. (2014). Lectures aren't just boring, they're ineffective, too, study finds. *Science.* https://www.science.org/content/article/lectures-arent-just-boring-theyre-ineffective-too-study-finds

Ballard, M. (2007). Drawing and questioning the syllabus. *National Teaching and Learning Forum, 16*(5), 5–6.

Ballen, C. J., Salehi, S., & Cotner, S. (2017). Exams disadvantage women in introductory biology. *PLoS ONE, 12*:e0186419. https://doi.org/10.1371/journal.pone.0186419

Ballen, C. J., Wieman, C., Salehi, S., Searle, J. B., & Zamudio, K. R. (2018). Enhancing diversity in undergraduate science: Self-efficacy drives performance gains with active learning. *CBE Life Sciences Education, 16*(4), ar56. https://doi.org/10.1187/cbe.16-12-0344

Barkley, E. F. (2009). *Student engagement techniques: A handbook for college faculty.* Jossey-Bass.

Barkley, E. F., & Major, C. H. (2018). *Interactive lecturing: A handbook for college faculty.* Jossey Bass/Wiley.

Barkley, E. F., & Major, C. H. (2022). *Engaged teaching: A handbook for college faculty.* K. Patricia Cross Academy.

Barkley, E. F., Major, C. H., & Cross, K. P. (2014). *Collaborative learning techniques: A handbook for faculty.* Jossey-Bass.

Barr, R. B., & Tagg, J. (1995). From teaching to learning—a new paradigm for undergraduate education. *Change: The Magazine of Higher Learning, 27*(6), 12–26, https://doi.org/ 10.1080/00091383.1995.10544672

Barrineau, N. W. (2001). Class preparation and summary note cards. *National Teaching and Learning Forum, 10*(4), 5–6.

Baumeister, R. F., & Vohs, K. D. (2018). Revisiting our reappraisal of the (surprisingly few) benefits of high self-esteem. *Perspectives on Psychological Science, 13*(2), 137–140. https://doi.org/10.1177/1745691617701185

Baugh, N. G., & Mellott, K. G. (1998). Clinical concept mapping as preparation for student nurses' clinical experiences. *Journal of Nursing Education, 37*(6), 253–256. https://doi.org/10.3928/0148-4834-19980901-06

Baughin, J. A., Brod, E. F., & Page, D. L. (2002). Primary trait analysis: A tool for classroom-based assessment. *College Teaching, 50*(2), 75–80. https://doi.org/10.1080/87567550209595879

Baume, D., & Baume, C. (2008). *Powerful ideas in teaching and learning.* Oxford Brookes University.

Baxter Magolda, M. B. (1992). *Knowing and reasoning in college: Gender-related patterns in students' intellectual development.* Jossey-Bass.

Bean, J. C. (2011). *Engaging ideas: A professor's guide to integrating writing, critical thinking, and active learning in the classroom* (2nd ed.). Jossey-Bass.

Beatriz, M. (2021). Ungrading: Why rating students undermines learning (and what to do instead). *International Journal for Educational Integrity, 17*(1). https://doi.org/10.1007/s40979-021-00077-7

Beaudry, J., & Wilson, P. (2010). Concept mapping and formative assessment: Elements supporting literacy and learning. In P. L. Torres & C. V. Marriott (Eds.), *Handbook of research on collaborative learning using concept mapping* (pp. 449–473). Information Science Reference.

Beichner, R. J., Saul, J. M., Abbott, D. S., Morse, J. J., Deardorff, D. L., Allain, R. J., Bonham, S. W., Dancy, M. H., & Risley, J. S. (2007). *The student-centered activities for large enrollment undergraduate programs (SCALE-UP) project.* http://www.per-central.org/document/ServeFile.cfm?ID=4517&DocID=183

Belbin, R. M. (2004). *Team roles at work.* Elsevier.

Benander, R., Denton, J., Page, D., & Skinner, C. (2000). Primary trait analysis: Anchoring assessment in the classroom. *Journal of General Education, 49*(4), 280–302. https://doi.org/10.1353/jge.2000.0025

Benford, R., & Lawson, A. E. (2001). *Relationships between effective inquiry use and the development of scientific reasoning skills in college biology labs.* Report to the National Science Foundation (Grant DUE 9453610).

Benton, S. L., & Young, S. (2018). *Best practices in the evaluation of teaching.* IDEA Paper No. 69. https://www.ideaedu.org/Portals/0/Uploads/Documents/IDEA%20Papers/IDEA%20Papers/IDEA_Paper_69.pdf

Bergtrom, G. (2006). Clicker sets as learning objects. *Interdisciplinary Journal of Knowledge and Learning Objects, 2.* http://ijklo.org/Volume2/v2p105-110Bergtrom.pdf

Berry, M. J., & Westfall, A. (2015). Dial D for distraction: The making and breaking of cell phone policies in the college classroom. College *Teaching, 63*(2), 62–71.

Berry, P., Thornton, B., & Baker, R. (2006). Demographics of digital cheating: Who cheats, and what we can do about it. In M. Murray (Ed.), *Proceedings of the Ninth Annual Conference of the Southern Association for Information Systems* (pp. 82–87). Jacksonville University, Davis College of Business.

Berry, W. (2008). Surviving lecture: A pedagogical alternative. *College Teaching, 56*(3), 149–153. https://doi.org/10.3200/CTCH.56.3.149-153

Beyers, C. (2008). The hermeneutics of student evaluations. *College Teaching, 56*(2), 102–106. https://doi.org/10.3200/CTCH.56.2.102-106

Bicen, H., & Haidov, R. (2021). A content analysis on articles using twitter in education. *Postmodern Openings, 12*(1 Suppl), 19–34. https://doi.org/10.18662/po/12.1Sup1/269

Biggs, J. (2003). *Teaching for quality learning at university* (2nd ed.). Society for Research into Higher Education and Open University Press.

Biktimirov, E. N., & Nilson, L. B. (2007). Adding animation and interactivity to finance courses with learning objects. *Journal of Financial Education, 33,* 35–47. https://www.jstor.org/stable/41948559

Bjork, E. L., & Bjork, R. A. (2011). Making things hard on yourself, but in a good way: Creating desirable difficulties to enhance learning. In M. A. Gernsbacher & J. Pomerantz (Eds.), *Psychology and the real world: Essays illustrating fundamental contributions to society* (2nd ed., pp. 56–64). Worth.

Bjork, R. A. (1994). Memory and metamemory considerations in the training of human beings. In J. Metcalfe & A. Shimamura (Eds.), *Metacognition: Knowing about knowing* (pp. 185–205). MIT Press.

Bjork, R. A. (2013). Desirable difficulties perspective on learning. In H. Pashler (Ed.), *Encyclopedia of the mind.* Sage. https://bjorklab.psych.ucla.edu/wp-content/uploads/sites/13/2016/07/RBjork_inpress.pdf

Bjork, R. A., & Bjork, E. L. (2020). Desirable difficulties in theory and practice. *Journal of Applied Research in Memory and Cognition, 9*(4), 475–479. https://doi.org/10.1016/j.jarmac.2020.09.003

Black, S., & Allen, J. D. (2019). Part 8: Academic help seeking. *The Reference Librarian, 60*(1), 62–76. https://doi.org/10.1080/02763877.2018.1533910

Bligh, D. A. (2000). *What's the use of lectures?* Jossey-Bass.

Bloom, B. (1956). *Taxonomy of educational objectives: The classification of educational goals. Vol. 1: Cognitive domain.* McKay.

Blue, T. (2003, March 14). *"I don't know HOW to read this book!"* Irascible Professor. http://irascibleprofessor.com/comments-03-14-03.htm

Blum, S.D. (2020). *Ungrading: Why rating students undermines learning (and what to do instead).* West Virginia University Press.

Blumenfeld, P. C., Soloway, E., Marx, R. W., Krajcik, J. S., Guzdial, M., &, Palincsar, A. (1991). Motivating project-based learning: Sustaining the doing, supporting the learning. *Educational Psychologist, 26*(3-4), 369–398. https://doi.org/10.1080/00461520.1991.9653139

Boice, B. (1996). Classroom incivilities. *Research in Higher Education, 37,* 456–486. https://doi.org/10.1007/BF01730110

Boice, R. (2000). *Advice for new faculty members: Nihil nimus.* Allyn & Bacon.

Bok, D. C. (2006). *Our underachieving colleges.* Princeton University Press.

Bonwell, C. C., & Eison, J. A. (1991). *Active learning: Creating excitement in the classroom* (ASHE-ERIC Higher Education Report No. 1). George Washington University, School of Education and Human Development.

Boswell, J. (1904/1791). *Life of Samuel Johnson.* Henry Frowde.

Botha, M., Dibb, B., & Frost, D. M. (2020). "Autism is me": An investigation of how autistic individuals make sense of autism and stigma. *Disability and Society, 37*(3), 427–453. https://doi.org/10.1080/09687599.2020.1822782

Boud, D., Lawson, R., & Thompson, D. G. (2013). Does student engagement in self-assessment calibrate their judgment over time? *Assessment and Evaluation in Higher Education, 38*(8), 941–956. https://doi.org/10.1080/02602938.2013.769198

Bowen, J. A. (2012). *Teaching naked: How moving technology out of your college classroom will improve student learning.* Jossey-Bass.

Bowman, N. A. (2011, April 11). *The validity of college seniors' self-reported gains as a proxy for longitudinal growth.* Paper presented at the Annual Meetings of the American Educational Research Association, New Orleans, LA.

Boyer, E. L. (1997). *Scholarship reconsidered: Priorities of the professoriate.* The Carnegie Foundation for the Advancement of Teaching.

Boyer Commission on Educating Undergraduates in the Research University. (1998). *Reinventing undergraduate education: A blueprint for America's research universities.* Carnegie Foundation for the Advancement of Teaching. https://files.eric.ed.gov/fulltext/ED424840.pdf

Bransford, J. D., Brown, A. L., & Cocking, R. R. (1999). *How people learn: Brain, mind, experience, and school.* National Academy Press.

Breslow, L. (2010, September/October). Wrestling with pedagogical change: The TEAL Initiative at MIT. *Change, 42,* 23–29.

Bright, A. (2016, Summer). The problem with story problems. *Rethinking Schools.* https://rethinkingschools.org/articles/the-problem-with-story-problems/

Brinkmann, A. (2003). Mind mapping as a tool in mathematics education. *Mathematics Teacher, 96,* 96–101.

Brockliss, L. (1996). Curricula. In H. de Ridder-Symoens (Ed.), *A history of the university in Europe* (Vol. II, 565–620.) Cambridge University Press.

Brookfield, S. D. (2012). *Teaching for critical thinking: Tools and techniques to help students question their assumptions.* Jossey-Bass.

Brookfield, S. D. (2017). *Becoming a critically reflective teacher* (2nd ed.). Jossey-Bass.

Brookfield, S. (2020, December 9). Adult ed reformer and anti-racist scholar Stephen Brookfield joins Antioch as distinguished scholar. *Common Thread: Antioch University News.* https://commonthread.antioch.edu/adult-ed-reformer-and-anti-racist-scholar-stephen-brookfield-joins-antioch-as-distinguished-scholar/

Brookfield, S. D., & Hess, M. E. (2021). *Becoming a white anti-racist: A practical guide for educators, leaders, and activists.* Stylus.

Brookfield, S. D., & Preskill, S. (2005). *Discussion as a way of teaching: Tools and techniques for democratic classrooms* (2nd ed.). Jossey-Bass.

Brookfield, S. D., & Preskill, S. (2016). *The discussion book: 50 great ways to get people talking.* Jossey-Bass.

Brookhart, S. M. (1999). *The art and science of classroom assessment: The missing part of pedagogy* (ASHE-ERIC Higher Education Report, 27(1)). George Washington University, Graduate School of Education and Human Development.

Brooks, D. C., & Gierdowski, D. C. (2021, April 5). *Student experiences with technology in the pandemic.* Educause. https://library.educause.edu/resources/2021/4/student-experiences-with-technology-in-the-pandemic

Brost, B. D., & Bradley, K. A. (2006). Student compliance with assigned reading: A case study. *Journal of Scholarship of Teaching and Learning, 6*(2), 101–111. https://eric.ed.gov/?id=EJ854930

Brown, K. (2021, December 21). *5 global issues to watch in 2022.* United Nations Foundation. https://unfoundation.org/blog/post/5-global-issues-to-watch-in-2022/

Brown, G. T. L., & Abdulnabi, H. H. A. (2017). Evaluating the quality of higher education instructor-constructed multiple-choice tests: Impact on student grades. *Frontiers in Education, 2*(24). https://doi.org/10.3389/feduc.2017.00024

Brown, P. C., Roediger III, H. L., & McDaniel, M. A. (2014). *Making it stick: The science of successful learning.* Belknap Press of Harvard University Press.

Brown, T., & Rose, B. (2008, November 19–21). *Use of metacognitive wrappers for field experiences.* Session presented at the National Association of Geoscience Teachers Workshops: The Role of Metacognition in Teaching Geoscience, Carleton College, Northfield, MN. http://serc.carleton.edu/NAGTWorkshops/metacognition/tactics/28926.html

Browne, M. N., & Keeley, S. M. (2010). *Asking the right questions: A guide to critical thinking* (9th ed.). Prentice Hall, Pearson.

Bruff, D. (2009). *Teaching with classroom response systems: Creating active learning environments.* Jossey-Bass.

Bruff, D. (2016). *Clickers.* Agile learning: Derek Bruff's blog on teaching and technology. http://derekbruff.org/?page_id=2

Buczynski, S., Ireland, K., Reed, S., & Lacanienta, E. (2012). Communicating science concepts through art: 21st-century skills in practice. *Science Scope, 35*(9), 29–35.

Budesheim, T. L., & Lundquist, A. R. (2000). Consider the opposite: Opening minds through in-class debates on course-related controversies. *Teaching of Psychology, 26,* 106–120. https://doi.org/10.1207/S15328023TOP2602_5

Budhai, S. S. (2020, May 11). *Fourteen simple strategies to reduce cheating on online examinations.* Faculty Focus. https://www.facultyfocus.com/articles/educational-assessment/fourteen-simple-strategies-to-reduce-cheating-on-online-examinations/

Bugeja, M. J. (2007, January 26). Distractions in the wireless classroom. *The Chronicle of Higher Education.* https://www.chronicle.com/article/distractions-in-the-wireless-classroom/

Burchfield, C. M., & Sappington, J. (2000). Compliance with required reading assignments. *Teaching of Psychology, 27*(1), 58–60.

Burgess, A., Matar, E., Roberts, C., Haq, I., Wynter, L., Singer, J., Kalman., E., & Bleasel, J. (2021). Scaffolding medical student knowledge and skills: Team-based learning (TBL) and case-based learning (CBL). *BMC Medical Education, 21,* 1–14. https://doi.org/10.1186/s12909-021-02638-3

Burgess, L. G., Riddell, P. M., Fancourt, A., & Murayama, K. (2018). The influence of social contagion within education: A motivational perspective. *Mind, Brain, and Education, 12*(4), 164–174. https://doi.org/10.1111/mbe.12178

Burt, D. (2010, December 1). Cheating confusion persists. *Yale Daily News.* http://yaledailynews.com/blog/2010/12/01/cheating-confusion-persists/

Butler, A. C., Marsh, E. J., Slavinsky, J. P., & Baraniuk, R. G. (2014). Integrating cognitive science and technology improves learning in a STEM classroom. *Educational Psychology Review, 26*(2), 331–340. https://doi.org/10.1007/s10648-014-9256-4

Calma, A., & Davies, M. (2020). Critical thinking in business education: Current outlook and future prospects. *Studies in Higher Education, 46*(11), 2279–2295. https://doi.org/10.1080/03075079.2020.1716324

Campus Compact. (2003). *Introduction to service-learning toolkit: Readings and resources for faculty* (2nd ed.). Author.

Campus Compact. (2012). *Creating a culture of assessment: 2012 annual member survey*. Author. https://digitalcommons.unomaha.edu/slcehighered/151/

Cardon, L. S. (2014). Diagnosing and treating millennial student disillusionment. *Change, 46*(6), 34–40. https://doi.org/10.1080/00091383.2014.969182

Carlile, O., & Jordan, A. (2005). It works in practice but will it work in theory? The theoretical underpinnings of pedagogy. In G. O'Neill, S. Moore, & R. McMullan (Eds.), *Emerging issues in the practice of university teaching* (pp. 11–25). All Ireland Society for Higher Education.

Carnes, M. C. (2014). *Minds on fire: How role-immersion games transform college*. Harvard University Press.

Carney, A. G., Fry, S. W., Gabriele, R. V., & Ballard, M. (2008). Reeling in the big fish: Changing pedagogy to encourage the completion of reading assignments. *College Teaching, 56*(4), 195–200. https://doi.org/10.3200/CTCH.56.4.195-200

Carrasco, M. (2021, October 26). Addressing the mental health of LGBTQ+ students. *Inside Higher Ed.* https://www.insidehighered.com/news/2021/10/26/lgbtq-students-face-sizable-mental-health-disparities

Carroll, J. (2003a, May 2). Dealing with nasty students: The sequel. *The Chronicle of Higher Education*, p. C5.

Carroll, J. (2003b, October 14). Constructing your in-class persona. *The Chronicle of Higher Education.* https://www.chronicle.com/article/constructing-your-in-class-persona/?cid2=gen_login_refresh&cid=gen_sign_in

Case, K., Bartsch, R., McEnery, L., Hall, S., Hermann, A., & Foster, D. (2008). Establishing a comfortable classroom from day one: Student perceptions of the reciprocal interview. *College Teaching, 56*(4), 210–214. https://doi.org/ 10.3200/CTCH.56.4.210-214

Casselman, Brock L., & Atwood, C. H. (2017, December 12). Improving general chemistry course performance through online homework-based metacognitive training. *Journal of Chemical Education, 94*(12), 1811–1821. https://doi.org/10.1021/acs.jchemed.7b00298

CAST. (2022). https://www.cast.org/

Cerra, P. P., Álvarez, H. F., Parra, B. B, & Cordera, P. I. (2022). Effects of using game-based learning to improve the academic performance and motivation in engineering studies. *Journal of Educational Computing Research.* https://doi.org/10.1177/07356331221074022

Cepeda, N. J., Pashler, H., Vul, E., Wixted, J. T., & Rohrer, D. (2006). Distributive practice in verbal recall tasks: A review and quantitative synthesis. *Psychological Bulletin, 132,* 354–380. https://doi.org/10.1037/0033-2909.132.3.354

Chambliss, D. F., & Takacs, C. G. (2014). *How college works.* Harvard University Press.

Chen, C. H., & Yang, Y. C. (2019). Revisiting the effects of project-based learning on students' academic achievement: A meta-analysis investigating moderators. *Educational Research Review, 26,* 71–81. https://doi.org/10.1016/j.edurev.2018.11.001

Chen, M., Ni, C., Hu, Y., Wang, M., Liu, L., Ji, X., Chu, H., Wu, W., Lu, C., Wang, S., Wang, S., Zhao, L., Li, z., Zhu, H., Wang, J., Xia, Y., & Wang, X.(2018). Meta-analysis on the effectiveness of team-based learning on medical education in China. *BMC Medical Education, 18*(77). https://doi.org/10.1186/s12909-018-1179-1

Chen, X. (2013). *STEM attrition: College students' paths into and out of STEM fields* (Statistical Analysis Report NCES2014-001). National Center for Education Statistics.

Cheplygina, V., Hermans, F., Albers, C., Bielczyk, N., & Smeets, I. (2020). Ten simple rules for getting started on Twitter as a scientist. *PLoS Computer Biology, 16*(2), e1007513. https://doi.org/10.1371/journal.pcbi.1007513

Chi, M. T. H., Glaser, R., & Rees, E. (1982). Expertise in problem solving. In R. Steinberg (Ed.), *Advances in the psychology of human intelligence* (pp. 7–76). Erlbaum.

Chiaramonte, P. (1994). The agony and the ecstasy of case teaching. *Reaching Through Teaching, 7*(2), 1–2.

Chickering, A. W., & Gamson, Z. F. (1987, March). Seven principles for good practice in undergraduate education. *AAHE Bulletin,* 3–7. http://files.eric.ed.gov/fulltext/ED282491.pdf

Chism, N. V. N. (2007). *Peer review of teaching: A sourcebook* (2nd ed.). Jossey-Bass.

Chrisler, J. C. (2013). Teaching about gender: Rewards and challenges. *Psychology of Men and Masculinity, 14*(3), 264–267. https://doi.org/10.1037/a0033260

Christensen Center. 2025 (n.d.). *Case method in practice.* Harvard Business School. http://www.hbs.edu/teaching/case-method-in-practice/

Cho, M., & Lim, S. (2017). Using regulation activities to improve undergraduate collaborative writing on wikis. *Innovations in Education and Teaching International, 54*(1), 53–61. http://dx.doi.org/10.1080/14703297.2015.1117009

Chun, M. (2010). Taking teaching to (performance) task: Linking pedagogical and assessment practices. *Change, 42*(2), 22–29. https://doi.org/10.1080/00091381003590795

Clark, J. (2008). PowerPoint and pedagogy: Maintaining student interest in university lectures. *College Teaching, 56*(1), 39–45. https://doi.org/10.3200/CTCH.56.1.39-46

Clayson, D. E. (2009). Student evaluations of teaching: Are they related to what students learn? A meta-analysis and review of the literature. *Journal of Marketing Education, 31*(1), 16–30. https://doi.org/10.1177/0273475308324086

Clayson, D. E., & Haley, D. A. (2011, Summer). Are students telling us the truth? A critical look at the student evaluation of teaching. *Marketing Education Review, 21*(2), 101–112. https://doi.org/10.2753/MER1052-8008210201 https://doi.org/10.1177/0273475312467339

Clayton, P. H., Bringle, R. G., & Hatcher, J. A. (Eds.). (2013). *Research on service-learning: Conceptual frameworks and assessment, Vol. 2A. Students and faculty.* Stylus.

Coffield, F., with Costa, C., Müller, W., & Webber, J. (2014). *Beyond bulimic learning: Improving teaching in further education.* Institute of Education Press.

Coffield, F., Moseley, D., Hall, E., & Ecclestone, K. (2004). *Learning styles and pedagogy in post-16 learning: A systematic and critical review.* Learning and Skills Research Centre.

Coggins, A., Zaklama, R., Szabo, R. A., Diaz-Navarro, C., Scalese, R. J., Krogh, K., & Eppich, W. (2021). Twelve tips for facilitating and implementing clinical debriefing programmes. *Medical Teacher, 43*(5), 509–517. https://doi.org/10.1080/0142159X.2020.1817349

Cohen, P. A. (1981). Student ratings of instruction and student achievement: A meta-analysis of multi-section validity studies. *Review of Educational Research, 51*(3), 281–309. https://doi.org/10.2307/1170209

Coghlan, S., Miller, T., & Paterson, J. (2021). Good proctor or "Big Brother"? Ethics of online exam supervision technologies. *Philosophy & Technology, 34*(4), 1581–1606. https://doi.org/10.1007/s13347-021-00476-1

Collins, R. L., Elliott, M. N., Berry, S. H., Kanouse, D. E., & Hunter, S. B. (2003). Entertainment television as a healthy sex educator: The impact of condom-efficacy information in an episode of Friends. *Pediatrics, 112*(5), 1115–1121. https://doi.org/10.1542/peds.112.5.1115

Comeford, L. (2022). Attendance matters! Supporting first year students' success. with a structured attendance policy. A practice report. *Student Success, 13*(2). https://doi.org/10.5204/ssj.2420

Cooke, A. N., & Halberstadt, A. G. (2021). Adultification, anger bias, and adults' different perceptions of Black and White children. *Cognition and Emotion, 35*(7), 1416–1422. https://doi.org/10.1080/02699931.2021.1950127

Coquyt, M. (2020). The effects of service-learning on the moral development of college students. *The Interactive Journal of Global Leadership and Learning, 1*(1). https://doi.org/10.55354/2692-3394.1000

Cornelius, T. L., & Owen-DeSchryver, J. (2008). Differential effects of full and partial notes on learning outcomes and attendance. *Teaching of Psychology, 35*(1), 6–12. https://doi.org/10.1080/00986280701818466

Cornelius-White, J. (2007). Learner-centered teacher-student relationships are effective: A meta-analysis. *Review of Educational Research, 77*(1), 113–143. https://doi.org/10.3102/003465430298563

Corrall, S. (2017). Developing a teaching philosophy statement. In *Workshop on Developing a Teaching Philosophy Statement,* 19 June 2017–19 June 2017, Technological Higher Education Association (THEA), Dublin, Ireland. http://d-scholarship.pitt.edu/32531/

Cortright, R. N., Collins, H. L., Rodenbaugh, D. W., & DiCarlo, S. E. (2003). Student retention of course content is improved by collaborative-group testing. *Advances in Physiology Education, 27*(3), 102–108. https://doi.org/10.1152/advan.00041.2002

Cox, R. D. (2011). *The college fear factor: How students and professors misunderstand one another.* Harvard University Press.

Cox, S.R., Rickard, M.K., & Lowery, C.M. (2022). The student evaluation of teaching: Let's be honest – who is telling the truth? *Marketing Education Review, 32*(1), 82–93. https://doi.org/10.1080/10528008.2021.1922924

Croizet, J. C., Désert, M., Dutrévis, M., & Leyens, J. P. (2001). Stereotype threat, social class, gender, and academic underachievement: When our reputation catches up to us and takes over. *Social Psychology of Education, 4*(3), 295–310. https://doi.org/10.1023/A:1011336821053

Crothers, B. (2020). *50 remote-friendly icebreakers: Quick and easy warmups and energizers for better meeting mojo.* Ben Crothers Publishing.

Crouch, C. E., & Mazur, E. (2001). Peer instruction: Ten years of experience and results. *American Journal of Physics, 69*, 970–977. https://doi.org/10.1119/1.1374249

Crutchfield, T. N., & Klamon, K. (2014). Assessing the dimension and outcomes of an effective teammate. *Journal of Education for Business, 89*(6), 285–291. https://doi.org/10.1080/08832323.2014.885873

Cuseo, J. B. (2002). *Igniting student involvement, peer interactions, and teamwork.* New Forums Press.

Cuseo, J. (2018). Student-faculty engagement. *New Directions in Teaching and Learning Special Issue: Student Engagement: A Multidimensional Perspective, 154*, 87–97. https://doi.org/10.1002/tl.20294

Dallimore, E. J., Hertenstein, J. H., & Platt, M. B. (2006). Non-voluntary class participation in graduate discussion courses: Effects of grading and cold-calling on student comfort. *Journal of Management Education, 30*(2), 354–377. https://doi.org/10.1177/1052562905277031

Dallimore, E. J., Hertenstein, J. H., & Platt, M. B. (2008). Using discussion pedagogy to enhance oral and written communication skills. *College Teaching, 56*(3), 163–170.

Dallimore, E. J., Hertenstein, J.H., & Platt, M. B. (2012). Impact of cold-calling on student voluntary participation. *Journal of Management Education, 37*(3), 305–341. https://doi.org/10.1177/1052562912446067

Daniels L. M., Goegan, L. D., & Parker, P. C. (2021). The impact of COVID-19 triggered changes to instruction and assessment on university students' self-reported motivation, engagement and perceptions. *Social Psychology of Education, 24*(1), 299–318. https://doi.org/10.1007/s11218-021-09612-3

Danielson, R. W., Grace, E., White, A. J., Kelton, M. L., Owen, J. P., Fisher, K. S., Martinez, A. D., & Mozo, M. (2022). Facilitating systems thinking through arts-based STEM integration. *Frontiers in Education, 7*, 915333. https://doi.org/10.3389/feduc.2022.915333

Darby, F. (2020, September 24). 7 ways to assess students online and minimize cheating. *The Chronicle of Higher Education.* https://www.chronicle.com/article/7-ways-to-assess-students-online-and-minimize-cheating

Daugherty, O. (2022, December). Americans' views on value of higher education hold steady, but fewer say it has a positive impact. *National Association of Student Financial Aid Administrations.* https://www.nasfaa.org/news-item/25634/Americans_Views_on_Value_of_Higher_Education_Hold_Steady_But_Fewer_Say_It_Has_Positive_Impact

Davachi, L., & DuBrow, S. (2015). How the hippocampus preserves order: The role of prediction and context. *Trends in Cognitive Sciences, 19*(2), 92–99. https://doi.org/10.1016/j.tics.2014.12.004

Davidson, H. (2008). *Hall Davidson Handouts.* http://www.halldavidson.com/

Davidson, N., & Major, C. H. (2014). Boundary crossings: Cooperative learning, collaborative learning, and problem-based learning. *Journal of Excellence on College Teaching, 25*(3&4), 7–55.

Davies, K. M. (2021) Aunt Becky goes rogue: De-celebrification and de-mothering in the college cheating scandal, Operation Varsity Blues, *Celebrity Studies*, 1–13. https://doi.org/10.1080/19392397.2021.1965894

Davis, B. G. (2009). *Tools for teaching* (2nd ed.). Jossey-Bass.

Davis, J. R., & Arend, B. D. (2013). *Facilitating seven ways of learning: A resource for more purposeful, effective, and enjoyable college teaching.* Stylus.

Deal, A. (2007, November). *Classroom response systems (Teaching with Technology White Paper).* https://www.cmu.edu/teaching/technology/whitepapers/ClassroomResponse_Nov07.pdf

Deans, T. (2019, January 20). Yes, your syllabus is way too long. *The Chronicle of Higher Education.* https://www.chronicle.com/article/yes-your-syllabus-is-way-too-long/

Deci, E. L., Koestner, R., & Ryan, R. M. (1999). A meta-analytic review of experiments examining the effects of extrinsic rewards on intrinsic motivation. *Psychological Bulletin, 125*(5), 627–668. https://doi.org/ 10.1037/0033-2909.125.6.627

Deci, E. L., & Ryan, R. M. (Eds.). (2002). *Handbook of self-determination research.* University of Rochester Press.

Dee, K. C. (2007). Student perceptions of high course workloads are not associated with poor student evaluations of instructor performance. *Journal of Engineering Education, 96*(1), 69–78. https://doi.org/10.1002/j.2168-9830.2007.tb00916.x

Dee, T. S., & Jacob, B. A. (2012). Rational ignorance in education: A field experiment in student plagiarism. *Journal of Human Resources, 47*(2), 397–434. https://doi.org/10.3368/jhr.47.2.397

DeJong, T., & Ferguson-Hessler, M. G. (1996). Types and quality of knowledge. *Educational Psychologist, 8*(2), 105–113. https://doi.org/10.1207/s15326985ep3102_2

Dennis, J. M., Phinney, J. S., & Chuateco, L. I. (2005). The role of motivation, parental support, and peer support in the academic success of ethnic minority first-generation college students. *Journal of College Student Development, 46*(3), 223–236. https://doi.org/10.1353/csd.2005.0023

Denton, A. W., & Veloso, J. (2018). Changes in syllabus tone affect warmth (but not competence) ratings of both male and female instructors. *Social Psychology of Education, 21*(4), 173–187. https://doi.org/10.1007/s11218-017-9409-7

Deslauriers, L., McCarty, L. S., Miller, K., Callaghan, K., & Kestin, G. (2019). Measuring actual learning versus feeling of learning in response to being actively engaged in the classroom. *PNAS, 116*(39), 19251–19257. https://doi.org/10.1073/pnas.1821936116

Deslauriers, L., Schelew, E., & Wieman, C. E. (2011). Improved learning in a large-enrollment physics class. *Science, 332*(6031), 862–864. https://doi.org/10.1126/science.1201783

Dey, S. (2021, August 27). *Reports of cheating at colleges soar during the pandemic.* NPR. https://www.npr.org/2021/08/27/1031255390/reports-of-cheating-at-colleges-soar-during-the-pandemic

DiMenna, M. (2019, April 4). *Why—and how—to build a sense of belonging on campus.* EAB. https://eab.com/insights/expert-insight/academic-affairs/why-and-how-to-build-a-sense-of-belonging-on-campus/

Dimitrov, N. (2009). *Western guide to mentoring graduate students across cultures.* Teaching Support Centre, University of Western Ontario, Canada. https://ir.lib.uwo.ca/cgi/viewcontent.cgi?article=1004&context=tsc-purple-guides

Dimock, M. (2019, January 17). *Defining generations: Where millennials end and Generation Z begins.* Pew Research Center. https://www.pewresearch.org/fact-tank/2019/01/17/where-millennials-end-and-generation-z-begins/

DiNatale, A. F., Repetto, C., Riva, G., & Villani, D. (2020). Immersive virtual reality in K-12 and higher education: A 10-year systematic review of empirical research. *British Journal of Educational Technology, 51*(6), 2006–2033. https://doi.org/10.1111/bjet.13030

Dinan, F. (2002). Chemistry by the case. *Journal of College Science Teaching, 32*(1), 36–41.

Dirkx, K., Joosten-ten Brinke, D., Arts, J., & van Diggelen, M. (2021). In-text and rubric-referenced feedback: Differences in focus, level, and function. *Active Learning in Higher Education, 22*(3), 189–201. https://doi.org/10.1177/1469787419855208

Dobrow, S. R., Smith, W. K., & Posner, M. A. (2011). Managing the grading paradox: Leveraging the power of choice in the classroom. *Academy of Management Learning and Education, 10*(2), 251–276. https://doi.org/10.5465/amle.10.2.zqr261

Dochy, F., Segers, M., Van den Bossche, P., & Gijbels, D. (2003). Effects of problem-based learning: A meta-analysis. *Learning and Instruction, 13*(5), 533–568. https://doi.org/10.1016/S0959-4752(02)00025-7

Donolato, E., Marci, T., Altoè, G., & Mammarella, I. C. (2020). Measuring test anxiety in primary and middle school children: Psychometric evaluation of the Test Anxiety Questionnaire for Children (TAQ-C).

Teaching of Psychology, 46(5), 839–851. https://doi.org/10.1027/1015-5759/a000556

Doolittle, P. E., & Siudzinski, R. A. (2010). Recommended syllabus components: What do higher education faculty include in their syllabi? *Journal on Excellence in College Teaching, 21*(3), 29–61.

Drake, R. (2009, February). Essay preparedness and student success. Poster session presented at the annual Lilly South Conference on College Teaching, Greensboro, NC.

Druckman, D., & Porter, L. W. (1991). Developing careers. In D. Druckman & R. A. Bjork (Eds.), *In the mind's eye: Enhancing human performance* (pp. 80–103). National Academy Press.

Duch, B. J., Groh, S. E., & Allen, D. E. (2001). *The power of problem-based learning*. Stylus.

Duda, G. (2014). The road to a project-based classroom. *Change, 46*(6), 42–45.

Duncan, N. (2007). Feed-forward: Improving students' use of tutors' comments. *Assessment and Evaluation in Higher Education, 32*(2), 271–283. https://doi.org/10.1080/02602930600896498

Dunlosky, J., Rawson, K., Marsh, E., Nathan, M., & Willingham, D. (2013). Improving students' learning with effective learning techniques: Promising directions from cognitive and educational psychology. *Psychological Science in the Public Interest, 14*(1), 4–58. https://doi.org/10.1177/1529100612453266

Dweck, C. S. (2007). *Mindset: The new psychology of success*. Random House.

Dweck, C. S. (2018). Reflections on the legacy of attribution theory. *Motivation Science, 4*(1), 17–18. https://doi.org/10.1037/mot0000095

Eagan, K., Hurtado, S., & Chang, M. (2010). *What matters in STEM: Institutional contexts that influence STEM bachelor's degree completion rates*. Paper presented at the annual meeting of the Association for the Study of Higher Education, Indianapolis, IN. https://www.heri.ucla.edu/nih/downloads/ASHE2010-What-matters-for-STEM-completion.pdf

Eagan, M. K., Lozano, J. B., Hurtado, S., & Case, M. H. (2013). *The American freshman: National norms fall 2013*. Los Angeles: Higher Education Research Institute, UCLA. http://www.heri.ucla.edu/monographs/TheAmericanFreshman2013.pdf

Eagan, M. K., Stolzenberg, E. B., Lozano, J. B., Aragon, M. C., Suchard, M. R., & Hurtado, S. (2014). *Undergraduate teaching faculty: The 2013–2014 HERI Faculty Survey*. Higher Education Research Institute, UCLA. http://heri.ucla.edu/monographs/HERI-FAC2014-monograph.pdf

Eddy, S. L., & Hogan, K. A. (2014). Getting under the hood: How and for whom does increasing course structure work? *Life Science Education, 13*(3), 453–468. https://doi.org/10.1187/cbe.14-03-0050

Edens, K. M. (2000). Preparing problem solvers for the 21st century through problem-based learning. *College Teaching, 48*(2), 55–60. https://doi.org/10.1080/87567550009595813

Ehrlichman, H., & Micic, D. (2012). Why do people move their eyes when they think? *Current Directions in Psychological Science, 21*(2), 96–100 https://doi.org/10.1177/0963721412436810

Ellis, D. (2006). *Becoming a master student* (11th ed.). Houghton Mifflin.

Esarey, J., & Valdes, N. (2020) Unbiased, reliable, and valid student evaluations can still be unfair. *Assessment & Evaluation in Higher Education, 45*(8), 1106–1120, https://doi.org/10.1080/02602938.2020.1724875

ETS Proficiency Profile. (2022). ETS® Proficiency Profile Optional Essay. https://www.ets.org/proficiencyprofile/about/essay/

Evans, T., Kensington-Miller, B., & Novak, J. (2021). Effectiveness, efficiency, engagement: Mapping the impact of pre-lecture quizzes on educational exchange. *Australasian Journal of Educational Technology, 37*(1), 163–177. https://doi.org/10.14742/ajet.6258

Eyler, J. (2022, March, 7). Grades are at the center of the student mental health crisis. *Inside Higher Ed.* https://www.insidehighered.com/blogs/just-visiting/grades-are-center-student-mental-health-crisis

Eyler J., & Giles, D. E., Jr. (1999). *Where's the learning in service-learning?* Jossey-Bass.

Ewing, A. M. (2012). Estimating the impact of relative expected grade on student evaluations of teachers. *Economics of Education Review, 31*(1), 141–154. https://doi.org/10.1016/j.econedurev.2011.10.002

Facione, P. A. (2011a). Measured reasons and critical thinking. The California Press.

Facione, P. A. (2011b). *Think critically.* Prentice Hall.

Facione, P. A. (2013). Critical thinking: What it is and why it counts. http://www.insightassessment.com/pdf_files/what&why2006.pdf

Facione, P. A., Facione, N. C., & Giancarlo, C. (2000). The disposition toward critical thinking: Its character, measurement, and relationship to critical thinking skills. *Journal of Informal Logic, 20*(1), 61–84. https://doi.org/10.22329/il.v20i1.2254

Facione, P. A., Facione, N. C., Riegel, F., Martini, J. G., Graca, M. D., & Crossetti, M. G. O. (2021). Holistic critical thinking in times of COVID-19 pandemic: Unveiling fundamental skills to clinical nurse practice. *Revista Gaúcha Enfermagem, 38*(3), e75576. https://doi.org/10.1590/1983-1447.2017.03.75576

Fadel, C. (2008). *Multimodal learning through media: What the research says.* Cisco Systems. http://www.cisco.com/web/strategy/docs/education/Multimodal-Learning-Through-Media.pdf

Faizan, N. D., Löffler, A., Heininger, R., Utesch, M., & Krcmar, H. (2019). Classification of evaluation methods for the effective assessment of simulation games: Results from a literature review. *International Journal of Engineering Pedagogy, 9*(1), 19–33. https://doi.org/10.3991/ijep.v9i1.9948

Falchikov, N., & Boud, D. (1989). Student self-assessment in higher education: A meta-analysis. *Review of Educational Research, 59*(4), 395–430. https://doi.org/10.3102/00346543059004395

Fasko, D. (2003, April). *Case studies and method in teaching and learning.* Paper presented at the Annual Meeting of the Society of Educators and Scholars, Louisville, KY.

Fast Company Staff. (2020). 25 moments in tech that defined the past 25 years. *Fast Company.* https://www.fastcompany.com/90565059/25-moments-in-tech-that-defined-the-past-25-years

Fawcett, J. M., Quinlan, C. K., & Taylor, T. L. (2012). Interplay of the production and picture superiority effects: A signal detection analysis. *Memory (Hove, England), 20*(7), 655–666. https://doi.org/10.1080/09658211.2012.693510

Featherly. K. (2014). The social club: Are Web 2.0 technologies the key to making distance learning truly effective? *Delta Sky,* 95–103.

Felder, R. M., & Brent, R. (2001). Effective strategies for cooperative learning. *Journal of Cooperation and Collaboration in College Teaching, 10*(2), 67–75. https://doi.org. 10.1021/bk-2007-0970.ch004

Feldman, K. A. (1989). The association between student ratings of specific instructional dimensions and student achievement: Refining and extending the synthesis of data from multisection validity studies. *Research in Higher Education, 30*(6), 583–645. https://doi.org/ 10.1007/BF00992392

Feldmann, L. J. (2001). Classroom civility is another of our instructor responsibilities. *College Teaching, 49*(4), 137–141. https://doi.org/10.1080/87567555.2001.10844595

Feldon, D. F. (2010). Why magic bullets don't work. *Change, 42*(2), 15–21. https://doi.org/10.1080/00091380903563043

Felege, C. J., & Ralph, S. G. (2019). Evaluating the efficacy of a student-centered active learning environment for undergraduate programs (SCALE-UP) classroom for major and non-major biology students. *Journal of Biological Education, 53*(1), 98–109. https://doi.org/10.1080/00219266.2018.1447001

Ferris, M. E. (2015, April 20). With Twitter, Statistics 101 takes flight. *The Chronicle of Higher Education.* https://www.chronicle.com/article/with-twitter-statistics-101-takes-flight/

Finelli, C. J., Nguyen, K., DeMonbrun, M., Borrego, M., Prince, M., Husman, J., Henderson, C., Shekhar, P., & Waters, C. K. (2018). Reducing student resistance to active learning: Strategies for instructors. *Journal of College Science Teaching, 47*(5), 80-91.

Finelli, C. J., Ott, M., Gottfried, A. C., Hershock, C., O'Heal, C., & Kaplan, M. (2008). Utilizing instructional consultations to enhance the teaching performance of engineering faculty. *Journal of Engineering Education, 97*(4), 397–411. https://doi.org/10.1002/j.2168-9830.2008.tb00989.x

Fink, L. D. (2013). *Creating significant learning experiences: An integrated approach to designing college courses* (2nd ed.). Jossey-Bass.

Fink, L. D. (2021). Toward learning-centered education in colleges and universities. *New Directions for Teaching and Learning, 166,* 7–16. https://doi.org/10.1002/tl.20447

Fink, L. D., & Fink, A. K. (Eds.). (2009). *New directions for teaching and learning: No. 119. Designing courses for significant learning: Voices of experience.* Jossey-Bass.

Finley, A. (2021). *How college contributes to workforce success: Employer views on what matters most.* Association of American Colleges & Universities and Hanover Research. https://www.tbr.edu/sites/default/files/media/2021/04/AACUEmployerReport2021.pdf

Fischman, J. (2009, March 16). Students stop surfing after being shown how in-class laptop use lowers test scores. *The Chronicle of Higher Education.* http://chronicle.com/blogs/wiredcampus/students-stop-surfing-after-being-shown-how-in-class-laptop-use-lowers-test-scores/457

Flanigan, A. E., & Titsworth, S. (2020). The impact of digital distraction on lecture note taking and student learning. *Instructional Science, 48,* 495–524. https://doi.org/10.1007/s11251-020-09517-2

Flavell, J. H. (1976). Metacognitive aspects of problem solving. In L. B. Resnick (Ed.), *The nature of intelligence* (pp. 231–236). Erlbaum.

Fletcher, J. A. (2018). Peer observation of teaching: A practical tool in higher education. *The Journal of Faculty Development, 32*(1), 51–64. https://doi.org/10.13140/RG.2.2.19455.82084

Foer, J. (2011). *Moonwalking with Einstein: The art and science of remembering everything.* Penguin. http://www.capitalessence.com/blog/wp-content/uploads/2011/12/Moonwalking_with_Einstein_-_Foer__Joshua.pdf

Foster, A. (2008, January 17). Despite skeptics, publishers tout new "fair use" agreements with universities. *The Chronicle of Higher Education.* https://www.chronicle.com/article/despite-skeptics-publishers-tout-new-fair-use-agreements-with-universities-414/

Foster, D. (2015). Private journals versus public blogs: The impact of peer readership on low-stakes reflective writing. *Teaching Sociology, 43*(2), 104–114. https://doi.org/10.1177/0092055X14568204

Fox, H. (1994). *Listening to the world: Cultural issues in academic writing.* National Council of Teachers of English. http://www-personal.umich.edu/~hfox/listening.pdf

Freeman, S., Eddy, S. L., McDonough, M., Smith, M. K., Okoroafor, N., Jordt, H., & Wenderoth, M. P. (2014). Active learning increases student performance in science, engineering, and mathematics. *Proceedings of the National Academy of Sciences USA, 111,* 8410–8415. http://www.pnas.org/content/111/23/8410.full.pdf+html

Frisby, B. N., & Martin, M. M. (2010). Instructor-student and student-student rapport in the classroom. *Communication Education, 59*(2), 146–164. https://doi.org/10.1080/03634520903564362

Fuentes, M. A., Zelaya, D. G., & Madsen, J. W. (2020). Rethinking the course syllabus: Considerations for promoting equity, diversity, and inclusion. *Teaching of Psychology, 48*(1), 69–79. https://doi.org/10.1177/0098628320959979

Fullilove, R. E., & Treisman, P. U. (1990). Mathematics achievement among African American undergraduates at the University of California, Berkeley: An evaluation of the mathematics workshop program. *The Journal of Negro Education, 59*(3), 463–478. https://doi.org/10.2307/2295577

Furey, W. (2020). The stubborn myth of "learning styles." *Education Next, 20*(3). https://www.educationnext.org/stubborn-myth-learning-styles-state-teacher-license-prep-materials-debunked-theory/

Gabriel, K. F. (2008). *Teaching unprepared students: Strategies for promoting success and retention in higher education.* Stylus.

Ganley, C. (2018, August 14). Are boys better than girls at math? *Scientific American.* https://www.scientificamerican.com/article/are-boys-better-than-girls-at-math/

Ganley, C. M., & Lubienski, S. T. (2016). Mathematics confidence, interest, and performance: Examining gender patterns and reciprocal relations. *Learning and Individual Differences, 47,* 182–193. https://doi.org/10.1016/j.lindif.2016.01.002

Gannon, K. (2018, September 12). How to create a syllabus: Advice guide. *The Chronicle of Higher Education.* https://www.chronicle.com/article/how-to-create-a-syllabus/

Garcia, E., Moizer, J., Wilkins, S., & Haddoud, M.Y. (2019). Student learning in higher education through blogging in the classroom. *Computers & Education, 136,* 61–74. https://doi.org/10.1016/j.compedu.2019.03.011

Garibay, J. C. (2015). *Creating a positive classroom climate for diversity.* UCLA Office of Diversity & Faculty Development. https://equity.ucla.edu/wp-content/uploads/2016/06/CreatingaPositiveClassroomClimateWeb-2.pdf

Gauci, S. A., Dantas, A. M., Williams, D. A., & Kenn, R. E. (2009). Promoting student-centered active learning in lectures with a personal response system. *Advanced Physiological Education, 33*(1), 60–71. https://doi.org/10.1152/advan.00109.2007

Gedalof, A. J. (1998). *Green guide: No. 1. Teaching large classes.* Society for Teaching and Learning in Higher Education.

Geddes, L. (2014, May 23). *How educators can get glowing course evaluations from students (even struggling students) in rigorous courses.* The Learnwell Projects. https://the-learnwellprojects.com/thewell/how-educators-can-get-glowing-course-evaluations-from-students-even-struggling-students-in-rigorous-courses/

Ghadirian, H., Salehi, K., & Ayub, A. F. M. (2019). Assessing the effectiveness of role assignment on improving students' asynchronous online discussion participation. *International Journal of Distance Education Technologies, 17*(1), 31–51. https://doi.org/10.4018/IJDET.2019010103

Gierdowski, D. C. (2019, October). *ECAR Study of Undergraduate Students and Information Technology, 2019.* Research Report. https://library.educause.edu/-/media/files/library/2019/10/studentstudy2019.pdf?la=en&hash=25FBB396AE482FAC3B765862BA6B197DBC98B42CECAR.

Gilmore, T. N., & Schall, E. (1996). Staying alive to learning: Integrating enactments with case teaching to develop leaders. *Journal of Policy Analysis and Management, 15*(3), 444–457. https://doi.org/10.1002/(SICI)1520-6688(199622)15:3<444::AID-PAM8>3.0.CO;2-I

Ginns, P. (2005). Meta-analysis of the modality effect. *Learning and Instruction, 15*(4), 313–331. https://doi.org/10.1016/j.learninstruc.2005.07.001

Giuliodori, M. J., Lujan, H. L., & DiCarlo, S. E. (2006). Peer instruction enhanced student performance on qualitative problem-solving questions. *Advances in Physiology Education, 30,* 168–173. https://doi.org/10.1152/advan.00013.2006

Glaser, R. (1991). The maturing of the relationship between the science of learning and cognition and educational practice. *Learning and Instruction, 1*(1), 129–144. https://doi.org/10.1016/0959-4752(91)90023-2

Glazer, F. S. (2011). Baby steps to blended: Introduction of a blended unit to a conventional course. In F. S. Glazer (Ed.), *Blended learning: Across the disciplines, across the academy* (pp. 31–58). Stylus.

Gobet, F., Lane, P. C. R., Croker, S., Cheng, P. C. H., Jones, G., Oliver, I., & Pine, J. M. (2001). Chunking mechanisms in human learning. *Trends in Cognitive Sciences, 5,* 236–243. https://doi.org/0.1016/S1364-6613(00)01662-4

Golden, S. (2017). *The use of augmented 3D holographic technology in higher education, increasing students' learning outcome scores: A mixed methods study.* ResearchGate-Working Paper. https://doi.org/10.13140/RG.2.2.11103.66729

Golding, T. L. (2008). Bonuses of a bonus assignment! *Teaching Professor, 22*(6), 5.

Goldstein, D. (2022, March 8). It's "alarming": Children are severely behind in reading. *The New York Times.* https://www.nytimes.com/2022/03/08/us/pandemic-schools-reading-crisis.html

Gonsalves, L. M. (2002). Making connections: Addressing the pitfalls of white faculty/black male student communication. *College Composition and Communication Online, 53,* 435–465.

Gonzalez, V., & Lopez, E. (2001). The age of incivility: Countering disruptive behavior in the classroom. *AAHE Bulletin, 55*(8), 3–6. https://www.aahea.org/articles/incivility.htm

Goodsett, M. (2020). Best practices for teaching and assessing critical thinking in information literacy online learning objects. *The Journal of Academic Librarianship, 46*(5). https://doi.org/10.1016/j.acalib.2020.102163

Goodson, L. (2005, March). *Content, presentation and learning activities* [Paper presentation]. 26th Annual Meeting of the Sharing Conference of the Southern Regional Faculty and Instructional Development Consortium, Lake Junaluska, NC, United States.

Goodspeed, J. (2021, August 24). *Support students' learning, and find the best video streaming sites for schools and classrooms.* Common Sense Education. https://www.commonsense.org/education/articles/teachers-essential-guide-to-showing-movies-and-videos-in-the-classroom

Gorichanaz, T. (2022). It made me feel like it was okay to be wrong: Student experiences with ungrading. *Active Learning in Higher Education.* https://doi.org/10.1177/14697874221093640

Grajek, S. (2020, October 2). *EDUCAUSE QuickPoll Results: IT Budgets, 2020–21.* Educause Review. https://er.educause.edu/blogs/2020/10/educause-quickpoll-results-it-budgets-2020-21

Granitz, N. A., Koernig, S. K., & Harich, K. R. (2009). Now it's personal: Antecedents and outcomes of rapport between business faculty and their students. *Journal of Marketing Education, 31*(1), 52–65. https://doi.org/10.1177/0273475308326408

Grant-Thompson, S., & Atkinson, D. (1997). Cross-cultural mentor effectiveness and African American male students. *Journal of Black Psychology, 23,* 120–134. https://doi.org/10.1177/00957984970232003

Grasgreen, A. (2012, March 16). Who cheats, and how. *Inside Higher Education.* https://www.insidehighered.com/news/2012/03/16/arizona-survey-examines-student-cheating-faculty-responses

Gray, M. J., Ondaatje, E. H., Fricker, R. D., & Geschwind, S. A. (2000). Assessing service-learning: Results from a survey of "Learn and Service American Higher Education." *Change, 32*(2), 30–39.

Gray, M. J., Ondaatje, E. H., & Zakaras, L. (1999). *Combining service and learning in higher education: Summary report.* Rand Corporation.

Griffiths, E. (2010). Clearing the misty landscape: Teaching students what they didn't know then, but know now. *College Teaching, 58*(1), 32–37. https://www.jstor.org/stable/25763411

Gruhn, D., & Cheng, Y. (2014). A self-correcting approach to multiple-choice exams improves students' learning. *Teaching of Psychology, 41*(4), 335–339. https://doi.org/10.1177/0098628314549706

Guo, J. (2019). The use of an extended flipped classroom model in improving students' learning in an undergraduate course. *Journal of Computing in Higher Education, 31*(2), 362–390. https://doi.org/10.1007/s12528-019-09224-z

Guo, S., & Jamal, Z. (2007). *Green guide: No 8. Cultural diversity and inclusive teaching.* Society for Teaching and Learning in Higher Education.

Guo, P., Saab, N., Post, L.S., & Admiraal, W. (2020). A review of project-based learning in higher education: Student outcomes and measures. *International Journal of Educational Research, 102,* 101506. https://doi.org/10.1016/j.ijer.2020.101586

Gurung, R. A. R., & Burns, K. (2018). Putting evidence-based claims to the test: A multi-site classroom study of retrieval practice and spaced practice. *Applied Cognitive Psychology, 33*(5), 732–743. https://doi.org/10.1002/acp.3507

Gurung, R. A. R., & Galardi, N. R. (2021). Syllabus tone, more than mental health statements, influence intentions to seek help. *Teaching of Psychology, 49*(3), 218–223. https://doi.org/10.1177/0098628321994632

Haak, D. C., HilleRisLambers, J., Pitre, E., & Freeman, S. (2011). Increased structure and active learning reduce the achievement gap in introductory biology. *Science, 332,* 1213–1216. https://doi.org/10.1126/science.1204820

Habanek, D. V. (2005). An examination of the integrity of the syllabus. *College Teaching, 53*(2), 62–64. https://doi.org/10.3200/CTCH.53.2.62-64

Habron, G., & Dann, S. (2002). Breathing life into the case study approach: Active learning in an introductory natural resource management class. *Journal on Excellence in College Teaching, 13*(2/3), 41–58. https://www.asec.purdue.edu/lct/HBCU/documents/Case_Study_Active_Learning_NRES.pdf

Hager, P. (1985, May 21). Magazine broke law, court says: Violation of copyright cited in Ford excerpts. *Los Angeles Times.* https://www.latimes.com/archives/la-xpm-1985-05-21-mn-7715-story.html

Hake, R. R. (1998). Interactive-engagement vs. traditional methods: A six thousand–student survey of mechanics test data for introductory physics courses. *American Journal of Physics, 66*(1), 64–74. https://doi.org/10.1119/1.18809

Hall, R. M., & Sandler, B. R. (1982). *The classroom climate: A chilly one for women?* Project on the Status and Education of Women. Association of American Colleges. https://files.eric.ed.gov/fulltext/ED215628.pdf

Halpern, D. F. (1999). Teaching for critical thinking: Helping college students develop the skills and dispositions of a critical thinker. *New Directions for Teaching and Learning, 1999*(80), 69–74. http://onlinelibrary.wiley.com/doi/10.1002/tl.v1999:80/issueto

Halpern, D. F. (2014). *Thought and knowledge: An introduction to critical thinking* (5th ed.). Erlbaum.

Halpern, D. F., & Associates. (1994). *Changing college classrooms.* Jossey-Bass.

Halpern, D. F., & Sternberg, R. J. (2020). An introduction to critical thinking: Maybe it will change your life. In R. J. Sternberg and D. F. Halpern (Eds.), *Critical thinking in psychology* (2nd ed., pp. 1–9). Cambridge University Press.

Halvorson, H. G. (2014). The key to great feedback? Praise the process, not the person. 99U. http://99u.com/articles/19442/the-key-to-great-feedback-praise-the-process-not-the-person

Handelsman, M. M. (2011, September 9). Is lecturing always unethical: Should, and can, professors keep their mouths closed? *Psychology Today.* https://www.psychologytoday.com/us/blog/the-ethical-professor/201109/is-lecturing-always-unethical

Hansen, E. J. (2011). *Idea-based learning: A course design process to promote conceptual understanding.* Stylus.

Hansen, M., & Quintero, D. (2017, August 10). Analyzing "the homework gap" among high school students. *Brookings.* https://www.brookings.edu/blog/brown-center-chalkboard/2017/08/10/analyzing-the-homework-gap-among-high-school-students/

Hanson, D. (2006). *Instructor's guide to process-oriented guided-inquiry learning.* Stony Brook University.

Hanson, M. (2022a, July 15). *Average cost of college textbooks.* Education Data Initiative. https://educationdata.org/average-cost-of-college-textbooks#:~:text=The%20average%20cost%20of%20college,the%202021%2D2022%20academic%20year.

Hanson, M. (2022b, July 26). *College enrollment & student demographic characteristics.* Education Data Initiative. https://educationdata.org/college-enrollment-statistics

Harrington, C. M., & Gabert-Quillen, C. A. (2015). Syllabus length and use of images: An empirical investigation of student perceptions. *Scholarship of Teaching and Learning in Psychology, 1*(3), 235–243. https://doi.org/10.1037/stl0000040

Harrington, C., & Thomas, M. (2018). *Designing a motivational syllabus: Creating a learning path for student engagement.* Stylus.

Harrington, C., & Zakrajsek, T. (2017). *Dynamic lecturing: Research-based strategies to enhance lecture effectiveness.* Stylus.

Hauer, K. E., Boscardin, C., Brenner, J. M., van Schaik, S. M., & Papp, K. K. (2020). Twelve tips for assessing medical knowledge with open-ended questions: Designing constructed response examinations in medical education. *Medical Teacher, 42*(8), 880–885. https://doi.org/10.1080/0142159X.2019.1629404

Hattie, J. (2009). *Visible learning: A synthesis of over 800 meta-analyses relating to achievement.* Routledge.

Hattie, J., Hodis, F. A., & Kang, S. H. K. (2020). Theories of motivation: Integration and ways forward. *Contemporary Educational Psychology, 61,* 101865. https://doi.org/10.1016/j.cedpsych.2020.101865

Hattie, J., & Timperley, H. (2007). The power of feedback. *Review of Educational Research, 77*(1), 81–112. https://doi.org/10.3102/003465430298487

Havlik, S., Pulliam, N., Malott, K., & Steen, S. (2020). Strengths and struggles: First-generation college-goers persisting at one predominantly white institution. *Journal of College Student Retention: Research, Theory & Practice, 22*(1), 118–140. https://doi.org/10.1177/1521025117724551

Heiner, C. E., Banet, A. I., & Wieman, C. (2014). Preparing students for class: How to get 80% of students reading the textbook before class. *American Journal of Physics, 82*(10), 989–996. https://doi.org/10.1119/1.4895008

Heller, P., & Hollabaugh, M. (1992). Teaching problem solving through cooperative grouping. Part 2: Designing problems and structuring groups. *American Journal of Physics, 60*(7), 637–644. https://doi.org/10.1119/1.17118

Hembree, R. (1988). Correlates, causes, effects, and treatment of test anxiety. *Review of Educational Research, 58*(1), 47–77. https://doi.org/10.3102/00346543058001047

Herman, J. H., & Nilson, L. B. (2018). *Creating engaging discussions: Strategies for "avoiding crickets" in any size classroom and online*. Stylus.

Herrando, C., & Constantinides, E. (2021). Emotional contagion: A brief overview and future directions. *Emotion Science: Frontiers in Psychology, 12,* 712606. https://doi.org/10.3389/fpsyg.2021.712606

Herreid, C. F. (2019). The chef returns: A recipe for writing great case studies. *Journal of College Science Teaching, 48*(3), 38–42. https://www.jstor.org/stable/26901281

Hertel, J. P., & Millis, B. J. (2002). *Using simulations to promote learning in higher education*. Stylus.

Hew, H. K. F., Bai, S., Dawson, P., & Lo, C. K. (2021). Meta-analyses of flipped classroom studies: A review of methodology. *Educational Research Review, 33.* https://doi.org/10.1016/j.edurev.2021.100393

Higdon, J., & Topaz, C. (2009). Blogs and wikis as instructional tools: A social software adaptation of just-in-time-teaching. *College Teaching, 57*(2), 105–110. https://doi.org/ 10.3200/CTCH.57.2.105-110

Higher Education Research Institute (2010). *Degrees of success: Bachelor's degree completion rates among initial STEM majors.* https://heri.ucla.edu/nih/downloads/2010-Degrees-of-Success.pdf

Hintz, M. M. (2005). Can problem-based learning address content and process? *Biochemistry and Molecular Biology Education, 33*(5), 363–368. https://doi.org/10.1002/bmb.2005.49403305363

Hmelo-Silver, C. E., Duncan, R. G., & Chinn, C. A. (2007). Scaffolding and achievement in problem-based and inquiry learning: A response to Kirschner, Sweller, and Clark (2006). *Educational Psychologist, 42*(2), 99–107. https://doi.org/10.1080/00461520701263368

Hobson, E. H. (2002). Assessing students' motivation to learn in large classes. *American Journal of Pharmaceutical Education, 56,* 82S.

Hobson, E. H. (2004). *Getting students to read: Fourteen tips* (IDEA Paper No. 40). Kansas State University, Center for Faculty Evaluation and Development.

Hockley, W. E. (2008). The picture superiority effect in associative recognition. *Memory & Cognition, 36*(7), 1351–1359. https://doi.org/10.3758/MC.36.7.1351

Hodges, L. C. (2015). *Teaching undergraduate science: A guide to overcoming obstacles to student learning.* Stylus.

Hoeft, M. E. (2012). Why university students don't read: What professors can do to increase compliance. *International Journal for the Scholarship of Teaching and Learning, 6*(2). https://doi.org/ 10.20429/ijsotl.2012.060212

Hoffman, E., Trott, J., & Neely, K. P. (2002). Concept mapping: A tool to bridge the disciplinary divide. *American Journal of Obstetrics and Gynecology, 187*(3), 41–43. https://doi.org/ 10.1067/mob.2002.127360

Hogan, K. A., & Sathy, V. (2022). *Inclusive teaching: Strategies for promoting equity in the college classroom.* West Virginia Press.

Hogan, M., & Young, K. (2021). Designing group assignments to develop groupwork skills. *Journal of Information Systems Education, 32*(4), 274–282. https://aisel.aisnet.org/cgi/viewcontent.cgi?article=1886&context=jise

Hostetter, C., & Savion, L. (2013). Metacognitive skills—why bother (and how)? *National Teaching and Learning Forum, 23*(1), 4–7.

Hottell, D. L., Martinez-Aleman, A., & Rowan-Kenyon, H. T. (2014). Summer bridge program 2.0: Using social media to develop students' campus capital. *Change, 46*(5), 34–38. https://doi.org/10.1080/00091383.2014.941769

Howard, D. R., & Miskowski, J. A. (2005). Using a module-based laboratory to incorporate inquiry into a large cell biology course. *Cell Biology Education, 4,* 249–260. https://doi.org/10.1187/cbe.04-09-0052

Howard, J. R. (2015). *Discussion in the college classroom: Getting your students engaged and participating in person and online.* Jossey-Bass.

Howard, M. G., Collins, H. L., & DiCarlo, S. E. (2002). "Survivor" torches "Who Wants to Be a Physician?" in the educational games ratings war. *Advances in Physiology Education, 26,* 30–36.

Hoyt, D. P., & Perera, S. (2000). *Teaching approach, instructional objectives, and learning* (IDEA Research Report No. 1). IDEA Center.

Hoyt, L. T., Cohen, A. K., Dull, B., Castro, E. M., & Yazdani, N. (2021). "Constant stress has become the new normal": Stress and anxiety inequalities among U.S. college students in the time of COVID-19. *Journal of Adolescent Health, 68*(2), 270–276. https://doi.org/10.1016/j.jadohealth.2020.10.030

Hu, S., Kuh, G., & Li, S. (2008). The effects of engagement in inquiry-oriented activities on student learning and personal development. *Innovative Higher Education, 33*(2), 71–81. https://doi.org/10.1007/s10755-008-9066-z

Huang, K. (2019). Design and investigation of cooperative, scaffolded wiki learning activities in an online graduate-level course. *International Journal of Educational Technology in Higher Education, 16*(1), 1–18. https://doi.org/10.1186/s41239-019-0141-6

Huang, L.-S. (2014, September 29). *Students riding on coattails during group work? Five simple ideas to try.* Faculty Focus. http://www.facultyfocus.com/articles/effective-teaching-strategies/students-riding-coattails-group-work-five-simple-ideas-try/

Huang, S., Capps, M., Blacklock P. J., & Garza, M. (2014). Reading habits of college students in the United States. *Reading Psychology, 35*(5), 437–467, https://doi.org/10.1080/02702711.2012.739593

Huang, Y-M., Trevisan, M., & Storfer, A. (2007). The impact of the "all-of-the-above" option and student ability on multiple choice tests. *International Journal for the Scholarship of Teaching and Learning, 1*(2). http://digital-commons.georgiasouthern.edu/ij-sotl/vol1/iss2/11

Hudspith, B., & Jenkins, H. (2001). *Green guide: No. 3. Teaching the art of inquiry.* Society for Teaching and Learning in Higher Education.

Hung, W., Bailey, J. H., & Jonassen, D. H. (2003). Exploring the tensions of problem-based learning: Insights from research. In D. S. Knowlton & D. C. Sharp (Eds.), *New directions for teaching and learning: No. 95. Problem-based learning in the information age* (pp. 13–24). Jossey-Bass.

Hunt, R. (2004). What is inkshedding? http://www.stthomasu.ca/~hunt/dialogic/whatshed.htm

Hurt, R. L. (2007). Advising as teaching: Establishing outcomes, developing tools, and assessing student learning. *NACADA Journal, 27*(2), 36–40. https://doi.org/10.12930/0271-9517-27.2.36

Husmann, P. R., & O'Loughlin, V. D. (2018). Another nail in the coffin for learning styles? Disparities among undergraduate anatomy students' study strategies, class performance, and reported VARK learning styles. *Anatomical Sciences Education, 12,* 6–19. https://doi.org/10.1002/ase.1777

Hussain, W., Spady, W. G., Khan, S. Z., Khawaja, B. A., Naqash, T., & Conner, L. (2021). Impact evaluations of engineering programs using ABET student outcomes. *IEEE Access, 9,* 46166–46190. https://doi.org/10.1109/ACCESS.2021.3066921

Hussein, M.A., Hassan H., & Nassef, M. (2019). Automated language essay scoring systems: a literature review. *PeerJ Computer Science, 5*:e208. http://doi.org/10.7717/peerj-cs.208

Hutton, P. A. (2006). Understanding student cheating and what educators can do about it. *College Teaching, 54*(1), 171–176. https://doi.org/10.3200/CTCH.54.1.171-176

Hyerle, D. (1996). *Visual tools for constructing knowledge.* Association for Supervision and Curriculum Development.

ICAI. (2020). *Facts and statistics.* International Center for Academic Integrity. https://academicintegrity.org/resources/facts-and-statistics

Ip, A., Morrison, I., & Currie, M. (2001). *What is a learning object, technically?* http://users.tpg.com.au/adslfrcf/lo/learningObject(WebNet2001).pdf

Ives, J., & Castillo-Montoya, M. (2020). First-generation college students as academic learners: A systematic review. *Review of Educational Research, 90*(2), 139–178. https://doi.org/10.3102/0034654319899707

Jackson, A. P., Smith, S. A., & Hill, C. L. (2003). Academic persistence among Native American college students. *Journal of College Student Development, 44*(4), 548–565. https://doi.org/10.1353/csd.2003.0039

Jalajas, D. S., & Sutton, R. I. (1984). Feuds in student groups: Coping with whiners, martyrs, saboteurs, bullies, and deadbeats. *Journal of Management Education, 9*(4), 94–102.https://doi.org/10.1177/105256298400900413

Jaleniauskiene, E., & Kasperiuniene, J. (2022). Infographics in higher education:A scoping review. *E-Learning and Digital Media.* https://doi.org/10.1177/20427530221107774

Jamet, E., Gonthier, C., Cohean, S., Colliot, T., & Erhel, S. (2020). Does multitasking in the classroom affect learning outcomes? A naturalistic study. *Computers in Human Behavior, 106,* 106264. https://doi.org/10.1016/j.chb.2020.106264

Jaramillo, J., Mello, Z. R., & Worrell, F. C. (2016). Ethnic identity, stereotype threat, and perceived discrimination among Native American adolescents. *Journal of Research on Adolescence, 26*(4), 769–775. https://doi.org/10.1111/jora.12228

Jaschik, S. (2009). Imagining college without grades. *Inside Higher Ed.* https://www.insidehighered.com/news/2009/01/22/imagining-college-without-grades#:~:text=At%20Fairhaven%2C%20students%20do%20not,and%20there%20is%20much%20discussion

Jassawalla, A. R., Malshe, A., & Sashittal, H. (2008). Student perceptions of social loafing in undergraduate business classroom teams. *Decision Sciences Journal of Innovative Education, 6*(2), 403–426. https://doi.org/10.1111/j.1540-4609.2008.00183.x

Jensen, J. D. (2011). Promoting self-regulation and critical reflection through writing students' use of electronic portfolio. *International Journal of ePortfolio, 1*(1), 49–60.

Johnson, D. W., & Johnson, R. T. (1989). *Cooperation and competition:Theory and research.* Interaction Books.

Johnson, D. W., Johnson, R. T., & Smith, K. A. (1991). *Active learning: Cooperation in the college classroom.* Interaction Books.

Johnson, D. W., & Johnson, R. T. (1992). Positive interdependence: Key to effective cooperation. In R. Hertz-Lazarowitz & N. Miller (Eds.), *Interaction in cooperative groups:The theoretical anatomy of group learning* (pp. 174–199). Cambridge University Press.

Johnson, D. W., Johnson, R. T., & Smith, K. A. (2014).The power of cooperative learning or university classes: The interrelationships among theory, research, and practice.

Journal of Excellence in College Teaching, 25(4). Available to subscribers at http://celt.muohio.edu/ject/archive.php

Johnson, R. T., & Johnson, D. W. (1994). An overview of cooperative learning. In J. Thousand, A. Villa, & A. Nevin (Eds.), *Creativity and collaborative learning* (pp. 31–44). Brookes Press.

Johnson, V. E. (2003). *Grade inflation:A crisis in college education.* Springer-Verlag.

Johnston, K. M. (2003). *"Why do I have to change the way I learn just to fit the way you teach?" Steps to creating a teaching philosophy statement.* Workshop conducted in the Michigan State University Teaching Assistant Program, East Lansing.

Johnston, P. (2005, August 10). Dressing the part. *The Chronicle of Higher Education.* http://chronicle.com/article/Dressing-the-Part/44918

Jonas, H., Etzel, S., & Barzansky, B. (1989). Undergraduate medical education. *Journal of the American Medical Association, 262*(8), 1011–1019.

Jones, E. B. (2004). Culturally relevant strategies in the classroom. In A. M. Johns & M. K. Sipp (Eds.), *Diversity in the classroom: Practices for today's campuses* (pp. 51–72). University of Michigan Press.

Jones, R. C. (2008). The "why" of class participation: A question worth asking. *College Teaching, 56*(1), 59–62. https://doi.org/10.3200/CTCH.56.1.59-64

Jones-Wilson, T. M. (2005). Teaching problem-solving skills without sacrificing course content: Marrying traditional lecture and active learning in an organic chemistry class. *Journal of College Science Teaching, 35*(1), 42–46.

Josephson Institute. (2012). *The ethics of American youth; 2012.* Character Counts! https://charactercounts.org/2012-report-card/

Junco, R., & Cotton, S. R. (2012). No A 4 U: The relationship between multitasking and academic performance. *Computers and Education, 59*(2), 505–514. https://doi.org/10.1016/j.compedu.2011.12.023

Junco, R., Heiberger, G., & Loken, E. (2010). The effect of Twitter on college student engagement and grades. *Journal of Computer Assisted Learning, 27*(2). https://doi.org/10.1111/j.1365-2729.2010.00387.x

Jung, C. G. (1964). *Psychological types: Or, the psychology of individuation* (H. Godwin Baynes, Trans.). Pantheon Books.

Justice, C., Rice, J., Warry, W., Inglis, S., Miller, S., & Sammon, S. (2007). Inquiry in higher education: Reflections and directions in course design and teaching methods. *Innovative Higher Education, 31*(4), 201–214.

Kalman, C. S. (2007). *Successful science and engineering teaching in colleges and universities.* Jossey-Bass/Anker.

Kalman, J., & Kalman, C. (1996). Writing to learn. *American Journal of Physics, 64,* 954–955. https://doi.org/10.1119/1.18279

Kalyuga, S. (2000). When using sound with a text or picture is not beneficial for learning. *Australian Journal of Educational Technology, 16*(2), 161–172. https://doi.org/10.14742/ajet.1829

Karabenick, S. A., & Dembo, M. H. (2011). Understanding and facilitating self-regulated help seeking. *New Directions for Teaching and Learning, 126,* 33–43. https://doi.org/10.1002/tl.442

Karpicke, J., & Blunt, J. (2011). Retrieval practice produces more learning than elaborative studying with concept mapping. *Science, 331*(6018), 772–775. https://doi.org/10.1126/science.1199327

Katayama, A. D. (1997, November). Getting students involved in note taking: Why partial notes benefit learners more than complete notes. Paper presented at the Annual Meeting of the Mid-South Educational Research Association, Memphis, TN.

Kaufman, A. (1985). *Implementing problem-based medical education.* Springer.

Kaufman, A., Mennin, S., Waterman, R., Duban, S., Hansbarger, C., Silverblatt, H., Obenshain, S.S., Kantrowitz, M., Becker, T., & Samet J. (1989). The New Mexico experiment: Educational innovation and institutional change. *Academic Medicine, 64,* 285–294. https://doi.org/ 10.1097/00001888-198906000-00001

Kaufmann, R., & Vallade, J. I. (2020). Exploring connections in the online learning environment: student perceptions of rapport, climate, and loneliness. *Interactive Learning Environments,* 1–15. https://doi.org/10.1080/10494820.2020.1749670

Kaupins, G. (2005). Using popular game and reality show formats to review for exams. *Teaching Professor, 19*(1), 5–6.

Kaur, A. (2021). "Dope syllabus": Student impressions of an infographic-style visual syllabus. *International Journal of the Scholarship of Teaching and Learning, 15*(2). https://doi.org/10.20429/ijsotl.2021.150206

Kaur, G., Rehncy, J., Kahal, K. S., Singh, J., Sharma, V., Matreja, P. S., & Grewal, H. (2020). Case-based learning as an effective tool in teaching pharmacology to undergraduate medical students in a large group setting. *Journal of Medical Education and Curricular Development, 7.* https://doi.org/10.1177/2382120520920640

Kelly, K., & Zakrajsek, T. (2020). *Advancing online teaching: Creating equity-based digital learning.* Stylus.

Kember, D. (2016). *Understanding the nature of motivation and motivating students through teaching and learning in higher education.* Springer. https://doi.org/10.1007/978-981-287-883-0_6

Kendricks, K., Nedunuri, K.V., & Arment, A. R. (2013). Minority student perceptions of the impact of mentoring to enhance academic performance in STEM disciplines. *Journal of STEM Education: Innovations and Research, 14*(2), 38–46. https://www.jstem.org/jstem/index.php/JSTEM/article/view/1783

Kennedy, A., & Navey-Davis, S. (2004). Inquiry-guided learning and the foreign language classroom. In V. S. Lee (Ed.), *Teaching and learning through inquiry: A guidebook for institutions and instructors* (pp. 71–79). Stylus.

Kennedy, F., & Nilson, L. B. (2008). *Successful strategies for teams: Team member handbook.* https://ctl.utexas.edu/sites/default/files/TeamworkHandbook-KennedyandNilson.pdf

Keyser, R. S., & Doyle, B. S. (2020). Clever methods students use to cheat and ways to neutralize them. *Journal of Higher Education Theory and Practice, 20*(16). https://doi.org/10.33423/jhetp.v20i16.3987

Kiewra, K. A. (1985). Providing the instructor's notes: An effective addition to student notetaking. *Educational Psychologist, 20*(1), 33–39. https://doi.org/10.1207/s15326985ep2001_5

Kiewra, K. A. (2005). *Learn how to study and SOAR to success.* Pearson Prentice Hall.

Kilpatrick, W. S. H. (1929). *The project method: The use of the purposeful act in the educative process.* Teachers College, Columbia University. https://archive.org/details/project methodus00kilpgoog/page/n2/mode/2up

Kim, G. M. (2021). What's in a name? language, identity, and power in English education. *English Education, 53*(3), 224–231.

Kimmel, R. M. (2002). Undergraduate labs in applied polymer science. In *Proceedings of the 2002 American Society for Engineering Education Annual Conference and Exposition (Session 1526).* American Society for Engineering Education.

Kinchin, I. M. (2000). Concept mapping in biology. *Journal of Biological Education, 34*(2), 61–68. https://doi .org/10.1080/00219266.2000.9655687

Kinchin, I. M. (2001). If concept mapping is so helpful to learning biology, why aren't we all using it? *International Journal of Science Education, 23*(12), 1257–1269. https:// doi.org/10.1080/09500690010025058

Kinchin, I. M. (2006). Developing PowerPoint handouts to support meaningful learning. *British Journal of Educational Technology, 37*(4), 647–650. https://doi.org/ 10.1111/j.1467-8535.2006.00536.x

King, A. (1993). From sage on the stage to guide on the side. *College Teaching, 41*(1), 30–35. http://www.jstor .org/stable/27558571

King, M., & Shell, R. (2002). Teaching and evaluating critical thinking with concept maps. *Nurse Educator, 27*(5), 214–216. https://doi.org/ 10.1097/00006223-20 0209000-00008

Kirschner, P. A., & Karpinski, A. C. (2010). Facebook and academic performance. *Computers in Human Behavior, 26*(6), 1237–1245. https://doi.org/10.1016/j .chb.2010.03.024

Kirschner, P. A., Sweller, J., & Clark, R. E. (2006). Why minimal guidance during instruction does not work: An analysis of the failure of constructivist, discovery, problem-based, experiential, and inquiry-based teaching. *Educational Psychologist, 41*(2), 75–86. https://doi .org/10.1207/s15326985ep4102_1

Kirschner, P. A., & van Merriënboer, J. J. G. (2013). Do learners really know best? Urban legends in education.

Educational Psychologist, 48(3), 169–183. http://dx.doi .org/10.1080/00461520.2013.804395

Klahr, D., & Nigam, M. (2004). The equivalence of learning paths in early science instruction: Effects of direct instruction and discovery learning. *Psychological Science, 15,* 661–667. https://doi.org/10.1111/j.0956-7976.2004.00737.x

Kloss, R. J. (1994). A nudge is best: Helping students through the Perry schema of intellectual development. *College Teaching, 42*(4), 151–158.

Knoll, A. R., Otani, H., Skeel, R. L., & Van Horn, K. R. (2017). Learning style, judgements of learning, and learning of verbal and visual information. *British Journal of Psychology, 108*(3), 544–563. http://dx.doi.org/ 10.1111/ bjop.12214

Kobrak, P. (1992). Black student retention in predominantly white regional universities: The politics of faculty involvement. *Journal of Negro Education, 61*(4), 509–530. https://doi.org/10.2307/2295368

Koh, A. (2015, January 28). Live-tweeting assignments: To use or not to use? *The Chronicle of Higher Education.* http://chronicle.com/blogs/profhacker/live-tweeting-assignments-to-use-or-not-to-use/

Kohn, A. (1993). *Punished by rewards: The trouble with gold stars, incentive plans, A's, praise, and other bribes.* Houghton Mifflin.

Kohn, A. (2018). *Punished by rewards: Twenty-fifth anniversary edition: The trouble with gold stars, incentive plans, A's, praise, and other bribes.* Houghton Mifflin.

Koljatic, M., Silva, M., & Sireci, S.G. (2021). College admission tests and social responsibility. *Educational Measurement: Issues and Practice, 40*(4), 22–27. https://doi .org/10.1111/emip.12425

Koncz, A., & Gray, K. (2022, February 15). *What attributes employers want to see on college students' resumes.* National Association of Colleges and Employers. https://www .naceweb.org/about-us/press/the-attributes-employers-want-to-see-on-college-students-resumes/

Kokotsaki, D., Menzies, V., & Wiggins, A. (2016). Project-based learning: A review of the literature. *Improving Schools, 19*(3), 267–277. https://doi.org/10.1177/13654 80216659733

Kozma, R. B., Russell, J., Jones, T., Marx, N., & Davis, J. (1996). The use of multiple linked representations to facilitate science understanding. In S. Vosniadou, E. DeCorte, R. Glaser, & H. Mandl (Eds.), *International perspectives on the design of technology-supported learning environments* (pp. 41–60). Erlbaum.

Kraft, K. (2008, November 20). *Using situated metacognition to enhance student understanding of the nature of science* [Session presentation]. National Association of Geoscience Teachers (NAGT) Workshops: The Role of Metacognition in Teaching Geoscience, Carleton College, Northfield, MN, United States. http://serc.carleton.edu/NAGTWorkshops/metacognition/kraft.html

Kramer, J., & Arnold, A. (2004). Music 200: "Understanding Music": An inquiry-guided approach to music appreciation. In V. S. Lee (Ed.), *Teaching and learning through inquiry: A guidebook for institutions and instructors* (pp. 41–50). Stylus.

Kraushaar, J. M., & Novak, D. (2010). Examining the effects of student multitasking with laptops during the lecture. *Journal of Information Systems Education, 21*(2), 241–251. http://jise.org/Volume21/n2/JISEv21n2p241.pdf

Kreitzer, R. J., & Sweet-Cushman, J. (2022). Evaluating student evaluations of teaching: A review of measurement and equity bias in SETs and recommendations for ethical reform. *Journal of Academic Ethics, 20*(1), 73–84. https://doi.org/10.1007/s10805-021-09400-w

Kress, G., Jewitt, C., Ogborn, J., & Charalampos, T. (2006). *Multimodal teaching and learning: The rhetorics of the science classroom*. Continuum.

Kristensen, E. (2007). *Teaching at the University of Ottawa: A handbook for professors and TAs* (5th ed.). University of Ottawa, Centre for University Teaching.

Kruger, J., & Dunning, D. (1999). Unskilled and unaware of it: How difficulties in recognizing one's own incompetence lead to inflated self-assessments. *Journal of Personality and Social Psychology, 77*(6), 1121–1134. https://doi.org/10.1037/0022-3514.77.6.1121

Kubitz, K. A. (2014). The evidence, please. In J. Sibley & P. Ostafichuk (Eds.), *Getting started with team-based learning* (pp. 45–61). Stylus.

Kuh, G. D. (2008). *High-impact educational practices: What they are, who has access to them, and why they matter*. Association of American Colleges & Universities.

Kuh, G. D., Kinzie, J., Schuh, J., Whitt, E., & Associates. (2005). *Student success in college: Creating conditions that matter*. Jossey-Bass.

Kuhn, T. S. (1970). *The structure of scientific revolutions* (2nd ed.). University of Chicago Press.

Kulhanek, A., Butler, B., & Bodnar, C. A. (2021). Motivating first-year engineering students through gamified homework. *Educational Action Research, 29*(5), 681–706. https://doi.org/10.1080/09650792.2019.1635511

Kulikowski, M. (2021, July 29). *NC state, NSF unveil institute focused on artificial intelligence and the future of education*. NC State University News. https://news.ncsu.edu/2021/07/nsf-funds-ai-institute/?utm_campaign=ucomm-engnc&utm_medium=newsletter&utm_source=insidehighered&utm_content=ai

Kumar, V., & Boulanger, D. (2020). Explainable automated essay scoring: Deep learning really has pedagogical value. *Frontiers in Education, 5,* 572367. https://doi.org/10.3389/feduc.2020.572367

Kustra, E. D. H., & Potter, M. K. (2008). *Green guide: No. 9. Leading effective discussions*. Society for Teaching and Learning in Higher Education.

Kuznekoff, J. H., & Titsworth, S. (2013). The impact of mobile phone usage on student learning. *Communication Education, 62*(3), 233–252. https://doi.org/10.1080/03634523.2013.767917

Lahner, F. M., Lörwald, A. C., Bauer, D., Nouns, Z. M., Krebs, R., Guttormsen, S., Fischer, M. R., & Huwendiek, S. (2018). Multiple true-false items: a comparison of scoring algorithms. *Advances in Health Sciences Education: Theory and Practice, 23*(3), 455–463. https://doi.org/10.1007/s10459-017-9805-y

Lancaster, T., & Cotarlan, C. (2021). Contract cheating by STEM students through a file sharing website: A Covid-19 pandemic perspective. *International Journal for Education Integrity, 17*(1). https://doi.org/10.1007/s40979-021-00070-0

Lang, J. M. (2008). *On course: A week-by-week guide to your first semester of college teaching*. Harvard University Press.

Lang, J. M. (2012, January 17). Metacognition and student learning. *The Chronicle of Higher Education*. https://www.chronicle.com/article/metacognition-and-student-learning/

Lang, J. M. (2013, October 13). *How can I use Twitter to improve teaching and learning?* Live broadcast of Magna Publications online seminar.

Lang, J. M. (2014). *Cheating lessons: Learning from academic dishonesty*. Harvard University Press.

Lang, J. M. (2019, January 4). How to teach a good first day of class. *The Chronicle of Higher Education.* https://www.chronicle.com/article/how-to-teach-a-good-first-day-of-class/

Lasry, N. (2008). Clickers or flashcards: Is there really a difference? *Physics Teacher, 46,* 242–244. https://doi.org/10.1119/1.2895678

Leamnson, R. (1999). *Thinking about teaching and learning: Developing habits of learning with first year college and university students.* Stylus.

Leamnson, R. (2000). Learning as biological brain change. *Change, 32*(6), 34–40. http://dx.doi.org/10.1080/00091380009601765

Leamnson, R. (2002). *Learning (your first job).* http://www.udel.edu/CIS/106/iaydin/07F/misc/firstJob.pdf

Leauby, B. A., & Brazina, P. (1998). Concept mapping: Potential uses in accounting education. *Journal of Accounting Education, 16*(1), 123–138.

Lee, J. J., & Mccabe, J. M. (2020). Who speaks and who listens: Revisiting the chilly climate in college classrooms. *Gender & Society, 35*(1), 32–60. https://doi.org/10.1177/0891243220977141

Lee, V. S. (Ed.). (2004). *Teaching and learning through inquiry: A guidebook for institutions and instructors.* Stylus.

Lee, V. S. (2011). The power of inquiry as a way to learning. *Innovative Higher Education, 36,* 149–160. https://doi.org/10.1007/s10755–010–9166–4

Lee, V. S. (2012). What is inquiry-guided learning? *New Directions for Teaching and Learning, 2012*(129), 5–14. https://doi.org/10.1002/tl.20002

Lempres, D. (2022). How has the pandemic changed the way educators think about homework? *EdSurge: Voices of Change.* https://www.edsurge.com/news/2022-01-19-how-has-the-pandemic-changed-the-way-educators-think-about-homework

Lertladaluck, K., Chutabhadikul, N., Chevalier, N., & Moriguchi, Y. (2020). Effects of social and nonsocial reward on executive function in preschoolers. *Brain and Behavior, 10*(9), e01763. https://doi.org/10.1002/brb3.1763

Levant, B., & Paolo, T. (2017). A between-exam review does not affect re-test performance of medical students in a two-test system. *Medical Science Educator, 27*(1), 29–32. https://doi.org/10.1007/s40670-016-0353-5

Levin, J. (2001). *Developing a learning environment where all students seek to excel.* Faculty workshop conducted at Clemson University, Clemson, SC.

Lewis, S. E., & Lewis, J. E. (2005). Departing from lectures: An evaluation of a peer-led guided inquiry alternative. *Journal of Chemical Education, 82*(1),135–139. https://doi.org/10.1021/ed082p135

Li, M., Frieze, I. H., Nokes-Malach, T. J., & Cheong, J. (2013). Do friends always help your studies? Mediating processes between social relations and academic motivation. *Social Psychology of Education, 16*(1), 129–149.

Light, R. J. (1990). *The Harvard Assessment Seminar, first report: Explorations with students and faculty about teaching, learning, and student life.* Harvard Graduate School of Education.

Light, R. J. (1992). *The Harvard Assessment Seminar, second report: Explorations with students and faculty about teaching, learning, and student life.* Harvard Graduate School of Education.

Lightner R., & Benander, R. (2018). First impressions: Student and faculty feedback on four styles of syllabi. *International Journal of Teaching and Learning in Higher Education, 30*(3), 443–453. https://files.eric.ed.gov/fulltext/EJ1199421.pdf

Lin, T-C. (2014, November 26). Using quizzes to improve students' learning. *Teaching Professor.* https://www.teachingprofessor.com/topics/grading-feedback/quizzes-exams/using-quizzes-to-improve-students-learning/

Livingston, R. W., Rosette, A. S., & Washington, E. F. (2012). Can an agentic Black Woman get ahead? The impact of race and interpersonal dominance on perceptions of female leaders. *Psychological Science, 23*(4), 354–358. https://doi.org/10.1177/0956797611428079

Locke, E. A., & Latham, G. P. (1990). *A theory of goal setting and task performance.* Prentice Hall.

Lockhart, J. W. (2020). A large and longstanding body: Historical authority in the science of sex. In L. D. Valencia-García (Ed.), *Far-right revisionism and the end of history* (pp. 359–386). Routledge.

Lockhart, J. W. (2021). Paradigms of sex research and women in stem. *Gender & Society, 35*(3), 449–475. https://doi.org/10.1177/08912432211001384

Lopez-Pastor, V., & Sicilia-Camacho, A. (2017). Formative and shared assessment in higher education: Lessons learned and challenges for the future. *Assessment & Evaluation in Higher Education, 42*(1), 77–97. https://doi.org/10.1080/02602938.2015.1083535

Lord, T., & Orkwiszewski, T. (2006). Didactic to inquiry-based instruction in a science laboratory. *American Biology Teacher, 68*(6), 342–345. https://doi.org/10.2307/4452009

Loukopoulos, L. D., Dismukes, R. K., & Barshi, I. (2009). *The multitasking myth.* Ashgate.

Lovett, M. C. (2008, January). *Teaching metacognition.* Presented at the annual meeting of the Educause Learning Initiative. https://events.educause.edu/ir/library/pdf/ELI08104.pdf

Lovett-Hooper, G., Komarraju, M., Western, R., & Dollinger, S. (2007). Is plagiarism a forerunner of other deviance? Imagined futures of academically dishonest students. *Ethics and Behavior, 17*(3), 323–336. https://doi.org/10.1080/10508420701519387

Luckie, D. B., Maleszewski, J. J., Loznak, S. D., & Krha, M. (2004). Infusion of collaborative inquiry throughout a biology curriculum increases student learning: A four-year study of "teams and streams." *Advances in Physiology Education, 28*(4), 199–209. https://doi.org/10.1152/advan.00025.2004

Lundberg, C. A., & Sheridan, D. (2015). Benefits of engagement with peers, faculty, and diversity for online learners. *College Teaching, 68*(1), 8–15. https://doi.org/10.1080/87567555.2014.972317

Lundeberg, M. A., Mogen, K., Bergland, M., Klyczek, K., Johnson, D., & MacDonald, E. (2002). Fostering ethical awareness about human genetics through multimedia-based cases. *Journal of College Science Teaching, 32*(1), 64–69.

Lundeberg, M. A., & Yadav, A. (2006a). Assessment of case study teaching: Where do we go from here? Part I. *Journal of College Science Teaching, 35*(5), 10–13.

Lundeberg, M. A., & Yadav, A. (2006b). Assessment of case study teaching: Where do we go from here? Part II. *Journal of College Science Teaching, 35*(6), 8–13.

MacDonald, L. T. (2013). *Letter to next semester's students.* On Course Workshops. http://oncourseworkshop.com/staying-course/letter-next-semesters-students/

Mack, V. L., & Udland, M. (2017). *Icebreakers 3: 67 no prep, no prop activities!* Shawnee Press.

Major, C., Harris, M., & Zakrajsek, T. (2021). *Teaching for learning: 101 intentionally designed educational activities to put students on the path to success* (2nd ed.). Routledge.

Major, C. H., & Palmer, B. (2001). Assessing the effectiveness of problem-based learning in higher education: Lessons from the literature. *Academic Exchange Quarterly, 5*(1), 4–9.

Mangurian, L. P. (2005, February). *Learning and teaching practice: The power of the affective* [Paper presentation]. Annual Lilly Conference on College Teaching South, Greensboro, NC, United States.

Mann, S., & Robinson, A. (2009). Boredom in the lecture theatre: An investigation into the contributors, moderators and outcomes of boredom amongst university students. *British Educational Research Journal, 35*(2), 243–258. https://doi.org/10.1080/01411920802042911

Marrs, K. A., & Novak, G. (2004). Just-in-time teaching in biology: Creating an active learner classroom using the Internet. *Cell Biology Education, 3*(1), 49–61. https://doi.org/10.1187/cbe.03-11-0022

Marsh, H. W. (1984). Students' evaluations of university teaching: Dimensionality, reliability, validity, potential biases, and utility. *Journal of Educational Psychology, 76,* 707–754. https://doi.org/10.1037/0022-0663.76.5.707

Marsh, H. W. (1987) Students' evaluation of university teaching: Research findings, methodological issues, and directions for future research. *International Journal of Educational Research, 11*(3), 253–388. https://doi.org/10.1016/0883-0355(87)90001-2

Marshall, J. (2010). Five ways to integrate: Using strategies from contemporary art. *Art Education, 63*, 13–19. https://doi.org/10.1080/00043125.2010.11519065

Marshall, K. (2015, January 5). How to curate your digital identity as an academic. *The Chronicle of Higher Education.* http://chronicle.com/article/How-to-Curate-Your-Digital/151001/

Martin, G. I. (2000). Peer carding. *College Teaching, 48*(1), 15–16.

Martin, H. H., Hands, K. B., Lancaster, S. M., Trytten, D. A., & Murphy, T. J. (2008). Hard but not too hard: Challenging courses and engineering students. *College Teaching, 56*(2), 107–113. https://doi.org/10.3200/CTCH.56.2.107-113

Marzano, R. J. (2003). *What works in schools: Translating research into action.* Association for Supervision and Curriculum Development.

Maslow, A. H. (1966). *The psychology of science: A reconnaissance.* Joanna Cotler Books.

Mastascusa, E. J., Snyder, W. J., & Hoyt, B. S. (2011). *Effective instruction for STEM disciplines: From learning theory to college teaching.* Jossey-Bass.

Maurer, T., & Longfield, J. (2013, October 4). *Improving reading compliance and quiz scores through the use of reading guides* [Panel presentation]. Annual Meetings of the International Society for the Scholarship of Teaching and Learning, Elon, NC, United States.

Mayer, R. E., (2002). Multimedia learning. *Psychology of Learning and Motivation, 41*, 85–139. https://doi.org/10.1016/S0079-7421(02)80005-6

Mayer, R. E. (2004). Should there be a three-strikes rule against pure discovery learning? The case for guided methods of instruction. *American Psychologist, 59*(1), 14–19. https://doi.org/10.1037/0003-066X.59.1.14

Mayer, R. E. (2005). Introduction to multimedia learning. In R. E. Mayer (Ed.), *The Cambridge handbook of multimedia learning* (pp. 1–15). Cambridge University Press.

Mayer, R. E. (2009). *Multimedia learning* (2nd ed.). Cambridge University Press.

Mayer, R. E., & Gallini, J. K. (1990). When is an illustration worth ten thousand words? *Journal of Educational Psychology, 82*(4), 715–726. https://doi.org/10.1037/0022-0663.82.4.715

Mayer, R. E., & Moreno, R. (2003). Nine ways to reduce cognitive load in multimedia learning. *Educational Psychologist, 38*(1), 43–52. https://doi.org/10.1207/S15326985EP3801_6

Mayo, L. (2019, May 30). Students, would you like fries with that? *Inside Higher Ed.* https://www.insidehighered.com/views/2019/05/30/students-should-stop-treating-faculty-expendable-opinion

Mazur, E. (1997). *Peer instruction: A user's manual.* Prentice Hall.

Mazur Group. (2008). *Publications: Peer instruction.* Mazur Group. https://mazur.harvard.edu/research-areas/peer-instruction

McCabe, D. L., Butterfield, K. D., & Treviño, L. K. (2012). *Cheating in college: Why students do it and what educators can do about it.* John Hopkins University Press.

McCabe, D. L. (2005). Cheating among college and university students: A North American perspective. *International Journal for Educational Integrity, 1*(1). https://doi.org/10.21913/IJEI.v1i1.14

McCoy, B. (2013). Digital distractions in the classroom: Student classroom use of digital devices for non–class related purposes. *Journal of Media Education, 4*(4), 5–14. http://en.calameo.com/read/000091789af53ca4e647f

McCoy, B. (2021). Why students cheat (it's not them–it's us). *Liberal Education, 107*(1), 46–51.

McCoy, B. R. (2016). Digital distractions in the classroom phase II: Student classroom use of digital devices for non-class related purposes. *Faculty Publications, College of Journalism & Mass Communications, 90.* http://digitalcommons.unl.edu/journalismfacpub/90

McCreary, C. L., Golde, M. F., & Koeske, R. (2006). Peer instruction in the general chemistry laboratory: Assessment of student learning. *Journal of Chemical Education, 83*(5), 804–810.

McDaniel, M. A., & Butler, A. C. (2010). A contextual framework for understanding when difficulties are desirable. In A. S. Benjamin (Ed.), *Successful remembering and successful forgetting: Essays in honor of Robert A. Bjork* (pp. 175–199). Psychology Press.

McDaniel, M. A., Howard, D. C., & Einstein, G. O. (2009). The read-recite-review study strategy: Effective and portable. *Psychological Science, 20*(4), 516–522. https://doi.org/10.1111/j.1467-9280.2009.02325.x

McDermott, L. C., & Shaffer, P. S. (2002). *Tutorials in introductory physics*. Prentice Hall.

McDermott, L. C., & Shaffer, P. S. (2011–2012). *Tutorials in introductory physics* (2nd ed.). Pearson.

McGaghie, W. C., McCrimmon, D. R., Mitchell, G., Thompson, J. A., & Ravitch, M. M. (2000). Quantitative concept mapping in pulmonary physiology: Comparison of student and faculty knowledge structures. *Advances in Physiology Education, 23*(1), 72–80. https://doi.org/10.1152/advances.2000.23.1.S72

McGuire, S. Y., with McGuire, S. (2015). *Teach students how to learn: Strategies you can incorporate in any course to improve student metacognition, study skills, and motivation*. Stylus.

McGuire, S. Y., with McGuire, S. (2018). *Teach yourself how to learn: Strategies you can use to ace any course at any level*. Stylus.

McGunagle, D., & Zizka, L. (2020). Employability skills for 21st-century STEM students: The employers' perspective. *Higher Education, Skills and Work-Based Learning, 10*(3), 591–606. https://doi.org/10.1108/HESWBL-10-2019-0148

McIntosh, M. (2010). *Professors—Assign numbers to your students and return assignments quickly and easily*. Ezine Articles. http://ezinearticles.com/?Professors—Assign-Numbers-to-Your-Students-and-Return-Assignments-Quickly-and-Easily&id=3799370

McIntosh, R. D., Fowler, E. A., Lyu, T., & Della Sala, S. (2019). Wise up: Clarifying the role of metacognition in the Dunning-Kruger effect. *Journal of Experimental Psychology: General, 148*(11), 1882–1897. https://doi.org/10.1037/xge0000579

McKeachie, W. J. (2002). *Teaching tips: Strategies, research, and theory for college and university teachers* (11th ed.). Houghton Mifflin.

Mealy, D. L., & Host, T. R. (1993). Coping with test anxiety. *College Teaching, 40*(4), 147–150. https://doi.org/10.1080/87567555.1992.10532238

Medina, J. (2008). *Brain rules*. Pear Press.

Mercader, D., Ion, G., & Diaz-Vicario, A. (2020). Factors influencing students' peer feedback uptake: Instructional design matters. *Assessment & Evaluation in Higher Education, 45*(8), 1169–1180. https://doi.org/10.1080/02602938.2020.1726283

Metiri Group. (2008). *Multimodal learning through media: What the research says*. Cisco Systems. http://www.cisco.com/web/strategy/docs/education/Multimodal-Learning-Through-Media.pdf

Meyers, S. A. (2009). Do your students care whether you care about them? *College Teaching, 57*(4), 205–210. https://doi.org/ 10.1080/87567550903218620

Meyers, S. A., Bender, J., Hill, E. K., & Thomas, S. Y. (2006). How do faculty experience and respond to classroom conflict? *International Journal of Teaching and Learning in Higher Education, 18*(3), 180–187.

Mezeske, B. (2009). *The Graduate* revisited: Not "plastics" but "metacognition." *Teaching Professor, 23*(9), 1.

Michaelsen, L. K., Knight, A. B., & Fink, L. D. (Eds.). (2004). *Team-based learning: A transformative use of small groups in college teaching*. Stylus.

Middendorf, J., & Kalish, A. (1996). The "change-up" in lectures. *National Teaching and Learning Forum, 5*(2), 1–4. https://tchsotl.sitehost.iu.edu/part3/Middendorf%20&%20Kalish.pdf

Mierson, S., & Parikh, A. A. (2000). Stories from the field: Problem-based learning from a teacher's and a student's perspective. *Change, 32*(1), 20–27. https://doi.org/10.1080/00091380009602705

Miller, K., Schell, J., Ho, A., Lukoff, B., & Mazur, E. (2015). Response switching and self-efficacy in peer instruction classrooms. *Physical Review Physics Education Research, 11*, 010104. https://doi.org/10.1103/PhysRevSTPER.11.010104

Miller, M. D. (2022, August 2). Ungrading light: 4 simple ways to ease the spotlight off points. *The Chronicle of Higher Education*. https://www.chronicle.com/article/ungrading-light-4-simple-ways-to-ease-the-spotlight-off-points

Millis, B. J. (1990). Helping faculty build learning communities through cooperative groups. In L. Hilsen (Ed.), *To improve the academy: Vol. 9. Resources for faculty, instructional, and organizational development* (pp. 43–58). New Forums Press.

Millis, B. J., & Cottell, P. G., Jr. (1998). *Cooperative learning for higher education faculty.* American Council on Education and Oryx Press.

Mills, J. E., & Treagust, D. F. (2003). Engineering education: Is problem-based or project-based learning the answer? *Australasian Journal of Engineering Education.* https://www.researchgate.net/publication/246069451_Engineering_Education_Is_Problem-Based_or_Project-Based_Learning_the_Answer

Mintz, S. (2022, January 8). Is literacy declining? *Inside Higher Ed.* https://www.insidehighered.com/blogs/higher-ed-gamma/literacy-declining

Mishra, P., & Koehler, M. J. (2006). Technological pedagogical content knowledge: A framework for integrating technology in teachers' knowledge. *Teachers College Record, 108*(6), 1017–1054. https://doi.org/10.1111/j.1467-9620.2006.00684.x

Missouri University S&T Library (2022, March 16). Library and learning resources. https://libguides.mst.edu/c.php?g=395171&p=2685087

Mitchell, K. M., & Martin, J. (2018). Gender bias in student evaluations. *Political Science & Politics, 51*(3), 648–652. https://doi.org/10.1017/S104909651800001X

Miyatsu, T., Nguyen, K., & McDaniel, M. A. (2018). Five popular study strategies: Their pitfalls and optimal implementations. *Perspectives on Psychological Science, 13*(3), 390–407. https://doi.org/10.1177/1745691617710510

Montgomery, K. (2002). Authentic tasks and rubrics: Going beyond traditional assessments in college teaching. *College Teaching, 50*(1), 34–39. https://doi.org/10.1080/87567550209595870

Montrosse-Moorhead, B., Ensminger, D. C., & Roseveare, C. (2022). *How do we teach and learn with cases?* In L. M. Kallemeyn, I. Bourgeois, & D. C. Ensminger, (Eds.), *New directions for evaluation: Special issue: Case-centered teaching and learning in evaluation* (pp. 53–67). American Evaluation Association.

Moore, E. (2013, January 7). *Adapting PowerPoint lectures for online delivery: Best practices.* Faculty Focus. http://www.facultyfocus.com/articles/online-education/adapting-powerpoint-lectures-for-online-delivery-best-practices/

Moore, S. (speaker). (2009). *Scott Moore: Using technology and collaboration to engage students (Video).* Center for Research on Learning and Teaching, University of Michigan. http://www.crlt.umich.edu/faculty/Thurnau/ThurnauVideos.php

Morad, R. (2022, March 11). Universities reimagine teaching labs for a virtual future. *EdTech.* https://edtechmagazine.com/higher/article/2022/03/universities-reimagine-teaching-labs-virtual-future

Moravec, M., Williams, A., Aguilar-Roca, N., & O'Dowd, D. K. (2010). Learn before lecture: A strategy that improves learning outcomes in a large introductory biology class. *CBE Life Sciences Education, 9*(4), 473–481. https://doi.org/10.1187/cbe.10-04-0063

Morehead, K., Dunlosky, J., & Rawson, K. A. (2019). How much mightier is the pen than the keyboard for note-taking? A replication and extension of Mueller and Oppenheimer. *Educational Psychology Review, 31*, 753–780. https://doi.org/10.1007/s10648-019-09468-2

Moreno, R. (2004). Decreasing cognitive load for novice students: Effects of explanatory versus corrective feedback in discovery-based multimedia. *Instructional Science, 32*(1–2), 99–113. https://doi.org/10.1023/B:TRUC.0000021811.66966.1d

Moro, C., Phelps, C., & Stromberga, Z. (2020). Utilizing serious games for physiology and anatomy learning and revision. *Advances in Physiology Education, 44*(3), 505–507. https://doi.org/10.1152/advan.00074.2020

Morris, P., & Sarapin. S. (2020). Mobile phones in the classroom: Policies and potential pedagogy. *Journal of Media Literacy Education, 12*(1), 57–69. https://doi.org/10.23860/JMLE-2020-12-1-5

Moy, J. R., Rodenbaugh, D. W., Collins, H. L., & DiCarlo, S. E. (2000). Who wants to be a physician? An educational tool for reviewing pulmonary physiology. *Advances in Physiology Education, 24*(1), 30–37. https://doi.org/10.1152/advances.2000.24.1.30

Mpofu, E. (2007). Service-learning effects on the academic learning of rehabilitation services students. *Michigan Journal of Community Service Learning, 14*(1), 46–52. http://hdl.handle.net/2027/spo.3239521.0014.104

Mueller, P. A., & Oppenheimer, D. M. (2014). The pen is mightier than the keyboard: Advantages of longhand over laptop note taking. *Psychological Science, 25*(6), 1159–1168. https://doi.org/10.1177/0956797614524581

Murrell, K. L. (1984). Peer performance evaluation: When peers do it, they do it better. *Journal of Management Education, 9*(4), 83–85. https://doi.org/10.1177/105256298400900411

Myers, C. B., & Myers, S. M. (2007). Assessing assessment: The effects of two exam formats on course achievement and evaluation. *Innovative Higher Education, 31,* 227–236. https://doi.org/ 10.1007/S10755-006-9020-X

Myers, S. A., Goldman, Z. W., Atkinson, J., Ball, H., Carton, S. T., Tindage, M, F., & Anderson, A. O. (2016). Student civility in the college classroom: Exploring student use and effects of classroom citizenship behavior. *Communication Education, 65*(1), 64–82. https://doi.org/ 10.1080/03634523.2015.1061197

Nabecker, S., Huwendiek, S., Theiler, L., Huber, M., Petroski, K., & Greif, R. (2021). The effective group size for teaching cardiopulmonary resuscitation skills: A randomized controlled simulation trial. *Resuscitation, 165,* 77–82. https://doi.org/10.1016/j.resuscitation.2021.05.034

Nadelson, S. (2007). Academic misconduct by university students: Faculty perceptions and responses. *Plagiary, 2*(2), 1–10. http://hdl.handle.net/2027/spo.5240451.0002.008

Nadolski, R. J., Kirschner, P. A., & van Merriënboer, J. J. G. (2005). Optimizing the number of steps in learning tasks for complex skills. *British Journal of Educational Psychology, 84,* 429–434. https://doi.org/10.1348/000709904X22403

Nadworny, E. (2019, October 5). *College students: How to make office hours less scary.* NPR. https://www.npr.org/2019/10/05/678815966/college-students-how-to-make-office-hours-less-scary

Najafi, F., Giovannucci, A., Wang, S. S.-H., & Medina, J. F. (2014). Coding of stimulus strength via analog calcium signals in Purkinje cell dendrites of awake mice. *eLife.* https://doi.org/10.7554/eLife.03663

Nancekivell, S. E., Shah, P., & Gelman, S. A. (2020). Maybe they're born with it, or maybe it's experience: Toward a deeper understanding of the learning style myth. *Journal of Educational Psychology, 112*(2), 221–235. https://doi.org/10.1037/edu0000366

Nancekivell, S. E., Xin Sun, S. A., & Priti, S. (2021). A slippery myth: How learning style beliefs shape reasoning about multimodal instruction and related scientific evidence. *Cognitive Science, 45*(10), e13047. https://doi.org/10.1111/cogs.13047

National Center for Education Statistics (2019). Indicator 23: Postsecondary graduation rates. *Status and trends in the education of racial and ethnic groups.* IES National Center for Education Statistics. https://nces.ed.gov/programs/raceindicators/indicator_red.asp#:~:text=The%206%2Dyear%20graduation%20rate%20was%20higher%20for%20females%20than,44%20percent%20for%20females%20vs

National Center for Education Statistics. (2022). College student employment. *Condition of Education.* U.S. Department of Education, Institute of Education Sciences. https://nces.ed.gov/programs/coe/indicator/ssa

National Science Foundation. (2016). *Science and engineering indicators* 2016. National Science Board. https://www.nsf.gov/statistics/2016/nsb20161/#/

National Survey of Student Engagement. (2007). *Experiences that matter: Enhancing student learning and success.* Indiana University, Center for Postsecondary Research and Planning.

NBME. (2020). *NBME item-writing guide: Constructing written test questions for the health sciences.* Author. https://www.nbme.org/sites/default/files/2020-11/NBME_Item%20Writing%20Guide_2020.pdf

Nelson, C. E. (2000). How can students who are reasonably bright and who are trying hard to do the work still flunk? *National Teaching and Learning Forum, 9*(5), 7–8.

Nemire, R. E. (2007). Intellectual property development and use for distance education courses: A review of law, organizations, and resources for faculty. *College Teaching, 55*(1), 26–30. https://doi.org/10.3200/CTCH.55.1.26-30

Nevin, J. A. (2012). Resistance to extinction and behavioral momentum. *Behavioural Processes, 90*(1), 89–97. https://doi.org/10.1016/j.beproc.2012.02.006

Nguyen, K. A., Borrego, M., Finelli, C. J., DeMonbrun, M., Crockett, C., Tharayil, S., Shekhar, P., Waters, C., & Rosenberg, R. (2021). Instructor strategies to aid implementation of active learning: A systematic literature review. *International Journal of STEM Education, 8*(9). https://doi.org/10.1186/s40594-021-00270-7

Nicol, D. (2010). From monologue to dialogue: Improving written feedback processes in mass higher education. *Assessment & Evaluation in Higher Education, 35*(5), 501–517. https://doi.org/10.1080/02602931003786559

Nilson, L. B. (2007). *The graphic syllabus and the outcomes map: Communicating your course.* Jossey-Bass.

Nilson, L. B. (2012). Time to raise questions about student ratings. In J. E. Groccia & L. Cruz (Eds.), *To improve the academy: Vol. 31. Resources for faculty, instructional, and organizational development* (pp. 213–227). Jossey-Bass.

Nilson, L. B. (2013a). *Creating self-regulated learners: Strategies for strengthening students' self-awareness and learning skills.* Stylus.

Nilson, L. B. (2013b). Measuring student learning to document faculty teaching effectiveness. In J. E. Groccia & L. Cruz (Eds.), *To improve the academy: Vol. 32. Resources for faculty, instructional, and organizational development* (pp. 287–300). Jossey-Bass.

Nilson, L. B. (2015). *Specifications grading: Restoring rigor, motivating students, and saving faculty time.* Stylus.

Nilson, L. B. (2021). *Infusing critical thinking into your course: A concrete, practical approach.* Stylus.

Nilson, L. B., & Goodson, L. A. (2018). *Online teaching at its best: Merging instructional design with teaching and learning research.* Jossey-Bass.

Nilson, L. B., & Weaver, B. E. (Eds.). (2005). *New directions for teaching and learning: No. 101. Enhancing learning with laptops in the classroom.* Jossey-Bass.

Nisbett, R. E. (1993). *Rules for reasoning.* Erlbaum.

Nixon-Cobb, E. (2005). Visualizing thinking: A strategy that improved thinking. *Teaching Professor, 19*(1), 3, 6.

Noppe, I. (2007). PowerPoint presentation handouts and college student learning outcomes. *International Journal for the Scholarship of Teaching and Learning, 1*(1). https://doi.org/10.20429/ijsotl.2007.010109

Norlock, K. J. (2016). Grading (anxious and silent) participation. *Teaching Philosophy, 39*(4), 483–505. https://philpapers.org/rec/NORGP-3

Norman, T. D. (2021). Teaching music online: Using Microsoft PowerPoint to create prerecorded lessons. *General Music Today, 34*(3), 45–51. https://doi.org/10.1177/1048371321996292

North Carolina State University Physics Education R&D Lab (2015). *About the SCALE-UP project.* https://www.ncsu.edu/per/scaleup.html

Nosich, G. M. (2012). *Learning to think things through: A guide to critical thinking across the curriculum* (4th ed.). Pearson/Prentice Hall.

Novak, G. M., Patterson, E. T., Gavrin, A. D., & Christian, W. (1999). *Just-in-time teaching: Blending active learning with web technology.* Prentice Hall.

Novak, J. D., & Gowin, B. D. (1984). *Learning how to learn.* Cambridge University Press.

Novak, J. M., Markey, V., & Allen, M. (2007). Evaluating cognitive outcomes of service-learning in higher education: A meta-analysis. *Communication Research Reports, 24*(2), 149–157. https://doi.org/10.1080/08824090701304881

Nückles, M., Roelle, J., Glogger-Frey, I., Waldeyer, J., & Renkl, A. (2020). The self-regulation-view in writing-to-learn: Using journal writing to optimize cognitive load in self-regulated learning. *Educational Psychology Review, 32,* 1089–1126. https://doi.org/10.1007/s10648-020-09541-1

Nuhfer, E., Harrington, R., Pasztor, S., & Whorf, S. (2014). Metadisciplinary awareness can illuminate the meaning, quality, and integrity of college degrees: Educating in fractal patterns XL. *National Teaching and Learning Forum, 23*(4), 9–11.

Nuhfer, E. B., & Knipp, D. (2003). The knowledge survey: A tool for all reasons. In C. Wehlburg & S. Chadwick-Blossey (Eds.), *To improve the academy: Vol. 21. Resources for faculty, instructional, and organizational development* (pp. 59–78). Anker.

Oakley, B., Brent, R., Felder, R. M., & Elhajj, I. (2004). Turning student groups into effective teams. *Journal of Student Centered Learning, 2*(1), 9–34. http://www4

.ncsu.edu/unity/lockers/users/f/felder/public/Papers/Oakley-paper%28JSCL%29.pdf

Ochnik, D., Rogowska, A. M., Kuśnierz, C., Jakubiak, M., Schütz, A., Held, M. J., Arzenšek, A., Benatov, J., Berger, R., Korchagina, E. V., Pavlova, I., Blažková, I., Aslan, I., Çınar, O., & Cuero-Acosta, Y. A. (2021). Mental health prevalence and predictors among university students in nine countries during the COVID-19 pandemic: A cross-national study. *Scientific Reports, 11*(1), 18644–18644. https://doi.org/10.1038/s41598-021-97697-3

O'Donovan, B. M., den Outer, B., Price, M., & Lloyd, A. (2021). What makes good feedback good? *Studies in Higher Education, 46*(2), 318–329. https://doi.org/10.1080/03075079.2019.1630812

Odom, C. D. (2002, April). *Advances in instructional physics laboratories at Clemson University.* Colloquium presented at the College of Engineering and Sciences, Clemson University, Clemson, SC.

Oliver, S., Marder, B., Erz, A., & Kietzmann, J. (2021). Fitted: The impact of academics' attire on students' evaluations and intentions. *Assessment & Evaluation in Higher Education, 47*(3), 390–410. https://doi.org/10.1080/02602938.2021.1921105

Oliver-Hoyo, M., & Allen, D. (2005). Attitudinal effects of a student-centered active learning environment. *Journal of Chemical Education, 82*(6), 944–949. https://doi.org/10.1021/ed082p944

Oliver-Hoyo, M., Allen, D., & Anderson, M. (2004). Inquiry-guided instruction. *Journal of College Science Teaching, 33*(6), 20–24.

Oliver-Hoyo, M., & Beichner, R. (2004). SCALE-UP: Bringing inquiry-guided methods to large enrollment courses. In V. S. Lee (Ed.), *Teaching and learning through inquiry: A guidebook for institutions and instructors* (pp. 51–69). Stylus.

Onodipe, G., Keengwe, J., & Cottrell-Yongye, A. (2020). Using learning management system to promote self-regulated learning in a flipped classroom. *Journal of Teaching and Learning with Technology, 9*(1). https://doi.org/10.14434/jotlt.v9i1.29375

Orlans, H. (1999). Scholarly fair use: Chaotic and shrinking. *Change, 31*(6), 53–60.

Ory, J. C., & Ryan, K. E. (1993). *Survival skills for college: Vol. 4. Tips for improving testing and grading.* Sage.

Oxford Learner's Dictionaries. (2022). *Syllabus.* https://www.oxfordlearnersdictionaries.com/us/definition/english/syllabus

Page, E. B. (2003). Project essay grade: PEG. In M. D. Shermis & J. C. Burstein (Eds.), *Automated essay scoring: A cross-disciplinary perspective* (pp. 43–54). Lawrence Erlbaum Associates Publishers.

Papadatou-Pastou, M., Touloumakos, A. K., Koutouveli, C., & Barrable, A. (2020). The learning styles neuromyth: When the same term means different things to different teachers. *European Journal of Psychology of Education, 36,* 511–531. https://doi.org/10.1007/s10212-020-00485-2

Pape-Lindstrom, P., Eddy, S., & Freeman, S. (2018). Reading quizzes improve exam scores for community college students. *CBE Life Sciences Education, 17*(2). https://doi.org/10.1187/cbe.17-08-0160

Parker, K., Graf, N., & Igielnic, R. (2019, January 17). *Generation Z looks a lot like millennials on key social and political issues.* Pew Research Center. https://www.pewresearch.org/social-trends/2019/01/17/generation-z-looks-a-lot-like-millennials-on-key-social-and-political-issues/

Parker, K., & Igielnic, R. (2020, May 14). *On the cusp of adulthood and facing an uncertain future: What we know about Gen Z so far.* Pew Research Center. https://www.pewresearch.org/social-trends/2020/05/14/on-the-cusp-of-adulthood-and-facing-an-uncertain-future-what-we-know-about-gen-z-so-far-2/

Pascarella, E. T., & Terenzini, P. T. (2005). *How college affects students: A third decade of research.* Jossey-Bass.

Pashler, H., McDaniel, M., Rohrer, D., & Bjork, R. (2009). Learning styles: Concepts and evidence. *Psychological Science in the Public Interest, 9*(3), 105–119. https://doi.org/10.1111/j.1539-6053.2009.01038.x

Patterson, R. W. (2015). *Can behavioral tools improve online student outcomes? Experimental evidence from a massive open online course.* Cornell Higher Education Research Institute. https://hdl.handle.net/1813/74637

Pauk, W. (2001). *How to study in college.* Houghton Mifflin.

Paul, R., & Elder, L. (2013a). *Critical thinking: Teaching students how to study and learn, Part III*. The Foundation for Critical Thinking. http://www.criticalthinking.org/pages/how-to-study-and-learn-part-three/515.

Paul, R., & Elder, L. (2013b). *The state of critical thinking today*. The Foundation for Critical Thinking. http://www.criticalthinking.org/pages/the-state-of-critical-thinking-today/523

Paul, R., & Elder, L. (2013c). *Universal intellectual standards*. The Foundation for Critical Thinking. http://www.criticalthinking.org/pages/universal-intellectual-standards/527

Paul, R., & Elder, L. (2013d). *Valuable intellectual traits*. The Foundation for Critical Thinking. http://www.critical-thinking.org/pages/valuable-intellectual-traits/528

Paul, R., Elder, L., & Bartell, T. (2013). *Study of 38 public universities and 28 private universities to determine faculty emphasis on critical thinking in instruction*. The Foundation for Critical Thinking. http://www.criticalthinking.org/pages/study-of-38-public-universities-and-28-private-universities-to-determine-faculty-emphasis-on-critical-thinking-in-instruction/598

Payette, P. R., & Brown, M. K. (2018). *Gathering mid-semester feedback: Three variations to improve instruction*. IDEA Paper #67. https://files.eric.ed.gov/fulltext/ED588349.pdf

Peirce, W. (2006). Strategies for teaching critical reading. https://sphweb.bumc.bu.edu/otlt/teachingLibrary/Teaching%20Activities/critical--reading.pdf

Peiser, J. (2018, April 30). It took 17 years: Freelancers receive $9 million in copyright suit. *The New York Times*. https://www.nytimes.com/2018/04/30/business/media/freelancers-digital-copyright-lawsuit.html

Perry, W. G. (1968). *Forms of intellectual and ethical development in the college years: A scheme*. Holt.

Perry, W. G. (1985). Different worlds in the same classroom. *Journal of the Harvard-Danforth Center: On Teaching and Learning, 1*, 1–17.

Persellin, D. C., & Daniels, M. B. (2014). *A concise guide to improving student learning: Six evidence-based principles and how to apply them*. Stylus.

Persson, H., Ahman, H., Yngling, A. A., & Gulliksen, J. (2015). Universal design, inclusive design, accessible design, design for all: Different concepts—one goal? On the concept of accessibility-historical, methodological and philosophical aspects. *Universal Access in the Information Society, 14*(4), 505–526. https://doi.org/10.1007/s10209-014-0358-z

Pew Research Center. (2021, April 27). Mobile Fact Sheet. https://www.pewinternet.org/fact-sheet/mobile/

Plotnick, E. (2001). A graphical system for understanding the relationship between concepts. *Teacher Librarian, 2*(4), 42–44.

Picklesimer, M. E., Buchin, Z. L., & Mulligan, N. W. (2019). The effect of retrieval practice on transitive inference. *Experimental Psychology, 66*(6), 377–392. https://doi.org/10.1027/1618-3169/a000467

Prégent, R. (1994). *Charting your course: How to prepare to teach more effectively*. Magna.

Premraj, D., Thompson, R. R., Hughes, L., & Adams, J. (2021). Key factors influencing retention rates among historically underrepresented students groups in STEM fields. *Journal of College Student Retention: Research, Theory & Practice, 23*(2), 457–478. https://doi.org/10.1177/1521025119848763

Preszler, R. W. (2009). Replacing lecture with peer-led workshops improves student learning. *Life Science Education, 8*(3), 182–192. https://doi.org/10.1187/cbe.09-01-0002

Prof, J. (2022, July 27). Why specifications grading deserves an A. *Inside Higher Ed*. https://www.insidehighered.com/advice/2022/07/27/specifications-grading-benefits-both-students-and-instructors-opinion

Prince, M. (2004). Does active learning work? A review of the research. *Journal of Engineering Education, 93*(3), 223–231. https://doi.org/10.1002/j.2168-9830.2004.tb00809.x

Prince, M., & Felder, R. M. (2006). Inductive teaching and learning methods: Definitions, comparisons, and research bases. *Journal of Engineering Education, 95*(2), 123–138. https://doi.org/10.1002/j.2168-9830.2006.tb00884.x

Prince, M., & Felder, R. M. (2007). The many faces of inductive teaching and learning. *Journal of College Science Teaching, 36*(5), 14–20. https://www.pfw.edu/offices/celt/pdfs/Inductive(JCST).pdf

Pryor, I. H., Hurtado, S., Saenz, V. B., Santos, J. L., & Korn, W. S. (2007). *The American freshman: Forty year trends.* Higher Education Research Institute, UCLA. http://www.heri.ucla.edu/PDFs/pubs/TFS/Trends/Monographs/TheAmericanFreshman40YearTrends.pdf

Puentadura, R. R. (n.d.). *An intro to SAMR: Building ladders.* Hippasus. http://hippasus.com/rrpweblog/archives/2020/01/AnIntroToSAMR_BuildingLadders.pdf

Quinn, D. M. (2020). Experimental evidence on teachers' racial bias in student evaluation: The role of grading scales. *Educational Evaluation and Policy Analysis, 42*(3), 375–392. https://doi.org/10.3102/0162373720932188

Quote Investigator. (n.d.). *Be kind; Everyone you meet is fighting a hard battle.* https://quoteinvestigator.com/2010/06/29/be-kind/

Race, P., & Pickford, R. (2007). *Making teaching work: "Teaching smarter" in post-compulsory education.* Sage.

Radosevich, D. J., Salomon, R., Radosevich, D. M., & Kahn, P. (2008). Using student response systems to increase motivation, learning, and knowledge retention. *Innovate, 5*(1). https://www.learntechlib.org/p/171457/

Raimondi, S. L., Bennett, K. F., Guenther, M. F., & Mineo, P. M. (2020). Guided homework assignments prepare students for flipped introductory biology classroom. *Journal of Microbiology & Biology Education, 21*(2). https://doi.org/10.1128/jmbe.v21i2.2089

Ramani, S., Könings, K. D., Ginsburg, S., & van der Vleuten, C. (2019). Twelve tips to promote a feedback culture with a growth mind-set: Swinging the feedback pendulum from recipes to relationships. *Medical Teacher, 41*(6), 625–631. https://doi.org/10.1080/0142159X.2018.1432850

Rao, C., Prasad, H. L. K., Sajitha, K., Permi, H., & Shetty, J. (2016). Item analysis of multiple choice questions: Assessing an assessment tool in medical students. *International Journal of Educational & Psychological Researchers, 2*(4), 201–204. https://doi.org/10.4103/2395-2296.189670

Raupach, T., de Temple, I., Middeke, A., Anders, S., Morton, C., & Schuelper, N. (2021). Effectiveness of a serious game addressing guideline adherence: Cohort study with 1.5-year follow-up. *BMC Medical Education, 21,* 1-9. https://doi.org/10.1186/s12909-021-02591-1

Reay, N. W., Li, P., & Bao, L. (2008). Testing a new voting machine question methodology. *American Journal of Physics, 76*(2), 171–178. https://doi.org/10.1119/1.2820392

Rebich, S., & Gauthier, C. (2005). Concept mapping to reveal prior knowledge and conceptual change in a mock summit course on global climate change. *Journal of Geoscience Education, 53*(4), 355–365. https://doi.org/10.5408/1089-9995-53.4.355

Reddish, E. F. (2003). *Teaching physics with the physics suite.* Wiley.

Redlawsk, D. P., Rice, T., & Associates. (2009). *Civic service: Service-learning with state and local government partners.* Jossey-Bass.

Redmond, B. F., & Perrin, J. J. (2014). *Goal setting theory.* PSYCH 484: Work Attitudes and Job Motivation, Pennsylvania State University. https://courses.worldcampus.psu.edu/welcome/psych484/001/common/wrapsyllabus

Regis, A., & Albertazzi, P. G. (1996). Concept maps in chemistry education. *Journal of Chemical Education, 73*(11), 1084–1088. https://doi.org/10.1021/ed073p1084

Remenick, L., & Bergman, M. (2021). Support for working students: Considerations for higher education institutions. *The Journal of Continuing Higher Education, 69*(1), 34–45. https://doi.org/10.1080/07377363.2020.1777381

Richmond, A. S., Morgan, R. K., Slattery, J. M., Mitchell, N. G., & Cooper, A. G. (2019). Project Syllabus: An exploratory study of learner-centered syllabi. *Teaching of Psychology, 46*(1), 6–15. https://doi.org/10.1177/0098628318816129

Reiner, C. M., Bothell, T. W., Sudweeks, R. R., & Wood. B. (2004). *Preparing effective essay questions: A self-directed workbook for educators.* New Forums Press.

Riener, C., & Willingham, D. (2010). The myth of learning styles. *Change, 42*(5), 32–35. https://doi.org/10.1080/00091383.2010.503139

Robinson, D. H., Katayama, A. D., DuBois, N. E., & Devaney, T. (1998). Interactive effects of graphic organizers and delayed review of concept application. *Journal of Experimental Education, 67*(1), 17–31. https://doi.org/10.1080/00220979809598342

Robinson, D. H., & Kiewra, K. A. (1995). Visual argument: Graphic organizers are superior to outlines in improving learning from text. *Journal of Educational Psychology, 87*(3), 455–467. https://doi.org/10.1037/0022-0663.87.3.455

Robinson, D. H., & Molina, E. (2002). The relative involvement of visual and auditory working memory when studying adjunct displays. *Contemporary Educational Psychology, 27*(1), 118–131. https://doi.org/10.1006/ceps.2001.1081

Rodgers, M. L. (1995). How holistic scoring kept writing alive in chemistry. *College Teaching, 43*(1), 19–22. https://doi.org/10.1080/87567555.1995.9925504

Rodriguez, J. G., Hunter, K. H., Scharlott, L. J., & Becker, N. M. (2020). A review of research on process oriented guided inquiry learning: Implications for research and practice. *Journal of Chemical Education, 97*(10), 3506–3520. https://doi.org/10.1021/acs.jchemed.0c00355

Rodriguez, M. C., & Albano, A. D. (2017). *The college instructor's guide to writing test items: Measuring student learning.* Routledge.

Roediger, H. L. III, & Butler, A. C. (2010). The critical role of retrieval practice in long-term retention. *Trends in Cognitive Sciences, 15*(1), 20–27. https://doi.org/10.1016/j.tics.2010.09.003

Roediger, H. L., III, & Karpicke, J. D. (2006). The power of testing memory: Basic research and implications of the educational practice. *Perspective on Psychological Science, 1*(3), 181–210. https://doi.org/10.1111/j.1745-6916.2006.00012.x

Rohrer, D., & Pashler, H. (2010). Recent research on human learning challenges conventional instructional strategies. *Educational Researcher, 39*(5), 406–412. https://doi.org/10.3102/0013189X10374770

Rohrer, D., Taylor, K., & Sholar, B. (2010). Tests enhance the transfer of learning. *Journal of Experimental Psychology: Learning, Memory, and Cognition, 36*(1), 233–239. https://doi.org/10.1037/a0017678

Romero, C. C. (2009). *Cooperative learning instruction and science achievement for secondary and early postsecondary students: A systematic review* (Publication No. 3374617) [Doctoral dissertation, Colorado State University]. ProQuest LLC.

Rowe, T. (2022, May 11). *How to catch a streaming pirate.* Reuters. https://www.reuters.com/legal/litigation/how-catch-streaming-pirate-2022-05-11/

Royce, A. P. (2000). *A survey of academic incivility at Indiana University: Preliminary report.* Bloomington: Indiana University, Center for Survey Research.

Royer, J., Cisero, C., & Carlo, M. S. (1993). Techniques and procedures for assessing cognitive skills. *Review of Educational Research, 63*(2), 201–243. https://doi.org/10.2307/1170473

Rudolph, M. J., Daugherty, K. K., Ray, M. E., Shuford, V. P., Lebovitz, L., & DiVall, M. V. (2019). Best practices related to examination item construction and post-hoc review. *American Journal of Pharmaceutical Education, 83*(7), 7204. https://doi.org/10.5688/ajpe7204

Rumore M. M. (2016). The course syllabus: Legal contract or operator's manual? *American Journal of Pharmaceutical Education, 80*(10), 177. https://doi.org/10.5688/ajpe8010177

Rybarczyk, B., Baines, A., McVey, M., Thompson, J., & Wilkins, H. (2007). A case-based approach increases student learning outcomes and comprehension of cellular respiration concepts. *Biochemistry and Molecular Biology Education, 35*, 181–186. https://doi.org/10.1002/bmb.40

Sam, A. H., Peleva, E., Fung, C. Y., Cohen, N., Benbow, E. W., & Meeran, K. (2019). Very short answer questions: A novel approach to summative assessments in pathology. *Advances in Medical Education and Practice, 10*, 943–948. https://doi.org/10.2147/AMEP.S197977

Sathy, V., & Moore, Q. (2020, July 14). Who benefits from the flipped classroom? Quasi-experimental findings on student learning, engagement, course perceptions and interest in statistics. In J. Rodgers (Ed.), *Teaching statistics and qualitative methods in the 21st century. Multivariate Analysis series.* Routledge.

Savaria, M., Monteiro, K. (2017). A critical discourse analysis of engineering course syllabi and recommendations for increasing engagement among women in

STEM. *Journal of STEM Education, 18*(1), 92–97. https://www.jstem.org/jstem/index.php/JSTEM/article/view/2217/1840

Schaffhauser, D. (2017, February 23). 9 in 10 students admit to cheating in college, suspect faculty do the same. *Campus Technology.* https://campustechnology.com/articles/2017/02/23/9-in-10-students-admit-to-cheating-in-college-suspect-faculty-do-the-same.aspx

Schau, C., & Mattern, N. (1997). Use of map techniques in teaching applied statistics courses. *American Statistician, 51,* 171–175. https://doi.org/ 10.1080/00031305.1997.10473955

Schell, J. (2012, September 4). *How one professor motivated students to read before a flipped class, and measured their effort.* Turn to Your Neighbor. https://peerinstruction.wordpress.com/2012/09/04/how-one-professor-motivated-students-to-read-before-a-flipped-class-and-measured-their-effort/

Schinske, J., & Tanner, K. (2014). Teaching more by grading less (or differently). *Cell Biology Education—Life Sciences Education, 13,* 159–166. https://doi.org/10.1187/cbe.cbe-14-03-0054

Schönwetter, D. J., Sokal, L., Friesen, M., & Taylor, L. L. (2002). Teaching philosophies reconsidered: A conceptual model for the development and evaluation of teaching philosophy statements. *International Journal for Academic Development, 7*(1), 83–97. https://doi.org/10.1080/13601440210156501

Schraw, G. (1998). Promoting general metacognitive awareness. *Instructional Science, 26*(1–2), 113–125. https://doi.org/10.1023/A:1003044231033

Schriver, J. L., & Kulynych, R. H. (2021). Do professor–student rapport and mattering predict college student outcomes? *Teaching of Psychology.* https://doi.org/10.1177/00986283211037987

Schroth, H. (2019). Are you ready for Gen Z in the workplace? *California Management Review, 61*(3), 5–18. https://doi.org/10.1177/0008125619841006

Schroeder, C. M., Scott, T. P., Tolson, H., Huang, T., & Lee, Y. (2007). A meta-analysis of national research: Effects of teaching strategies on student achievement in science in the United States. *Journal of Research in Science Teaching, 44*(10), 1436–1460. https://doi.org/10.1002/tea.20212

Schroeder, N. L., Nesbit, J. C., Anguiano, C. J., & Adesope, O. O. (2018). Studying and constructing concept maps: A meta-analysis. *Educational Psychology Review, 30,* 431–455. https://doi.org/10.1007/s10648-017-9403-9

Schröter, E., & Röber, M. (2021). Understanding the case method: Teaching public administration case by case. *Teaching Public Administration, 40*(2), 258–275. https://doi.org/10.1177/01447394211051883

Schuman, R. (2014, August 26). Syllabus Tyrannus: The decline and fall of the American university is written in 25-page course syllabi. *Slate.* http://www.slate.com/articles/life/education/2014/08/college_course_syllabi_they_re_too_long_and_they_re_a_symbol_of_the_decline.html

Schwartz, B., Tatum, H., & Hageman, M. (2013). Undergraduate perceptions of and responses to academic dishonesty: The impact of honor codes. *Ethics & Behavior, 23,* 463–476. https://doi.org.10.1080/10508422.2013.814538

Scott, H., Fawkner, S., Oliver, C. W., & Murray, A. (2017). How to make an engaging infographic? *British Journal of Sports Medicine, 51*(16), 1183–1184. https://doi.org/10.1136/bjsports-2016-097023

Scott, K. C. (2021). A review of faculty self-assessment TPACK instruments (January 2006 – March 2020). *International Journal of Information and Communication Technology Education, 17*(2), 118–137. http://doi.org/10.4018/IJICTE.2021040108

Seesholtz, M., & Polk, B. (2009, October 10). Two professors, one valuable lesson: How to respectfully disagree. *The Chronicle of Higher Education.* http://chronicle.com/article/Two-Professors-One-Valuable/48901/

Seldin, P., Miller, J. E., & Seldin, C. A. (2010). *The teaching portfolio: A practical guide to improved performance and promotion/tenure decisions.* Jossey-Bass.

Semetko, H. A., & Scammell, M. (2012). *The Sage handbook of political communication.* Sage.

Sera, L., & McPherson, M. L. (2019). Effect of a study skills course on student self-assessment of learning skills and strategies. *Currents in Pharmacy Teaching and*

Learning, 11(7), 664–668. https://doi.org/10.1016/j.cptl.2019.03.004

Shadle, S.E., Marker, A., & Earl, B. (2017). Faculty drivers and barriers: Laying the groundwork for undergraduate STEM education reform in academic departments. *International Journal of STEM Education, 4*(8), 1–13. https://doi.org/10.1186/s40594-017-0062-7

Shank, J. D. (2014). *Interactive open educational resources: A guide to finding, choosing, and using what's out there to transform college teaching.* Jossey-Bass.

Sharkey, L., Overmann, J., & Flash, P. (2007). Evolution of a course in veterinary clinical pathology: The application of case-based writing assignments to focus on skill development and facilitation of learning. *Journal of Veterinary Medical Education, 34*(4), 423–430. https://doi.org/ 10.3138/jvme.34.4.423

Shekhar, P., Borrego, M., DeMonbrun, M., Finelli, C., Crockett, C., & Nguyen, K. (2020). Negative student response to active learning in STEM classrooms: A systematic review of underlying reasons. *Journal of College Science Teaching, 49*(6), 45-54. https://www.jstor.org/stable/27119215

Shulman, L. S. (1986). Those who understand: Knowledge growth in teaching. *Educational Researcher, 15*(2), 4–14. http://www.jstor.org/stable/1175860

Sibley, J., & Ostafichuk, P. (Eds.), with Roberson, B., Franchini, B., & Kubitz, K. A. (2014). *Getting started with team-based learning.* Stylus.

Siegel-Stechler, K. (2021). Teaching for citizenship: Instructional practices and open classroom climate. *Theory and Research in Social Education, 49*(4), 570–601. https://doi.org/10.1080/00933104.2021.1966560

Silberman, M. (1994). *Active learning: 101 strategies to teach any subject.* Allyn & Bacon.

Simpson, E. H., & Balsam, P. D. (2016). The behavioral neuroscience of motivation: An overview of concepts, measures, and translational applications. *Current Topics in Behavioral Neurosciences, 27*, 1–12. https://doi.org/10.1007/7854_2015_402

Singleton-Jackson, J. A., Jackson, D. L., & Reinhardt, J. (2010). Students as consumers of knowledge: Are they buying what we're selling? *Innovative Higher Education, 35*(4), 343–358.

Sipiyaruk, K., Gallagher, J. E., Hatzipanagos, S., & Reynolds, P. A. (2017). Acquiring critical thinking and decision-making skills: An evaluation of a serious game used by undergraduate dental students in dental public health. *Technology, Knowledge and Learning, 22*, 209–218. http://dx.doi.org/10.1007/s10758-016-9296-6

Slatta, R. W. (2004). Enhancing inquiry-guided learning with technology in history courses. In V. S. Lee (Ed.), *Teaching and learning through inquiry: A guidebook for institutions and instructors* (pp. 93–102). Stylus.

Slaughter, M. H., Lindstrom, J. H., & Anderson, R. (2020). Perceptions of extended time accommodations among postsecondary students with disabilities. *Exceptionality.* https://doi.org/10.1080/09362835.2020.1727339

Slunt, K. M., & Giancarlo, L. C. (2004). Student-centered learning: A comparison of two different methods of instruction. *Journal of Chemical Education, 81*(7), 985–988.

Skinner, B. H. (1974). *About behaviorism.* Vintage Books.

Smith, D. J., & Valentine, T. (2012). The use and perceived effectiveness of instructional practices in two-year technical colleges. *Journal of Excellence in College Teaching, 23*(1), 133–161.

Smith, K.A. (1994). Cooperative learning: Making "groupwork" work. *New Directions in Teaching and Learning, 67*, 71–82. http://www.linqed.net/media/28435/1-useful-for-reading-Cooperative-Learning-Making-Groupwork-Work.pdf

Smith, M. K., Jones, F. H., Gilbert, S. L., & Wieman, C. E. (2013). The classroom observation protocol for undergraduate STEM (CIPUS): A new instrument to characterize university STEM classroom practices. *Life Sciences Education, 12*(4), 618–627. https://doi.org/10.1187/cbe.13-08-0154

Soufi, N. E., & See, B. H. (2019). Does explicit teaching of critical thinking improve critical thinking skills of English language learners in higher education? A critical review of causal evidence. *Studies in Educational Evaluation, 60*, 140–162. https://doi.org/10.1016/j.stueduc.2018.12.006

Spady, W.G. (1994). *Outcome-based education: Critical issues and answers.* American Association of School Administrators.

Spence, L. D. (2001). The case against teaching. *Change, 33* (6), 10–19. https://doi.org/10.1080/00091380109601822

Spencer, S. J., Steele, C. M., & Quinn, D. M. (1999). Stereotype threat and women's math performance. *Journal of Experimental Social Psychology, 35*(1), 4–28. https://doi.org/10.1006/jesp.1998.1373

Springer, L., Stanne, M. E., & Donovan, S. S. (1999). Effects of small-group learning on undergraduates in science, mathematics, engineering, and technology: A meta-analysis. *Review of Educational Research, 69*(1), 21–51. https://doi.org/10.3102/00346543069001021

Sproule, R. (2002). The underdetermination of instructor performance by data from the student evaluation of teaching. *Economics of Education Review, 21*(3), 287–295.

Starr, C. R., & Simpkins, S. D. (2021). High school students' math and science gender stereotypes: Relations with their STEM outcomes and socializers' stereotypes. *Social Psychology of Education, 24*, 273–298. https://doi.org/10.1007/s11218-021-09611-4

Steele, C. M. (1997). A threat in the air. *American Psychologist, 52*, 613–629. https://doi.org/10.1037//0003-066X.52.6.613

Steele, C. M., & Aronson, J. (1995). Stereotype threat and the intellectual test performance of African Americans. *Journal of Personality and Social Psychology,* 69(5), 797–811. https://doi.org/10.1037//0022-3514.69.5.797

Steiner, S., Holley, L. C., Gerdes, K., & Campbell, H. E. (2006). Evaluating teaching: Listening to students while acknowledging bias. *Journal of Social Work Education, 42*(2), 355–376. https://doi.org/10.5175/JSWE.2006.200404113

Stenson, M. (2022). Implementing ungrading in undergraduate exercise physiology. *The FASEB Journal, 36* (Suppl 1). https://doi.org/10.1096/fasebj.2022.36.S1.R6135

Stevens, D. D., & Cooper, J. E. (2009). *Journal keeping: How to use reflective writing for learning, teaching, professional insight and positive change.* Stylus.

Stevens, D. D., & Levi, A. J. (2012). *Introduction to rubrics: An assessment tool to save grading time, convey effective feedback, and promote student learning* (2nd ed.). Stylus.

Stim, R. (2019). *Getting permission: Using & licensing copyright-protected materials online & off.* Nolo Publishing.

Stommel, J. (March 11, 2018). *How to ungrade.* Jesse Stomme. https://www.jessestommel.com/how-to-ungrade/

Stork, E., & Hartley, N. T. (2009). Classroom incivilities: Students' perceptions about professors' behaviors. *Contemporary Issues in Education Research, 2*(4), 13–24. https://doi.org/10.19030/cier.v2i4.1066

Strauss, V. (2018, November 15). Where in the world are teachers most respected? Not in the U.S., a new study shows. *The Washington Post.* https://www.washingtonpost.com/education/2018/11/15/where-world-are-teachers-most-respected-not-us-new-survey-shows/

Strobel, J., & van Barneveld, A. (2009). When is PBL more effective? A meta-synthesis of meta-analyses comparing PBL to conventional classrooms. *Interdisciplinary Journal of Problem-Based Learning, 3*(1), 44–58. https://doi.org/10.7771/1541-5015.1046

Stroebe, W. (2020). Student evaluations of teaching encourages poor teaching and contributes to grade inflation: A theoretical and empirical analysis. *Basic and Applied Social Psychology, (42)*4, 276–294. https://doi.org/10.1080/01973533.2020.1756817

Student Assessment of Learning Gains (SALG) survey instrument. (n.d.). http://www.salgsite.org

Su, S.-F. (2021). Exploring students' attitudes toward university e-textbooks: Experiences, expectations, and preferences. *Journal of Librarianship and Information Science.* https://doi.org/10.1177/09610006211020096

Suarez, J., & Martin, A. (2001). Internet plagiarism: A teacher's combat guide. *Contemporary Issues in Technology and Teacher Education [online serial], 1*(4). https://citejournal.org/volume-1/issue-4-01/current-practice/article2-htm-20/

Sullivan, C. S., Middendorf, J., & Camp, M. E. (2008). Engrained study habits and the challenge of warm-ups in just-in-time teaching. *National Teaching and Learning Forum, 17*(4), 5–8.

Supiano, B. (2020, October 21). Students cheat. How much does it matter?: As the pandemic continues, the debate grows louder. *The Chronicle of Higher Education*. https://www.chronicle.com/article/students-cheat-how-much-does-it-matter

Suskie, L. (2009). *Assessing student learning: A common sense guide* (2nd ed.). Jossey-Bass.

Suyo-Vega, J. A., Meneses-La-Riva, M. E., Fernández-Bedoya, V. H., Polonia A.dC., Miotto, A.I., Alvarado-Suyo, S. A., Ocupa-Cabrera, H. G., & Alarcón-Martínez, M. (2022). Mental health projects for university students: A systematic review of the scientific literature available in Portuguese, English, and Spanish. *Frontiers in Sociology.* 7:922017. https://doi.org/10.3389/fsoc.2022.922017

Svensson, J., Axén, A., Andersson, E. K., & Hjelm, M. (2021). Nursing students' experiences of what influences achievement of learning outcomes in a problem-based learning context: A qualitative descriptive study. *Nursing Open, 8*(4), 1863-1869. https://doi.org/10.1002/nop2.842

Svinicki, M. (2004). *Learning and motivation in the postsecondary classroom.* Anker.

Svinicki, M. (2014). In note-taking, quantity and quality both count (or more is better but better is also better). *National Teaching and Learning Forum, 23*(5), 11–12.

Svinicki, M., & McKeachie, W. J. (2013). *McKeachie's teaching tips: Strategies, research, and theory for college and university teachers.* Wadsworth.

Swauger, S. (2020, April 20) *Our bodies encoded: Algorithmic test proctoring in higher education.* Hybrid Pedagogy. https://hybridpedagogy.org/our-bodies-encoded-algorithmic-test-proctoring-in-higher-education/

Sweet, M., & Michaelsen, L. K. (2012). *Team-based learning in the social sciences and humanities: Group work that works to generate critical thinking and engagement.* Stylus.

Sweller, J. (1988). Cognitive load during problem solving: Effects on learning. *Cognitive Science: A Multidisciplinary Journal, 12*(2), 257–285. https://doi.org/10.1207/s15516709cog1202_4

Tai-Seale, T. (2001). Liberating service-learning and applying new practice. *College Teaching, 49*(1), 14–18. https://doi.org/10.1080/87567550109595839

Talbert, R. (2015, March 15*). Three critical conversations started and sustained by flipping learning.* Faculty Focus. http://www.facultyfocus.com/articles/effective-teaching-strategies/three-critical-conversations-started-sustained-flipped-learning/

Tanner, K. D. (2012). Promoting student metacognition. *Life Sciences Education, 11*(2), 113–120. https://doi.org/10.1187/cbe.12-03-0033

Taricani, E. M., & Clariana, R. B. (2006). A technique for automatically scoring open-ended concept maps. *Educational Technology Research and Development, 54*(1), 65–82. https://doi.org/ 10.1007/s11423-006-6497-z

Tatum, H. E. (2022). Honor codes and academic integrity: Three decades of research. *Journal of College and Character, 23*(1), 32–47. https://doi.org/10.1080/2194587X.2021.2017977

Tatum, H. E., Schwartz, B. M., Hageman, M. C., & Koretke, S. L. (2018). College students' perceptions of and responses to academic dishonesty: An investigation of type of honor code, institution size, and student-faculty ratio. *Ethics & Behavior, 28*(4), 302–315. https://doi.org/10.1080/10508422.2017.1331132

Tavits, M., & Pérez, E. O. (2019). Language influences mass opinion toward gender and LGBT equality. *Proceedings of the National Academy of Sciences of the United States of America, 116*(34), 16781–16786. https://www.jstor.org/stable/26850543

Tayce, J. D., Saunders, A. B., Keefer, L., & Korich, J. (2019). The creation of a collaborative, case-based learning experience in a large-enrollment classroom. *Journal of Veterinary Medical Education, 48*(1), 14–20. https://doi.org/10.3138/jvme.2019-0001

Taylor, A. K., & Kowalski, P. (2014). Student misconceptions: Where do they come from and what can we do? In V. A. Benassi, C. E. Overton, & C. M. Hakala (Eds.), *Applying science of learning in education: Infusing psychological science into the curriculum* (pp. 259–273). Division 2, American Psychological Association, Society for the Teaching of Psychology. http://teachpsych.org/ebooks/asle2014/index.php

Taylor, H. C., & Russell, J. T. (1939). The relationship of validity coefficients to the practical effectiveness of tests in selection: Discussion and tables. *Journal of Applied Psychology, 23*(5), 565–578. https://doi.org/10.1037/h0057079

Terada, Y. (2020, May 4). *A powerful model for understanding good tech integration.* Edutopia. https://www.edutopia.org/article/powerful-model-understanding-good-tech-integration

Tharayil, S., Borrego, M., Prince, M., Nguyen, K.A., Shekhar, P., Finelli, C.J., & Waters, C. (2018). Strategies to mitigate student resistance to active learning. *International Journal of STEM Education, 5*(7). https://doi.org/10.1186/s40594-018-0102-y

Theall, M., & Franklin, J. (1999). What have we learned? A synthesis and some guidelines for effective motivation in higher education. In M. Theall (Ed.), *New directions for teaching and learning: No. 78. Motivation from within: Encouraging faculty and students to excel* (pp. 97–109). Jossey-Bass.

Theobald, E. J., Hill, M. J., Tran, E., Agrawal, S., Arroyo, E. N., Behling, S., Chambwe, N., Cintrón, D. L., Cooper, J. D., Dunster, G., Grummer, J. A., Hennessey, K., Hsiao, J., Iranon, N., Jones, L., Jordt, H., Keller, M., Lacey, M. E., Littlefield, C. E., Lowe, A., Newman, S., . . ., Freeman, S. (2020). Active learning narrows achievement gaps for underrepresented students in undergraduate science, technology, engineering, and math. *Proceedings of the National Academy of Sciences, 117*(12), 6476–6483. https://doi.org/10.1073/pnas.1916903117

Thomas, C. L., Cassady, J. C., & Finch, W. H. (2018). Identifying severity standards on the Cognitive Test Anxiety Scale: Cut score determination using latent class and cluster analysis. *Journal of Psychoeducational Assessment, 36*(5), 492–508. https://doi.org/10.1177/0734282916686004

Thomas, J. W. (2000). *A review of research on project-based learning.* Autodesk Foundation.

Thomason, A. (2014, September 3). Your 3 worst classroom distractions (and how to deal with them). *The Chronicle of Higher Education.* http://chronicle.com/blogs/ticker/your-3-worst-classroom-distractions-and-how-to-deal-with-them/85255

Thompson, B. (2002, June 21). If I quiz them, they will come. *The Chronicle of Higher Education*, p. B5.

Tigner, R. B. (1999). Putting memory research to good use: Hints from cognitive psychology. *College Teaching, 47*(4), 149–152. https://doi.org/10.1080/87567559909595807

TIMSS 2019 U.S. Highlights Web Report (NCES 2021-021). (2019). U.S. Department of Education. Institute of Education Sciences, National Center for Education Statistics. https://nces.ed.gov/timss/results19/index.asp

Tindell, D. R., & Bohlander, R. W. (2012). The use and abuse of cell phones and text messaging in the classroom: A survey of college students. *College Teaching, 60*(1), 1–9. https://doi.org/10.1080/87567555.2011.604802

Toker, S., & Baturay, M. H. (2019). What foresees college students' tendency to use Facebook for diverse educational purposes? *International Journal of Educational Technology in Higher Education, 16*(9). https://doi.org/10.1186/s41239-019-0139-0

Tools for Inclusive Teaching. (2021, January 15). University of Southern California, Rossier School of Education. https://rossier.usc.edu/news-insights/news/tools-inclusive-teaching

Treisman, U. (2013). A conversation with Uri Treisman. *Journal of Mathematics Education at Teachers College, 3*(2), 6–11. https://journals.library.columbia.edu/index.php/jmetc/article/view/743/189

Treme, J. (2018). Classroom debates: Using speed rounds to encourage greater participation, *College Teaching, 66*(2), 86–87. https://doi.org/10.1080/87567555.2017.1416330

Trujillo-Jenks, L., & Rosen, L. (2015, May 27). *Fostering student learning through the use of debates.* Faculty Focus. http://www.facultyfocus.com/articles/instructional-design/fostering-student-learning-through-the-use-of-debates/

Tufte, E. (1983). *Visual explanations: The visual display of quantitative information.* Graphics Press.

Turnitin. (2014). *Instructor feedback writ large: Student perceptions on effective feedback.* White paper. https://go.turnitin.com/paper/student-perceptions-on-effective-feedback

Tversky, B. (1995). Cognitive origins of conventions. In F. T. Marchese (Ed.), *Understanding images* (pp. 29–53). Springer-Verlag.

Tversky, B. (2001). Spatial schemas in depictions. In M. Gattis (Ed.), *Spatial schemas and abstract thought* (pp. 79–111). MIT Press.

Umbach, P. D., & Wawrzynski. M. R. (2005). Faculty do matter: The role of college faculty in student learning and engagement. *Research in Higher Education, 46,* 153–184. http://dx.doi.org/10.1007/s11162-004-1598-1

University of Minnesota Libraries. (2015). *Copyright information and resources.* https://www.lib.umn.edu/copyright/

U.S. Bureau of Labor Statistics. (2022, April 18). Fitness trainers and instructors. *Occupational Outlook Handbook.* https://www.bls.gov/ooh/personal-care-and-service/fitness-trainers-and-instructors.htm

Uttl, B., White, C. A., & Gonzalez, D. W. (2017). Meta-analysis of faculty's teaching effectiveness: Student evaluation of teaching ratings and student learning are not related. *Studies in Educational Evaluation, 54,* 22–42. https://doi.org/10.1016/j.stueduc.2016.08.007

Vahedi, Z., Zannella, L., & Want, S. C. (2021). Students' use of information and communication technologies in the classroom: Uses, restriction, and integration. *Active Learning in Higher Education, 22*(3), 215–228. https://doi.org/10.1177/1469787419861926

von der Embse, N., Jester, D., Roy, D., & Post, J. (2018). Test anxiety effects, predictors, and correlates: A 30-year meta-analytic review. *Journal of Affective Disorders, 227,* 483–493. https://doi.org/10.1016/j.jad.2017.11.048

Vander Schee, B. A. (2009). Do students really know their academic strengths? *Teaching Professor, 23*(7).

van der Zanden, P. J. A. C., Denessen, E., Cillessen, A. H. N., & Meijer, P. C. (2018). Domains and predictors of first-year student success: A systematic review. *Educational Research Review, 23,* 57–77. https://doi.org/10.1016/j.edurev.2018.01.001

Van Eynde, D. F., & Spencer, R. W. (1988). Lecture versus experiential learning: Their differential effects on long-term memory. *Organizational Behavior Teaching Review, 12*(4), 52–58. https://doi.org/10.1177/105256298801200404

Vekiri, I. (2002). What is the value of graphical displays in learning? *Educational Psychology Review, 14*(3), 261–312. https://doi.org/10.1023/A:1016064429161

Vella, J. (1994). *Learning to listen, learning to teach: The power of dialogue in educating adults.* Jossey-Bass.

Vlachopoulos, D., & Makri, A. (2017). The effect of games and simulations on higher education: a systematic literature review. *International Journal of Educational Technology in Higher Education, 14,* 22. https://doi.org/10.1186/s41239-017-0062-1

Vroom, V. (1964). *Work and motivation.* Wiley.

Vojtek, B., & Vojtek, R. (2000). Technology: Visual learning—This software helps organize ideas and concepts. *Journal of Staff Development, 21*(4).

Vought, R. T. (2019). *Charting a course for success: America's strategy for STEM education.* White House Office. https://www.hsdl.org/?abstract&did=826425

Wahleithner, J.M. (2020). The high school – college disconnect: Examining first-generation college students' perceptions of their literacy preparation. *Journal of Adolescent & Adult Literacy, 64*(1), 19–26. https://doi.org/10.1002/jaal.1057

Walker, L., & Warfa, A. M. (2017). Process oriented guided inquiry learning (POGIL®) marginally effects student achievement measures but substantially increases the odds of passing a course. *PLoS One, 12*(10). https://doi.org/10.1371/journal.pone.0186203

Walsh, L. L., Lichti, D. A., Zambrano-Varghese, C. M., Borgaonkar, J. S. S., Moon, S., Wester, E. R., & Callis-Duehl, K. L. (2021). Why and how science students in the United States think their peers cheat more frequently online: Perspectives during the COVID-19 pandemic. *International Journal for Educational Integrity, 17*(23). https://doi.org/10.1007/s40979-021-00089-3

Walls, J. K., & Hall, S. S. (2017). A focus group study of African American students' experiences with classroom discussions about race at a predominantly White university. *Teaching in Higher Education, 23*(1), 47–62. https://doi.org.10.1080/13562517.2017.1359158

Walvoord, B. E. (2014). *Assessing and improving student writing in college: A guide for institutions, general education, departments, and classrooms.* Jossey-Bass.

Walvoord, B. E., & Anderson, V. J. (2010). *Effective grading: A tool for learning and assessment* (2nd ed.). Jossey-Bass.

Wandersee, J. (2002a). Using concept circle diagramming as a knowledge mapping tool. In K. Fisher, J. Wandersee, & D. Moody (Eds.), *Mapping biology knowledge* (pp. 109–126). Springer Netherlands.

Wandersee, J. (2002b). Using concept mapping as a knowledge mapping tool. In K. Fisher, J. Wandersee, & D. Moody (Eds.), *Mapping biology knowledge* (pp. 127–142). Springer Netherlands.

Watson, C. E., & Hagood, T. C. (2018). *Playing to learn with reacting to the past: Research on high impact, active learning practices*. Palgrave MacMillan.

Waugh, C. K., & Gronlund, N. E. (2012). *Assessment of student achievement* (10th ed.). Pearson.

Webb, N. G., & Barrett, L. O. (2014). Student views of instructor-student rapport in the college classroom. *Journal of the Scholarship of Teaching and Learning, 14*(2), 15–28. https://doi.org/ 10.14434/josotl.v14i2.4259

Weimer, M. (2013). *Learner-centered teaching: Five key changes to practice* (2nd ed.). Jossey-Bass.

Weinberg, B. A., Fleisher, B. M., & Hashimoto, M. (2007). *Evaluating methods of evaluating instruction: The case of higher education* (NBER Working Paper No. 12844). http:// www.nber.org/papers/w12844

Weinberg, B. A., Hashimoto, M., & Fleisher, B. M. (2009). Evaluating teaching in higher education. *Journal of Economic Education, 40*(3), 227–261. https://doi.org/ 10.3200/JECE.40.3.227-261

Weiner, B. (2018). The legacy of an attribution approach to motivation and emotion: A no-crisis zone. *Motivation Science, 4*(1), 4–14. https://doi.org/10.1037/mot0000082

Wergin, J. F. (1988). Basic issues and principles in classroom assessment. In J. H. McMillan (Ed.), *New directions for teaching and learning: No. 34. Assessing students' learning* (pp. 5–17). Jossey-Bass.

West, D. C., Pomeroy, J. R., & Park, J. K. (2000). Critical thinking in graduate medical education: A role for concept mapping assessment? *Journal of the American Medical Association, 284*(9), 1105–1110. https://doi.org/ 10.1001/jama.284.9.1105

Wheeler, L. B., Palmer, M., & Aneece, I. (2019). Students' perceptions of course syllabi: The role of syllabi in motivating students. *International Journal for the Scholarship of Teaching and Learning, 13*(3), 7. https://doi.org/10.20429/ijsotl.2019.130307

Whimbey, A., & Lochhead, J. (1999). *Problem solving and comprehension*. Erlbaum.

Wieman, C. E. (2007). Why not try a scientific approach to science education? *Change, 39*(5), 9–15. https://doi .org/10.3200/CHNG.39.5.9-15

Wieman, C. E. (2014). Large-scale comparison of science teaching methods send clear message. *Proceedings of the National Academy of Sciences USA, 111*(23), 8319–8320. http://www.pnas.org/content/111/23/8319 .full.pdf+html

Wieman, C. (2015). A better way to evaluate undergraduate teaching. *Change, 47*(1), 6–15. https://doi.org/10.1 080/00091383.2015.996077

Wieman, C., & Gilbert, S. L. (2014). The Teaching Practices Inventory: A new tool for characterizing college and university teaching in mathematics and science. *Life Sciences Education, 13*, 552–569. https://doi.org/ 10.1187/cbe.14-02-0023

Wieman, C. E., Perkins, K., & Gilbert, S. (2010). Transforming science education at large research universities: A case study in progress. *Change, 42*(2), 7–14. https://doi.org/10.1080/00091380903563035

Wigfield, A., & Eccles, J. (2000). Expectancy-value theory of achievement motivation. *Contemporary Educational Psychology, 25*(1), 68–81. https://doi.org/10.1006/ceps .1999.1015

Wiggins, G., & McTighe, J. (2005). *Understanding by design* (2nd ed.). Pearson.

Williams Ware, K. S., Watters, S. O., & Wang, C. (2021). Student perceptions of a cardiac skills laboratory using a just-in-time teaching approach. *Journal of Nursing Education, 60*(8), 472–475. https://doi.org/ 10.3928/01484834-20210723-02

Willingham, D. T. (2005, Summer). Do visual, auditory, and kinesthetic learners need visual, auditory, and kinesthetic instruction? *American Educator*. http:// www.readingrockets.org/article/do-visual-auditory-and-kinesthetic-learners-need-visual-auditory-and-kinesthetic-instruction

Willingham, D. T. (2007, Summer). Critical thinking: Why is it so hard to teach? *American Educator*, 8–19. aft .org/sites/default/files/periodicals/Crit_Thinking.pdf

Willingham, D. (2018). Ask the cognitive scientist: Does tailoring instruction to "learning styles" helps students learn? *American Educator*. https://www.aft.org/ae/summer2018/willingham

Wilson, J. H., & Ryan, R. G. (2013). Professor-student rapport scale: Six items predict student outcomes. *Teaching of Psychology, 40*(2), 130–133. https://doi.org/10.1177/0098628312475033

Wilson, J. H., & Taylor, K. W. (2001). Professor immediacy as behaviors associated with liking students. *Teaching of Psychology, 28,* 136–138.

Wilson, K., & Korn, J. H. (2007). Attention during lectures: Beyond ten minutes. *Teaching of Psychology, 34*(2), 85–89. https://doi.org/10.1080/00986280701291291

Winget, M., & Persky, A. M. (2022). A practical review of mastery learning. *American Journal of Pharmaceutical Education,* 8906. https://doi.org/10.5688/ajpe8906

Winne, P. H., & Nesbit, J. C. (2010). The psychology of academic achievement. *Annual Review Psychology, 61,* 653–678. https://doi.org/10.1146/annurev.psych.093008.100348

Winstone, N. E., Nash, R. A., Rowntree, J., & Parker, M. (2017). It'd be useful, but I wouldn't use it: Barriers to university students' feedback seeking and recipience, *Studies in Higher Education, 42*(11), 2026–2041, https://doi.org/10.1080/03075079.2015.1130032

Wirth, K. R. (n.d.). *Reading reflections.* The Role of Metacognition in Teaching Geoscience: Topical Resources. http://serc.carleton.edu/NAGTWorkshops/metacognition/activities/27560.html

Wirth, K. R., & Perkins, D. (2008, November 20). *Knowledge surveys.* Session presented at the National Association of Geoscience Teachers (NAGT) Workshops: The Role of Metacognition in Teaching Geoscience, Carleton College, Northfield, MN. http://serc.carleton.edu/NAGTWorkshops/assess/knowledgesurvey/

Witherby, A. E., & Tauber, S. K. (2019). The current status of students' notetaking: Why and how do students take notes? *Journal of Applied Research in Memory and Cognition, 8*(2), 139–153. https://doi.org/10.1016/j.jarmac.2019.04.002

Wlodkowski, R. J. (1993). *Enhancing adult motivation to learn: A guide to improving instruction and increasing learner achievements.* Jossey-Bass.

Wolcott, S. K. (2006). *Steps for better thinking, Steps for better thinking performance patterns; Templates for designing assignment questions.* https://wolcottlynch.com/educator-resources

Wright, M., & Hill, L. H. (2015). Academic incivility among health sciences faculty. *Adult Learning, 26*(1), 14–20. https://doi.org/10.1177/1045159514558410

Wurdinger, S., & Qureshi, M. (2015). Enhancing college students' life skills through project-based learning. *Innovative Higher Education, 40*(2), 297–286. https://doi.org/10.1007/s10755-014-9314-3

Wycoff, J. (1991). *Mind mapping: Your personal guide to exploring creativity and problem solving.* Berkley Books.

Yadav, A., Shaver, G. M., Meckl, P., & Firebaugh, S. (2014). Case-based instruction: Improving students' conceptual understanding through cases in a mechanical engineering course. *Journal of Research in Science Teaching, 51,* 659–677. https://chsdoi.org/10.1002/tea.21149

Yardley, J., Rodríguez, M. D., Bates, S. C., & Nelson, J. (2009). True confessions? Alumni's retrospective reports on undergraduate cheating behaviors. *Ethics and Behavior, 19*(1), 1–14. https://doi.org/10.1080/10508420802487096

Yoon, G., Duff, B. R. L., & Bunker, M. P. (2021). Sensation seeking, media multitasking, and social Facebook use. *Social Behavior and Personality, 49*(1), 1–7. https://doi.org/10.2224/sbp.8918

Young, J. R. (2003, August 8). Sssshhh. We're taking notes here. Colleges look for new ways to discourage disruptive behavior in the classroom. *Chronicle of Higher Education,* p. A29.

Young, J. R. (2004, November 12). When good technology means bad teaching. *The Chronicle of Higher Education.* https://www.chronicle.com/article/when-good-technology-means-bad-teaching/

Young, J. R. (2009, November 22). Teaching with Twitter: Not for the faint of heart. *The Chronicle of Higher Education.* http://chronicle.com/article/Teaching-With-Twitter-Not-/49230/

Young, J. R. (2010, March 28). High-tech cheating abounds, and professors bear some blame. *The Chronicle of Higher Education.* http://chronicle.com/article/High-Tech-Cheating-on-Homework/64857/

Zakrajsek, T. (2014). Developing learning in faculty: Seeking expert assistance from colleagues. In P. L. Eddy (Ed.), *Connecting learning across the institution: New Directions in Higher Education, No. 16*, 63-73. Jossey-Bass.

Zakrajsek, T. (2015). I get by with a little help from my friends: Leveraging the expertise of colleagues. *Scholarly Teacher.* https://www.scholarlyteacher.com/post/leveraging-expertise-of-colleagues

Zakrajsek, T. (2017, April 13). Students who don't participate in class discussions: They are not all introverts. *The Scholarly Teacher.* https://www.scholarlyteacher.com/post/students-who-dont-participate-in-class-discussions

Zakrajsek, T. (2018). Reframing the lecture versus active learning debate: Suggestions for a new way forward. *Education in the Health Professions, 1*(1), 1–3. https://www.ehpjournal.com/text.asp?2018/1/1/1/242551

Zakrajsek, T. (2019, June 26). Analyzing student end of course written comments. *The Scholarly Teacher.* https://www.scholarlyteacher.com/post/analyzing-student-end-of-course-written-comments

Zakrajsek, T. (2021, August 17). *Teaching so everyone learns: Concepts and tips for a more inclusive classroom.* Belmont University: Teaching enter August Workshops. https://repository.belmont.edu/tc_workshops/8

Zakrajsek, T. (2022). *The new science of learning: How to learn in harmony with your brain* (3rd ed.). Stylus.

Zander, R. S., & Zander, B. (2000). *The art of possibility: Transforming professional and personal life.* Harvard University Business Press.

Zeilik, M., Schau, C., Mattern, N., Hall, S., Teague, K. W., & Bisard, W. (1997). Conceptual astronomy: A novel model for teaching postsecondary science courses. *American Journal of Physics, 6*(10), 987–996. https://doi.org/10.1119/1.18702

Zhonggen, Y. (2019). A meta-analysis of use of serious games in education over a decade. *International Journal of Computer Games Technology*: 4797032, 8 pages. https://doi.org/10.1155/2019/4797032

Zimmaro, D. (2022). *Constructed-response items.* Routledge. https://doi.org/10.4324/9781138609877-REE29-1

Zimmerman, B. J., Moylan, A., Hudesman, J., White, N., & Flugman, B. (2011). Enhancing self-reflection and mathematics achievement of at-risk students at an urban technical college. *Psychological Test and Assessment Modeling, 53*(1), 141–160.

Zlotkowski, E. (Ed.). (1998). *Successful service-learning programs: New models of excellence in higher education.* Jossey-Bass.

Zull, J. E. (2002). *The art of changing the brain: Enriching the practice of teaching by exploring the biology of learning.* Stylus.

Zull, J. E. (2011). *From brain to mind: Using neuroscience to guide change in education.* Stylus.